Handbook on Food

Handbook on Food

Demand, Supply, Sustainability and Security

Edited by

Raghbendra Jha
Canberra, ACT, Australia

Raghav Gaiha
Cambridge, MA, USA

Anil B. Deolalikar
Riverside, CA, USA

Edward Elgar
Cheltenham, UK • Northampton, MA, USA

© Raghbendra Jha, Raghav Gaiha and Anil B. Deolalikar 2014
© Chapter 5, FAO (Food and Agriculture Organization of the United Nations)

All rights reserved. No part of this publication may be reproduced, stored in a retrieval system or transmitted in any form or by any means, electronic, mechanical or photocopying, recording, or otherwise without the prior permission of the publisher.

Published by
Edward Elgar Publishing Limited
The Lypiatts
15 Lansdown Road
Cheltenham
Glos GL50 2JA
UK

Edward Elgar Publishing, Inc.
William Pratt House
9 Dewey Court
Northampton
Massachusetts 01060
USA

A catalogue record for this book
is available from the British Library

Library of Congress Control Number: 2013951842

This book is available electronically in the ElgarOnline.com Economics Subject Collection, E-ISBN 978 1 78100 429 6

ISBN 978 1 78100 428 9 (cased)

Typeset by Servis Filmsetting Ltd, Stockport, Cheshire
Printed and bound in Great Britain by T.J. International Ltd, Padstow

Contents

About the editors		vii
List of contributors		viii
Preface		xii

1	Overview: Handbook on Food: Demand, Supply, Sustainability and Security Raghbendra Jha, Raghav Gaiha and Anil B. Deolalikar	1
2	The political economy of food security: a behavioral perspective C. Peter Timmer	22
3	Shocks to the system: monitoring food security in a volatile world Derek Headey, Olivier Ecker and Jean-Francois Trinh Tan	41
4	Food price inflation, growth and poverty Shikha Jha and P.V. Srinivasan	72
5	Transmission of global food prices, supply response and impacts on the poor David Dawe	100
6	The financialization of food commodity markets Christopher L. Gilbert and Simone Pfuderer	122
7	Financialisation of food commodity markets, price surge and volatility: new evidence Kritika Mathur, Nidhi Kaicker, Raghav Gaiha, Katsushi S. Imai and Ganesh Thapa	149
8	Dietary shift and diet quality in India: an analysis based on the 50th, 61st and 66th rounds of NSS Raghav Gaiha, Nidhi Kaicker, Katsushi S. Imai, Vani S. Kulkarni and Ganesh Thapa	177
9	Dietary change, nutrient transition and food security in fast-growing China Jing You	204
10	Poverty nutrition traps Raghbendra Jha, Katsushi S. Imai and Raghav Gaiha	246
11	The political economy of dietary allowances C. Sathyamala	260
12	Economic prosperity and non-communicable disease: understanding the linkages Ajay Mahal and Lainie Sutton	278

13 Trade, food and welfare   325
    Alexandros Sarris

14 Enhancing food security: agricultural productivity, international trade and
    poverty reduction   353
    Peter Warr

15 Best-fit options of crop staples for food security: productivity, nutrition and
    sustainability   381
    Jill E. Gready

16 Emissions of greenhouse gases from agriculture and their mitigation 422
    Francesco N. Tubiello and Josef Schmidhuber

17 Land degradation, water scarcity and sustainability   443
    Manab Das, Debashish Goswami, Anshuman and Alok Adholeya

18 Viability of small-scale farms in Asia   462
    Keijiro Otsuka

19 Food entitlements, subsidies and right to food: a South Asian perspective 482
    Simrit Kaur

20 Global middle class and dietary patterns: a sociological perspective 515
    Vani S. Kulkarni

Index   539

About the editors

Raghbendra Jha is Rajiv Gandhi Chair Professor of Economics and Executive Director, Australia South Asia Research Centre at the Australian National University. He has previously taught at Columbia University and Williams College in the United States, Queen's University in Canada, the University of Warwick in the UK, and the Delhi School of Economics, IIM Bangalore and the Indira Gandhi Institute of Development Research in India. He has been a consultant to many organizations including the ADB, the World Bank, WIDER, IFAD, DFID, UNESCAP, UNRISD and the Government of India.

Raghav Gaiha is a former Professor of Public Policy at the University of Delhi, Faculty of Management Studies. He has also served as a visiting fellow/scholar at various institutions, including Harvard, MIT, Stanford, Yale, Penn and the University of Cambridge. He is currently a Visiting Fellow at the Australian National University. He has been a consultant with the World Bank, ADB, FAO, ILO, IFAD and WIDER.

Anil B. Deolalikar is Professor Economics and Associate Dean of Social Sciences for the College of Humanities, Arts and Social Sciences at the University of California, Riverside, USA. He has published extensively on poverty, health, education and social protection in developing countries, has held visiting appointments at major universities and has consulted widely for many international organizations.

Contributors

Alok Adholeya, PhD, Director at The Energy and Resources Institute (TERI), New Delhi, India, is largely devoted to finding and developing ways to harness the power of microbes to increase the productivity of crop plants, to restore degraded lands and remediate contaminated soil. He has published over 60 research papers in reputed national and international journals.

Anshuman, Associate Director, Water Resources Division at TERI, has worked in the water sector for the last 15 years. His key qualifications include an M. Tech. in energy and environmental management from the Indian Institute of Technology, New Delhi, India. His expertise includes integrated water resource management, water use efficiency and water quality, amongst others.

Manab Das is currently a fellow at TERI, New Delhi, India. He obtained his PhD in environmental science from ISM, Dhanbad, India. He has made significant contributions to reclamation of disturbed lands due to industrial activities. He has published several research papers and book chapters on bioremediation aspects of contaminated lands.

David Dawe is a senior economist in the Agricultural Development Economics Division of FAO, based in the Regional Office for Asia and the Pacific in Bangkok. He works on agricultural and food policy analysis, with a special emphasis on the rice economies of Asia. He is also an editor for the journal *Global Food Security*.

Olivier Ecker is a research fellow in the Development Strategy and Governance Division at the International Food Policy Research Institute (IFPRI). Olivier is an economist specializing in development strategy and policies for poverty reduction and food and nutrition security in the Middle East, North Africa and sub-Saharan Africa. He has also worked as a research associate in the Department of International Agricultural Trade and Food Security at the University of Hohenheim, Germany.

Christopher L. Gilbert is Professor of Econometrics at the University of Trento, Italy. His doctorate is from Oxford and he has held teaching positions at Oxford, London (Queen Mary and Birkbeck) and the Free University, Amsterdam. He has worked on food issues for the EU, FAO, UNCTAD and the World Bank.

Debashish Goswami, a fellow at TERI, has a PhD in water resources engineering from the University of Illinois at Urbana-Champaign, USA. His expertise includes hydrology, agricultural water quality, groundwater modeling, irrigation and drainage.

Jill E. Gready is a research professor in the John Curtin School of Medical Research at the Australian National University and Head of the Computational and Conceptual Biology Group. She has been a junior research fellow of Wolfson College, Oxford; a Queen Elizabeth II Fellow and NHMRC Principal Research Fellow at Sydney

University; and a Fulbright Fellow at Scripps Clinic, La Jolla, USA. Her current work focuses on improving the performance of the enzyme Rubisco for crop development. She is a fellow of the Royal Australian Chemical Institute and holder of its Adrien Albert Award and Masson Medal.

Derek Headey is a research fellow in the Poverty, Health and Nutrition Division at the International Food Policy Research Institute (IFPRI). A development economist, his research encompasses a wide range of issues, including development strategies, agricultural development, poverty and nutrition, structural change and demography. He has published in leading scientific journals.

Katsushi S. Imai is an associate professor in Development Economics at the University of Manchester. He previously taught at Oxford and the University of London. He has published widely on risk, vulnerability and poverty dynamics of households in developing countries and on evaluations of anti-poverty programmes.

Shikha Jha is Principal Economist at the Economics and Research Department of Asian Development Bank. She has published widely on fiscal policies, government expenditure, social safety nets and economics of food markets. Her research and operational experience covers several countries in South Asia, South East Asia, East Asia and Central Asia.

Nidhi Kaicker, has submitted her PhD dissertation to Delhi University and is currently an assistant professor at Ambedkar University in New Delhi. She has published papers in the *Journal of Policy Modeling*, and contributed chapters to two books forthcoming from Oxford University Press. She has served as a consultant with IFAD. Her research interests include financial markets, agriculture, nutrition and poverty and financial econometrics.

Simrit Kaur is Professor of Economics at the Faculty of Management Studies, University of Delhi, India. Her areas of interest include privatization, productivity, agricultural policy and food security. Dr Kaur has acted as an advisor to several organizations, such as Ministry of Finance (India), OECD, IFAD and FAO.

Vani S. Kulkarni, a postdoctoral fellow in sociology at Yale University. She has a PhD with distinction from the University of Pennsylvania. She has held research fellowships and taught at Penn, Harvard and Yale, and has been a consultant to the United Nations. Her work lies at the intersection of racial caste inequality, health, decentralized governance, gender, culture and social theory.

Ajay Mahal is the Alan and Elizabeth Finkel Chair of Global Health at the School of Public Health and Preventive Medicine and an adjunct professor of economics at Monash University. His current research is on the economics of health, with a specific focus on the design and evaluation of health systems.

Kritika Mathur is currently pursuing her doctoral research at the Faculty of Management Studies, Delhi University. She completed her Masters in economics from Jamia Millia Islamia, New Delhi. She has taught development economics and macroeconomics at Jesus and Mary College, Delhi University. Her areas of research interest include: commodity markets, game theory and financial econometrics.

Keijiro Otsuka is Professor of Economics at the National Institute for Policy Studies in Tokyo. He has held positions at Tokyo Metropolitan University, the International Rice Research Institute, the International Food Policy Research Institute and the World Bank. He has conducted a large number of case studies on agricultural development in Asia and sub-Saharan Africa.

Simone Pfuderer is a PhD student in economics and management at the University of Trento, Italy. She previously worked for the UK Department for Environment, Food and Rural Affairs, initially as a statistician and later as an economist. She has an MSc in economics (York) and in official statistics (Southampton).

Alexandros Sarris has been Professor of Economics, University of Athens, Greece, since 1982. He has also taught at the University of California, Berkeley, USA, and has been Director of the Trade and Markets Division of FAO. He has authored more than 15 books and monographs, and more than 70 journal and book articles on various issues of international trade and development.

C. Sathyamala is a public health physician and an epidemiologist, currently pursuing a doctorate in development studies at the International Institute of Social Studies (Den Haag), Erasmus University, The Netherlands. Her research interests include political economy of health, medical ethics and environmental health.

Josef Schmidhuber is the Head of FAO's Global Perspective Studies Unit. He is coauthor of 'World agriculture: towards 2015/2030', FAO's long-term perspective of global agriculture. He was a lead author of the chapter on agriculture of the Fourth Assessment Report of the International Panel on Climate Change (IPCC) and member of the International Taskforce on Commodity Risk Management. His research has been widely published in leading scientific journals.

P.V. Srinivasan is an Evaluation Specialist at the Independent Evaluation Department of the Asian Development Bank. He has published extensively on issues related to poverty, food security and public finance. He has been consultant to several international organizations including the World Bank, the Asian Development Bank, the African Development Bank and the Food and Agricultural Organization.

Lainie Sutton is a researcher at the School of Public Health and Preventive Medicine at Monash University. With a background in biomedical science and public health, she is interested in research questions related to international health and health inequalities. Prior to her current assignment, she spent nearly one year working on health sector issues in China.

Ganesh Thapa is a Regional Economist at the International Fund for Agricultural Development (IFAD). He has a PhD in agricultural economics from Cornell University, USA. His areas of research include smallholder agriculture, food security, rural poverty and risks and vulnerability of the rural poor.

C. Peter Timmer is a non-resident fellow at the Center for Global Development (CGD). Now retired from teaching, he is the Thomas D. Cabot Professor of Development Studies, *emeritus*, at Harvard University. Prior to joining CGD, Timmer was Dean of the Graduate School of International Relations and Pacific Studies at UC–San Diego.

In addition to his faculty positions in three schools at Harvard, Timmer has also held professorships at Cornell and Stanford. Timmer's work focuses on four broad topics: the nature of 'pro-poor growth' and its application in Indonesia and other countries in Asia; the supermarket revolution in developing countries and its impact on the poor (both producers and consumers); the structural transformation in historical perspective as a framework for understanding the political economy of agricultural policy; and the functioning of the world rice market.

Jean-Francois Trinh Tan has been a senior research assistant in the Development Strategy and Governance Division at the International Food Policy Research Institute (IFPRI) since 2011. His research focuses on issues related to food security, poverty reduction, agriculture and conflict in sub-Saharan Africa, South East Asia, and the Middle East and North Africa regions.

Francesco N. Tubiello is a climate change scientist with interests in the terrestrial carbon cycle, with a focus on impacts, adaptation and mitigation strategies for agriculture and forestry; food security; sustainability of energy use; and methodologies for greenhouse gas emission mitigation. His research work has been funded by NOAA, NSF, NASA, UNDP, UNFCCC and OECD. He is lead author of the IPCC WGII report on climate change and a UNFCCC expert for CDM and JI projects under the Kyoto Protocol. He is a graduate of NYU and Columbia University.

Peter Warr is Head of the Arndt-Corden Department of Economics and John Crawford Professor of Agricultural Economics in the College of Asia and the Pacific at the Australian National University. His current research is on the relationship between economic policy, technological change and poverty incidence, especially in South East Asia.

Jing You is a lecturer in the School of Agricultural Economics and Rural Development at Renmin University of China and an external research associate affiliated to the Brooks World Poverty Institute at the University of Manchester, UK. Her primary research area is development economics with a focus on China. Her research has appeared in leading international journals, such as *Oxford Bulletin of Economics and Statistics*, *China Economic Review*, *Journal of Policy Modeling* and *Journal of International Economics*.

Preface

The United Nations estimated that, on Thursday 11 July 2013, the world population reached 7.2 billion people. The Food and Agricultural Organization (FAO), a subsidiary of the UN, estimated that, during 2010–12 870 million, or one in eight, people were chronically hungry. Of these, 852 million lived in developing countries (and comprised 15 per cent of their population). Looking forward, the United States Census Bureau predicts a global population of 9.4 billion by 2050. Much of this increase will be concentrated in developing regions.

For the first time in human history, more than one-half of the world's population is living in cities. This trend is global. Yet, it is most prevalent in the developing world. The United Nations estimates that by 2050, the world's population will exceed nine billion. That will be 2.3 billion more than 30 years earlier. The urban population in developing countries is set to rise from 2 to 4 billion over the same period. That means virtually all of the growth in global population in the decades ahead will take place in cities in the developing world. This adds an important new dimension to food security as faster growth of urban incomes and more diversified diets call for higher food yields and different composition of food production, and integration of smallholders into high-value chains.

Ensuring adequate food and nourishment to this large population is a pressing economic and even security challenge. Asymmetric distribution of population growth, rapid urbanization and changes in diets are all occurring concurrently with strains on the supply of food as evidenced, among others, by the challenge of climate change with associated impact on productivity of agriculture, particularly in developing countries. Addressing this multi-dimensional challenge requires research (and action) from a multi-disciplinary perspective going beyond economics.

The present volume is designed to provide the first such integrated approach. It includes chapters written by leading experts and promising young scholars in several areas including, among others, the political economy of food, the transmission of global food price shocks, the implications of financialization of food markets, the impacts of prosperity on food demand and on non-communicable diseases, the role of international trade in addressing food insecurity, the challenge posed by greenhouse gas emissions from agriculture and land degradation, labour market implications of severe undernutrition, viability of small scale farms (where most of the food in developing countries is grown) and strategies to augment food availability.

In compiling such a *Handbook*, one is liable to run up a long list of debts. Our thanks are due to the various authors of this volume who took the time and effort to write such insightful chapters and revise them in light of comments from editors and others. We are grateful to management and staff at Edward Elgar Publishing, particularly Alex Pettifer, for their consistent support and understanding. At the ANU we are grateful to Stephanie Hancock for her administrative support.

Finally, all views expressed in this volume are those of the respective authors.

# 1. Overview: Handbook on Food: Demand, Supply, Sustainability and Security
Raghbendra Jha, Raghav Gaiha and Anil B. Deolalikar

1.1 INTRODUCTION: GLOBAL FOOD PRICE SURGE: THEN AND NOW

In a 2012 report, IFAD (International Fund for Agricultural Development), WFP (World Food Programme) and FAO (Food and Agriculture Organization of the United Nations) argue that in 2010–12 as many as 870 million people (or 12.5 per cent of the global population) were nutritionally deficient in energy. This figure was certainly adversely affected by the food price spiral of 2007–08. A recent and continuing surge in food prices portends another crisis. Nevertheless, there are some striking differences between the food crisis of 2007–08 and the present. One is that the latter is more pervasive (not only have prices of wheat and maize risen sharply but also those of sugar, among other food commodities). A second important difference is that the present surge is largely a result of supply shocks – weather is a more important factor this time than in 2008, reducing production and stocks. A third difference is that, although trade policy responses are associated with price spikes, the former had a more important role in the earlier crisis.

Some critical inputs into agriculture such as oil also affect food prices. Oil affects food prices through supply and demand channels.[1] On the supply side oil and oil-related costs are a substantial component of production costs of food and non-food crops. Agriculture is second only to transportation in its oil-use intensity, implying high sensitivity of marginal costs to oil prices. The effect of rising oil prices is reinforced by surges in fertiliser prices, most of which are based on energy products, such as natural gas. In fact, energy costs could account for up to 90 per cent of the fertiliser cost (e.g. nitrogen fertiliser). Moreover, the bulky nature of food grains implies that their prices are heavily influenced by transport costs. As rise in energy prices pre-dates that in food prices, the causality is likely to run from energy prices to food prices and not the other way around.[2]

Demand factors further contributed to food price spiral. Of particular importance is biofuel demand (Headey and Fan, 2010; Timmer, 2010).[3] In recent times when oil prices have exceeded US$60 a barrel, biofuels become more competitive, especially if such high oil prices are expected to persist. Recent studies (cited in Headey and Fan, 2010) show that the diversion of the US maize crop from food to biofuel uses is the largest source for international biofuel demand and the largest source of demand-induced price pressure.[4]

Biofuels are a major new source of demand in maize and vegetable oil markets, and so they are a potentially important factor in explaining price rises in these markets. But the knock-on effects on other food commodities are significant as well. In the United States, for example, expansion of maize area by 23 per cent in 2007 resulted in a 16 per cent decline in soya-bean area and a price rise of 75 per cent between April 2007 and

April 2008. In Europe, other oilseeds displaced wheat for the same reason (Headey and Fan, 2010).

There is a high degree of correlation between food and oil prices.[5] The increases in oil price in the first quarter of 2012 are a result of both shortages and rising demand, particularly from the industrial sector in China.

Heightened volatility in food prices is also the result of localised weather problems, for instance, onion prices soared in India in November–December 2010, following unseasonal heavy rains. Evidence also points towards the role of speculators in exaggerating the rally in food prices.[6] Commodity derivatives are seen as an important portfolio-hedging instrument since the returns in commodity sector are uncorrelated with the returns on other assets.[7] This financialisation of commodities may not be a source of food inflation; however, it does play an important role in the short-term volatility in food prices (World Bank, 2011a).[8] High oil prices, strong demand for crops from the biofuel sector, depleting stockpiles of food-grains and lower production are also responsible for the food price surge. No less important are protectionist policies adopted by many exporting nations, and expansionary monetary policies. Moreover, as markets are increasingly integrated, economic shocks in international markets get transmitted to domestic markets quickly but pass-through effects vary greatly (Timmer, 2010).

Recent evidence suggests that most major cereal producers, including both consumer nations and exporter nations, responded positively to spiralling food prices in 2007–08 (Fuglie and Nin-Pratt, 2012).

The exporters are distinguished on the basis that they export more than 10 per cent of their production. The major consuming nations increased their production of maize by 16.8 per cent during 2007–08 and 2008–09, of rice by 12.4 per cent, and of wheat by 8.5 per cent. The response in China and India was particularly strong as they increased public agricultural spending by 25–30 per cent in 2008. The response from major exporting nations was even stronger, especially for maize and wheat production, which increased by 25–30 per cent. Rice production grew less as it is dominated by smallholders.

There were other constraining factors for rice. First, rice prices rose with a lag. Second, in most rice producing countries, protectionist government policies limited incentives to produce more. Third, Asian rice producers are much more dependent on fertilisers than smallholders from other regions. In countries where fertilisers were highly subsidised and/or their export was restricted, fertiliser price did not rise much (as in China and India) and the supply response was quite high.

1.2 IMPACT OF GLOBAL PRICE RISE ON DOMESTIC PRICES

What is crucial for understanding the impacts of global food price surge is transmission to domestic prices. As a recent Asian Development Bank (ADB, 2011) study emphasises, several factors determine this transmission. For food importing countries, the key factors are the exchange rate, trade policies and the speed of adjustment. For countries that are not so dependent on food imports, market conditions – local crop conditions, supply costs and policy measures – matter more. Available evidence suggests that international grain prices and domestic prices move in tandem. In fact, in some cases, domestic prices rise faster.

Between June 2010 and February 2011, global rice prices increased by 16.8 per cent. But domestic rice prices, since June 2010, rose by 21.4 per cent in Bangladesh, 21.6 per cent in Indonesia and 36.7 per cent in Vietnam. By contrast, the increases were lower (between 13.5 per cent and 10.3 per cent) in Sri Lanka, Pakistan, China and Thailand; and decreased in the Philippines (the price of well-milled rice fell by 0.9 per cent) and Cambodia (by 10.5 per cent).

Wheat prices are a different story. International prices rose by 99.6 per cent in the 8 months to February 2011, but domestic prices in Asia generally did not exceed 70 per cent. In the Kyrgyz Republic, for example, local wheat prices rose by about 67 per cent, in Bangladesh by 50 per cent, and in India, China and Pakistan by 10–20 per cent.

Since food is assigned a high weight in consumer price indices (about 59 per cent in Bangladesh, over 46 per cent in India and 40 per cent in Vietnam), food price inflation is associated with general inflation. In Vietnam, for example, inflation was in double digits (about 12 per cent in January 2011), in part due to higher food prices (about 15 per cent).

But higher food prices also induce a positive supply response. Recent evidence suggests that most major cereal producers – including both consumer nations and exporter nations – responded positively to spiralling food prices in 2007–08.

The exporters are distinguished on the basis that they export more than 10 per cent of their production. The major consuming nations increased their production of maize by 16.8 per cent during 2007–08 and 2008–09, of rice by 12.4 per cent and of wheat by 8.5 per cent. The response in China and India was particularly strong as they increased public agricultural spending by 25–30 per cent in 2008. The response from major exporting nations was even stronger – especially for maize and wheat production, which increased by 25–30 per cent. Rice production grew less as it is dominated by smallholders.

There were other constraining factors for rice. First, rice prices rose with a lag. Second, in most rice producing countries, protectionist government policies limited incentives to produce more. Third, Asian rice producers are much more dependent on fertilisers than smallholders from other regions. In countries where fertilisers were highly subsidised and/or their export was restricted, fertiliser price did not rise much (as in China and India) and the supply response was quite high.

Supply response is impeded by transport and other input costs. Transport costs have risen because of rising fuel prices, cutting into producers' profits. Also, given lack of data on farm gate prices, it is not straightforward to assess what fractions of retail prices are transmitted to the former – especially smallholders.

1.3 IMPACT OF PRICE RISE ON GROWTH, POVERTY AND INEQUALITY

There are short-run growth and poverty effects.

Two scenarios are considered in the ADB study (2011) for ten selected Asian countries: in the first scenario, worldwide food prices rise by 30 per cent in 2011 and decline by 5 per cent in 2012; and in the second, in addition to the rise in food prices, the oil price rises by 30 per cent in 2011, and declines by 3.1 per cent in 2012.[9]

In the first scenario, GDP growth in some food-importing countries will decrease by up to 0.6 percentage points in 2011. By contrast, in food exporting countries, higher global food prices are associated with growth acceleration. In Thailand, for example, the GDP growth accelerates slightly. In several countries (India, Indonesia and Malaysia), the growth impacts are likely to be stronger in 2012, as the economies take time to adjust to exogenous shocks in food prices.

Under the second scenario, the GDP impacts are more pronounced, with growth deceleration of up to 1.5 percentage points in 2011 and 0.8 percentage points in 2012. In the Philippines, for example, the GDP growth slows down by 1.2 percentage points in 2011, and 0.9 percentage points in 2012, since it is a net importer of both food and oil.

Should these simulation results be taken at face value? We are inclined to the view that these exaggerate the slowing down of growth if yield increases occur in response to total factor productivity (TFP) growth. So, even if agricultural investment suffers under a tight monetary stance, TFP growth may be sustained through more efficient use of water, fertiliser and other resources (Fuglie, 2010; IFAD, 2011).[10]

An increase in food prices adversely affects the poor since they spend a large proportion of their income on food items. In response, the poor tend to take remedial actions: switching over to less nutritious and cheaper diets, cutting down on their children's (especially girls') food intake, and reducing expenditure on non-food items such as health and education of children. In extreme situations, the poor are also forced to sell their assets such as livestock. Although food prices have been increasing since 2000, they increased at a more rapid pace between 2006 and 2007–08 when prices of major cereals surged very rapidly. Asia and the Pacific countries experienced varying spikes in these prices. These spikes have been due to a combination of both short-term (such as droughts, trade restrictions, and speculation and hoarding) and long-term factors (such as declining yield growth, inadequate investments in infrastructure and linkages with other commodity markets such as energy markets).

Although there are alarming estimates of the impact of food price inflation on poverty – a World Bank estimate of the increase in the number of poor globally, for example, ranges from 75 million to 105 million (World Bank, 2008) – more plausible and insightful estimates are reported in a recent study by the ADB (2008), taking supply responses to higher food prices into account. An important finding obtained from simulations for China and Indonesia is that the negative effects of food price inflation (e.g. higher incidence of poverty and increase in income inequality) are dampened by the positive supply response in rural areas. The comparison is interesting as China is a net food exporter while Indonesia is a net food importer. China gains from rising global food prices. Specifically, the largest gains accrue to households dependent on agriculture. Not only does the head-count index of poverty decline but so does the Gini index of income inequality, more than compensating for the unfavourable effects in urban areas. The results for Indonesia, however, differ. Although higher global food prices result in higher consumer prices, appreciation of the exchange rate and a loss of competitiveness of Indonesian exports, and a lowering of real GDP, the food crops sub-sector expands. Not surprisingly, therefore, the overall head-count of poverty rises but slightly.

Two recent studies (ADB, 2011; World Bank, 2011b) offer assessments of the impact of the recent and continuing food price surge. Both are alarmingly high. The main findings of the ADB (2011) study are given below. Changes in poverty are a pure price effect in the sense nominal incomes are held constant. There are two implicit assumptions: one is that wages adjust with a lag; and the second is delayed supply response. While both seem consistent with empirical evidence, it must be emphasized that the short-term results may be larger than longer-term effects.[11]

Using the poverty cut-off of $1.25 per day (purchasing power parity, PPP, 2005) and assuming that domestic food prices rise by 10 per cent, the simulations show that the number of poor in selected Asian countries rises by 64.4 million or the percentage of poor rises by 1.9 points.[12] With higher food price increases of 20 and 30 per cent, the percentage of poor rises by 3.9 points and 5.8 points, respectively.[13] As the poverty gap ratio captures both increases in the number of poor, and deterioration in their standards of living, this is the more comprehensive measure. With domestic food prices rising by 10 per cent, 20 per cent and 30 per cent, the poverty gap ratio rises by 1.4, 2.7 and 4.1 percentage points, respectively.

1.4 IMPACT ON REAL FACTOR INCOMES

Additional simulations focus on the impact of a 10 per cent increase in the price of a staple food in a small sample of countries (FAO, 2008). Households are classified across different characteristics (net market position, income quintile, sources of income). The main findings are: (1) urban consumers lose in Bangladesh, Pakistan and Vietnam; (2) in both rural and urban areas, the poorest quintiles are the worst affected; (3) even in some countries where rural households gain on average, such as Vietnam and Pakistan, the poorest of the poor suffer a welfare loss; (4) disaggregating quintiles of households by landownership, the poor landless are likely to be worse-off. In Bangladesh, for example, the welfare loss of the landless is as high as 3.5 per cent in the bottom quintile; in Vietnam, the average loss of the landless is 1.8 per cent, as against 2.7 per cent of the bottom 40 per cent. Classifying households into agricultural 'specialisers' – households that derived more than 75 per cent of their income from farming – an interesting finding is that their welfare improves. In Bangladesh, for example, the average welfare of agricultural specialisers – comprising 10 per cent of the rural sample – increases by 1.7 per cent (1.3 per cent in the bottom quintile, 1.8 in the top). In Vietnam too, the richer agricultural specialisers gain around 2.2–2.3 per cent.[14] Finally, welfare effects vary between male- and female-headed households. Specifically, in most urban, rural and national samples, female-headed households record greater proportional losses (or smaller proportional gains) than male-headed households. A key explanation is that female-headed households fail to benefit from agricultural income generating activities due to their limited access to land, credit and markets (e.g. Bangladesh, Vietnam and Pakistan).

A more recent study of countries in the Greater Mekong sub-region offers a rich and insightful analysis of how food producers, consumers and wage labourers were affected by the food price crisis (Sombilla et al., 2010). While higher rice prices were welfare reducing, the favourable supply responses were weakened by higher input prices. Wage labourers lost. In Cambodia, for example, in terms of the rice wage equivalent, the average wages during the crisis were lower. In rural coastal region, the daily rice wage equivalent fell from 4.67 kg in June 2007 to 3.84 kg in June 2008; in the rural plains, it fell from 5.75 kg to 4.77 kg; and in rural Cambodia as a whole, from 5.09 kg to 4.43 kg. For those surviving at bare subsistence, such reductions imply substantial welfare loss.

A policy concern is quick transmission of rising food prices to farm gate prices – especially for smallholders – and easy access to markets. If impediments to market access are removed, the sales of smallholders increase more than proportionately to those of wealthy farmers (Shilpi and Umali-Deininger, 2007). So, given a timely and an adequate supply response, the rise in poverty may be considerably lower than predicted without such a response.[15]

1.5 EFFECT ON NUTRITION AND LABOUR MARKET PARTICIPATION

If there are nutritional shocks as a result of the food price surge, poverty–nutrition traps (henceforth PNTs) cannot be ruled out (Jha et al., 2009).

The effect of nutritional intake on labour productivity and wage rates, an important area for research for economists and nutritionists, found initial expression in the form of the efficiency wage hypothesis. It postulated that in developing countries, particularly at low levels of nutrition, workers are physically incapable of doing hard manual labour. Hence their productivity is low which then implies that they get low wages, have low purchasing power and, therefore, low levels of nutrition, completing a vicious cycle of deprivation. These workers are unable to save very much so their assets – both physical and human – are minimal. This reduces their chances of escaping the PNT.[16]

So instead of nutritional deprivation as an effect of income loss, the focus shifts to nutritional adequacy as a precondition for participation in labour market activities. Even if some succeed in participating, their wage earnings will not allow them to escape the PNT. Indeed, a mild labour shock (e.g. associated with a crop shortfall) would worsen their plight, as the risk of loss of employment would be considerably higher. In particular, female workers are more prone to PNT than male workers, and there is a persistent gender inequality in rural India. They find that improving nutrient intakes can have significant effects on rural wages and, therefore, on the possibility of breaking PNT as well as reducing poverty. Thus public policy should concentrate urgently on providing direct nutritional supplements to the nutritionally deprived in addition to pursuing direct poverty alleviation policies.

Estimates of obesity are alarming. Recent projections indicate that globally in 2005 about 1.6 billion (age 15+ years) were overweight and at least 400 million were obese. Besides, at least 20 million children under the age of 5 years are overweight globally. By 2015, 2.3 billion adults are likely to be overweight and more than 700 million will be obese. Once considered a problem only in high-income countries, excess weight and obesity are emerging as a major health concern in low- and middle-income countries (WHO, 2006).[17]

Excess weight and obesity are a manifestation of energy imbalance between calories consumed and calories expended. Broadly, the underlying causal factors include (1) dietary shifts towards higher intake of energy-dense foods that are high in fat and sugars but low in vitamins, minerals and other micronutrients; (2) decreased physical activity due to the increasingly sedentary nature of many forms of work; (3) faster and less strenuous modes of transportation, and growing urbanisation.

Excess weight and obesity are associated with higher risks of cardiovascular disease (mainly heart disease and stroke), diabetes, musculoskeletal disorders – especially osteoarthritis – and some cancers (endometrial, breast and colon). Childhood obesity, on the other hand, is associated with a higher risk of premature death and disability in adulthood.

Many developing countries are confronted by a 'double burden' of malnutrition in which undernutrition and obesity exist side-by-side within the same country, same community and, not infrequently, in the same household (Gaiha et al., 2010).[18] This double burden is attributable to inadequate pre-natal, infant and child nutrition followed by exposure to high fat, energy-dense, micronutrient-deficient foods and lack of physical activity (Caballero, 2005; WHO, 2006).

While the relentless battle against poverty and hunger continues, the double burden of undernutrition and obesity, a new phenomenon particularly in middle-income developing countries, that afflicts millions has barely received careful attention. Underweight children and obese adults are two manifestations of this scourge.

The emergence of the double burden is symptomatic of the dietary transition underway in developing countries as a result of growing prosperity and urbanisation. Diets are shifting from traditional foods towards low-cost energy-dense foods, and physical activity patterns are becoming less strenuous and more sedentary. The excess energy from these foods may affect children and adults within the same household differently. Children may use up the excess energy and still remain underweight while adults are more likely to gain weight. Intrahousehold food allocation biases between adults and children, and between males and females, compound these effects.[19]

The upsurge in the numbers of the overweight and obese portends higher risks of chronic non-communicable diseases (NCDs). The burden of chronic diseases has risen sharply in India, accounting for 53 per cent of all deaths and 44 per cent of disability-adjusted life years in 2005. Worse, many of these deaths occur at early ages and the number of potentially productive years lost due to deaths from cardiovascular disease in the age group of 35–64 years (9.2 million years lost in 2000) is the highest in the world. By 2030, it is expected to touch 17.9 million years.[20]

1.6 DIETARY TRANSITION AND POLICY IMPLICATIONS THEREOF

While growing prosperity and associated life-style and dietary changes are irreversible, a pessimistic reading of the rising burden of diet-related NCDs must be avoided. Although the health policy challenge remains – arising from the conflict between policies that reduce undernutrition and those designed to curb obesity – there is now better awareness of interventions that reduce both. These include promoting breast-feeding, improving the nutritional status of women of reproductive age and reducing foetal growth retardation. Moreover, their costs are a fraction of treating the much larger numbers likely to suffer from chronic ailments in the near future.

A defining characteristic of transformation of emerging economies in the Asia-Pacific region – especially India, China and Indonesia, among others – has been a dietary transition. As their food markets integrate globally and communication improves, diet transitions become unavoidable resulting in a move away from inferior to superior foods and a substitution of traditional staples by primary food products that are more prevalent in Western diets. These shifts are reflected in higher consumption of proteins, sugars, fats and vegetables.[21]

Some of the underlying factors behind this dietary transition are expansion of the middle class, higher female participation in labour markets, emergence of nuclear two-income families, a sharp age divide in food preferences (with younger age groups more susceptible to new foods advertised in the media), and rapid growth of supermarkets and fast-food outlets (Gaiha and Thapa, 2008; Deolalikar, 2010; Timmer, 2010).

The health implications of the dietary transition are unclear. A more varied and nutritionally balanced diet and higher levels of food hygiene are associated with better health. But there is a trade-off as more energy-dense foods are linked to higher incidence of diet-related NCDs such as diabetes, coronary heart disease and certain types of cancer. Although India lags behind other developing countries in the epidemiological transition – decline in infectious disease mortality is compensated increasingly by higher mortality from chronic degenerative NCDs – there is some evidence of this transition taking place.

In view of the above-mentioned tradeoff some policy recommendations can be made. In particular, enhancing awareness of healthy diets is a must. As consumer preferences for flavour, packaging and variety evolve in complex ways in a context of rapidly integrating food markets, a careful scrutiny of measures (e.g. labelling of food quality, consumer awareness campaigns through the media and other channels) designed to influence consumer food choice is imperative.

1.7 INCREASING FOOD OUTPUT

The world population is expected to be about 9.1 billion in 2050. With increasing urbanisation and high-income levels, food production must increase by 70 per cent to meet the food demand in 2050.[22] Since the scope for net increase in arable land is highly limited (especially in Asia and the Pacific Region), 90 per cent of this additional food requirement has to be met through increases in yields in areas with intensive agriculture. Availability of fresh water resources for food production is declining fast and may worsen due to climate change. Since South Asia, and East Asia and the Pacific are slated to experience food deficits in domestic production and increased dependence on food imports by 2030, the pressure to maintain food security would be reflected in intensive exploitation of natural resources (land, water, forestry and fish production). Most poor in these sub-regions are located in ecologically fragile environments that are already experiencing further deterioration. Utmost attention, therefore, should be paid to the sustainability of natural resources used in the intensification of agriculture.

Much recent literature draws attention to slowing cereal yields (WDR, 2008). Combined yield of rice, wheat and maize in developing countries grew at 2 per cent per annum during 1970–90 and about 1 per cent per annum during 1990–2007. But this is not sufficient to argue that agricultural productivity growth decelerated sharply. One major limitation of this measure is that it lumps together a wide range of intensification processes.

The TFP growth analysis, however, points to a different story.[23] In developing regions, productivity growth accelerated in the 1980s and in the subsequent decades. Input growth slowed but remained positive. China sustained exceptionally high TFP growth rates since the 1980s. Few other countries and sub-regions in Asia-Pacific also performed well (Fuglie, 2010).

TFP performance in developing countries is strongly correlated with national investments in 'technology capital' a measure of a country's ability to develop and extend improved technology to farmers. Countries that failed in this respect lagged behind others. So there is a case for higher spending on agricultural research. However, there are long time lags between research investments and productivity growth.

Another important insight relates to supply response to higher food prices. The slowdown in growth rate of agricultural capital formation was in part a consequence of a long spell of unfavourable prices facing producers, resulting in capital moving out of agriculture. The incentives offered by spiralling food prices are likely to accelerate agricultural growth and dampen food price inflation.

Within the agricultural sector, sub-sectors comprising livestock and fisheries have made considerable progress. Attention may be drawn to the factors leading to high production of some of the high-value products. It may be added that in China, fishery exports doubled during the 1990s but these were not more than 8 per cent of the total production for that decade. Domestic demand, rather than exports, fuelled an increase in production (Gulati et al., 2007). For instance, milk production in India increased because of a shift in the composition of food away from cereals. Changes in technology and the sale of commercial production in poultry have adversely affected household production in Cambodia, Laos, Vietnam and Indonesia. This may have reduced production for self-consumption.

Biotechnology – especially GMOs – offers new opportunities for enhancing yields and livelihoods. Some of the big challenges, however, are: (1) developing varieties that can perform well under conditions of drought, flood, heat and salinity; (2) strengthening biosafety assessment; and (3) making smallholders aware of the risks and benefits of GMOs. These enormous tasks need substantial finances and scientific talent, and public–private collaboration (Pender, 2008).

1.8 SUSTAINABILITY OF FOOD OUTPUT

There are serious sustainability concerns too.

Degradation of land adds to the crisis of declining yields. In South East Asia and the Pacific (SEAP) sub-region, loss of top soil due to water and wind erosion is 15.7 per cent and 5.4 per cent, respectively. The loss of grain production due to land degradation in China between 1985 and 1989 is estimated to be 60 per cent, mostly caused by flooding, drought and soil erosion. The estimated annual cost of soil degradation is 7 per cent of GDP originating from agriculture in South Asia. For the SEAP sub-region as a whole, the estimated loss varies from 1 to 7 per cent of agriculture GDP. Water-logging is also an important cause of salinity in the SEAP sub-region, and has affected about 7 per cent of arable land. Heavy use of chemical fertilisers has led to contamination of ground water. Another major concern for sustainability is the growing scarcity of water for agriculture, caused primarily by overexploitation of ground water resources in the SEAP sub-region. In the North China plains, the water table has fallen by one metre a year due to heavy dependence on tube well irrigation. In southern India, the situation is extremely alarming since the ground water levels have declined by 25–30 m in a decade (Pender, 2008).

Most of the overexploitation of ground water is occurring due to faulty policies such as absence of or weak regulatory measures for use of ground water and public provision of cheap electricity and diesel in the form of heavy subsidies for drawing ground water (Gulati and Narayanan, 2003).

Increased production of livestock has contributed to pollution of water resources and is also responsible for the overconsumption of water and rising demand for feed/coarse cereals. The increase in meat production in China between 1994 and 2004 (i.e. from 45 million to 74 million tonnes) led to rising demand for feedgrains. As a result, 70 per cent of the increased exports (the trade in soybeans doubled in this period) of soybeans went to China (World Bank, 2008).

Climate change scenarios paint a grim picture and reinforce the concerns for sustainable natural resource use. Asia and the Pacific Region encompasses a wide spectrum of farming agro-ecosystems – dry wheat producing areas (Central Asia) and wet rice producing ones (South East Asia). The region is likely to face extreme weather conditions, including a higher probability of floods and droughts.

While the search for effective mitigation mechanisms continues, it must be combined with adaptation. The latter, of course, deserves greater attention than it has received. Since the 'world's appetite for emissions reductions has been revealed to be chronically weak', it is imperative 'to find ways of adapting to many possible future climates' (*The Economist*, 25 November, 2010).

Poor countries need assistance as they lack the financial resources, technical expertise and political institutions for such endeavours. Moreover, they are more vulnerable to the risks of climate change as they depend more on agriculture that is so closely tied to weather. Crops are sensitive to changes in patterns of rainfall and peak temperature, and also the pests and diseases that attack them.

Adaptation calls for not just expanded research into improved crop yields and tolerance of temperature and water scarcity, but also research into management of pests, soil conservation and cropping patterns that enhance their resilience.[24] There is also a case for weather insurance which will pay not when crops fail but when specific climatic events occur (e.g. rainfall below a set level).[25]

There is a shift from the traditional supply chains characterised by many traders and intermediaries and face-to-face interactions between agents, towards chains with fewer links and more impersonal dealings. Supermarket chains offer better deals to farmers, higher prices and greater certainty of selling the produce, along with credit and technical assistance in certain cases. However, farmers are also obliged to meet stringent quality requirements and adhere to food safety standards. Supermarkets prefer dealing with a few large farmers rather than many small farmers. Organising small farmers is a challenge. Further, in response to changes in dietary habits and lifestyle, and liberalisation of retail trade, supermarkets with global links are emerging fast. Smallholders' participation in supply chain/supermarkets can be made profitable if the government plays the role of not only providing public goods (infrastructure, food safety standards and favourable environment for enforcing contracts) but also a proactive role in collaboration with forward-looking private players in providing inputs and transferring technology to smallholders. These initiatives, combined with suitable trade negotiations, can be helpful in overcoming the threats that global trade poses to smallholders.

1.9 FOOD ENTITLEMENTS, SUBSIDIES AND RIGHT TO FOOD

In India's context, as also elsewhere, there are strong advocates of the Right to Food Act (RTF), passed by the Parliament of India in 2013, given pervasive hunger and child malnutrition. So, while identification of key analytical issues draws upon the debate in India, the implications are more general.

Besides, there are legal compulsions. Article 21 (the fundamental 'right to life') of the Indian Constitution encompasses the right to food while Article 47 of the Directive Principles directs the state to 'regard the raising of the level of nutrition and the standard of living of its people . . . as among its primary duties', and India being a signatory to various international treaties on these issues. Finally, the Supreme Court has issued several orders on fulfilment of food entitlements (Khera, 2010).

We delineate a perspective on the RTF that differs from the vast literature that has emerged around it in recent years.[26]

The RTF as an enforceable claim to a minimum quantity of food of a certain quality carries with it correlated duties, particularly of the state.[27] These include the duty to avoid loss of the means of subsistence, and to provide for the subsistence of those unable to provide for their own (Shue, 1980). Much, of course, will depend on the specific form of the right to food, the corresponding duties/obligations and the implementation mechanisms.

In practical terms, RTF translates into food entitlements, that is, enforceable claims on the delivery of food. These entitlements could be based on trade, production and employment.

Since RTF does not involve state provision of food except under special circumstances of failures of duties to avoid and protect, and natural disasters, in an important sense it could be viewed as a right to policies (or, as 'a right to a right') that enables individuals to produce or acquire minimum food requirements (Osmani, 2000). This may yield useful insights into whether non-fulfilment of the right to food is due to insufficiency of public resources or due to policies followed or both.

From this perspective, recent debates on the National Food Security Bill have concentrated on a rigid interpretation of the RTF as being confined mostly to state provision of food.

Although estimates of the subsidy involved differ, it is likely that the fiscal burden will be unsustainable. More importantly, given the waste involved (it takes Rs 6 of Public Distribution System (PDS) expenditure to transfer a rupee of real income), it is not even clear if this is the best way of fulfilling RTF. If, instead, more sensible policies are pursued that aim to augment low productivity in agriculture, avoid market imperfections that come in the way of remunerative farm gate food prices and expand livelihood options, fulfilment of food entitlements may be far less costly. In fact, an analysis based on the 61st round of the National Sample Survey (NSS) yields two robust insights: the higher the agricultural wage rate, the lower is the demand for rural public works; and the lower the food price, the lower is the demand for subsidised food (Gaiha et al., 2009). A crucial requirement is a clear enunciation of time-bound objectives and a coherent policy framework. Although not specific to the right to food, what really matters is the effective use of resources in enforcement. As experience accumulates – both juridical and policy related – these costs may decline substantially (Gaiha, 2003).

Hence, contrary to assertions that RTF is both 'undefinable' and 'undeliverable', it was argued that it is evolving slowly into an enforceable right. Some of the arguments against it are exaggerated, if not mistaken. More significantly, its potential for enabling governments to do what they should by providing a strong foundation for their poverty alleviation programmes and policies, and for sharpening the focus of civil society organisations as active agents in such programmes is substantial. While realisation of this right is likely to be slow, difficult and uncertain, it would be a mistake to discard it on the ground that 'too many rights may well make a wrong' (*The Economist*, 2001, p. 20).

1.10 OUTLINE OF THE VOLUME

In his chapter 'The political economy of food security: a behavioral perspective', C. Peter Timmer makes three basic points. First, from a political economy perspective, food security is intimately connected to volatility of staple food prices. Second, policy makers respond to this connection by focusing policy attention and fiscal resources on preventing and coping with volatile food prices, but these resources have opportunity costs in terms of slower long-run economic growth. And third, policy makers are right to do this, because their political constituents have deep, visceral responses to volatile food prices, especially to food price spikes, that are based in behavioural psychology. The empirical regularities of behavioural economics, especially *loss aversion, time inconsistency, other-regarding preferences, herd behaviour, and framing of decisions*, present significant challenges to traditional approaches to food security. The formation of price expectations, hoarding behaviour and the welfare losses from highly unstable food prices all depend on these behavioural regularities. A new theoretical underpinning to political economy analysis is needed that incorporates this behavioural perspective, with psychology, sociology and anthropology all likely to make significant contributions.

In their chapter 'Shocks to the system: monitoring food security in a volatile world', Derek Headey, Olivier Ecker and Jean-Francois Trinh Tan argue that monitoring food security is an increasingly important goal in development given predictions of persistently high food prices, continued uncertainty in the global economy, and the potential for increased frequency of natural disasters. Yet the 2007–08 food crisis revealed the development community's inability to gauge the impacts of economic shocks on food security. For assessing the crisis' global impact, it relied on simulation analyses combined with unreliable indicators that led to grave miscalculations of the number of affected people. This chapter reviews the literature on the welfare effects of major economic shocks – particularly of food price spikes – and discusses common approaches and indicators for assessing the impact on food security and nutrition. Based on empirical evidence from past crises it evaluates the validity and reliability of different types of food security indicators in gauging the impact. The chapter concludes by outlining some means of improving food security measurement for a better monitoring of future food crises.

In their chapter 'Food price inflation, growth and poverty', Shikha Jha and P.V. Srinivasan explore the implications of high and volatile global food prices for economic growth and poverty, and discuss policy choices available to developing countries in Asia in dealing with uncertain supplies and rising and fluctuating food prices. As the poor cope with rising prices by depleting assets and switching to less nutritious foods they fall further into a PNT. Food price increases contribute to general inflation by putting pressure on wages. By reducing household expenditures on education and health, they adversely affect productivity and growth. Tight monetary policy could hurt growth further in the context of supply constraints. While in the short run a judicious mix of trade and buffer stock policies can help stabilise prices, in the long run improving agricultural productivity requires investment in research and modern technology. International policy coordination can help avoid panic driven protectionist policies, integrate markets and reduce global food imbalances.

In his chapter 'Transmission of global food prices, supply response and impacts on the poor', David Dawe shows that price transmission from world markets to domestic markets during the world food crisis of 2007–08 was less than complete. But domestic price increases were nevertheless typically large, with domestic prices in early 2008 being about 40 per cent higher in real terms than in early 2007. Transmission across countries was heterogeneous. Some countries (e.g. China, India, Indonesia) that were not too dependent on imports (or exports) used trade policies to insulate themselves from the world price shock and contain domestic price increases, and these policies exacerbated the shocks experienced by other countries. But countries that were dependent on imports for a substantial share of domestic consumption generally experienced larger domestic price increases. The evidence from household surveys indicates that high food prices generally hurt the poor, although the poverty impact in any particular country will depend on the net trade status of that country and the distribution of land (and thus marketable surplus). The poverty impact of high food prices is likely to be worse in food-importing countries and in countries with an unequal distribution of land.

In their chapter 'The financialization of food commodity markets', Christopher L. Gilbert and Simone Pfuderer quantify the extent of financialisation of food commodity markets over the period since 2000 and analyse the impacts of this process. They look specifically at food price bubbles, price volatility and price comovement. They reject the view that financialisation has been responsible for high and volatile food commodity prices but also reject the view that financialisation has not had any effects on these markets. Trades originated by financial actors, and specifically index investors, can move prices but tend typically to be volatility reducing. The widely commented increased comovement, which relates to oil prices but not to equity prices, appears more likely to have resulted from the use of food commodities as biofuels feedstocks than from financialisation.

In their chapter 'Financialisation of food commodity markets, price surge and volatility: new evidence,' Kritika Mathur, Nidhi Kaicker, Raghav Gaiha, Katsushi S. Imai and Ganesh Thapa argue that recent literature points towards the role of speculators in exaggerating the rally in food prices, over and above that explained by the fundamentals of demand and supply. Some studies argue that futures market speculation can only be blamed for the increasing food prices if it is accompanied by hoarding. With this background, the issues that the present chapter deals with are: (1) assessing the impact of indices such as the S&P500 and MSCI on commodity prices; and (2) tracing the volatility patterns in commodity prices, and linking volatility in commodity markets to these variables. Their results show a negative relationship between the commodity market returns and the Dollex, and a positive relationship between commodity market returns and crude oil price returns. The impact of equity markets, inflation and emerging market performance on commodity markets is weak. They also find some evidence of reverse causality or mutual endogeneity, for instance, causality from Goldman Sachs Commodity Index (GSCI), Standard and Poor's Stock Market Index (S&P500) and West Texas Intermediate (WTI) to Morgan Stanley Capital International Index (MSCI), Consumer Price Index (CPI) to WTI, and MSCI, S&P500 to the US-dollar denominated Bombay Stock Exchange Index (Dollex). They also study the causal relationships between the volatility of returns on macroeconomic variables and commodity markets, using the cross-correlation function and Granger causality tests. The results confirm unidirectional relationship from (volatilities of) GSCI to S&P500, from GSCI to MSCI, and from Dollex to GSCI. But there is also evidence of a two-way causality between Inflation and GSCI (volatilities). Thus, the case for financialisation of commodity/food markets driving commodity/food returns and their volatility rests on weak foundations, leaving the door open for the pivotal role of supply–demand fundamentals.

In their chapter 'Dietary shift and diet quality in India: an analysis based on the 50th, 61st and 66th rounds of NSS', Raghav Gaiha, Nidhi Kaicker, Katsushi S. Imai, Vani S. Kulkarni and Ganesh Thapa examine changes in diets in India over the period 1993–2009. Diets have shifted away from cereals towards higher consumption of fruits, vegetables, oils and livestock products. Using household level data, a food diversity index (FDI) is constructed, based on five food commodities. Significant price effects that vary over time are confirmed, as are income/expenditure effects. Over and above these effects, more sedentary life styles and less strenuous activity patterns played a significant role in shaping dietary patterns. An important finding is the slowing down of dietary transition in the more recent sub-period 2004–09. Clues relate to weakening or strengthening of food price, expenditure and life-style effects over time. Using an instrumented measure of FDI in the second stage, and all other exogenous variables, its effects on nutrients' intakes are analysed. A common finding that food diversity is associated with better quality diet and higher intakes of nutrients is not corroborated. While there is a reduction in calorie intake, there are increases in protein and fat intakes. A case is made for the provision of public goods, nutrition labelling, regulation of food standards, consumer awareness of healthy diets, food fortification and supplementation, and active involvement of the private sector in adhering to the regulatory standards and nutritional norms.

In her chapter 'Dietary change, nutrient transition and food security in fast-growing China' Jing You analyses food security issues in China against the background of fast and consistent economic growth over more than three decades. Along with a better economic situation, the country has also undergone changes in food consumption – not only changing structures of diets but also the increasing quantity of food to feed the larger and richer population. This chapter reviews food issues in China at the micro and macro levels, respectively. At the micro level, it draws upon large-scale household surveys and summarises findings on both rural and urban individuals' structural changes of food consumption, including responsiveness of tastes and food consumption behaviour to income and food prices, the contradiction between improved economic status and unimproved nutrient intake, and changes in eating decisions. At the macro level, it takes stock of the recent literature and the up-to-date data. It discusses the challenges of food security facing China, including both domestic production and import pressures. The chapter concludes with current policy and possible improvement.

In their chapter 'Poverty nutrition traps' Raghbendra Jha, Katsushi S. Imai and Raghav Gaiha argue that while economic growth has been associated with poverty reduction, it has often been observed that such poverty reduction has largely benefitted people living just below the poverty line and not those who are well below it and severely deprived, particularly in terms of nutrition. Particularly at low levels of nutrition, workers are physically incapable of doing hard manual labour. Their productivity tends to be low, which then implies that they get low wages, have low purchasing power and, therefore, low levels of nutrition, completing a vicious cycle of deprivation, i.e., they are caught in a PNT. These workers are unable to save very much and so their assets – both physical and human – are minimal, i.e. they are obliged to work to maintain the minimum living standard for their survival. A principal reason for the existence of poverty traps and the particular problem of PNT is the fact that workers have very few assets apart from their labour. Consequently, they are obliged to work under circumstances that perpetuate their poverty/hunger. Any long-term solution to the problem of poverty traps must, therefore, involve augmentation of worker assets so that they are not obliged to work under unfavourable conditions. These conditions require both positive and negative public policy initiatives.

In her chapter 'The political economy of dietary allowances', C. Sathyamala argues that there is an assumption that dietary recommendations, including norms for nutritional requirements, have been arrived at through an impartial inquiry. While revising of dietary norms is to be expected as advances are made in nutritional science, recommendations of dietary allowances become a contested territory. Depending on particular contexts, recommendations have been scaled up or scaled down to suit the needs of the state and capital. Use of calorie counts has taken the focus away from the need to provide for a diet with all the necessary, equally important nutrients in appropriate quantities for optimal health, irrespective of costs. This chapter, based on a review of literature, presents key shifts in the development of nutrition from the late-nineteenth century, to support the assertion that nutritional recommendations are very much shaped by the socio-political contexts in which they are formulated.

In their chapter 'Economic prosperity and non-communicable disease: understanding the linkages', Ajay Mahal and Lainie Sutton maintain that the period since World War II has seen global GDP per capita increase by nearly three times and improved life expectancy in most countries around the world. However, this period has also been characterised by the growth of NCDs. Nearly 25.5 million die of NCDs annually, 80 per cent of the deaths occurring in low- and middle-income countries. One perspective has been to view NCDs as a collateral damage of affluence, presumably necessitating no more than a better measure of economic performance and possibly policy action directed to address market failures associated with their spread. Another approach, however, views low economic and social status as a key driver of NCDs necessitating urgent attention to inequalities. A large empirical literature on these issues has been repetitive and unclear in its basis for policy suggestions, especially on the causal linkages running from income to health. The chapter attempts to disentangle existing literature on this subject, listing key stylised facts about the global NCD epidemic, its relationship to economic performance; the theoretical basis of the two-way causality between incomes and NCDs, the emerging literature for developing countries and new empirical work assessing causal links from income to NCDs and their risk factors.

In his chapter 'Trade, food and welfare', Alexandros Sarris discusses how agricultural trade and trade policy affect food security. Trade and trade policy affect food security, but whether open economies are more likely to achieve food security depends on how trade and trade policy interact with the domestic markets that affect those that are food insecure. A closed economy while insulated from external shocks, is more vulnerable to domestic shocks. On whether a country can trust global food markets to deliver food commodities when needed and at reasonable cost, the answer is, in general, yes. However, there are occasions, when international markets become excessively unstable and unreliable. History suggests that such occurrences are very infrequent. On what countries that face food security problems do, the review suggests that a drive towards complete self-sufficiency is almost never the answer, and some degree of adequate domestic productive food capacity is wise.

In his chapter 'Enhancing food security: agricultural productivity, international trade and poverty reduction', Peter Warr argues that food security is a meaningful concept because of the special characteristics of food as a commodity. It is argued here that food security is enhanced by three factors: reductions in the real price of food; reductions in poverty incidence; and establishment of effective food social safety nets. Food price reductions depend heavily on agricultural productivity improvement, which occurs through research and extension and through investments in rural infrastructure. Reductions in poverty incidence are a central determinant of food security because under most circumstances only the poor suffer from food insecurity. By increasing the real purchasing power of the poor they can be self-insulated against food insecurity. Establishing effective food social safety nets is necessary because some groups lie outside the reach of the forces of economic growth and poverty reduction, requiring special help with regard to food. Emergency food safety nets are also required in case of natural or anthropogenic disasters.

In her chapter 'Best-fit options of crop staples for food security: productivity, nutrition and sustainability', Jill E. Gready argues that food is a primal need and all people have a right to sufficient nutritious food to sustain life and health. Food security represents public concerns and responsibilities of governments for food provision. Food insecurity, on the other hand, embodies the anxieties of people most at risk of being unable to obtain sufficient affordable, safe and nutritious food reliably. She identifies and attempts to integrate, the disparate factors limiting food production, but more importantly vulnerabilities and risks for reliable production in an increasingly uncertain world, climatically and resource constrained. She provides an objective framework to define best-bet choices of staple food crops and options to improve their productivity, sustainably and reliably with minimal resource and labour inputs and farming-system complexity. Its aim is to simultaneously assure food security and minimise food insecurity. Her analysis suggests that although a step change in plant productivity, analogous to the Green Revolution is necessary, its starting point should not be the current *status quo* and vested interests of national, international and commercial agriculture. She suggests alternative staple crops better fit-for-purpose: more nutritious, better adapted and more resilient to harsh unreliable growing conditions, more efficient users of resources (land, water, fertiliser, labour), and ecologically sustainable. She outlines why photosynthetic improvement is the best-bet option to increase intrinsic crop yield and resilience to adverse growing conditions and minimise resource use, and how such improved crops should be deployed to maximise their advantages, especially under increasing atmospheric CO_2 and higher temperatures, and drought. The goal must be to minimise food insecurity, provide stable pathways out of poverty and reduce the crippling effects of 'hidden hunger' (malnutrition).

In their chapter 'Emissions of greenhouse gases from agriculture and their mitigation', Francesco N. Tubiello and Josef Schmidhuber argue that greenhouse gas (GHG) emissions from agriculture – including crop and livestock production – forestry and associated land-use changes (AFOLU) are responsible for a significant fraction of global anthropogenic emissions, up to 25 per cent according to the latest estimates of the FAO. The estimates stem from a complete time-series of emission statistics for the period 1961–2010, made at country-level by using FAOSTAT activity data and the GHG methodology endorsed by the United Nations Framework Convention on Climate Change (UNFCCC) and developed by the International Panel on Climate Change (IPCC). In particular, from 2000 to 2010, agricultural emissions increased by 1.1 per cent annually, reaching 5.3 Gt CO_2-eq. yr^{-1} in 2010. Current global agricultural emissions are larger than those from net deforestation, and higher than those from the entire transport sector. They are dominated by emissions from livestock production, application of synthetic fertilisers and rice cultivation. In terms of mitigation measures and their linkages with key rural development dimensions, recent literature indicates that supply-side measures – such as changes in crop and grassland management – might either enhance or have negative societal impacts on food security. By contrast, demand-side measures – such as reduced waste or reduced demand for livestock products – could more decisively contribute to both food security and GHG abatement. In fact, demand-side measures offer greater potential abatement, with a range of 1.5–15.6 Gt CO_2-eq. yr^{-1}, compared to supply-side measures, ranging 1.5–4.3 Gt CO_2-eq. yr^{-1}. Given the complexity of land-based mitigation challenges, as well as the multiple repercussions they may have on many key societal outcomes, these mitigation options for agriculture need to be considered and implemented in a complementary fashion. Supply-side measures could be implemented immediately, focusing on those that spur increased efficiency of production, i.e. more agricultural product per unit input and less natural resources used per commodity output. For demand-side measures, their potential will likely depend on successful introduction of appropriate policy aiming at maximising co-benefits with improved environmental quality and human development issues.

In their chapter 'Land degradation, water scarcity and sustainability', Manab Das, Debashish Goswami, Anshuman and Alok Adholeya argue that land degradation and water scarcity are factors that have direct negative consequences on the general status of the ecosystems and their inhabitants. Excessive anthropogenic activities in agriculture, forestry and industrial sectors have resulted in a significant negative effect on soil health and water sustainability. Producing food to feed everyone well, including the 2 billion additional people expected to inhabit the earth by mid-century, will place greater pressure on available water and land resources. In response to the degrading land and water resources, an efficient and sustainable development strategy is warranted. Efficient water management supported by suitable policies are required to meet the increased demands for food, water and material goods of a growing global population, while at the same time protecting the ecological services/functions provided by natural water ecosystems. Similarly, sustainable land management (SLM) practices which are based on three main principles, viz. increased land productivity, improved livelihood and improved ecosystem, could be an effective strategy to cope with land degradation.

In his chapter 'Viability of small-scale farms in Asia', Keijiro Otsuka begins with the observed inverse relationship between farm size and productivity that is oftentimes found in developing countries, particularly in South Asia, which indicates that small farms are more efficient than large farms. In other words, the optimum farm size is small in low-wage economies, because labour-intensive, small-scale production systems are more cost-effective than capital-intensive, large-scale farms. This is clearly the case for subsistence farming where major staples, such as rice, wheat and maize, are grown using manual methods. However, as wage rate increases, capital-using larger farms become more efficient. Indeed, the positive correlation between farm size and productivity tends to emerge in high-wage areas in Asia. Yet, the average farm size in Asia is small and generally declining over time. This study argues that unless significant farm size expansion takes place in high-performing Asian countries, the production cost of farming will increase, leading to declining comparative advantage in agriculture in Asia.

In her chapter 'Food entitlements, subsidies, and right to food: a South Asian Perspective', Simrit Kaur, in addition to analysing several dimensions of food (in)security in South Asia, tests a specific hypothesis, i.e. whether India's food subsidy programme (PDS) has a significant price dampening effect. As theoretical predictions of the price effects are ambiguous, an empirical investigation of the same has considerable policy significance – especially in the context of ongoing food crisis and the National Food Security Ordinance (NFSO). The econometric analysis suggests that the share of PDS in food availability, like the revamping of PDS in 1997, has no significant price dampening effect. Results also indicate that inflation in India is driven more by external than domestic factors. Within domestic factors, supply bottlenecks drive prices more than excess demand. As an illustrative case study, she also reviews the NFSO, and whether it is amenable to extension to other developing countries where the state provides food to the vulnerable.

In her chapter 'Global middle class and dietary patterns: a sociological perspective', Vani S. Kulkarni argues that shifts in food preference, consumption and dietary patterns among middle classes have been quite dramatic so much so that the meaning of 'middle-classness' is traced through the *ontology of diet consumption*. Although consumption patterns, including dietary consumption patterns, are reflection of life styles and perceptions, and a certain habitus (Bourdieu, 1984, 1990; Wacquant, 2004), the phenomenon is dominantly analysed in terms of the scientific model and the economic perspective. Economic affluence and implications for nutrition are certainly important drivers of dietary consumption pattern, and hence necessary to analyse. Nevertheless, these analyses are not *sufficient* to gain a comprehensive understanding of diet behaviour of the middle class. This is because the consumption patterns of middle classes are embedded within a much

Overview 19

broader social context and social relations that influence dietary consumptions and are influenced by it. The social context includes the phenomenon of symbolised identities, psychological and emotional conditions, memories, historical traditions and 'the local configuration of social relations which comprise social structures such as class, race, and gender; institutional practices, collective and individual behaviour, and intersecting personal biographies' (Poland et al., 2006, p. 60). As dietary patterns become increasingly diversified and the size and nature of the middle class becomes ever more heterogeneous, it behoves a more detailed inquiry into the relationship between dietary patterns of the middle class and the economic, social and cultural processes. This chapter is just such an enquiry. It also emphasises why and how the various aspects of dietary patterns of the middle class are relationally connected. It, therefore, proposes a sociological approach to the study of dietary consumption patterns of the middle class.

NOTES

1. This draws upon Headey and Fan (2010), several recent influential writings of Timmer, especially Timmer (2010), and IFAD (2011).
2. Mathur et.al. in this volume contest this contention.
3. In an influential work, Wright (2011) argues that no special tools are necessary for analysing grain price volatility and that the balance between consumption, available supply and stocks remains relevant for any analysis of such volatility.
4. In an emphatic comment, Timmer (2010) adds another dimension. He observes, 'The emergence of biofuels as a commercially viable use of food-grains and vegetable oils not only raises the level of demand that agricultural resources and productivity must meet, but it also links the prices of energy to foodstuffs. There has long been a partial link between energy prices and food prices through production costs, but this demand side link has more troubling implications. In particular, energy prices have been more volatile for decades. A price link between energy and food implies that this volatility will extend to food prices in the future' (p. 6).
5. As a recent World Bank report (2011a) observes, links between crude oil and agricultural markets have become stronger since 2005, with the pass-through elasticity rising from 0.22 for the pre-2005 period to 0.28 through 2009. Dawe, in this volume, has some interesting results for Asian countries.
6. For confirmation of role of speculators in the food crisis of 2007–08, see Timmer (2010) and Imai et al. (2008). Gilbert in this volume has a more nuanced view.
7. Wright (2011) and Mathur et al. (this volume) produce evidence against this argument. Wright, in particular, rules out speculation and argues that food price spikes are a result of supply–demand fundamentals. In fact, every episode of price spikes that he analysed since the 1970s displayed a low stock-to-use ratio and, given that, even a mild supply shock caused a huge price impact.
8. As the World Bank report (2011a) points out, much of the recent increase in commodity financial transactions has occurred in the futures markets, including for maize and wheat. This is largely driven by demand is from index funds holding and continuously rolling over future positions in commodity markets, without taking physical delivery. The extent to which these inflows affect spot prices, however, remains debatable. This mechanism has been questioned in recent studies, including Mathur et al. (this volume).
9. The simulations are done with the Oxford Economics global model. It assumes that the economies in Asia will take a tight monetary stance to prevent domestic inflation getting worse, but higher interest rates will curb investment, and higher consumer prices will restrict consumption. These two together will curb growth.
10. See Imai et.al. (2013).
11. For details, see Imai et. al (2013).
12. Global food prices rose by more than 30 per cent in the first 2 months of 2011, relative to the previous year, and domestic food inflation in Asia averaged 10 per cent (ADB, 2011).
13. The World Bank (2011b) study computes the expected domestic price changes and the associated increases in the cost of living for net consumers and profits of net producers. Using the poverty cut-off of $1.25, while in half the sample, the increase was 0.5 percentage points, in a few countries the increases were much larger (in Tajikistan the increase was 3.6 percentage points and in Pakistan it was 1.9 percentage points).

By contrast, poverty fell in Vietnam, as a large fraction of poor households is net producers of rice and benefits from higher prices.
14. A negative correlation between rice prices and nutritional status was observed in Bangladesh and Indonesia (Torlesse et al., 2003; Block et al., 2004).
15. There is an important caveat, however. If food price volatility rises, as it has in the recent surge, it could dampen investment in augmenting supply (Gaiha and Thapa, 2006; World Bank, 2011a).
16. See Dasgupta and Ray (1986, 1987). Srinivasan (1994) offers a cogent critique.
17. See Popkin et. al. (2012).
18. See also Gaiha et. al. (2013).
19. See Popkin et. al. (2012).
20. See Gaiha et.al. (2013).
21. See Pingali (2007).
22. This is net biofuel demand.
23. TFP growth refers to growth in yields controlling for the effects of growth of inputs. The primary driver of TFP is technological improvement.
24. For details, see Gaiha and Mathur (2010).
25. For a review of weather-based insurance, see Gaiha and Thapa (2006).
26. This draws upon Gaiha (2003) and our more recent research on related issues. See also Jha et. al. (2013).
27. For an elaboration, see Gaiha (2003).

REFERENCES

Asian Development Bank (ADB) (2008), *Asian Development Outlook Update 2008*.
Asian Development Bank (ADB) (2011), Global food price inflation and developing Asia. March 2011. Manila, the Philippines: ADB.
Block, S., L. Keiss, P. Webb, S. Kosen, R. Moench-Pfanner, M.W. Bloem and C.P. Timmer (2004), Macro shocks and micro outcomes: child nutrition during Indonesia's crisis. *Economics and Human Biology*, **2**(1), 21–44.
Bourdieu, P. (1984), *Distinction: A Social Critique of the Judgement of Taste*. London: Routledge.
Bourdieu, P. (1990), The scholastic point of view. *Cultural Anthropology*, **5**(2), 380–91.
Caballero, B. (2005), International nutrition. In C. Duggan, J.B. Watkins and W.A. Walker (eds), *Nutrition in Pediatrics 4: Basic Science. Clinical Applications*. Toronto: B.C. Decker Inc., pp. 195–204.
Dasgupta, P. and D. Ray (1986), Inequality as a determinant of malnutrition and unemployment: theory. *Economic Journal*, **96**, 1011–1034.
Dasgupta, P. and D. Ray (1987), Inequality as a determinant of malnutrition and unemployment: policy. *Economic Journal*, **97**, 177–88.
Deolalikar, A. (2010), The middle class in Asia: emerging trends and patterns and their implications. Paper presented at a Workshop on the Asian Middle Class, Asian Development Bank, 27–28 May.
The Economist (2001), The politics of human rights. Righting wrongs. 18 August, 18–20. Available at: http://www.economist.com/displaystory.cfm?story_id=739385. Accessed 10 January 2013.
The Economist (2010), Adapting to climate change: facing the consequences. 25 November. Available at: http://www.economist.com/node/17572735. Accessed 28 October 2013.
Food and Agricultural Organization (FAO) (2008), Soaring food prices: facts, perspectives, impacts and actions required. High-level conference on world food security: the challenges of climate change and bioenergy. HLC/08/INF/1. Available at http://www.fao.org/home/en/. Accessed 12 March 2013.
Fuglie, K.O. (2010), Total factor productivity in the global agricultural economy: evidence from FAO data. In J.M. Alston, B.A. Babcock and P.G. Pardey (eds), *Shifting Patterns of Agricultural Production and Productivity Worldwide*, Ames, IA: The Midwest Agribusiness Trade Research and Information Centre, Chapter IV.
Fuglie, K.O. and A. Nin-Pratt (2012), A changing global harvest. *2012 Global Food Policy Report*. Washington DC: IFPRI, Chapter 2.
Gaiha, R. (2003), Does the right to food matter? *Economic and Political Weekly*, October 4.
Gaiha, R. and G. Thapa (2006), *Natural Disasters, Agricultural Investment and Productivity in Developing Countries*. Rome: APR, IFAD.
Gaiha, R. and G. Thapa (2008), Supermarkets, smallholders and livelihoods in selected Asian countries. In R. Jha (ed.), *The Indian Economy Sixty Years After Independence*. London: Palgrave Macmillan.
Gaiha, R., V.S. Kulkarni, G. Thapa and K. Imai (2009), Wages, prices and anti-poverty interventions in rural India. Mimeo.

Gaiha, R., R. Jha and V.S. Kulkarni (2010), Obesity, affluence and urbanisation in India. ASARC Working Paper 2010/10, Canberra: ANU.
Gaiha, R. and S. Mathur (2010), Commentary on does research reduce poverty? Assessing the impact of policy-oriented research in agriculture. *IDS Bulletin*, **41**(6).
Gaiha, R., R. Jha and V. Kulkarni (2013), *Diets, Malnutrition and Disease: The Indian Experience*. New Delhi: Oxford University Press.
Gulati, A. and S. Narayanan (2003), *The Subsidy Syndrome in Indian Agriculture*. New Delhi: Oxford University Press.
Gulati, A., N. Minot, C. Delgado and S. Bora (2007), Growth in high value agriculture in Asia and the emergence of vertical links with farmers. In J. Swinnen (ed.), *Global Supply Chains, Standards and the Poor*, Wallingford: CABI Publishing, 91–108.
Headey, D. and S. Fan (2010), *Reflections on the Global Food Crisis*. Washington DC: IFPRI.
IFAD (2011), Agriculture-pathways to prosperity in Asia and the Pacific. Mimeo. IFAD, Asia and the Pacific Division, Rome.
IFAD, WFP and FAO (2012), *The State of Food Insecurity in the World*. Rome: IFAD, WFP and FAO.
Imai, K.S., R. Gaiha and G. Thapa (2008), Foodgrain stocks, prices and speculation. Brooks World Poverty Institute Working Paper 6408, University of Manchester, UK.
Imai, K., Gaiha, R., Thapa, G. And A. Ali (2013), Supply response to food price changes in Asian Countries. In M. Aoki, T. Kuran, and G. Roland (eds), *Institutions and Comparative Economic Development: The IEA 2011 Conference Volume No. 150–1*. New York: Palgrave Macmillan, pp. 313–31.
Jha, R., R. Gaiha and A. Sharma (2009), Calorie and micronutrient and poverty nutrition traps in rural India. *World Development*, **37**(5), 982–91.
Jha, R., R. Gaiha, M. Pandey and N. Kaicker (2013), Food subsidy, income transfer and the poor: a comparative analysis of India's public distribution system in India's states. *Journal of Policy Modeling*, **35**(3), 887–908.
Khera, R. (2010), India's Right to Food Act: beyond the rhetoric. *India in Transition*, 7 July.
Osmani, S. (2000), Human rights to food, health and education. *Journal of Human Development*, **1**(2), 273–98.
Pender, J. (2008), *Agriculture Technology Choices for Poor Farmers in Less Favoured Areas of South and South East Asia*. Rome: APR, IFAD.
Pingali, P. (2007), Westernisation of Asian diets and the transformation of food systems: implications for research and policy. *Food Policy*, **32**(3), 281–98.
Poland, B., K. Frohlich, R. Haines, E. Mykhalovskiy, M. Rock and R. Sparks (2006), The social context of smoking: the next frontier in tobacco control? *Tobacco Control*, **15**(11), 59–63.
Popkin, B.M., L.S. Adair and S.W. Ng (2012), Global nutrition transition and the pandemic of obesity in developing countries. *Nutrition Reviews*, **70**(1), 3–21.
Shilpi, F. and D. Umali-Deininger (2007), Where to sell? Market facilities and agricultural marketing. Policy Research Working Paper 4455, World Bank, Washington DC.
Shue, H. (1980), *Basic Rights*. Princeton, NJ: Princeton University Press.
Sombilla, M.A., D.B. Antiporta, A.M. Balisacan and R.W. Dikitanan (2010), Policy implications to food price crisis and their implications: the case of Greater Mekong sub-region countries. Report submitted to Asia and the Pacific Division, IFAD, Rome.
Srinivasan, T.N. (1994), Destitution: a discourse. *Journal of Economic Literature*, **32**, 1842–1855.
Timmer, C.P. (2010), Reflections on Food Crises Past, *Food Policy*, vol. 35(1), 1–11.
Torlesse, H., L. Kiess and M.W. Bloem (2003), Association of household rice expenditure with child nutritional status indicates a role for macroeconomic food policy in combating malnutrition. *Journal of Nutrition*, **133**(5). 1302–1325.
Wacquant, L. (2004), *Body and Soul: Ethnographic Notebooks of an Apprentice Boxer*, New York: Oxford University Press.
World Development Report (WDR) (2008), *Agriculture for Development*. The World Bank: Washington DC.
WHO (2006), WHO Child Growth Standards: length/height for age, weight for age, weight for length, weight for height. Available at: http://www.ncbi.nlm.nih.gov/pubmed/16817681.
World Bank (2008), *World Development Report 2008*. Washington DC: World Bank.
World Bank (2011a), *Responding to Global Food Price Volatility and Its Impact on Food Security*. Report prepared for Development Committee meeting on 16 April, 2011, World Bank, Washington DC.
World Bank (2011b), *Food Price Watch*. Washington DC: World Bank.
Wright, B. (2011), The economic of grain price volatility. *Applied Economics Perspectives and Policy*, **33**(1), 32–58.

2. The political economy of food security: a behavioral perspective*
C. Peter Timmer

This chapter makes three basic points. First, from a political economy perspective, food security is intimately connected to volatility of staple food prices. Second, policy makers respond to this connection by focusing policy attention and fiscal resources on preventing and coping with volatile food prices, but these resources have opportunity costs in terms of slower economic growth in the long run. And third, policy makers are right to do this, because their political constituents have deep, visceral responses to volatile food prices, especially to food price spikes, that are based in behavioral psychology. The basic argument of the chapter is that new understanding from behavioral economics provides a solid foundation for a political economy of food security that moves away from the narrow assumptions of neoclassical economics, especially trade theory, to a more realistic framework that identifies why the vast majority of consumers and producers want stable food prices. From this understanding flows a much clearer approach to how and when to stabilize food prices.

2.1 INTRODUCTION

What does price volatility have to do with food security?[1] It is widely agreed in the development community that, in general: (1) price *spikes* hurt poor consumers; (2) price *collapses* hurt farmers; and (3) price *risks* reduce investments, including by smallholder farmers for agricultural modernization.

But food price volatility also has a deeper and more insidious impact: it slows down economic growth and the structural transformation that is the pathway out of rural poverty. Thus food price volatility hurts the poor in both the short run and the long run.

People are not food secure until they *think* they are food secure. This basic reality of behavioral psychology adds an important expectational dimension to the traditional definition of food security. For example, the US position paper for the 1996 World Food Conference, provides a standard definition (USDA, 1996: 2):

> Food security exists when all people at all times have physical and economic access to sufficient food to meet their dietary needs for a productive and healthy life. Food security has three dimensions: AVAILABILITY of sufficient quantities of food of appropriate quality, supplied through domestic production or imports; ACCESS by households and individuals to adequate resources to acquire appropriate foods for a nutritious diet; and UTILIZATION of food through adequate diet, water, sanitation, and health care.

The new *behavioral dimension* is dynamic, and is important to food policy because it helps policy analysts better understand how to prevent future food crises. Although not common – on average there are three world food crises per century – food crises do enormous damage to the poor when they hit. Equally devastating, food crises almost always give rise to anti-market and anti-trade policies in a 'beggar my neighbor' approach to building national food reserves at the expense of trade. National food autarky has not been a reliable way to improve food security or broader economic welfare in the long run, and this is likely to be increasingly true in the future if climate change adds to production variability, requiring greater trade to even out supplies across countries.

Preventing food crises through better understanding of their fundamental causes, thus allowing implementation of better food policies, should be a high priority for food policy analysts. Once a food crisis hits, coping with its consequences becomes the main task at hand, with emergency food aid and other forms of safety nets hastily brought into play. But preventing food crises in the first place, *especially by preventing sharp spikes in food prices*, is obviously a superior alternative if a way can be found to do it. Understanding the behavioral dimensions of food security is an important step in learning how. This chapter seeks to integrate new insights from behavioral economics into an understanding of why governments should stabilize basic food grain prices. With a better understanding of 'why', it is possible to suggest better approaches to 'how'.

The argument here is that unstable food prices are undesirable for two separate reasons. First, it is increasingly recognized that highly volatile staple grain prices have serious consequences for economic welfare, especially for the poor (Timmer, 1986, 1989, 1991b; World Bank, 2005; Timmer and Dawe, 2007; IFPRI, 2008). Second, and the new argument in this chapter, unstable food prices universally evoke a visceral, hostile response among producers and consumers alike. This response has deep behavioral foundations – the experimental and psychological literature shows clearly that individuals strongly prefer stable to unstable environments (Kahneman and Tversky, 1979; Tversky and Kahneman, 1986).[2]

Although this behavioral response is part of the reason that individuals tend to be risk averse, the implications are actually more profound. It is conceptually possible to hedge the risks from unstable food prices, or to mitigate their welfare consequences for the poor using safety nets, but there are no markets in which to purchase stability in food prices directly. The message is clear. Citizens would willingly go to the market to buy food price stability, but such a market does not exist. Food price stability is a public good, not a market good.[3] Understandably then, citizens turn to the political market instead. *Only political action and public response from governments can provide stable food prices.* Thus food becomes a political commodity, not just an economic commodity.

Governments that fail to stabilize food prices have failed in the provision of a quite basic human need that is rooted in behavioral psychology – the need for a stable environment. Governments that are successful in stabilizing food prices are usually rewarded politically; witness the landslide victories for Prime Minister Singh in India and of President Yudhoyono in Indonesia in early 2009. Both candidates campaigned openly on their ability to bring their countries through the world food crisis with minimal impact on domestic food prices.

The trick, of course, is to provide stability in domestic food prices at low cost to economic growth and participation by the poor. By and large, Asia has figured out how to do this as a domestic endeavor, but with large negative spillovers to world markets

24 *Handbook on food*

(Timmer, 2009e). African countries do not have a viable strategy for stabilizing their domestic food prices, and the continent suffers even more from the volatility in world markets transmitted from the Asian approach to food price stabilization (Jayne, 2009).

The challenge to the development profession is twofold: (1) to help Asia find more efficient ways to stabilize their domestic food prices, especially for rice, with fewer spillovers to world markets, and (2) to help Africa find a way to stabilize their domestic food prices without introducing serious distortions to their food economies or retarding the development of an efficient private food marketing sector.

2.2 A FRAMEWORK FOR UNDERSTANDING FOOD SECURITY

Especially when a long-run perspective is needed, it is useful to have an organizing framework for understanding how the essential components of food security relate to each other. In what is otherwise an extremely complicated food system, this framework should be as simple as possible (but no simpler, to quote Albert Einstein). The framework used here divides the world into issues facing policy makers in the short run (e.g. 1–2 years) versus the long run (5–10 years or longer), and at the macro, economy-wide level versus at the household, or individual level (see Figure 2.1).

The policy objective in this simple framework is for all households to have reliable and sustainable access to nutritious and healthy food. Thus 'food security' is achieved by ending up in the bottom right box of the matrix. The starting point, however, is the upper left box of the matrix, where policy makers deal primarily with macro-level issues in the short run. To the extent they are concerned about the welfare of poor households, in the short run the best they can do is stabilize food prices and send transfer payments – via

	Short run	Long run
Macro	Rice price stability and the role of rice reserves and international trade. Budget costs of safety nets to protect the poor, and impact of these transfers.	Policies for creating inclusive economic growth, including fiscal policy, management of price stability, the exchange rate and the role of international trade.
Micro	Receipts from safety nets (including from the government), vulnerability to price shocks, and resilience in the face of other shocks to household welfare.	Sustained poverty reduction and reliable access to nutritious and healthy food. This is the definition of *sustainable food security*.

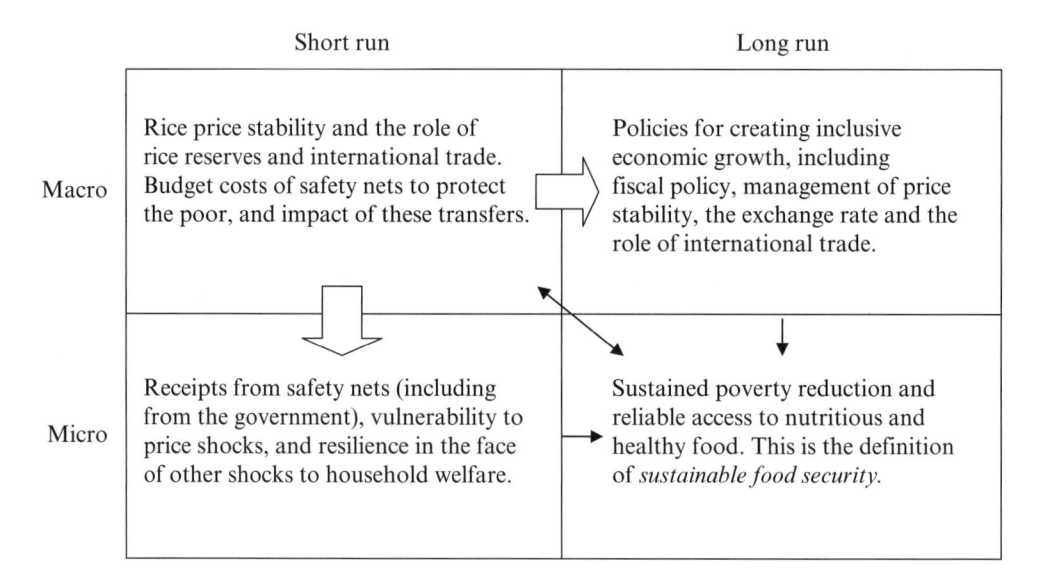

Figure 2.1 *Basic framework for understanding food security issues in Asia*

safety net mechanisms – to those households most affected during a food crisis when prices rise sharply.

In an ideal world, policy makers could use economic mechanisms under their control to shift households directly to the long-run objective, the lower right box where sustainable food security is achieved. In return, policy makers would receive political support for this achievement, hence the two-way diagonal arrow connecting the upper left and lower right boxes. The diagonal arrow reflects a technocratic view of the world where policy makers take informed actions on behalf of public objectives and are rewarded when they succeed.

In fact, market economies, and politics, do not work that way. Policy makers at the macro level must implement long-run measures to stimulate inclusive, pro-poor economic growth and sustain that growth for decades in order to have a measurable impact on poverty, via the small vertical arrow connecting the upper right box to the lower right box. These long-run measures are reflected in the broad arrow from the upper left to the upper right, but it is hard to concentrate the political and financial resources needed to make this arrow an effective mechanism to stimulate economic growth if most policy attention, and fiscal resources, are being devoted to short-run crises.

Simultaneously, and creating tensions for the policies favoring long-run growth, policy makers must also find enough resources, and efficient transfer mechanisms, to ensure that the poor do not fall into irreversible poverty traps during times of economic crisis, including food crises. These transfers can impose substantial fiscal costs and hence challenge the necessary investments for long-run growth. Design and implementation of these transfers involves human and political capital that also has real opportunity costs to the growth process. Thus a focus on the broad downward arrow is necessary to ensure the continued viability and participation of poor households, but these activities have opportunity costs in terms of economic growth.

When the global economic economy is reasonably stable, and when food prices are well behaved, policy makers can concentrate their political and financial capital on the process of long-run, inclusive growth. Keeping the poor from falling into irreversible poverty traps is easier and less costly in a world of stable food prices, and the poor are able to use their own resources and entrepreneurial abilities to connect (via the small horizontal arrow) to long-run, sustainable food security for themselves. With success in achieving the objectives in the upper right and lower left boxes, market forces gradually – over decades – bring the poor above a threshold of vulnerability and into sustained food security (connecting macro to micro and short-run to long run). The country has then managed the 'escape from hunger' that Fogel documented for Europe and America in the late-eighteenth and early-nineteenth centuries, and which a number of Asian countries have managed in the twentieth century (Fogel, 1991, 1994; Timmer, 2004, 2005a).

By contrast, a world of heightened instability – in global finance and the world food economy – forces policy makers to concentrate their resources in the upper left box, where they are trying to stabilize domestic food prices and keep the poor from slipping deeper, irreversibly, into poverty. Important as this effort is, it clearly comes at the expense of significant progress out of the short-run box on the upper left, both to the right and from top to bottom. From this perspective, volatility is a serious impediment to achieving long-run food security. In a world of greater instability, induced by climate change, by new financial arrangements, even by the pressures from new political voices, food security is likely to suffer.

The first step toward fixing this is to understand how the world of food security has changed in the past several decades. The starting point – where we've come from – reflects a broad political mandate in Asia to feed both urban and rural populations, the contributions of a technological revolution in rice (and wheat) that made this possible, and the role of rapid, inclusive economic growth in giving Asian households access to the food in their fields and markets (Timmer, 2005b). What's changed is the structural transformation driven by these processes and the role of rice in the economy – Asia is now richer, more urban, better connected and much better fed (Timmer, 2009a). Asia's food marketing system is also being transformed before our eyes, as modern supply chains and supermarkets change the nature of farm-market-consumer interactions (Reardon et al., 2012). Finally, climate change really does seem upon us, with greatly increased uncertainty about weather patterns and corresponding increases in instability of production. As noted above, volatility is a real problem for food security.

2.3 STABILIZING RICE PRICES AS AN APPROACH TO FOOD SECURITY

The food crisis of 2007–08 caught most of the countries in Asia unprepared for a sudden spike in food prices, especially the price of rice. The panicked response of both rice importing and exporting countries is testimony to the continued political importance of rice, but also to how little long-run strategic planning has gone into the formation of rice policy in Asia, and its relationship to food security.

Food security in Asia has traditionally been defined as having stable prices for rice in the major urban markets of a country. The world market was used as an instrument to defend this goal, with imports and exports controlled by government authorities tasked to defend stable prices (Timmer, 1996). That approach to food security made sense when a third of the economy was dependent on rice production, marketing, and consumption, and well over half of daily caloric intake in some countries came from rice. Except for a few important exceptions – Bangladesh, for example, still gets more than half its calories from rice – that world no longer exists. But the mindset still exists, and it is time for an update.

Part of the updating requires a clearer recognition of who consumes rice. Increasingly, rice is consumed by the poor, who usually must buy most of their rice in rural and urban markets. Almost by definition, having a surplus of rice to sell to the market raises a family above the poverty line in most Asian countries. This reality, of course, makes rice more, not less, important to food security in Asia, but it also makes a mockery of the strategy of most Asian countries of keeping rice prices stable by keeping them high, well above long-run levels in world markets.

When *food security* is equated with *food self-sufficiency*, this strategy may make sense, because it is easier to stabilize domestic food prices using domestic production – stimulated by high prices – than to follow and depend on the world market for rice, with its great price volatility. But this strategy forces poor consumers to pay high prices for rice, and it increases considerably the degree of poverty in a country. Self-sufficiency in rice is a political strategy, not a poverty strategy. If countries were more open to rice trade, they would be richer, not poorer. The big question is how to make such openness possible when policy makers and the general public distrust the world rice market, for reasons that are easy to understand (Timmer, 2009e).

The two most recent world food crises – in 1972–73 and 2007–08 – provide important lessons on the importance of understanding behavior of a wide range of economic agents in the food system if future crises are to be avoided. In particular, understanding how price expectations for basic food grains are formed by farmers, traders and consumers, and how these agents act on those expectations, is critical to knowing what policy actions will stabilize food prices and keep consumers more food secure (Timmer, 2009a, c).

Other behavioral dimensions important to the food system are also being revealed by recent empirical research. Much behavioral research has focused on 'irrational' responses to risk, especially in financial decision making. The relevance to rural credit schemes, micro-credit programs, and the design of commitment mechanisms for effective savings instruments are obvious. Less obvious, perhaps, is the time-inconsistent behavior of Kenyan farmers with respect to fertilizer purchases. Standard intensification programs, even with subsidies, seem to be ineffective in the face of such behavior (Duflo et al., 2008).

The purpose of this chapter is to apply insights from the emerging literature on the behavioral foundations of public economics to food policy analysis (see Bernheim and Rangel, 2005). The proximate goal of food policy analysis has always been to improve food security at both the macro (market stability) level and the micro (household access) levels (Timmer et al., 1983).[4]

To accomplish this goal, of course, food policy needs to influence behavior of food system participants. A richer understanding of behavioral economics offers the hope of more effective policy instruments, and improved food security. Except in rare circumstances, the straightforward way to prevent a food crisis is to have rapidly rising labor productivity through economic growth, keep food prices stable, while maintaining access by the poor. The formula is easier to state than to implement, especially on a global scale, but it is good to have both the objective – reducing short-run spikes in hunger – and the deep mechanisms – pro-poor economic growth and stable food prices – clearly in mind.[5] A coherent food policy seeks to use these mechanisms, and others, to achieve a sustained reduction in chronic hunger over the long run while preventing spikes in hunger in the short run.

On a global basis, it is impossible to reduce hunger in the short-run or the long-run without providing adequate supplies of rice that are accessible to the poor. Perhaps two-thirds of the world's poor consume rice as their staple food, and they live mostly in Asia. It should be no surprise that many of the lessons on how to stabilize staple grain prices come from food price policies designed and implemented in Asia (Timmer, 1986, 1989, 1991b).

2.4 UNDERSTANDING THE BEHAVIORAL DIMENSIONS OF FOOD CRISES

The empirical regularities of behavioral economics, especially *loss aversion, time inconsistency, other-regarding preferences, herd behavior* and *framing of decisions*, present significant challenges to traditional approaches to food security. The formation of price expectations, hoarding behavior and the welfare losses from highly unstable food prices all depend on these behavioral regularities. At least when they are driven by speculative bubbles, market prices for food staples (and especially for rice, the staple food of over 2 billion people), often lose their efficiency properties and the normative implications assigned by trade theory. Theoretical objections to government efforts to stabilize food prices thus have reduced saliency, although operational, financing, and implementation problems remain important, even critical. A new theoretical underpinning to political economy analysis is needed that incorporates this behavioral perspective, with psychology, sociology and anthropology all likely to make significant contributions.

The formation of rice prices in world markets has long interested scholars and policy makers.[6] Nearly half the world's population consumes rice as a staple food and it is typically produced by small farmers using highly labor-intensive techniques. Rice is mostly consumed where it is produced, with international trade less than 30 million metric tons (mmt) out of a global production of nearly 440 mmt (milled rice equivalent) – only 7–8 percent of rice produced crosses an international border.[7] Still, the world market for rice provides essential supplies to importing countries around the world, and the prices set in this market provide signals to both exporting and importing countries about the opportunity cost of increasing production and/or consumption. It is disconcerting to exporters and importers alike if these market signals are highly volatile.

Part of the longstanding interest in the world rice market has been precisely because it has been so volatile. The coefficient of variation of world rice prices has often been double that of wheat or corn for decades at a time. Understanding this volatility has been difficult because much of it traces to the residual nature of the world rice market, as both importing and exporting countries stabilize rice prices internally by using the world rice market to dispose of surpluses or to meet deficits via imports. Thus supply and demand in the world market are a direct result of political decisions in a large number of countries. Rice is a very political commodity (Timmer and Falcon, 1975).

But volatility in rice prices is also driven by the structure of rice production, marketing and consumption in most Asian countries, that is, by the industrial organization of the rice economy. Hundreds of millions of small farmers, millions of traders, processors and retailers, and billions of individual consumers all handle a commodity that can be stored for well over a year in a consumable form. The price expectations of these market participants are critical to their decisions about how much to grow, to sell, to store and to consume. Because there are virtually no data available about either these price expectations or their marketing consequences, the world rice market operates with highly incomplete and imperfect information about short-run supply and demand factors. In this, rice is a very different commodity from the other basic food staples, wheat and maize.[8]

When the political dimensions and the different market structure for rice are integrated into actual price formation, the scope for extreme volatility is clear. Understanding the proximate causes of unstable rice prices requires understanding both factors, and how they contribute to the formation of price expectations on the part of market participants. These expectations can drive 'destabilizing speculative behavior' among millions, even billions, of market participants, such that price formation seems to have a large, destabilizing, speculative component.[9] If so, and price behavior late in 2007 and early 2008 shows that this is a serious problem, what stabilizing activities might be taken to make the world rice market a more reliable venue for imports and exports, with price signals that reflect long-run production costs and consumer demand rather than short-run panicked behavior? Understanding the behavioral foundations of formation of price expectations will be critical to answering this question.

Understanding the formation of price expectations requires a sequence of steps, each linked to the others by basic mechanisms of price formation. Simple supply and demand models are a start. The difference between short-run responses to price changes, and those responses after full adaptation is possible in the long run, is crucial and the semi-empirical model developed in Timmer (2009a) highlights the importance of these differences for understanding current prices. History matters.

But storage and price expectations also become important for storable commodities in the short run – the length of time the commodity can be stored – a year or so for rice. A model of the 'supply of storage', a staple of commodity market analysis for more than half a century, is useful in understanding the factors affecting price expectations, and price formation, in the short run. This model is very powerful in its ability to explain hoarding behavior and subsequent impact on prices.

The link between the supply of grain held in storage and prices in both spot and futures markets has long been the subject of analytical attention (Working, 1933, 1948, 1949; Keynes, 1936; Kaldor, 1939; Telser, 1958, Brennen, 1958; Cootner, 1960, 1961; Weymar, 1968; Williams and Wright, 1991). The basic 'supply of storage' model that has emerged from this theoretical and empirical work is the foundation for understanding short-run price behavior for storable commodities (Houthakker, 1987). It stresses the inter-related behavior of speculators and hedgers as they judge inventory levels in relation to use. The formation of price expectations is the key to this behavior.

The supply of storage model is less successful in explaining the impact on spot market prices of futures market prices that are driven by 'outside' speculators, i.e. those who have no interests in owning the actual commodity but are investing solely on the basis of expected price changes on futures markets. The role of outside speculators in commodity price formation is an old debate, although one that has usually not included rice because of the thinness of rice futures markets. The potential of outside speculators to induce destabilizing price formation is a major element of this debate. The controversy over the role of 'outside' speculators – investors who are not active participants in the commodity system – has many precursors in the history and analysis of commodity price formation on futures markets (see, for example, the Telser–Keynes debate reviewed by Cootner, 1960).[10]

Traders who follow closely the specifics of the commodity know that inventories (especially relative to actual use for consumption) are the key to price formation, once the harvest/supply situation for the crop is established. Clearly, the analytics of price behavior for oil or metals begin to look quite different from the analytics of food commodities at this stage, as seasonal production and the inherent need to store the commodity for daily use throughout the year drive inventory behavior via the supply of storage.

Typically, commodities for which inventory data are reasonably reliable tend to have their short-run prices driven by unexpected supply behavior, whereas commodities with poor data on inventories, especially where significant inventories can be in the hands of millions of small agents – farmers, traders, consumers – tend to have their extremes in price behavior generated by rapidly changing price expectations themselves, and consequent hoarding or dis-hoarding of the commodity.

The *short-run price dynamics* for rice thus look significantly different from wheat or corn, partly because of the different industrial organization of the respective commodity systems. There are surprisingly few studies of individual commodity systems that are set within this broader macroeconomic and organizational framework (see Timmer, 1987, for an exception). The world food crisis in 2008 provides ample rationale for major new studies within this framework for all of the major food commodities (Sarris et al., 2009).

2.5 WHY THE DIFFERENCE IN MARKET STRUCTURE FOR RICE MATTERS IN SHORT-RUN PRICE FORMATION

Experience with world rice prices since 2007 illustrates the importance of market structure to short-run price dynamics. As concerns grew in 2007 that world food supplies were limited and prices for wheat, corn and vegetable oils were rising, several Asian countries reconsidered the wisdom of maintaining low domestic stocks for rice.[11] The Philippines, in particular, tried to build up their stocks to protect against shortages going forward. Of course, if every country – or individual consumer – acts the same way, the hoarding causes a panic and extreme shortage in markets, leading to rapidly rising prices. Even US consumers are not immune from this panic, as the 'run' on bags of rice at Costco and Sam's Club in April 2008 indicated. Such price panics have been fairly common over the past 50 years, but the hope was that deeper markets, more open trading regimes, and wealthier consumers able to adjust more flexibly to price changes had made markets more stable.[12] It turns out this was wishful thinking, as the price record for rice shows.

After an acceleration started in October 2007 of the gradual price increases seen for half a decade, concern over the impact of higher rice prices in exporting countries, especially India, Vietnam and Thailand, started to translate into talk, and then action, on export controls.[13] Importing countries, especially the Philippines, started to scramble for supplies. Fears of shortages spread and a cumulative price spiral started that fed on the fear itself.

The trigger for the panic was provided by inter-commodity price linkages. In India, the 2007 wheat harvest was damaged by drought and disease – as in so many other parts of the world. Thus the national food authority had less wheat for public distribution. Importing as much wheat as in 2006 (nearly 7 mmt) would be too expensive (both economically and politically) because of the high wheat price in world markets, so the food authority announced it needed to retain more rice from domestic production.

Barriers were put on rice exports in October – India is usually the second largest rice exporter in the world, 5 mmt in 2007 – and eventually an outright ban on exports of non-Basmati rice from India was announced in February 2008. Other rice-exporting countries followed, as rice prices started to spike.

The newly elected government in Thailand did not want consumer prices for rice to go up, and the commerce minister openly discussed export restrictions from Thailand – the world's largest rice exporter, 9.5 mmt in 2007. On March 28, 2008, rice prices in Thailand jumped $75 per metric ton (mt). Prices continued to skyrocket until it cost over $1100 per mt in April. This is the stuff of panics.

Low and declining rice stocks have been held accountable for the rising prices, with the argument that rice consumption has outpaced rice production for a number of years since 2000 (a mathematical inevitability if rice stocks are falling). Rice stocks in China have come down over the past decade, but that was a sensible response to growing reliance on trade as the buffer, and to lower prices in world markets. There has been little change in rice stocks in the rest of the world – indeed, the stocks-to-use ratio has been rising since 2005 (Timmer, 2009e). Holding rice stocks in tropical conditions is extraordinarily expensive, so a smoother flow of rice internationally reduces this wasteful stockholding.

Now that the exporting countries are clearly willing to put bans on rice exports to protect their own consumers, nearly all countries will have increased incentives to resort to domestic stockpiles. That is a real tragedy for poor consumers and for economic growth – capital tied up in funding inventories is not very productive in stimulating productivity growth.

The *psychology of hoarding behavior* is important in explaining why rice prices suddenly shot up starting in late 2007. Financial speculation seems to have played only a small role (partly because futures markets for rice are very thinly traded). Instead, decisions by millions of households, farmers, traders and some governments sparked a sudden surge in demand for rice and changed the gradual increase in rice prices from 2002 to 2007 into an explosion (Timmer, 2012). This was 'precautionary' demand even if not 'speculative' demand, to use the language Keynes (1936) used in the early debate over the role of speculative demand in the supply of storage – *panicked hoarding caused the rice price spike*.

Fortunately, a speculative run based on herd psychology can be ended by 'pricking the bubble' and deflating expectations. Once the price starts to drop, the psychology reverses on hoarding behavior by households, farmers, traders and even governments. When the government of Japan announced in early June, after considerable international urging, that it would sell 300 000 tons of its surplus 'WTO (World Trade Organization)' rice stocks to the Philippines, prices in world rice markets started to fall immediately (Mallaby, 2008; Slayton and Timmer, 2008). By late August, medium quality rice for export from Vietnam was available for half what it sold for in late April, as dis-hoarding gained momentum.[14]

2.6 THE BEHAVIORAL DYNAMICS OF PREVENTING FOOD CRISES

Preventing food crises requires two separate, but integrated, approaches – a *market-oriented approach* to economic growth and structural transformation, and a *stabilization approach* to policy initiatives that prevent sharp price spikes for staple foods. Both approaches require a behavioral perspective, and neither can work without the other.

The pathway of structural transformation is long and hard. It is easy to get sidetracked or to miss the path altogether. The endpoint – an agricultural sector that is a small share of a large economy – is easily confused with a development strategy that squeezes agriculture from the start. Such a strategy has always been a catastrophe. Because of the unreliability of market prices in the short run as signals for long-run investments, both governments and private firms easily miss the importance of investing in higher agricultural productivity, better food safety standards, or social responsibility (Timmer, 2009b).

Changing income distribution is an important part of the problem. Even if the structural transformation goes smoothly, most rural households find growth in their incomes lagging behind growth in urban incomes. Changing *relative* incomes in rural and urban areas drive political dynamics, and the nearly universal tendency to increase agricultural protection during a successful structural transformation is easily understandable from the viewpoint of behavioral economics, thus explaining much of the 'empirical' political economy of food prices.[15]

Successful structural transformations have always been primarily a market-driven process. Markets process billions of pieces of information on a daily basis to generate price signals to all participants – no other form of institutional organization has evolved that is capable of the necessary information processing required for individuals and firms to make efficient allocation and investment decisions, and thus to raise long-run productivity. Without reasonably efficient markets, we are all doomed to poverty.

The dilemma, of course, is that markets sometimes (or often, depending on political perspective and analytical training) fail at tasks that society regards as important, such as poverty reduction, nutritional well-being or food price stability, even employment generation. We now understand that these failures are not just for technical reasons – externalities, spillovers, monopoly power or asymmetric information, for example – but also have deep behavioral roots, based in loss aversion, widespread norms of fairness and the regularity of 'other-regarding preferences'. Fixing them is not easy unless these root causes are incorporated into the policy analysis, design, and interventions (an example is in Thaler and Benartzi, 2004). That said, a number of behavioral regularities are well documented, and building them into policy design simply requires paying attention. Norms of 'fairness', for example, are easy to build into food subsidy schemes – even when they conflict with economists' sense of efficiency. The *Raskin* program of rice distribution to the poor in Indonesia, for example, has struggled with the 'losses' to rice distributed by village leaders on the basis of a 'fairness' mechanism rather than a 'poverty' mechanism. Knowing that such an approach was inevitable from the start would have significantly improved the performance of this program.

These are lessons not just for food security, but more broadly for many firms involved in the development process. Firms that cannot rely solely on market signals to provide accurate guidance on pricing levels, quality standards, or investments to promote social responsibility, for example, will need input from a diverse array of 'micro' specialists in medicine, psychology, sociology and anthropology, and from 'macro' specialists in history, climatology, geography and ethics. It is far from clear how these inputs can be coordinated and evaluated, but the need for a broader science of evaluation is clear.

Beyond market failures, there are several problems with the process of structural transformation in the short- and medium-term. A health and nutrition transition seems to accompany structural transformation, but with lags and significant sectoral differences. Not all of the transitional impact is positive: significant increases in obesity, and accompanying chronic diseases, are linked to both the higher incomes and larger urban populations that come with successful structural transformation, as evidence from China and India is making apparent (Webb and Block, 2012).

Technical change, which is stimulated by high food prices, has paradoxically been the long-run mechanism for generating low food prices and better nutrition for the poor. There is considerable debate over the impact of cheap food, a processing-oriented commercial food sector and urban lifestyles, on the rising tide of obesity. But again, the temporal disconnect between the poor losing access to food in the short run because of high prices, and a positive long-run technological response, requires public understanding and intervention, in the nutrition arena as well as in preventing food crises. By necessity, the poor live in the short run, but must place their hope for an escape from poverty in long-run forces that are mediated by efficient markets. The time inconsistent behavior of most individuals and policymakers means this dilemma is very difficult to resolve.

2.7 PREVENTING FOOD CRISES THROUGH UNDERSTANDING AND ACTION

Food crises have important short-run and long-run consequences for the welfare of the poor. Poverty traps and irreversible effects from childhood malnutrition (learning, stature, mortality) stem from even temporary loss of access to food. Markets are usually not the best mechanism for preventing these problems in the first place, or alleviating them once they happen. Markets are crucial in the medium to long run as the institutional vehicles for raising productivity of poor workers, but sudden spikes in food prices that cut off these workers from access to food supplies reflect serious market failures. *Price stability is not a routine market outcome.*

It should be recognized, of course, that high food prices also offer opportunities, for surplus producers, both at the farm level and at the national level. High food prices provide incentives for technical change, which paradoxically has been the long-run mechanism for generating low food prices and better nutrition for the poor. But again, the temporal disconnect between the poor losing access to food in the short run, and a positive long-run technological response, requires public understanding and intervention. By necessity, the poor live in the short run, but must place their hope for an escape from poverty in long-run forces.

A policy dialogue on these issues over the past quarter century has shown significant progress. First, the need for rapid growth in agricultural productivity, with substantial participation by small farmers where they are a significant part of the production structure, is increasingly recognized by macro policy makers as a key element in the overall development strategy. Finance ministers, with their hands on fiscal policy and public investment allocations, central bankers, with their hands on exchange rates and money supplies, and heads of planning agencies, with their hands on strategic approaches and sectoral resource allocations, understand now their own stakes in a healthy rural economy (Timmer, 2009d).

In return, food and agricultural planners increasingly understand that real wages in rural areas depend fundamentally on real wages in the urban economy. Real food prices for farmers and consumers are conditioned by the rate of inflation and by exchange rates. Investments in rural infrastructure require budget allocations. Trade policy has direct and indirect effects on rural incentives. The need for a 'macro food policy' has never been clearer.

As always, this macro food policy must encompass consumption, production, marketing/trade and the macro economy (with new roles for financial markets as they connect to commodity markets). Analytically, modeling all of these dimensions is intractable, which is why the way forward continues to be on the intuitive rather than the quantitative front. In the policy business, 'three facts beat a theory' is true most of the time, but a really compelling story wins every time.

How can this intuitive understanding be built? The answer involves a combination of theory, history, quantitative analysis and experience. Different analysts will bring different combinations to bear, and differences in individual temperament, training and hands-on opportunities probably mean that a variety of combinations can work. But no single component alone will make for effective policy analysis and advising.

2.8 ANALYTICAL UNDERSTANDING

A 'vision' of an interconnected food system is the starting point for a deeper analytical understanding of how it works and, especially, how it would respond to external shocks, technical change and policy initiatives. *Building a vision is an intuitive and pedagogical process.* Some analysts see the interconnections most clearly in the context of general equilibrium theory, now a standard tool in all macroeconomists' kit. Others find the equilibrium of ecological systems a guidepost. Whatever the underlying framework, understanding how markets process billions of pieces of information on a daily basis to generate price signals to all participants is absolutely crucial to building this food policy vision. Markets cannot solve all of society's problems, and sometimes make them worse. But no other form of institutional organization has evolved that is capable of the necessary information processing required for individuals and firms to make efficient allocation and investment decisions, and thus to raise long-run productivity. Without reasonably efficient markets, we are all doomed to poverty.

The dilemma, of course, is that markets often fail at tasks that society regards as important, such as poverty reduction or food price stability. Fortunately, relatively simple analytical tools and models are available that cast light on these market failures and point the way toward appropriate government interventions to solve them. Not all market failures are susceptible to successful government interventions – effective risk-sharing mechanisms would be high on the list – but historical experience demonstrates that public action against poverty and food price volatility can be effective in both the short run and the long run.

2.9 MECHANISM DESIGN

The key to effective public action is to get the 'mechanism design' right. That is, policy initiatives must worry about the incentive structures set up so that they are compatible both with respect to government budgetary and bureaucratic capacity and with respect to self-interested behavior on the part of market participants who are exposed to the results of policy changes. This may seem an arcane and theoretical point (and worthy of the Nobel Prize in Economics in 2007), but failure to think through the nature of incentives being set up by policy initiatives is almost a sure way to guarantee an unsuccessful outcome.

Equally, policy design needs to be clear on whether the initiative is meant to be a temporary palliative for the problem at hand, or a long-run cure. There is nothing wrong with palliatives, especially if they build support for longer-run approaches that solve the problem. But it is important not to confuse palliatives with cures. Thus, bridges between short-run approaches and long-run impact become the essence of successful food policy design and implementation.

These bridges will be built from 'real' policy instruments, not 'theoretical' ones. The distinction lies in understanding how realistic the assumptions are that underlie the expected behavioral responses to policy initiatives. A policy that assumes poor people have unimpeded access to financial markets to hedge risks will fail. But equally, a policy that assumes poor people will not change their consumption behavior in the face of price subsidies will also be challenged by unexpected results.

In the end, food policy initiatives must stress the importance of economic growth that includes the poor, and rising labor productivity for unskilled workers. Without these long-run economic dynamics working reasonably smoothly, food policy becomes an exercise in permanent, and expensive, palliatives.

2.10 KNOWING WHAT NOT TO DO: THE POLITICAL ECONOMY OF UNINTENDED CONSEQUENCES

Good intentions do not inevitably lead to good outcomes. The concern for appropriate mechanism design is one reflection of this potential disconnect, but that concern is primarily a technical one. A broader concern is at issue here – the potential (indeed, likely) disconnect between political rhetoric and effective public action. The problem is that political rhetoric can generate expectations that cannot be met, with subsequent loss of credibility (and hope). Since credibility is often crucial to successful implementation of government policies, especially in short-run price stabilization activities, this loss is potentially serious.

In the original *Food Policy Analysis* (Timmer et al., 1983), we tried to dodge this issue by noting in the preface that it was 'beyond the scope of this book to structure meaningfully the political issues of food policy'. Understandable as that stance may have been at the time, when the economics of food policy were also poorly developed, the intervening three decades have amply demonstrated the primacy of politics in the design and implementation of food policy, a point deepened by our new understanding of the behavioral foundations of this political primacy. Unfortunately, there is no equivalent to *Food Policy Analysis* in the political science literature, perhaps because 'all politics is local' (to quote a famous American congressional leader, Tip O'Neil).

Without clear guidelines, then, on how to implement effective food policies, the best that can be done is to review what those policies need to accomplish. A way must be found to link short-run political imperatives with long-run economic realities. Democratic societies have the best historical track record at building and maintaining this link, but the deep institutions needed for democracies to fulfill this task take time to build.

A way must be found to make markets work to deliver long-run growth. No alternative exists to organizing economies around market-based transactions if societies are to reach their goals of greater material welfare and broad political freedom. Markets produce both. But markets also fail in important social tasks. Responsible governments must find a way to prevent those failures through careful regulation and to fix them when innocent workers and consumers cannot participate in the promises of market outcomes.

Thus finding a way for governments to deliver effective and efficient safety nets as both a moral and political imperative – to allow markets to deliver on these promises – becomes the essence of policy making. Governments, like the poor, live in the short run. Their vision and strategic design for inclusive, long-run growth must survive the day-to-day challenges of managing power. 'Stability' would seem to be essential to building this bridge between short-run political imperatives and long-run performance – stability in food prices, in the macroeconomy, in the political arena. Within a reasonably stable environment, competitive politics then offer a mechanism for the political economy of food security to meet these challenges.

NOTES

* This paper has been prepared as a chapter for the *Handbook on Food*, edited by Raghbendra Jha, Raghav Gaiha and Anil Deolalikar, to be published by Edward Elgar in 2013. It draws on a body of my own work over the past several years, much of which has been stimulated by the world food crisis in 2007–08 and follow-on events. An early version of the ideas developed here appeared as Timmer, 2012. I thank the editors for very helpful comments on an earlier draft.

1. It is useful to distinguish between 'variance' in food prices, a standard statistical measure of price movements around an average or a trend, and which often has a substantial degree of predictability because of seasonal patterns and links to storage levels, and 'volatility' in food prices, which emphasizes unforeseen spikes and crashes. Somewhat confusingly, 'instability' is often used both ways. For the arguments being made here, volatility is the important concept, and a more formal definition is not necessary.

2. Bernheim and Rangel (2005), in a review of 'behavioral public economics', stress the seriousness of the challenge from behavioral economics to mainstream welfare analysis, which is based on the principal of revealed preferences. If revealed preferences from choices about consumption, income generation, and time allocation, for example, are not 'really' what individuals prefer, as the experimental evidence from behavioral economics suggests, the normative foundations of consumer theory no longer hold. Without these foundations, such stalwarts of applied welfare analysis as consumer surplus no longer have a theoretical basis. The consequences are obvious for the arguments in this paper: models that international economists use to prove the existence of 'gains to trade' no longer hold, and theoretical arguments against stabilizing prices also disappear.

3. Of course, markets are the arena in which food prices are formed. Private sector participants, buyers and sellers, interact to produce a market price. Markets that are highly liquid, transparent, with many participants, tend to have more stable prices than thin, opaque markets with only a handful of buyers or sellers. Clearly, investments by the private sector in market development can help stabilize prices over the long term, but these investments never have price stability as their objective, and consumers have no mechanism for directing these investments toward that goal. The classic analysis of this conundrum is Newbery and Stiglitz (1981), with Timmer (1986, 1989) providing a rejoinder in terms of appropriate government interactions on behalf of stabilizing food prices.

4. It has been 30 years since *Food Policy Analysis* (Timmer et al., 1983) was published, and more than 35 years since the initial outline for the book was circulated among the authors. It is fair to say that the volume has been very influential in thinking about food policy issues since its publication, and it remains in use as a textbook for a number of university courses. Although long out of print, the volume remains available on-line: http://www.stanford.edu/group/FRI/indonesia/documents/foodpolicy/front-toc.fm.html.

5. 'Pro-poor growth' is a nebulous concept, easier to measure *ex post* than to plan for *ex ante*. But countries have planned explicit pro-poor growth development strategies and implemented them successfully. The best documented case is Indonesia (Timmer, 2004), but much of East and Southeast Asia followed rural-based, pro-poor development strategies until manufactured exports became the main engine of wage growth for unskilled labor.
6. The early standard works are Wickizer and Bennett (1941) and Barker and Herdt (with Beth Rose) (1985). This section of the chapter draws on Timmer (2009a).
7. Information on the world rice market is available at http://usda.mannlib.cornell.edu/usda/ers/89001.
8. This difference was pointed out clearly in Jasny's classic study of *Competition Among Grains* (Jasny, 1940). He justifies his exclusion of rice from the study with the following observation: 'The Orient is a world by itself, with its own climate, diet, and economic and social setup, and this makes it easy for us to omit it. The inclusion of rice would mean the discussion of two worlds. The writer would be satisfied to have mastered one' (p. 7). The sharp difference between rice-based economies and those based on wheat or corn is also stressed by Bray (1986) and Oshima (1987).
9. The emphasis here on *destabilizing* expectations and subsequent speculative price behavior is meant to contrast with the normally *stabilizing* role that routine speculative activities play. Unless speculators buy during the harvest, store grain and sell during the short season, seasonal price movements would be much larger than they are without these normal speculative activities. Of course, seasonal prices must rise from their harvest lows to their peak just before the new harvest, or these stabilizing speculative investments would not be made. It is difficult to define precisely the difference between stabilizing and destabilizing speculation. Even agents who engage entirely in the financial derivatives of commodities, such as futures, options and swaps, can contribute to the liquidity of the underlying markets and thus help support the stabilizing function of speculation. But when herd behavior sets in and most financial speculation is in only one direction, the potential to generate bubbles and less stable prices is clear. Much more analytical and empirical work needs to be done on the role of financial instruments as they influence commodity prices in spot markets (Robles et al., 2009).
10. A workshop at FAO/Rome on 26–27 October 2009, reviewed this debate in detail. See Gilbert (2009), Jayne (2009), Gross (2009), and Dart (2009) for a variety of contrasting views, and the rapporteur's report by Sarris et al. (2009) for a synthesis of the divergent views of the participants.
11. What follows is a very brief overview of the 'fire' in the world rice market from late 2007 until mid-2008. See Slayton (2009) for a detailed analysis and chronology.
12. The prospect of more stable markets for rice from these forces was raised in Timmer (1991a).
13. It is almost amusing that Indonesia announced a ban on rice exports early in 2008, before its main rice harvest started in March. Historically, Indonesia has been the world's largest rice *importer*, surpassed only recently by the Philippines, and no one in the world rice trade was looking to Indonesia for export supplies. But there was a rationale to the announcement by the Minister of Trade – it signaled that Indonesia would not be needing imports and was thus not vulnerable to the skyrocketing prices in world markets. The calming effect on domestic rice market participants meant that little of the hoarding behavior seen in Vietnam and the Philippines was evidenced in Indonesia. *This is a clear example where government policy acted successfully to stabilize market expectations and generate the desired behavioral response.*
14. As further evidence that *psychology* was driving prices in the world rice market rather than *fundamentals*, it was the *announcement* by the Prime Minister of Japan that rice supplies would be available to the Philippines, not their actual shipment, that pricked the price bubble and started the rapid decline in rice prices. As of late-2009, Japan has actually not shipped any rice to the Philippines, or any other country seeking rice imports (Slayton, 2009).
15. See Lindert (1991) for a summary of the empirical regularities in agricultural policy that cannot be explained by standard neoclassical economics. These include a bias against both imports and exports, an urban bias in poor countries when farmers are a majority of the population, and a rural bias when urban consumers are a majority of the population.

REFERENCES

Barker, R. and R.W. Herdt (with B. Rose) (1985), *The Rice Economy of Asia*. Washington, DC: Resources for the Future.
Bernheim, B.D. and A. Rangel (2005), Behavioral public economics: welfare and policy analysis with non-standard decision-makers. NBER Working Paper No. W11518. Available at SSRN: http://ssrn.com/abstract=776006.

Bray, F. (1986), *The Rice Economies: Technology and Development in Asian Societies*. Oxford, UK: Basil Blackwell.
Brennan, M.J. (1958), The supply of storage. *American Economic Review*, **48**(1), 50–72.
Cootner, P.H. (1960), Returns to speculators: Telser vs Keynes, *Journal of Political Economy*, **68** (August), 396–404.
Cootner, P.H. (1961), Common elements in futures markets for commodities and bonds. *American Economic Review*, **31** (May), 173–83.
Dart, S. (2009), Financial speculators and commodity market instability. Paper presented to the Experts' Meeting on Institutions and Policies to Manage Global Market Risks and Price Spikes in Basic Food Commodities by the FAO Trade and Markets Division, 26–27 October 2009 at FAO Headquarters, Rome.
Duflo, E., M. Kremer and J. Robinson (2008), How high are rates of return to fertilizer? Evidence from field experiments in Kenya, *American Economic Review: Papers and Proceedings*, **98**(2), 482–88.
Fogel, R.W. (1991), The conquest of high mortality and hunger in Europe and America: timing and mechanisms. In P. Higonnet, D.S. Landes and H. Rosovsky (eds), *Favorites of Fortune: Technology, Growth, and Economic Development since the Industrial Revolution*. Cambridge, MA: Harvard University Press, pp. 35–71.
Fogel, R.W. (1994), Economic growth, population theory, and physiology: the bearing of long-term processes on the making of economic policy [Nobel Prize Lecture], *American Economic Review*, **84**(3) (June), 369–95.
Gilbert, C. (2009), Understanding spikes and speculation in agricultural commodity markets. Paper presented to the Experts' Meeting on Institutions and Policies to Manage Global Market Risks and Price Spikes in Basic Food Commodities by the FAO Trade and Markets Division, 26–27 October 2009 at FAO Headquarters, Rome.
Gross, A. (2009), The role of agricultural commodity exchanges in market price volatility in developing countries. Paper presented to the Experts' Meeting on Institutions and Policies to Manage Global Market Risks and Price Spikes in Basic Food Commodities by the FAO Trade and Markets Division, 26–27 October 2009 at FAO Headquarters, Rome.
Houthakker, H. (1987), Futures trading. In J. Eatwell, M. Milgate and P. Newman (eds), *The New Palgrave: A Dictionary of Economics, Volume 2*. London, UK: Macmillan Press Ltd, pp. 447–49.
IFPRI (2008), High food prices: the what, who, and how of proposed policy actions. Washington, DC: International Food Policy Research Institute, May.
Jasny, N. (1940), *Competition Among Grains*. Stanford University, CA: Food Research Institute.
Jayne, T. (2009), Market failures and food price spikes in Southern Africa. Paper presented to the Experts' Meeting on Institutions and Policies to Manage Global Market Risks and Price Spikes in Basic Food Commodities by the FAO Trade and Markets Division, 26–27 October 2009 at FAO Headquarters, Rome.
Kahneman, D. and A. Tversky (1979), Prospect theory: an analysis of decision under risk. *Econometrica*, **47**, 269–91.
Kaldor, N. (1939), Speculation and economic stability. *Review of Economic Studies*, **VII** (October), 1–27.
Keynes, J.M. (1936), *The General Theory of Employment, Interest, and Money*. New York, NY: Harcourt Brace Publishing.
Lindert, P.H. (1991), Historical patterns of agricultural policy. In C.P. Timmer (ed.), *Agriculture and the State: Growth, Employment and Poverty in Developing Countries*. Ithaca, NY: Cornell University Press, pp. 29–83.
Mallaby, Sebastian (2008), Rice and baloney: irrational policies the world over are making the food crisis worse. *The Washington Post*, A–17 (18 May).
Newbery, D.M.G. and J.E. Stiglitz (1981), *The Theory of Commodity Price Stabilization: A Study in the Economics of Risk*. Oxford: Clarendon Press.
Oshima, H.T. (1987), *Economic Growth in Monsoon Asia: A Comparative Study*. Tokyo, Japan: University of Tokyo Press.
Reardon, T., B. Minten and K.Z. Chen (2012), *The Quiet Revolution in Staple Food Value Chains in Asia: Enter the Dragon, the Elephant, and the Tiger*. Manila: Asian Development Bank.
Robles, M., M. Torero and J. von Braun (2009), When speculation matters. IFPRI Issue Brief 57 (February), International Food Policy Research Institute, Washington DC.
Sarris, A., A.A. Gurkan and R.W. Cummings, Jr (2009), Conclusions and the way forward. Paper presented to the Experts' Meeting on Institutions and Policies to Manage Global Market Risks and Price Spikes in Basic Food Commodities by the FAO Trade and Markets Division, 26–27 October 2009 at FAO Headquarters, Rome.
Slayton, T. (2009), Rice crisis forensics: how Asian governments carelessly set the world rice market on fire. Working Paper No. 163, Center for Global Development, Washington DC.

Slayton, T. and C.P. Timmer (2008), Japan, China and Thailand can solve the rice crisis – but US leadership is needed. CGD Notes (May), Center for Global Development, Washington DC.

Telser, L.G. (1958), Futures trading and the storage of cotton and wheat. *Journal of Political Economy*, **66** (June), 233–55.

Thaler, R. and S. Benartzi (2004), Save more tomorrow: using behavioral economics to increase employee saving. *Journal of Political Economy*, **112**(1), S164–187.

Timmer, C. Peter (1986), *Getting Prices Right: The Scope and Limits of Agricultural Price Policy*. Ithaca, NY: Cornell University Press.

Timmer, C.P. (ed.) (1987), *The Corn Economy of Indonesia*. Ithaca, NY: Cornell University Press.

Timmer, C.P. (1989), Food price policy: the rationale for government intervention. *Food Policy*, **14**(1) (February), 17–27.

Timmer, C.P. (1991a), Food price stabilization: rationale, design, and implementation. in D.H. Perkins and M. Roemer (eds), *Reforming Economic Systems*. Cambridge, MA: Harvard Institute for International Development, Harvard University, pp. 219–48.

Timmer, C.P. (ed.) (1991b), *Agriculture and the State: Growth, Employment, and Poverty in Developing Countries*. Ithaca, NY: Cornell University Press.

Timmer, C.P. (1996), Does BULOG stabilize rice prices in Indonesia? Should it try? *Bulletin of Indonesian Economic Studies* (Canberra), **32**(2) (August), 45–74.

Timmer, C.P. (2004), The road to pro-poor growth: Indonesia's experience in regional perspective. *Bulletin of Indonesian Economic Studies*, **40**(2) (August), 177–207.

Timmer, C.P. (2005a), Food security and economic growth: an Asian perspective. H.W. Arndt Memorial Lecture, Australian National University, Canberra (November 22). *Asian-Pacific Economic Literature*, **19**, 1–17.

Timmer, C.P. (2005b), Agriculture and pro-poor growth: an Asian perspective. Working Paper No. 63, Center for Global Development, Washington DC.

Timmer, C.P. (2009a), Rice price formation in the short run and the long run: the role of market structure in explaining volatility. Center for Global Development Working Paper 172, May, 1–46.

Timmer, C.P. (2009b), *A World Without Agriculture: The Structural Transformation in Historical Perspective*, Wendt Memorial Lecture. Washington DC: American Enterprise Institute.

Timmer, C.P. (2009c), Reflections on food crises past: Viewpoint. *Food Policy*, online 17 October at http://dx.doi.org/10.1016/j.foodpol.2009.09.002.

Timmer, C.P. (2009d), Preventing food crises using a food policy approach. *Journal of Nutrition. Supplement: The Impact of Climate Change, the Economic Crisis, and the Increase in Food Prices on Malnutrition*, November, pp. S1–S5.

Timmer, C.P. (2009e), Management of rice reserve stocks in Asia: Analytical issues and country experiences. Paper presented to the Experts' Meeting on Institutions and Policies to Manage Global Market Risks and Price Spikes in Basic Food Commodities by the FAO Trade and Markets Division, 26–27 October 2009 at FAO Headquarters, Rome.

Timmer, C.P. (2012), Behavioral dimensions of food security. *Proceedings of the National Academy of Sciences (PNAS), Agricultural Development and Nutrition Security* Special Feature, 31 July 2012, **109**(31), 12315–12320.

Timmer, C.P. and W.P. Falcon (1975), The political economy of rice production and trade in Asia. In L.G. Reynolds (ed.), *Agriculture in Development Theory*, New Haven, CT: Yale University Press, pp. 373–408.

Timmer, C.P., W.P. Falcon and S.R. Pearson (1983), *Food Policy Analysis*. Baltimore, MD: Johns Hopkins University Press for the World Bank. Available at: http://www.stanford.edu/group/FRI/indonesia/documents/foodpolicy/fronttoc.fm.html.

Timmer, C.P. and D. Dawe (2007), Managing food price instability in Asia: a macro food security perspective. *Asian Economic Journal*, **21**(1) (March), 1–18.

Tversky, A. and D. Kahneman (1986), Rational choice and the framing of decisions. *Journal of Business*, **59**(4), 5251–5278.

USDA (United States Department of Agriculture) (1996), The US contribution to world food security. The US position paper prepared for the World Food Summit, United States Department of Agriculture, Washington DC, 3 July.

Webb, P. and S. Block (2012), Transition trade-offs: underweight and obesity in the structural transformation of developing economies. *Proceedings of the National Academy of Sciences (PNAS)*, Agricultural Development and Nutrition Security Special Feature, 31 July, **109**(31), 12309–12314.

Weymar, F.H. (1968), *The Dynamics of the World Cocoa Market*. Cambridge, MA: MIT Press.

Wickizer, V.D. and M.K. Bennett (1941), *The Rice Economy of Monsoon Asia*. Stanford, CA: Food Research Institute, Stanford University, in cooperation with the Institute of Pacific Relations.

Williams, J.C., and B.D. Wright (1991), *Storage and Commodity Markets*. Cambridge: Cambridge University Press.

Working, H. (1933), Price relations between July and September wheat futures at Chicago since 1885. *Wheat Studies*, **9** (March), 187–238.
Working, H. (1948), Theory of the inverse carrying charge in futures markets. *Journal of Farm Economics*, **30** (February), 1–28.
Working, H. (1949), The theory of the price of storage. *American Economic Review*, **31** (December), 1254–1262.
World Bank (2005), *Managing Food Price Risks and Instability in an Environment of Market Liberalization*, Washington DC: Agriculture and Rural Development Department Report No. 32727–GLB.

3. Shocks to the system: monitoring food security in a volatile world

Derek Headey, Olivier Ecker and Jean-Francois Trinh Tan

3.1 INTRODUCTION

The 2007–08 food crisis revealed a number of flaws in the global food system, including our ability to monitor the welfare impacts of rising food prices, or other economic shocks for that matter. Early on in the crisis, economists resorted to simulation models to predict the impacts of higher food prices on poverty, following Deaton's (1989) net benefit ratio approach. These partial simulation analyses predicted very negative impacts of higher food prices on poverty (e.g. Dessus et al., 2008; Ivanic and Martin, 2008; de Hoyos and Medvedev, 2009), though subsequent surveys showed that – at the global level, at least – poverty and subjective food insecurity both fell (Headey, 2013). Whilst the discrepancy between simulation models and historical data can be reconciled – particularly by the surprisingly strong economic growth in the developing world – the fundamental inability of existing monitoring systems to gauge short-run changes in food insecurity is clearly of some concern. In addition to the persistence of high and volatile food prices, a weak global economy leaves many developing countries vulnerable to recession, and large scale natural disasters may well becoming increasingly common with the onset of climate change (IPCC, 2012). In short, developing countries are highly exposed to shocks, but our ability to gauge the welfare impacts of these shocks is quite limited (Headey and Ecker, 2013).

This chapter will therefore review a relevant sparse literature on the theory and measurement of food security in the context of major economic shocks. We adopt a standard definition of food security as existing 'when all people, at all times, have physical, social, and economic access to sufficient, safe, and nutritious food to meet their dietary needs and food preferences for an active and healthy life' (FAO, 1996: par. 1). In practice, food security is measured by a wide range of indicators, though these can be classed into various types, such as those pertaining to calorie consumption, poverty, dietary diversity, nutritional outcomes and self-reporting (subjective or experiential) indicators. We also note that a related concept to food security is nutrition security. A key difference between the two concepts is that nutrition outcomes are significantly influence by health factors and child care practices. Moreover, nutrition security understandably tends to focus more emphasis on the welfare of young children and mothers, given the well-established hypothesis that growth faltering typically occurs in the first 'thousand days' of life (Victora et al., 2009). Despite a clear distinction between health and nutrition security, the intricate interactions between food, health and nutrition mean that nutritional monitoring is highly relevant to the issue at hand.

In terms of 'major economic shocks', our review of the literature obviously focuses on food price spikes – particularly the 2007–08 crisis and subsequent price hikes – but since that literature is rather sparse we extend our review to research on other major economic shocks, particularly the Indonesian financial crisis of 1998. That crisis is relevant both for the nature of the crisis (possessing elements of both a food price crisis and a financial crisis), but also because it remains probably the most surveyed crisis in economic history.

Our ultimate objective goes beyond assessing the state of the existing literature, however. First, we have the ambitious objective of trying to improve our understanding of how economic shocks (or different types of shocks) affect economic welfare. There are tremendous complexities in doing so, which are discussed in Sections 3.2 and 3.3. Section 3.2 provides a conceptual discussion of how we might expect households to respond to major economic shocks. Section 3.3 focuses on simulation analyses of food price changes and some of the question marks surrounding their key assumptions.

A second and quite related objective is to understand which food security indicators are most valid (relevant) and reliable in gauging the impacts of shocks. This is also a difficult task, particularly given the lack of high-frequency data. Though we believe our review of survey-based monitoring of food security during shocks (in Section 3.4) does provide some tentative conclusions on this front.

And finally, our concluding section has the objective of outlining some means of improving food security measurement, based on the findings under the first and second objectives. As others have noted (e.g. Barrett, 2010), crises bring opportunities as well as threats. The food price crises of 2007–08 and 2011–12 have refocused attention on food security issues, which suggests that there is a political opportunity to improve the measurement of food security. So our concluding remarks discuss how that opportunity might best be seized.

3.2 THEORETICAL CONSIDERATIONS ON THE BEHAVIORAL RESPONSE TO ECONOMIC SHOCKS

Before delving into the empirics of food security measurement during shocks, it behooves us to step back and consider theoretical issues regarding behavioral responses to shocks. Specifically, we focus on the nature of shocks, economic supply and demand issues, and coping behaviors more generally.

3.2.1 Food Crises

A food crisis might be defined as any situation which threatens the food security of a sizeable share of the population (as opposed to idiosyncratic shocks to the household). The underlying shock from which this threat emerges, however, could take many different forms and play out in many different ways. Traditional concerns in developing countries have largely focused on shocks to agricultural production, such as droughts, floods or pestilence, though in many countries even seasonal shortfalls are a perennial concern. While such shocks appear to be related to availability, Sen (1982) famously showed that the real problem in such situations was not typically a lack of food, but a lack of access to food. In other words, shortfalls in availability translated into sharp price increases, which reduced the affordability of food for the poor. Thus, from a certain perspective, even natural disasters share a common characteristic to food inflation induced by international price hikes, though the impacts on farming households (i.e. the producers of food) may be quite different, since they will often benefit from higher international prices. A second implication is that the change in real food prices can be a good indicator of the size of a shock, particularly in the absence of reliable and timely data on production shortfalls. However, it certainly cannot always be assumed that food price changes are a sufficient indicator of the size of a shock, particularly in major economic downturns wherein wages may be decreasing and unemployment increasing. Indonesia's economic crisis is a case in point, since unemployment rose sharply in addition to the large hike in food prices. Furthermore, food price changes may partially be anticipated in the run-up of a foreseeable food crisis (such as after consecutive droughts), so that price changes do not fully reflect the size of the shock.

In addition to the source of a food crisis, we note that timing matters. Some economic shocks are extremely sudden. Indonesia's economic crisis in 1998 was effectively initiated by the devaluation of the rupiah, which led to huge domestic price changes over a matter of days and weeks. The 2007–08 food crisis involved a more gradual increase in real food prices over 2006 and 2007, and then a sharp acceleration in 2008. Despite this acceleration, it seems likely that the price increases in previous years allowed for some supply response, since global food production in 2008 was indeed markedly higher than previous years (Headey et al., 2010). The duration of a crisis also has implications for coping behavior on the demand side. A household may be able to ride out a month or two of much higher prices (for example, by depleting stocks), but 6 months of higher prices may exhaust all available coping mechanisms.

In summary, food crises can differ in terms of their underlying causes, their general severity, and the speed of their onset and duration of their existence. These somewhat trivial observations nevertheless have important implications for behavioral responses during crises and for the measurement of food security. For example, sudden onset crises may greatly limit the scope for adjustment, thus precluding coping behaviors that might be available in other settings. Similarly, sudden onset crises may require either regular high frequency surveys, or survey procedures that can be implemented very quickly.

3.2.2 Economic Theories of Consumer Behavior

Standard economic theories of consumer behavior in response to shocks largely focus on the theory of demand, or the utility (revealed preference) framework. In a static framework in which no major livelihood adjustments are possible, the impact of real price changes (including income or wage changes) influences households according to their net benefit ratio, the distribution of price changes (which prices change and by how much in relative terms), and the various elasticities of demand (own-price, cross-price and income elasticities).

As long as they are accurately estimated, these elasticities may well describe various coping behaviors. For example, one issue we will return to again is the notion that, in the face of large price increases in staple foods, people actually tend to concentrate consumption more on staple foods, and less on higher value foods, and they tend to substitute more expensive staple foods with cheaper ones of lower quality. This result is plausibly explained in conventional demand terms as the result of own-price and income elasticities of demand for staple foods, and much higher own-price and income elasticities of demand for non-staple foods and high-quality staple foods.[1] Cross-price elasticities can also describe coping behaviors. For example, in times of low prices poor people may prefer wheat and rice (which are often imported) to coarser grains (e.g. maize) or other local staples (e.g. cassava, sorghum, plantain), and high-quality to low-quality staple food varieties/types (e.g. long-grain to short-grain, polished to non-polished rice). But when prices increase they switch back to cheaper sources of calories and to local varieties for which prices tend not to increase as sharply. Arguably one further explanation of consumption patterns during food crises is that many poor people at least produce and store some of their own food. Thus when food prices increase, they may rely more on own-consumption than on market purchases, which further influences the pattern of dietary changes during food crises.

One implication of the analysis above is that calorie consumption alone may be a poor indicator of changes in food security, since dietary diversity is the more reactive measure when consumers are switching from higher value foods to ever more basic staples. However, one could go even further and argue that total expenditure is a more comprehensive measure of possible changes in consumption and consumption patterns. For example, a fall in education expenditure or enrollment might also be a relevant means of maintaining food intake in the face of price increases.

3.2.3 Theory and Evidence on Coping Mechanisms

One implication of the points made above is that simulation analyses – such as those following the net-benefit ratio approach – may be quite accurate in gauging the welfare impacts of higher prices, provided that the elasticities in question are accurately estimated.[2] Though, the literature on coping behaviors suggests that households may use other means to minimize the adverse impacts of shocks, not all of which are adequately identified by demand elasticities. Such behaviors typically include things like working longer hours, reallocating labor between farm and nonfarm activities, withdrawing children from school, temporary migration, cutting-down on meal sizes or frequency and selling off household assets (Corbett, 1988; Dercon, 2002; Skoufias, 2003a). These coping behaviors raise important questions for all indicators of food and nutrition security: To what extent is food security maintained at the expense of education, health or childcare practices? And, to what extent are coping behaviors location- or context-specific?

3.3 SIMULATION APPROACHES TO GAUGING THE IMPACTS OF FOOD AND FINANCIAL CRISES

In the 2007–08 food crisis the first research on the impacts of the crisis relied on simulation analyses, most of which adopted Deaton's (1989) net benefit approach to estimate the impacts on household expenditure and poverty. A second approach adopted by the USDA (and indirectly by FAO) used a global trade model to estimate the impacts of higher food prices on calorie deprivation (Shapouri et al., 2009). In this section we review both of these approaches, before discussing some of their weaknesses.

3.3.1 Calorie Deprivation Simulations

For many years now, the FAO has principally monitoring global food insecurity – or 'hunger' – by estimating the proportion of national populations that do not achieve minimum calorie requirements. This approach has long been criticized for a number of reasons beyond the scope of the current chapter (Smith 1998; Svedberg, 1999, 2002; Gabbert and Weikard 2001; Nube 2001; FAO, 2002). However, one pertinent issue at hand is that the FAO approach did not allow for estimating the impacts of the shocks in 2007–08 because of delays in data collection. Hence they relied on a USDA trade model (Shapouri et al., 2009) for low-income countries to derive some basic estimates of changes in hunger. The USDA uses cross-country elasticities of per capita income with respect to per capita calorie availability (calculated from the FAO food balance sheets), along with income distribution data from the World Bank. It then incorporates these elasticities into a partial equilibrium global trade and production model that includes elements like a food demand function. However, the model is still weak on the food access dimension, with no incorporation of domestic food inflation. Moreover, as the authors of the USDA report note, if countries draw down on stocks or receive more food aid, then the model may underestimate food availability (Shapouri et al., 2009).[3] As for estimating the impacts of the financial crisis following the 2007–08 food crisis USDA based these on International Monetary Fund (IMF) projections from February 2009 on lost growth in export earnings and capital inflows for 2009. A 'lost exports' scenario puts the increase in hunger at 63 million people, while the 'lost exports plus lost capital flow' model puts it even higher at 97 million. Such large numbers are mainly driven by the fact that early IMF estimates projected that Asian countries would suffer most from lost export earnings and capital inflows because their baseline growth in these indicators was so strong. So Asia accounts for about half of the 97 million additional hungry people, for example. In retrospect, these IMF projections were too bleak for Asia. Indeed, updated USDA (2011) estimates of food consumption for 2007–08 and 2008–09 show that, relative to 2005–06, food consumption was at the same level or higher in all Asian regions, with only a very slight decline of −0.7 percent in rice consumption in East Asia (Table 3.1).[4]

We would cautiously argue that these hunger models are at least far too crude to reliably predict the impact of access shocks, such as a rise in international food prices.[5] The results of the USDA model also seem to contradict USDA data on consumption trends, reported in Table 3.1. These data show that cereal availability for food consumption did not decline substantially in any Asian region. Overall, then, Table 3.1 does not suggest that there was a major food availability shock in any populous region. Similar trends were observed in the Asian financial crisis of 1998 (FAO, 2002), which raises concerns about whether indicators focused on food availability and calorie availability specifically are well suited to gauging the impacts of shocks. As we will outline in Section 3.4, FAO data on the Indonesian financial crisis in 1998 actually seem consistent with household survey data, since both show that there was no observable decline in calorie consumption. Instead, there were increases in poverty and reductions in dietary diversity.

Table 3.1 *Availability of major cereals in 2007–08 and 2008–09 relative to 2005–06 (percentage change)*

Region	Maize		Wheat		Rice		Any major declines?
	2007–08	2008–09	2007–08	2008–09	2007–08	2008–09	
Caribbean	1.1%	0.9%	7.7%	1.4%	10.0%	3.6%	no
Central America	13.4%	13.4%	−3.0%	−3.3%	3.3%	5.2%	wheat only
South America	4.8%	9.6%	2.3%	2.7%	0.6%	4.6%	no
East Asia	16.3%	18.5%	−0.1%	−0.5%	−0.7%	3.6%	no
South Asia	−4.7%	10.8%	9.6%	4.8%	6.6%	8.0%	maize only
Southeast Asia	12.5%	20.8%	3.6%	4.5%	5.1%	4.5%	wheat only
Sub-Saharan Africa	5.0%	16.3%	−11.0%	3.8%	5.2%	10.5%	wheat only
North Africa	15.0%	30.0%	6.0%	9.7%	1.7%	15.6%	no
Middle East	9.2%	9.2%	1.4%	3.4%	−1.1%	2.7%	no
Former USSR	5.7%	11.7%	−0.4%	0.1%	−2.4%	−6.7%	rice only
Other Europe	−4.1%	−4.1%	−4.6%	−5.5%	16.2%	6.8%	maize and wheat
European Union	−10.3%	0.7%	−0.7%	3.0%	20.1%	10.3%	maize only
North America*	40.0%	56.4%	1.9%	1.1%	4.5%	5.5%	no

Notes:
Data generally run from July in year t to June in year $t + 1$. Note that all data are aggregate.
* In the case of maize and wheat we have used non-feed consumption data, which includes industrial uses such as biofuels. This explains the sharp increase in North American maize consumption.

Source: USDA (2011).

3.3.2 Poverty/Expenditure Simulations

Are poverty and expenditure simulation techniques any better? A number of studies followed Deaton (1989) in estimating changes in household disposable income as a function of whether a household is a net consumer or net producer of food. In this approach the estimated change in welfare is a function of the net benefit ratio (NBR) and the change in prices (ΔP):

$$\Delta W_{Food} = \Delta P_{Food} * NBR_{Food} = \Delta P_{Food} * (Y_{Food} / Y_{total} - C_{Food} / C_{total}),$$

where Y_{Food} / Y_{total} is the ratio of food sales and own-production to total household monetary income, and $CR = C_{Food} / C_{total}$ is the ratio of food expenditure and own-consumption to total household expenditure. Notice that, by definition, own-production equals own-consumption, and because each enters into Y_{Food} / Y_{total} and C_{Food} / C_{total}, respectively, the consumption of food produced by the household is netted out of the NBR. Prior to the 2008 food crisis, there were relatively few applications of this approach to the analysis of food crises, with Friedman and Levinsohn's (2002) study of the Indonesian financial crisis being a prominent exception. Since 2008, however, a plethora of studies have emerged. Ivanic and Martin (2008) conducted an analysis for nine developing countries, and Zezza et al. (2008) for 11 countries, while Dessus et al.

(2008) and de Hoyos and Medvedev (2009) conducted an analysis for 73 developing countries. More recently, Ivanic et al. (2011) studied the poverty impacts of the price changes in 2010–11 for 28 countries. While the two 73-country studies are certainly quite comprehensive, Dessus et al. (2008) covered only urban areas, and de Hoyos and Medvedev's (2009) coverage of rural areas was based on an imputation of rural nonfarm income shares for the majority of their sample. Moreover, the datasets of both studies still excluded China (which has 25 percent of the developing world's population), so coverage was still not truly global.

These caveats aside, a consistent result from these studies is that the vast majority of countries analysed are estimated to see increases in poverty when real food prices increase. At the global scale, the largest impact was estimated by de Hoyos and Medvedev (2009), with an additional 155 million people thrown into poverty by higher food prices. The main results of these studies are summarized in Table 3.2, along with various details of the data and methods, including a quick review of strengths and weaknesses of the analyses.

Given the grim prognostications made by these studies, it is important to consider their relative strengths and weaknesses. First, a general strength of this approach is that at least it starts to bring in some microeconomic foundations, though the papers in question vary in the extent to which they do so. But certainly the distinction between net food consumers and producers is a useful one, as is the potential incorporation of food substitution, wage adjustments and changes in non-food prices. Nonetheless, household surveys also offer important policy-relevant insights on which types of households are affected most: rural–urban discrepancies; vulnerability of smallholder farmers and female-headed households; and so on. Second, these estimates can be produced relatively quickly from the net benefit approach provided the data are ready. Indeed, further improvements in the collection of houschold surveys – particularly in agricultural modules through the Living Standards Measurement Surveys–Integrated Surveys on Agriculture (LSMS–ISA) project led by the World Bank – will further expand the capacity of these models to yield timely predictions about the impacts of economic shocks.

Bearing these strengths in mind, there are also important limitations of the net benefit-based models, as pointed out by Headey and Fan (2008, 2010). First, they expressed some skepticism related to the predominant finding of the simulations that higher food prices raise rural poverty. For example, many rural nonfarm activities relate directly to the processing, transporting or sale of food, and there is a large literature showing strong effects of farm-based economic growth on rural nonfarm incomes (Haggblade et al., 2007). This suggests that first-round effects on farm incomes, even if accrued to the non-poor, could have beneficial spillover effects on farm and nonfarm wages, which could well accrue to the poor. The evidence on wage adjustments to higher food prices is limited, however, with some papers only discerning an adjustment in the long run, but others finding some impact in the short run (see Headey and Ecker, 2013, for a review). Ivanic and Martin (2008) partly allowed for some wage effects through a partial equilibrium adjustment, but the majority of partial equilibrium simulation approaches do not incorporate these more indirect causal pathways.

Headey and Fan (2010) also suggested that household surveys may overestimate net food consumption given recall biases. For example, production and consumption

Table 3.2 Overview of cross-country studies on the effects of rising food prices in recent food crises

Source	Sample	Scope	Assumed price shocks	Impacts of price shocks*	Strengths	Limitations
Ivanic and Martin, 2008	9 LDCs from several regions	Rural and urban areas	1. 10% 2. 20% 3. real world price shocks between 2005 and 2007	Poverty declines in two LDCs and increases in seven, including all three African countries from a 25% price increase.	The study was produced very quickly (April 2008) in response to high demand. The study adjusted for wage impacts as a robustness test.	The study does not model demand elasticities or supply responses. The extrapolation to the global sample is questionable.
Wodon et al., 2008	12 West African LDCs	Consumers and producers	1. 25% increase 2. 50% increase	Poverty increases in all cases (but varies a lot) from a 25% price increase.	As above.	As above, but a more limited number of food items are considered. Wage adjustments are not considered.
Dessus, Herrera and de Hoyos, 2008	73 LDCs	urban areas	1. 10% increase 3. 20% increase 4. 30% increase	20 countries are found to be vulnerable, with an average increase in poverty of 4.5 percentage points from a 25% price increase.	As above, but the study covers a large number of countries.	The study only examines urban areas, assumes that food expenditure shares and food/nonfood price elasticities are the same in all countries. It does not model sophisticated demand or supply responses.

Study	Countries	Area	Price data	Results	Strengths	Weaknesses
de Hoyos and Medvedev, 2011	73 LDCs	Rural and urban areas	Observed increases in relative food inflation from Jan. 2005 to Dec. 2007	Poverty increases by about 2.4 percentage points, or 155.6 million people, with East Asia (113.5 m) and South Asia (27.7 m) accounting for the majority.	The first study that covers rural and urban areas in a large number of countries. Unlike most previous studies, it uses observed price changes rather than assumed price changes.	The analysis required imputation of food expenditure shares and agricultural income shares for most of the sample.
Ivanic, Martin and Zaman, 2011	28 LDCs	Rural and urban areas	A combination of observed price increases and estimated price increases	Poverty increases by about 0.8 percentage points, or 44 million people, using an extrapolation to the global level.	The study incorporates more detailed price changes than previous studies, including changes in cash crop prices. It also models substitution effects.	The study does not include wage adjustments. Some of the found price impacts are unintuitive, such as a substantial poverty impact of higher sugar prices. The extrapolation to the global sample is questionable.

Notes:
LDCs = least-developed countries.
* For Ivanic and Martin (2008), Wodon et al. (2008), and Dessus et al. (2008), we report the price shocks of a 25 percent price increase. The other two papers mostly use actual price data, so this issue is not relevant.

Source: Constructed by the authors.

questions cover different recall periods (such as 1 year versus 1 week, respectively). This creates the potential for a bias rather than just random error. For example, longer recall periods of production could lead to underreporting of food production, while a shorter recall period for consumption could fail to pick up food received in kind. Recent work has found that the method of estimating food consumption has significant impacts on estimates (Beegle et al., 2012b), suggesting that estimation of net food consumers versus producers could indeed be biased by differences in the consumption and production modules of household surveys. However, analogous work on production modules did not find significant recall bias (Beegle et al., 2012a). Even so, the measurement of net benefit ratios is by no means straightforward.

Finally, virtually all of these simulation exercises asked a very specific question of their models: 'What would happen to poverty if food prices went up by a certain percent, assuming no other prices change (and all other factors stay constant, too)?' This assumption, however, is a particularly strong one in times of crises, and, additionally, the adopted perspective itself limits the relevance of simulation tools to pure food security monitoring by ignoring potential changes in many other factors of (economic) well-being other than food prices.[6] Actually, the period from 2005 to the present has seen many other economic events. For example, non-food commodity prices were also increasing rapidly, which constituted a secondary source of inflation that may have hurt the poor in some cases (Arndt et al., 2008; Passa Orio and Wodon, 2008), but benefited them in other cases. Indeed, since most developing countries are net commodity exporters, the rapid increase in commodity prices since the mid-2000s has been a significant factor in driving economic growth in much of the developing world, including Africa. Headey (2013) shows that economic growth – particularly in the most populous developing countries – plausibly explains why recent evidence suggests that food security at the global level was not as seriously impacted by higher food prices as was first thought. This point should make us wary of interpreting simulations results as equivalent to actual monitoring exercises. The former have their uses, and certainly yield insights into causal pathways, but they are far from being a substitute for more timely survey-based monitoring mechanisms.

3.4 SURVEY BASED EVIDENCE ON THE IMPACTS OF SHOCKS

The principal reason that simulation-based approaches were so popular and useful in assessing the impacts of the 2007–08 and 2010–11 food crises was that sufficiently high-frequency survey data were simply not available. Household economic surveys, as well as demographic and health surveys, are large and expensive exercises that are typically only conducted in any given country on a 4–5 year basis. In this section we therefore explore what household surveys retrospectively have to say about the impacts of shocks. We begin with the 2007–08 food crisis, and then turn to a review of the welfare impacts of Indonesia's 1998 financial crisis, since this was a major economic shock that was unusually well surveyed. Hence it is something like a natural experiment from a methodological point of view. Finally, we look at research on other shocks, including natural disasters in various regions.

3.4.1 Survey Evidence on the 2007–08 Food Crisis

The only global study to date based on surveys carried out before, during, and after the 2007–08 food crisis and with broad country coverage is Headey's (2013) analysis of the Gallup World Poll (GWP) data. Beginning in 2005–06, Gallup started conducting relatively small but nationally representative surveys in around 150 countries, with the intention of conducting one survey per year. These surveys mostly include subjective data, including a question about experiences of hunger over the past 12 months, and another about problems affording food over the last 12 months. Headey (2013) showed that the latter indicator potentially yields valid data on trends in food insecurity, insofar as the indicator is explained by real GDP growth, with an elasticity that is commensurable to poverty-growth elasticities. However, he also raised concerns about response biases in the cross-section related to differences in reference frames. In particular, he found some evidence suggestive of an education bias, in the form of unusually high self-reported food insecurity in some countries with high education levels and relatively low monetary poverty (such as Sri Lanka). He also raised concerns about measurement error, especially in the first round of the GWP (2005–06), and particularly in China.

Bearing these caveats in mind, the spatial and temporal coverage of the GWP allowed Headey (2013) to produce the only survey-based estimates of changes in global (or near-global) food security. Somewhat controversially, these showed a reduction in subjective food insecurity at the global level over 2006–08 of around 132 million people (that is almost the total opposite of de Hoyos and Medvedev's (2009) estimate). Several sensitivity analyses also showed either a substantial decline in subjective food insecurity or, at worst, no change over 2007–08. Within this global result, however, there were large regional variations, with the bulk of the reduction in subjective food security occurring in India, such that several other regions seeing moderate increases in subjective food insecurity (see Table 3.3). Headey (2013) explained these results by suggesting that strong economic growth – particularly in some of the largest developing countries – was fueling nominal income gains that largely exceeded food price increases. Moreover, many large developing countries were able to minimize the transmission of global food price inflation into domestic markets, particularly India and China.

Despite relying on trends in subjective indicators from relatively small surveys, Headey's results were later validated to some extent by the World Bank's most recent poverty estimates, which showed declining poverty from 2005 to 2008 at the global level, and in every region. These results further suggest that rapid real income growth sufficed to offset the largely negative effects of higher food prices on poverty.

We know of only one other multi-country study on the impacts of the food crisis, namely by Sanogo (2009). This study examined changes in the food consumption score (FCS) of the World Food Programme (WFP) – an indicator of diversity and the frequency of food groups consumed within a 7-day recall period. However, the study only measured changes in the FCS in six countries, all of which were recipients of food aid, so inferences drawn from this study should not be extended to the global level. Nonetheless, the timing of the surveys was highly relevant, since all were conducted from April to August of 2008 – a period of very high food price increases, which were compared to baselines from previous years. Interestingly, the FCS proved quite responsive to food

52   Handbook on food

Table 3.3   Regional trends in self-reported food insecurity (percentage prevalence)

Developing region	# obs.	2005–06 surveys (pre-crisis)	2008 surveys (food crisis)	2009 surveys (financial crisis)
8 most populous developing countries*	8	32.7	28.0	30.6
Sub-Saharan Africa	14	55.8	54.6	57.2
West Africa, coastal	4	48.5	51.3	58.0
West Africa, Sahel	5	59.6	49.2	55.2
Eastern and southern Africa	5	57.8	62.8	58.6
Latin America and Caribbean	15	33.2	36.4	35.7
Central America, Caribbean	7	38.4	41.4	40.3
South America	8	28.6	32.0	31.6
Middle East (including Turkey)	3	19.7	26.0	21.3
Transition countries	13	31.9	30.2	34.6
Eastern Europe	6	21.8	19.7	25.8
Central Asia	7	40.6	39.1	42.1
Asia	12	28.8	29.0	30.8
East Asia	7	30.1	30.6	32.7
South Asia	5	26.8	26.8	28.6

Note: * 'Big and fast growing' includes India, Indonesia, Brazil, Pakistan, Bangladesh, Nigeria, Mexico and Vietnam, but excludes China.

Source: Headey (2013).

price changes, as indicated in Table 3.4, summarizing Sanogo's (2009) results. In fact, dietary diversity indicators seem to be cost-effective indicators for measuring the food security impacts of shocks (Headey and Ecker, 2013), as we will also show below when looking at the 1998 Indonesian financial crisis.

3.4.2   Insights from the 1998 Indonesian Economic Crisis[7]

Given the limited survey-based evidence on the impacts of the 2007–08 food crisis, it is pertinent to examine the performance of different survey instruments and indicators in the context of other crises. Ideally we want to provide a 'fair race' between alternative indicators as gauged by their responsiveness to a common shock of sufficient magnitude. By far the best such example of a major economic shock that was widely and thoroughly surveyed was the Indonesian economic crisis of 1998.[8] While underlying economic imbalances were the deeper cause of the crisis, the proximate trigger for the crisis was the devaluation of the rupiah by 68 percent in January of 1998. That devaluation in turn caused various other ripple effects, including loss a sharp spike in food prices, loss of consumer and investor confidence and public spending cutbacks. This 'financial' crisis also coincided with a significant shock to food production in the form of the El Niño drought, with rice production falling by 8 percent in 1998. The magnitude of the economic shock is well gauged by a number of very stark statistics: GDP fell by 14 percent between 1997 and 1998, and wages fell by 36 percent in urban areas and 32 percent in rural areas (Bresciani et al., 2002).[9] The crisis was associated with rapid surges in the

Table 3.4 Summary of a six-country study on the impacts of the 2007–08 food crisis on the prevalence of food insecurity according to WFP's Food Consumption Score

Country	Shock	Period	Indicator	Outcomes (change in prevalence)
Afghanistan	Food price increase: e.g. wheat by 110% and rice by 61% from 2007 to 2008, as a result of the global crisis and drought	2007–2008	Poor food consumption	Increase by 20%
			Mean food expenditure share	Increase by 95%
Ethiopia (Addis Ababa only)	Food price increase: e.g. maize by 147%, wheat by 74% and sorghum by 133% between 2007 a 2008	Jan. 2008–July 2008	Poor food consumption	Increase from 3% to 5%
			Borderline food consumption	Increase from 9% to 22%
Liberia	Food price increase (not quantified)	Dec. 2006–June 2008	Poor food consumption	Increase from 4% to 8%
			Good food consumption	Decrease from 64% to 40%
Niger	Food price increase: e.g. rice by 18% sorghum by 17% and millet by 12%	Dec. 2007–July 2008	Poor food consumption	Increase from 18% to 36%
Pakistan	Food price increase: e.g. wheat flour by 40%	2007–2008	Poor food consumption	Increase from 23% to 28%

Note: * WFP classifies food (in)secure households into three categories according to the Food Consumption Score (FCS): households with poor food consumption (FCS <= 21), borderline food consumption (FCS = 21.5–35), and acceptable food consumption (FCS > 35) (Wiesmann et al., 2009).

Source: Sanogo's (2009) analysis of the WFP Emergency Food Security Assessment surveys.

price of food, especially a 195 percent increase in the country's key staple food, rice. Table 3.5 provides an overview of the price hikes of main foods.

Hence, the 1998 Indonesian economic crisis shared important characteristics with both the 2008 food crisis – that is large and sudden increases in staple food prices and fertilizer – and the subsequent financial crisis – that is rising unemployment and reduced wages.[10] In addition, no crisis other than the 1998 Indonesian crisis was so exhaustively studied in terms of the sheer number of surveys carried out and the wide variety of indicators used to gauge changes in food security. Major surveys carried out before, during and after the crisis include the government's National Socio-Economic Surveys (SUSENAS), two large-scale panel surveys (the Indonesian Family Life Surveys (IFLS) and the 100 Villages Surveys), and – somewhat uniquely – the high-frequency Nutrition and Health Surveillance System (NSS) surveys, which were conducted on a monthly basis. Table 3.6 summarizes the results of our literature review on the response of various food and nutrition indicators to the 1998 Indonesian economic crisis. There are four important findings that can be garnered from this synthesis.

Table 3.5 Nominal price increases of selected foods in Indonesia from January 1997 to October 1998

Food	Mean price increase (%)
Rice	195
Other staples	138
Fish	89
Meat	97
Dairy products and eggs	117
Vegetables	200
Pulses, tofu and tempeh	95
Fruits	104
Oils	122
Sugar, coffee and tea	143
Prepared food and beverages	81

Source: Friedman and Levinsohn (2002), based on SUSENAS and BPS data from urban markets in 27 provinces.

First, results for food security and nutritional outcomes are not wholly consistent across studies and generally quite sensitive to measurement issues. Specifically the high-frequency surveys of the NSS and Hartini et al.'s (2002, 2003a, b) surveys – which were repeatedly conducted before and after the start of the crisis – suggest (mostly) negative and larger impacts on food security compared to the SUSENAS, IFLS and 100 Villages Surveys. Estimates based on NSS data show that the prevalence of thinness among mothers and underweight among children under 3 years of age increased by about 3 percentage points in Central Java (de Pee et al., 2000; Block et al., 2004), while micronutrient deficiencies – particularly anemia and vitamin A deficiency among women and young children – also rose sharply (Bloem et al., 1998; Kiess et al., 2000; Block et al., 2004). Particularly striking are estimates by Block et al. (2004) that an additional 16 percent of children under 5 years of age became anemic due to the crisis.[11] The underlying cause of this appears to be sharp decreases in consumption of relatively expensive and nutritious foods – especially eggs, milk and meat (Bloem et al., 1998; Kiess et al., 2000; Hartini et al., 2003a; Block et al., 2004).

In contrast, studies based on SUSENAS data often suggest an improvement of food and nutrition security. For example, Ngwenya and Ray (2007) found that the prevalence of undernourishment (hunger) sharply declined from 1996 to 2002 by 43 percentage points in rural areas and even 62 percentage points in urban areas,[12] and Waters et al. (2004) estimated that the prevalence of underweight among children under five dropped nationwide by almost three percentage points from 1995 to 1998 and more than one percentage point to 1999. Kusnanto (2002), however, found some significant increases in underweight prevalence from 1992 to 1998 in a regional disaggregation of SUSENAS data.

Studies using data from the IFLS – the only panel survey – consistently reveal increasing poverty but mostly decreasing food and nutrition insecurity (including compensating substitution effects in household expenditure patterns). Frankenberg et al. (1999)

Table 3.6 Response of FNS indicators to the 1998 Indonesian economic crisis: summary

Data	Ref.#	Time period	Indicator	Outcomes
SUSENAS	(1)	1996–2002	Undernourishment	Decrease from 71.6% to 28.2% in rural areas and from 86.4% to 24.2% in urban areas
			Poverty	Decrease from 64.3% to 20.5% in rural areas but increase from 39.5% to 47.1% in urban areas
	(4)	1992, 1995, 1998, 1999	Underweight among children aged 0–5 years	Decrease from 37.7% to 32.6%, 29.8% and 28.5%
IFLS	(6)	1997–1998	Per capita expenditure (mean)	Decrease by 24% countrywide, 13% in rural areas and 34% in urban areas
			Expenditure patterns (mean)	In rural and urban areas, increase in total food expenditures (6–8%) and especially staple food expenditures (29–59%) particularly in urban areas, and decrease in expenditures for meat (18–22%) and non-food items including health (14–40%), education (8–24%), clothing (16–32%) and housing (15–21%), particularly in rural areas
			Poverty	Increase from 11.0% to 19.9% countrywide, from 12.4% to 23% in rural areas and from 9.2% to 15.8% in urban areas
100 Villages Survey	(8)	Aug. 1998– Dec. 1998– May 1999	Stunting among children aged 0–9 years	Decrease from 50.0% to 47.3%
			Wasting among children aged 0–9 years	Decrease from 8.4% to 5.0%
			Thinness among adults aged 18+ years (BMI<18 kg/m^2)	Increase from 13.6% to 15.4%
			Self-assessed household food shortage in preceding months	Decrease from 17.6% to 14.8% and 12.4%
NSS*	(9)	Dec. 1996– July 1998	Underweight among children aged 0–3 years	Increase from 27% to 30%
			Thinness among mothers	Increase from 14.4% to 17.4%
	(10)	Before Jan. 1996– after May 1998	Thinness among mothers	Increase from 14.9% to 17.7%
			Thinness among adolescents aged 12–15 years	No significant change

Table 3.6 (continued)

Data	Ref.#	Time period	Indicator	Outcomes
	(11)	Dec 1996–Mar.1998	Wasting among children aged 0–3 years	Significant increase in most zones
			Thinness among mothers	Significant increase in most zones
			Mothers/children who did not consume eggs/milk in the past week	Decrease
	(12)	Jun. 1996–Jun. 1998	Mothers who did not eat eggs in the past week	Increase from <1% to 7.6%
			Mothers and children who did not consume any vitamin A from retinol sources in the past 24 hours	Increase from 34–36% to 47–52%
Small-scale, cross-sectional surveys	(13)	Before Sep. 1997–after Nov. 1997	Food intake among pregnant women (mean)	In rural and urban areas, decrease in intakes of animal foods (16–61%), especially eggs (10–92%) and chicken (79–80%), particularly in urban areas. For all other food groups, reverse intake changes in rural and urban areas
	(14)	1998	Self-assessed household food insecurity and its manifestations during the past 12 months	Food insecurity or uncertainty: 94.2%Weight losses: 11%

Notes:
See Tables 3A.1–3A.4 in the Appendix for the complete overview and paper references.
Undernourishment is measured as the proportion of people with calorie consumption below 2100 kcal/day.
Child stunting, wasting and low weight is measured as proportion of children with HAZ, WHZ and WAZ below −2, respectively.
Thinness among adults and adolescents is measured as proportion of persons with BMI below 18.5 kg/m², if not specified otherwise.
* Reported results are based on data from Central Java only.

estimated that poverty increased by about 10 percentage points from 1997 to 1998 with a slightly higher increase in rural areas than urban areas, which is consistent with Poppele et al.'s (1999) findings.[13] Over the same period the prevalence of stunting and wasting among children under 9 years of age decreased by about 3 percentage points each (Frankenberg et al., 1999), and anemia prevalence dropped by almost 2 percentage points; but the prevalence of thinness among adults increased by almost 2 percentage points. The study also examined coping strategies and found that households reduced non-food expenditures, increased total food expenditures, and shifted consumption patterns from more expensive, micronutrient-rich foods to cheaper calorie-dense foods (Frankenberg et al., 1999). Accordingly an increasing number of households reported less food shortages after having faced the first shocks of the crisis. From mid-1998 to the end of 1998 the prevalence of households having experienced food shortages declined by about 3 percentage points nationwide and additionally by more than 2 percentage points to mid-1999.

A second conclusion is that the prevalence of thinness among mothers and wasting in young children seem to be good indicators for assessing the nutritional outcomes of economic shocks. The NSS studies suggest that the prevalence of mothers with low BMI and the prevalence of moderate and severe wasting among children under 3 years were responsive to the crisis. The finding on maternal thinness is further strengthened by Frankenberg et al.'s (1999) study showing slight increases in thinness prevalence among all adults. Moreover the evidence is consistent with the hypothesis that, within households, mothers buffer children's food and nutrient intakes through restricting their own food intake (Block et al., 2004). Given that child wasting is a measure of acute malnutrition, it should be particularly responsive to shocks and therefore a good crisis monitoring indicator; though the empirical evidence does not provide strong support for that. The prevalence of moderate and severe wasting and low weight – influenced by wasting – among children under 3 years significantly increased in (most of) Central Java during the rise of the crisis (Bloem et al., 1998; Block et al., 2004). Contradictory results in Frankenberg et al.'s (1999) IFLS study may be explained by the protective behavior of mothers and also by the unusual step of averaging over children aged 0–9 years. The prevalence of anemia was found to be a highly responsive indicator, but its utilization in large-scale surveys becomes costly because of the blood samples needed for detection.

Third, dietary diversity indicators seems to be much better suited than calorie availability indicators for gauging crisis impacts on food and nutrient adequacy. A stark result from several studies using different surveys (Frankenberg et al., 1999; Hartini et al., 2003a, b; Skoufias, 2003b; Ngwenya and Ray, 2007) is that in the face of much higher food prices – including price increases of rice by nearly 200 percent and other staples by nearly 140 percent, staple food consumption levels and calorie intakes were largely maintained, whilst dietary diversity declined considerably. The NSS survey-based studies, for example, showed that the consumption of eggs and milk was reduced (Bloem et al., 1998; Kiess et al., 2000) as well as the consumption of vitamin A-rich animal foods (Kiess et al., 2000). This is consistent with the findings on the 2007–08 food crisis reported by Sanogo (2009), as well as another study using high-frequency NSS data in Bangladesh (Torlesse et al., 2003). Indeed this study demonstrated that higher rice prices are not only associated with decreasing dietary diversity but also that decreased dietary diversity leads to child malnutrition.

58 *Handbook on food*

3.5 IMPLICATIONS FOR IMPROVING THE MEASUREMENT OF FOOD SECURITY

This chapter has reviewed attempts to gauge the impact of food price volatility on food security. As we noted in our introduction, improving the monitoring of food security – particularly our capacity to gauge the impacts of shocks – is an increasingly important goal given predictions of persistently high food prices, continued uncertainty in the global economy, and the potential for increased frequency of natural disasters. This review has demonstrated, however, that there are significant shortcomings in our existing capacity to gauge the impacts of these various types of shocks. In the 2007–08 food crisis the development community primarily relied on simulation analyses. As predictive tools, these simulations appear to have erred, despite their insights into the channels by which food price might influence household welfare. Of course, there may be means by which these simulation tools can be improved (namely, more surveys, better data, and more realistic assumptions in the models), but simulation techniques will probably never be an adequate substitute for real time data. How, then, can we improve the monitoring of food security for the purposes of gauging shocks? We discuss three inter-related steps that might reap substantial dividends in this regard.

3.5.1 Scaling Up and Homogenizing the Most Cost-effective Indicators

This review has clearly demonstrated that dietary diversity indicators are highly reactive to shocks, since in the presence of food inflation (including inflation of staple foods), poor people increasingly switch to cheaper and cheaper sources of calories. Some important research shows that this can have serious nutritional consequences, even if total calorie consumption is maintained. This suggests that dietary diversity indicators are well suited to gauging shocks, which is reaffirming news for the World Food Programme, as it has increasingly relied on its Food Consumption Score (FCS) to gauge food security. However, it has also been shown that dietary diversity scores are surprisingly good predictors of household calorie consumption (Ruel, 2003; Wiesmann et al., 2009), since people tend to diversify their diets once their hunger is satiated. Another benefit is that dietary diversity can be asked about individuals – such as mothers and children – which greatly enhances their nutritional relevance. In addition to these benefits, dietary diversity indicators are also relatively cheap to collect since the simplest types only entail answering yes or no to questions about the consumption of basic food types. So relative to detailed household expenditure questionnaires, they are quick to complete.

3.5.2 Better Coordination Between Agencies

Whilst many agencies measure nutrition and dietary outcomes in their surveys, there is currently little coordination in terms of the timings of surveys and in the types of variables collected. For example, although dietary diversity indicators appear to be useful measures of food security, different agencies measure dietary diversity in different ways, and no agency has yet measured dietary diversity in a manner that is clearly comparable across countries. Ideally, every developing country should have surveys every 3–5 years that cover the inter-related areas of food consumption, health and nutritional outcomes, and which measure food security in a common manner. This level of frequency and inter-agency coordination would serve multiple purposes. First, it would allow for cross-country comparisons, thus guiding development agencies in the allocation of their resources. Second, it would allow for more accurate monitoring of trends, to better differentiate countries that are achieving their development goals and countries that are lagging behind. And third, whilst this level of frequency will not typically suffice to pick up the impacts of shocks, they would at least provide a relevant baseline for 'emergency surveys' that could be mobilized when shocks do strike.

3.5.3 Scaling Up High Frequency Surveys

In this chapter we referred to some important research from high frequency surveys, particularly the nutrition surveillance systems (NSS) surveys of Indonesia (e.g. Block et al., 2004), and Bangladesh (Torlesse et al., 2003). High-frequency surveys – provided they are of sufficient quality – are the best means of gauging the impacts of shocks, including the often important effects of seasonality on food security. In Bangladesh the NSS, in fact, proved extremely useful in identifying the areas most affected by the 1998 floods. And in both Indonesia and Bangladesh we have observed that high-frequency data tells us a much richer story about the timeline of economic shocks.

That said, these kinds of high frequency surveys are not cheap. The NSS in Bangladesh is estimated to cost around US$1 million a year, but this figure could often be greater in a typical African country context with higher transportation costs. Hence, it arguably makes more sense to target high-frequency surveys in countries that are the most vulnerable to natural disasters, and most dependent on food aid and other humanitarian relief funds (Headey and Ecker, 2013).[14] Given that the WFP and other humanitarian relief agencies would be the primary beneficiaries of this kind of monitoring system, they would be natural agents for coordination and implementation, along with more technically oriented partners such as the World Bank, FAO, and national statistical agencies. In fact, the WFP has already implemented this kind of survey in a few settings, but financial constraints appear to be a significant factor in preventing the expansion of this approach. More funding – and for that essential cooperation with other partners – would therefore be needed to scale up the use of these surveys.

Despite the increased costs, we conjecture that the benefits of this system would ultimately exceed the costs by a healthy margin. Why so? First, information communication technologies (ICTs) will surely have a substantive effect in reducing the costs of data collection, and in improving the timeliness of their dissemination. The World Bank, for example, is experimenting with high-frequency surveys in South Sudan using tablets, which reduce the cost and greatly increase the timeliness of data processing. Second, the exposure of developing countries to shocks may well be increasing. Climate change research suggests that many already vulnerable regions could be much more exposed to these shocks in the future (IPCC, 2012). For example, recent climate research in the Horn of Africa suggest droughts have already become more common on the back of a much warmer India Ocean, and will continue to do so in the future (Funk et al., 2008). Yet the data that feed into the monitoring of recurrent and increasingly severe droughts in that region – including the exceptionally severe drought of 2011 – are infrequently collected and more conjectural than they need to be.[15] Highly vulnerable regions such

60   *Handbook on food*

as the Horn of Africa, to which many millions of dollars of humanitarian assistance are directed on annual basis, surely merit better monitoring of food and nutrition security.

NOTES

1. Note that the level of disaggregation of the food group classification in food demand estimations matters for detecting substitution effects (Subramanian and Deaton, 1996). For example, substitutions between different varieties/types of rice (of different quality) cannot be captured, if the food group 'rice' is not disaggregated accordingly.
2. The latter is somewhat open to debate, since most elasticities are estimated with cross-sectional data rather than panel data. Nevertheless, cross-sectional elasticities certainly demonstrate a plausible pattern of results.
3. Also critical is the fact that the USDA model pertains only to 70 low-income countries and thus excludes some huge middle-income countries, including China, Brazil and Mexico. This would appear to explain why FAO applied the proportional change in the 'global' USDA hunger figures rather than the country-level changes.
4. A variation of the USDA and FAO approaches was developed in a World Bank research paper by Tiwari and Zaman (2010). The authors estimated a cross-country Engel curve in order to quantify the amount of income needed to obtain minimum calorie requirements, estimated cumulative density functions for income, and then assumed an own-price calorie elasticity of -0.5. They then shocked the model with a food price surge and an economic growth downturn. The food price shock was an assumed food price increase (for example, 25 percent) rather than an observed one, which influenced calorie availability through the own-price elasticity. The financial crisis shock was the difference between pre-financial crisis forecast growth rates and post-financial crisis forecast growth rates. Again, we note that it has subsequently turned out that developing countries were mostly not hard hit by the financial crisis, especially China and India (IMF 2010). Moreover, the food price effect almost entirely hinged on the assumed own-price calorie elasticity of -0.5, a figure applied to the global dataset but based on estimates from only three developing countries.
5. Of the three hunger models, the USDA model is certainly the most sophisticated. It is also important to note two other features of the USDA model. First, in our view its estimates should be considered as upper-bound estimates because countries can respond to higher international food prices by altering their trade policies (for example, reducing tariffs) or by releasing stocks. Hence many countries may not import international food inflation as the model suggests. Second, USDA conducted its model relatively early on when the full impacts of the financial crisis in developing countries were estimated by the IMF to be quite dire. Re-estimating the USDA model with more recent data could well show more muted impacts on hunger.
6. Another concern relevant to some of the early simulation exercises was that they incorporated price shocks that are an assumed proportion of international price increases rather the actual price increases observed in domestic markets. (The study by de Hoyos and Medvedev (2009) is an important exception since it used domestic food inflation relative to nonfood inflation.) However, Headey and Fan (2008) and others documented large variation in domestic food inflation across countries. In addition, whether the simulated poverty increases in response to food price surges are accurate depends on whether the food supply responses are rapid and large. Although high food prices are a strong incentive for farmers to boost agricultural productivity, substantial poverty-reducing effects resulting from agricultural productivity are unlikely to be substantial in the short run, particularly in sub-Saharan Africa (Fuglie, 2011).
7. Note that we also explored research on other crises, but in addition to encountering very few studies, the survey instruments used to study these crises were less than ideal, particularly the lack of high-frequency surveys.
8. This crisis was often called a financial crisis, though this term is arguably misleading. Indeed economic imbalances and a devaluation of the currency was a principal cause of what ensued, but there was a significant weather shock and the rapid surge in food prices was not characteristic of financial crises elsewhere. We therefore prefer the broader term 'economic crisis'.
9. There were only fairly marginal increases in unemployment (though there is disagreement across sources), suggesting that wage declines were the primary means for labor markets to absorb the shock.
10. There was some controversy over the exact impact of the crisis. Initial reports on the 1998 Indonesian crisis indicated catastrophic welfare losses, whereas subsequent empirical studies tended to find more moderate impacts that were nevertheless large by any other standard (Frankenberg et al., 1999).

11. Block et al.'s (2004) prevalence estimations account for cohort effects which all other cross-sectional studies ignore.
12. There is also a discrepancy between undernourishment and poverty estimates in Ngwenya and Ray's study (2007): while undernourishment was considerably less prevalent in 2002 than in 1996 in both rural and urban areas, the prevalence of poverty increased by almost 8 percentage points in urban areas but dropped by about 44 percentage points in rural areas over the same time period.
13. Differences in the poverty estimates reported by Ngwenya and Ray (2007) and Frankenberg et al. (1999) mainly result from using different poverty lines.
14. See Barrett (2010) for a very similar argument. He tends to use the phrase 'sentinel surveys', but this is a semantic difference only.
15. In the 2011 drought in the Horn of Africa, it was estimated by major humanitarian agencies (such as UN-OCHA, WFP and USAID) that around 14 million people in four countries were in need of humanitarian assistance. In fact, it is quite difficult to ascertain how these specific numbers were obtained. However, the WFP was extremely helpful in sharing details of their methods. Specifically, they typically use Emergency Food Security Assessments (EFSA) for crisis situations, and their handbook on conducting EFSAs is available on the web (www.wfp.org/content/emergency-food-security-assessment-handbook). We were informed that EFSAs vary a lot by context in terms of being rapid or in-depth, quantitative or qualitative data, and in terms of what information is collected and what existing data are available. For example, an EFSA in Bangladesh primarily relied on focus group interviews and some collected of market price data. Interestingly, that EFSA also used some baseline data from the Bangladesh NSS. EFSAs in South Sudan and Senegal had more quantitative data, but the nature of this data varied substantially across the two countries. In South Sudan the WFP were utilizing sentinel sites, as well as a range of other household survey and census data. In Senegal a relatively small survey of 552 households was conducted in affected areas. Our perception is that this flexible approach is sensible given existing data constraints and limited resources, but our argument is that more high-frequency data could and should be collected in all but the most volatile environments. Indeed, high-frequency surveys should also be thought of as a capacity building instrument for the countries involved.

REFERENCES

Arndt, C., R. Benfica, N. Maximiano, A.M.D. Nucifora and J.T. Thurlow (2008), Higher fuel and food prices: impacts and responses for Mozambique. *Agricultural Economics*, **39** (2008 supplement), 497–511.
Barrett, C.B. (2010), Measuring food insecurity. *Science*, **327**(5967), 825–28.
Beegle, K., C. Carletto and K. Himelein (2012a), Reliability of recall in agricultural data. *Journal of Development Economics*, **98**(1), 34–41.
Beegle, K., J. De Weerdt, J. Friedman and J. Gibson (2012b), Methods of household consumption measurement through surveys: experimental results from Tanzania. *Journal of Development Economics*, **98**(1), 3–18.
Block, S.A., L. Kiess, P. Webb, S. Kosen, R. Moench-Pfanner, M.W. Bloem and C.P. Timmer (2004), Macro shocks and micro outcomes: child nutrition during Indonesia's crisis. *Economics and Human Biology*, **2**(1), 21–44.
Bloem, M., R. Tjiong, F.S. Graciano, S. Mayang and S. de Pee (1998), Nutrition and health-related issues resulting from Indonesia's crisis: summary and recommendations. Helen Keller International Special Report.
Bresciani, F., G. Feder, D.O. Gilligan, H.G. Jacoby, T. Onchan and J. Quezon (2002), Weathering the storm: the impacts of the east Asian crisis on farm households in Indonesia and Thailand. *World Bank Research Observer*, **17**(1), 1–20.
Cameron, L. (2000), The Residency Decision of Elderly Indonesians: A Nested Logit Analysis, *Demography*, **37**(1), 17–27.
Corbett, J. (1988), Famine and household coping strategies. *World Development*, **16**(9), 1099–1112.
de Hoyos, R. and D. Medvedev (2009), Poverty effects of higher food prices: a global perspective. Policy Research Working Paper No. 4887, Washington DC: The World Bank.
de Pee, S., M.W. Bloem, M. Sari, D.D. Soekarjo, R. Tjiong, S. Kosen, Muhilal and Satoto (2000), Indonesia's crisis causes considerable weight loss among mothers and adolescents. *Malaysian Journal of Nutrition*, **6**, 203–14.
Deaton, A. (1989), Rice prices and income distribution in Thailand: a non-parametric analysis. *Economic Journal*, **99**, (Conference), 1–37.
Dercon, S. (2002), Income risk, coping strategies, and safety nets. *World Bank Research Observer*, **17**(2), 141–66.

Dessus, S., S. Herrera and R. de Hoyos (2008), The impact of food inflation on urban poverty and its monetary cost: Some back-of-the-envelope calculations. *Agricultural Economics*, **39**, (Supplement), 417–129.
FAO (1996), *Declaration on World Food Security*. Proceedings of The World Food Summit. Rome: Food and Agriculture Organization.
FAO (2002), Summary of proceedings. Paper presented at Measurement and Assessment of Food Depreviation and Undernutrition, 26–28 June, Rome.
Frankenberg, E., D. Thomas and K. Beegle (1999), The real costs of Indonesia's economic crisis: preliminary findings from the Indonesia Family Life Survey. Santa Monica: RAND.
Friedman J. and J. Levinsohn (2002), The distributional impacts of Indonesia's financial crisis on household welfare: a 'rapid response' methodology. *World Bank Economic Review*, **16**(3), 397–423.
Fuglie, K.O. (2011), Agricultural productivity in sub-Saharan Africa. In D.R. Lee and M.D. Ndule (eds), *The Food and Financial Crises in Sub-Saharan Africa: Origins, Impacts and Policy Implications*. Oxford: CABI, pp. 152–53.
Funk, C., M.D. Dettinger, J.C. Michaelsen, J.P. Verdin, M.E. Brown, M. Barlow and A. Hoell (2008), Warming of the Indian Ocean threatens eastern and southern African food security but could be mitigated by agricultural development. *Proceedings of the National Academy of Sciences*, **105**(32), 11081–86.
Gabbert, S. and H.P. Weikard (2001), How widespread is undernourishment? A critique of measurement methods and new empirical results. *Food Policy*, **26**, 209–28.
Haggblade, S., P. Hazell and T. Reardon (2007), *Transforming the Rural Nonfarm Economy*. Baltimore, MD: John Hopkins University Press.
Hartini, T.N.S., A. Winkvist, L. Lindholm, H. Stenlund, A.Surjono and M. Hakimi (2002), Energy intake during economic crisis depends on initial wealth and access to rice fields: the case of pregnant Indonesian women. *Health Policy*, **61**, 57–71.
Hartini, T.N.S., A. Winkvist, L. Lindholm, H. Stenlund, V. Persson, D.S. Nurdiati and A. Surjono (2003a), Nutrient intake and iron status of urban poor and rural poor without access to rice fields are affected by the emerging economic crisis: the case of pregnant Indonesian women. *European Journal of Clinical Nutrition*, **57**, 654–66.
Hartini, T.N.S., A. Winkvist, L. Lindholm, H. Stenlund and A. Surjono (2003b), Food patterns during an economic crisis among pregnant women in Purworejo District, Central Java, Indonesia. *Food and Nutrition Bulletin*, **24**(3), 256–67.
Headey, D. (2013), The impact of the global food crisis on self-assessed food security. *World Bank Economic Review*, **27**(1), 1–27.
Headey, D. and O. Ecker (2013), Rethinking the measurement of food security: from first principles to best practice. *Food Security*, **5**(3), 327–43.
Headey, D. and S. Fan (2008), Anatomy of a crisis: the causes and consequences of surging food prices. *Agricultural Economics*, **39** (Supplement), 375–91.
Headey, D. and S. Fan (2010), *Reflections on the Global Food Crisis: How Did it Happen? How Has it Hurt? And How Can We Prevent the Next One?* Washington DC: International Food Policy Research Institute (IFPRI).
Headey, D., S. Fan and S. Malaiyandi (2010), Navigating the perfect storm: reflections on the food, energy, and financial crises. *Agricultural Economics*, **41**(s1), 217–28.
IMF (2010), *World Economic Outlook – October 2010*, Washington DC: International Monetary Fund.
IPCC (2012), *Managing the Risks of Extreme Events and Disasters to Advance Climate Change Adaptation*. Cambridge University Press, New York: Intergovernmental Panel on Climate Change.
Ivanic, M. and W. Martin (2008), Implications of higher global food prices for poverty in low-income countries. *Agricultural Economics* **39**(s1), 405–16 (supplement).
Ivanic, M., W. Martin and H. Zaman (2011), *Estimating the Short-Run Poverty Impacts of the 2010–11 Surge in Food Prices*. Policy Research Working Paper 5633, World Bank, Washington DC.
Kiess, L., R. Moench-Pfanner, M.W. Bloem, S. de Pee, M. Sari and S. Kosen (2000), New conceptual thinking about surveillance: using micronutrient status to assess the impact of economic crises on health and nutrition. *Malaysian Journal of Nutrition*, **6**, 223–32.
Kusnanto, H. (2002), Regional differences in the impact of the economic crisis and social safety net on child nutrition in Indonesia. Takemi Fellow Working Papers.
Ngwenya. E. and R. Ray (2007), Changes in Indonesian food consumption patterns and their nutritional implications. UTAS Discussion paper 2007–06, Department of Economics and Finance, University of Tasmania, Hobart.
Nube, M. (2001), Confronting dietary energy supply with anthropometry in the assessement of undernutrition prevalence at the level of countries. *World Development*, **29**(7), 1275–1289.
Passa Orio, J.C. and Q. Wodon (2008), Impact of higher food prices on cost of living: assessing multiplier effects using social accounting matrices. Mimeo, World Bank, Washington DC.
Poppele, J., S. Sumarto, and J. Pritchett (1999), *Social Impacts of the Indonesian Crisis: New Data and Policy Implications*. Jakarta: Social Monitoring and Early Response Unit.

Ruel, M. (2003), Operationalizing dietary diversity: a review of measurement issues and research priorities. *Journal of Nutrition*, **133**, 3911S–3926S.
Saadah, F., H. Waters and P. Heywood (1999), Indonesia, Undernutrition in Young Children, World bank Watching Brief, East Asia and Pacific Region No. 1.
Sanogo, I. (2009), The global food price crisis and household hunger: a review of recent food security assessments. *Humanitarian Exchange*, **42**, 8–12.
Sen, A. (1982), *Poverty and Famines: An Essay on Entitlements and Deprivation*, Oxford: Clarendon Press.
Shapouri, S., S. Rosen, B. Meade and F. Gale (2009), *Food Security Assessment, 2008–09*, Outlook Report No. GFA-20, Washington DC: United States Department of Agriculture.
Skoufias, E. (2003a), Economic crises and natural disasters: coping strategies and policy implications. *World Development*, **31**(7), 1087–1102.
Skoufias, E. (2003b), Is the calorie–income elasticity sensitive to price changes? Evidence from Indonesia. *World Development*, **31**(7), 1291–1307.
Smith, L.C. (1998), Can FAO's measure of chronic undernourishment be strengthened? *Food Policy*, **23**(5), 425–45.
Studdert, L., E. Frongillo and P. Valois (2001), Household Food Insecurity Was Prevalent in Java during Indonesia's Economic Crisis. *Journal of Nutrition*, **131**, 2685–91.
Subramanian, S. and A. Deaton (1996), The demand for food and calories. *Journal of Political Economy*, **104**(1), 133–62.
Svedberg, P. (1999), 841 million undernourished?. *World Development*, **27**(12), 2081–2098.
Svedberg, P. (2002), Undernutrition overestimated. *Economic Development and Cultural Change*, **51**(1), 5–36.
Tiwari, S. and H. Zaman (2010), The impact of economic shocks on global undernourishment. Policy Research Working Paper Series with number 5215, World Bank, Washington DC.
Torlesse, H., L. Kiess and M.W. Bloem (2003), Association of household rice expenditure with child nutritional status indicates a role for macroeconomic food policy in combating malnutrition. *The Journal of Nutrition*, **133**(5), 1320–1325.
USDA (2011), PS&D online database. Available at: http://www.fas.usda.gov/psdonline/psdQuery.aspx (accessed 4 March).
Victora, C.G., M. de Onis, P. Curi Hallal, M. Blössner and R. Shrimpton (2009), Worldwide timing of growth faltering: revisiting implications for interventions. *Pediatrics*, **2010**(125), 473–80.
Waters, H., F. Saadah, S. Surbaktiand and P. Heywood (2004), Malnutrition in Indonesian children, 1992–1999. *International Journal of Epidemiology*, **33**(3), 589–95.
Wiesmann, D., L. Bassett, T. Benson and J. Hoddinott (2009), Validation of the World Food Programme's Food Consumption Score and alternative indicators of household food security. IFPRI Discussion Paper 00870, International Food Policy Research Institute (IFPRI), Washington DC.
Wodon, Q., C.P. Tsimpo, G. Backiny-Yetna, F.A. Joseph and H. Coulombe (2008), Measuring the potential impact of higher food prices on poverty: summary evidence from West and Central Africa. Mimeo. The World Bank, Washington DC.
Zezza, A., B. Davis, C. Azzarri, K. Covarrubias, L. Tasciotti and G. Anriquez (2008), *The Impact of Rising Food Prices on the Poor*. Rome: Food and Agriculture Organization.

APPENDIX

Table 3A.1 Response of food security and nutrition indicators to the 1998 Indonesian economic crisis based on data from the Indonesian Socio-Economic Survey (SUSENAS)

Source	Ref.#	Time period	Indicator	Outcomes	Comments and conclusions
Ngwenya and Ray (2007)	(1)	1996–2002	Calorie consumption (mean) Undernourishment Poverty	Rural areas: Increase by 44% Urban areas: Increase by 80% Rural areas: Decrease from 71.6% to 28.2% Urban areas: Decrease from 86.4% to 24.2% Rural areas: Decrease from 64.3% to 20.5% Urban areas: Increase from 39.5% to 47.1%	Dietary diversity improved as a greater share of household total calorie consumption was from animal products and vegetables.
Skoufias (2003b)	(2)	Feb. 1996– Feb. 1999	Income and price elasticities	The income elasticity with respect to total calorie consumption was slightly increased. The calorie–income elasticity for cereals increased while the calorie–income elasticity for other food groups decreased.	Households substituted away from more expensive, micronutrient-rich foods towards cheaper staple foods as prices increase (which was consistent with the observed coping strategies).
Friedman and Levinsohn (2002)	(3)	1996	Compensating variations in expenditure patterns (based on simulations)	The crisis had affected all types of households, while the urban poor were hardest hit. The capacity of rural households to produce food allowed them to buffer the effects high food inflation to a certain extent.	Since the effects of the crisis on income and wages have not been considered, the total impact of the crisis cannot be adequately estimated.

Waters et al. (2004)	(4)	1992–1995–1998–1999	Underweight among children aged 0–5 years	Both sexes: Decrease from 37.7% to 32.6%, 29.8% and 28.5% Females: Decrease from 33.9% to 30.3%, 27.2% and 26.7% Males: Decrease from 41.5% to 34.9%, 32.3% and 30.1%	There have been no measurable effects of the crisis on child low weight.
Saadah et al. (1999)	(5)	1992–1998	Underweight in children aged 0–5 years	Both sexes: Decrease from 34.7% to 29.8% Females: Decrease from 30.9% to 26.9% Males: Decrease from 38.3% to 32.6% Rural areas: Decrease from 38% to 32% Urban areas: Constant at 27%	Inconsistency in the 1998 prevalence rates with Ref. (4) emerges from using different child growth reference populations. Decrease of national prevalence rates is due to decreases in rural areas.

Notes:
Data description: SUSENAS is an annual, nationally representative cross-section household survey.
Undernourishment is measured as the proportion of people with calorie consumption below 2100 kcal/day. Childlow weight is measured as proportion of children with WAZ below −2.

Table 3A.2 Response of food security and nutrition indicators to the 1998 Indonesian economic crisis based on data from the Indonesian Family Life Survey (IFLS) and the 100 Villages Survey

Source	Ref.#	Time period	Indicator	Outcomes	Comments and conclusions
Frankenberg et al. (1999)*	(6)	1997–1998	Per capita expenditure (mean)	Decrease by 24% countrywide, 13% in rural areas and 34% in urban areas	The dietary quality declined as households substitute their consumption toward more staple food and less animal products. To mitigate the crisis' impact on food consumption overall, households cut back on critical non-food expenditures such as for health, education, housing and clothing and spent more on food. Differences in poverty estimates from Ref. (1) mainly occur from different cutoff levels.
			Expenditure patterns (mean)	Rural areas: Increase in total food expenditures (6%) and especially expenditures for staples (29%) and vegetables (13%); decrease in expenditures for meat (22%), oil (8%) and dairy products (1%); decrease in all non-food expenditures, including expenditures for health (40%), clothing (32%), education (24%), housing (21%), transport (16%), household goods (12%), alcohol/tobacco (9%) and recreation (7%) Urban areas: Increase in total food expenditures (8%) and especially expenditures for staples (59%), oil (50%) and dairy products (2%); decrease in expenditures for meat (18%) and vegetables (4%); increase in expenditures for alcohol/tobacco (41%) and transport (1%); decrease in expenditures for recreation (21%), household goods (17%), clothing (16%), housing (15%), health (14%) and education (8%)	
			Poverty	Increase from 11.0% to 19.9% countrywide, from 12.4% to 23.0% in rural areas and from 9.2% to 15.8% in urban areas	

			Stunting among children aged 0–9 years	Decrease from 50.0% to 47.3%
			Wasting among children aged 0–9 years (WHZ<−1)	Decrease from 36.8% to 35.9%
			Wasting among children aged 0–9 years	Decrease from 8.4% to 5.0%
			Thinness among adults aged 18+ years (BMI<18kg/m²)	Increase from 13.6% to 15.4%
			Anemia among persons aged 1+ years (hemoglobin <12mg/dl)	Decrease from 34.8% to 30.5%
Poppele et al. (1999)**	(7)	Jul.–Aug. 1998	Expenditure patterns (mean)	Increase in food expenditures by 14% and decrease in non-food expenditures by 28%
			Poverty	Increase from 11.0% to 18.6%
Cameron (2000)**	(8)	Aug. 1998– Dec. 1998– May 1999	Self-assessed household food shortage in preceding months	Decrease from 17.6% to 14.8% and 12.4%	There was no evidence of deterioration in children's health or negative impact on children's well-being.

Notes:
Data description: The IFLS is a nationally representative household panel survey with two data collection waves per survey round; the baseline wave of the second IFLS was conducted from Aug. to Dec. 1997 and the follow-up wave from Aug. to Dec. 1998. The 100 Villages Survey is a household panel survey of villages across Indonesia with four survey rounds conducted between May 1997 and May 1998.
*, ** Based on data from the IFLS and 100 Villages Survey, respectively. Child stunting and wasting is measured as proportion of children with HAZ and WHZ below −2, respectively, if not specified otherwise.

Table 3A.3 Response of food security and nutrition indicators to the 1998 Indonesian economic crisis based on data from the Nutrition Surveillance System (NSS)

Source	Ref#	Time period	Indicator	Results	Comments and conclusions
Block et al. (2004)*	(9)	Dec. 1996–Jul. 1998	Underweight among children aged 0–3 years	Increase from 27% to 30%	Maternal anemia increased statistically significantly, too.
			Thinness among mothers	Increase from 14.4% to 17.4%	
			Anemia among children aged 0–5 years	Increase from 52% to 68%	
de Pee et al. (2000)*	(10)	Before Jan. 1996 – after May 1998	Thinness among mothers	Increase from 14.9% to 17.7%	Since mothers tend to reduce their own food intake before that of their children and husbands, maternal BMI is an early-impact
			Thinness among adolescents aged 12–15 years	No significant change among boys and girls	
Bloem et al. (1998)	(11)	Dec. 1996–Mar. 1998	Wasting among children aged 0–3 years	No increase in S. Kalimantan and S. Sulawesi. Significant increase in most zones of Central Java	Results from Central Java indicate that intake of relatively expensive, micronutrient-rich foods, maternal thinness, wasting in children aged 0–3 years and child and maternal hemoglobin concentration are responsive to the crisis.
			Thinness among mothers	No increase in S. Kalimantan and S. Sulawesi. Significant increase in most zones of Central Java	
			Mothers and children who did not eat eggs in the past week	Mothers, urban S. Kalimantan: Increase from ≈3% to ≈7%. Mothers, rural S. Sulawesi: Increase from ≈3% to ≈22%. Children, urban S. Kalimantan: Increase from ≈0% to ≈5%. Children, rural S. Sulawesi: Increase from ≈0% to ≈13%. Mothers and children, East and Central Java: Decrease (no estimates reported)	
			Mothers and children who did not drink milk in the past week	Mothers, urban S. Kalimantan: Increase from ≈18% to ≈41%. Mothers, rural S. Sulawesi: Increase from ≈38% to ≈78%	

Kiess et al. (2000)*	(12)	Jun. 1996–Jun. 1998	Anemia among non-pregnant women and children	Children, urban S. Kalimantan: Increase from ≈16% to ≈43% Children, rural S. Sulawesi: Increase from ≈40% to ≈77% Mothers and children, East and Central Java: Decrease (no estimates reported) Mothers, Central Java: Increase from ≈20% to ≈29% Children, Central Java: Increase from ≈39% to ≈65%	Anemia and vitamin A deficiency appear to be very sensitive to changes in dietary quality (unlike child anthropometrics). The authors also argue that maternal wasting (thinness) is a better indicator of food accessibility than child wasting.
			Nightblindness among mothers and children	Mothers, Central Java: Increase from ≈0.2% to ≈0.5% Children, Central Java: Increase from ≈0.08% to ≈0.21%	
			Anemia among non-pregnant women and children aged 0–2 years	Women: Increase from ≈23% to ≈29% Children: Increase from ≈52% to ≈70%	
			Nightblindness among mothers and children aged 18–35 months	Mothers: Increase from ≈0.15% to ≈0.27% Children: Increase from ≈0% to ≈0.05%	
			Mothers who did not eat eggs in the past week	Increase from <1% to 7.6%	
			Mothers and children who did not consume any vitamin A from retinol sources in the past 24 hours	Mothers: Increase from 34% to 52% Children: Increase from 36% to 47%	

Notes:
Data description: NSS is a high-frequency, cross-sectional survey for Central Java (and East Java, South Sulawesi and South Kalimantan), comprising eight survey rounds between Dec. 1995 and Dec. 1998.
* Based on data from Central Java only.
Undernourishment is measured as the proportion of people with calorie consumption below 2100 kcal/day. Child wasting and low weight is measured as proportion of children with WHZ, and WAZ below −2, respectively, if not specified otherwise. Thinness among adults and adolescents is measured as the proportion of persons with BMI below 18.5 kg/m². Anemia among non-pregnant women and children is measured as the proportion of women or children with a hemoglobin concentration below 12 mg/dl and 11 mg/dl, respectively.

Table 3A.4 Response of food security and nutrition indicators to the 1998 Indonesian economic crisis based on data from small-scale, regional food intake and adequacy surveys

Source	Ref#	Time period	Indicator	Outcomes	Comments and conclusions
Hartini et al. (2002, 2003a, 2003b)*	(13)	Before Sep. 1997– after Nov. 1997	Food intake among pregnant women (mean)	Rural areas: Increase in intakes of rice (12%), sugar (7%), nuts and pulses (5%), fruits (5%) and vegetables (4%); decrease in intakes of non-rice staple foods (21%), animal foods (16%), chicken (80%), eggs (10%) and fats and oils (5%) Urban areas: Increase in intakes of non-rice staple foods (3%), decreases in intakes of animal foods (61%), eggs (92%), chicken (79%), fruits (56%), sugar (21%), nuts and pulses (14%), rice (5%) and vegetables (2%),; no change in intakes of fats and oils	There might be a potential bias due to seasonality effects.
			Nutrient intake among pregnant women (mean)	Rural areas: Increase in intakes of vitamin A (14%), protein (7%), iron (7%) and calcium (4%); decrease in intakes of fat (22%) and carbohydrates (8%) Urban areas: Decrease in intakes of calcium (33%), iron (29%), fat (22%), protein (15%), carbohydrates (9%) and vitamin A (6%)	

			Mid-upper arm circumferences among poor, pregnant women (mean)	Rural areas: Increase by insignificant 3% Urban areas: Decrease by insignificant 3%
			Iron status among pregnant women (median serum ferritin concentration)	Rural areas: Increase by 12% Urban areas: Decrease by 48%
Studdert et al. (2001)**	(14)	1998	Self-assessed household food insecurity and its manifestations during the past 12 months	Food insecurity or uncertainty: 94.2% Weight losses: 11%	There is no validation with alternative indicators of food insecurity.

Notes:
Data description: Small-scale, cross-sectional food intake and adequacy surveys.
* Based on data from six cross-sectional 24-hour dietary recall surveys with women pregnant in the second trimester from Purworejo District in Central Java between 1996 and 1998 ** Based on data from a cross-sectional survey of mothers with children under 5 years from Java between July and September 1998.

4. Food price inflation, growth and poverty*
Shikha Jha and P. V. Srinivasan

4.1 INTRODUCTION

Recent episodes of sharp spikes in global food prices and their increasing volatility have raised concerns worldwide about inflation, growth, hunger and poverty. By adding to inflationary pressures, food price increases hinder economic growth and enhance macroeconomic vulnerability. Low-income households, the most vulnerable to food price increases, are forced to adjust their consumption and switch to cheaper and less nutritious foods. The resulting undernourishment has grave implications, especially for children, affecting their health, cognitive abilities and lifetime earnings. By eroding real household incomes, elevated prices entail a major setback for the progress toward the Millennium Development Goals (MDGs) linked to food and nutrition. At the same time, high prices increase the cost of food-based safety net programs to protect the poor. By adding to the subsidy burdens of governments the prices impact on the country's fiscal position, which might fuel inflation even more. Moreover, global price shocks cause fluctuations in international terms of trade.

Developing Asia is particularly impacted by food price inflation. Although it remains the fastest-growing region in the world, its growth has slowed significantly since the occurrence of global food, fuel and financial crises. Yet it has to feed two-thirds of the world's hungry people who live in the region and whose numbers are on the rise. High food prices pushed millions of people in developing Asia into poverty (ADB, 2011a). Plentiful of food supplies over the last 50 years made possible by technological advances allowed the region to provide inexpensive food to its populations. However, the slowing of growth in agricultural yields coupled with rising demand for food driven by population dynamics and increasing incomes in emerging economies is threatening food security and economic stability. Extreme movements and rapid rise in food prices over the last half a decade have not only brought uncertainty regarding food supplies but have also affected prospects for growth and poverty in the region. This chapter explores the causes and consequences of high and fluctuating global food prices, their implications for economic growth and poverty, and the policy choices available to developing countries in Asia.

The plan of the chapter is as follows. The next section discusses the phenomenon of the nascent resurgence in global food price inflation. It presents recent trends in food price movements globally and in developing Asia and reviews the causes of food price increases and volatility, including factors responsible at the domestic and global levels. Section 4.3 assesses the pass through of world prices to domestic markets. The next section analyzes the channels by which food price inflation impacts on general inflationary process and economic growth. Section 4.5 discusses the impact of high food prices on poverty in Asia. Section 4.6 reviews alternative policy choices to respond to food price shocks and their effectiveness in developing Asian economies. The final section provides concluding remarks.

4.2 RESURGENCE IN GLOBAL FOOD PRICE INFLATION

The old concern of rising food prices has resurfaced in recent years. Movements in global food prices over the last half a century can be roughly divided into three sub-periods (Jha and Rhee, 2012). The first sub-period saw almost flat prices from 1960 to 1972 (Figure 4.1). The next three decades formed another sub-period of a horizontal trend though at a higher plane, as the food crisis of early 1970s lifted prices up, and brought in much greater variability. The third sub-period, starting from the early part of this millennium, witnessed the prices drifting up swiftly. Sharp surges from 2006–07 led to rice, wheat and palm oil prices doubling in 2007–08 relative to 1999–2000. The most dramatic increase occurred in rice. From April 2001 to September 2007, Thai 100 percent B rice steadily doubled from US$170 per ton to US$335 per ton. Within the next 7 months, by April 2008, the price further tripled to over US$1000 per ton (Dawe and Slayton, 2011). The food price index in 2007 and 2008 was 26 and 68 percent higher, respectively, than the index in 2006.

As demand growth raced ahead of supply, grain inventories were depleted rapidly to cover the gaps (Figure 4.2). Diminishing global stocks of rice, corn and wheat – from 350 million metric tons in 2000 down to only 200 million metric tons in 2007 – were indicative that production growth fell below the consumption rate. Real and anticipated food shortages in countries led to implementation of protectionist trade policies. Increases in export price not only reflected lower production but also imposition of price controls to keep the demand low as a strategy to rebuild stocks. More recent data suggest that by 2009, as global food markets calmed down, total stocks of rice, corn and wheat were built up way above the 2007 levels and crossed 400 million metric tons in 2012.

Food prices are not only increasing, but also their volatility has become more pronounced since 2006. Although, in real terms, prices in the 2007–08 episode were way below those observed in 1974, price volatility (as measured by standard deviation) in 2008 was higher than that in 1974. When markets normalized in the aftermath of the food crisis, global food prices settled down to trend levels in 2009. However, this reversion to trend was short lived and the prices started climbing again from mid-2010 due to supply disruptions caused by adverse weather conditions across the globe. While in 2008 the price increases were mainly concentrated in grain crops, the 2010–11 increases were more broad based across agricultural commodities affecting sugar, edible oils, beverages, animal products and cotton (Global Monitoring Report, 2012). Since then the trend has been much steeper. The most recent spike occurred in mid-2012 caused by an unparalleled heat wave and drought in the United States, insufficient rain in Eastern Europe and weak monsoon rains in India.

Long-term trends in inflation-adjusted commodity prices suggest the commodity boom is not yet over (Figure 4.1). Growing urbanization and increased production of biofuels has resulted in greater competition for limited agricultural land. Such factors, coupled with increasing costs of production due to high oil and other input prices are likely to sustain a long-term rise in food prices. In general, the trend of rising food prices and their growing volatility are attributed to both demand and supply-side causes and to long-term and short-term factors, which influence the formation of price expectations. Rising demand for food, feed and fuels, speculative investments in commodity markets

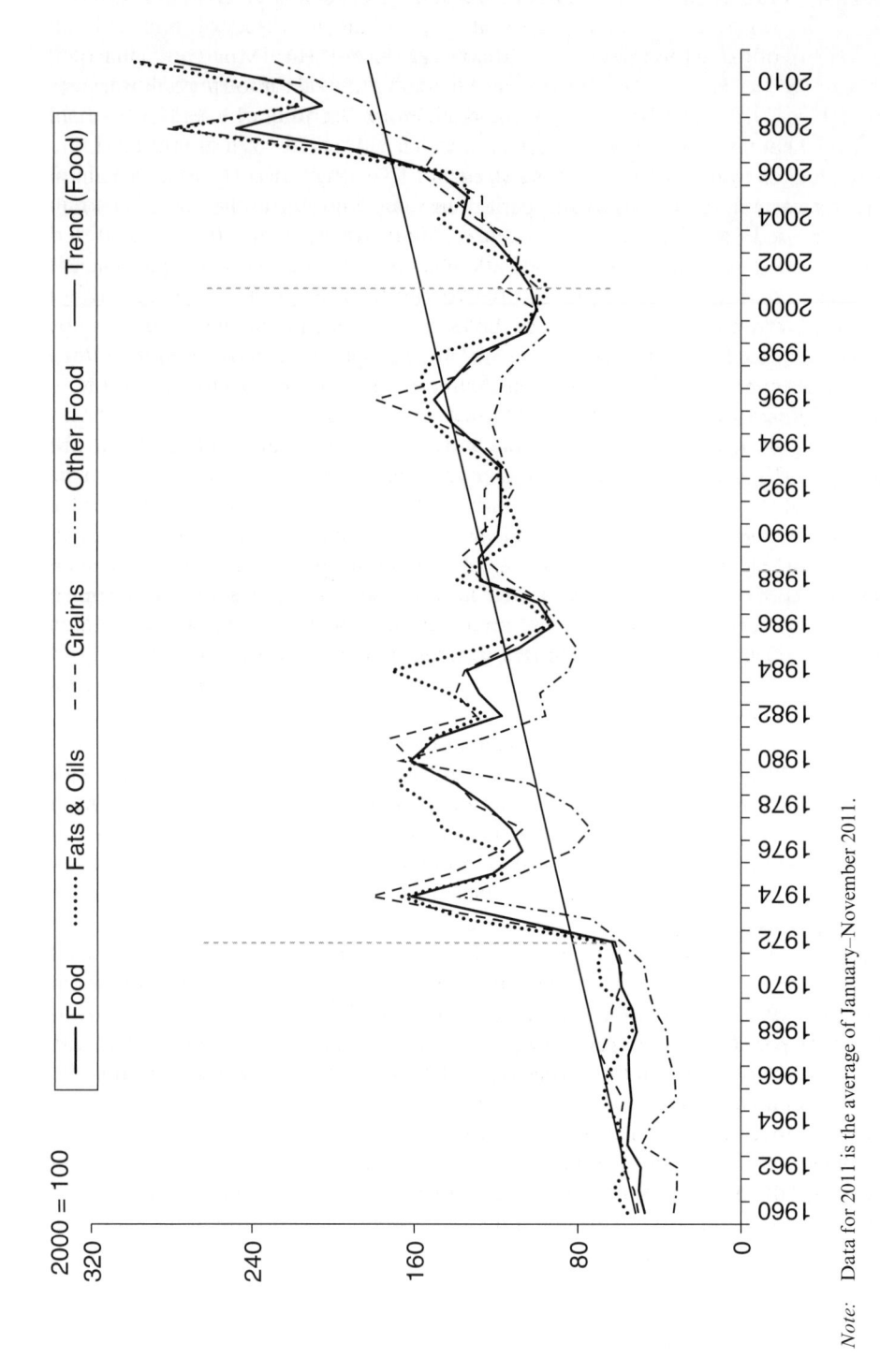

Note: Data for 2011 is the average of January–November 2011.

Source: World Bank. Commodity Price Data (Pink Sheet). Http://www.worldbank.org (accessed 6 December 2011).

Figure 4.1 Structural shifts in food price indices, 1960–2011

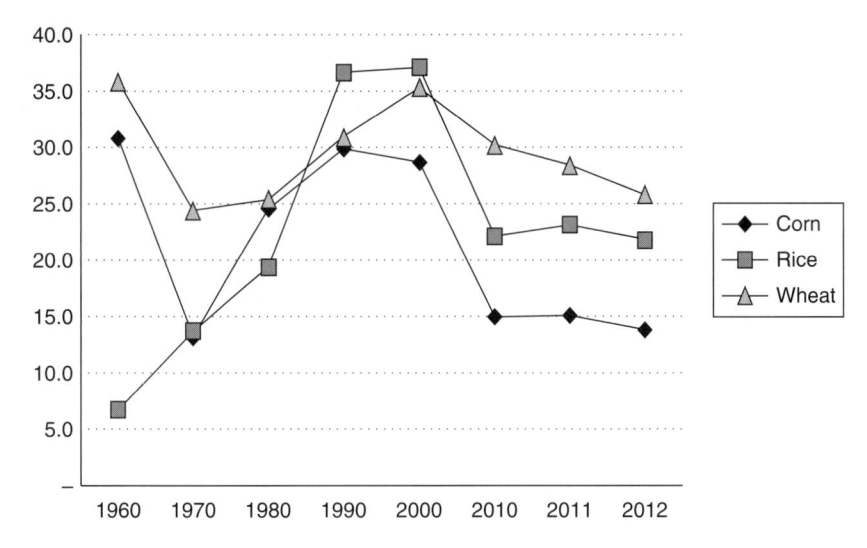

Source: US Department of Agriculture, http://www.usda.gov (accessed 27 November 2012).

Figure 4.2 Stock-to-use ratios of grains, percent

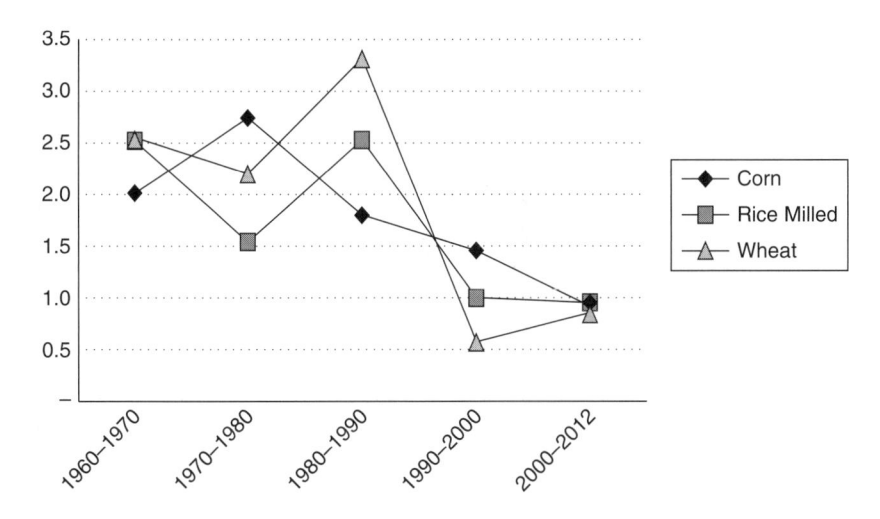

Source: US Department of Agriculture, http://www.usda.gov (accessed 27 November 2012).

Figure 4.3 Growth in food crop yields at the global level

and restrictive trade policies have all been identified as major contributory factors rising prices.

Demand for food on a global basis has been increasing steadily for decades. Until the 2000s, food production increases outpaced demand causing a downward trend in food prices but then this trend reversed and production was unable to keep up with rising demand (UN-ESCAP, 2009). A major underlying supply-side factor in the long term is low and falling growth in agricultural yields (Figure 4.3), combined with declining

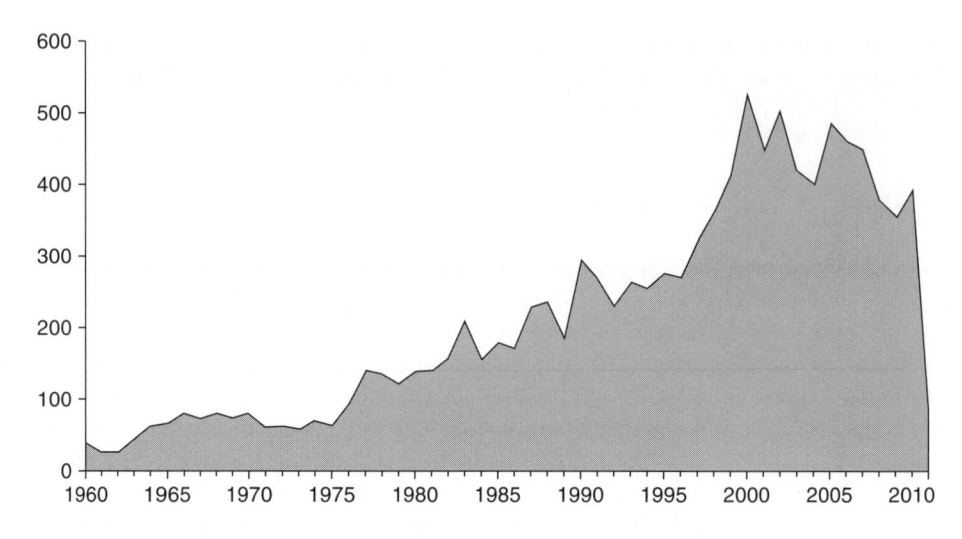

Source: The International Disaster Database, www.emdat.be (accessed 30 August 2011).

Figure 4.4   Growing frequency of natural disasters, 1960 to 2011

agricultural investment. While the global production frontier in agriculture has advanced rapidly, agricultural total factor productivity growth in all developing regions has been falling further behind the frontier. Indeed, low agricultural labor productivity and persistent gaps in yield have become critical binding constraints in improving food production in developing Asia. Average yields of staples rice and wheat in much of the region remain far below potential levels (ADB, 2011a). Only three developing Asian countries among the top 10 rice producers in the world – PRC, Viet Nam and Indonesia – were able to surpass average global yields over the past decade. In the case of wheat, PRC is the only country in the region that exceeded average global yields over the last 10 years.

Studies analysing factors behind the sudden food price rise in 2007–08 have attributed the episode also to short-term production shocks from adverse weather such as droughts and floods (see, e.g., Abbot et al., 2008; ADB, 2008; Rosegrant et al., 2008; and Gilbert, 2010). The frequency of natural disasters has increased, with more occurring in Asia (Figure 4.4). Their average occurrence in the region during 2000–09 was 156 against the worldwide total of 371. Over the last half a century between 2001 and 2010, of the world total, the region accounted for 90 percent of the people affected, 65 percent of those killed and 38 percent of economic damages, exceeding its share of world GDP (UN–ESCAP, 2011a). Climate change seems to be an important factor behind the increasing frequency of occurrence of weather-related natural disasters.

Increasing demand pressure from rapid growth of affluent populations and steadily rising incomes in emerging economies has surfaced as an important contributor to global food price pressures. With rising incomes, consumers worldwide have shifted their consumption patterns away from traditional foods towards more resource intensive diets such as poultry and meats (Figure 4.5). The latter foods require increasing amounts of expensive cereal crops (wheat, corn, soy) as animal feed in comparison with direct food consumption. For example, production of 1 kg of beef requires 8 kg of grain on

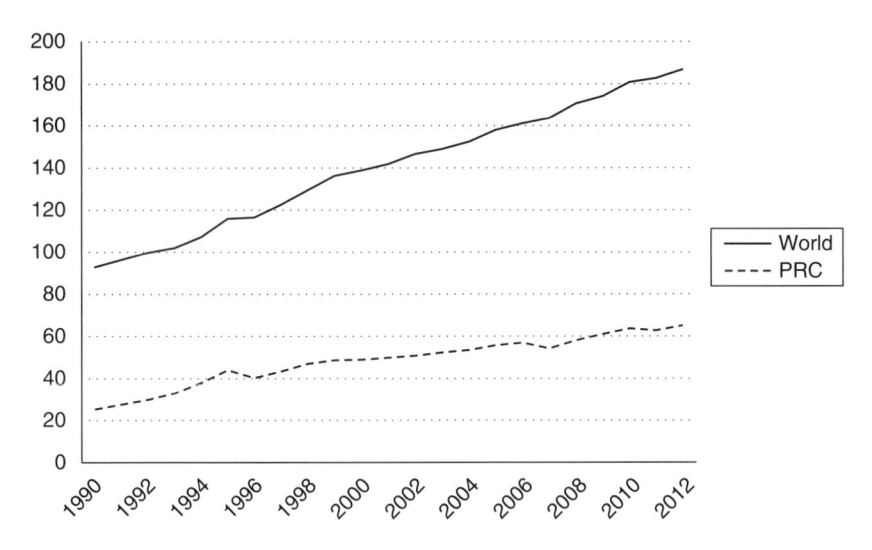

Source: US Department of Agriculture, http://www.usda.gov (accessed 27 November 2012).

Figure 4.5 Pork and chicken production in developing Asia

average (UN–ESCAP, 2009). In large-scale commercial systems, feed constitutes 60–70 percent of the cost of poultry production (Ravindran, 2010). Shifting consumption patterns in the region means that growing meat consumption in countries like China, the world's largest meat consumer, will continue unabated even as the economy slows. This trend will expand its import demand for corn and soybeans, which are fed to pigs and chicken. Indeed, China is the largest buyer of soybeans in the world. Soybeans and corn prices shot to record levels in mid-2012 following the worst drought in half a century in the United States, a major producing country. This pushed global food prices up by 10 percent. Any imbalance in China's meat economy will thus significantly affect the global food price system.

Fuel and non-fuel prices, in general, and fuel and food prices, in particular, are moving much more closely than observed in the past, reflecting closer interlinks between their markets (Figure 4.6). On the one hand, increase in fuel prices such as diesel, oil and electricity leads to higher cost of energy-based agricultural inputs such as irrigation, fertilizers and transport. On the other hand, rising oil prices make the production of biofuels more attractive (Figure 4.7). While crops such as corn and sugar are diverted from direct consumption to produce ethanol; soybean and palm oil are employed as key raw materials in the production of biodiesel. All these interactions contribute to higher food prices.

The closer movement of food and energy prices resulting in increasing diversion of food crops as fuel inputs can be traced to biofuel mandates led by advanced economies. Although Brazil, the United States and the EU dominate biofuel production, over 50 countries have adopted policies to promote biofuels, spurred by agricultural and agro-industrial lobbies, and global climate change and biodiversity conventions. The US biodiesel production exceeded 1 billion gallons of fuel by the end of 2011, while production of ethanol reached close to 14 billion gallons.[1] The use of corn in ethanol production increased from 6.5 percent of global corn production in 2000–01 to 40 percent in 2010–11

78 *Handbook on food*

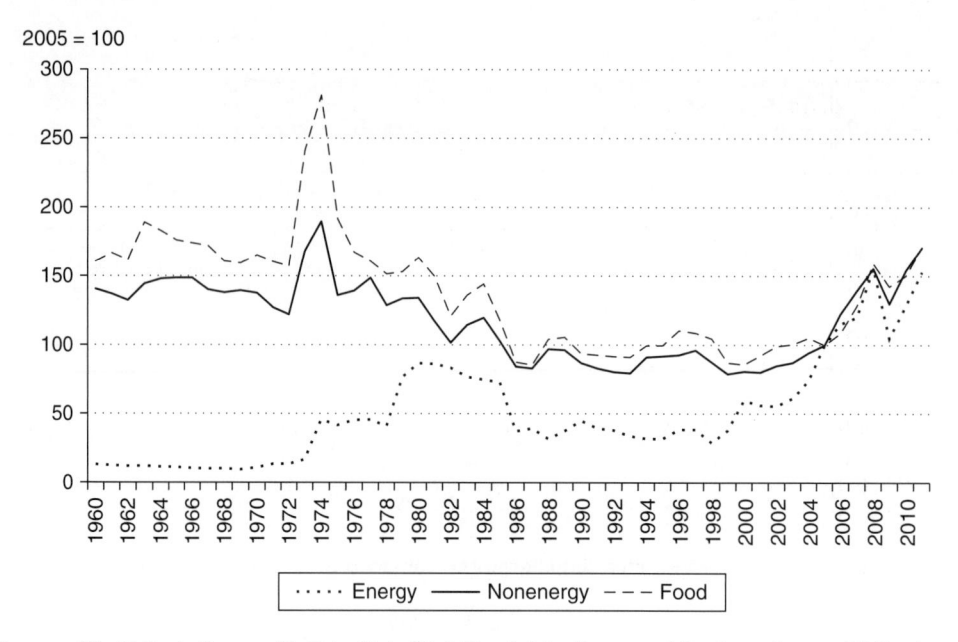

Source: World Bank, Commodity Price Data (Pink Sheet), http://www.worldbank.org (accessed 7 October 2012).

Figure 4.6 Long-term movement of real commodity prices

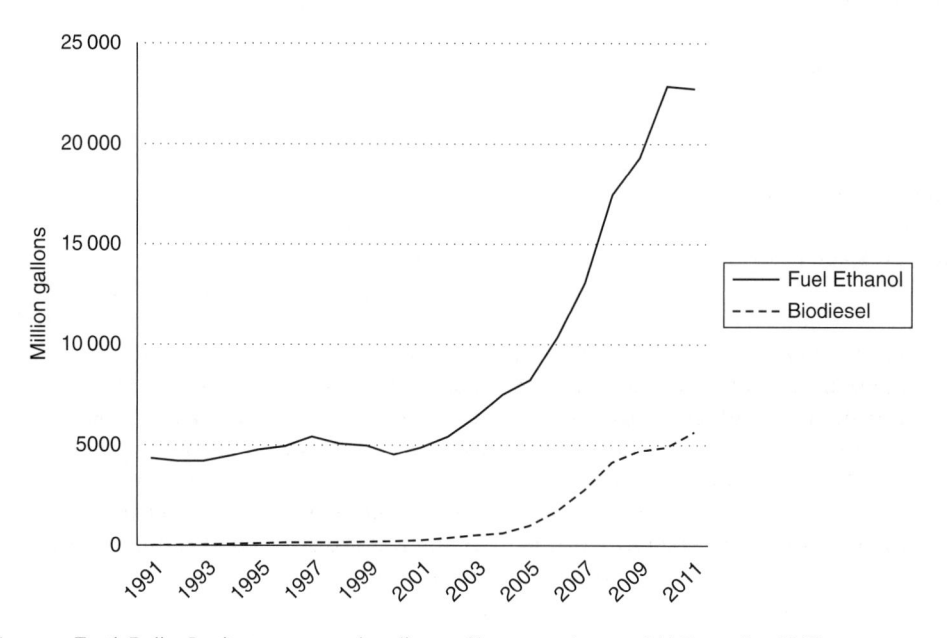

Source: Earth Policy Institute, www.earth-policy.org/datacenter (accessed 11 December 2012).

Figure 4.7 World biofuel production

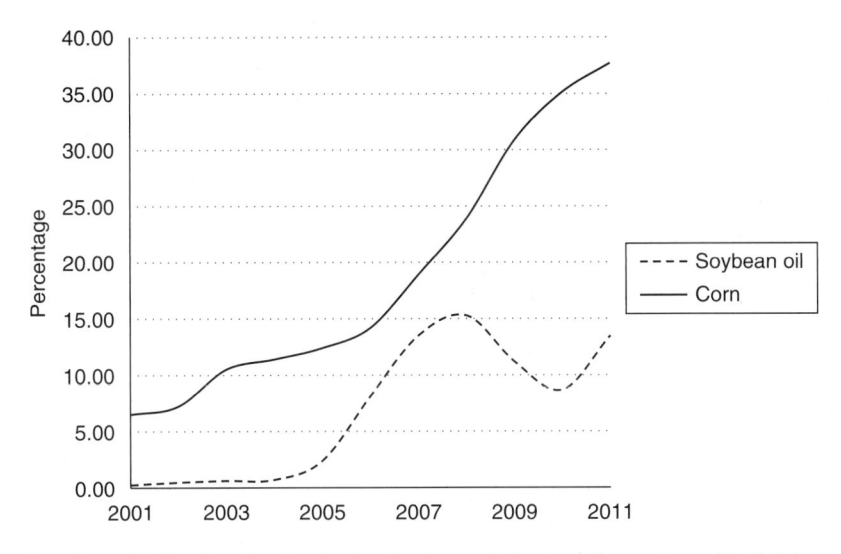

Figure 4.8 Percentage of crop production used in biofuels (United States)

(Figure 4.8).² Similarly, the percentage of soybean oil production used in biodiesel increased from 0.25 percent in 2000–01 to 13.5 percent in 2010–11, contributing to the lift in soybean prices above their 2008 levels. Higher biofuel production spurred palm oil production and exports by some Asian countries (Figure 4.9). Food importing developing countries are particularly vulnerable to food price rises.

There has been a concern that over the past decade excess funds flowed into agricultural commodities, linking price movements to market sentiment. However, the literature is still divided on whether speculation was partly responsible for commodity price volatility in 2007–08. Some believe that excess liquidity, for example from loose monetary policy of advanced economies, reallocation of investment portfolios from stock markets and increased demand for commodities as an important tradable asset class may have amplified the extent of the price surge (Baffes, 2011). They argue that given the globally low interest rates and weak earning opportunities from stock or property markets, financial capital moved to commodities in search of higher profits. Hernandez and Torero (2010) find using Granger causality tests that changes in futures prices do influence spot prices and suggest that disproportionate spikes in grain spot prices can be prevented through policies that influence price movements in the futures exchanges.

In contrast, Headey and Fan (2008) note that despite their co-movement there is no causal relationship between spot and futures prices of agricultural commodities. Others argue that episodes of low and high food price volatility are a recurrent phenomenon. If markets are efficient, trading in commodity futures could actually contribute to price stability. However, markets are not always efficient; and speculation, hoarding and hysteria may have the potential to generate price bubbles. Timmer (2009) conducted Granger causality analysis for a wide range of financial and commodity markets and came to the conclusion that although speculative behavior on the part of large investment and hedge

80 *Handbook on food*

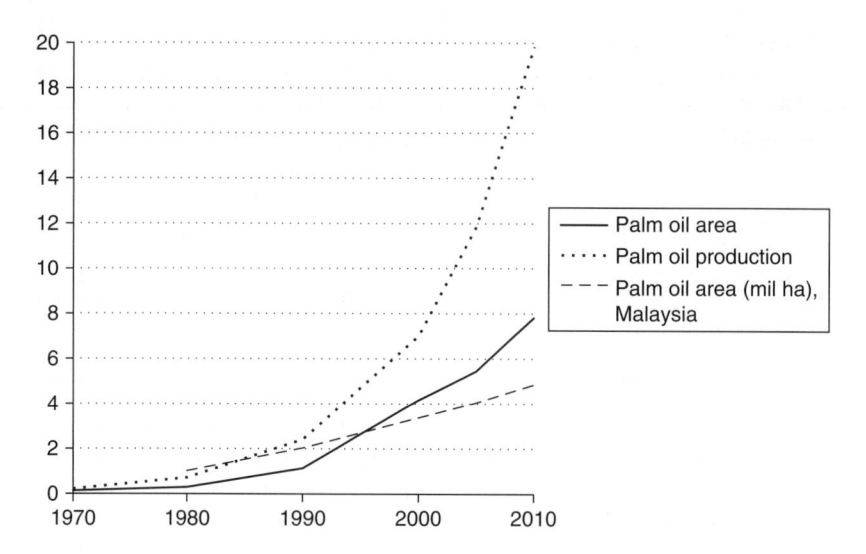

Source: Obidzinski et al. (2011); http://www.ecologyandsociety.org/vol17/iss1/art25/; Malaysian Palm Oil Board. http://bepi.mpob.gov.my/ (accessed 11 December 2012).

Figure 4.9 Palm oil area (million hectares) and production (million tons) in Indonesia and Malaysia

funds was responsible for the spike in food prices in 2007, the links between financial markets and commodity markets are observed only for short periods of time and there are no really long term relationships. Using data on the four agricultural commodities traded on the Chicago Board of Trade, Gilbert (2008) tested empirically if index-based investment has any persistent effect on commodity futures prices. He found that overall there is weak evidence for the belief that commodity investment was a major factor in the commodity price boom during 2007–08, although it is possible that in specific markets at particular periods of time such activity might produce substantial and persistent effect on prices.

Apart from exogenous weather related shocks, recent food price shocks have been attributed to endogenous shocks due to policy responses (Figure 4.10). The sharp surges in prices since 2008 were not only exacerbated by but also perpetuated protectionist policies such as export bans by major food producing countries and panic buying by large importing countries to buffer the impact. See, for example, Timmer (2008), Gilbert and Morgan (2010), Abbot (2011), Dawe and Slayton (2011), Martin and Anderson (2011), Wright (2011), Giordani et al. (2012), and Jha et al. (2012).

The rice market is especially vulnerable to price shocks since, unlike wheat and maize, a relatively small proportion of world rice production (7 percent) is traded (Table 4.1). The top four Asian exporters account for over two-thirds of exports (Figure 4.11). Whereas wheat and maize trade is driven by surpluses in rich and large countries with abundant land, most large rice producing countries (except for Thailand, the largest rice exporter) are relatively poor and have small surpluses or deficits relative to consumption. The small volume of rice trade relative to total production and consumption is sometimes attributed to aggressive promotion of consumption of locally produced food

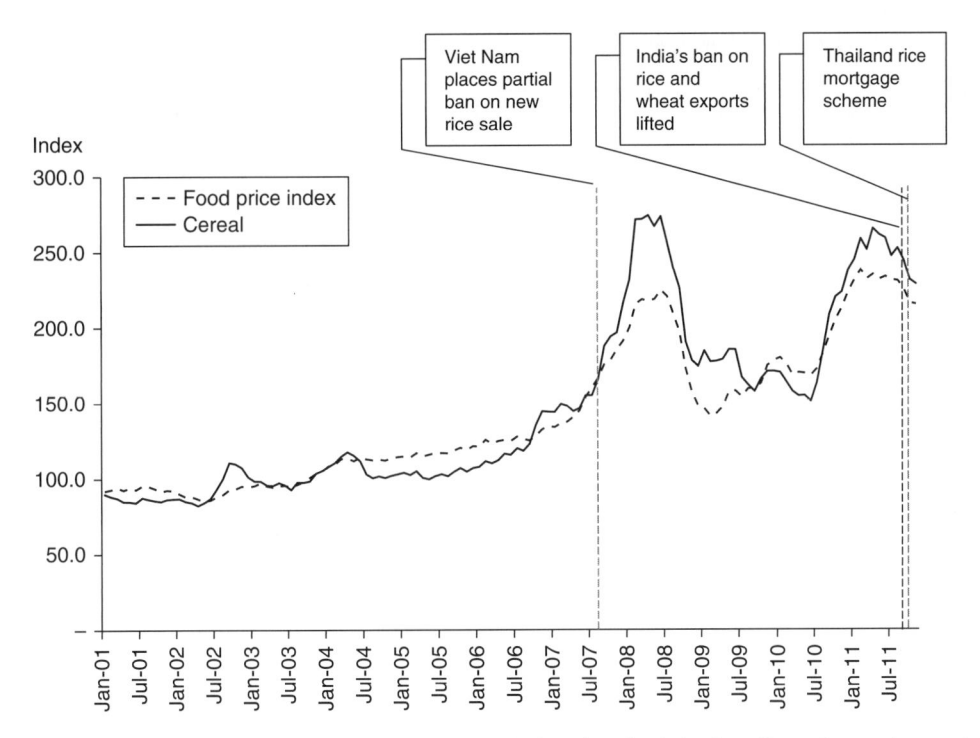

Figure 4.10   Food price index and cereal prices, 2001–2011

through adoption of sustainable and organic agricultural practices. The large domestic markets in major rice producing countries create the capacity to absorb their agricultural production and leave very little marketable surplus for international trade, unless the commodities are specifically intended for the export market.

4.3   WORLD FOOD PRICE TRANSMISSION TO DOMESTIC MARKETS

As discussed in the previous section, food price shocks in a country can be caused either by local output fluctuations or disruptions in global food markets. Globalization has brought about increased trade in agricultural commodities and as a result crop failures in one country can affect supply conditions in other regions. In a free trade scenario, the difference between prices in two spatially separated markets equals the cost of transportation of the commodity from one market to the other. The markets are integrated and demand or supply shocks in one market will have an equal impact on price in the other market. In the real world, however, trade is not fully liberalized and the impacts of world prices on domestic markets and of domestic prices on world markets are not symmetric. Domestic price changes due to local factors such as supply shocks from bad weather and

82 *Handbook on food*

Table 4.1 World rice market

	Production[a]	Supply[b]	Utilization	Trade[c]	Ending stocks[d]	World stock-to-use ratio	Major exporters' stock-to-disappearance ratio[e]
	(million tonnes)					(percent)	
2001–02	400.6	551.1	405.3	28.2	143.1	35.3	25.6
2002–03	380.8	523.9	404.8	27.6	119.7	29.2	15.6
2003–04	393.4	513.1	409.5	26.8	105.5	25.5	15.7
2004–05	406.9	512.4	413.0	29.7	100.0	23.8	13.5
2005–06	424.2	524.2	419.1	29.0	105.5	24.6	16.1
2006–07	428.5	534.1	425.6	32.0	106.5	24.5	15.4
2007–08	440.1	546.6	434.6	29.9	113.7	25.6	17.5
2008–09	458.4	572.0	444.4	29.6	128.4	28.6	21.7
2009–10	456.0	584.3	448.7	31.5	134.7	29.2	20.8
2010–11	466.6	601.3	460.4	34.3	140.6	29.8	20.2
2011–12	480.4	621.0	471.3	33.8	149.8	32.0	21.3

Notes:
a. Production data refer to the calendar year of the first year shown. Rice production is expressed in milled terms.
b. Production plus opening stocks.
c. Trade data refer to exports based on a July/June marketing season for wheat and coarse grains and on a January/December marketing season for rice (second year shown).
d. May not equal the difference between supply and utilization due to differences in individual country marketing years.
e. Major grain exporters are Argentina, Australia, Canada, the EU, and the United States; major rice exporters are India, Pakistan, Thailand, the United States, and Viet Nam. Disappearance is defined as domestic utilization plus exports for any given season.

Source: Food and Agriculture Organization of the United Nations. http://www.fao.org/worldfoodsituation/wfs-home/csdb/en/ (accessed 17 January 2011).

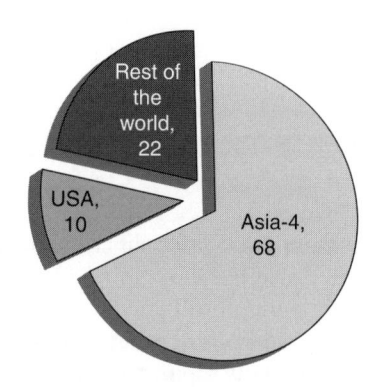

Note: Asia-4: India, Pakistan, Thailand, Viet Nam; 2011 export shares.

Source: Foreign Agricultural Service, US Department of Agriculture. http://www.fas.usda.gov/psdonline/psdResult.aspx (accessed 3 May 2012).

Figure 4.11 Dominance of Asian rice producers in the export market

natural calamities, political uncertainty and changing patterns of household demand may not fully be reflected in international prices except perhaps for large exporting countries. Domestic prices in countries with a small share of world exports do not have a noticeable influence on world prices (Ghoshray, 2006; Minot, 2010). Similarly, as world prices rise steeply or fluctuate widely, these changes may not automatically transmit to domestic prices.

Domestic food prices fluctuate more widely in low-income and landlocked countries, which are typically less integrated with international markets, than in middle-income countries and those countries, which have much better access to seas and ports (World Bank, 2011). The pass through of world price movements to domestic markets tends to be larger in emerging and developing economies than in advanced economies. Additionally, transmission from international prices to domestic prices is greater for countries that are more open to trade and for countries that either rely on imports to meet a large proportion of their consumption or are large exporters of grain.

Several researchers have estimated the elasticity of transmission of international prices to domestic markets (for some early estimates see, e.g., Nerlove, 1972, and Tyers and Anderson, 1992). Recent estimates of short-run elasticities in Asian economies over the last two decades range from a low of 0.5 for rice and wheat to 0.7 for soybean (Table 4.2). The unweighted average across key agricultural products is 0.6, suggesting that within one year, a little over half the movement in international prices is transmitted domestically. In 2011, global food prices increased by 24 percent while domestic food inflation for a number of regional economies averaged about 10 percent. This implies that about 40 percent of the increase in global food prices got transmitted to domestic food prices in developing Asia.

A number of factors drive a wedge between domestic and international prices, including tariffs, quotas, exchange rates, domestic price support; transaction costs arising from poor infrastructure, transportation and communication services; and existence of close substitutes that make import demand more elastic. Dawe (2008), for example, notes in

Table 4.2 Short-run (one-year) price transmission elasticities, 1985–2010

	Rice	Wheat	Maize	Soybean	Sugar	Unweighted average
Bangladesh	0.42	0.26			0.04	0.24
China	0.56	0.55	0.47	0.66	0.83	0.61
India	0.44	0.43	0.53	1.00	0.08	0.50
Indonesia	0.58		0.71	0.55	0.46	0.58
Pakistan	0.20	0.29	0.12		0.14	0.19
Philippines	0.32		0.22		0.25	0.26
Sri Lanka	0.29					0.29
Thailand	1.00		0.79	0.14	0.75	0.67
Vietnam	0.57				0.28	0.43
Global average	0.51	0.58	0.63	0.73	0.43	0.58

Note: The estimates are the proportion of a change in the international price that is transmitted to the domestic market of a country within a year, as reflected in the producer price.

Source: Anderson et al. (2013).

84 *Handbook on food*

the case of seven economies in developing Asia that a large part of the increases in world cereal prices was neutralized by real depreciation of the US dollar. He finds that between the fourth quarter of 2003 and the fourth quarter of 2007 the increase in real domestic rice prices was about a third of the increase in real US dollar world market price. To keep domestic prices stable, typically governments insulate their markets by restrictive trade policies. Import restrictions such as tariffs and tariff rate quotas diminish the opportunities for spatial arbitrage and prevent international price changes from being proportionately transmitted to domestic prices. When world prices are high, export restrictions create distortions and deprive domestic producers of the gains from higher export prices thereby suppressing the supply response and exacerbating the problem of high world prices. There is evidence that food price volatility was higher in periods when trade was impeded, such as during the two World Wars and at the time of the breakdown of the Bretton Woods regime in the 1970s. Domestic price support policies too may weaken the relationship between world and domestic prices. For example, if domestic price floor is set above the level of world price, fall in the latter will have no effect on domestic price. Since consumers and producers in individual countries in general face prices different from world prices, they will adjust only partially to changes in world prices so that necessary adjustments in world supply and demand that would have otherwise occurred will not take place.

Since the global food crisis, local food prices across Asian economies are not only diverging but are also delinked from global food prices. As Figures 4.12a and b show, domestic rice and wheat prices in many economies largely followed the movement in international grain prices in the past. However, since 2008 the effect is muted compared

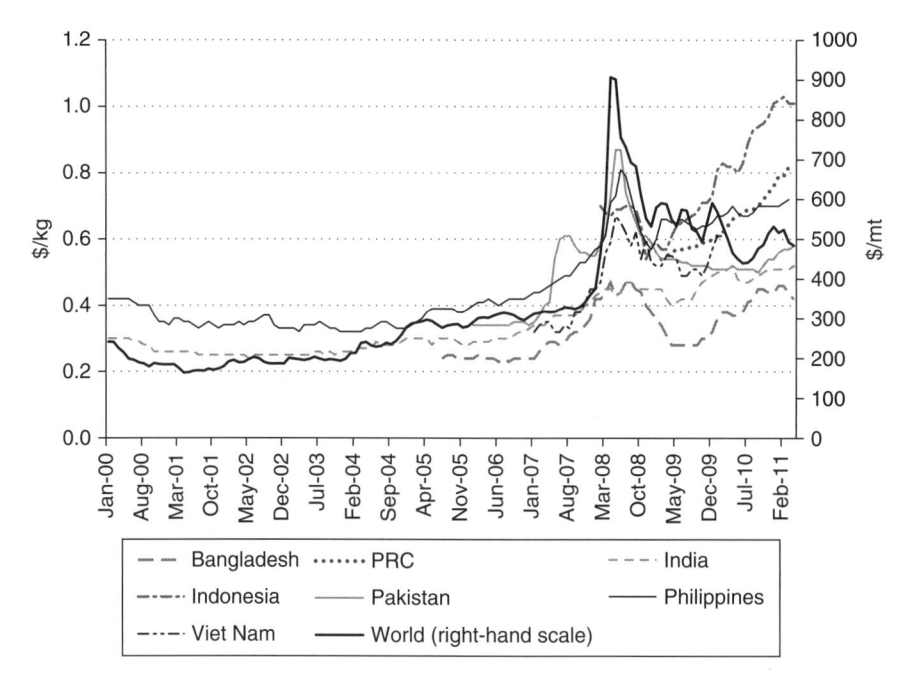

Figure 4.12a Divergence between local prices in Asia and world prices since 2008 – rice

Figure 4.12b Divergence between local prices in Asia and world prices since 2008 – wheat

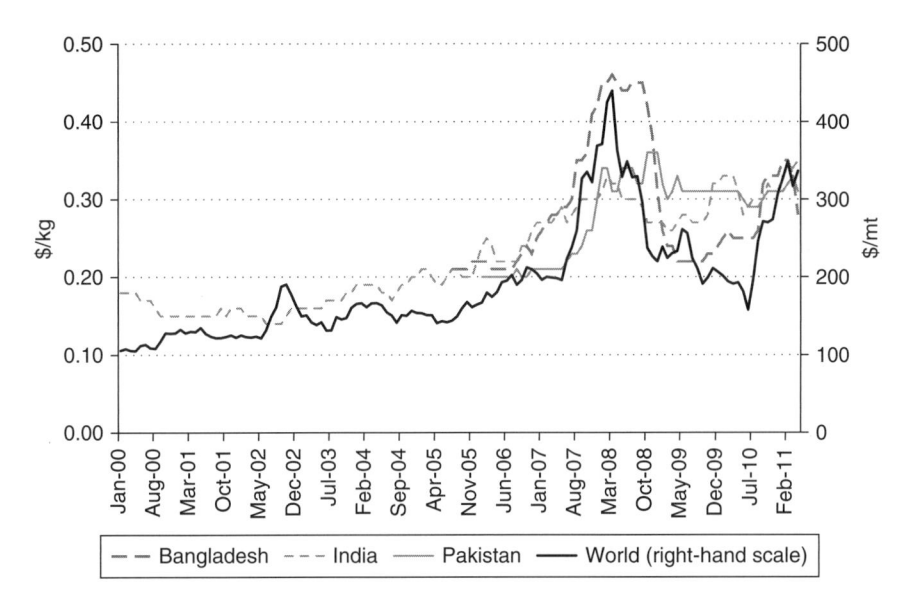

to the situation that would have occurred had the countries allowed full price transmission. Although barriers to free trade tend to reduce price pass through from international to domestic prices, opening up to trade can reduce domestic price volatility. In the case of sub-Saharan Africa, for example, it is seen that price volatility of internationally tradable commodities such as wheat, rice and cooking oil has been low compared to the non-tradable ones like maize and cowpeas. Trade restrictions can also have a direct spillover effect on global prices. In the case of India, a large player in the world rice and wheat markets, Srinivasan and Jha (2001) show that unilateral trade liberalization by the country can bring about not only greater domestic but also greater world price stability because of the large size of its trade. Antitrade policies are a typical example of a zero-sum game with poor countries like the sub-Saharan African economies (which import more than half of their rice from Asia) being most adversely affected.

4.4   IMPACTS ON INFLATION AND GROWTH

Food price inflation is of great concern to Asia's developing economies because with a large weight of food in the Consumer Price Index (CPI), food price shocks give rise to inflationary pressures (Table 4.3 and Figure 4.13). For example, for the ASEAN countries Cambodia, Indonesia, Malaysia, Philippines, Thailand, and Viet Nam, the average food share is close to 40 percent compared to under 15 percent for the United States and Eurozone and below 26 percent for Japan. Undoubtedly, high food prices have contributed heavily to general inflation in Asia because of the high share of food in the CPI. In 2011, the effect was particularly noticeable in Bangladesh, PRC, Sri Lanka

Table 4.3 *Food weights in consumer price index baskets (%) developing Asia*

Economy	Share (%)
Bangladesh	58.84
India	46.19
Sri Lanka	45.50
Cambodia[a]	44.78
Pakistan[b]	40.34
Viet Nam	39.93
Philippines[a]	38.98
Indonesia[c]	36.20
Thailand[a]	33.01
Malaysia[a]	30.30
China, People's Rep. of[b]	30.20
Hong Kong, China	26.67
Taipei, China	26.08
Singapore[a]	22.05
Korea, Rep. of[a]	14.04

Notes:
a. Includes nonalcoholic beverages.
b. Includes beverages.
c. Includes beverages and tobacco.

Source: ADB (2011b, Table 1.4.1).

and Thailand where food price inflation accounted for more than 60 percent of the CPI inflation.

In general, the effects on headline inflation are larger in emerging and developing economies than in advanced economies as in the former group the food share of CPI is larger (IMF, 2011). Walsh (2011) shows that food price shocks are more persistent in developing economies compared to advanced economies. That is, in poorer countries the second-round effects of high food inflation can be significant and not quickly reversed as in rich countries. He argues that persistent food price shocks are likely to feed into inflationary expectations and policymakers cannot afford to ignore this fact if inflationary expectations are to be kept in control. Mishra and Roy (2011), using Indian data, show that food price shocks are as persistent as non-food price shocks and that there is significant pass-through from food to non-food inflation rates. Al-Eyd et al. (2012) find in the case of four central Asian countries that global food price inflation has a strong and significant short-run effect on headline inflation. Sustained rise in food prices gives rise to second-round inflationary pressures when wages are renegotiated and adjusted to protect the purchasing power of wage earners. Higher wages translate into higher production costs, which further influence consumer prices. Food price increases also indirectly affect production costs of goods such as meats and biofuel that use food as inputs, feed and fodder.

Examining the inflationary effects of commodity price shocks for several countries, Gelos and Ustyugova (2012) find that the median long-term impact of a 10 percentage point food price shock is a 0.2 percentage point increase in domestic inflation for

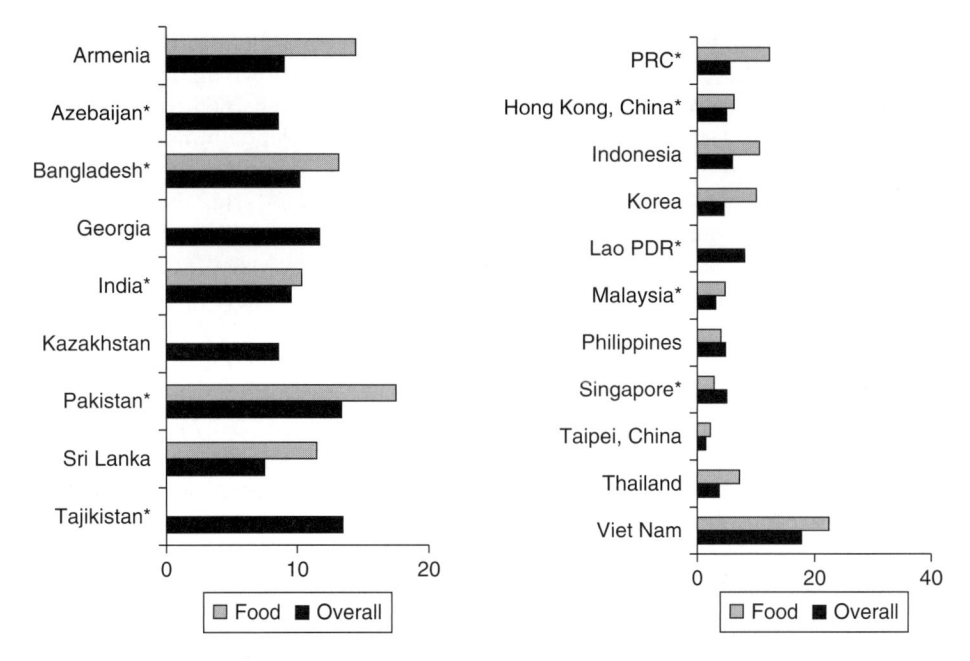

Note: * January–July 2011 (%, year on year).

Source: CEIC Data Company (accessed 30 August 2011).

Figure 4.13 Contribution of food to inflation in developing Asia

advanced economies and about four times larger for emerging and developing economies. The extent to which food price shocks impact on inflation of course depends on price controls and other policies followed by governments. The above study finds that higher central bank autonomy and better governance are associated with a smaller inflationary impact of commodity price shocks. It also finds that impact on inflation is higher in a high inflation environment. Model simulations by ADB (2008) show that if the 57.4 percent increase in world food prices in the first quarter of 2008 was maintained till the end of the fourth quarter, it would have resulted in a rise in Asian regional inflation rate by 1.65 percentage points. The resulting interest rate increases would have reduced consumption and investment and impacted growth by almost 1 percentage point. It is estimated that if the global food and oil price hikes seen in early 2011 persisted for the remainder of that year, GDP growth in some developing Asian countries could have been reduced by up to 1.5 percentage points (ADB, 2011a).

By affecting economic growth food price movements create winners and losers. The channels of such effects work through a consumption effect, an inflation effect, among others (Hadass and Williamson, 2001; IMF, 2012; UN–ESCAP, 2012). The consumption effect works by forcing families to allocate a larger share of their expenditure on food, thereby reducing consumption of non-food items such as education, health, clothing and entertainment, dampening overall consumer spending and hence reducing growth. Many low-income economies suffer from what Schultz (1953) called the 'food problem' where a critically large fraction of household income is spent on food, resulting in 'high food drain'. In the poorest countries, where people spend up to two-thirds of their daily income on food, higher food prices impact consumption, bear down on demand, growth and social stability. Indeed, examining four super-cycles during 1865 to 2009 ranging between 30–40 years each, Erten and Ocampo (2012) argue that commodity prices are directly related to phases of prosperity and stagnation. In particular, non-oil prices were driven by the resurgence of demand for food and raw materials during the industrialization and urbanization phases of major economies.

The inflation effect of food prices on growth is caused by wage indexation. Other channels through which growth is affected include policies aimed at controlling inflation. Central banks may hike interest rates to control the upward pressure on prices, which in turn could slow down growth by reducing investment demand. Or, they may not be able to cut rates to stimulate growth due to inflationary pressures. Growth can also be impacted through the effect of high prices on government budgets. As food prices go up, the subsidy costs and costs of safety net programs such as school meal and other feeding programs increase, leaving less for growth oriented government expenditure and other development expenditures.

The direction of causality between inflation and growth is not usually obvious. In an overheating economy economic growth tends to create inflationary pressures due to supply constraints. However, in a demand-constrained economy moderate levels of inflation can have stimulating effect on growth. When nominal wages adjust with a lag, rising prices lead to greater profits and increased investment. As the economy approaches full employment, the inflationary situation can worsen creating a negative effect on economic growth. Inflation has a negative effect on growth especially when the level of inflation exceeds a certain threshold. Khan and Senhadji (2001) estimate this threshold to be 11–12 percent for developing countries. In a more recent study, Jha and Dang (2012) examine the relationship between inflation variability and growth and find a negative relationship between the two for developing countries when the rate of inflation exceeds 10 percent. Indeed, in 2011, a number of South Asian countries faced double-digit inflation or close to those levels. In most of these countries high budget deficits and accommodative monetary policy contributed to high inflation.

Volatility in food prices can be bad for economic growth because it creates risk that inhibits private agricultural investment and threatens farm incomes. Using quarterly data for 113 developing countries over 1957–97, Dehn (2000) shows that per capita growth rates are significantly reduced by large negative commodity price shocks. In contrast, greater food price stability contributes to faster economic growth by reducing price risk, encouraging investment, and reducing political instability (Global Monitoring Report, 2012). By reducing vulnerability of the poor to price shocks, stability also stimulates investment in human capital, contributing further to economic growth.

4.5 THE POVERTY IMPACT

Price rise and volatility hurt the poor most as a great majority of them have less of a buffer in terms of savings, their ability to borrow is limited and they have lower access to land, capital markets, production and marketing support. To maintain food consumption in the face of a price surge, poor and vulnerable households resort to use of their limited savings, borrowing by pawning valuables, and selling of assets, which are difficult to rebuild or re-acquire. Such short-term coping mechanisms have long-term negative impacts on their livelihoods and may even be irreversible (FAO, 2012).

In general, poor households in developing Asia spend as much as 60 percent to 70 percent of their total income on food (ADB, 2011a). For female-headed and landless households the figure is as high as 80 percent (FAO, 2012). Sudden increases in food prices can therefore play havoc with the wellbeing of the poor and near-poor households (Global Monitoring Report, 2012). Since food cannot be substituted with other goods, its high contribution to general inflation adds further to the misery of the poor. Continued rise in food prices could push the near poor and other vulnerable households into poverty, reversing the trend of the progress made in reducing poverty in a region where about 1.7 billion are living on less than $2 a day, and over 800 million struggling on less than $1.25 a day. It is estimated that, based on $1.25 a day poverty line, a 10 percent increase in domestic food prices could risk creating additional 64 million poor people, or increasing the percentage of poor by almost 2 points in developing Asia (Figure 4.14). Or equivalently, the price rise. Within the ASEAN countries, a 10 percent increase in food prices is projected to lead to an increase of 7.91 million persons in the number of poor below the $1.25 a day poverty line (ADB 2011a). Higher food prices not only increase the number of the poor but also reduce the living standards of those already living below the poverty line. The 10 percent increase in domestic food prices in developing Asia will also result in an increase of 1.4 percentage points in the poverty gap ratio, affecting 6.8 million poor people.

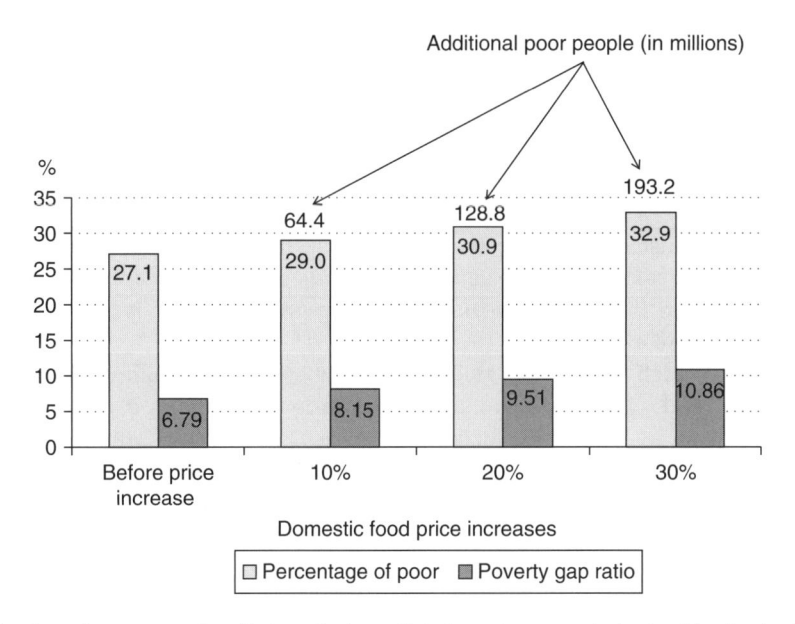

Note: The chart shows pure price effects or the immediate impact on poverty due to rising food prices. The assumption is that household nominal incomes do not change during the inflationary period.

Source: ADB (2011a).

Figure 4.14 Impact of high food prices on poverty

An increase in food prices in the second half of 2010 was responsible for keeping close to 20 million people in developing Asia in poverty who otherwise would be out of poverty (UN–ESCAP, 2011b). In low- and middle-income countries across the world, food price increases pushed about 44 million more people into poverty in 2011 in comparison with 105 million in 2008 (Ivanic et al., 2011). By the end of 2012, an additional 31 million people in low-income countries may have become poor with higher food prices (IMF, 2011). Food price inflation would also raise the likelihood of chronic poverty for those already poor, trapping them in the cycle of poverty. Compton et al. (2010) reviewed the impact of the 2007–08 food price shocks on the poor and concluded that the main impact of food price shocks was the increasing depth of poverty in the already poor rather that the number of people falling below the poverty line.

Spikes in food prices have an adverse impact on the poor's food intake as well as their expenditures on non-food essentials. Even the smallest price fluctuation is enough to force poor people to make difficult decisions on where to devote their scant resources. More disposable income spent on food means less is available for other essential needs such as health, education and other critical necessities. Nutrition is sacrificed when these households shift to cheaper low-quality food in the face of high prices. Food price shocks could thus worsen the prevalence of hunger and malnutrition because both the quantity and quality of food consumed is reduced (FAO, 2012). As many as 105 countries of the 144 monitored are not expected to reach MDG 4 (child mortality), while 94 are off track on MDG 5 (maternal mortality) (Global Monitoring Report, 2012). If food prices remain high, more children are likely to become undernourished with serious long-term consequences. In particular, girls are likely to be affected more than boys due to inherent biases in intra-household food distribution. According to the efficiency wage hypothesis, nutritional deficiency reduces labor productivity and raises the risk of fall in earnings. The poor thus fall into the familiar poverty–nutrition trap whereby low nutrition implies low productivity, which in turn implies low wages and low purchasing power, which again implies low levels of nutrition. Women are in particular vulnerable to this trap through reduced labor market participation. Jha et al. (2009) for example, find empirical evidence for the existence of poverty-nutrition trap in the case of rural India by considering intakes of calories as well as micronutrients such as carotene and thiamine. In particular, they find that female workers are more prone to the poverty–nutrition trap compared to male workers.

The impact of high food prices on the poor may vary with their status as net food buyers or net food sellers. Most of the urban poor are net food buyers and hence negatively affected by food price increases. Unless they buy more than what they sell, rural households that produce and sell food crops should benefit from price increases. However, poor households in rural communities are not all net food sellers. In South Asia, for example, 70–80 percent of rural households are net buyers of rice and wheat (World Bank, 2010). In Bangladesh, in 2000, 91 percent of the rural poor were net buyers of food (UN-ESCAP, 2011b). In fact, large sections of rural population engaged in producing commercial crops or working in non-farm activities as wage laborers or artisans are vulnerable to high food prices. Small farmers in developing economies do not have enough land and capital to produce a significant marketable surplus to take advantage of higher prices. To benefit from price increase they need to raise their productivity, either through intensive production, more crops per year, or through increase in crop yields.

Aside from the direct effects on net sellers and net buyers of food, poverty impact depends on how price changes affect labor markets in production (rural) and consumption (urban) areas. Polaski (2008), for example, argues that if rising food prices cause farmers to expand production and hire additional farm labor, it benefits other farmers, including landless workers and tenants and those in off-farm employment with small-scale traders and other support industries. Thus, through an increase in wage rate and employment, it is possible for rural poor to benefit from high food prices, even if they are net demanders of food (Ravallion, 1990). Similarly, if food prices go down and reduce the profitability of farm investment, laborers from rural areas may migrate to seek employment in urban centers. This influx can contribute to the supply of labor and therefore lower wages.

4.6 POLICY CHOICES FOR DEVELOPING ASIA

Stagnating growth in crop yields and increasing demand pressures suggest that high food prices are likely to persist in the future, making it vital for countries to not only address long-term agricultural productivity issues but also adopt short-term measures to shield the poor. Clearly, policy responses that address the trend growth in food prices would differ from those that deal with price volatility. The long-term trend growth in food prices is a result of decreasing yield growth combined with increasing demand growth whereas short-term spikes in prices are caused by cyclical phenomenon and temporary shortages. Policy response to the 2008 global food crisis by different countries included macro and sector level measures to counter food price inflation such as price controls, export bans, higher subsidies for food imports and consumption, and crackdowns on hoarders and speculators.

Large and sustained increases in food prices can be contained in the long run by ensuring that agricultural production keeps pace with demand. Measures to increase food supply include supply-augmenting policies that encourage agricultural investment, use of modern technology and improvements in agricultural practices for better yields. ADB (2011a) estimates show that if the yields in the six major rice-producing countries (India, Bangladesh, Thailand, Myanmar, the Philippines and Brazil) that are below the global mean could be raised to just the world average, global rice production would increase by over 10 percent. If their yield could rise significantly to match the maximum global yield, worldwide rice production would enormously expand by 170 percent. Like rice, wheat yields in eight major producing countries are lower than the global mean. These countries could add over 10 percent to total world wheat production by augmenting their yields to the latter level and multiply global wheat production by more than three times if they could raise their yields to the world's maximum level observed during the last decade (ADB, 2011a). Both rice and wheat thus hold the promise of significant jump in yields with modern technology and better farming practices.

Policies for the long term need to not only focus on increasing productivity but also do so in an environmentally sustainable way. This would require rationalizing input subsidies so that benefits are restricted to poor farmers and resources such as land and water, which are increasingly becoming scarce commodities, are not overexploited. Improved food availability also necessitates reductions in post harvest losses. Agricultural research, extension and efficient management of inputs to agriculture can help improve productivity, increase yields and avoid food shortages in the long run. Investment in supply-chain infrastructure (processing, storage, transport) can help reduce post-harvest losses and wastage of perishable inputs and outputs. Speedier responses to food supply disruptions can be made possible through improvements in trade infrastructure and development of institutions to improve market information and to provide grading, labeling and standardizing facilities.

As a part of their long-term development strategies another important area is for countries to invest more in disaster risk reduction. The causes and impacts of natural disasters are not always limited to national boundaries. Growing interdependence among countries implies that floods or droughts in one country can have a wider impact affecting food supply globally. Regional cooperation is a good avenue for countries to build early warning systems and effectively respond to disasters. This point was highlighted in the G20 recommendations which also included, among other things, improving agricultural production and productivity by giving special attention to smallholders; strengthening agricultural research and innovation through coordinated research efforts of national and international agricultural research institutions; enhancing market information and transparency; and improve the functioning of agricultural commodities' derivatives markets. International cooperation is thus essential in reducing the risks of food insecurity.

Policies to tackle short-term fluctuations in food supply and prices include trade and buffer stock policies aimed at stabilizing prices and safety net programs to protect the poor. Following the price shocks in 2008, many countries implemented trade barriers and began focusing on inward-looking self-sufficiency initiatives. As many as 30 exporting countries imposed export restrictions while 84 importing countries reduced food taxes and tariffs (IMF, 2008). Major importing countries displayed panic herd reaction by putting in place policies to increase reliance on self-sufficiency. For example, Brunei Darussalam raised its self-sufficiency target from 3 percent to 60 percent while the Philippines aimed for 100 percent self-sufficiency in rice by 2015. The Republic of Korea removed import tariffs on maize and soymeal among other items. Indonesia suspended temporarily import duty on wheat, soybean and feed products. The Philippines allowed duty-free import of wheat; and India allowed duty free imports of rice, wheat, pulses and edible oils. There were also temporary suspensions of exports from exporting countries. For example, major exporting countries like Thailand and India imposed bans on rice exports to protect local consumers. India imposed ban on onion exports, Bangladesh on rice and Pakistan on wheat exports.[3]

Countries implemented protectionist policies without fully realizing their direct spillover effect on global prices. Since export bans reduce export supply and subsidies on imports increase import demand, the net result of trade measures involving taxing or banning of exports by exporting countries and subsidizing of imports by importing countries is a reinforcement of price hikes at the global level. Martin and Anderson (2011) found that between 2006 and 2008, insulating behavior of governments caused 45 percent of the increase in global rice price and 30 percent in global wheat price. However, most of these measures were reversed as the situation improved and policies were maintained in line with the long-term objective of raising food security through support to domestic production. Instead of an outright ban on trade, policies such as variable tariffs and quotas are more effective mechanisms for managing risks of volatile commodity prices for individual economies.

When a crisis occurs at a global level, disruptions to international trade in food grains are very much likely as observed recently. This has prompted a number of countries to increase the size of their food reserves. A combination of trade and buffer stock policies would be a better option than either of the two policies to stabilize prices. The policies chosen by a country are dictated by its particular circumstances. If the country is a net importer of food grains it could mitigate the impact of world price rise either by adjusting its import tariffs or subsidies or through depletion of its buffer stocks. If the country is a net exporter of food grains it could mitigate the impact of a world price increase through adjusting its export tax/subsidies or through release from stocks. Countries that are self sufficient in meeting their consumption needs and are infrequent exporters or importers of food grains could use a mix of buffer stock policies and trade tax/subsidies. However, excessive involvement of the government in the storage and distribution of grains would typically crowd out private traders from the grain markets and add to fiscal costs. Although adverse impact of price shocks on growth and poverty can be mitigated through price stabilization, prices need to be stabilized at levels that are neither too low to discourage private investment and production nor too high to hurt poor consumers.

In general, trade liberalization can help avoid market distortions, advance efficient agricultural production in the long term and boost global growth. However, international trade agreements that restrict countries from using protectionist policies can expose them to greater instability arising from volatile international markets (Stiglitz, 2012). Thus, countries may retain short-term flexibility in choosing appropriate policies to protect them from exposure to external vulnerability even though such short-term actions by individual countries may aggravate global price volatility.

Regional cooperation can bring forth stronger market integration, strengthen international policy coordination and help in the collection and dissemination of data reflecting on current and future global market situation. Regional coordination can help prevent panic buying by importing countries and hasty bans on exports by exporting countries and avoid aggravation of global price volatility. Another area with promising scope for regional cooperation is the renewed interest in setting up international food reserves to reduce the risk of food insecurity (von Braun and Torero, 2008). Past experiences with international commodity agreements have been disappointing (Gilbert, 2010). Regional emergency reserves such as the International Emergency Food Reserve established by WFP in the 1970s, ASEAN reserves of 1979 and SAARC Food Security Reserve in the 1980s failed. The failure can be attributed to a small size of reserves, contributions tied to specific commodities and emergencies, high expenses, lack of funds for the secretariat, and ineffective institutional mechanisms such as incompatible bilateral negotiations between exporters and importers (Wright, 2009; Briones, 2011). Regional coordination on emergency reserves may work if the emergency is limited to only a few countries and the reserves are adequate so that concerted action by affected countries would become feasible. ASEAN+3 countries have held discussions regarding a coordinated effort for joint stockholding program for rice with firmly agreed rules for buying and selling (Briones, 2011).

As linkages between the energy and agricultural sectors have strengthened through the promotion of biofuels, attempts to expand production of bio-ethanol and biodiesel must not be at the expense of food production. The close co-movement of food and energy prices raises the danger of volatility in one commodity price spilling over to other commodities, for example, from wheat to rice or from fuel to food, as seen over the duration of 2011.

In response to growing inflationary pressures from food prices, governments across the region tightened monetary policy over the course of 2011 and 2012. In economies where inflation was a pressing concern, such as China, India and Viet Nam, interest rates were raised. However, for many other countries, such as Malaysia, the Republic of Korea and Thailand, inflation was not yet a major issue; nevertheless, to counter growing price pressures, those economies too started to raise interest rates. Such monetary tightening places added pressure on growth. In India, for example, where the policy rates were raised by over ten times between January 2010 and October 2011 in an effort to control high inflation rates, the growth momentum slowed considerably. Much of the rest of Asia experienced similar slowdowns in growth subsequently. In the face of slowing growth, many Asian economies turned to fiscal expansion again after it was witnessed following the global financial crisis in 2008. At the same time, to tame inflationary expectations arising from second-round effects of food price inflation, central banks adopted a tight monetary policy stance. This may however, dampen investment and consumption and slow growth further, presenting a policy dilemma to governments and central bankers in the region.

When domestic supply factors or external factors like global food price rise cause inflation, raising interest rates may not be effective in controlling inflation. This might even worsen the impact on the poor. Reducing inflation through this policy can cause unemployment among the workers who are already suffering from high food prices and amounts to 'adding insult to injury' (Siglitz, 2012). The poor can be protected from the adverse effects of high prices by strengthening social safety nets. In the wake of the global food crisis, countries adopted subsidies for storage of grains (India) and subsidies on inputs such as diesel (Kazakhstan), credit (Pakistan, Viet Nam) and chemical fertilizers (India and Pakistan). Several governments took steps to increase grain procurement by raising support prices for farmers (e.g., China, India, Pakistan, Philippines and Thailand).[4] The IMF (2008) estimated that for 43 net food importers, the rise in their average food bill from the 2008 food crisis was 0.8 percent of their 2008 GDP. The extent of such social protection would depend on the fiscal room available to the government, its administrative capacity as well as existence of systems that target the poor and vulnerable that can be scaled up easily during a crisis. In countries such as India, poor management of the food grain economy is leading to ironic situations where poor go hungry when food grain stocks with the government are in plenty. While the government has been encouraging food grain production by offering a high support price to the farmers, it has not been able to distribute the grains procured to the poor effectively due to problems with delivery mechanisms of the public distribution system such as leakages and targeting errors.

While governments have a useful role in ensuring food security to their populations, improving the efficiency of government expenditure can maximize societal payoff. In general, efficiency of government spending can be improved by targeting subsidies only to those most in need as opposed to general price subsidies, which disproportionately benefit the non-poor. Instead of across the board tax exemptions and tariff reductions it is desirable to restrict these measures to commodities that are consumed mostly by the poor. Use of information technology makes it possible to reduce leakages in transfers to poor households by switching from distribution of food in kind to electronic cash transfers (see, e.g., Adato and Hoddinott, 2010). Such efficiency improvements would enable governments to focus more on public investments in agricultural research and development, rural transport and communications that help overcome underinvestment due to positive externalities. The alternative of cash transfers however is not free from problems. In rural areas, for example, as in the case of India most of the poor do not have bank accounts and are not literate enough to use smart cards; and moreover the retail market network may be inadequate for people to purchase their requirements.

Speculation may be playing a role in increasing price volatility but the extent and mechanism through which it does this requires further study. Since the role of speculation in futures markets for food commodities can be contested, efforts to reduce speculation might yield unintended and undesirable consequences. Instead of blocking markets it is better to adopt market-based solutions to deal with price volatility. While removing policy distortions would encourage private participation in marketing and investment there is a need for regulation and supervision of agricultural financial markets to curb speculative activities. Possible short term actions to deal with speculative activities and *financialization* of food commodities include strengthening of market regulation and surveillance, greater policy dialogue to coordinate national policies, and strengthening the ability of the private sector to access market-based hedging instruments.

4.7 CONCLUDING OBSERVATIONS

This chapter reviewed recent trends in food prices, their causes and impact on growth and poverty. It explored the channels through which food price inflation affects general inflation and economic growth. The chapter discussed policy responses by developing Asian economies to rising and volatile food prices since the food price crisis in 2008 and the policy choices available to them.

While the price volatility observed in mid-2000s is due to both demand and supply factors, the long run trend of rising prices appears to be a result of slowing growth in agricultural yields combined with a rising demand for food, feed and green fuels. Increasing growth rates in emerging markets have led to rising demand for high value food and for meats which gave rise to increasing feed demand for grains. At the same time biofuel mandates in developed countries diverted food crops to the production of bioethanol and biodiesel.

Food price inflation causes direct increases in headline inflation due to the high weight given to food in the CPI, particularly in developing economies. It can lead to second-round effects through the wage–price nexus creating inflationary expectations. These effects are particularly higher in a high inflation environment. Though inflation at mild levels can be conducive to economic growth, beyond certain levels it has a negative impact. While monetary tightening is the usual mechanism used to control inflation, its effectiveness depends on other macroeconomic conditions in the economy.

Policies aimed at controlling inflation should be based on its underlying causes. Monetary policy tightening could hurt growth when inflation is due to supply-side factors as in the case of food crises. Price controls used to protect consumers are not in the interests of producers and can have a negative impact on productivity and growth. While net sellers of food are better off due to higher food prices, even net buyers in rural areas might benefit if the increased profits induce expanded production creating additional employment and possibly increasing wages.

High and volatile food prices pose a challenge for developing countries' fight against poverty and achievement of other development goals. Some of them have seen reversal in the gains made in terms of poverty reduction. Adverse nutritional impact particularly on children has long-term consequences for human capital development. This is partly the reason why governments insulate their domestic food prices from fluctuations in world market prices.

To avoid contributing to inflationary pressures public spending on safety net programs has to be well targeted and focused on vulnerable groups. Programs to address the adverse impact on the poor need to be flexible and reversible without making a long-term dent on the fiscal situation. There is a need for a check on increase in the volume of subsidies through better targeting to help the genuinely needy and subsidies that minimize market price distortion.

Increasing productivity and resilience of food production should be the priority for the long-term, especially for developing countries dependent on volatile international markets. Structural adjustments that are needed to secure food supplies include measures to improve crop productivity, increased investments in infrastructure such as irrigation and food transport, and stronger market integration. A higher pass-through of international prices through less restrictive trade policies/barriers would provide better price signals to improve efficiency of farmers triggering productivity and output increases in the long run.

Closer cooperation at the regional and global level is essential in increasing food productivity through coordinated efforts by national and international research institutes; in mitigating the risks of climate related natural disasters and in reducing risks from financial derivatives markets through regulation.

NOTES

* The authors are grateful to Professor Raghbendra Jha and an anonymous referee for thoughtful comments. The views expressed in this chapter are those of the authors and do not necessarily reflect the views and policies of the Asian Development Bank (ADB), or its Board of Governors, or the governments they represent. ADB does not guarantee the accuracy of the data included in this publication and accepts no responsibility for any consequence of their use.
1. http://www.biodiesel.org/production/production-statistics; http://www.eia.gov/biofuels/issuestrends/.
2. http://www.ers.usda.gov/data-products/us-bioenergy-statistics.aspx.
3. For other examples, see Jones and Kwiecinski (2010), ADB (2011a) and FAO and others (2011).
4. See Freire et al. (2012) for a compilation of food-related policy measures adopted by countries in the Asia-Pacific to control food price inflation.

REFERENCES

Abbot, P.C. (2011), Export restrictions as stabilization responses to food crisis. *American Journal of Agricultural Economics*, **94**(2), 428–34.

Abbot, P.C., C. Hurt and W.E. Tyner (2008), *What's Driving Food Prices?* Oak Brook, IL: Farm Foundation.

Adato, M. and J. Hoddinott (eds) (2010), *Conditional Cash Transfers in Latin America*, Baltimore, MD: Johns Hopkins University Press for IFPRI.

ADB (2008), Food prices and inflation in developing Asia: is poverty reduction coming to an end? Manilla: Economics and Research Department, ADB.

ADB (2011a), *Global Food Price Inflation and Developing Asia*. Manila: Asian Development Bank, March.

ADB (2011b), *Asian Development Outlook 2011*. Manila: Asian Development Bank, April.

Al-Eyd, A., D. Amaglobeli, B. Shukurov and M. Sumlinski (2012), Global food price inflation and policy responses in Central Asia. IMF Working Paper WP/12/86.

Anderson, K., S. Jha, S. Nelgen and A. Strutt (2013), Re-examining policies for food security in Asia. *Food Security*, **5**, Springer. Available at: http://www.springerlink.com/openurl.asp?genre=article&id=doi:10.1007/s12571-012-0237-5.

Baffes, J. (2011), The long-term implications of the 2007–08 commodity-price boom, *Development in Practice*, **21**(4–5), 517–25.

Briones, R.M. (2011), Regional cooperation for food security: the case of emergency rice reserves in the ASEAN plus three. ADB Sustainable Development Working Paper Series No. 18. Manila: Asian Development Bank.

Compton, J., Steve Wiggins and Sharada Keats (2010), *Impact of the Global Food Crisis on the Poor: What is the Evidence?* London: Overseas Development Institute.

Dawe, D. (2008), Have recent increases in international cereal prices been transmitted to domestic economies? The experience in seven large Asian countries. ESA Working Paper No. 08-03, Agricultural Development Economics Division, The Food and Agriculture Organization of the United Nations, Rome.

Dawe, D. and T. Slayton (2011), The world rice market in 2007/08. In A. Prakash (ed.), *Safeguarding Food Security in Volatile Global Markets*. Rome: FAO, pp. 164–74.

Dehn, J. (2000), Commodity price uncertainty and shocks: implications for economic growth. Centre for the Study of African Economies, Department of Economics, University of Oxford, WPS/2000-10.

Erten, B. and J.A. Ocampo (2012), Super-cycles of commodity prices since the mid-nineteenth century. UN-DESA Working Paper No. 110ST/ESA/2012/DWP/110, February.

FAO (Food and Agriculture Organization) (2012), *Statistical Yearbook, World Food and Agriculture*. Rome: FAO, Part 2, pp. 104–106.

FAO, IFAD, OECD, WFP, World Bank, WTO, UNCTAD, IFPRI and UN HLTF (2011), Price volatility in food and agricultural markets: policy responses. Policy Report for the G-20s Agricultural Ministerial meeting, Paris, 22–23 June, Rome: FAO, June 2.

Freire C., A. Hasan and M.H. Malik (2012), High food prices in Asia-Pacific: policy initiatives in view of supply uncertainty and price volatility. MPDD working papers WP/12/01, UN Economic and Social Commission for Asia and the Pacific.

Gelos, G. and Y. Ustyugova (2012), Inflation responses to commodity prices: how and why do countries differ? IMF Working Paper WP/12/225.

Ghoshray, A. (2006), Long-run relationship between US and Argentine maize prices. *Journal of Agribusiness*, **24**(1), 79–92.

Gilbert, C.L. (2008), Commodity speculation and commodity investment. Discussion Paper No. 20, Department of Economics, University of Trento, Italy.

Gilbert, C. (2010), *An Assessment of International Commodity Agreements for Commodity Price Stabilization*, Paris: OECD.

Gilbert, C.L. and C.W. Morgan (2010), Food price volatility. *Philosophical Transactions of The Royal Society B*, **365**, 3023–3034.

Giordani, P.E., N. Rocha and M. Ruta (2012), Food prices and the multiplier effect of export policy. Staff Working Paper ERSD-2012-08, Economic Research and Statistics Division, World Trade Organization, Geneva.

Global Monitoring Report (2012), Food prices, nutrition and the millennium development goals. World Bank and International Monetary Fund, Washington DC.

Hadass, Y.S. and J.G. Williamson (2001), Terms of trade shocks and economic performance 1870–1940: Prebisch and Singer revisited. NBER Working Paper 8188.

Headey, D. and S. Fan (2008), Anatomy of a crisis: the causes and consequences of surging food prices. *Agricultural Economics*, **39**(supplement), 375–91.

Hernandez, M. and M. Torero (2010), Examining the dynamic relationship between spot and future prices of agricultural commodities. Discussion Paper 00988, Markets, Trade and Institutions Division, International Food Policy Research Institute, Washington DC.

IMF (2008), *Food and Fuel Prices – Recent Developments, Macroeconomic Impact, and Policy Responses: An Update*. Washington DC: IMF.

IMF (2011), *Managing Global Growth Risks and Commodity Price Shocks – Vulnerabilities and Policy Challenges for Low-Income Countries*. Washington DC: IMF.

IMF (2012), *Managing Global Growth Risks and Commodity Price Shocks Vulnerabilities and Policy Challenges for Low-Income Countries*. Washington DC: Strategy, Policy and Review Department, IMF.

Ivanic, M., W. Martin and H. Zaman (2011), Estimating the short-run poverty impacts of the 2010–11 surge in food prices. Policy Research Working Paper 5533, World Bank, Washington DC, April.

Jha, R. and T.N. Dang (2012), Inflation variability and the relationship between inflation and growth. *Macroeconomics and Finance in Emerging Market Economies*, **5**(1), 3–17.

Jha, S. and C. Rhee (2012), Distributional consequences and policy responses to food price inflation in Developing Asia. In R. Arezki, C.A. Pattillo, M. Quintyn and M. Zhu (eds), *Commodity Price Volatility and Inclusive Growth in Low-income Countries*. Washington DC: International Monetary Fund, Chapter 14.

Jha, R., R. Gaiha and A. Sharma (2009), Calorie and micronutrient deprivation and poverty nutrition traps in rural India. *World Development*, **37**(5), 982–91.

Jha, S., K. Kubo and B. Ramaswami (2012), International trade and risk sharing in the global rice market: the impact of foreign and domestic supply shocks. Paper presented at ADB-CIDA Symposium on Food Security in Asia and the Pacific: Key Policy Issues and Options, 17–18 September 2012, Vancouver, Canada.

Jones, D. and A. Kwiecinski (2010), Policy responses in emerging economies to international agricultural commodity price surges. OECD Food, Agriculture and Fisheries Working Paper No. 34, Paris.

Khan, M.S. and A.S. Senhadji (2001), Threshold effects in the relationship between inflation and growth. IMF Staff Papers, **48**(1).

Martin W. and K. Anderson (2011), Export restrictions and price insulation during commodity price books. *American Journal of Agricultural Economics*, **94**(2), 422–27.

Minot, N. (2010), Transmission of world food price changes to African markets and its effect on household welfare. Food Security Collaborative Working Paper No. 58563, Department of Agricultural Food and Resource Economics, Michigan State University.

Mishra, P. and D. Roy (2011), Explaining inflation in India: the role of food prices. In S. Shah et al. (eds), *India Policy Forum*, Volume 8. National Council of Applied Economic Research India Policy Forum, New Delhi, and Brookings Institution, Washington DC.

Nerlove, M. (1972), Lags in economic behavior. *Econometrica*, **40**(2), 221–52.

Obidzinski, K., R. Andriani, H. Komarudin and A. Andrianto (2011), Environmental and social impacts of oil palm plantations and their implications for biofuel production in Indonesia. *Ecology and Society*, **17**(1), 25.

Polaski, S. (2008), Rising food prices, poverty and the Doha Round. *Policy Outlook*, Carnegie Endowment for International Peace.

Ravallion, M. (1990), Rural welfare effects of food price changes under induced wage responses: theory and evidence for Bangladesh. *Oxford Economic Papers*, **42**, 574–85.

Ravindran, V. (2010), Poultry feed availability and nutrition in developing countries. *Poultry Development Review*. Food and Agriculture Organization, United Nations.

Rosegrant, M.W., T. Zhu, S. Msangi and T. Sulser (2008), Global scenarios for biofuels: impacts and implications. *Review of Agricultural Economics*, **30**, 495–505.

Schultz, T.W. (1953), *The Economic Organization of Agriculture*. New York: McGraw-Hill.

Srinivasan, P.V. and S. Jha (2001), Liberalised trade and domestic price stability: the case of rice and wheat in India. *Journal of Development Economics* **65**(2), 417–41.

Stiglitz, J. (2012), Essay on commodity price volatility and inclusive growth. In R. Arezki, C.A. Pattillo, M. Quintyn and M. Zhu (eds), *Commodity Price Volatility and Inclusive Growth in Low-income Countries*. Washington DC: International Monetary Fund.

Timmer, C.P. (2008), Causes of high food prices. ADB Economics Working Paper Series, 128, Manila, Asian Development Bank.

Timmer, C.P. (2009), Did speculation affect world rice prices? ESA Working Paper No. 09–07, The Food and Agricultural Organization of the United Nations (FAO), Rome.

Tyers, R. and K. Anderson (1992), *Disarray in World Food Markets: A Quantitative Assessment*. Cambridge and New York: Cambridge University Press.

UN-ESCAP (2009), *Sustainable Agriculture and Food Security in Asia and the Pacific*, Bangkok: United Nations Economic and Social Commission for Asia and the Pacific.

UN-ESCAP (2011a), *Statistical Yearbook for Asia and the Pacific 2011*. Available at: http://www.unescap.org/stat/data/syb2011/II-Environment/Natural-disasters.asp.

UN-ESCAP (2011b), Rising food prices and inflation in the Asia-Pacific region: causes, impact and policy response. Macroeconomic Policy and Development Division Policy Briefs, No.7, United Nations – Economic and Social Commission for Asia and the Pacific.
UN-ESCAP (2012), *Economic and Social Survey of Asia and the Pacific 2012: Pursuing Shared Prosperity in an Era of Turbulence and High Commodity Prices*. Bangkok: UN-ESCAP.
von Braun, J. and M. Torero (2008), Implementation of physical and virtual international food security reserves to protect the poor and prevent market failure. International Food Policy Research Institute, October.
Walsh, J.P. (2011), Reconsidering the role of food prices in inflation. IMF Working Paper WP/11/71 Washington DC.
World Bank (2010), *Food Price Increases in South Asia: National Responses and Regional Dimensions*. Washington DC: South Asia Region, The World Bank.
World Bank (2011), *Food Price Watch*. Poverty Reduction and Economic Management (Prem) Network, Washington DC, November.
Wright, B. (2009), International grain reserves and other instruments to address volatility in grain markets. Policy Research Working Paper 5028. The World Bank, Washington DC.
Wright, B. (2011), The economics of grain price volatility. *Applied Economic Perspectives and Policy*, **33**(2), 32–58.

5. Transmission of global food prices, supply response and impacts on the poor*
*David Dawe****

5.1 INTRODUCTION

There has been substantial discussion of what happened (and why) on world food markets between 2006 and 2008, and more recently, in 2010 and 2011 (Piesse and Thirtle, 2009; Gilbert, 2010; Headey and Fan, 2010; Timmer, 2010; Headey, 2011; OECD–FAO, 2011; Wright and Cafiero, 2011, to cite just a few). This chapter will not discuss those important issues, but will focus instead on two main 'downstream' topics. First, and primarily, the degree to which world price movements were transmitted to domestic farm and retail prices (and why), because neither farmers nor consumers interact directly with world markets. Second, a review of how food prices affect poverty in different types of countries.

5.2 DOMESTIC STAPLE FOOD PRICES INCREASED SUBSTANTIALLY IN MOST COUNTRIES DURING THE 2006–08 FOOD PRICE CRISIS

The transmission of world prices to domestic prices was quite heterogeneous across countries and commodities, with policies having a strong influence on this transmission. These policies will be discussed below, but before doing that some aggregate estimates of increases in domestic staple food prices will be presented. Staple food prices are examined instead of the food component of the consumer price index (CPI) because the basket used to calculate food price inflation is not representative of the expenditure patterns of the poor.

In order to examine trends in domestic staple food prices, monthly indices of domestic rice, wheat and maize prices during the period January 2007 to December 2011 were constructed. These indices include 50, 30 and 39 countries for rice, wheat and maize, respectively, and include all countries for which data were available from FAO (2012). All prices are in local currency terms and are deflated by the national CPI.

The choice of currency in which to analyse domestic price movements can make a substantial difference in some situations. For example, between January 2005 and December 2007, domestic rice prices in the Philippines increased by more than 40 per cent in US dollar terms, but were nearly constant in local currency terms (Figure 5.1).

---

* The views expressed in this chapter are those of the author(s) and do not necessarily reflect the views or policies of the Food and Agriculture Organization of the United Nations.
** Excellent research assistance from Ali Doroudian and Cristian Morales-Opazo was much appreciated.

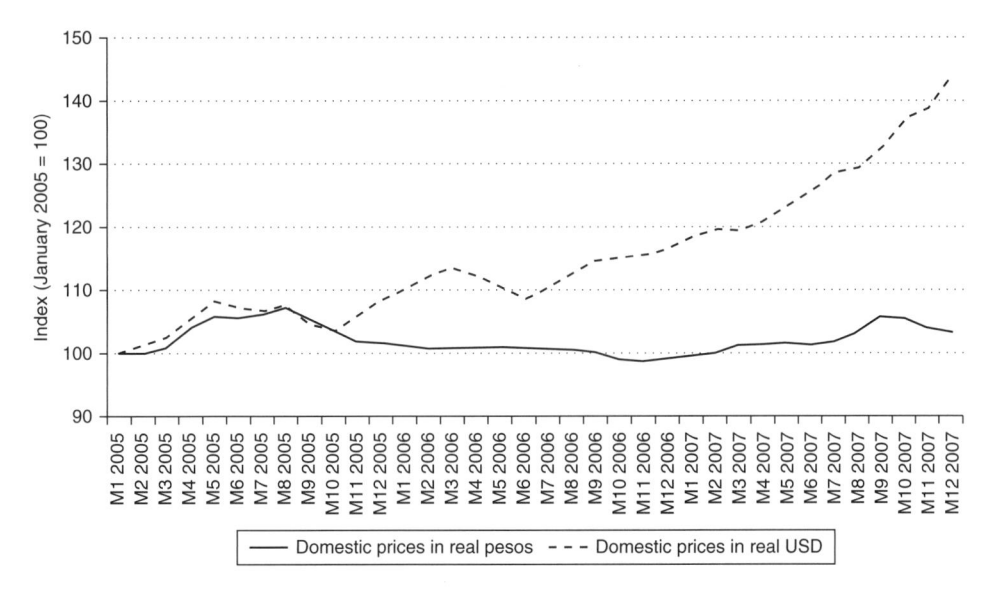

Figure 5.1 Rice prices in the Philippines, January 2005 to December 2007

The difference was due to an appreciation of the real peso–dollar exchange rate during this period. While it sometimes makes sense to analyse prices in US dollar terms, food security and poverty are affected by local currency prices, so local currency prices are used throughout this chapter unless otherwise mentioned.

Within a given country for a given staple food, nominal price data are often available for multiple locations, multiple qualities, multiple levels of the marketing chain (i.e. wholesale and retail), or some combination thereof. In order to avoid skewing the results, only one price series for each of rice, wheat and maize in any given country is included (e.g. both wheat and wheat flour from the same country would not be included, or rice wholesale and retail).

When data are available for multiple locations, multiple qualities or multiple marketing levels for a given staple food in a given country, a set of ordered selection criteria are needed in order to choose which data series to analyse. The first criterion was to use, whenever possible, retail price data, the justification being that these are the prices paid by consumers. However, if no retail price data were available for a particular case study, wholesale prices, which are usually linked quite closely to retail prices, were used. In the case of wheat, if there were data for both wheat and wheat flour, data on wheat flour were used. In the case of maize, data on tortillas were used if available, but if not, data on maize flour were used. If data for neither of those two commodities were available, data on maize grain were used.

The next criterion was based on quality. The lowest quality available was used, on the grounds that lower qualities are more important for the poor. That being said, prices of different qualities generally seemed to move broadly together within the same country.

The third criterion was to use national average prices when available. When national average prices were unavailable, an unweighted average of price in all the markets in the given country for which data were available was used.

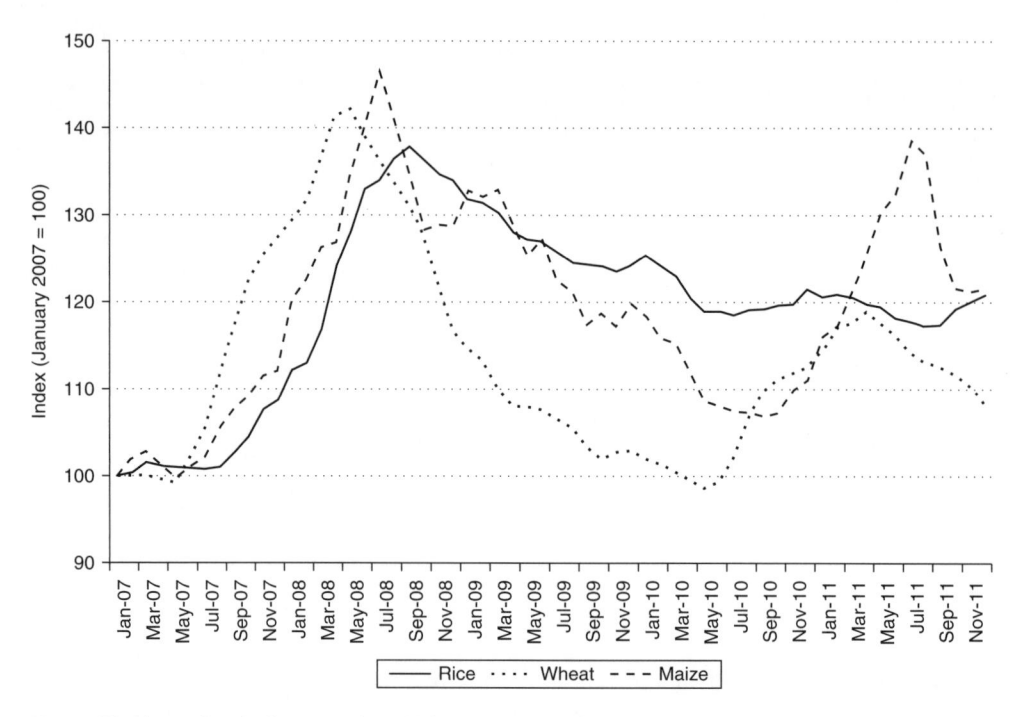

Note: The domestic price is set equal to 100 in January 2007 for all countries, and the index value for subsequent months is equal to the average index value across all countries.

Source: Underlying raw data: FAO (2012).

Figure 5.2 Domestic price indices for rice, wheat and maize, January 2007 to December 2011

The indices for domestic rice, wheat and maize prices are shown in Figure 5.2. Generally speaking, there were strong surges in domestic prices in 2007–08. In the middle of 2008, domestic rice, wheat and maize prices were each, on average across countries, about 40 per cent higher (after adjusting for inflation) than they were in January 2007. Other studies (e.g. Robles and Torero, 2010; Minot, 2011) have also reached the conclusion that there was substantial transmission of prices from world markets to domestic markets during the crisis. While transmission is often weak in normal times, transmission was stronger during the world food crisis.

Note that after the collapse of international cereal prices in the second half of 2008, domestic prices eventually began to decline substantially in most countries. By the second quarter of 2010, domestic prices (after adjusting for inflation) had returned to January 2007 levels for wheat, although maize prices were still about 10 per cent higher than in January 2007. Domestic rice prices were even higher, with prices on average 19 per cent higher than in January 2007. The pattern of changes in domestic prices across cereals was similar to that on world markets, as world rice prices increased the most between January 2007 and the second quarter of 2010.

In the 2010–11 cereal price surge, which began in the third quarter of 2010, trends in domestic prices were also similar to those on world markets. Domestic prices increased sharply for both wheat and maize, but not for rice, for which the world price did not increase at that time.

Using annual averages, in 2008 domestic prices (adjusted for inflation) in the same sample of countries as used in Figure 5.2 were on average 25, 21 and 26 per cent higher for rice, wheat and maize, respectively, than in 2007. Although much less than the changes experienced on world markets, these increases must have had a substantial impact on the purchasing power of at least some segments of the poor. In countries such as Bangladesh, Malawi and Viet Nam, the poor often spend 35 per cent or more of their income on staple foods. Thus, in 2008, poor consumers who did not produce staple foods experienced a decline in real income of approximately 9 per cent (equal to a budget share of 35 per cent multiplied by a price increase of about 25 per cent).[1] Not surprisingly, the volatility of domestic prices also increased during the crisis, reaching a peak for all three cereals in 2008 or early 2009 (Figure 5.3; measured as the unweighted average volatility across countries). Domestic price volatility for maize is consistently higher for maize than for rice or wheat.

The changes in domestic prices shown in Figure 5.2 are useful in the sense that they give an indication of average price changes across countries, each one of which has

Note: Volatility of domestic prices is calculated as the standard deviation of the logarithm of (P_t/P_{t-1}) over the previous 12 months. Countries included are the same as those in Figure 5.2.

Source: Raw data: FAO (2012).

Figure 5.3 Price volatility for domestic rice, wheat and maize prices, 2007–11

104 *Handbook on food*

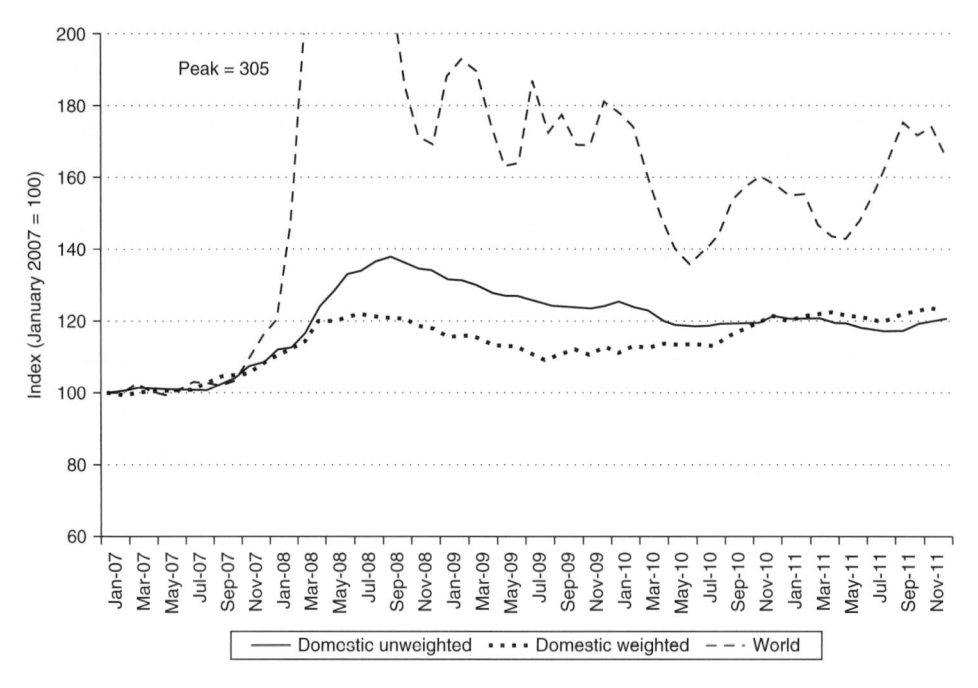

Note: Country weights are shares in global rice consumption (by calories), scaled to sum to one. Countries included in the index account for 81 percent of developing country rice consumption.

Figure 5.4a   Inflation-adjusted rice price indices, 2007–10

a different combination of trade policies, exchange rate movements, infrastructure, import dependence and other factors that are important for determining the ultimate degree of transmission. The indices are misleading, however, in terms of thinking about global food security because price changes in all countries are implicitly given equal importance (each index shown is a simple average of indexes across countries). An alternative is to weight each country by its share in global dietary energy intake of that particular staple food (with the sum of the weights scaled to 1 in order to account for the facts that high-income countries are excluded from the calculation by design and price data are not available for all developing countries). Figures 5.4a, b and c show how the weighted average index compares to world prices and the unweighted index (copied from Figure 5.2).

Compared to the unweighted index, the price changes in the weighted index were generally smaller in 2008, especially for rice and wheat. This is because rice and wheat prices in China and India, the world's two largest consumers of staple foods, were largely stable during the crisis due to trade controls (see below).

Comparing 2008 with 2007, weighted average prices increased by 16, 7 and 26 per cent for rice, wheat and maize, respectively. Using the share of each of the three major cereals in developing country energy intake as weights (with rice being the most important and maize the least), there was a weighted average cereal price increase in 2008 of 14 per cent (compared to 2007). This calculation only includes the three major cereals – it excludes other cereals and roots and tubers, for which there are fewer available price data.

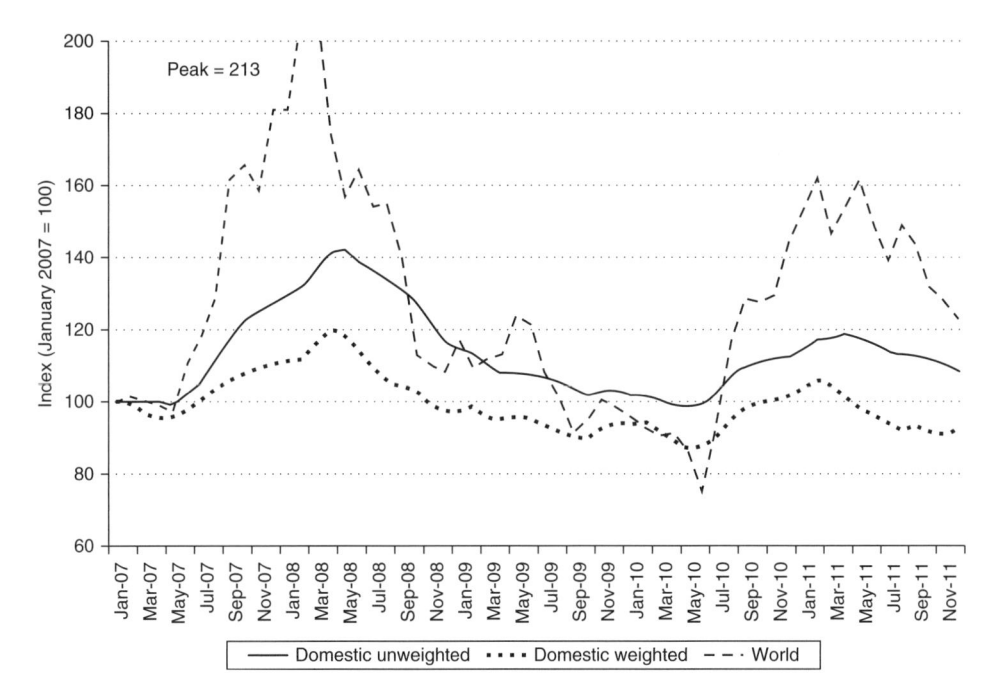

Note: Country weights are shares in global wheat consumption (by calories), scaled to sum to one. Countries included in the index account for 42 percent of developing country wheat consumption.

Figure 5.4b   Inflation-adjusted wheat price indices, 2007–10

5.3   TRADE POLICIES HAD AN IMPORTANT EFFECT ON PRICE TRANSMISSION

Price transmission from world markets to domestic markets is affected by several factors, including transport costs, countries' levels of self-sufficiency, exchange rates and domestic shocks. But trade policy is perhaps the most fundamental determinant of the extent to which world price shocks pass through to domestic markets. Trade policy interventions were relatively common in developing countries during the world food crisis, with at least 55 countries using trade policy instruments to mitigate the impacts of the world food crisis of 2006–08 (Demeke et al., 2009).

In particular, the key factor that affects price transmission is the degree to which the government determines the volume of trade (either exports or imports), as opposed to allowing the private sector to make the decision. Government control might be applied formally, through a fixed quota, or informally, through ad-hoc determination of quotas that vary in response to external events. Export quotas can reduce pass-through of high world prices to the domestic economy, while import quotas can prevent the pass-through of low world prices.

During the world food crisis of 2006–08, domestic prices of rice and wheat were very stable in China, India and Indonesia because of government controls on exports of these

106 *Handbook on food*

Note: Country weights are shares in direct global maize consumption (by calories), scaled to sum to one. Countries included in the index account for 53 percent of direct developing country maize consumption.

Figure 5.4c Inflation-adjusted maize price indices, 2007–10

crops (Fang, 2010; Gulati and Dutta, 2010; Saifullah, 2010; see Figure 5.5 for China). These controls are in place even in normal times (although the magnitude of the quota varies with events) and were not implemented specifically in response to the crisis. It is important to note that while trade controls in China did prevent transmission from world markets, China has maintained a generally open trade policy in the sense that domestic rice prices are at most times similar to those on world markets – the government does not systematically force domestic rice prices to be substantially above or below world prices (Huang et al., 2009).

In addition to trade controls, another key feature of these three countries is that they were not heavily reliant on imports during this time. As a result, a cessation of trade did not lead to higher domestic prices. For a country that is heavily reliant on imports, domestic prices must increase along with world prices, unless the government is willing to subsidize imports. For example, China is heavily reliant on soybean imports. Furthermore, the government does not control trade in that commodity. As a result, domestic prices of soybean in China surged in 2007 and 2008 (Figure 5.6).

Not all countries with export controls are able to successfully stabilize domestic prices, however. Viet Nam, for example, restricted rice exports in the early months of 2008 (Hoang Ngan, 2010). Even though domestic supplies were more than enough to feed the population, domestic retail prices soared by 50 per cent in only 5 weeks in April–May 2008. In this case, it seems that there was an element of generalized panic and hoarding

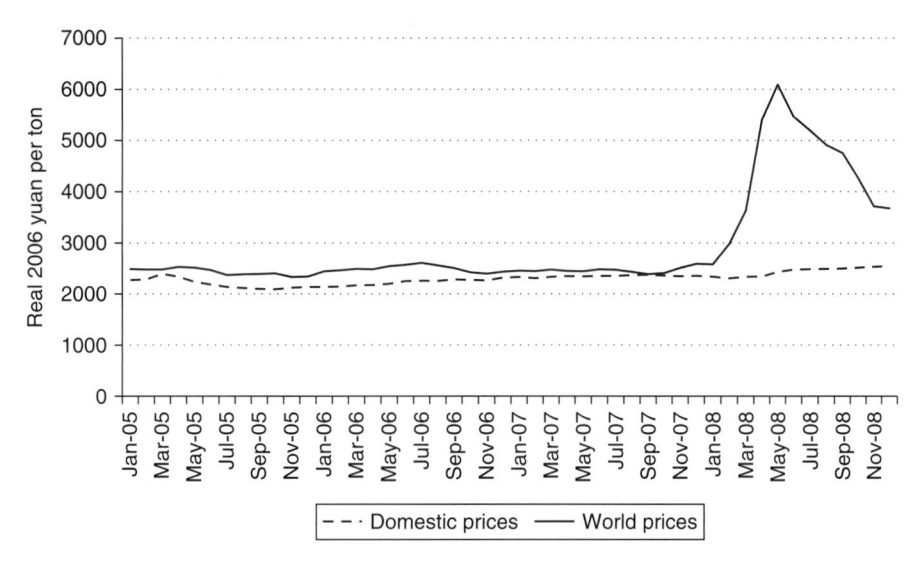

Source: Fang (2010).

Figure 5.5 Domestic rice prices in China and international rice prices, 2005–08

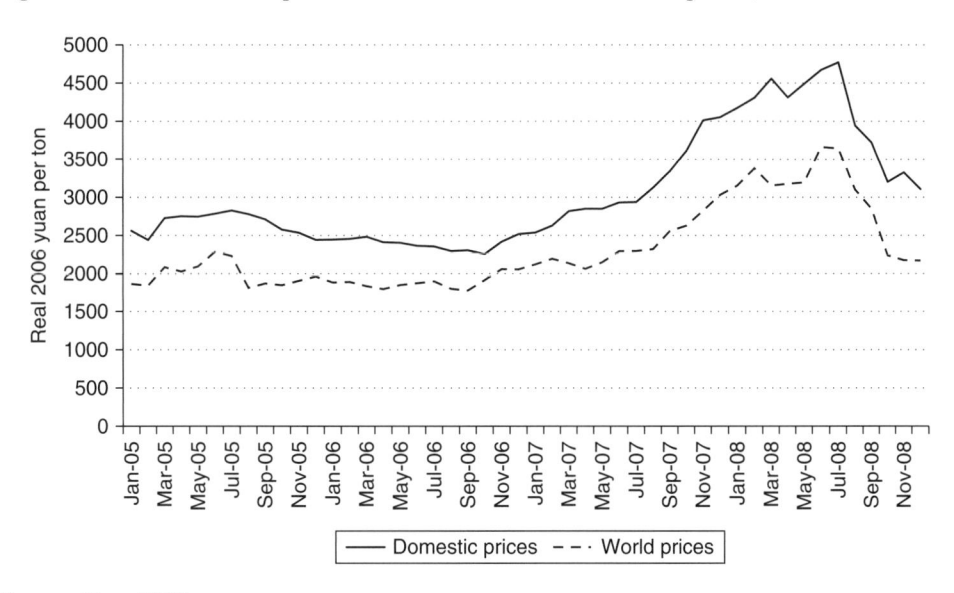

Source: Fang (2010).

Figure 5.6 Domestic soybean prices in China and international soybean prices, 2005–08

on the part of traders, consumers and farmers (Timmer, 2010). Government policies such as export taxes also changed frequently, adding to uncertainty and risk for traders.

The Philippines also had trade controls in place before and during the rice price crisis, but domestic prices surged there during 2008. Again, panic and hoarding likely played a key role. Statements by government officials seemed to encourage the notion that there was a shortage, despite the fact that domestic production had reached record levels in 2007 and the upcoming dry season harvest (which accounts for nearly half of annual production) was forecast to reach record levels (as it in fact eventually did). For example, one official suggested that all restaurants should cut their servings of rice in half, and the President publicly pursued a memorandum of understanding (MOU) with Thailand to arrange for additional imports. In Indonesia, by contrast, government officials emphasized that public distributions would be increased, and that no exports would be allowed (unless public stocks reached a very high level of 3 million tons). Such government statements likely have a key role to play in determining the extent of speculative behaviour by the millions of farmers, traders and consumers in the region.

The other main tool of trade policy, import tariffs or export taxes, in many cases will not impede transmission of world price shocks to domestic markets unless the tariff/tax is varied in response to changes in world prices. A constant import tariff will raise the domestic price of food (and an export tax will lower it), but if the private sector is allowed to choose the amount they import at a given tariff, changes in world prices will often be completely transmitted to domestic prices until world prices or the tariff get so high that there are no more imports.

Nevertheless, a high import tariff (or other trade measure that raises domestic prices) can reduce price transmission, although there are important measurement issues to consider. A high pre-existing tariff will affect measured price transmission in at least two ways. First, even if price transmission as measured in currency units per ton is not affected by a tariff, price transmission as measured in percentage terms will be affected because of a level effect, i.e. the same absolute change in currency units per ton will be a smaller percentage change if the initial price was higher due to trade restrictions. Reinforcing this effect is the fact that as world prices rise, eventually they become so high that domestic prices cease to be determined by the world price plus tariff (plus transport costs), but rather are determined by the intersection of domestic supply and demand. This point is reached after a smaller increase in domestic prices if domestic prices were initially high.

To give a concrete example, rice prices in the Dominican Republic were much higher than in neighbouring countries before the crisis, as the government used (and still uses) import quotas and other measures to influence domestic prices (Quezada, 2013). During the crisis, domestic prices increased just 11 per cent from 2007 to 2008 (in nominal United States dollars) while prices in neighbouring countries increased by between 26 per cent (Costa Rica) and 59 per cent (El Salvador). But the reduced transmission during the crisis came at the cost of much higher prices before the crisis. Indeed, despite lower transmission during the crisis, the level of rice prices in the Dominican Republic at the peak of the crisis was similar to those in neighbouring countries (Figure 5.7). In the longer-term sense, then, transmission was not reduced – it was just moved forward in time. And when world prices fell, domestic prices in the Dominican Republic did not.

Even when controls on trade volumes (or variable tariffs) do serve to stabilize domestic prices, there are costs to such policies. In terms of losses to the domestic economy, there are short-run static efficiency losses from not allowing domestic prices to follow

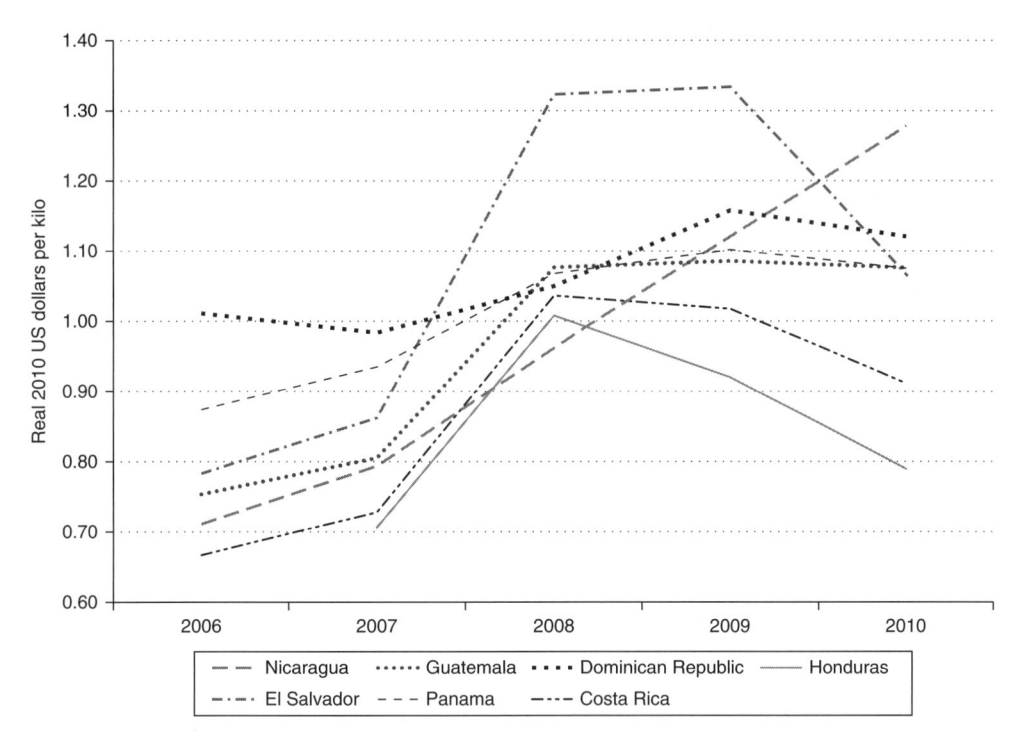

Figure 5.7 Domestic rice prices in Central America and the Caribbean (USD per ton), 2006–2010

world price movements. Supply response is impeded during price spikes and there are losses in export revenue. A high tariff can shield an economy from international price fluctuations, but might result in higher domestic price volatility due to domestic supply shocks. In addition to the losses imposed on the domestic economy, export restrictions also result in world prices being higher and more volatile than they would otherwise have been, imposing costs on other countries.

On the other hand, excessive short-term volatility can reduce the information content of prices and lead to medium-term dynamic efficiency losses (Timmer and Dawe, 2007), so it is not clear that following world price movements at all times maximizes economic efficiency. Furthermore, while supply response may be impeded during price spikes, if farmers are also protected from price declines, trade controls might augment supply response at other times. Thus, price stabilization need not reduce farm production in the medium-run, and it might even increase it if the uncertainty and risk facing farmers is reduced (Subervie, 2008).

In addition to their effects on price volatility, trade policies also affect the level of prices. Higher domestic prices, in most cases, tend to increase the level of poverty (see below). In addition, if a country has higher prices for staple foods than do its neighbours it may lose competitiveness in labour-intensive industries, as it will be forced to raise wages to compensate for higher food prices. This might reduce non-farm employment opportunities, cutting off a key pathway out of poverty.

5.4 FARMGATE PRICES AND PROFITS INCREASED DURING THE WORLD FOOD CRISIS

The above analysis focused solely on consumer (wholesale or retail) prices. But price transmission to the farmgate is also important. If farmgate prices do not increase, there will be no supply response.

While there are many anecdotal stories of retail prices increasing while farmgate prices did not, hard data on farmgate prices are essential to address this issue in a convincing manner. Farm price data are not as readily available as data on consumer prices, so it is not sensible to construct aggregate domestic price indices as was done in Figure 5.2. Nevertheless, there is some evidence to draw upon. The percentage increases in farmgate prices for rice, wheat and maize were very similar to those in consumer prices in several Asian countries (Bangladesh, China, Indonesia, Philippines, Thailand) between 2003 and 2008 (Dawe, 2010; Hossain and Deb, 2010). In Tanzania, farmgate prices for maize followed a similar pattern to consumer prices from 2007 to 2008 (Maltsoglou and Khwaja, 2010), and longer-term data from Burkina Faso for both white and yellow maize also show similar movements at producer and consumer levels (FAO, 2011). Farmgate prices for maize in Kenya also increased substantially during the world food crisis (Höffler and Owuor Ochieng, 2009). Based on this evidence (summarized in Figure 5.8), it appears that farmgate prices usually increase when consumer prices increase.

Theoretically, higher farmgate prices should lead to a positive supply response, and this is shown to be the case empirically by Imai et al. (2012) for a wide range of commodities in Asia. But supply response is also affected by changes in input prices – Imai et al. (2012) estimate that the elasticity of production with respect to fertilizer price

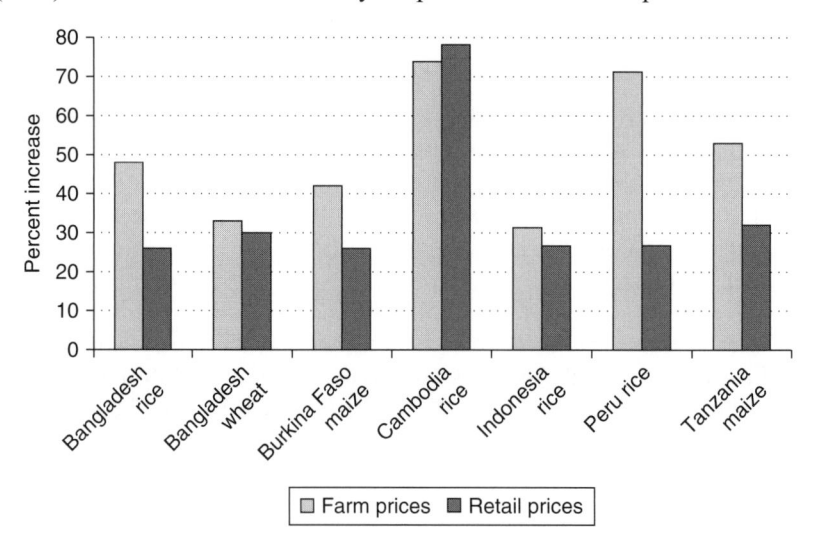

Notes: Based on inflation-adjusted prices. Price changes for Bangladesh wheat are from 2003 to 2006 and for Tanzania maize are from 2007 to 2008.

Source: National statistical agencies.

Figure 5.8   Per cent increase in real farmgate and retail prices, 2003–2008

is about −0.3 for rice and maize. Between 2004 and 2008, world prices for nitrogen, phosphorus and potassium fertilizers all increased by more than world grain prices. The price of urea, a prime source of nitrogen and one of the most widely used fertilizers, more than quadrupled in real terms from 2001 to 2008. To the extent that these higher world input prices were passed on to farmers, they reduced farm profitability and hence potential supply response. However, the extent to which fertilizer prices cancelled out farmgate price increases is probably less than commonly believed.

In traditional production systems that use little fertilizer, higher fertilizer prices have little impact on profitability. However, even in intensive production systems that use large quantities of fertilizer, the cost of fertilizer used is much less than the gross value of the crop produced, and it is the relative magnitude of these two quantities that determines the net impact of fertilizer price changes on profitability. For example, across a range of high-yielding Asian irrigated rice systems in six countries, the value of fertilizer applied was typically about 8 per cent of the gross value of production in 1999 (Moya et al., 2004). This implies that a doubling of fertilizer prices would raise production costs by 8 per cent of the value of production (assuming no change in fertilizer use), which in turn means that an increase in output prices of just 8 per cent would maintain profitability at a constant level. Even a further doubling (i.e. a four-fold increase in total, as happened on world urea markets) would require just a 32 per cent increase in output prices to fully compensate for the increased cost. Of course, if fertilizer prices increase substantially over the longer term and the cost of fertilizer becomes closer to the gross value of production, larger and larger increases in output prices will be required to compensate.

This general pattern is evident in Table 5.1, which shows the evolution of production costs and returns for winter–spring rice in An Giang province in the Mekong River Delta of Viet Nam. Between 2007 and 2008, fertilizer costs more than doubled, seed costs nearly doubled, labour costs increased substantially and yields fell, but a 57 per cent increase in paddy prices was enough to lead to an increase in profits of 34 per cent. Profits from rice production in Bangladesh in 2007–08 more than doubled compared with the previous year (Descargues, 2011). Not surprisingly, they subsequently fell in each of the next two years, although even in 2009–10 they were comparable to those in 2005–06.

Table 5.1 Production costs and returns, winter–spring paddy in An Giang Province, Viet Nam, 2007 and 2008

Item	2007	2008	% change
Seed	484	936	93
Fertilizer	3269	6691	105
Labour	3116	4765	53
Other costs	2928	2941	0
Yield (kg)	6100	5792	−5
Paddy price (VND/kg)	2350	3700	57
Profit	4538	6097	34

Note: VND = Vietnamese dong. Prices, costs and profits shown in thousands of Vietnamese dong per hectare.

Source: Adapted from Hoang Ngan (2010).

Thus, while the impact of changes in fertilizer and fuel prices will vary across different types of production system, in many cases it will take only a small increase in output prices to compensate for even a large increase in fertilizer prices. In other words, an increase in the ratio of fertilizer price to output price does not necessarily imply a decline in profitability.

Indeed, during the world food crisis, it appears that supply response was quite substantial in a number of developing countries. Comparing 2008 with 2007, cereal production increased by 6.2 per cent in OECD countries, 8.2 per cent in the BRICS, and 7.2 per cent in the rest of the world. Headey et al. (2010) and Imai et al. (2012) also conclude that supply response to the price surge during the world food crisis was substantial.

5.5 CHANGES IN MARKETING MARGINS DURING THE WORLD FOOD CRISIS

Given that farm prices increased in several Asian rice economies during the crisis, it is interesting to explore the magnitude of that increase relative to the increase in wholesale prices. Equivalently, what happened to marketing margins during the food crisis? Did farm prices increase as much as wholesale prices?

If markets are functioning well, one might expect percentage changes in farm and wholesale prices during the crisis to be similar. Such an expectation makes an implicit assumption about marketing behaviour, however, namely that margins are constant in proportional terms (this would be consistent with mark up pricing by a constant percentage). In nominal terms, and over the long haul, this is likely to be at least approximately the case, as changes in nominal domestic farm and wholesale prices are predominantly determined by monetary policies (of course, changes in technology or market structure could lead to different percentage changes at different levels of the marketing system).

In the short term, however, such an assumption is much less likely to be true. Timmer (1974) points out that of all the different marketing costs involved in moving a commodity from farm to wholesale markets, only interest and insurance charges are necessarily incurred in percentage terms. Other costs are more likely to be incurred on a per ton basis, e.g. transport costs. Speculative behaviour, discussed earlier, can also induce changes in marketing margins by increasing price risk (Timmer, 2010); possible examples of the impact of such behaviour in the Philippines and Thailand in 2007–08 for rice are given below. During the 2006–08 crisis, movements in farm and wholesale food prices were not primarily due to monetary policies, but rather to short-term shocks to supply and demand. Under these circumstances, there is no reason to expect that proportional changes in farm and wholesale prices will be equal, as marketing margins are not subject to the same shocks as farm and wholesale prices.

Figure 5.8 shows that, between 2003 and 2008, percentage increases in real retail prices were less than percentage increases in real farm prices in six of the seven cases analysed, often by substantial amounts. Such a pattern does not necessarily mean that markets are not functioning well (notice that farm price increases in percentage terms are larger, not smaller, than percentage increases in wholesale prices in this sample). In fact, this pattern is consistent with different marketing behaviour, namely that marketing margins are approximately constant in real absolute (currency units per ton) terms. In such cases,

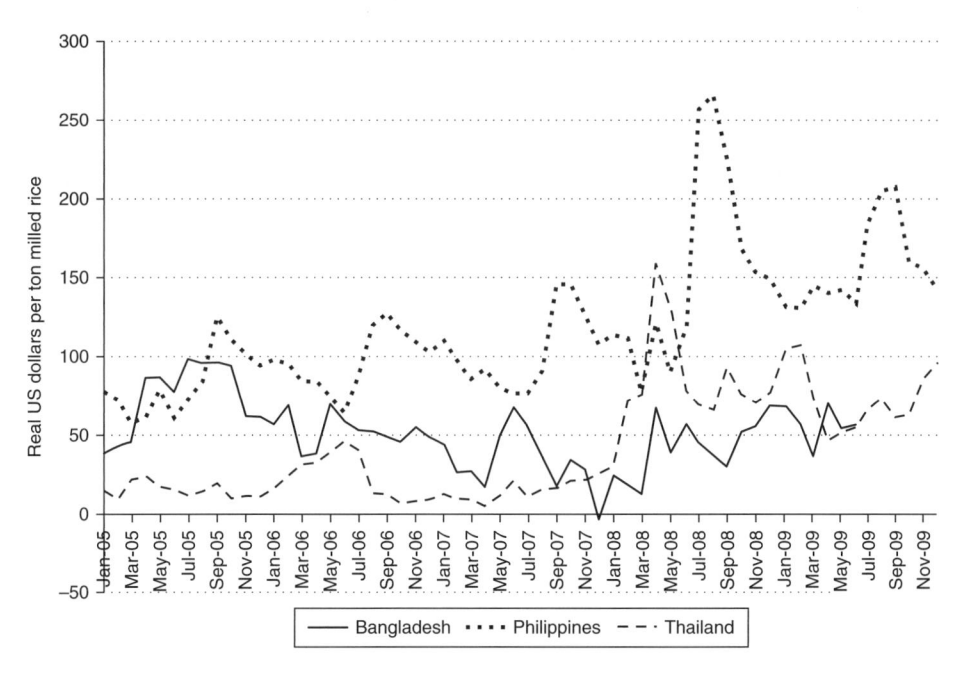

Figure 5.9 Real rice marketing margins in Bangladesh, the Philippines and Thailand, 2005–09

farm prices will increase by more in percentage terms simply because they start from a lower base, i.e. farm prices are below wholesale prices. They would also be likely to fall more in percentage terms if there was surplus production.

To examine the behaviour of marketing margins in more detail, we look at three large Asian countries (Bangladesh, the Philippines and Thailand) where domestic rice prices increased during the crisis and for which monthly data on both farm and wholesale/retail prices are available for several years. In all three countries, retail prices rose sharply in 2008. Figure 5.9 shows that marketing margins in Bangladesh in real USD per ton were essentially constant before and after the crisis, albeit with some fluctuations. In the Philippines and Thailand, however, there was a sharp increase, starting in February 2008 in Thailand and several months later in the Philippines in July of that year. The sharp increase does not necessarily support a model of constant margins in proportional terms, however. During the period 2005–07 in Thailand, wholesale prices were 6 per cent above farm prices on average, but this differential increased to 16 per cent during 2008–09. In the Philippines, retail prices were 26 per cent above farm prices during January 2005 to June 2008, but from July 2008 to December 2009 the differential increased to 37 per cent. Thus, in the Philippines and Thailand, marketing margins increased in both absolute and percentage terms in the midst of the crisis.

It is not clear why margins increased so substantially in the Philippines and Thailand, but it is possible that it was due to the increased risk facing traders in the volatile environment at that time. Many traders agree on a selling price for rice before they secure supplies, in order to reduce the risk of purchasing supplies and being unable to sell them. But when prices were increasing rapidly in early 2008, this business strategy led to increased risks on another front, namely that traders could not secure supplies at a price that would allow a profit, because prices had gone up substantially after the selling price was negotiated but before the supplies had been secured. Indeed, many traders lost money on some deals or were forced to renegotiate in order to avoid large losses (Hill, 2008). In the wake of such episodes, traders may have felt compelled to raise the selling price substantially in order to be sure that they could deliver at a profit. Such wider margins are a cost of price volatility.

It is interesting to note that, looking at a longer time series of prices in the Philippines, marketing margins increased sharply on one other occasion. Just as in 2008 (when farm to retail margins rose 35 per cent compared to 2007), margins rose 16 per cent in 1995 (compared to 1994) when prices rose sharply. On the earlier occasion, the sharp price increase was not due to events on world markets, but because the government decided to import only small quantities in the belief that self-sufficiency had been achieved. The main point is that when prices rise sharply, uncertainty may also increase, and the added risk facing traders is translated into wider margins.

Another possibility is that, at least in 2008, higher fuel prices led to substantially greater marketing costs. If higher oil prices were the main driving force behind higher marketing margins for rice, then they should have led to similar increases for white maize, given that rice and maize are both grains with similar marketing systems. But marketing margins for white maize in the Philippines declined at this time, suggesting that the increased margins were not due to some macroeconomic factor such as high oil prices, but were rather specific to the rice market. In essence, data on maize margins allow us to control for macroeconomic factors that should be common to all grains.

5.6 THE IMPACT OF HIGHER FOOD PRICES ON POVERTY

Given the importance of rice in Asia in both production and consumption, this section of the chapter focuses on the impact of higher rice prices on poverty. However, some evidence on the impact of higher food prices more generally will also be discussed – it does not fundamentally alter the general conclusions reached with respect to rice.

In order to understand the importance of higher rice prices for welfare, poverty and food security, it is first important to distinguish between net rice producers and net rice consumers. A net rice producer is someone for whom total sales of rice to the market exceed total purchases of rice from the market, whereas, for a net rice consumer, the reverse is true. Net rice consumers will generally be hurt by higher rice prices, while net rice producers will benefit. It is also true that whether a given household is a net rice producer or consumer depends on market prices. Higher prices will discourage consumption, encourage more production and possibly convert some households from net consumers to net producers. Lower prices could do the opposite.

The concepts of net rice producers and consumers are quite distinct from rural and urban. Although nearly all urban dwellers are net rice consumers, not all rural dwellers are net rice producers. In fact, very small farmers and agricultural labourers are often net consumers of rice, as they do not own enough land to produce enough rice for their family. These landless rural households are often the poorest of the poor. Although some of these labourers work on rice farms and are occasionally paid in rice, surveys show that they do not earn enough rice to sell a surplus on the market. Instead, they need to purchase rice on markets and are likely to benefit from lower prices.

The importance of the rural landless varies greatly from country to country. In many large countries, such as India, Indonesia, Bangladesh and the Philippines, the landless constitute a significant portion of the rural population. In Indonesia, 45% of rural households on Java do not own any land, and another 20 per cent own less than 0.25 ha (BPS, 1996). In the Philippines, the landless constitute 13 per cent of the agricultural labour force, and are one of the poorest groups in the countryside, with income 30 per cent lower than that of rice farmers (Dawe et al., 2006). They are less common in Thailand (where population density is lower), China and Viet Nam (due to comprehensive land reforms).

Another important group of poor rice consumers is rural dwellers who own land, but use it to grow nonrice crops. They would benefit from cheaper rice prices. In Indonesia, many farmers plant maize, cassava and soybeans. In the Philippines, maize and coconut are important crops grown by poor smallholders, with maize farmers being particularly poor.

Higher rice prices will substantially hurt poor net rice consumers because rice is typically a larger share of expenditures for the poor (Dawe et al., 2010). In such circumstances, rice price increases can have important effects on effective purchasing power, even if they do not directly affect nominal income per se. As one example, Block et al. (2004) found that, when rice prices increased in Indonesia in the late 1990s, mothers in poor families responded by reducing their dietary energy intake in order to better feed their children, leading to an increase in maternal wasting. Furthermore, purchases of more nutritious foods were reduced in order to afford the more expensive rice. This led to a measurable decline in blood haemoglobin levels in young children (and in their mothers), thus increasing the probability of developmental damage. A negative correlation between rice prices and nutritional status has also been observed in Bangladesh (Torlesse et al., 2003).

On the other hand, farmers who are net food producers are likely to benefit from higher prices, which, other things being equal, will tend to increase their incomes. Since many farmers are poor, higher prices could help to alleviate poverty and improve food security. However, it must also be kept in mind that farmers with more surplus production to sell will benefit more from high prices than farmers who have only a small surplus to sell. Further, in many (but not all) contexts, farmers with more land tend to be better off than farmers with only a little land, so it may be that poorer farmers will not receive the bulk of the benefits from higher food prices. In the Philippines, the top quintile of rice farmers has per capita income 15 times that of the bottom quintile, and accounts for 44 per cent of the total marketed surplus, compared with just 6 per cent for the bottom quintile. Since high rice prices benefit farmers only when they have a surplus to sell, most of the benefits of higher prices go to farmers who are in the top half of the national income distribution (Dawe et al., 2006). In Thailand, Poapongsakorn (2010) showed that the bottom quintile of rice farmers ranked according to income received only about 4.5 per cent of the benefits of the paddy pledging programme that seeks to increase farm prices. One reason for this (just as in the Philippines) is that the poorest farmers do not have irrigated land, and thus produce less.

In principle, it is important to take account of second-round effects and cross-price elasticities in estimating welfare impacts of food price changes. For staple foods such as rice, however, these effects are likely to be less important, because income elasticities, own-price elasticities and cross-price elasticities are all relatively low (Wood et al., 2012). Thus, Wood et al. (2012) found that welfare effects from changes in tortilla prices in Mexico were similar regardless of whether one estimated the changes using first-order approximations, second-order approximations or compensating variation (this was not true for non-staple commodities).

Another potentially important effect of rice prices works through labour markets. Higher rice prices, by stimulating the demand for unskilled labour in rural areas, can result in a long-run increase in rural wages, thereby benefiting wage labour households in addition to self-employed farmers. Ravallion (1990), using a dynamic econometric model of wage determination and data from the 1950s to the 1970s, concluded that the average landless poor household in Bangladesh loses from an increase in the rice price in the short run (due to higher consumption expenditures), but gain slightly in the long run (after 5 years or more). This is because, in the long run, as wages adjust, the increase in household income (dominated by unskilled wage labour) is large enough to exceed the increase in household expenditures on rice. However, this study used relatively old data, from when rice farming was a larger sector of the economy and thus had a more profound impact on labour markets. Rashid (2002), using co-integration techniques and updating the data used by Ravallion (1990), found that, since the mid-1970s, rice prices in Bangladesh no longer have a significant effect on agricultural wages. McCulloch (2008) found no evidence that higher real rice prices were correlated with higher real rural wages in Indonesia. On the other hand, some more recent research implies that the labour-market channel is worthy of more study. For example, real wages in Bangladesh rose substantially in 2007 and 2008, in the wake of substantial increases in real rice prices (Hossain and Deb, 2010). Lasco et al. (2008) also found an effect of rice prices on agricultural wages in the Philippines. Polaski (2008) used a general equilibrium model of the Indian economy and found that higher rice prices lead to reduced poverty. This conclusion is due to its assumption that higher rice prices will lead to large increases in agricultural employment, which is important to the poor. It is not clear, however, how large the magnitude of employment with respect to prices is in actual practice – more research would be helpful in this area.

The net effect of higher food prices on welfare and poverty at the country level will thus depend upon socioeconomic structures and the national net trade position (as well as labour-market outcomes). Positive impacts of higher prices are much more likely in exporting nations, since a greater percentage of households are probably net producers. Thus, Ivanic and Martin (2008) found that higher rice prices reduce poverty in Viet Nam and Pakistan. The result for Viet Nam agrees with that from Minot and Goletti (1998), although it differs from that in Zezza et al. (2008). In Viet Nam, the factors that may contribute to a positive outcome of higher prices are a relatively equal distribution of land and the large share of production (about 20 per cent) that is exported. In Pakistan, the share of production that is exported is even higher than in Viet Nam (about 40 per cent) because rice is not the staple food, so it is not surprising that higher prices reduce poverty there. Thailand also exports a large share of production (about 40 per cent since 1990), and Deaton (1989) and Warr (2001) found that high rice prices reduce poverty there as well. On the other hand, similar results do not necessarily hold for all exporters at all times. Using more recent data and a different methodology, Warr (2008) found that higher rice prices increase poverty in Thailand, a surprising result given the large share of rice production that is exported. In this case, it would appear that most of the benefits from higher prices must go to larger farmers with a large marketed surplus who are not poor (see Poapongsakorn, 2010).

Among rice importers, the results are more uniformly negative. Warr (2005) found that higher rice prices increase poverty in Indonesia, as did McCulloch (2008), and similar results were found for Bangladesh and Nepal by Zezza et al. (2008). Balisacan (2000) also found that the poorest deciles of the income distribution in the Philippines were net rice consumers, and would thus be harmed by higher rice prices. Ivanic and Martin (2008) found that higher rice prices increased poverty in Cambodia (which was a rice importer in 2004, the year to which the analysis pertains). Sahn's (1988) analysis of Sri Lanka also strongly suggests that high prices hurt the poor. He notes that, in the lowest income quartile in rural areas, 91 per cent of households are net buyers of rice. In addition, he estimates that, among producer households in the bottom quartile, an increase in rice prices at both farm-gate and retail levels would reduce food energy intake even after taking into account the positive effect of higher prices on farm income. Outside Asia, Ivanic and Martin (2008) found that higher rice prices increased poverty in Bolivia, Nicaragua, and Madagascar (all three of which are importers). In Madagascar, Barrett and Dorosh (1996) find that 'the roughly one-third of rice farmers who fall below the poverty line have substantial net purchases of rice, suggesting important negative effects of increases in rice prices on household welfare.' This finding only concerns rice farmers with land, and ignores the rural landless who are even poorer and are also net purchasers of rice. The authors go on to state that 'the poorest rice farmers are quite vulnerable to an increase in the price of their principal crop . . . Conversely, the largest, wealthiest 10% or so of farmers stand to benefit significantly from rice price increases.' Simulation results from Wodon et al. (2008) also suggest that higher rice prices have adverse effects on poverty in Western and Central Africa, which is not surprising given that most of these countries are large importers.

Among the studies reported above, Ivanic and Martin (2008) is the only one that attempted to take into account labour-market responses. Their simulation results with and without labour market effects were similar.

Studies for other foods in other parts of the world are generally consistent with the above observations. Ivanic and Martin (2008) found that higher food prices increased poverty in seven of the nine countries studied, with Peru and Viet Nam being the only exceptions. The reasons for the beneficial effects in Viet Nam were elaborated earlier, and the beneficial effects in Peru were very small. Zezza et al. (2008) found that the poor were hurt by higher prices in all 11 countries studied, with the exception of rural dwellers in Viet Nam. This study did not examine labour-market effects, but did incorporate supply and demand responses, and found that high prices still hurt the poor. Robles and Torero (2010) found that higher food prices increased poverty in four Latin American countries, and Wood et al. (2012) found that higher prices harmed the poor in Mexico. In the cases of Uruguay (Estrades and Ines Terra, 2012) and Brazil (de Souza Ferreira Filho, 2008), however, both of which are large food exporters, higher food prices led to a reduction in overall poverty.[2] These latter two studies used CGE approaches.

To summarize, it appears that the effects of higher rice prices on poverty are generally negative in countries where rice is the staple food. This tendency is mitigated, or even reversed, in countries where large shares of domestic production are exported (as in Viet Nam). However, it is not the case that higher prices always reduce poverty in exporters (as shown by Warr (2008) for Thailand); it also depends on socioeconomic structures such as the distribution of land across income classes. Labour-market effects will also tend to reduce the negative impact of higher prices on poverty, although the limited research available suggests that these effects are not particularly strong.

5.7 SUMMARY

Price transmission from world markets to domestic markets during the world food crisis was less than complete from a markets point of view, but the transmission that did occur was substantial from a food security point of view. Furthermore, transmission across countries was very heterogeneous. Generally speaking, there were three types of countries (FAO, 2011).

The first group of countries used trade restrictions as the main instrument to prevent price transmission in staple food markets. Examples include China, India and Indonesia. This allowed them to shelter their food markets from the international turbulence. Generally speaking, these policies required few financial resources to implement, although export restrictions do result in lost revenues from an opportunity cost point of view. Unfortunately, the export restrictions exacerbated price increases in international markets and compounded the impacts of food shortages in import-dependent countries.

The second group of countries may have benefited from higher prices, as they are exporters of staple foods – Thailand and Viet Nam, two large rice exporters, are examples. Their incomes generally rose with higher prices even if some of the profits were partially reduced by higher prices for inputs such as fertilizer, seeds or fuel. Higher staple food prices may also reduce poverty in these countries, as in Viet Nam, which has a relatively equal distribution of land. The evidence on whether higher rice prices reduce poverty in Thailand is mixed.

The third group comprises countries that generally depend on food imports. They were exposed to higher international prices for food commodities, were typically without sufficient stocks, and did not have the budgetary resources to protect the food security of the poor adequately. These countries bore the brunt of the crisis. Many African countries fall into this category, as do several Asian countries.

Roughly speaking, there may have been a 4–5 per cent increase in undernourishment due to a price shock of 15 per cent instead of 5 per cent (i.e. compared to the Tiwari and Zaman (2010) baseline of a 5 per cent increase in food prices). It is not possible to estimate the impact of the price shock because the baseline in Tiwari and Zaman (2010) is a 5 per cent increase in food prices, not a 0 per cent increase.

The above estimates for undernourishment are based on energy intake alone, and are likely to be relatively low because the calorie–price elasticity is likely to be relatively low (i.e. consumers may defend energy intake but reduce dietary diversity and cut expenditure on other items such as investments in health care and education). Thus, in terms of poverty, the effects are likely to have been larger. Ivanic and Martin (2008) estimated an increase in extreme poverty of 105 million people due to the 2008 price shock (they did not consider income growth in their analysis, so their estimates are estimates of the price shock, not estimates of what happened in 2008). In retrospect, their estimate was probably too high, because they used a high estimate of price transmission (66 per cent) to come up with this number. In their defence, they made their estimate at an early stage of the crisis, without the benefit of data on the actual extent of price transmission.

For the price spike in the second half of 2010, when world maize and wheat prices surged, Ivanic et al. (2011) estimate an increase in extreme poverty of 44 million people due to the price spike. This estimate does not take into account income growth, and relies on actual price increases in a number of countries for which household income and expenditure survey (HIES) data were available. This approach of coupling actual data on country specific price increases with country specific HIES data is probably the best that can be done.[3]

Freire and Isgut (2011) estimated the impact on poverty in the Asia and Pacific region of the price spikes from 2009 to 2010 using a methodology similar to that in Ivanic et al. (2011), except that instead of using HIES, they used data from the Global Income Distribution Dynamics (GIDD) database. This database does not include data on net sales and net purchase positions of households, however, so the authors made some assumptions about these parameters. They estimated that price increases in 2010 increased poverty by 19.4 million people in the Asia-Pacific region, compared to a counterfactual of no increases in real prices. Actual poverty was estimated to have declined in 2010 due to income growth, but the decline was less than what would have occurred had real prices not increased.

NOTES

1. This is an upper bound on the true effect, as substitution into other foods will occur. These substitution effects are very small for staple foods, however (Wood et al., 2012).
2. Estrades and Ines Terra (2012), however, found an increase in extreme poverty due to higher food prices.
3. Ideally, it would be desirable to determine how much of the domestic price increase was due to world price increases, but to do this on a country by country basis would be a huge (and problematic) task.

REFERENCES

Balisacan, A. (2000), Growth, inequality and poverty reduction in the Philippines: a re-examination of evidence. Quezon City, Philippines: University of the Philippines.
Barrett, C.B. and P.A. Dorosh (1996), Farmers' welfare and changing food prices: nonparametric evidence from rice in Madagascar. *American Journal of Agricultural Economics*, **78**(3), 656–69.
Block, S., L. Kiess, P. Webb, S. Kosen, R. Moench-Pfanner, M.W. Bloem and C.P. Timmer (2004), Macro shocks and micro outcomes: child nutrition during Indonesia's crisis. *Economics & Human Biology*, **2**(1), 21–44.
BPS (Badan Pusat Statistik) (1996), Population of Indonesia: results of the 1995 intercensal population survey. Jakarta, Indonesia: BPS Publication.
Dawe, D. (2010), Cereal price transmission in several large Asian countries during the global food crisis. *Asian Journal of Agriculture and Development*, **6**(1), 1–12.
Dawe, D., P. Moya and C. Casiwan (eds) (2006), *Why Does the Philippines Import Rice? Meeting the Challenge of Trade Liberalization*. Los Baños (Philippines): International Rice Research Institute (IRRI) and Philippine Rice Research Institute (PhilRice).
Dawe, D., S. Block, A. Gulati, J. Huang and S. Ito (2010), Domestic rice price, trade and marketing policies.

In S. Pandey, D Byerlee, D Dawe,. A Dobermann, S. Mohanty, S. Rozelle, and B. Hardy (eds), *Rice in the Global Economy: Strategic Research and Policy Issues for Food Security*. Los Baños (Philippines): IRRI, pp. 379–407.

Deaton A. (1989), Rice prices and income distribution in Thailand: a non-parametric analysis. *Economic Journal*, **99**(Supplement), 1–37.

Demeke, M., G. Pangrazio and M. Maetz (2009), Country responses to the food security crisis: nature and preliminary implications of the policies pursued. FAO Initiative on Soaring Food Prices. Available at: ftp://ftp.fao.org/docrep/fao/011/ak177e/ak177e00.pdf.

Descargues, S. (2011), *Impact of Food Price Volatility on Incomes and Investment of Smallholder Farmers in Bangladesh*. Rome: FAO.

De Souza Ferreira Filho, J.B. (2008), The world food price increase and Brazil: opportunity for all?. Paper presented at the II Regional Meeting on Computable General Equilibrium (CGE) Modeling: Contributions to Economic Policy in Latin America and the Caribbean. San José, Costa Rica, November 2008.

Estrades, C. and M. Inés Terra (2012), Commodity prices, trade, and poverty in Uruguay. *Food Policy*, **37**, 58–66.

Fang, C. (2010), How China stabilized grain prices during the global price crisis. In D. Dawe (ed.), *The Rice Crisis: Markets, Policies and Food Security*. London and Rome: Earthscan and FAO, Chapter 13.

FAO (2011), *State of Food Insecurity in the World. How Does International Price Volatility Affect Domestic Economies and Food Security?* Rome: FAO.

FAO (2012), GIEWS Food price data and analysis tool. Available at: http://www.fao.org/giews/pricetool2/.

Freire, C. and A. Isgut (2011), High food and oil prices and their impact on the achievement of MDG1 in Asia and the Pacific. MPDD Working Paper 11/18, United Nations Economic and Social Commission for Asia and the Pacific (UNESCAP).

Gilbert, C.L. (2010), How to understand high food prices. *Journal of Agricultural Economics*, **61**, 398–425.

Gulati, A. and M. Dutta (2010), Rice policies in India in the context of the global rice price spike. In D. Dawe (ed.), *The Rice Crisis: Markets, Policies and Food Security*. London and Rome: Earthscan and FAO, Chapter 14.

Headey, D. (2011), Rethinking the global food crisis: the role of trade shocks. *Food Policy*, **36**(2), 136–46.

Headey, D. and S. Fan (2010), Reflections on the global food crisis: how did it happen? How has it hurt? And how can we prevent the next one? IFPRI Research Monograph 165, Washington, DC: International Food Policy Research Institute.

Headey, D., S. Malaiyandi and S. Fan (2010), Navigating the perfect storm: reflections on the food, energy and financial crises. *Agricultural Economics*, **41**(s1), 217–28.

Hill B. (2008), Shaking the invisible hand. *Rice Today*, **7**(4), 26–31.

Hoang Ngan, P. (2010), The Vietnamese rice industry during the global food crisis. In D. Dawe (ed.), *The Rice Crisis: Markets, Policies and Food Security*. London and Rome: Earthscan and FAO, pp. 219–32.

Höffler, H. and B.W. Owuor Ochieng (2009), High commodity prices: who gets the money? A case study on the impact of high food and factor prices on Kenyan farmers. Berlin, Heinrich-Boell-Foundation. Available at: http://www.boell.de/downloads/worldwide/HighFoodPrices-WhoGetsTheMoney_Kenya.pdf.

Hossain, M. and U. Deb (2010), Volatility in rice prices and policy responses in Bangladesh. In D. Dawe (ed.), *The Rice Crisis: Markets, Policies and Food Security*. London and Rome: Earthscan and FAO, pp. 91–108.

Huang J., Y. Liu, W. Martin and S. Rozelle (2009), Changes in trade and domestic distortions affecting China's agriculture. *Food Policy*, **34**, 407–16.

Imai, K.S., R. Gaiha, G. Thapa and A. Ali (2012), Supply response to food price changes in Asian countries. In M. Aoki, T. Kuran and G. Roland (eds), *Institutions and Comparative Economic Development*, New York: Palgrave Macmillan.

Ivanic, M. and W. Martin (2008), Implications of higher global food prices for poverty in low-income countries. *Agricultural Economics*, **39**, 405–16.

Ivanic, M., W. Martin and H. Zaman (2011), Estimating the short-run poverty impacts of the 2010–11 surge in food prices. Policy Research Working Paper 5633, World Bank, Washington DC.

Lasco, C.D., R.J. Myers and R.H. Bernsten (2008), Dynamics of rice prices and agricultural wages in the Philippines. *Agricultural Economics*, **38**, 339–48.

Maltsoglou, I. and Y. Khwaja (2010), Bioenergy and food security: the BEFS analysis for Tanzania. Environment and Natural Resources Management Working Paper 35, FAO, Rome.

McCulloch, N. (2008), Rice prices and poverty in Indonesia. *Bulletin of Indonesian Economic Studies*, **44**(1), 45–63.

Minot, N. (2011), Transmission of world food price changes to markets in sub-Saharan Africa. IFPRI Discussion Paper 01059, International Food Policy Research Institute, Washington DC.

Minot, N. and F. Goletti (1998), Rice export liberalization and welfare in Vietnam. *American Journal of Agricultural Economics*, **80**(4), 738–49.

Moya, P.F., D. Dawe, D. Pabale, M. Tiongco, N.V. Chien, S. Devarajan, A. Djatiharti, N.X. Lai,

L. Niyomvit, H.X. Ping, G. Redondo and P. Wardana (2004), The economics of intensively irrigated rice in Asia. In A. Dobermann, C. Witt and D. Dawe (eds), *Increasing the Productivity of Intensive Rice Systems through Site-specific Nutrient Management*. Enfield, NH, and Los Baños, Philippines: Science Publishers and International Rice Research Institute, pp. 29–58.

OECD–FAO (2011), Agricultural Outlook 2011. Available at: http://www.agri-outlook.org.

Piesse, J. and C. Thirtle (2009), Three bubbles and a panic: an explanatory review of recent food commodity price events. *Food Policy*, **34**(2), 119–29.

Poapongsakorn, N. (2010), The political economy of Thai rice price and export policies in 2007–08. In D. Dawe (ed.), *The Rice Crisis: Markets, Policies and Food Security*. London and Rome: Earthscan and FAO, pp. 191–208.

Polaski, S. (2008), Rising food prices, poverty, and the Doha Round. Carnegie Endowment for International Peace, *Policy Outlook*, May. Available at: www.carnegieendowment.org/files/polaski__food_prices.pdf (accessed 18 March 2010).

Quezada, N. (2013), Policy responses to the 2007–2008 food price swing and their impact on domestic prices in the Dominican Republic. In E. Krivonos and D. Dawe (eds), *Food Policy in Latin America During the World Food Crisis*. Rome: FAO.

Rashid, S. (2002), Dynamics of agricultural wage and rice price in Bangladesh: a re-examination. Markets and Structural Studies Division Discussion Paper No. 44, International Food Policy Research Institute, Washington DC.

Ravallion, M. (1990), Rural welfare effects of food price changes under induced wage responses: theory and evidence for Bangladesh. *Oxford Economic Papers*, **42**(3), 574–85.

Robles, M. and M. Torero (2010), Understanding the impact of high food prices in Latin America. *Economica*, **10**(2), 117–64.

Sahn, D. (1988), The effect of price and income changes on food-energy intake in Sri Lanka. *Economic Development and Cultural Change*, **36**(2), 315–40.

Saifullah, A. (2010), Indonesia's rice policy and price stabilization programme: managing domestic prices during the 2008 crisis. In D. Dawe (ed.), *The Rice Crisis: Markets, Policies and Food Security*. London and Rome: Earthscan and FAO, Chapter 6.

Subervie, J. (2008), The variable response of agricultural supply to world price instability in developing countries. *Journal of Agricultural Economics*, **59**(1), 72–92.

Timmer, C. P. (1974), A model of rice marketing margins in Indonesia. *Food Research Institute Studies*, **XIII**(2), 145–167.

Timmer, C.P. (2010), Reflections on food crises past. *Food Policy*, **35**, 1–11.

Timmer, C.P. and D. Dawe (2007), Managing food price instability in Asia: a macro food security perspective. *Asian Economic Journal*, **21**(1), 1–18.

Tiwari, S. and H. Zaman (2010), The impact of economic shocks on global undernourishment. World Bank Policy Research Working Paper 5215. The World Bank Poverty Reduction and Economic Management Network, Poverty Reduction and Equity Unit. Available at: http://www-wds.worldbank.org/servlet/WDSContentServer/WDSP/IB/2010/02/23/000158349_20100223161348/Rendered/PDF/WPS5215.pdf (accessed 31 October 2013).

Torlesse, H., L. Kiess and M.W. Bloem (2003), Association of household rice expenditure with child nutritional status indicates a role for macroeconomic food policy in combating malnutrition. *Journal of Nutrition*, **133**(5), 1320–1325.

Warr, P. (2001), Welfare effects of an export tax: Thailand's rice premium. *American Journal of Agricultural Economics*, **83**(4), 903–920.

Warr, P. (2005), Food policy and poverty in Indonesia: a general equilibrium analysis. *Australian Journal of Agricultural Research Economics*, **49**(4), 429–51.

Warr, P. (2008), World food prices and poverty incidence in a food exporting country: a multi-household general equilibrium analysis for Thailand. *Agricultural Economics*, **39**, 525–37.

Wodon, Q., C. Tsimpo, P. Backiny-Yetna, G. Joseph, F. Adoho and H. Coulombe (2008), Potential impact of higher food prices on poverty: summary estimates for a dozen west and central African countries, World Bank Policy Research Working Paper No. 4745, World Bank, Washington DC.

Wood, B.D.K., C.H. Nelson and L. Nogueira (2012), Poverty effects of food price escalation: the importance of substitution effects in Mexican households. *Food Policy*, **37**(1), 77–85.

Wright, B. and C. Cafiero (2011), Grain reserves and food security in the Middle East and North Africa. *Food Security*, **3**(S1), S61–S76.

Zezza, A., B. Davis, C. Azzarri, K. Covarrubias, L. Tasciotti and G Anriquez (2008), The impact of rising food prices on the poor. ESA Working Paper 08–07, FAO, Rome. Available at: ftp://ftp.fao.org/docrep/fao/011/aj284e/aj284e00.pdf.

6. The financialization of food commodity markets
Christopher L. Gilbert and Simone Pfuderer

6.1 INTRODUCTION

There is a widespread perception that financialization may have contributed to the 2008 food price spike. This perception has been stimulated by pronouncements by prominent politicians and leading market commentators. Here we cite three instances:

- French President Sarkozy asked in 2011, 'Speculation, panic and lack of transparency have seen prices soaring. Is that the world we want?'[1]
- A 2009 US Senate Subcommittee report examined 'excessive speculation' in the wheat market (United States Senate Permanent Subcommittee on Investigations, 2009). The subcommittee report was particularly concerned by the growth of index-based investment which it termed 'index speculation'.
- Hedge fund manager Michael Masters (2008) argued in evidence before a second Senate subcommittee that index-based investment both raised the levels of commodity prices and, by consuming liquidity, increased volatilities.

In the old days, it was widely believed, commodity futures markets in general and food commodity markets in particular, were populated by commodity market professionals. These professionals comprised three groups.

- Firms with a direct involvement in the physical commodity market ('commercials') who wished to offset their price exposure on the physical market by hedging on the futures market. The principal members of this group were supply chain intermediaries such as grain elevator companies.
- Large ('non-commercial') speculative funds which had no direct involvement in the physical market but nevertheless were habitual participants in the specific markets in which they operated. This group included funds operated by the (then) relatively small Commodity Trade Advisors (CTAs) who specialized in commodity as distinct from financial futures. While very many of these funds were technical traders, i.e. they traded on the basis of some form of trend identification procedure, a smaller proportion traded on the basis of their assessment of the supply and demand balance in the physical market (i.e. on market fundamentals).
- Small ('non-commercial') speculative funds and individual traders.

From around 1990, commodity futures markets started to witness an influx of financial actors who were new to commodity futures. These included investment banks, hedge funds, pension funds and the entirely new group of index traders. Members of this new group often were motivated by different considerations than were traditional speculators, for example portfolio diversification, and they also adopted different trading strategies, for example taking positions in a commodity, say corn, rather than a specific commodity future, say the Chicago Board of Trade (CBT) December corn contract.

A consequence of this influx is that some traditional market participants found it more difficult to read market developments. In the situation, for example, in which a market was moving towards excess supply and a build-up of stocks implying a likely price fall, financial traders might nevertheless move the market upwards by taking long positions as an inflation hedge. Alternatively, another group of financial actors might see the commodity price as low relative to its long-run value and take long positions in the expectation of eventual reversion towards the mean. Futures markets were seen becoming separate from underlying physical markets. In a discussion of the impact of commodity funds on the London cocoa futures market, Gilbert (1994) wrote 'the funds may appear as an outside, non-fundamental and possibly unnecessary intrusion into what is primarily a physical market'.

This gives us a broad characterization of financialization in terms of the influx of speculative and investment money into the commodity futures markets (Mayer, 2011). This definition is less than completely satisfactory since some of these financial institutions will have numbered among the traditional large non-commercial category of traders, and because hedging by commercial traders has generally grown by the same order of magnitude as non-commercial activity. More hedge funds exist now than 20 years ago and it is therefore unsurprising that there is greater hedge fund participation in commodity futures.

A narrower characterization of financialization results from the distinction between investing or speculating in commodities and investing in the 'commodity asset class'. Traditional speculators saw themselves as investing in particular commodity futures on the basis that these offered attractive prospective returns. Some of the new financial actors, by contrast, saw themselves in commodities as a class either because commodities in general offered attractive prospective returns, or simply as a means of diversifying a portfolio of equities and bonds and thereby obtaining a higher prospective return for the same risk (or equivalently a lower risk with the same prospective return).

The perspective that commodities form a distinct asset class, similar to equities, fixed interest and real estate asset classes, supposes that the return behaviour of the different commodities is fairly homogeneous in the sense that it may be spanned by a small number of representative positions. Specifically, this requires that the class have a unique risk premium which is not replicable by combining other asset classes (see Scherer and He, 2008). Given this premise, then provided that commodities exhibit sufficiently high returns and sufficiently low correlations with other asset classes, it follows that, when added to portfolio, the overall risk-return characteristics of the portfolio improve (see Bodie and Rosansky, 1980; Jaffee, 1989; Gorton and Rouwenhorst, 2006; and for a summary, Woodward, 2008).

Two characteristics of this new type of investor differentiate them from traditional speculators. The first is that they take positions in commodities in general rather than in specific commodities. Second, their positions are almost invariably long whereas traditional speculators will take long or short positions according to their perception of the underlying price trends. These differences led Gilbert (2010a, b) to describe the new class of commodity actors as investors as distinct from speculators.

This chapter is structured as follows. Section 6.2 documents the growth in financialization of food commodity markets since 2000, distinguishing between the broader and narrower concepts introduced above. In section 6.3, we discuss the evidence for bubbles in food prices. In section 6.4, we look at the evidence relating to possible impacts of financial traders on food price levels. Section 6.5 documents the rise in food price volatility and examines whether this may have been caused by financialization. Then, in section 6.6, we look at the contemporaneous rise in the co-movement of food commodity prices and crude oil prices and equity returns. Section 6.7 concludes.

6.2 THE EXTENT OF FINANCIALIZATION

We first consider growth of financialization on the broader of the two definitions in section 6.1. The Bank for International Settlements publishes semiannual statistics on the notional value of outstanding commodity derivative positions. The first column of Table 6.1 reports these figures for alternate years. The figures relate to futures and swap positions in all commodity futures excluding gold and other precious metals.[2] The figures show rapid growth in the dollar values of these positions from 2004 to 2008 followed by a subsequent fall back to lower levels from the end of 2008. Even after this fall, the outstanding contract value remains three times that of 2004, prior to the big rise.

In part, of course, this rise in values reflects the rise in prices over the same period. We obtain an approximation to the quantum of positions by deflating by an appropriate commodity price index (here, the average of the International Monetary Fund (IMF) non-fuel commodity price index and energy price index – see Table 6.1, column 2). The overall picture is unchanged by deflation. The implied total quantity of outstanding positions nearly trebled between 2004 and 2006 and then redoubled between 2006 and 2008. Subsequently, it has fallen back to a level which nevertheless remains substantially higher than that prevailing in 2004.

The figures reported in Table 6.1 relate to all commodity futures contracts with the exception of precious metals. Energy commodities, in particular crude oil, are the most important commodity contracts by value and the growth in overall positions seen in

Table 6.1 Total commodity futures and swap positions ($bn)

	Nominal	2005 values
1998	137.8	246.6
2000	159.3	234.1
2002	271.5	438.4
2004	480.7	580.5
2006	2153.4	1709.7
2008	7474.2	3626.4
2010	1470.1	1015.6
2012	1595.9	942.1

Notes:
Figures relate to the end of June. Source for column 1: BIS, *Detailed tables on semi-annual OTC derivatives statistics at end-June 2012*, Table DT19. The reported figures are for total forwards and swaps and exclude gold and other precious metals. Column 2 gives these notional values deflated by the average of the IMF non-fuel commodity price and energy price indices (2005 = 100), IMF, *International Financial Statistics*.

Table 6.2 Open interest, Chicago grains and oilseed contracts

	Corn	Soybeans	Wheat
1998	301 399	133 659	118 612
2000	431 659	156 455	131 555
2002	424 811	191 074	97 871
2004	577 335	183 456	144 525
2006	1 329 400	351 200	461 737
2008	1 366 107	476 188	349 615
2010	1 133 201	440 453	455 011
2012	1 057 772	767 737	412 616

Notes:
Contracts of 5000 bushels. Figures relate to the final trading day of June of the respective years.

Source: CFTC, *Commitments of Traders* reports.

Table 6.1 is likely to be driven by growth in positions in energy futures and swaps. Nevertheless, the same pattern is seen in food commodity markets. Irwin and Sanders (2012a) show that the fast growth in trading volume and open interest on the Chicago grains markets commenced in 2004. They attribute this growth to increased market access and greater liquidity arising out of the move from pit to electronic trading. Table 6.2 reports the growth in open interest (i.e. the number of futures contracts outstanding) in the three important CBT grains and oilseeds markets – those for corn (maize), soybeans and soft wheat. The CBT market is the most important world market for each of these three commodities and these CBT prices are generally taken as reference prices in both domestic United States and in international commerce.

The table shows the rapid growth in outstanding positions in both the corn and wheat markets from around 2004 peaking in the 3 years 2006–08.[3] In both cases open interest fell back in 2009 but recovered to reach new peaks in the (northern hemisphere) winter of 2010–11.[4] Differently from the all commodity pattern seen in Table 6.1, the rapid growth in outstanding positions in these two grains started somewhat later (around the mid decade) and the high 2007–08 levels were maintained even after the financial crisis and through the subsequent recession.

The growth path of open interest in soybeans, the major oilseed traded on world markets, is different again and shows a broadly steady growth throughout the period under consideration. In the late 1990s, the Chicago soybean and wheat markets were of comparable size (in terms of contracts traded) while the corn market was significantly larger. By 2012, the soybean market had grown to become 50 per cent larger than the wheat market.

Starting from June 2006, the Commodity Futures Trading Commission (CFTC) which regulates all US futures markets, has published information on the composition of outstanding positions. The CFTC *Commitments of Traders* (COT) reports distinguish positions held by

- producers and merchants
- swap dealers

- money managers (typically hedge funds, pension funds)
- other reporting traders (commodity funds, such as Commodity Trade Advisors, and rich individuals), and
- non-reporting traders (typically, large farmers and small speculators).[5]

The producers and merchants category corresponds to the 'commercial' category of traders who have a direct interest in the physical commodity industry. While it is not possible to infer the motivation of particular trades from the nature of a trader's business, it is natural to think that the bulk of the producers' and merchants' trades are hedges. Instead, the remaining three categories of reporting traders correspond broadly to the non-commercial group in that they have little or no involvement in the physical commodity. It is not the case that all trades undertaken by these three groups of traders are speculative or investment trades – swap providers, for example, will see their futures positions as offsetting price exposure taken on by writing swaps for their clients.[6] However, if these clients are non-commercial, as will usually be the case, the swap dealer's hedge may be taken as proxying a speculative or investment trade by the client. Broadly, therefore, we can regard the producers and merchants category as commercial traders, who will typically be hedgers, and the remaining four categories as non-commercial traders, either directly or indirectly driven predominantly by speculative or investment motives.

It has long been recognized that futures markets require a balance of hedgers and speculators (see, for example, Edwards and Ma, 1992, chapter 7). In commodity futures markets, hedgers are almost invariably net long the physical commodity and hence have a net short futures position.[7] In the absence of speculators, they could not all find counterparties. Speculators take positions in the hope of making profits. In the absence of hedgers, net speculative profits would be zero (negative after trading costs). By paying a risk premium, hedgers ensure the profitability (in an average or expected sense) of speculation. A premise of much of the discussion of financialization is that the large increase in futures trading in food commodities witnessed over the past decade has been driven by financial institutions. This view is difficult to sustain since, at least in terms of net positions, hedging and speculation inevitably grow together.

Table 6.3 illustrates this issue in relation the CBT corn market, the most important of the US agricultural futures market, for the final Tuesday of June from 2006 to 2012. Producers and merchants were invariably net short and swap dealers invariably net long as are the other reporting group on the particular dates considered. Money manager positions show the greatest variability. The non-reporting category of small traders is consistently net short suggesting that their positions may be dominated by farmers' hedge trades. Table 6.2 shows a rapid growth in outstanding positions between 2006 and 2008. From Table 6.3, we can see both a large increase in the net producers and merchants short position and in the long positions taken by money managers and the other reporting category. It is not clear from this information whether financialization resulted in an increase in hedging or whether an increase in hedging increased the prospective profitability of commodity speculation and drew in a greater volume of speculative funds.

Granger-causality analysis is a standard technique used by time series econometricians to disentangle causal relationships (see, for example, Stock and Watson, 2003, chapter 12). The test asks whether knowledge of the past history of a candidate causal variable

Table 6.3   Net positions (number of contracts), CBT corn futures

	Producers and merchants	Swap dealers	Money managers	Other reporting	Non-reporting
27-Jun-06	−410 966	350 607	88 171	65 612	−93 424
26-Jun-07	−500 967	335 943	138 557	87 368	−60 901
24-Jun-08	−577 800	350 337	220 321	119 408	−112 266
30-Jun-09	−225 853	221 106	94 106	18 944	−108 303
29-Jun-10	−263 825	383 214	−19 821	29 649	−129 217
28-Jun-11	−459 248	199 850	225 301	96 114	−62 017
26-Jun-12	−316 713	266 433	104 215	23 266	−77 201

Note: Positions relate to the final Tuesday of June.

Source: CFTC, *Commitments of Traders* reports.

C helps, in a statistically robust sense, forecast an effect variable *E*. If so, the investigator may conclude that there is a causal relationship (possibly indirect) between *C* and *E* which, given time's arrow, must be from *C* to *E* (since there cannot be causal links from the present to the past). We can use this approach to examine whether commercial hedging behaviour causes or is caused by the activities of financial institutions.

The results of this investigation, using data from July 2006 to December 2012, are summarized in Figure 6.1 for the three main CBT grain and oilseed contracts. In each case, causation is seen to run from changes in producer and merchant positions to changes in money manager positions implying that changes in hedging drive changes in financialization. The results are more mixed for the two other categories but it remains true that the majority of the causal relationships detected are from producers and merchants and to the financial transactors.[8] These results suggest that, notwithstanding the global character of financialization, the influx of financial actors into the food commodity markets over the past decade has in large measure been driven by the requirements of commercial hedgers to find counterparties.

Up to now we have focused on the broad definition of financialization as influx of investment money. The narrower definition looks instead at the influx of money into commodity markets from only those, non-traditional, investors who consider commodities as an asset class. These investors take long position across the range of commodities, generally by replicating one of the main tradable commodity futures indices.[9] Regulators

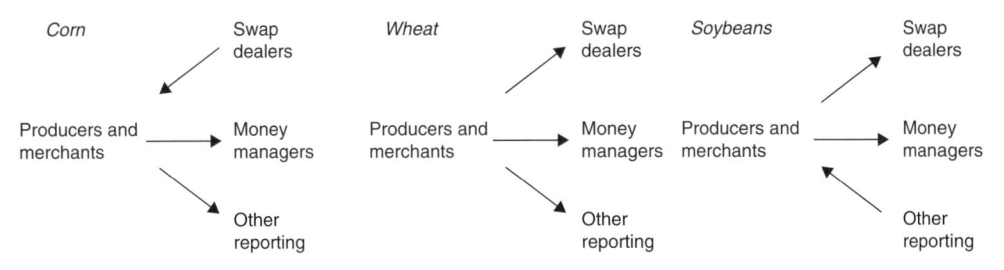

Figure 6.1   Causal relationships between positions, CBT grains markets

128   *Handbook on food*

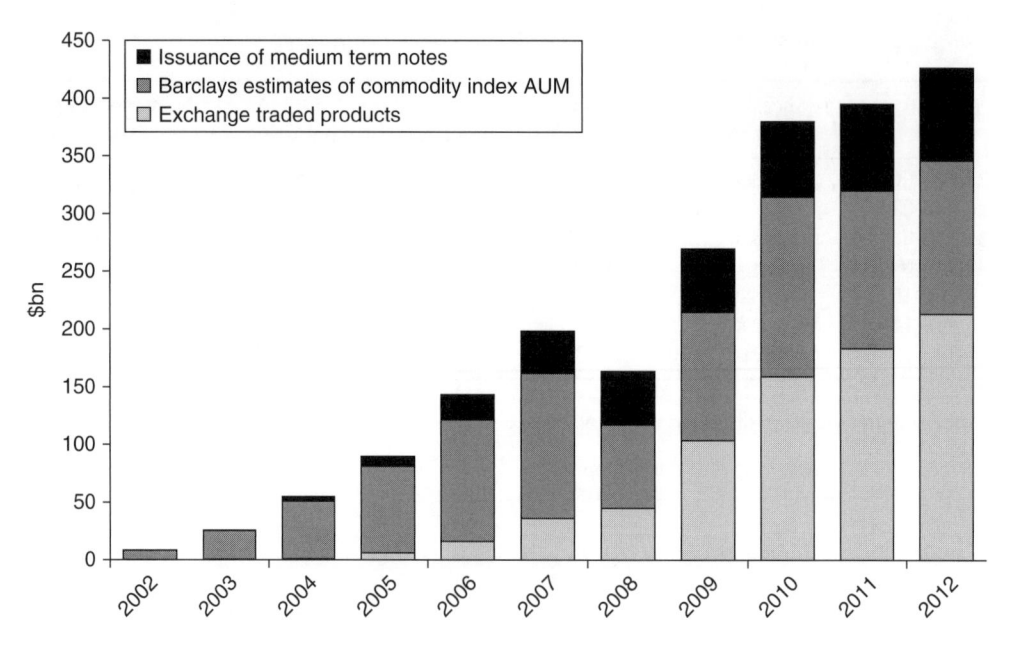

```
■ Issuance of medium term notes
▨ Barclays estimates of commodity index AUM
□ Exchange traded products
```

Source: Barclays Capital. We are grateful to Kevin Norrish for making these data available.

Figure 6.2   Total assets invested in commodity products 2002 to 2012 ($bn)

only started to compile and disseminate information on the size of index-related positions once these became controversial. The CFTC started to monitor positions in US markets from 2004 although information in the public domain starts in 2006. Figure 6.2, which gives estimates of assets under management (AUM) in commodity index products, derives from numbers made available by Barclays Capital and extends back to 2002. Investment in commodity index products has risen rapidly over the last 10 years from close to zero to over 400 billion dollars. The only year-on-year fall was recorded between 2007 and 2008. The increase in the following year more than made up for the decrease in index related products the previous year and the rapid increase continued between 2009 and 2010. These figures relate to all index related investment of which food commodities are only a relatively small share, as commodity index products are dominated by energy markets.

The CFTC has published data on positions held by commodity index traders (CIT) at close on Tuesdays on a weekly basis in the 12 most important US agricultural futures markets starting from 2006.[10] Table 6.4 shows CIT net positions on the last Tuesday of June for CBT corn, wheat and soybeans from 2006 to 2012. Comparing the three markets, net CIT positions are highest in the CBT corn market but the share of long positions held by CITs is highest in the CBT wheat market. In all three markets, the commodity index trader positions represented a sizeable share of total long positions over the period, generally between 20 per cent and 35 per cent in the corn and soybean markets and between just under 40 per cent and 50 per cent in the wheat market.

The data in Table 6.4 do not show any clear trends or patterns. However, in all three markets, net CIT positions and the shares increased between June 2007 and June 2008

Table 6.4 Net CIT positions (number of contracts) and shares of total long positions

	CBT Corn		CBT Wheat		CBT Soybeans	
	Net Positions	Share of Total	Net Positions	Share of Total	Net Positions	Share of Total
27-Jun-06	418 882	26.6%	199 467	39.3%	114 050	27.7%
26-Jun-07	362 737	22.6%	174 380	38.1%	144 448	22.4%
24-Jun-08	428 310	22.9%	179 228	48.1%	168 857	28.6%
30-Jun-09	305 167	27.5%	151 964	44.4%	137 088	26.9%
29-Jun-10	469 750	33.6%	215 461	46.7%	170 909	33.4%
28-Jun-11	378 124	26.3%	208 626	45.1%	171 893	27.7%
26-Jun-12	383 854	28.8%	195 655	43.6%	150 193	18.9%

Note: Positions and shares relate to final Tuesday of June.

Source: CFTC, *Commitment of Traders* reports.

and between June 2009 and June 2010.[11] Both of these years were followed by falls in CIT net positions and falls in the share of CIT positions in two out of the three markets. Between June 2010 and June 2012, the commodity index traders' share of total long positions in the soybean market fell substantially from 33.4 per cent to 18.9 per cent, which was mainly due to a large increase in total long positions.

6.3 FOOD PRICE BUBBLES[12]

A number of commentators have suggested that the past two decades have come to be dominated by a series of bubbles caused by excessive market exuberance during to so-called Great Moderation, by relatively loose monetary control as central banks moved from money supply rules to inflation targeting and by low interest rates initially after 9/11 and subsequently in the post-Lehman period. Caballero, Fahri and Gourinchas (2008a, b) see recent financial crises as linking global financial asset scarcity and global imbalances to the rise in US real estate prices, the subsequent subprime crisis and the 2007–08 spike in commodity prices. They model bubble creation followed by collapse as money migrates from sector to sector. In line with this story, Gilbert (2010c) argued that world money supply has been a major determinant of changes in food commodity prices over a 40-year period.

Bubbles may be generated by 'loose money' but we need to ask how this is transmitted into food commodity prices. A possible mechanism is as follows (other possible routes are discussed later in the section). A chance rise in a commodity price, perhaps generated by a large purchase by a financial institution, may lead uninformed traders to believe that market fundamentals have become more positive. Not having detailed market information themselves, they attempt to infer the information that others may have by working backwards from observed price changes. The result may be that the initial purchase attracts a further influx of money leading to a further rise taking the price further away from its equilibrium value. Informed traders will know that the price is now out of line with fundamentals but may be wary of taking a contrarian position, either because there is now too much money on the buy side or because they have short reporting horizons and cannot afford to carry a loss until the market comes right (De Long et al., 1990). It is often remarked that the easiest way to go bankrupt in a financial market is to be right but to be right too early.

It is frequently objected that food commodity prices cannot move significantly away from the level implied by supply and demand equilibrium since that would imply accumulation or disaccumulation of stocks and consequential price correction. The argument is correct in the sense that no bubble can persist indefinitely. However, for annual crop commodities, production responses to higher prices can only come with a new harvest and consumption responses to price rises take time as price changes feed through the food processing and distribution chain. The stock correction mechanism will therefore do little to prevent a bubble over a period of weeks or even months. Since the first major documented price bubble was in an agricultural market (tulips in seventeenth century Holland),[13] it would be unwise to dismiss the possibility of food price bubbles in the more recent past.

The key feature of any bubble is that price follows an explosive path. Explosions can easily be heard even at a distance and explosive price behaviour is therefore in principle easy to detect although it is difficult to do this in a statistically robust manner. However, since bubbles can only persist for a limited period of time, any bubble-affected time series must exhibit discontinuities in its behaviour. Standard tests, for example those based on the Augmented Dickey–Fuller (ADF) non-stationarity test,[14] may therefore fail to detect even visually evident periodically collapsing bubbles (Evans, 1991). Bubble tests are therefore tests for such discontinuities.

There are two strands to the empirical bubble literature. The first, initiated by Hall, Psaradakis and Sola (1999), Psaradakis, Sola and Spagnolo (2001) and Schaller and van Noorden (2002), adopts a Markov-switching approach to identify periods associated with bubble-type behaviour. Brooks and Katsaris (BK, 2005) extend the Schaller and van Noorden (2002) model to allow for three regimes – a dormant regime where the price follows a stationary trend, an explosive regime and a collapsing regime. These models were all developed in relation to macroeconomic (money, exchange rates, price) and stock market variables. Shi and Arora (2012) apply the BK model to the West Texas Intermediate (WTI) crude oil price and find evidence for a bubble in crude oil prices in 2008. However, to the best of our knowledge this approach has yet to be applied to agricultural commodity prices.

The Markov-switching approach to bubble identification estimates a probability associated with each state (dormant, explosive and, in the BK model, collapsing) for each date in the sample. Bubble periods are therefore identified only in a probabilistic sense. The alternative approach to bubble modelling, developed by Phillips, Wu and Yu (PWY, 2011), adopts a classical approach with the result that, at any level of significance, a given period is either a bubble or a normal period. Gilbert (2010b) reports the results of application of the PWY procedure to the Chicago corn, soybeans and wheat markets using both monthly average data and daily data over the sample January 2000 to June 2009 and January 2006 to December 2008. There is no evidence of bubbles in the three food commodities using monthly data but the daily tests yield evidence for a bubble in soybean prices in the first three months of 2008.

There are (at least) two reasons why bubbles apparent at a high data sampling frequency (e.g. daily) may fail to be detected at a more coarse frequency (e.g. monthly). First, Figuerola-Ferretti, Gilbert and McCrorie (2012a) show that if the tests at different sampling frequencies are to be mutually significant, it will be necessary to use different critical values in the two cases. Second, PWY impose a condition that to qualify as a bubble, the sequence of explosive observations must satisfy a minimum duration condition. The length of this duration is somewhat arbitrary but the criterion used by PWY (the rounded natural log of the sample length) implies a minimum length which, on monthly data, will typically be between 4 and 7 months while on daily data this may be between 10 and 20 days. It is evidently possible that a bubble which is sufficiently long to be identified as a bubble on daily data may fail to be so identified on monthly data. Consequently, short duration bubbles (froth?) may not be apparent using low frequency data.

Figuerola-Ferretti, Gilbert and McCrorie (FGM, 2012b) revisit the issue of food price bubbles and employ the PWY procedure using daily, weekly and monthly data from January 2000 to December 2011 with critical values adjusted for sample length and frequency. They consider five grains (corn, oats, rough rice and both hard and soft wheat), two oilseed contracts (soybeans and soybean oil), three meat contracts (feeder cattle, live cattle and lean hogs) and three 'soft' commodities (cocoa, coffee and sugar).[15] They find that the clearest bubble definition is obtained with weekly data.[16] Table 6.5, which is adapted from Table 3 in FGM, summarizes bubble identification results for these 13 food commodities in relation to three periods: 2000–06, 2007–08 and 2009–11. Looking at the 2007–08 'food price spike' period, bubbles are identified for four of the five grains

Table 6.5 Food price bubble periods

		Pre-2007	2007–08	Post-2008
Grains	Corn	No bubble	Daily, weekly and monthly	Test unavailable
	Soft wheat	No bubble	Daily and monthly	No bubble
	Hard wheat	Daily and weekly (2002)	* Daily, weekly and monthly	Test unavailable
	Oats	Weekly (2001)	No bubble	No bubble
	Rough rice	No bubble	Daily, weekly and monthly	Test unavailable
Oils and oilseeds	Soybeans	Daily and weekly (2004)	* Daily	No bubble
	Soybean oil	Daily and weekly (2004)	* Daily and weekly	No bubble
Livestock	Feeder cattle	No bubble	No bubble	No bubble
	Live cattle	No bubble	No bubble	No bubble
	Lean hogs	No bubble	No bubble	No bubble
Softs	Cocoa	Daily and weekly (2002)	No bubble	No bubble
	Coffee	Daily (2001)	No bubble	No bubble
	Sugar	Daily and weekly (2000)	No bubble	No bubble

Notes:
The table lists bubbles identified by the PWY procedure at the 90% critical value distinguishing three time periods: 2000–06, 2007–08 and 2009–11. The test procedure terminates once a bubble has been identified and any subsequent bubbles are only identified if the bubble identified by the PWY procedure is classified as non-robust. In those cases, indicated by an asterisk (*), a subsequent bubble may be identified using the Phillips and Yu (2011) procedure. In those cases in which a bubble has been classified as robust, the bubble test is subsequently unavailable.

Source: The table is adapted from Table 3 in Figuerola-Ferretti et al. (2012b).

Table 6.6   Estimated bubble inflation (2007–08 bubbles)

		Daily	Weekly	Monthly
Grains	Corn	6.7%	19.2%	17.1%
	Soft wheat	12.6%	No bubble	70.3%
	Hard wheat	11.8%	19.7%	86.0%
	Rough rice	25.6%	33.2%	36.4%
Oils and oilseeds	Soybeans	6.0%	No bubble	No bubble
	Soybean oil	12.6%	23.3%	No bubble

Notes:
The table reports the price change from the period (day, week or month) prior to the estimated bubble start date to the estimated bubble end date. Bubble start and end dates are taken from the basic PWY estimates. The longest bubble period is selected from those estimated at 2.5%, 5% and 10% (typically implying 10%).

Source: FGM, Table 5.

(oats being the exception) and for both the soybean and soybean oil contracts but for none of the meat or 'soft' contracts.[17]

FGM also estimate the extent of price inflation over bubble periods in 2007–08. Their results are reported in Table 6.6 (adapted from Table 4 of FGM). Inflation is of the order of 10 per cent to 30 per cent but substantially higher than this for the long bubbles (August 2007 to February 2008) estimated for wheat prices at the monthly data frequency.

There are three important points to make about these estimated bubbles. The first is that financialization is only one of several factors which can lead to the emergence of bubbles and there is nothing explicit in these studies which links the emergence of bubbles to the increased trading of commodity derivatives generally or index-based investment in particular.[18] The oats and rough rice contracts are crucial in this regard. These are both thinly traded contracts which have little relevance to world markets and attract only very slight interest from financial institutions. Index-based investment in these two contracts is negligible. If financialization were the only explanation for commodity price bubbles, we should not expect to find bubbles for either of these two grains. Although this negative expectation is confirmed for oats, there is strong evidence for a 2007–08 price bubble in rough rice.[19]

The second important qualification is that price bubbles may derive from sharp and unexpected movements in supply and demand fundamentals, especially during periods of relatively low stocks. Models of competitive storage can explain the general price patterns seen in many commodity markets – long periods of lower prices interrupted by sharp price peaks in periods of stockouts. Cafiero et al. (2011) argue that models of competitive storage can explain the order of magnitude of volatility and autocorrelations in many commodity markets. The end-2007 and early 2008 bubbles which FGM identify in the two wheat contracts, soybean oil and rough rice, are susceptible to very straightforward fundamental explanations in terms of supply problems at that time and concerns about the emergence of such problems when global stocks were relatively low. While it is possible that speculation and other financial factors may have played some role in these bubbles, it does not seem necessary to go beyond market fundamentals. A tentative conclusion may be that, while financialization may have played a role in determining the apparently explosive character of price movements during the 2007–08 food price spike, there is little evidence that it was the major driver of these changes.

The third qualification refers to the econometric methodology which remains in a state of evolution. The PY procedure, which was employed by FGM in relation to the results reported here in Tables 6.5 and 6.6, suffers from the fact that results may not be robust to the choice of sample start date and that the procedure cannot cope with multiple bubbles. Phillips, Shi and Yu (2012) have suggested a modified procedure which appears to overcome both these problems. Figuerola-Ferretti, Gilbert and McCrorie (2012c) have applied this procedure to non-ferrous metals prices but we are not aware of any application to food commodity prices.

6.4 FINANCIALIZATION AND THE LEVEL OF FOOD PRICES

There is a large literature which asks whether trades initiated by financial transactors with no direct interest in the physical markets may shift prices away from fundamental price levels. A number of possible mechanisms leading to price movements that are unrelated to market fundamentals have been suggested. Nissanke (2012) asserts, for example, 'There is growing evidence that the unprecedented magnitude of swings and excessive volatility in commodity prices over the past decade can be seen as a reflection of the ever increasing linkages between activities in commodity and financial markets.' She goes on to quote Maizels (1994) as implying that 'Through this process of financialization . . . the volatility in commodity markets and financial markets can feed on each other and constitute an inbuilt mechanism of destabilization and uncertainty . . .'. These preoccupations are echoed in much popular and political discussion. However, the data-based evidence fails to arrive at such an alarmist conclusion.

If financially instigated futures market purchases are large in relation to the total size of a market, they may eat into the market order book and push prices upwards (see Scholes, 1972; Shleifer, 1986; and Holthausen et al., 1987). We should therefore not be surprised if we find that CIT trades have an impact on US agricultural futures prices and indirectly also spot prices (see Hernandez and Torero, 2010; Acharya et al., 2012; and Sockin and Xiong, 2012). However, these weight-of-money or liquidity effects should be transient and hence evaporate fairly quickly. Nevertheless, this may not be true if other, uninformed, market participants interpret the resulting price movement as conveying information about underlying market fundamentals or about the likelihood of future large purchases (see, for example, O'Hara, 1995; Stoll, 2000; and de Jong and Rindi, 2009).

Following the practice in the financial economics market microstructure literature (O'Hara, 1995), UNCTAD (2009) distinguishes three types of traders. Informed traders base their position taking in commodity markets on information about market fundamentals. Uninformed traders do not collect information about market conditions but base their trading instead on past and current prices. Noise traders base their position taking on strategic considerations unrelated to the specific commodity market conditions. Index investors whose involvement in commodity markets is based on portfolio diversification considerations are one example of noise traders. When the number of noise traders and uninformed traders is large and when informed traders face limits to arbitrage, prices might not revert to fundamental values in the short term. In such a situation it can be even rational for informed traders to follow the trend away from fundamentals (de Long et al., 1990).[20] The concern that financial investors have moved prices away from fundamentals has been examined in the specific context of whether index investment may have impacted food price levels in particular during the 2008 food price spike – the Masters Hypothesis. This relates to the bubbles discussion in section 6.3.

The now large academic literature has looked at this impact issue mainly in relation to commodity index (CIT) positions. Commodity futures price returns and CIT positions are generally positively correlated.[21] Using the weekly CIT position data from the CTFC, over the period from 2006 to 2011 the contemporaneous correlation for the CBT corn, wheat and soybean markets were 0.145, 0.179 and 0.368, respectively.[22] It is not possible, however, to infer causality from CIT positions to prices since causation could also be from prices to CIT positions – high prices could attract CIT investment – or the positive association could be indirect through a third variable. As explained in section 6.2, Granger-causality analysis is a standard technique to investigate causal relationships and has become the most widely employed method used in the academic literature to examine the impact of asset market trades on price and, specifically, the impact of CIT position impacts on agricultural commodity futures prices.

A large number of studies have used Granger-causality analysis to examine the impact of index of CIT trading. The results are predominantly negative although there are important exceptions to this. Among the negative results, Stoll and Whaley (2010), using data from the complete set of 12 agricultural markets included in the Supplemental report CFTC Commitment of Traders reports (the *Supplementals*), only find evidence of Granger-causality from positions to prices over the period from 2006 to 2009 in the cotton market. Similarly, Sanders and Irwin (2011a), who use the same *Supplementals* data but extended back to 2004 and 2005 fail to find Granger-causality for the grains they examine (corn, soybeans, soft and hard wheat). Capelle-Blancard and Coulibaly (2011) use the same data over 2006–10 for the 12 *Supplementals* food commodities within a systems framework. This can increase efficiency and hence test power by exploitation of the cross-equation residual correlations. No evidence is found that commodity index positions Granger-cause prices in the majority of the markets with the exception of the live cattle market before September 2008 and the cocoa market for the period between September 2008 and December 2010. Sanders and Irwin (2011b) also adopt a systems approach using swap provider positions over the 2006 and 2009 period.[23] They do not find Granger-causality in agricultural markets. Hamilton and Wu (2012) take a slightly different approach and examine whether changes in nominal CIT exposure Granger-cause price changes. Their results are negative. Mayer (2012) analyses price effects of index positions together with those of money managers in four agricultural (wheat, maize, soybeans and soybean oil) and four non-agricultural markets over the period June 2006 to June 2009. He finds Granger-causality from index positions to prices in two of the agricultural (soybeans and soybean oil) and two of non-agricultural markets while for money managers Granger-causality is only found in the maize market.

This battery of negative results supports the conclusion that there is indeed no causal impact from CIT trading to futures returns and that the small number of contrary results reflect sampling error. However, these studies fail to explain how the positive contem-

Table 6.7   Granger-Causality test results (CIT positions) – 2006 to 2011

CBT corn	Absolute	Yes (5%)
	Normalized	Yes (5%)
CBT wheat	Absolute	No
	Normalized	No
KCBT wheat	Absolute	No
	Normalized	No
CBT soybeans	Absolute	No
	Normalized	Yes (10%)
CBT soybean oil*	Absolute	Yes (5%)
	Normalized	Yes (5%)
CME feeder cattle	Absolute	No
	Normalized	No
CME live cattle	Absolute	Yes (10%)
	Normalized	Yes (5%)
CME lean hogs	Absolute	No
	Normalized	Yes (5%)

Notes:
The table reports the results of Granger-causality tests over the period 6 January 2006 to 27 December 2011 (313 weekly observations). Lag lengths, equal for the causal and effect variables, were chosen on the basis of the Akaike Information Criterion (AIC) and vary across commodities (see Gilbert and Pfuderer, 2012, for details). The table states whether or not absence of Granger-causality was rejected and the significance level of the rejection.
* CIT positions in soybean oil are relatively small. However, the soybean oil market is closely linked to the soybean market through the so-called 'crush spread'. The results reported in Table 6.7 relate changes in the soybean oil price to changes in both soybean and soybean oil CIT positions.

Source: Gilbert and Pfuderer (2012).

poraneous correlation between returns and position changes arises. It must be expected that, in a liquid financial market, any price impact of position changes will be immediate. However, in Granger-causality analysis the analyst is limited to looking at lagged reactions. Many of the studies quoted above have focused primarily on the most actively traded markets (corn, soybeans and the two wheat markets). Gilbert and Pfuderer (2012) conjecture that such lagged reactions are more likely to be evident in illiquid markets. They perform Granger-causality tests for eight grains and livestock markets over the period 2006 to 2011 using two different measures of index positions,

Table 6.7 summarizes the Gilbert and Pfuderer (2012) results. They use both an absolute measure (net long positions) and a normalized measure (share of long positions held by index investors). Among the four most active contracts, there is evidence Granger-causality for corn and (at the 10 per cent significance level) soybeans. Among less active contracts, Granger-causality is found for soybean oil and the two cattle contacts. Similarly, Aulerich, Irwin and Garcia (2012), who have access to the CFTC's daily Large Traders Reporting System database and who use daily position change data within a system framework, establish Granger-causality for the feeder cattle, lean hogs and Kansas City Board of Trade wheat markets.

Contemporaneous position change-return correlations differ little between the markets in which Granger-causality is established and those in which it is not. This suggests that changes in index positions may, after all, drive food price changes but that Granger-causality is not always sufficiently powerful to establish this. Gilbert and Pfuderer (2012) conjecture that it is more likely that Granger-causality will be found in less liquid market. Their results, together with those of Aulerich et al. (2012), lend support to this hypothesis. If CIT positions impact prices in less liquid markets, they may also do so in more liquid markets. In liquid markets, the impact would happen in a shorter period of time and thus would manifest itself in contemporaneous correlations. As noted before, contemporaneous correlations between measures of prices movement and measures of index investment are generally positive in agricultural futures markets, which is in line with our conjecture.[24]

Two final qualifications are in order. First, Granger-causality analysis tests for the presence of a causal relationship but cannot be used to quantify its importance. It is therefore not possible to move directly from a positive Granger-causality finding to an estimate of the size of the causal impact for which purpose one needs a more fully specified model. Gilbert (2010b) estimated the impact of CIT positions on CBT corn, soybean and wheat prices as between 12 per cent and 15 per cent over the first 6 months of 2008. Second, as emphasized by Gilbert (2010c), index investment may be an important channel by which information about market fundamentals becomes impounded in prices. There is thus no necessary reason to regard a financially driven price change as non-fundamental.

6.5 FINANCIALIZATION AND FOOD PRICE VOLATILITY

In popular discussion, it is often stated that a price is volatile when what is intended is that it is high relative to some past value. Instead, in academic discourse, volatility is a measure of the directionless extent of the variability of that price. This can be the price standard deviation, either in levels or in logarithms, and possibly after detrending. In the finance literature volatilities are the return standard deviations which can be approximated by the standard deviation of logarithmic price changes. This definition avoids problematic issues of trend estimation. In periods in which prices are high they are often also volatile since both are symptomatic of tight market conditions. Nevertheless, prices can be high without being volatile, for example when they result from supply restrictions in a cartelized market. The impact on financialization of food price volatility is therefore not necessarily the same as that on price levels.

Gilbert and Morgan (2010, 2011) used monthly data to analyse the volatility of 19 food commodities over the 40-year period 1970–2009. Volatility had only increased in a statistically significant manner over the second half of the period (1990–2009) relative to the first two decades for 2 of the 19 commodities (bananas and rice) whereas it had decreased significantly for 9 of the commodities. This reflects the fact that the food price rises of 1972–74 were in general much larger than those in 2007–08. Figure 6.3 updates the numbers in Gilbert and Morgan (2010, 2011) with data for two additional years. The figure graphs the standard deviation of monthly logarithmic price changes over the two 6-year periods 2000–05 and 2006–11.[25] It is arranged in increasing order of the difference between 2000–06 and 2007–11 volatilities. Dark bars indicate cases where the change in volatility is statistically significant (on the basis of a standard F test for equality of two

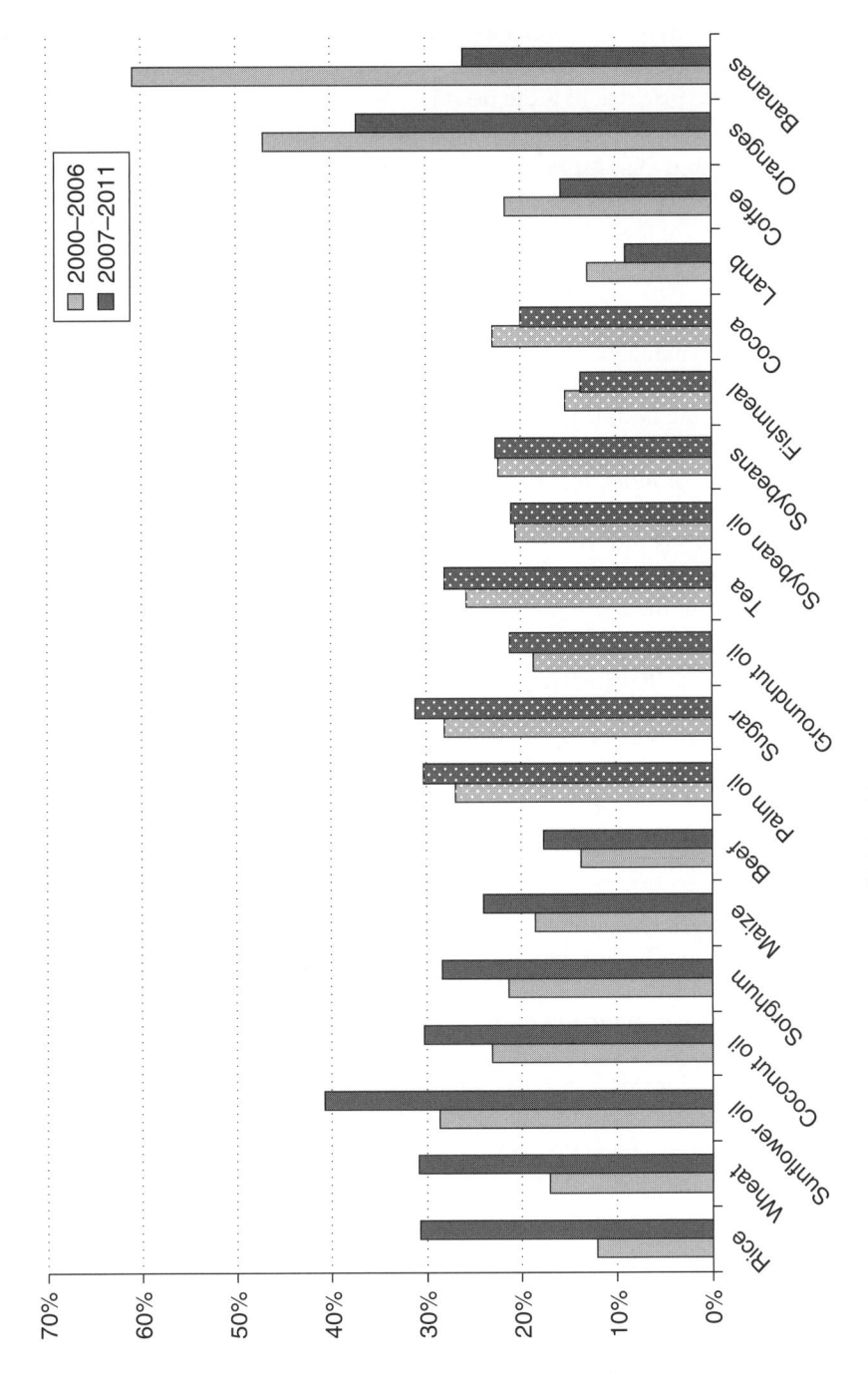

Figure 6.3 Food price volatilities, 2000–06 and 2007–11

variances). There are statistically significant increases for 7 of the same 19 food commodities and decreases for only 4. The increases are concentrated on the grains. Beef (dependent on maize feed) also shows a volatility increase as does sunflower oil. What we appear to have witnessed is an increase in the volatility of grains prices but not a general increase in that of food prices across the board.

It is natural to ask whether these increases in price volatility might be associated with financialization. This inference is problematic on the basis that there are no active futures markets in rice, sunflower oil or coconut oil, all of which have seen volatility increases, but there are active markets in palm oil, sugar, soybeans, soybean oil and cocoa, where the change in volatility is seen as not statistically significant, and in coffee, where volatility has declined.[26] The concentration of volatility increases among the grains and oilseed commodities suggests an explanation which differentiates between this group of food commodities and the remainder.

Masters (2008) argued that index investment both raised the levels of commodity prices, and by consuming liquidity, increased volatilities. We have already discussed the Masters Hypothesis in terms of level effects in section 6.5. Gilbert (2012) refers to possible volatility impacts of index investment as the Masters Volatility Hypothesis. From a theoretical standpoint, the impact of financialized trading might either be volatility increasing, as Masters maintained, or volatility reducing. Large trades will be volatility increasing if they eat into the order book leading to (possibly transient) price movements. They will be volatility reducing if transactors trade in such a way as to accommodate commercial counterparties thereby reducing the price movement resulting from large hedge trades. In the former case, these transactions reduce market liquidity while in the latter case, they increase it.

A number of authors have employed Granger-causality analysis to examine the impact of changes in the positions taken by financial transactors, and specifically index investors, on the volatility of food commodity prices. Brunetti and Büyükşahin (2009) find a negative association between changes in swap dealer positions and changes in volatility in energy markets but not in the corn market. Sanders and Irwin (2011b) report that rises in CIT positions tend to lead falls in price volatility across a range of agricultural futures markets but hesitate to state that the former cause the latter. Gilbert (2012), who embeds the Granger-causality methodology within a Generalized AutoRegressive Conditional Heteroscedasticity (GARCH; see Bollerslev, 1986) framework, finds that swap dealer, money manager and other reporting position changes do not have any discernible volatility impact. Nevertheless, CIT position changes do Granger-cause either or both cash and futures volatility changes in all five markets examined (corn, soybeans, soybean oil, soft and hard wheat). These effects are volatility reducing. The Masters Volatility Hypothesis is therefore emphatically rejected for US grains and vegetable oils markets.

These results imply that index-based trades have generally been accommodating and that their impact has been volatility reducing. The Masters (2008) view is that index-based investment is passive. It is possible that this is indeed true of the pension funds and other large institutional investors which initiate these trades. However, both index providers and direct index investors may trade on the basis of their index positions, for example by trading calendar spreads or writing options, and this would be sufficient to explain the negative volatility impact.

Overall, we can conclude that food price volatility has risen but this does not appear to be directly linked with the increased presence of financial actors in food commodity futures markets. To the extent that financialized trading does have an impact on food price volatility, it is volatility reducing.

6.6 PRICE CO-MOVEMENT

A number of authors have emphasized the increased co-movement of food prices (and indeed of commodity prices generally) with crude oil prices, stock market returns and exchange rate changes over the recent past. There is little dispute in relation to the facts. Büyükşahin, Haigh and Robe (2010) document that the correlation between equity and commodity returns increased sharply in the latter part of 2008 following the Lehman collapse. UNCTAD (2011) reports that the rolling correlation between crude oil returns and returns on the S&P 500 equity index has grown steadily since 2004. Tang and Xiong (2012) find similar rises in the rolling correlations between crude oil returns and both agricultural and non-agricultural commodity futures prices. Bicchetti and Maystre (2012) use high frequency data to document a jump in the moving correlation in the returns on various commodity futures (including CBT corn, soybeans and wheat, CME live cattle and ICE sugar) and S&P 500 futures returns. Gilbert and Mugera (2012) show that the conditional correlations, generated from a multivariate Dynamic Conditional Correlation (DCC) GARCH model (see Engle, 2002), between daily returns on WTI crude oil and respectively CBT corn, soybeans and wheat rose sharply from around 2006.

Here, we illustrate these rising correlations using the same monthly data employed in relation to the volatility changes charted in Figure 6.3. Figure 6.4 charts the correlations in the logs of the monthly averages of the same set of food commodity prices and log changes in the Brent crude oil price.[27] The commodities are organized in descending order of 2007–11 crude oil correlation. Dark colours indicate statistically significant increases in correlation (at the 5 per cent significance level).

The comparison is dramatic. With the single exception of bananas, price changes are all positively correlated with changes in the price of crude oil in the later period while in the earlier period they are small and so not exhibit any consistent sign. The correlation increases are statistically significant for all the grains except rice, all the oilseeds and additionally for lamb. This is the same broad group of food commodities for which the volatility increases were seen as significant (see Figure 6.3).

Figure 6.5 repeats the same exercise substituting S&P industrial returns for crude oil price changes. The same pattern of increased correlations emerges but in this case, the 2007–11 correlations are generally lower (except for coconut oil) and fewer of the correlation increases are statistically significant.

The correlations reported in Figures 6.4 and 6.5 demonstrate that the increase in co-movement with crude oil price has been more dramatic than that with share prices. Since changes in crude oil prices are themselves correlated with equity returns, it seems possible that co-movement of food commodity prices with equity prices, stressed by Büyükşahin, Haigh and Robe (2010) and Bicchetti and Maystre (2012) may be largely accounted for as an indirect impact of changes in crude oil prices. Table 6.8, which reports the partial correlations of food commodity prices and respectively crude oil prices and equity returns demonstrates that this is indeed correct. The partial correlations of food

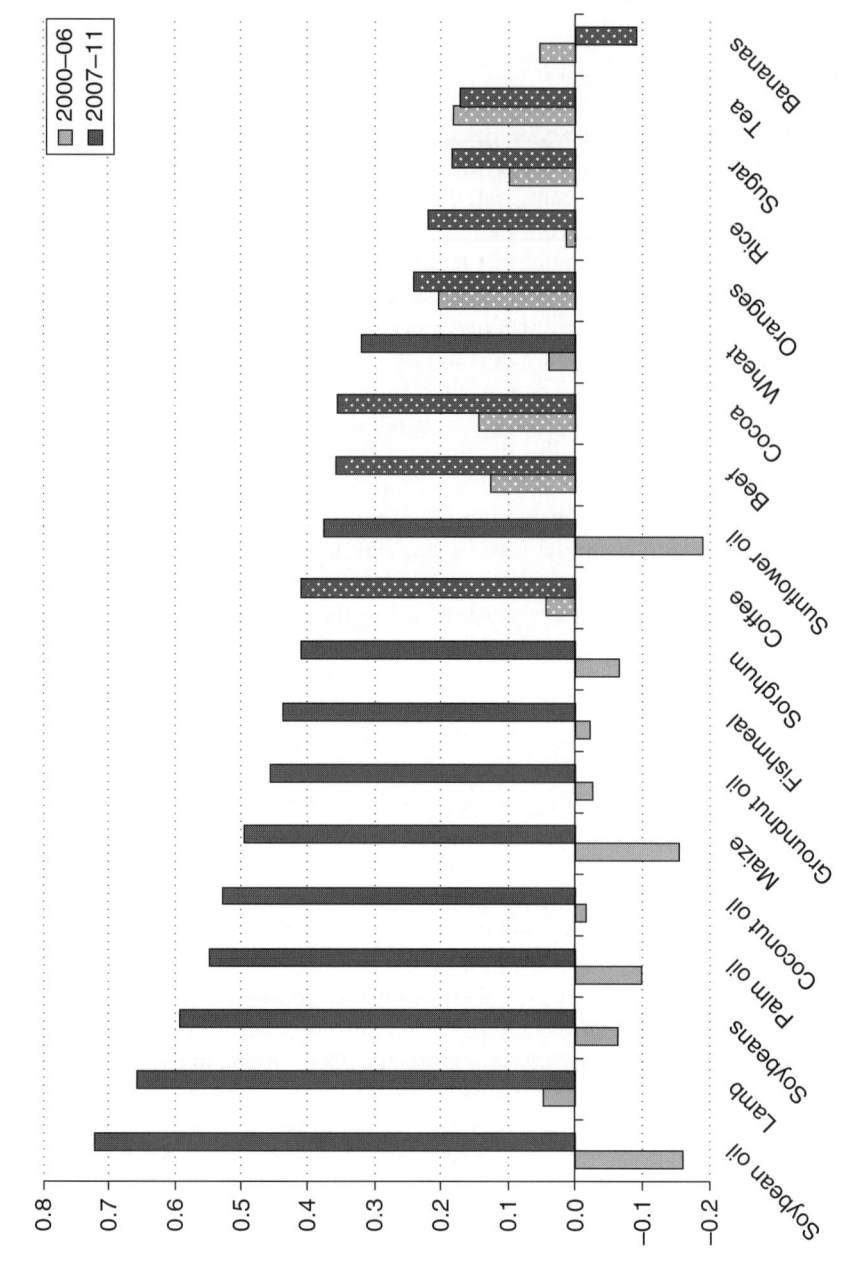

Figure 6.4 Correlations, changes in food and crude oil (Brent) Prices, 2000–06 and 2007–11

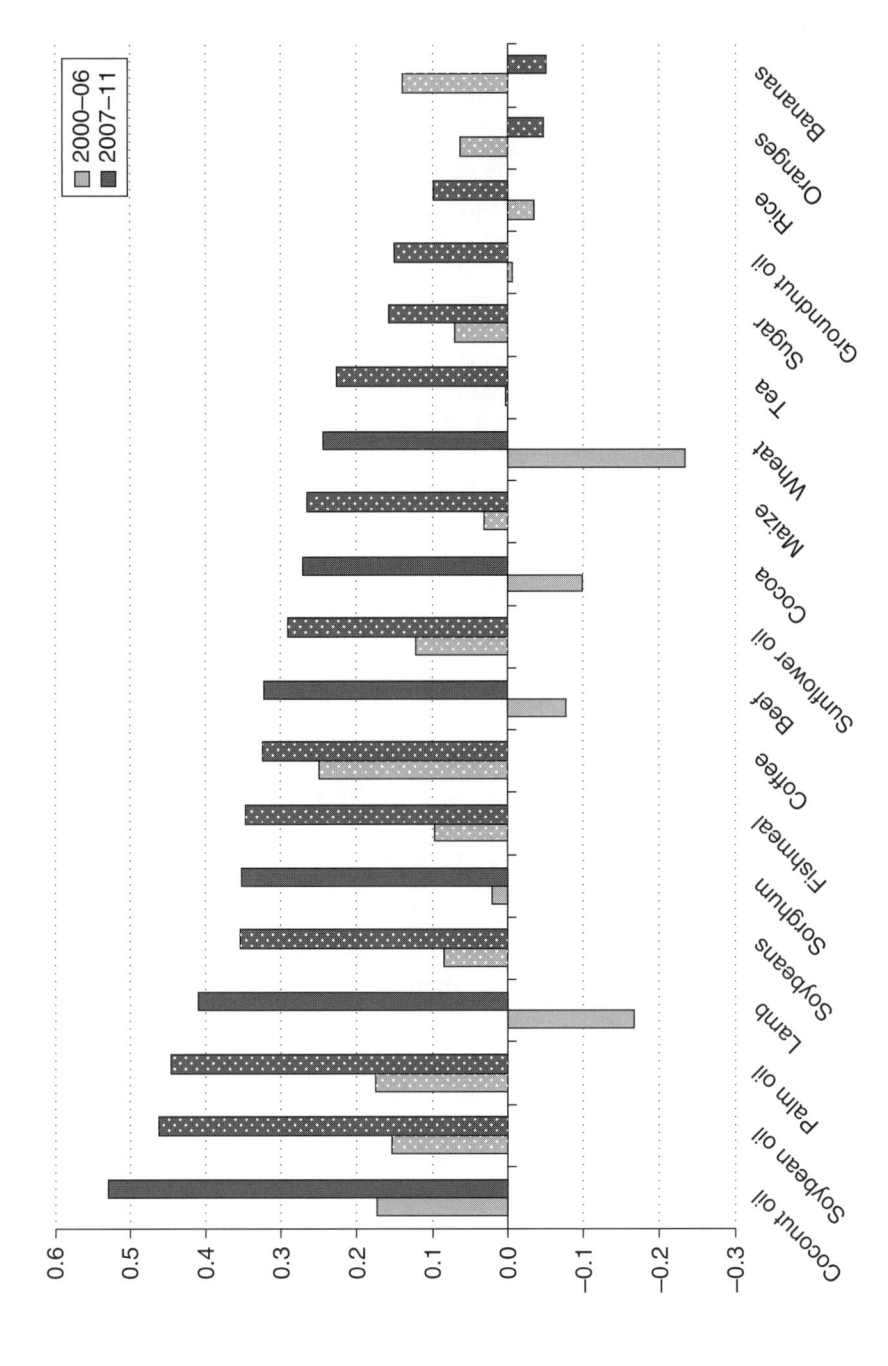

Figure 6.5 Correlations, changes in food prices and S&P returns, 2000–06 and 2007–11

Table 6.8 Partial correlations

	Brent crude		S&P Industrials	
	2000–06	2007–11	2000–06	2007–11
Cocoa	0.1277	0.2615	−0.0762	0.2615
Coffee	0.0883	**0.3007**	**0.2604**	0.1428
Tea	0.1833	0.0686	0.1058	0.1673
Sugar	0.1105	0.1204	0.0889	0.0794
Oranges	**0.2163**	**0.3013**	0.1068	−0.1934
Bananas	0.0768	−0.0755	0.0500	0.0000
Beef	0.1131	0.2387	0.0566	0.1808
Lamb	0.0200	**0.5739**	−0.1616	0.1304
Wheat	0.0000	0.2360	**−0.2313**	0.1058
Rice	0.0624	0.1944	0.0100	−0.0100
Maize	−0.1513	**0.4343**	0.0000	0.0283
Sorghum	−0.0624	**0.2879**	0.0100	0.1903
Soybeans	0.0500	**0.5138**	0.0742	0.0900
Coconut oil	0.0141	**0.3604**	0.1726	**0.3633**
Soybean oil	−0.1378	**0.6392**	0.1288	0.1764
Groundnut oil	−0.0283	**0.4441**	−0.0100	−0.0964
Palm oil	−0.0707	**0.4199**	0.1606	0.2410
Sunflower oil	−0.1720	**0.2782**	0.0933	0.1304
Fishmeal	0.0000	**0.3245**	0.0943	0.1694
Average	0.0232	0.3117	0.0491	0.1135

Notes:
Columns 1 and 2 give the partial correlations of the change in the row price and Brent crude, holding the S&P Industrials indexconstant. Columns 3 and 4 give the partial correlations of the change in the row price and the S&P Industrials index, holding the Brent crude price constant. Bold face indicates statistical significance at the 95% level.

commodity prices and equity returns, holding crude oil prices constant, showed only a modest increase between 2000–06 and 2007–11 (Table 6.8, columns 3 and 4) while that between food commodity and crude oil prices, holding share prices constant, rose sharply (Table 6.8, columns 1 and 2).

It is therefore the increased co-movement of food commodity crude oil prices which requires explanation, as emphasized by UNCTAD (2011), Tang and Xiong (2012) and Gilbert and Mugera (2012).Two rival explanations are available. Tang and Xiong (2012) see this as a financialization effect. According to their view, the increased correlation arises as index investors buy or sell 'on block' the entire range of commodity futures included in the two major commodity indices of which crude oil is the single most important by index weight. They claim that the co-movement is greater for commodities included in indices than for those less liquidly contracts outside the indices. Figure 6.5 fails to bear out this contention with respect to the co-movement of food commodity and crude oil prices. The alternative view, stressed by Gilbert and Mugera (2012), is that the co-movement arises instead from the biofuels link whereby the profitability of diverting grains (essentially corn) into ethanol production and vegetable oils (largely oil seed rape and palm oil) into the production of biodiesel. This explanation, which has nothing to do with financialization, can explain why the volatility rises documented in section 6.5 and the rises in oil price co-movement documented here are concentrated on grains and vegetable oils. It is also consistent with the finding that index investment tends to be volatility reducing.

6.7 CONCLUSIONS

The food commodity financialization literature is characterized by two opposing views. On the one hand, much popular opinion sees financialization, and in particular speculation, as the major driver of recent high food prices and the rise in food price volatility. This view has been shared by some important politicians and legislators who point the finger specifically at index-based investment which, they suggest, should be limited or tightly regulated. At the other extreme, a major strand of the academic literature minimizes the impact of financialization on food commodity markets. The food commodity markets have absorbed the large inflows from financial transactors without any problem. According to this view there is no abuse to be regulated. The truth lies somewhere between these two positions.

Bubbles are seen as emblematic of financialization. The academic literature characterized bubbles in terms of episodes of explosive price movements. We have reported evidence of explosive price behaviour in some food commodity markets (mainly in grains and oilseeds) in 2007 and 2008. Nevertheless, financialization is only one explanation of explosive behaviour which could also be generated by sharp changes in market fundamentals. That may have been the case in the 2007–08 grains and oilseeds markets as supply problems and concerns about the emergence of such problems existed at the time in which case financialization may have been no more than a facilitating factor.

The extensive literature which examines the impact of index investment on food commodity futures prices relies on Granger-causality analysis. In general, few causal impacts have been found although we argue that these impacts are clearer on less actively traded markets, particularly meats. Nevertheless changes in index investor positions are strongly correlated with contemporaneous changes in food prices. We suggest that the failure of much of the academic literature to see price impacts is because the Granger causality methodology lacks sufficient power to detect these, in particular if used, as is standard, with data at the weekly frequency. However, even if there are impacts, there is no implication that these are quantitatively important.

A smaller literature looks at possible impacts of financialization on food price volatility. The volatility of grains and vegetable oils prices has increased over recent years, but this is not true of food price volatility more generally. There is no evidence that links this increase to financialization and indeed index investment in food commodity futures markets appears to be volatility reducing.

Finally, we have examined the increased co-movement of food commodity prices with the crude oil price and with equity returns. The increased co-movement with oil prices is robust and general while the increased co-movement with equity prices, which is in any case less clearly defined, disappears once one controls for the oil price. We argue that this phenomenon may be better explained by the biofuels link between oil prices and grains and oilseed prices than by financialization.

In summary, financialization has been an important element in the recent evolution of food commodity markets and may have impacted prices over recent years including during the price rises in 2007 and 2008. Grains and oilseeds markets, in particular, have experienced bubbles and volatility increases, and though financialization is one possible explanation, other explanations seem more likely as main explanations for these phenomena. Speculation, in particular index investment, has tended to reduce food price volatility and is probably not responsible for the increased co-movement of food and crude oil prices.

NOTES

1. *The Guardian*, 17 June 2011.
2. We exclude options positions since many of these will have been offset by futures positions resulting in potential double counting.
3. Corn (Tuesday) open interest peaked at 1 523 926 contracts on 20 February 2007 and again at 1 488 009 contracts on 22 April 2008. Wheat (Tuesday) open interest peaked at 482 008 contracts on 1 August 2006 and then subsequently at 462 934 contracts on 8 February 2008.
4. Corn (Tuesday) open interest peaked at 1 719 814 contracts on 15 February 2011. Wheat (Tuesday) open interest reached a new peak of 562 198 contracts on 8 February 2011.
5. The COT data is collected under the CFTC's mandate to monitor large positions. The 'other reporting' positions are too small to be of interest for this purpose but brokers are nevertheless required to report the aggregate of such small positions. Prior to June 2006, the CFTC used a much coarser classification of commercials, large non-commercials and non-reporting traders. However, this classification had ceased to be very informative given that many financial institutions, in particular swap providers and some money managers, were classified as commercial on the basis that they were hedging positions taken by non-commercial clients – see CFTC (2006).
6. In a vanilla fixed for floating commodity swap, the client agrees to pay the swap provider a fixed dollar sum and will receive in exchange a sum contingent on the price of a commodity or commodity index at the swap maturity date (or dates). This generates a short exposure for the provider in the sense that, the higher the commodity or index price, the more he is obliged to pay to the client under the swap contract. The provider will therefore have an incentive to hedge out this exposure by taking a long position in the commodity future (or in the basket of futures corresponding to the index).
7. Stockholders, who typically operate on slender margins, will have short futures positions. Food processing companies, who have a short exposure to the physical and who therefore may be expected to take a long futures position, may remain unhedged on the basis that adverse price changes can be passed through to final consumers.
8. Sample: 11 July 2006 to 24 December 2012 (338 weekly observations). Tests are carried out within an ADL(3,3) reducing symmetrically to an ADL(2,2) and ADL(1,1) with selection on the basis of the Akaike Information Criterion (AIC). The results reported in Figure 6.1 use a 5 per cent critical value. (With a 10 per cent critical value, the relationship between the other reporting and producer and merchants groups becomes bidirectional for wheat.) Tests cannot be taken as independent since position changes sum to zero across trading categories and position changes are correlated across the three markets considered.
9. The S&P GSCI and the Dow Jones-UBS indices are the most common commodity futures indices. The former is the more widely tracked. It gives a high weighting to energy commodities and only a low weight to agricultural commodities. The Dow-Jones UBS index caps sectoral shares, including that of energy, at one third and hence gives greater weight to food commodities.
10. Not all positions in the CIT category track the main commodity indices. The CFTC have also published Index Investment Data since end of 2007 initially on a quarterly basis and since June 2010 on a monthly basis. See Irwin and Sanders (2012b) and Sanders and Irwin (2012) for discussion of the index investment data.
11. Irwin and Sanders (2011) have access to data on CIT positions for 2004 and 2005 that are not publically available. They show that net positions held by commodity index traders grew rapidly in all three of these markets over these 2 years.
12. We are grateful to Rod McCrorie for comments on the initial draft of this section.
13. Krelage (1942), Dash (1999).
14. See, for example, Stock and Watson (2003, chapter 12).

15. Hard wheat is traded on the Kansas City Board of Trade (KCBT). Cocoa, coffee and sugar are traded on the InterContinental Exchange (ICE). The remaining contracts are traded on either the CBT or Chicago Mercantile Exchange (CME), both part of the CME Group.
16. Many food price bubbles are too short to be visible on monthly data. With daily data, bubble identification can be imperilled by individual days in which the price corrects within a more extended explosive period. The PY procedure cannot cope with these minor corrections – see Gilbert (2010b).
17. The PWY procedure terminates once a bubble has been identified and is therefore blind to subsequent bubbles. FGM discuss various ways of circumventing this problem. One approach is to search for bubbles using different levels of significance. A second relies on the Phillips and Yu (PY, 2011) modification of the PWY procedure. PY note that the results obtained by applying the PWY procedure may not be robust to the sample start date. In those cases in which the PY procedure reveals a bubble identified by the PWY procedure to be non-robust, it is possible to proceed to identify a second possible bubble using the PY procedure. Bubbles identified in this way are marked with an asterisk in the table. In the remaining cases in which the PWY test is judged robust, no test is available post-2008.
18. FGM investigate whether bubble incidence is related to index-based investment. They fail to find any association.
19. The 2007–08 rice price spike is authoritatively discussed in Christiaensen (2009) and Dawe and Slayton (2010, 2011).
20. See UNCTAD (2009) and Mayer (2011, 2012) for a more detailed discussion.
21. Gilbert and Pfuderer (2012); Stoll and Whaley (2010); Sanders et al. (2009).
22. Correlation for corn is significant at the 5 per cent level and those for wheat and soybeans at the 1 per cent level.
23. In agricultural markets, there is substantial overlap between CIT and swap provider positions (Sanders et al., 2010).
24. CIT position changes tend to be positively autocorrelated. Supposing there is a positive causal link from current position changes to returns, Granger-causality analysis sees this through the indirect link from lagged position changes via the current change. The strength of that relationship will depend on the degree of position change autocorrelation which may be higher is less active markets.
25. Volatilities are reported on an annualized basis by multiplying the standard deviation of monthly logarithmic price changes by $\sqrt{12}$. Source for data: IMF, *International Financial Statistics* except coffee: International Coffee Organization (ICO indicator price).
26. There are futures markets for rice in Bangkok and Chicago. Trading volume on the Bangkok market is low and it tends to follow rather than lead commercial transactions (Gilbert, 2011). The Chicago (CBT) rough rice market also trades relatively small volumes and is relevant only in the US domestic rice trade. Palm oil futures are traded in Kuala Lumpur.
27. The WTI price has traditionally been taken as the reference price for crude oil. The NYMECX WTI contract prices crude oil at Cushing (OK). Limitations of storage capacity at Cushing resulted in WTI moving to a substantial discount to the Brent seaborne crude oil price during 2010–12. It is this seaborne price which is of greater relevance in international oil commerce. With two exceptions (bananas and groundnut oil) the 2007–11 correlations charted in Figure 6.3 would be lower if WTI were substituted for Brent.

REFERENCES

Acharya, V.V., L.A. Lochstoer and T. Ramadorai (2012), Limits to arbitrage and hedging: evidence from commodity markets. NYU Working Paper No. FIN-08-027, NYU Stern School of Business Research Paper Series.
Aulerich, N.M., S.H. Irwin and P. Garcia (2012), Bubbles, food prices, and speculation: evidence from the CFTC's daily Large Trader Data files. Paper prepared for presentation at the NBER Conference on Economics and Food Price Volatility, Seattle, 15–16 August 2012.
Bicchetti, D. and N. Maystre (2012), The synchronized and long-lasting structural change on commodity markets: evidence from high frequency data. Manuscript, Geneva, UNCTAD.
Bodie, Z. and V.I. Rosansky (1980), Risk and return in commodity futures. *Journal of Portfolio Management*, **4**, 26–29.
Bollerslev, T. (1986), Generalized autoregressive conditional heteroskedasticity. *Journal of Econometrics*, **31**, 307–327.
Brooks, C. and A. Katsaris (2005), A three-regime model of speculative behaviour: modelling the evolution of the S&P 500 composite index. *Economic Journal*, **115**, 767–797.

Brunetti, C. and B. Büyükşahin (2009), Is speculation destabilizing? Working Paper, Carey Business School, Johns Hopkins University, Baltimore, MD.
Büyükşahin, B., M.S. Haigh and M.A. Robe (2010), Commodities and equities: ever a 'market of one'?. *Journal of Alternative Investments*, **12**, 76–95.
Caballero, R.J., E. Fahri and P-O Gourinchas (2008a), Financial crash, commodity prices and global imbalances. Brookings Papers on Economic Activity, Fall, 1–55.
Caballero, R.J., E. Fahri and P-O Gourinchas (2008b), An equilibrium model of 'global imbalances' and low interest rates. *American Economic Review*, **92**, 358–393.
Cafiero, C., E.S.A. Bobenrieth, J.R.A.Bobenrieth and B.D. Wright (2011), The empirical relevance of the competitive storage model. *Journal of Econometrics*, **162**, 44–54.
Capelle-Blancard, G. and D. Coulibaly (2012), Index Trading and agricultural commodity prices: a panel Granger causality analysis. *Working Paper*, 2011–28, Paris, CEPII.
CFTC (2006), *Commission Actions in Response to the 'Comprehensive Review of the Commitments of Traders Reporting Program'*, CFTC, Washington DC, 21 June 2006.
Christiaensen, L. (2009), Revisiting the global food architecture. Lessons from the 2008 crisis. *Review of Business and Economics*, **54**, 345–361.
Dash, M. (1999), *Tulipomania*. London: Weidenfield and Nicolson.
Dawe, D. and T. Slayton (2010), The world rice market crisis of 2007–08. In D. Dawe (ed.), *The Rice Crisis*. London: Earthscan, pp.15–28.
Dawe, D. and T. Slayton (2011), The world rice market in 2007–08. In A. Prakash (ed.), *Safeguarding Food Security in Volatile Global Markets*. Rome: FAO, pp.171–81.
de Jong, F. and B. Rindi (2009), *The Microstructure of Financial Markets*. Cambridge: Cambridge University Press.
De Long, J.B., A. Shleifer, L.H. Summers and R.J. Waldman (1990), Positive feedback investment strategies and destabilizing rational expectations. *Journal of Finance*, **45**, 379–395.
Edwards, F.M. and C.W. Ma (1992), *Futures and Options*. New York: McGraw-Hill.
Engle, R.F. (2002), Dynamic conditional correlation: a simple class of multivariate generalized autoregressive conditional heteroskedasticity models. *Journal of Business and Economic Statistics*, **20**, 339–350.
Evans, G.W. (1991), Pitfalls in testing for explosive bubbles in asset prices. *American Economic Review*, **81**, 922–930.
Figuerola-Ferretti, I., C.L. Gilbert and J.R McCrorie (2012a), Recursive tests for explosive behavior and bubbles: extending the Phillips–Wu–Yu methodology to varying data spans and sampling intervals. Manuscript, University of St. Andrews, UK.
Figuerola-Ferretti, I., C.L. Gilbert and J.R McCrorie (2012b), Understanding commodity futures prices: fundamentals, financialization and bubble characteristics. Manuscript, University of Trento, Italy.
Figuerola-Ferretti, I., C.L. Gilbert and J.R McCrorie (2012c), Testing for bubbles in LME metals prices. Manuscript, Universidad Carlos III de Madrid, Spain.
Gilbert, C.L. (1994), *Commodity Fund Activity and the World Cocoa Market*. London: London Commodity Exchange.
Gilbert, C.L. (2010a), Commodity speculation and commodity investment. *Commodity Market Review*, 2009–10, 25–46.
Gilbert, C.L, (2010b), Speculative influence on commodity prices 2006–08. Discussion Paper, 197, Geneva: UNCTAD.
Gilbert, C.L. (2010c), How to understand high food prices. *Journal of Agricultural Economics*, **61**, 398–425.
Gilbert, C.L. (2011), Grains pass-through, 2005–09. In A. Prakash (ed.), *Safeguarding Food Security in Volatile Global Markets*. Rome: FAO, pp.127–148.
Gilbert, C.L. (2012), Testing the Masters Volatility Hypothesis: speculative impacts on agricultural price volatility. Manuscript, University of Trento, Italy.
Gilbert, C.L. and C.W. Morgan (2010), Food price volatility. *Philosophical Transactions of the Royal Society*, **B 365**, 3023–3034.
Gilbert, C.L. and C.W. Morgan (2011), Food price volatility. In I. Piot-Lepetit and R. M'Barek (eds), *Methods to Analyse Agricultural Commodity Price Volatility*. Berlin: Springer, pp.45–62.
Gilbert, C.L. and H.K. Mugera (2012), Biofuels or financialization: explaining the increased correlation between grains and crude oil prices. Manuscript, University of Trento, Italy.
Gilbert, C.L. and S. Pfuderer (2012), Index funds do impact agricultural prices. Paper presented at the Money, Macro and Finance Study Group Workshop on Commodity Markets, Bank of England, London, 25 May 2012.
Gorton, G. and K.G. Rouwenhorst (2006), Facts and fantasies about commodity futures. *Financial Analysts Journal*, **62**, 47–68.
Hall, S.G., Z. Psaradakis and M. Sola (1999), Detecting periodically collapsing bubbles: a Markov-switching unit root test. *Journal of Applied Econometrics*, **14**, 143–54.

Hamilton, J.D. and J.C. Wu (2012), Effects of index-fund investing on commodity futures prices. Working Paper, Department of Economics, University of California, San Diego.
Hernandez, M. A. and M. Torero (2010), Examining the dynamic relation between spot and futures prices of agricultural commodities. In Rapsomanikis and Sarris (eds), *Commodity Market Review 2009–10*, pp. 47–86, Rome: FAO.
Holthausen, R.E., R. Leftwich and D. Mayers (1987), The effects of large block transactions on security prices: a cross-sectional analysis. *Journal of Financial Economics*, **19**, 237–67.
Irwin, S.H. and D.R. Sanders (2011), Index funds, financialization, and commodity futures markets. *Applied Economic Perspectives and Policy*, **33**, 1–31.
Irwin, S.H. and D.R. Sanders (2012a), Financialization and structural change in commodity futures markets. *Journal of Agricultural and Applied Economics*, **44**, 371–96.
Irwin, S.H. and D.R. Sanders (2012b), Testing the masters hypothesis in commodity futures markets. *Energy Economics*, **34**, 256–269.
Jaffee, J.F. (1989), Gold and gold stocks as investments for institutional portfolios. *Financial Analysts Journal*, **45**, 53–60.
Krelage, E.H. (1942), *Bloemenspeculatie in Nederland*. Amsterdam: van Kampen and Zoon.
Maizels, A. (1994), The continuing commodity crisis of developing countries. *World Development*, **22**, 1685–1695.
Masters, M.W. (2008), Testimony before the US Senate Committee of Homeland Security and Government Affairs, Washington DC, 20 May 2008.
Mayer, J. (2011), Financialized commodity markets: the role of information and policy issues. *Économie Appliquée*, **44**, 5–34.
Mayer, J. (2012), The growing financialisation of commodity markets: divergences between index investors and money managers. *Journal of Development Studies*, **48**, 751–767.
Nissanke, M. (2012), Commodity market linages in the global financial crisis: excess volatility and development impacts. *Journal of Development Studies*, **48**, 732–750.
O'Hara, M. (1995), *Market Microstructure Theory*. Oxford: Blackwell.
Phillips, P.C.B. and J. Yu (2011), Dating the timeline of financial bubbles during the subprime crisis. *Quantitative Economics*, **2**, 455–491.
Phillips, P.C.B., S-P. Shi and J. Yu, (2012), Testing for multiple bubbles. Cowles Foundation Discussion Paper, 1843, Yale University, New Haven, CT.
Phillips, P.C.B., Y. Wu and J. Yu (2011), Explosive behavior in the 1990s Nasdaq: when did exuberance escalate asset values? *International Economic Review*, **52**, 210–226.
Psaradakis, Z., M. Sola and F. Spagnolo (2001), A simple procedure for detecting periodically collapsing rational bubbles. *Economics Letters*, **24**, 317–323.
Sanders, D.R. and S.H. Irwin (2011a), New evidence on the impact of index funds in US grain futures markets. *Canadian Journal of Agricultural Economics*, **59**, 519–532.
Sanders, D.R. and S.H. Irwin (2011b), The impact of index funds in commodity futures markets: a systems approach. *Journal of Alternative Investments*, **14**, 40–49.
Sanders, D.R. and S.H. Irwin (2012), Measuring index investment in commodity futures markets. Working Paper, Department of Agricultural and Consumer Economics, University of Illinois at Urbana, Champaign, IL.
Sanders, D.R., S.H. Irwin and R.P. Merrin (2009), Smart money: the forecasting ability of CFTC large traders in agricultural futures markets. *Journal of Agricultural and Resource Economics*, **34**, 276–296.
Sanders, D.R., S.H. Irwin and R.P. Merrin (2010), The adequacy of speculation in agricultural futures markets: too much of a good thing?. *Applied Economic Perspectives and Policy*, **32**, 77–94.
Schaller, H. and S. van Noorden (2002), Fads or bubbles?. *Empirical Economics*, **27**, 335–362.
Scherer, V. and L. He (2008), The diversification benefits of commodity futures indexes: a mean-variance spanning test. In F.J. Fabozzi, R. Füss and D.G. Kaiser (eds), *The Handbook of Commodity Investing*. Hoboken, NJ: Wiley, pp. 241–265.
Scholes, M. (1972), The market for securities: substitution versus price pressure and the effects of information on share prices. *Journal of Business*, **45**, 179–211.
Shi, S-P. and V. Arora (2012), An application of models of speculative behaviour to oil prices. *Economics Letters*, **115**, 469–472.
Shleifer, A. (1986), Do demand curves for stocks slope down? *Journal of Finance*, **41**, 579–590.
Sockin, M. and W. Xiong (2012), Feedback effects of commodity futures prices. Working Paper, Princeton University, Princeton, NJ.
Stock, J.H. and M.W. Watson (2003), *Introduction to Econometrics*. Boston, MA: Addison-Wesley.
Stoll, H.R. (2000), Friction. *Journal of Finance*, **55**, 1479–1514.
Stoll, H.R. and R.E. Whaley (2010), Commodity index investing and commodity futures prices. *Journal of Applied Finance*, **20**, 7–46.

Tang K. and W. Xiong (2012), Index investment and financialization of commodities. *Financial Analysts Journal*, **68**, 54–74.
UNCTAD (2009), Trade and development report. United Nations, New York and Geneva.
UNCTAD (2011), *Price Formation in Financialized Commodity Markets: The Role of Information*. New York and Geneva: United Nations.
United States Senate Permanent Subcommittee on Investigations (2009), Excessive speculation in the wheat market. Majority and. Minority Report, US Senate, Washington DC, 24 June 2009.
Woodward, J.D. (2008), Commodity futures investments: a review of strategic motivations and tactical opportunities. In F.J. Fabozzi, R. Füss and D.G. Kaiser (eds), *The Handbook of Commodity Investing*. Hoboken, NJ: Wiley, pp. 56–86.

7. Financialisation of food commodity markets, price surge and volatility: new evidence*
Kritika Mathur, Nidhi Kaicker, Raghav Gaiha, Katsushi S. Imai and Ganesh Thapa

7.1 INTRODUCTION

Food prices have been rising sharply the world over since July 2010. Although food prices have been increasing since 2000, they increased at a faster pace between 2006 and 2007–08 when prices of major cereals surged very rapidly. After the peak in prices in 2008, good harvests helped the prices to fall back. However, adverse weather conditions in several food exporting countries affected supplies, and there was another food price crisis in 2010. These spikes have been due to a combination of both short-term (such as droughts and trade restrictions) and long-term (such as declining productivity and inadequate investments in infrastructure) factors. Another factor is the deep integration between agricultural commodity markets and other markets in the world. For instance, rising crude oil prices have led to an increase in agriculture prices in two ways: rising inputs costs (such as oil-based fertilizers and transportation), and increased demand for agricultural crops for alternate energy sources such as biofuels.

Many analysts claim that speculation and hoarding further fuelled the price rise. Recent studies (Hernandez and Torero, 2010; Mayer, 2012; Nissanke, 2012) point towards the role of speculators in exaggerating the rally in food prices, over and above that explained by the fundamentals of demand and supply. Commodity derivatives are seen as an important portfolio-hedging instrument since the returns in commodity sector are uncorrelated with the returns on other assets. This financialization of commodity markets may not be a source of food inflation; however, it does play an important role in the short-term volatility in food prices.

As a World Bank report (2011) points out, much of the recent increase in commodity financial transactions has occurred in the futures markets, including for maize and wheat. This is largely driven by demand from index funds holding and continuously rolling over futures positions in commodity markets, without taking physical delivery. The extent to which these inflows affect spot prices, however, remains debatable.

In the context of food prices, speculation may take two forms – hoarding of commodities during shortages in anticipation of a further price rise, and investments into commodity futures or options. Investments in futures have led to prices being out of line with fundamental values. Moreover, futures prices have also been volatile. Some studies argue that futures market speculation can only be blamed for the increasing food prices if it is accompanied by hoarding. Moreover, it is expected that over the next few years, energy price volatility will translate into food price volatility.

With this background, we address the following issues in this chapter: (1) assessing the impact of macroeconomic variables on commodity prices; and (2) tracing the volatility patterns in commodity prices, and linking volatility in commodity markets to macroeconomic factors. The scheme is as follows. In the next section, we review recent literature addressing these issues. Our study builds on to the extant literature by examining not just the impact of macroeconomic factors on commodity prices, but also highlights a bicausal relationship between them. The third section gives an overview of the time series data characterizing commodity market returns. The statistical tests pertaining to the data and methodological issues are covered in section 7.4. To address the issue of reverse causality that may exist between macroeconomic factors and commodity prices, we use a vector autoregression framework. Empirical results are analysed in section 7.5, and section 7.6 concludes.

7.2 LITERATURE REVIEW

Recent literature on commodity price movements yields mixed results.

Tang and Xiong (2009) empirically study the futures contracts of 28 commodities and segregate the analysis into indexed and non-indexed commodities. They examine the difference in co-movements of indexed and non-indexed commodities by studying the correlations between a commodity return and return on oil. Comparison of the average 1-year correlation of indexed and non-indexed commodities for the period from 1973 till 2009 suggests that indexed non-energy commodities faced greater volatility compared to non-indexed commodities. This study also suggests that the average correlation in commodities is found to be higher in the United States than in China.

Gorton and Rouwenhorst (2006) construct an equally weighted performance index of commodity futures to investigate the impact of macroeconomic variables on return of commodity futures for the period from 1959–2004. They examine the correlation of stocks (total return index of SP500 stocks) with returns on commodity futures at various frequencies – quarterly, annual and at intervals of 5 years. Even though the correlation between returns on commodity futures and stocks is found to be negative for quarterly, 1-year and 5-year intervals, it remains weak. Using the CPI Index, the authors analyse the relationship between inflation and commodity futures returns. They find a positive correlation which is larger at longer intervals (yearly or 5 yearly) than shorter intervals (monthly or quarterly). Greer (2000) uses returns of asset class from 1970 to 2000 and is able to conclude that there is a negative correlation between returns on commodities and stocks and bonds. He also shows that there is positive correlation between returns on asset class and inflation. Erb (2006) points out that inflation can explain variations in returns on some commodity futures.

Silvennoinen and Thorp (2013) use DSTCC-GARCH[1] models to assess the changes in correlation of commodity futures returns, stocks and bonds due to changes in observable financial variables and time. The authors use price of futures contracts for 24 commodities for the period from May 1990 to July 2009. Weekly commodity futures returns are calculated. Returns of stock price indices of the United States, UK, Germany, France and Japan, and changes in Dollex are utilized in the study. The authors conclude that the level of correlations between commodity futures returns and US stock index returns increased over time. Buyuksahin (2010) employs the Standard and Poor Index of 500 companies (S&P 500) and Goldman Sachs Commodity Index (GSCI) returns and finds that simple correlation between the two during the period June 1992 to June 2008 is almost zero but rolling correlations fluctuate substantially in the chosen period of study. But for the overall period, on using dynamic correlation technique and recursive cointegration, the relation between stock and commodity indices does not vary.

In several important contributions, Wright (2011) and Bobenrieth (2010), among others, have employed a competitive storage model to shed light on foodgrain price spikes. The main argument is: given the substitutability between wheat, rice and corn in the global market for calories, when aggregate stocks decline to minimal feasible levels, prices become highly sensitive to small shocks, consistent with the economics of storage behaviour. Higher stocks when prices fall reduce the dispersion of price and prevent steeper price slumps. Disposal of stocks when supplies are scarcer reduces the severity of price spikes. Given sufficiency of speculative capital, storage can eliminate negative price spikes but can moderate positive price spikes only as long as stocks are available. When stocks are used up, aggregate use must match an almost fixed supply in the short run.

Most recent explanations of commodity price surges/spikes have relied on 'bubbles'. These imply that price rises at the rate of interest, or at a higher 'explosive' rate, for a sustained period, followed by a sharp slump and a period of quiescence (Wright, 2011). Bubbles are noticed only after a sequence of price run-up and crash has been completed, often viewed as incompatible with market fundamentals.

Our preceding literature review focused on cash inflow and commodity price spikes. Wright (2011) is deeply sceptical of this link primarily on the ground that there is no evidence suggesting that this cash increased grain stocks during the price spikes in 2007–08. If the excess cash caused a bubble, it must have reduced consumption and increased food stocks. But in 2007–08, stocks in the global markets were close to minimal levels as prices spiked.

There is in fact evidence of massive storing by exporter governments denying their stocks to the global market by restricting supply to protect their domestic consumers. Following the announcement by India of banning of rice exports to protect its consumers from a wheat shortfall, other exporters followed suit while importers resorted to panic buying. The important point here is that charges against private hoarders and financiers of excessive hoarding are misplaced as huge stocks held off the market are overlooked, especially by China.

In 2007–08 the aggregate stocks of wheat, rice and corn were at minimal levels, lower than the amount than would have been observed without mandated diversions of grain and oilseeds for biofuels. Lack of stocks rendered the markets vulnerable to regional weather problems, the boost to biofuel demand from the oil price hike in 2007–08, and the long Australian drought. Moreover, the demand for biofuel was expected to increase in the future, and using stocks of wheat, rice and corn to dampen prices would have been irresponsible and would have lead to rise in their prices in the future. Supplies were adequate to meet food demands without food price hikes but for panic reactions of food exporters and importers.

The effect of spillovers from the financial markets to the commodity markets during the global financial crisis on developing economies has been investigated by Nissanke (2012). The author analyses the price movement of agricultural commodities, crude oil and minerals over the period January 2010 to July 2011. The rise in price level of commodities during 2002–08 is attributed to the increase in demand from industrial emerging economies. Inventory management is also found to be a determining factor leading to sharp increases in crops such as rice, wheat and maize in 2007–08. Apart from demand supply factors, Nissanke observes that the rise in price of commodities is a result of participation of financial investors as there was a marked jump in the volume of trading of derivatives in 2005. This aspect has been dealt with in detail by Mayer (2012). Aulerich et al. (2013) argue that the bubble in agricultural commodity prices is not an outcome of index fund investment. Their study uses bivariate Granger causality to investigate the dynamics between position of index traders and agricultural futures prices for the period from January 2004 to September 2009.

Financial investors are categorized into index traders and money managers. Money managers operate hedge funds with short-term horizons, by taking positions on both side of the commodity market, they earn profits from a rise as well as a fall in the commodity prices, whereas index traders take long-term positions without physically taking delivery of the commodities. Mayer argues that efficient market hypothesis fails in commodity markets due to factors other than market fundamentals of demand and supply and due to positions taken up by financial investors also called the 'weight of money effect'. Using the Commodity Futures Trading Commission (CFTC) weekly Commitments of Traders (COT) reports, he studies positions of index traders and non-commercial traders (excluding index traders) focusing on eight commodities namely – soybeans, soybean oil, wheat, maize, gold, copper, crude oil and natural gas. The author finds correlations in positions and prices of commodities during subperiods. Regression analysis is performed to study the determinants of the positions taken by index traders and non-commercial traders, with the explanatory variables comprising spot returns, roll returns, volatility, interest rate, correlation with equity market, expected inflation and dollar index. The results suggest that position of index traders are influenced by roll returns while positions of non-commercial traders are influenced by spot returns of commodities. He attributes speculation to diversification objectives since correlation in equity and commodity market is found to be negative and significant in the period from January 1999 and December 2004. Whereas in the period from January 2005 to June 2008, positions taken up by investors are found to be positively related to movements in equity markets. Granger Causality tests are conducted on the positions taken by index traders and money managers with the prices of the eight commodities. The results of Granger causality tests conducted in the study refute the Efficient Market Hypothesis since a significant impact of index traders positions is found on the price level of commodities and not vice versa.

7.3 COMMODITY PRICE MOVEMENTS

The movement in the futures prices of various commodities have been very volatile in recent times. The futures price of rough rice increased slightly from US$7.5 in 1990 to US$8.16 in 1991, and came down in 1992. Following a gradual increase, there was a slight decline in the latter half of the decade. Since 2001, the futures price of rough rice has been going up, with a major spike in 2008. If we see Figure 7.1, for each commodity, there has been a stable movement in prices prior to 2007, and a very pronounced price spike is seen in the year 2008, followed by massive volatility.

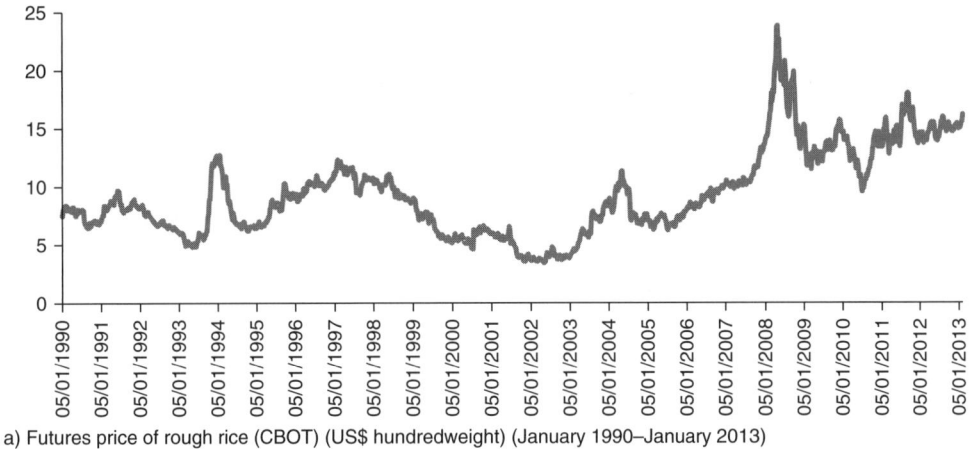

a) Futures price of rough rice (CBOT) (US$ hundredweight) (January 1990–January 2013)

b) Futures price of soybean (CBOT) (USc/bu) (January 1990–January 2013)

c) Futures price of corn (CBOT) (USc/bu) (January 1990–January 2013)

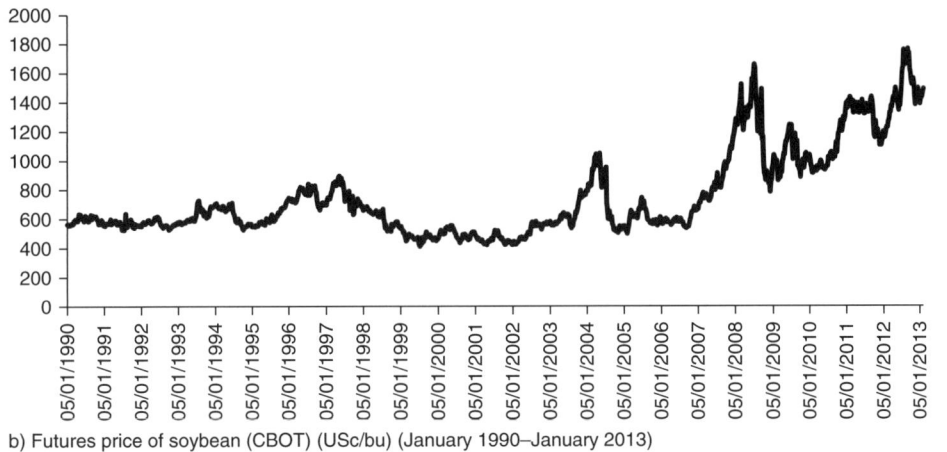

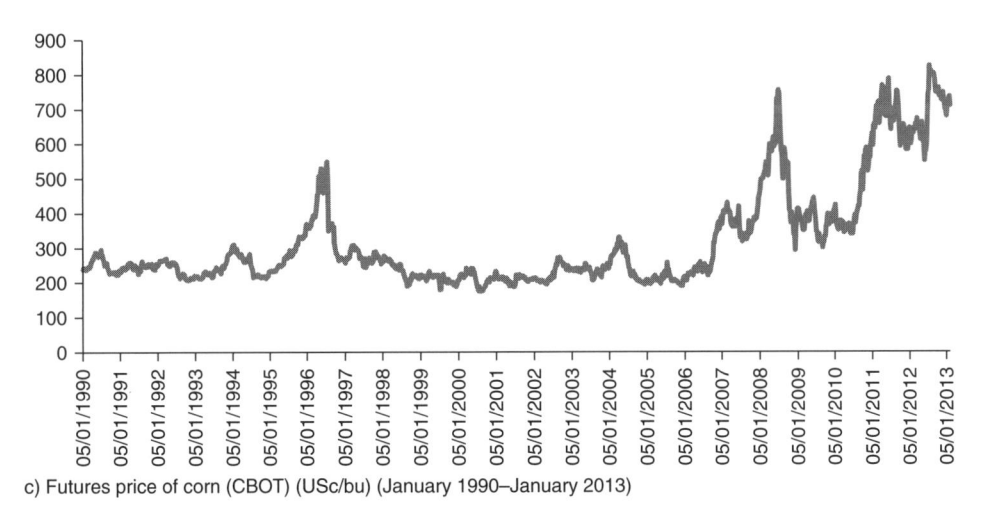

Figure 7.1 Futures price movements

154 *Handbook on food*

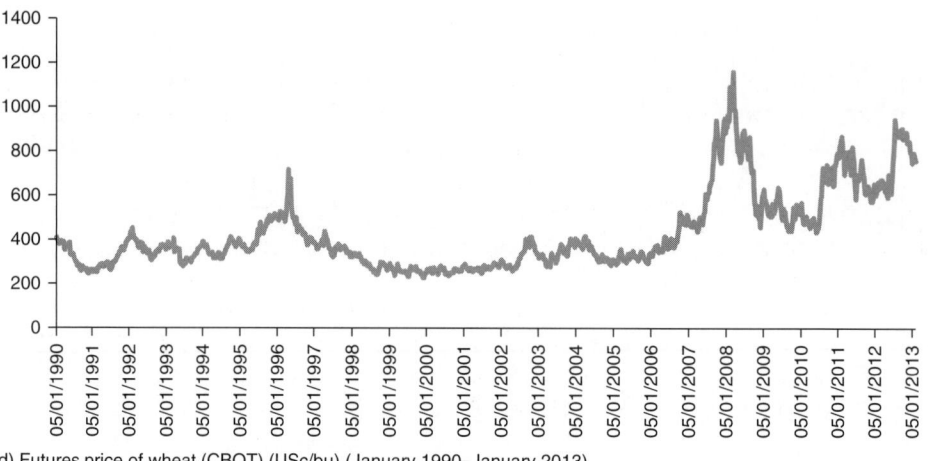

d) Futures price of wheat (CBOT) (USc/bu) (January 1990–January 2013)

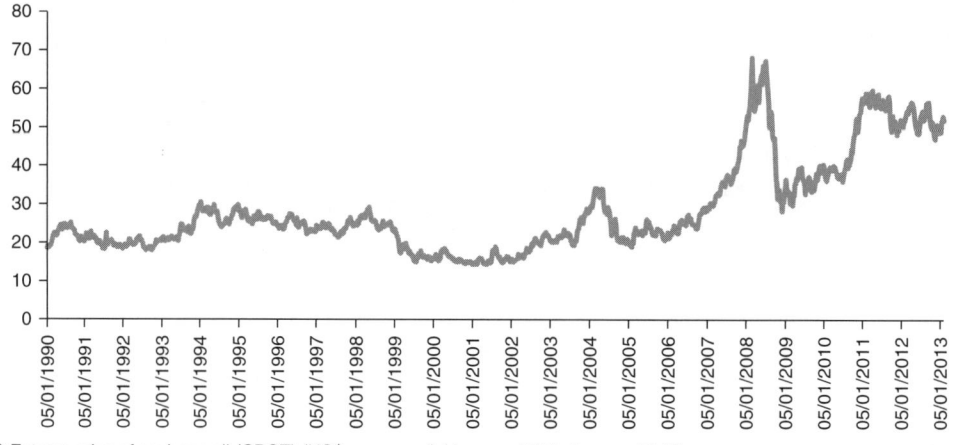

e) Futures price of soybean oil (CBOT) (US$ per pound) (January 1990–January 2013)

Figure 7.1 (continued)

The futures price of soybean was 564 USc/bushel in January 1990 and continued to remain below 894.25 USc/bushel until May 1997. From then, the price remained below 800 USc/bushel until a spike in soybean price was experienced in January 2004 when it rose to 835.25, resulting from a supply shortage of the commodity. A marked rise in price of soybean took place in 2007 and 2008 and continued to rise until reaching a peak of 1658 USc/bushel in July 2008 which was accompanied by rise in price of crude oil. The price spike has been attributed to financialization of commodities (Masters and White, 2008). The commodity in question experienced a sharp fall in the second half of 2008 and prices have continued to remain volatile since then. Another spike was observed in soybean prices in August 2012 when prices rose to more than 1750 USc/bushel.

Corn also faced similar movements in price. Corn prices remained below 300 USc/bushel in the first half of 1990s. In 1996, corn prices experienced a sharp rise, reaching a peak of 548 USc/bushel in July 1996 due to low stocks, a result of low production of corn in the preceding years. Following the spike, prices continued to fall until 1999 and remained in the range of 200–300 USc/bushel until 2008. In 2008, prices shot up, and reached a peak of 754.75 USc/bushel in June 2008, followed by a decline in price in the second half of 2008 reaching to as low as 293.5 USc/bushel. Prices remained volatile in 2010, succeeded by a peak in corn prices in April 2011 and another spike in July 2012, reaching a level of 824.5 USc/bushel.

The movement in price of hard winter wheat traded on Kansas City Board of Trade (KCBT) and price of hard red spring wheat traded on Minneapolis Grain Exchange (MGE) is similar from 1990 to 2013. Both the varieties of wheat faced a rise in 1996. This was followed by low fluctuation in price level until 2003, when a rise in price level can be observed in both the types of wheat. Prices began to rise in the beginning of 2008 and reached peak levels (1217 USc/ bushel – KCBT wheat and 1944 USc/bushel – MGE Wheat) in February–March 2008. Price of wheat has continued to remain volatile since the beginning of the crisis.

7.4 DATA AND METHODOLOGY

7.4.1 Data

The data used in this study are the returns on the GSCI, Morgan Stanley Commodities Index (MSCI, which is an indicator of the performance of emerging economies), SP500 (which taps the equity market performance), Dollex Index (to capture the exchange rates changes), inflation rate as measured by the consumer price index (CPI) and crude oil price captured by the price of West Texas Intermediate (WTI). The definitions of the variables used in the econometric analysis are provided in the Appendix. The notations used for the *monthly returns* on these variables are GSCI, MSCI, S&P 500, Dollex, CPI, and WTI, respectively.[2] Table 7.1 gives the summary statistics of the monthly returns on these variables. The statistics include mean returns/growth, standard deviation, skewness, kurtosis, autocorrelation and Portmanteau Q test. Mean returns suggest a more or less stable regime if we look at the complete period; but these may be very volatile. A commonly used measure to estimate volatility is the standard deviation of returns/growth. The returns on CPI (inflation rate) and WTI are more volatile than the returns on commodity markets and other macroeconomic variables. The returns on GSCI, MSCI and S&P 500 are negatively skewed, suggesting that the values lower than the mean are farther from it than those higher than the mean. The coefficient of kurtosis is greater than 3, implying a fat-tailed distribution.

When there is correlation or dependence between observations that are close in time, the disturbance process exhibits autocorrelation or serial correlation. The larger the absolute value of autocorrelation, the more highly autocorrelated are the disturbances. Since we suspect the presence of autocorrelation[3] in the time series, we use estimated residuals to diagnose it using the Q-statistic.[4] Figure 7.2 shows the serial dependence of various series. The significant value of the Portmanteau's Q statistic provides evidence of strong dependencies in the distribution of returns and justifies the use of autoregressive filters and conditional heteroscedasticity models.

We further examine the properties of our data by testing for stationarity. A stationary

Table 7.1 Summary statistics (monthly returns)

	GSCI	MSCI	SP500	CPI	WTI	Dollex
Mean	0.0010	0.0015	0.0013	2.4321	0.0011	0.0000
Standard Deviation	0.0297	0.0305	0.0238	0.8277	0.0508	0.0117
Skewness	−0.8640	−0.8173	−0.7436	1.0071	−0.8811	0.2088
Kurtosis	7.4003	9.1493	9.8295	5.3933	8.6073	3.7552
Autocorrelation						
p1	0.000	0.000	0.000	0.000	0.000	0.000
p2	0.000	0.000	0.000	0.000	0.000	0.000
p3	0.000	0.000	0.000	0.000	0.000	0.000
p4	0.000	0.000	0.000	0.000	0.000	0.000
p5	0.000	0.000	0.000	0.000	0.000	0.000
p6	0.000	0.000	0.000	0.000	0.000	−0.001
p7	−0.038	0.068	−0.079	0.991	−0.098	−0.002
p8	0.000	0.000	0.000	0.000	0.000	0.000
p9	0.000	0.000	0.000	0.000	0.000	0.000
p10	0.000	0.000	0.000	0.000	0.000	0.000
p11	0.000	0.000	0.000	0.000	0.000	0.000
p12	0.000	0.000	0.000	0.000	0.000	0.000
p13	0.000	0.000	0.000	0.000	0.000	0.000
p14	0.030	0.137	0.061	0.981	−0.022	0.036
p15	0.000	0.000	0.000	0.000	0.000	0.000
p16	0.000	0.000	0.000	0.000	0.000	0.000
p17	0.000	0.000	0.000	0.000	0.000	0.000
p18	0.000	0.000	0.000	0.000	0.000	0.000
p19	0.000	0.000	0.000	0.000	0.000	0.000
p20	0.000	0.000	0.000	0.000	0.000	0.001
Pormanteau's Q(20)	2.742	27.503	11.595	2255.8	11.844	1.532

time series is one whose statistical properties such as mean, variance and autocorrelation remain constant overtime. If a series has a long-term trend, and tends to revert to the trend line (such a series is known as *trend stationary series*), it may be possible to stationarize it by de-trending the series. A *difference stationary series* is one whose statistical properties are not constant overtime even after de-trending, and it has to be transformed into a series of period-to-period changes (also known as first differences). We examine the stationarity of the various time series using unit root test – Augmented Dicky–Fuller (ADF) test[5] and the Phillips–Perron (PP) test (Wooldridge, 2006).[6] The results are shown in Table 7.2.

The null hypothesis of presence of unit root in the series is rejected for all the series, and thus, the returns exhibit stationarity. These are *difference stationary* series as the first difference of the logarithmic transformation of values is used to calculate returns/growth rates.

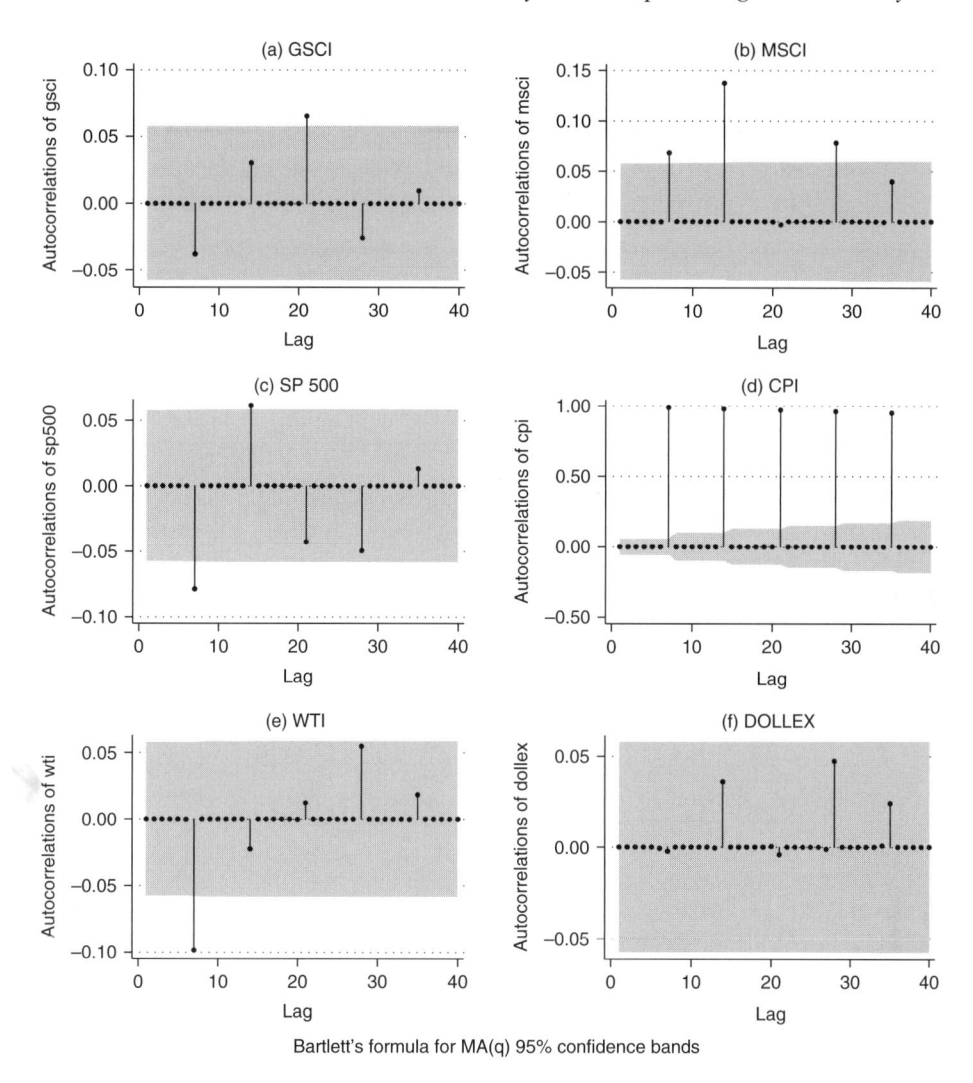

Food commodity markets, price surge and volatility 157

Figure 7.2 Autocorrelations

7.4.2 Methodology

The first objective of this chapter is to assess the impact of macroeconomic variables on commodity prices. Towards this objective, we use regression analysis to examine the effects of the various economic variables, following Tang and Xiong (2012) – the performance of emerging market economies as captured by MSCI, equity market performance as measured by the S&P 500, inflation rate, oil price as measured by the WTI and exchange rate captured by the Dollex – on commodity markets in general, captured by the GSCI, and then on individual commodity prices. In addition to the explanatory variables, we use time dummies, to examine the impact of the financial and food crises on commodity market returns.

Table 7.2 Tests for stationarity

	Augmented Dicky–Fuller Test for Unit Root			Phillip–Perron Test for Unit Root		
	Test statistic Z(t)	5% critical value	Mackinnon p-value for Z(t)	Test statistic Z(Rho)	5% critical value	Mackinnon p-value for Z(t)
GSCI	−23.705	−2.860	0.0000	−1262.765	−14.100	0.0000
MSCI	−20.236	−2.860	0.0000	−1222.470	−14.100	0.0000
S&P500	−23.586	−2.860	0.0000	−1256.093	−14.100	0.0000
CPI	−4.118	−2.860	0.0009	−10.587	−14.100	0.0000
WTI	−25.925	−2.860	0.0000	−1274.636	−14.100	0.0000
Dollex	−23.161	−2.860	0.0000	−1212.072	−14.100	0.0000

Since the variables in the macroeconomic framework are integrated, we use a VAR (value at risk) framework to capture the relation between each of the macroeconomic variables and commodity market returns in a dynamic setting. The VAR approach models every endogenous variable in the system as a function of lagged values of itself as well as of all the other endogenous variables in the system (Sims, 1980; Watson, 1994; Stock and Watson, 2001).

A reduced form of the VAR (bivariate) model can be represented as follows:

$$\Delta Z_{1t} = \Delta x_{1t} = \omega_1 + A_{11}(L)\Delta x_{1t-1} + A_{12}(L)\Delta x_{2t-1} + \varepsilon_{1t}$$

$$\Delta Z_{2t} = \Delta x_{2t} = \omega_2 + A_{21}(L)\Delta x_{1t-1} + A_{22}(L)\Delta x_{2t-1} + \varepsilon_{2t}$$

where x_i are the endogenous variables, ω_i are the intercept terms, L is the lag operator, such that $A_{11}(L) = \alpha_{11}(0) + \alpha_{11}(1)L + \alpha_{11}(2)L^2 + \ldots + \alpha_{11}(p)L^p$, p is the number of lags included in the VAR models and $L^i x_t = x_{t-i}$, and ε_i are the error terms (Binswanger, 2004).

The VAR model requires variables to be stationary. Since each variable in our study is stationary (at the level of first difference of logarithm), we use a VAR framework to assess the impact of the macroeconomic variables (returns or growth rates) on commodity returns, and the reverse causality.

The second objective of this study is to trace the volatility patterns in commodity prices, and link volatility in commodity markets to macroeconomic factors. Since the volatility of many economic time series is not constant through time, conditional heteroscedasticity models are used to estimate the volatility of commodity returns, and other macroeconomic variables, and the causal relationships between the predicted variances are assessed using cross-correlation functions and vector autoregression models.

Traditional homoscedastic models are not appropriate when using data for commodity prices, because of the presence of conditional heteroscedasticity (Mandelbrot, 1963; Baillie and Bollerslev, 1990; Lamoureux and Lastrapes, 1990a, b). The volatility of many economic time series is not constant through time. For instance, stock market volatility exhibits clustering, i.e. large deviations from the mean tend to be followed by even larger deviations, and small deviations tend to be followed by smaller deviations. The Autoregressive Conditional Heteroscedasticity (ARCH), and its extension, Generalised

Autoregressive Conditional Heteroscedasticity (GARCH) address this time dependent volatility as a function of observed time volatility (Black, 1976; Engle, 1982; Bollerslev, 1986; Bollerslev et al., 1992, 1994; Chiang and Doong, 2001). The ARCH[7] models the variance of a regression model's disturbance as a linear function of lagged values of the squared regression disturbances. The GARCH model, in addition, includes lagged values of the conditional variance. A standard GARCH (p,q) model may be written as:

$$y_t = x_t\delta + \varepsilon_t \text{(conditional mean)}$$

$$\sigma_t^2 = \omega + \sum_{i=1}^{p}\alpha_i\varepsilon_{t-i}^2 + \sum_{j=1}^{q}\beta_j\sigma_{t-j}^2 \text{(conditional variance)}$$

where α_i are the ARCH parameters and β_j are the GARCH parameters. In a GARCH model, an Autoregressive Moving Average (ARMA) process can also be added to the mean equation (Hamilton, 1994; Enders, 2004).

A drawback of the ARCH and GARCH models is the failure to address the problem of asymmetry. Both of these models imply a symmetric impact of innovations, i.e. whether the shock is positive or negative makes no difference to the expected variance. However, many economic time series, particularly stock market returns, exhibit an asymmetric effect, i.e. a negative shock to returns generates more volatility than a positive shock. Nelson (1991) addresses the asymmetry problem in GARCH by employing an Exponential Generalised Autoregressive Conditional Heteroscedasticity model (E-GARCH). The conditional volatility equation for an E-GARCH(p, q) model is as follows:

$$\ln(\sigma_t^2) = \omega + \sum_{i=1}^{p}\alpha_i|z_{t-i}| + \gamma_i z_{t-i} \sum_{j=1}^{q}\beta_j \ln(\sigma_{t-j}^2) \text{ where } z_t = \varepsilon_t/\sigma_t$$

The presence of leverage effect can be tested by the hypothesis $\gamma_i = 0$. The impact is asymmetric if $\gamma_i \neq 0$. If $\gamma_i > 0$, the volatility tends to rise when the shock is positive, and if $\gamma_i < 0$, the volatility tends to fall. We use an E-GARCH model to calculate the volatility of various time series, and also experiment with various conditional heteroscedastic models (with and without autoregressive coefficients), and the best-fit model is selected on the basis of the log likelihood ratio test.

Having estimated the variance using the conditional heteroscedasticity models for all the variables, we study the causal relationships between these using the cross-correlation function (Cheung and Ng, 1996). The cross-correlation function is implemented as follows. In the first stage, the time-varying variance is modelled using conditional heteroscedasticity. In the second stage, the resulting squared residuals are standardized by their conditional variances, and the cross-correlation function of these squared residuals is used to test the null hypothesis of no causality in variance (Constantinou et al., 2005). The cross-correlation function is used by Cheung and Ng (1996) to study the causal relationships between the NIKKEI 225 and the S&P 500 stock price indices.

Since the variables in the macroeconomic framework are integrated, the predicted volatility of any of them should affect others. Thus, we use a VAR framework to capture this relationship. After estimating the VAR model, impulse response functions (IRFs) are derived from the estimates. An impulse response function measures the effect of a shock to an endogenous variable on itself or on another endogenous variable

160   Handbook on food

(Lutkepohl, 1993; Hamilton, 1994). We then employ Granger causality tests to find whether there exists any relationship between macroeconomic variables and commodity returns, and the direction of causality.

7.5 RESULTS

The following subsections analyse the empirical results based on the methodology discussed earlier. The results pertaining to the first objective (relationship between commodity market returns and macroeconomic factors) are given in section 7.5.1 for commodity markets and individual commodities. As discussed previously, variables in the macroeconomic framework may be integrated. Hence, we use a VAR framework to capture the relation between each of the macroeconomic variables and commodity market returns. The results for the second objective, linking volatilities in various variables, are given in section 7.5.2.

7.5.1 Relationship Between Commodity Market Returns and Macroeconomic Factors

Impact of economic factors on commodity market returns

To assess the impact of economic factors on the commodity market returns, we regress the return on GSCI on S&P 500, MSCI (an emerging markets index), CPI, exchange rates (using Dollex) and crude oil price (using WTI). We experiment with two alternate specifications: (1) in the first, we take a single time dummy; (2) in the second, we take three time dummies.

In Table 7.3, in Column A, we take a single time dummy that takes the value 1 for the years 2007–10 (covering the food and financial crises) and 0 otherwise. This dummy is interacted with each of the explanatory variables, to see the varying impacts over time of the macroeconomic factors. In Column B, the time dummy takes the value 1 for the period September 2008 to June 2010 (financial crisis) and 0 otherwise.

Table 7.3   Impact of macroeconomic factors on commodity markets (specification 1)

DEPENDENT VARIABLE: GSCI	Column A			Column B		
Time Dummy	−0.001	(−0.23)	–	0.002	(0.24)	–
MSCI	0.035	(1.34)	–	0.044	(1.78)	*
*Interaction: Time Dummy*MSCI*	0.253	(3.41)	***	0.376	(3.78)	***
S&P 500	0.037	(1.22)	–	0.022	(0.75)	–
*Interaction: Time Dummy*S&P500*	−0.104	(−1.61)	–	−0.110	(−1.28)	–
Dollex	−0.187	(−4.27)	***	−0.210	(−5.01)	***
*Interaction: Time Dummy*Dollex*	−0.129	(−0.87)	–	0.021	(0.1)	–
CPI	−0.001	(−0.99)	–	−0.001	(−1.48)	–
*Interaction: Time Dummy*CPI*	0.000	(0.2)	–	−0.003	(−0.65)	–
Crude Oil Price (WTI)	0.454	(28.43)	***	0.469	(29.94)	***
*Interaction: Time Dummy*WTI*	0.010	(0.19)	–	−0.071	(−1.25)	–
Constant	0.002	(1.04)	–	0.002	(1.69)	–

Table 7.4 *Impact of macroeconomic factors on commodity markets (Specification 2)*

DEPENDENT VARIABLE: GSCI		Coefficient	
T1 (June 2006 to August 2008)	0.003	(0.19)	–
T2 (September 2008 to June 2010)	0.002	(0.33)	–
T3 (July 2010 to June 2011)	0.006	(1.18)	–
MSCI	0.036	(1.34)	–
Interaction: T1*MSCI	0.029	(0.5)	–
Interaction: T2*MSCI	0.384	(3.83)	***
Interaction: T3*MSCI	−0.057	(−0.39)	–
S&P 500	0.034	(1.1)	–
Interaction: T1*S&P500	−0.112	(−1.31)	–
Interaction: T2*S&P500	−0.122	(−1.41)	–
Interaction: T3*S&P500	0.209	(1.53)	–
Dollex	−0.181	(−4.05)	***
Interaction: T1*Dollex	0.066	(0.41)	–
Interaction: T2*Dollex	−0.008	(−0.04)	–
Interaction: T3*Dollex	−0.058	(−0.41)	–
CPI	−0.001	(−0.91)	–
Interaction: T1*CPI	−0.001	(−0.17)	–
Interaction: T2*CPI	−0.003	(−0.69)	–
Interaction: T3*CPI	−0.005	(−1.06)	–
Crude Oil Price (WTI)	0.448	(27.58)	***
Interaction: T1*WTI	0.178	(3.81)	***
Interaction: T2*WTI	−0.050	(−0.88)	–
Interaction: T3*WTI	0.110	(1.8)	*
Constant	0.002	(0.99)	–

Our results show a negative relationship between the commodity market returns and the Dollex, and a positive relationship between commodity market returns and crude oil price returns. The impact of equity markets and inflation on commodity markets is weak except when interacted with time. As suggested by the results in the second panel, emerging markets performance has a positive impact on commodity markets, and this relationship became stronger in the years of the financial crisis. Surprisingly, the overall impact of the two time dummies is insignificant.

In Table 7.4, we experiment with an alternate specification with three time dummies: T1 which takes the value 1 for the period June 2006 to August 2008 (food price crisis) and 0 otherwise, T2 which takes the value 1 for the period September 2008 to June 2010 (financial crisis), T3 which takes the value 1 for the period July 2010 to June 2011 (food price spikes), and each of these dummies in specific cases is interacted with the explanatory variables. The results are similar to those in Table 7.3 – a negative relationship between the commodity market returns and the Dollex, and a positive relationship between commodity market returns and crude oil price returns. The impact of equity markets, emerging markets and inflation on commodity markets is weak. An additional finding is that the oil price impacts become stronger in the periods of the two food crises. This is consistent with our introductory remarks on the food–energy nexus. Moreover, compared to Table 7.3, MSCI has a weak coefficient.

162 *Handbook on food*

Impact of economic factors on individual commodity returns
In the second set of exercises, we take individual commodity returns, instead of the commodity market index, i.e. the GSCI. We regress returns on various commodities (corn, soyabean, Kansas wheat and Minnesota wheat) on S&P 500 (equity markets index), MSCI (an emerging markets index), CPI (to capture inflation), exchange rates (using Dollex) and crude oil price (using WTI). Our specification uses three time dummies: T1 which takes the value 1 for the period June 2006 to August 2008 (food price crisis) and 0 otherwise, T2 which takes the value 1 for the period September 2008 to June 2010 (financial crisis), T3 which takes the value 1 for the period July 2010 to June 2011 (food price spikes), and each of these dummies in specific cases is interacted with the explanatory variables, to check the varying impacts overtime. The results are given in Table 7.5. We use different specifications for the four commodities.

For each of the commodities, T3 has a significant positive impact. This implies that the returns were higher in the period of the recent food price spike, i.e. July 2010 to June 2011. There is no significant relationship between equity market performance and returns on the various commodities. In case of Kansas wheat and corn, a significant positive relationship is found between the returns, and the indicator of emerging markets performance. The returns on corn and Minnesota wheat are negatively related to the returns on Dollex, and this relationship weakens during the recent financial crisis, and the food price surge following it. A positive relationship is observed between returns on both types of wheat and inflation rates, with the effect weakening in the wake of the second food price crisis.

Bidirectional relationship between commodity market returns and macroeconomic factors
We use a vector autoregression (VAR) framework to capture the relation between macroeconomic variables and commodity market returns in a dynamic setting. The Schwartz Bayesian Information Criterion (SBIC) is used to determine the appropriate lag length for the VAR framework. The variables that we use in our VAR are (1) returns on GSCI, (2) returns on MSCI, (3) returns on S&P 500, (4) inflation rate based on CPI, (5) returns on the WTI (representing oil prices) and (6) returns on the Dollex index. The lag length obtained for each of the variables, using SBIC is 1. The results of the VAR are given in Table 7.6.

As may be seen from the table above, there is some evidence of reverse causality or mutual endogeneity, for instance, causality from GSCI, S&P 500 and WTI to MSCI, CPI to WTI and from MSCI, S&P500 to Dollex. We also performed a similar analysis taking individual commodity returns instead of the composite GSCI. Some evidence of mutual endogeniety between these variables is found. There is also, in some cases, reverse causality from commodity return to macroeconomic factors, for example, from soybean return to the Dollex index.[8]

7.5.2 Relationship between Volatility in Commodity Markets and Other Markets

Traditional homoscedastic models are not appropriate when using data for commodity prices, because of the presence of conditional heteroscedasticity. Having tested for the presence of ARCH effect,[9] the appropriate lag length for the mean equation is calculated using the Akaike Information (AIC) criterion. The order of E-GARCH (p,q) is estimated using diagnostic tests, t-values and the log likelihood ratio of

Table 7.5 Impact of macroeconomic factors on individual commodity returns

DEPENDENT VARIABLE = Commodity Returns	Corn			Soyabean		
T1 (June 2006 to August 2008)	−0.025	(−0.7)	–	0.050	(1.55)	–
T2 (September 2008 to June 2010)	0.009	(0.6)	–	−0.011	(−0.77)	–
T3 (July 2010 to June 2011)	0.090	(5.06)	***	0.030	(1.86)	*
S&P 500	0.050	(0.8)	–	−0.043	(−0.75)	–
Interaction: T1*S&P500	−0.244	(−1.14)	–	0.180	(0.92)	–
Interaction: T2*S&P500	0.086	(0.53)	–	0.147	(0.98)	–
Interaction: T3*S&P500	−0.477	(−1.34)	–	−0.311	(−0.94)	–
MSCI	0.084	(1.69)	*	−0.004	(−0.08)	–
Interaction: T1*MSCI	0.164	(1.06)	–	−0.095	(−0.66)	–
Interaction: T2*MSCI	−0.020	(−0.15)	–	0.096	(0.77)	–
Interaction: T3*MSCI	0.286	(0.82)	–	0.377	(1.18)	–
Dollex	−0.208	(−2.15)	**	0.071	(0.8)	–
Interaction: T1*Dollex	−0.533	(−1.39)	–	−0.201	(−0.57)	–
Interaction: T2*Dollex	−1.026	(−3.36)	***	1.034	(3.67)	***
Interaction: T3*Dollex	−1.089	(−2.45)	**	1.007	(2.45)	**
Crude (WTI)	0.024	(1.03)	–	−0.008	(−0.36)	–
Interaction: T1*Crude (WTI)	0.197	(2.2)	**	0.098	(1.19)	–
Interaction: T2*Crude (WTI)	0.022	(0.42)	–	0.083	(1.75)	*
Interaction: T3*Crude (WTI)	0.043	(0.33)	–	0.054	(0.45)	–
CPI	0.001	(0.97)	–	−0.001	(−0.44)	–
Interaction: T1*CPI	0.013	(0.92)	–	−0.016	(−1.22)	–
Interaction: T2*CPI	−0.005	(−0.55)	–	0.007	(0.85)	–
Interaction: T3*CPI	−0.073	(−4.51)	***	−0.022	(−1.49)	–
Constant	−0.004	(−1.15)	–	0.003	(0.83)	–

Kansas wheat			Minnesota wheat		
0.048	(1.18)	–	0.051	(1.36)	–
0.008	(0.48)	–	0.008	(0.5)	–
0.073	(3.54)	***	0.065	(3.41)	***
−0.052	(−0.72)	–	−0.063	(−0.94)	–
0.071	(0.29)	–	0.202	(0.88)	–
0.061	(0.32)	–	−0.036	(−0.21)	–
−0.052	(−0.13)	–	0.151	(0.39)	–
0.116	(2)	**	0.070	(1.31)	–
−0.136	(−0.75)	–	−0.120	(−0.72)	–
−0.059	(−0.37)	–	0.081	(0.55)	–
0.626	(1.55)	–	0.492	(1.32)	–
−0.170	(−1.51)	–	−0.198	(−1.9)	*
−0.300	(−0.68)	–	−0.044	(−0.11)	–
−1.559	(−4.39)	***	−1.079	(−3.28)	***
−1.135	(−2.19)	**	−0.641	(−1.34)	–
0.041	(1.52)	–	0.027	(1.1)	–
−0.027	(−0.26)	–	−0.044	(−0.46)	–
0.137	(2.29)	**	0.137	(2.48)	**
−0.112	(−0.74)	–	−0.091	(−0.65)	–

Table 7.5 (continued)

	Kansas wheat			Minnesota wheat	
0.003	(1.87)	*	0.002	(1.65)	*
−0.018	(−1.1)	−	−0.020	(−1.31)	−
−0.006	(−0.57)	−	−0.007	(−0.7)	−
−0.063	(−3.34)	***	−0.052	(−2.99)	***
−0.008	(−1.85)	*	−0.006	(−1.51)	−

Table 7.6 VAR results

DEPENDENT VARIABLE →	GSCI	MSCI	S&P 500	CPI	WTI	Dollex
No. of Obs			1147			
Log Likelihood			15437.34			
Chi²	6.7021	16.3103	10.0650	198745.4	17.9370	9.2505
P>chi²	0.3493	0.0122	0.1219	0.0000	0.0064	0.1600
Lags of						
GSCI (L1)	−0.004	−0.105	−0.051	−0.007	0.154	−0.036
	(−0.08)	(−1.81)*	(−1.12)	(−0.06)	(1.6)	(−1.6)
MSCI (L1)	0.020	0.012	−0.017	0.039	0.004	0.032
	(0.52)	(0.3)	(−0.54)	(0.47)	(0.06)	(2.06)**
S&P 500 (L1)	−0.030	0.126	−0.063	−0.122	−0.074	−0.036
	(−0.63)	(2.54)**	(−1.63)	(−1.2)	(−0.9)	(−1.87)*
CPI (L1)	−0.002	0.000	0.000	0.991	−0.003	0.001
	(−1.97)**	(0.29)	(0.37)	(444.37)***	(−1.65)*	(1.41)
WTI (L1)	−0.024	0.069	0.032	−0.054	−0.172	0.018
	(−0.75)	(2.14)**	(1.25)	(−0.81)	(−3.21)***	(1.47)
Dollex (L1)	0.050	−0.018	−0.076	0.138	−0.019	0.001
	(0.63)	(−0.22)	(−1.21)	(0.83)	(−0.14)	(0.02)
Constant	0.006	0.001	0.001	0.020	0.008	−0.001
	(2.25)	(0.21)	(0.29)	(3.44)	(1.83)	(−1.36)

alternate specifications. Based on the post-estimation diagnostic tests, we choose the following models: E-GARCH(1,1) for GSCI, AR(2)EGARCH(1,2) for MSCI, AR(1) EGARCH(1,1) for S&P 500, ARCH(1) for CPI, EGARCH(1,1) for WTI and E-GARCH(1,1) for Dollex.

Table 7.7 gives the parameters of the conditional heteroscedasticity models for all the six variables. The significance of the γ coefficients suggests the presence of leverage effects. The positive values for the various variables suggest that positive shocks generate more volatility than negative shocks. This is surprising, especially in the case of commodity markets, but given the fairly long time series studied, there might be variations from one time period to the other. The coefficient α captures the symmetric effect, and the coefficient β measures the persistence in conditional volatility.

Based on the parameters estimated according to the conditional heteroscedastic

Table 7.7 Parameter estimates of conditional heteroscedastic models

Model	E-GARCH (1,1)	AR(2) EGARCH (1,2)	AR(1) EGARCH (1,2)	ARCH(1)	EGARCH (1,1)	EGARCH (1,1)
	GSCI	MSCI	S&P 500	CPI	WTI	DOLLEX
No. of obs.	1154	1154	1154	1148	1154	1154
Wald chi^2	–	29.18***	10.04***	–	–	–
$\pi 0$	0.000	0.001	0.001	2.285	0.000	0.000
	(0.39)	(1.45)	(2.74)***	(591.51)***	(0.12)	(0.03)
$\pi 1$	–	0.120	−0.098	–	–	–
		(3.58)***	(−3.17)***			
$\pi 2$	–	0.116	–	–	–	–
		(3.93)***				
$\alpha 1$	0.025	−0.169	−0.208	1.021	−0.026	−0.003
	(2.08)**	(−7.35)***	(−10.13)***	(10.39)***	(−1.35)	(−0.23)
$\gamma 1$	0.183	0.269	0.266	–	0.214	0.125
	(8.22)***	(7.30)***	(7.12)***		(7.99)***	(4.44)***
$\beta 1$	0.982	0.431	0.456	–	0.941	0.974
	(171.3)***	(4.41)***	(3.61)***		(50.47)***	(72.59)***
$\beta 2$	–	0.495	0.485	–	–	–
		(5.15)***	(3.82)***			
ω	−0.129	−0.536	−0.461	0.002	−0.353	−0.236
	(−3.12)***	(−5.56)***	(−5.23)***	(8.08)***	(−3.07)***	(−1.97)**
Max LL	2540.297	2563.018	2878.249	−472.101	1896.374	3521.541

Notes:
π_i are the autoregressive parameters, α_i are the ARCH / EARCH parameters, γ_i are the symmetric parameters of EARCH, β_i are the GARCH / EGARCH parameters and ω is the constant.
*** significance at 1%, ** significance at 5%, and * significance at 10% levels.

models, the volatility of the various macroeconomic variables and stock market returns are calculated. Tables 7.8 and 7.9 report the cross-correlations between volatility of stock market returns and macroeconomic variables for 20 leads and 20 lags. Table 7.8 reports the results for causality in the variance. Table 7.9 reports the results for causality in mean (negative lags denote lags of the macro variables, and positive lags denote lags of GSCI).

Causality in variance runs from volatility in MSCI to volatility in GSCI (at lag 0, 1), from volatility in S&P 500 to volatility in GSCI (at lags 0, 1, 8), from volatility in CPI to volatility in GSCI (at lags 1, 12), from volatility in WTI to volatility in GSCI (at lags 0, 15) and from Dollex volatility to GSCI volatility (at lags 16). Causality in variance runs from volatility in GSCI to volatility in MSCI (at lags 0), from volatility in GSCI to volatility in S&P 500 (at lags 0, 1, 13), from volatility in GSCI to volatility in CPI (at lag 5, 9, 10), from volatility in GSCI to volatility in WTI (at lags 0, 1, 3, 8, 9), and from volatility in GSCI to volatility in Dollex (at lags 0, 1). Therefore, we see in some cases, reversal of causality in volatility.

Table 7.8 Causality of variance

Correlation between GSCI and	MSCI	S&P500	CPI	WTI	Dollex
−20	−0.0255	−0.0247	0.0117	0.0138	−0.0036
−19	−0.0122	−0.0288	0.0323	−0.0363	−0.017
−18	−0.0205	−0.0242	0.0181	−0.0192	−0.0445
−17	−0.0034	0.0009	0.024	0.0064	0.0436
−16	−0.0401	−0.0256	0.007	0.0164	0.057**
−15	0.014	0.0184	−0.0133	−0.0526*	−0.0347
−14	−0.0281	−0.0179	−0.0066	0.0024	−0.0202
−13	0.0072	−0.0308	0.0138	−0.0136	−0.0241
−12	−0.019	0.0204	−0.0478*	−0.002	−0.0145
−11	−0.0352	−0.0167	−0.0005	−0.0134	−0.0082
−10	−0.0233	−0.0101	−0.0264	0.0253	−0.0305
−9	0.0235	0.0213	0.0125	−0.0151	0.0335
−8	0.0273	0.0626**	−0.0313	0.0369	0.0271
−7	0.0184	0.0317	−0.0454	0.0067	0.0033
−6	0.0071	0.0084	0.0207	−0.0098	0.0221
−5	−0.0012	0.0166	−0.0123	−0.0238	0
−4	−0.0011	−0.0131	0.0064	−0.0016	−0.0337
−3	0.019	0.0002	0.0299	−0.0351	−0.033
−2	0.0211	0.0151	0.1319	−0.0124	0.027
−1	0.0574**	0.0483*	−0.0236**	0.0092	0.049*
0	0.1879***	0.2446***	0.0239	0.7397***	0.1617***
1	0.0419	0.0736***	0.0112	0.0638**	0.0645***
2	−0.0058	−0.0116	0.02	0.0072	0.0164
3	0.0235	0.0044	−0.0281	−0.0439*	0.0286
4	0.0285	0.0437	0.038	−0.0103	−0.027
5	0.0393	0.0141	0.0632**	0.0156	0.0332
6	−0.011	−0.0279	0.0059	0.0206	−0.0138
7	0.0442	−0.0075	−0.001	0.0003	−0.0044
8	0.0066	0.0119	0.025	0.0539*	−0.0425
9	−0.0121	−0.0057	0.0644**	0.0524*	0.0376
10	−0.0339	−0.0111	−0.0448*	0.0201	0.0332
11	0.0466	−0.0061	0.012	0.0081	0.008
12	0.0046	0.0234	−0.0202	0.0021	−0.0242
13	0.0255	0.0803***	−0.0145	0.0117	0.0193
14	0.021	−0.0173	0.0022	0.0326	0.0052
15	0.0023	−0.0395	0.0241	−0.0354	0.0161
16	−0.0329	−0.0157	0.0086	0.0042	−0.0219
17	−0.0014	0.0257	0.0091	0.0375	−0.0065
18	−0.0403	−0.0111	−0.0337	−0.0168	0.0306
19	−0.0042	0.031	0.0212	−0.0107	−0.0126
20	0.0123	0.0142	−0.0006	0.0331	0.0274

Notes:
*** significance at 1%, ** significance at 5%, and * significance at 10% levels.
Negative lags indicate lags of the macroeconomic variables, and positive lags indicate lags of the stock return.

Table 7.9 Causality of mean

Correlation between GSCI and	MSCI	S&P500	CPI	WTI	Dollex
−20	−0.019	0.0112	−0.0458*	0.0107	0.0344
−19	0.0613**	0.0265	−0.0424	−0.0102	−0.0321
−18	0.0282	−0.0285	−0.0566**	−0.0123	−0.0238
−17	0.0414	0.0545*	−0.0553**	−0.015	−0.0005
−16	0.0057	−0.0367	−0.0388	0.0255	0.0167
−15	0.0267	0.0398	−0.0417	−0.0087	0.052*
−14	0.032	0.0391	−0.0465*	0.025	−0.024
−13	0.0428	−0.0335	−0.0454*	0.0191	−0.0616***
−12	0.0077	−0.0231	−0.0566**	−0.013	0.0308
−11	−0.0118	0.0169	−0.0585**	−0.0003	−0.0194
−10	0.0533*	0.0081	−0.0647**	−0.0168	0.0374
−9	0.0103	0.0039	−0.0609**	0.011	0.0494*
−8	0.044	0.0754***	−0.0611**	0.0174	−0.0172
−7	0.0255	−0.0084	−0.0531*	−0.0341	0.0208
−6	−0.0078	0.0345	−0.0631**	−0.0017	−0.06**
−5	−0.0004	−0.0277	−0.0532*	0.0069	0.031
−4	0.0196	−0.0025	−0.045	−0.0173	−0.0095
−3	0.0009	0.0282	−0.0622**	0.0209	0.0037
−2	0.0763***	0.0651**	−0.0731**	0.0132	−0.0126
−1	0.0034	−0.0048	−0.046	−0.0156	0.0018
0	0.2171***	0.167***	−0.042	0.8539***	−0.1995***
1	0.011	−0.001	−0.0537*	0.0077	−0.0487*
2	−0.0366	−0.0774***	−0.0305	0.0344	−0.02
3	−0.0079	−0.0181	−0.02	0.0177	−0.0574**
4	−0.037	−0.0406	−0.0206	−0.0117	−0.0356
5	−0.0144	0.0115	−0.0494*	−0.0195	−0.0314
6	−0.008	−0.0184	−0.048*	0.0217	0.0321
7	0.0582**	0.0573**	−0.029	−0.0406	−0.0436
8	0.035	0.0081	−0.036	0.0539*	−0.0361
9	−0.0561*	0.0126	−0.0275	−0.0077	0.0293
10	−0.037	−0.0071	−0.0197	−0.0148	−0.0265
11	−0.0284	0.0123	−0.0287	−0.0094	0.0679**
12	0.0253	−0.0321	−0.0174	−0.0289	−0.0143
13	−0.022	0.0051	−0.0022	0.0134	−0.0216
14	0.0291	0.0342	−0.0334	0.0164	−0.0149
15	−0.0054	−0.0072	−0.0166	0.0315	−0.0116
16	0.0129	0.0126	−0.024	0.0198	−0.01
17	−0.0603**	−0.0572**	−0.0116	−0.0219	−0.0145
18	0.0026	−0.0757***	−0.0253	0.0022	−0.0301
19	−0.027	−0.012	−0.0148	−0.0043	−0.0156
20	0.0048	0.005	−0.0094	−0.0128	0.0159

Notes:
*** significance at 1%, ** significance at 5%, and * significance at 10% levels.
Negative lags indicate lags of the macroeconomic variables, and positive lags indicate lags of the stock return.

Table 7.9 reports the results for causality in mean. Causality in mean runs from MSCI to GSCI (at lag 0, 2, 10, 19), S&P 500 to GSCI (at lag 0, 2, 8, 17), CPI to GSCI (at lags 2, 3, 5–14, 17, 18, 20), WTI to GSCI (at lag 0) and Dollex to GSCI (at lags 0, 6, 9, 13, 15). Causality in mean runs from GSCI to MSCI (at lags 0, 7, 9, 17), GSCI to S&P 500 (at lag 0, 2, 7, 17, 18), GSCI to CPI (at lags 1, 5, 6), GSCI to WTI (at lags 0, 8) and GSCI to Dollex (at lags 0, 1, 3, 11). Thus, there are mixed patterns of causality with a few reversals depending on lags.

The predicted variance for each of the macroeconomic variables and commodity returns are used in a VAR framework, to assess the causality that exists between them, and the direction of causality. The results of the VAR model are given in Table 7.10. To estimate the appropriate lag length of the VAR model, we use the SBIC. The lag length obtained using this criterion is 2 for the relationship between volatility in MSCI and volatility in GSCI, 2 for the relationship between volatility in S&P 500 and volatility in GSCI, 1 for the relationship between volatility in CPI and volatility in GSCI, 2 for the relationship between volatility in WTI and volatility in GSCI, and 1 for the relationship between volatility in Dollex and volatility in GSCI.

Examination of statistics in the following tables suggest that volatility in commodity market returns has an impact on the volatility in returns of MSCI, crude prices and Dollex. In the case of MSCI, there is a reverse causality as well. There is also a significant (unidirectional) relationship between volatilities in equity market returns, and volatilities in commodity market returns.

In our impulse response function (IRFs), we see the impact of a 1 unit positive shock to one variable on the other IRFs. The graphs of and forecast error variance decomposition (FEVDs) are given in Figure 7.3. We employ Granger causality tests to find whether there exists any relationship between macroeconomic variables and stock returns, and the direction of causality. In the Granger test of causality, lags of one variable enter into the equation for the other variable. The Granger causality results are given in Table 7.11. The key findings are summarized below:

- The relationship between volatilities in GSCI and MSCI is unidirectional, the direction being from the former to the latter. A shock to GSCI results in a negative response in MSCI for two periods, followed by a positive response, and after a series of fluctuations, takes the value above its positive equilibrium in the next five periods. The process of returning to the equilibrium value is gradual, and take up to 100 periods.
- The relationship between volatilities in GSCI and S&P 500 is also unidirectional, the direction being from the former to the latter. A shock to GSCI results in a small negative response in S&P500, followed by a positive response for the next 20 periods. There is a gradual adjustment process which brings the value back to equilibrium from its positive high, which takes more than 100 periods.
- No significant relationship is found between GSCI volatility and CPI volatility, hence, we do not report or comment on the IRFs
- The relationship between volatilities in GSCI and WTI is bidirectional. A shock to GSCI generates a positive response in WTI which continues for about 25 periods, and then starts declining towards the equilibrium value, which is a long but

Table 7.10 Vector autoregression results

(a) Impact of commodity market return on macroeconomic variables

	MSCI	S&P 500	CPI	WTI	Dollex
No. of Obs	1152	1152	1153	1152	1153
Log Likelihood	15931.34	16205.7	8243.865	15869	20102.21
Chi2	2871.959	2494.931	24891.87	9921.638	16088.25
P>chi2	0.0000	0.0000	0.0000	0.0000	0.0000
Lags of GSCI					
1	−0.166	−0.018	5.236	0.880	0.001
	(−1.71)*	(−0.23)	(0.34)	(6.04)***	(1.75)*
2	0.178	0.049		−0.697	
	(1.87)*	(0.65)		(−4.74)***	
Constant	0.000	0.000	0.012	0.000	−0.000
	(3.53)***	(2.82)***	(0.66)	(3.53)***	(4.08)***

Notes:
*** significance at 1%, ** significance at 5%, and * significance at 10% levels.

(b) Impact of macroeconomic variables on commodity market returns

	MSCI	S&P 500	CPI	WTI	Dollex
No. of Obs					
Log Likelihood					
Chi2	25078.9	25438.69	24058.01	24496.69	24037.39
P>chi2	0.0000	0.0000	0.0000	0.0000	0.0000
Lags of Macroeconomic variables					
1	0.024	0.013	−0.000	−0.001	0.026
	(3.09)***	(1.23)	(−1.01)	(−0.07)	(0.26)
2	0.011	0.044		−0.009	
	(1.38)	(4.18)***		(−1.02)	
Constant	0.000	0.000	0.000	−0.000	0.000
	(1.52)	(2.35)**	(3.03)***	(3.83)***	(1.27)

Notes:
*** significance at 1%, ** significance at 5%, and * significance at 10% levels.

gradual process, and takes more than 100 periods. A shock to WTI generates an initial negative response in GSCI, and then there is a positive movement towards the equilibrium value.

- The relationship between volatilities in GSCI and Dollex is unidirectional, the direction being from the latter to the former. A shock to Dollex generates a positive response in GSCI which persists for about 50 periods, and then starts declining towards the equilibrium value, which is a long but gradual process, and takes more than 200 periods.

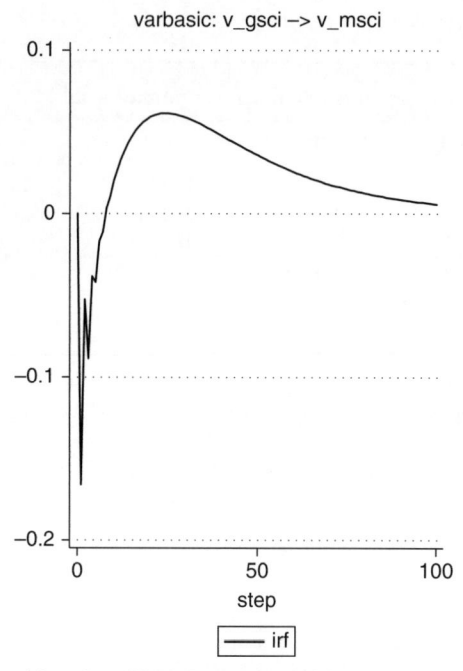

a) Impulse: GSCI, Response: MSCI

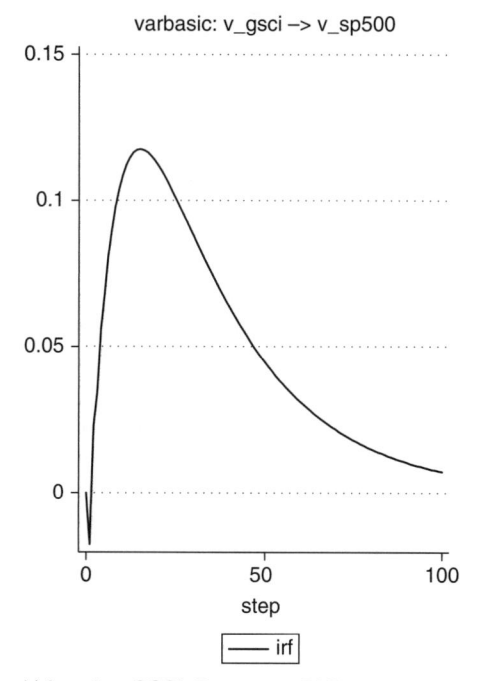

b) Impulse: GSCI, Response: S&P 500

Figure 7.3   Impulse response functions

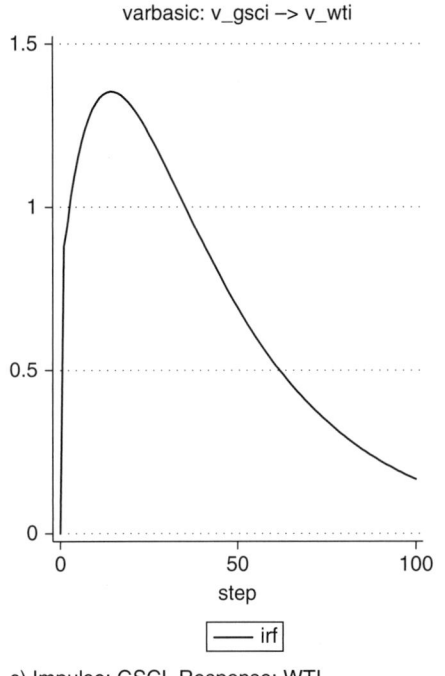

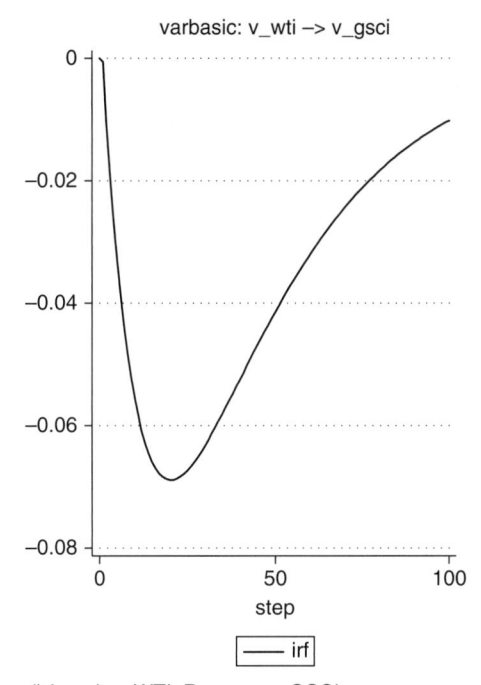

c) Impulse: GSCI, Response: WTI

d) Impulse: WTI, Response: GSCI

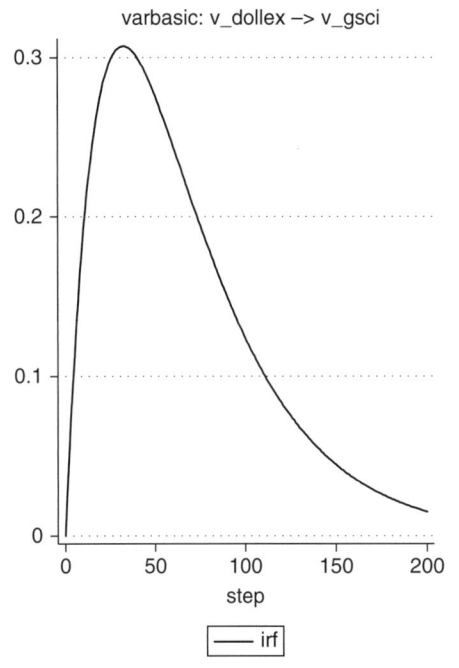

e) Impulse: Dollex, Response: GSCI

Figure 7.3 (continued)

Table 7.11 Granger causality results

Null Hypothesis	Chi²	Prob>Chi²
Volatility in GSCI does not Granger cause volatility in MSCI	32.403	0.000***
Volatility in MSCI does not Granger cause volatility in GSCI	3.6599	0.160
Volatility in GSCI does not Granger cause volatility in S&P 500	48.648	0.000***
Volatility in S&P 500 does not Granger cause volatility in GSCI	2.87	0.238
Volatility in GSCI does not Granger cause volatility in CPI	1.0118	0.314
Volatility in CPI does not Granger cause volatility in GSCI	0.11439	0.735
Volatility in GSCI does not Granger cause volatility in WTI	6.1144	0.047**
Volatility in WTI does not Granger cause volatility in GSCI	49.417	0.000***
Volatility in GSCI does not Granger cause volatility in Dollex	0.068	0.794
Volatility in Dollex does not Granger cause volatility in GSCI	3.0588	0.080*

Notes:
*** significance at 1%, ** significance at 5%, and * significance at 10% level.

7.6 CONCLUDING OBSERVATIONS

The present study builds on the extant literature on financialization of commodity markets, and assesses the impact of macroeconomic factors on commodity prices, linking both returns and volatility to each other in a dynamic set up.

Our results show a negative relationship between the commodity market returns and the Dollex, and a positive relationship between commodity market returns and crude oil price returns. The impact of equity markets, inflation and emerging market performance on commodity markets is weak. Since the variables in the macroeconomic framework are integrated, we use a VAR framework to capture the relation between each of the macroeconomic variables and commodity market returns in a dynamic setting. We find some evidence of reverse causality or mutual endogeneity, for instance, causality from GSCI, S&P 500 and WTI to MSCI, CPI to WTI, and MSCI, S&P 500 to Dollex. A similar analysis is also performed using individual commodity returns (for corn, soyabean, Chicago wheat and Kansas wheat) instead of the composite GSCI.

There are also causal relationships, obtained using the cross-correlation function and Granger causality tests, between the volatility of returns on macroeconomic variables and volatility of return on commodity markets. Our results confirm a unidirectional relationship from (volatilities of) GSCI to S&P 500, from GSCI to MSCI, and from Dollex to GSCI. There is also evidence of a two-way causality between inflation and GSCI (volatilities).

In conclusion, serious doubts are raised about the findings confirming a strong link between financialization of commodity/food markets and food prices and their volatility. Although there is evidence of causality from indices such as S&P 500 and MSCI to commodity/food returns and their volatility, there is also evidence of reversal of causality in which commodity/food returns drive S&P 500 and MSCI. Macro factors such as inflation and the dollar exchange rate Granger cause commodity/food returns while the latter also cause the former. A two-way causality between commodity/food returns volatility and these indices is confirmed, as also between macro factors and commodity/food volatility. Taken together, the case for financialization of commodity/food markets driving commodity/food returns and their volatility rests on weak foundations, leaving the door open for the pivotal role of supply–demand fundamentals.

NOTES

* This study was funded by the Asia and Pacific Division of IFAD. We are grateful to its Director, Hoonae Kim, for her support and encouragement. Gaiha would like to acknowledge the support of W. Fawzie, David Bloom and Peter Berman for the invitation to spend the summer at the Department of Global Health and Population, Harvard School of Public Health, where the first draft was produced. He would also like to acknowledge the benefit of advice from C. Peter Timmer, Brian Wright, R. Jha and T. Elhaut. The views expressed, however, are personal and not necessarily of the institutions to which the authors are affiliated.
1. Double Smooth Transition Conditional. Correlation. For details, refer to Silvennoinen and Thorp (2013).
2. Throughout this chapter we use commodity returns for GSCI, and other macroeconomic variables/returns on other markets for MSCI, S&P 500, Dollex, CPI and WTI. For definitions, refer to Appendix 1.
3. Autocorrelation is calculated as $r_k = \frac{\sum_{t=k+1}^{T}(y_t - \bar{y})(y_{t-k} - \bar{y})}{\sum_{t=1}^{T}(y_t - \bar{y})^2}$, where k is the number of lags, and y_t is the return at time t (Campbell et al., 1997; Greene, 2008).
4. The Box Pierce Q-statistic, later refined by Ljung-Box is calculated as $Q = T(T+2)\sum_{k=1}^{p}\frac{r_k^2}{T-k}$, where p is the number of autocorrelations that are squared and summed (Campbell et al., 1997).
5. The Augmented Dicky–Fuller test fits the model of the form $\Delta y_t = \alpha + \beta y_{t-1} + \delta t + \zeta_1 \Delta y_{t-1} + \zeta_2 \Delta y_{t-2} + \cdots + \zeta_k \Delta y_{t-k} + \varepsilon_t$, testing for the null hypothesis $\beta = 0$. The lag length k is determined using Akaike Information Criterion (AIC) and Schwartz/Bayesian Information Criterion (BIC). The information criterion offers the same conclusion – lag length of 1.
6. The Phillip–Perron (PP) unit root test fits the following model originally proposed by Dicky and Fuller $y_t = \alpha + \rho y_{t-1} + \delta t + \mu_t$. This specification poses the problem of serial correlation. Hence the ADF test which uses lags of first difference of y_t was an improvisation over this. Phillip–Perron use the original Dicky–Fuller statistics which have been made robust to serial correlation by using Newey–West heteroscedasticity and autocorrelation consistent covariance matrix estimator. The default lag of 8 given by Newey–West (integer part of $4*(N/100)^{2/9}$) is used.
7. Engle (1982) assumed that the error term in the ARCH model follows a normal distribution. However, recent studies have found that the distribution of stock returns has a high skewness, implying that extreme values occur more frequently, thus permitting the use of distributions that can have fatter tails than the normal distribution – Student's t distribution or the generalized error distribution.
8. Details available on request.
9. This is done using Engle's Lagrange multiplier test for the presence of autoregressive conditional heteroscedasticity (Adkins and Hill, 2011).

REFERENCES

Adkins, L. and R. Hill (2011), *Using Stats for Principles of Econometrics*. New York: John Wiley & Sons.
Aulerich, N., S. Irwin and P. Garcia (2013), Bubbles, food prices, and speculation: evidence from the CFTC's daily large trader data files. NBER working paper no. 19065. Available at: http://www.nber.org/papers/w19065.
Baillie, R. and T. Bollerslev (1990), A multivariate generalized ARCH approach to modeling risk premia in forward foreign exchange market. *Journal of International Money Finance*, **9**, 309–24.
Binswanger, M. (2004), How important are fundamentals? Evidence from a structural VAR model for the stock markets in the US, Japan and Europe. *Journal of International Financial Markets, Institutions and Money*, **14**, 185–201.
Black, F. (1976), Studies of stock price volatility changes. *Proceedings of the American Statistical Association, Business*, 177–81.
Bobenrieth, E.B. (2010), Stocks-to-use ratios and prices as indicators of vulnerability to spikes in global cereal markets. Mimeo.

Bollerslev, T. (1986), Generalized autoregressive conditional heteroscedasticity. *Journal of Econometrics*, **31**, 307–27.
Bollerslev, T., R. Chou and K. Kroner (1992), ARCH modeling in finance. *Journal of Econometrics*, **52**, 5–59.
Bollerslev, T., R.F. Engle and D. Nelson (1994), ARCH models. In R. Engle and D. McFadden (eds), *Handbook of Econometrics* (Vol. IV). New York: Elsevier, pp. 2959–3038.
Buyuksahin, B.M. (2010), Commodities and equities: ever a 'market of one'? *Journal of Alternative Investments*, **12**, 76–95.
Campbell, J., A. Lo and A. MacKinlay (1997), *The Econometrics of Financial Markets*. Princeton, NJ: Princeton University Press.
Cheung, Y. and L. Ng (1996), A causality-in-variance test and its application to financial market prices. *Journal of Econometrics*, **72**, 33–48.
Chiang, T. and S. Doong (2001), Empirical analysis of stock returns and volatility: evidence from seven Asian stock markets based on TAR-GARCH model. *Review of Quantitative Finance and Accounting*, **17**, 301–318.
Constantinou, E., R. Georgiades, A. Kazandjian and G. Kouretas (2005), *Mean and Variance Causality between the Cyprus Stock Exchange and Major Equities Markets*. Nicosia, Cyprus: Cyprus Research Promotion Foundation.
Enders, W. (2004), *Applied Econometric Time Series* (2nd edn). New York: Wiley.
Engle, R. (1982), Autoregressive conditional heteroscedasticity with estimates of the variance of United Kingdom inflation. *Econometrica*, **50**, 987–1007.
Erb, C. (2006), The strategic and tactical value of commodity futures. *Financial Analysts Journal*, **62**(2), 69–97.
Gorton, G. and K.G. Rouwenhorst (2006), Facts and fantasies about commodity futures. *Financial Analysts Journal*, **62**(2), 47–68.
Greene, W. (2008), *Econometric Analysis* (6th edn). New York: Prentice Hall.
Greer, R. (2000), The nature of commodity index returns. *Journal of Alternative Investments*, **3**(1), 45–53.
Hamilton, J. (1994), *Time Series Analysis*. Princeton, NJ: Princeton University Press.
Hernandez, M. and M. Torero (2010), Examining the dynamic relationship between spot and future price of agricultural commodities. Discussion Paper 988, IFPRI, Washington DC.
Lamoureux, C. and W. Lastrapes (1990a), Persistence in variance, structural change, and the GARCH model. *Journal of Business Economics and Statistics*, **8**, 225–34.
Lamoureux, C. and W. Lastrapes (1990b), Heteroskedasticity in stock return data: volume versus GARCH effects. *Journal of Finance*, **55**, 221–29.
Lutkepohl, H. (1993), *Introduction to Multiple Time Series Analysis*. New York: Springer.
Mandelbrot, B. (1963), The variation of certain speculative prices. *Journal of Business*, **36**, 394–419.
Masters, M.W. and A.K. White (2008), The accidental Hunt brothers: how institutional investors are driving up food and energy prices. Special Report. Available at: http://www.loe.org/images/content/080919/Act1.pdf.
Mayer, J. (2012), The growing financialisation of commodity markets: divergences between index investors and money managers. *Journal of Development Studies*, **48**(6), 751–67.
Nelson, D. (1991), Conditional heteroskedasticity in asset returns: a new approach. *Econometrics*, **59**, 347–70.
Nissanke, M. (2012), Commodity market linkages in the global financial crisis: excess volatility and development impacts, *Journal of Development Studies*, **48**(6), 732–50.
Silvennoinen, A. and S. Thorp (2013), Financialization, crisis and commodity correlation. *Journal of International Finance*, **24**, 42–65.
Sims, C. (1980), Macroeconomics and reality. *Econometrica*, **48**, 1–49.
Stock, J. and M. Watson (2001), Vector autoregressions. *Journal of Economic Perspectives*, **15**(4), 101–15.
Tang, K. and W. Xiong (2012), Index investing and the financialization of commodities. *Financial Analysts Journal*, **68**(6), 54–74.
Watson, M. (1994), Vector autoregressions and cointegrations. In R. Engle and D. McFadden (eds), *Handbook of Econometrics Volume 14*. Amsterdam: Elsevier, Chapter 47.
Wooldridge, J.M. (2006), *Introductory Econometrics*. Mason, OH: Thomson.
World Bank (2011), *Responding to Global Food Price Volatility and Its Impact on Food Security*. Report prepared for the Development Committee meeting on 16 April 2011.
Wright, B. (2011), The economics of grain price volatility. *Applied Economic Perspectives and Policy*, **33**(1), 32–58.

APPENDIX: DEFINITIONS OF VARIABLES USED IN THE STUDY

The **S&P GSCI** is designed to be a 'tradable' index, providing investors with a reliable and publicly available benchmark for investment performance in the commodity markets. The index comprises the principal physical commodities that are traded in active, liquid futures markets. In addition to numerous related and sub-indices calculated on a single component and multi-currency basis, thematic baskets such as biofuel and petroleum are available.

MSCI Emerging Market Index is a free float-adjusted market capitalization index that is designed to measure equity market performance in the global emerging markets. It measures equity market performance in 21 global emerging markets, covering large and mid-cap securities in all industries in the following countries: Brazil, Chile, Columbia, Mexico, Peru, Czech Republic, Egypt, Hungary, Morocco, Poland, Russia, South Africa, Turkey, China, India Indonesia, Korea, Malaysia, Philippines, Taiwan and Thailand. The Bloomberg ticker symbol for this index is MXEF.

WTI Crude Future (Bloomberg ticker for generic futures series is CL1) traded on NYMEX has a futures contract size of 1000 barrels. The delivery point is Cushing, Oklahoma, USA. Light, sweet crudes are preferred by refiners because of their low sulphur content and relatively high yields of high-value products such as gasoline, diesel fuel, heating oil and jet fuel.

CPI represents changes in prices of all goods and services purchased for consumption by urban households. User fees (such as water and sewer service) and sales and excise taxes paid by the consumer are also included. Income taxes and investment items (stocks, bonds and life insurance) are not included.

DOLLEX currency is a weighted geometric mean of the dollar's value compared only with 'baker' of six other major currencies which are euro (57.6% weight), Japanese yen (13.6%), pound sterling (11.9% weight), Canadian dollar (9.1% weight), Swedish krona (4.2% weight), Swiss franc (3.6% weight). It can be traded on Intercontinental Exchange.

For the commodities, weekly closing price of generic futures series (includes near month futures contract) has been downloaded from Bloomberg. We have used weekly prices to calculate weekly returns (log difference of prices) for each of the four commodities.

Soybean (Bloomberg ticker of generic futures: S1) traded on Chicago Board of Trade with a contract size of 5000 bushels. The deliverable grade for soybeans is #2 Yellow at contract price, #1 Yellow at a 6 USc/bushel premium, #3 Yellow at a 6 USc/bushel discount. The soybean price is quoted in US cents per bushel. The contract months for CBOT Soybean futures are January, March, May, July, August, September and November.

Corn (Bloomberg ticker of generic futures: C1) traded on Chicago Board of Trade with a contract size of 5000 bushels and calls for the delivery #2 yellow corn. The corn price is quoted in US cents per bushel. The contract months for the Chicago Board of Trade corn future are March, May, July, September and December.

Kansas Wheat (Bloomberg ticker of generic futures: KW1) traded on Kansas City Board of Trade with a contract size of 5000 bushels. The price of the futures contract is quoted in US cents per bushel. The deliverable grade of the futures include #2 at contract price with a maximum of 10 IDK per 100 grams; #1 at a 1.5-cent premium.

Minnesota Wheat (Bloomberg Ticker of generic futures: MW1) traded on Minneapolis Grain Exchange with a contract seize of 5000 bushels. The deliverable grade for the contract is No. 2 or better Northern Spring Wheat with a protein content of 13.5% or higher, with 13% protein deliverable at a discount. The contract months are March, May, July, September (new crop) and December.

Rough Rice (Bloomberg ticker of generic futures: RR1) traded on Chicago Board of Trade with a contract size of 2000 hundredweight (cwt.). The deliverable grade is US #2 or better long grain rough rice with a total milling yield of not less than 65 per cent, including head rice of not less than 48 per cent. Rough rice can be used to produce five different types of rice – hulls, bran, brown rice, whole-kernel milled rice and brokens (broken-kernel milled rice). The contract months for CBOT rough rice future are January, March, May, July, September and November.

Wheat (Bloomberg ticker of generic futures: W1) traded on Chicago Board, contract calls for the delivery of #2 Soft Red Winter at contract price, #1 Soft Red Winter at a 3 USc premium and other deliverable grades. The wheat price is quoted in US cents per bushel. The contract months for CBOT Wheat futures are March, May, July, September and December.

Soybean oil (Bloomberg ticker of generic futures: B01) traded on Chicago Board of Trade, has a contract size of 60 000 pounds (lbs). The deliverable grade of soybean oil includes crude soybean oil meeting exchange-approved grades and standards. The price is quoted in US cents per pound. The contract months for the commodity are January, March, May, July, August, September, October and December.

8. Dietary shift and diet quality in India: an analysis based on the 50th, 61st and 66th rounds of NSS*
Raghav Gaiha, Nidhi Kaicker, Katsushi S. Imai, Vani S. Kulkarni and Ganesh Thapa

8.1 INTRODUCTION

India is currently undergoing a rapid economic and demographic transformation. Since 1980, average living standards have experienced a sustained and rapid rise. The gross domestic product per capita has risen by 230 per cent; a trend rate of 4 per cent annually. Life expectancy has risen from 54 years to 69 years while the (crude) birth rate fell from 34 to 22 per thousand between 1980 and 2008. Rapid economic growth has been accompanied by rising urbanisation. Between 1980 and 2000, the share of the urban population rose from 23 to 28 per cent. By 2030, it is likely to be as high as 41 per cent.

Rapid economic growth, urbanisation and globalisation have resulted in dietary shifts in Asia, away from staples and increasingly towards livestock and dairy products, fruits and vegetables, and fats and oil. Besides, current consumption patterns seem to be converging towards a Western diet (Pingali, 2004, 2006; Popkin et al., 2012).[1]

These dietary changes reflect interaction of demand and supply factors.[2] The demand factors include: rapid income growth and urbanisation, bringing about new dietary needs; and, more generally, growing affluence and life-style changes. Expansion of the middle class, higher female participation, the emergence of nuclear two-income families, a sharp age divide in food preferences (with younger age groups more susceptible to new foods advertised in the media) underlie the demand. As incomes rise, exposure to the global 'urban' eating patterns increases. Recent evidence also points to greater reliance of smaller and poorer households on street foods. Urban slums often mimic the branded products of fast food outlets (Pingali, 2004). On the supply side, the main factors associated with the availability of food are: closer integration of global economies, severing of the link between local production and availability of food; liberalisation of foreign direct investment, with a new role of multinational corporations – especially supermarkets and fast-food outlets,[3] and a sharp reduction in freight and transportation costs (Pingali, 2006).

Often diet diversity is taken to be synonymous with diet quality. In a recent contribution (Rashid et al., 2011), for example, one of the two measures of diet quality is diet diversity. The latter is defined as the number of different foods or food groups consumed over a given reference period. It is rationalised that increasing the variety of foods across and within groups ensures adequate intake of essential nutrients that promote good health. In fact, it is pointed out that there is a strong positive association between diet diversity and nutrient adequacy (Ruel, 2002).[4] A major limitation, however, of the studies reviewed by Ruel (2002) is that diet diversity is not adjusted for its endogeneity (in other words, it is the outcome of a choice). Hence the favourable effects of diet diversity on various nutrition indicators are suspect. But another study (FAO, 2012) takes a broader view that dietary changes in the past two decades have had both positive and negative impacts on nutrition. On the positive side, the quality of diets at the aggregate global level has improved, and nutritional outcomes have improved in most parts of the world.[5] On the negative side, diets increasingly contain more energy-dense, semi-processed foods, saturated fats and sugars. These dietary shifts/changes are associated with an increase in overnutrition and obesity. The latter are causally linked to higher prevalence rates of non-communicable diseases (NCDs) such as diabetes, cardiovascular disease and cancer. So whether the nutritional implications are positive or negative is essentially an *empirical* issue. This is what the present study aims to examine, overcoming a major methodological weakness of extant studies (i.e. lack of adjustment for endogeneity of diet or food diversity).

The health implications of the dietary transition are unclear but the growing risk of NCDs ought not to be overlooked (Bloom and Cafeiro, 2012). Although India lags behind other developing countries in the epidemiological transition – decline in infectious disease mortality increasingly compensated for by higher mortality from chronic degenerative NCDs – there is some evidence of this transition taking place. Estimated deaths from NCDs are projected to rise from 3.78 million in 1990 (40.46 per cent of all deaths) to 7.63 million in 2020 (66.70 per cent of all deaths). Worse, about a quarter of the deaths are occurring in the 35–64 age group in urban areas (Kulkarni and Gaiha, 2010).[6]

In a comprehensive study, Mahal et al. (2009) demonstrate that NCDs constitute a major economic burden in India. They report high levels of out-of-pocket spending by households with members suffering from NCDs, limited levels of insurance coverage (including subsidised public services) and the income losses that befall affected households. Associated with these costs are risks of catastrophic spending and impoverishment, and, of course, macro impacts.[7]

Although undernutrition still afflicts the world, dietary excess and related chronic diseases are increasing globally, aggravating the burdens on national budgets and institutions. Dealing with all forms of malnutrition (deficiencies as well as excess of calories and fats) poses a major challenge for governments and individuals (Kennedy et al., 2011).

The most recent round (66th round corresponding to the year 2009–10) of the National Sample Survey (NSS) provides new insights into the consumption and expenditure behaviour of households. Together with the 50th and 61st rounds of the NSS, the 66th round data allow analysis of changes in food consumption behaviour in the past two decades and their nutritional implications. Our analysis is based mostly on unit record data collected for these rounds of the NSS (corresponding to 1993–94, 2004–05 and 2009–10, respectively).[8]

8.2 SCHEME

We first examine recent evidence on how prevalent eating out is and amounts spent, as these are closely linked to dietary diversification (Timmer, 2010). We then report our findings on changing dietary patterns of Indian households, based on three rounds of the NSS. Broadly, dietary transition is characterised by a substitution of traditional staples by primary food products that are more prevalent in western diets. To capture dietary transition, we construct an index of dietary or food diversification (FDI) and examine the changes in food diversity over the period 1993–2009.[9] This is followed by a demand theory based analysis of changes in the food consumption basket of Indian households and their nutritional implications. Finally, concluding observations are made from a broad policy perspective.

8.3 EATING OUT

From the perspective of dietary transition as discussed above, we give below a distillation of our findings on eating out, based on an analysis of a nationwide household survey, *India Human Development Survey 2005* (IHDS), conducted jointly by the University of Maryland and the National Council of Applied Economic Research. Our focus is on the socioeconomic status of households eating out, and their spatial distribution.[10] Eating out refers to meals or snacks served in restaurants, roadside eating places, tea and snack shops and street vendors.

Eating out is pervasive, going by the fact that about 30 per cent of the households did so. A large majority of those eating out (about 42 per cent) spent under Rs 99 per month, and about a quarter spent over Rs 200 per month (at 2004–05 prices) (Figure 8.1). Eating out is a feature not just of the metros or urban areas, but also of urban slums and rural areas, though it is less pervasive in the last two areas. In the six largest metros (Mumbai, Delhi, Kolkata, Chennai, Bangalore and Hyderabad), about 34 per cent of the households ate out, as compared to about 27 per cent elsewhere. Over 47 per cent of the former spent Rs 200 or more per month on eating out, and less than one quarter of the latter did so. Eating out is thus more pervasive among the metro residents, who also spend larger amounts.

About 25 per cent of the Scheduled Castes (SCs), about 27 per cent of the Scheduled Tribes (STs), and about 31 per cent each of the Other Backward Castes (OBCs) and Others ate out. Even some of the most deprived and socially excluded groups – especially the SCs and STs – have switched from traditional staples to fast foods and opted for greater variety in food consumption. This is further corroborated when the sample is

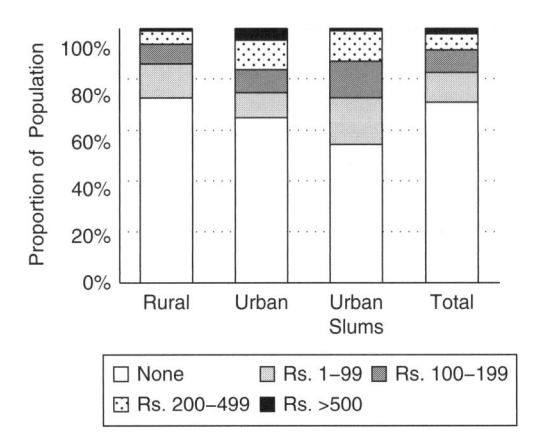

Source: Authors' calculations based on IHDS (2005).

Figure 8.1 Amounts spent on eating out in 2005

180   *Handbook on food*

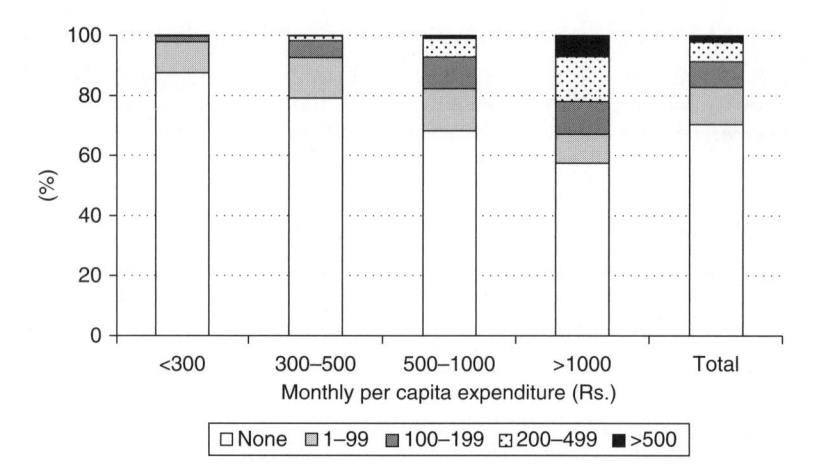

Figure 8.2   Distribution of household expenditure on eating out by monthly per capita expenditure (Rs)

split into the poor and non-poor households using the official poverty line. While a much larger proportion of the non-poor households (about 32 per cent) ate out, that of the poor (about 12.5 per cent) was far from negligible. A more disaggregated classification of the households into four MPCE classes (less than Rs 300, between Rs 300–500, between Rs 500–1000, and greater than Rs 1000) further *dispels* any doubts that eating out as a manifestation of dietary transition is mostly *a middle-class phenomenon* (Figure 8.2).

About 22 per cent of the households eating out had MPCE below Rs 500, with the majority (about 78 per cent) from the lower- and upper-middle income classes (i.e. between Rs 500–1000, and greater than Rs 1000). Within the low-income households too (less than Rs 500), the share of those eating out was 18 per cent, and 36 per cent among the lower- and upper-middle income households. Also, there are differences in the distribution of expenditure on eating out disaggregated by family type (i.e. whether it is a nuclear or a joint family; Figure 8.3).

Using an econometric model, we obtain additional insights into the *marginal* contribution of household traits and locational characteristics.[11] The results show that location of households, their demographic and caste characteristics and, above all, their relative affluence determine both the decision to eat out, and, conditional on it, the amounts spent. Metro and non-metro urban locations induce eating out, relative to the rural. SCs and STs have a lower propensity to eat out relative to Others, and OBCs are more likely to eat out. Over and above these effects, the higher the ratio of per capita expenditure to the poverty cut-off expenditure – as a measure of affluence – the higher is the probability of such households eating out.

Amounts spent on eating out vary with location. Households located in both metros and non-metro urban locations are likely to spend larger amounts on eating out, relative to rural areas. Between the metros and non-metros, households in the former are likely to spend much larger amounts. SCs, STs and OBCs are likely to spend lower amounts relative to Others. The higher the number of adult males in paid employment in the age group 25–45 years, and of females in the older age-group, >45 years, the greater is the

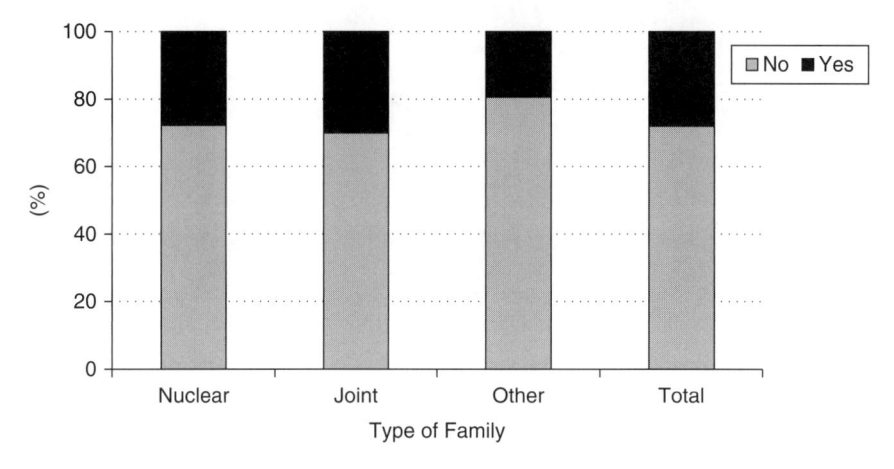

```
                              100
                               80
                               60
                          (%)
                               40
                               20
                                0
                                    Nuclear      Joint      Other      Total
                                               Type of Family
```

Source: Authors' calculations based on IHDS (2005).

Figure 8.3   Distribution of households eating out by family type

amount spent. The effect of higher per capita expenditure relative to the poverty line is large and significant, confirming that the more affluent are not just likely to eat out more often but also likely to spend larger amounts. Somewhat surprisingly, the higher the share of salary in household income, the lower is the amount spent. By contrast, the higher the share of business income, the larger is the amount spent.

Thus, our analysis broadly confirms the important role of urbanisation, demographic changes, expansion of the middle class and its growing affluence in eating out, or, more generally, consumption of snacks, beverages and precooked meals. To the extent that even more deprived sections are not immune to these evolving dietary patterns, and, given their limited access to medical care and dietary awareness, the health outcomes may well be a lot grimmer than often acknowledged.

8.4   CHANGES IN DIETS

Let us first consider changes in consumption of various food items in rural and urban areas between 1993 and 2009. For details, refer to Figure 8.4 below and Table 8A1.1 in Appendix 1.

There was a sharp reduction in cereal consumption between 1993 and 2009 – 15 per cent in rural areas and 12 per cent in urban areas. While the reduction was more drastic in the first period (1993–94 to 2004–05) in rural areas, as compared to the second (2004–05 to 2009–10), in urban areas, the rate of reduction was almost equal in both the periods.

In both rural and urban areas, pulses/nuts/dry fruits recorded a sharp drop between 1993 and 2004. While it continued to decline in urban areas (although at a lesser rate), it increased substantially in the rural areas. The consumption of sugar decreased too, in both the periods and in both the sectors – rural and urban.[12] By contrast, intakes of vanaspati oil rose sharply in both rural and urban areas, especially in the first period. The consumption of milk and milk products increased, and, more substantially, for

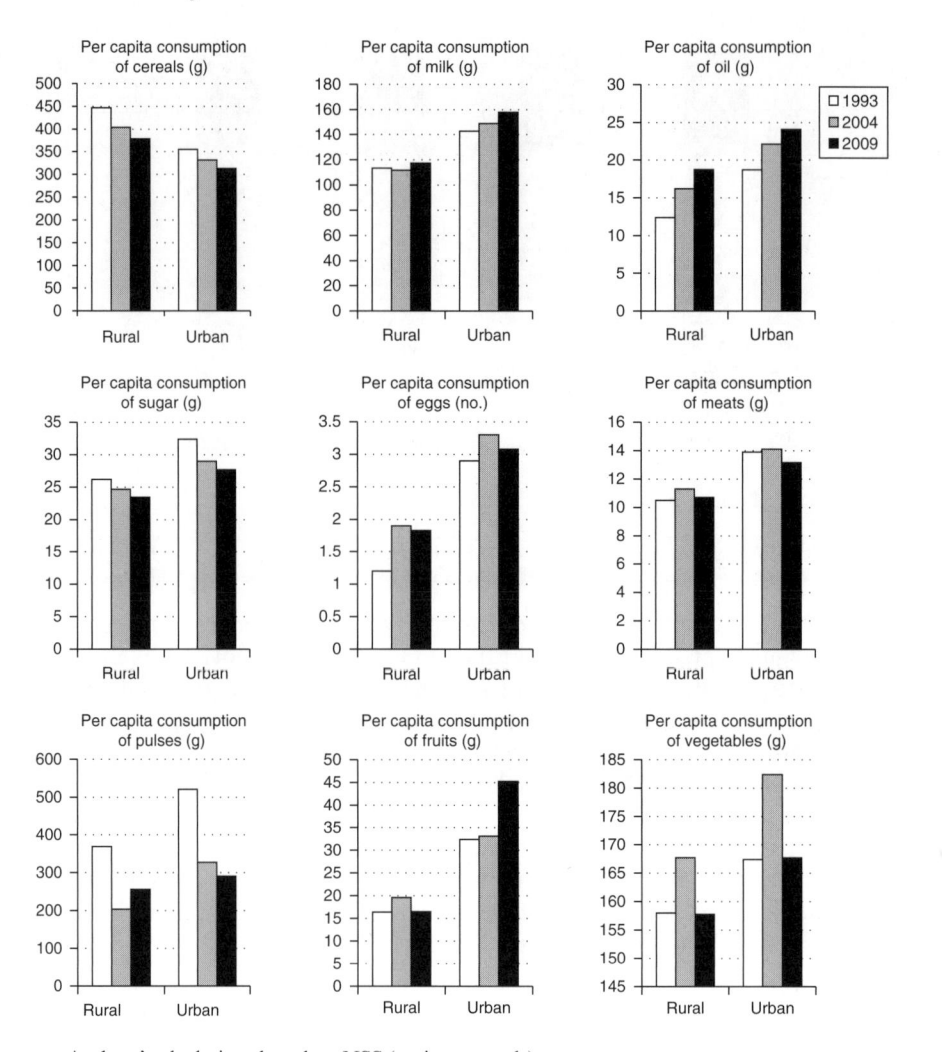

Source: Authors' calculations based on NSS (various rounds).

Figure 8.4 Changes in diets (1993–2009)

urban areas (by about 10 per cent between 1993 and 2009), especially in the second period. Intakes of meat/fish/poultry increased slightly in rural areas (by 2 per cent) and declined in urban areas (by 5 per cent) between 1993–2009. Vegetable intakes increased moderately in the first period in both rural and urban areas, but declined by an equal amount in the second, leaving the intakes largely unchanged between 1993 and 2009. Fruit consumption increased substantially in the urban areas, especially in the second period. There are marked differences in the intakes of various food commodities among various income classes too (refer to Table 8A1.2 in Appendix 1).[13]

Thus food composition/diet changed considerably in both rural and urban areas over the period 1993–2009.[14] The key features are a reduction in intakes of staples (cereal and pulses) and an increase in intakes of more energy dense foods, particularly fats (as seen in the

Dietary shift and diet quality in India: an analysis 183

increased intake of vanaspati oil). But dietary transition slowed down in the second period (2004–05 to 2009–10) compared to the first (1993–94 to 2004–05) – as seen in the reduction in the rate of decrease in staples consumption and rate of increase in oil consumption.

As these dietary shifts are linked to intakes of calories, proteins and fats with varying importance, an investigation of how food consumption patterns changed in response to changes in income and food prices, among other changes, is necessary.

8.5 DIET DIVERSIFICATION

To capture diversification in diets, i.e. a move from a cereal-dominated diet to more variety in food consumption basket, we use a Food Diversity Index (FDI). The FDI is calculated as the sum of squares of the shares of the various food items in the food consumption basket.

Algebraically,

$$FDI_{it} = \sum_{j=1}^{5} S_{jit}^2$$

where FDI_{it} is the food diversity index for household i at time period t, S_{jit} is the share of *j*th commodity in the food consumption basket. This is similar to the Herfindahl index used to measure the competitiveness of an industry. High value of the index implies a monopolistic market (or, in our case, a more *concentrated* food basket) and low value implies a nearly perfectly competitive market (in our case, a more *diverse* food basket).[15] We use five food groups to construct the FDI: (1) cereals and pulses; (2) milk, milk products, eggs and meats; (3) oil; (4) sugar; and (5) fruits and vegetables. Figure 8.5 shows the

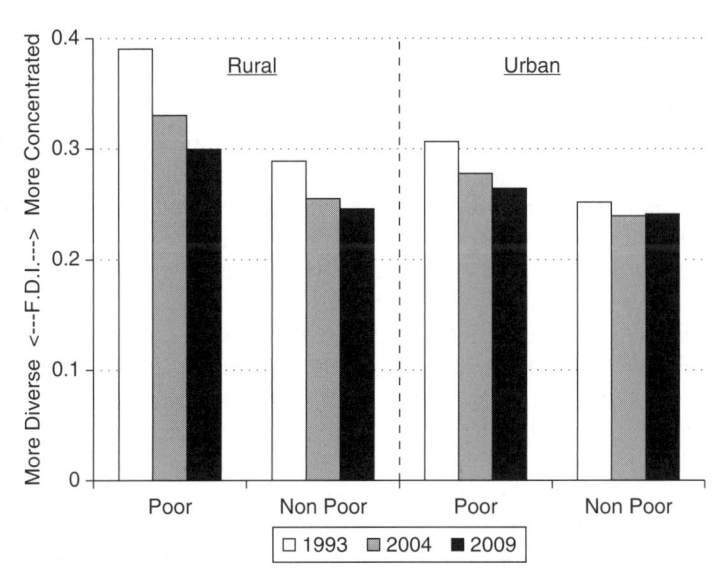

Source: Authors' calculations based on various rounds of NSS.

Figure 8.5 Food Diversity Index (1993–2009)

variation in FDI for rural and urban areas between 1993 and 2009, and for the poor and the non-poor, separately.

The poor in both rural and urban areas had less diverse diets than the corresponding non-poor. For both the poor and non-poor, the food basket became more diverse (the Herfindahl index decreased) but with stark differences. In the rural areas, food diversity increased at a faster rate for the poor (15 per cent decline in the index as against 12 per cent among the non-poor) during 1993–2004. This diversification slowed down during 2004–09 among both the poor and non-poor (9 per cent and 4 per cent decline in the index, respectively). The change in urban areas was slower (increase in diversity by 9 per cent for the poor and 5 per cent for the non-poor between 1993–2004). Between 2004–09, the diets of the poor continued to diversify, albeit at a slower rate (5 per cent), and somewhat surprisingly became less diversified among the non-poor.

8.6 DEMAND THEORY BASED EXPLANATION OF CHANGES IN DIETS

8.6.1 Methodology

We report our findings on changing dietary patterns of Indian households, based on an analysis of the 1993, 2004 and 2009 household surveys conducted by the NSS. Estimation at the household level is preferred as there is greater variation in expenditure levels than found in grouped data. An instrumental variable regression estimation (IV) is used.[16] First, a *reduced* form demand relation is used in which the dependent variable is the Food Diversity Index (FDI), as defined earlier, and the right side/explanatory variables include prices of food commodities, income, household characteristics such as proportion of adults, educational level, caste, location, and the general environment (e.g. lifestyle changes, health environment).[17] The latter are sought to be captured through two dummy variables. D_t^1 is a dummy variable that takes the value 1 for 2004 and 0 otherwise, and another time dummy D_t^2 that takes the value 1 for 2009 and 0 otherwise (to allow for changes in factors other than food prices and expenditure over time), two regional dummies, RD^1 and RD^2, denoting BIMARU (Bihar, Madhya Pradesh, Rajasthan and Uttar Pradesh) and coastal states, respectively, and whether a household belongs to the middle class or not denoted by CD_{it} based on whether it owns consumer durables (e.g. TV) and an error term.

As dietary transition is closely linked to the emergence of the middle class (Pingali, 2004, 2006; Deolalikar, 2010; Popkin et al., 2012), the latter serves as an instrument for the diet/food diversity equation. It must be emphasized that our choice of the instrument is guided by the consideration that this variable directly influences diet composition (through, for example, more frequent eating out), and, through changes in diet composition, nutrient intakes. As shown later, validity of this instrument is corroborated.[18]

The regional dummies for BIMARU and coastal states are justified on the grounds that the first subset is among the poorest while the latter are among the more prosperous. An innovative feature of this specification is that both price and expenditure variables are interacted with time to allow for changes in their coefficients over time.[19]

In the second stage, calories consumed per capita per day, calories$_{it}$, and two other nutrients, protein and fats, are successively regressed on all exogenous variables in the reduced form except the instrument.[20]

We have pooled our sample over time (1993, 2004 and 2009) and do our analysis at all-India level. Some distinctive features of the demand functions estimated are: (1) use of food commodity prices whose effects vary over time; (2) household characteristics such as size, proportion of adults, education level and caste affiliation; and (3) time-related changes such as less strenuous activity levels and healthier environments, through two time dummies.

8.6.2 Results

The instrumental variable regression (IV) results for calories are discussed below (Table 8A2.1),[21] followed by those on protein (Table 8A2.2) and then on fats (Table 8A2.3).

Calories

Let us first examine the factors underlying the variation in FDI.[22] Our strategy here is to first summarise the regression results and then comment on their elasticities that are comparable across explanatory variables.

Going by the results in Table 8A2.1, higher price of cereals and pulses increased food diversity.[23] This effect is magnified when interacted with the two time dummies, implying that the effect is larger. Higher prices of milk/meat/eggs reduced food diversity but this effect weakened over time (that is, in 2004 and 2009 relative to that in 1993). Higher prices of fruits and vegetables increased food diversity, but this was diminished by the time effects. Higher oil prices increased food diversity despite a weakening of this effect over time. Higher sugar price also increased diet diversity but at a diminished rate over time.

Our measure of income/expenditure is relative to the poverty cut-off point. Greater (relative) affluence is associated with greater food diversity even though this effect weakened over time, especially between 2004–09.

Larger households displayed lower food diversity given the proportion of adults and dependency burden. This is a pure size effect as proportions of adults and dependency burden are held constant. Higher education of both adult males and females was associated with greater diet diversity. The caste variables include STs and a residual group of Others, with the SCs as the omitted group. Both STs and Others displayed greater food diversity relative to the SCs.

Urban households displayed greater food diversity relative to the rural. Both BIMARU and Coastal states consumed more diversified diets relative to the omitted states.

The middle class (instrument) variable was associated with greater food diversity relative to others (who did not own consumer durables).

As food prices and expenditure are interacted with time dummies, elasticities of food diversity (instead of FDI with a sign reversal) with respect to these variables, as also with respect to middle class affiliation, are computed. These are reported in Table 8A2.4. They allow comparisons of magnitudes of their effects in an intuitive way, which is complicated by interaction effects with time dummies.

The elasticity of food diversity with respect to price of cereals (including pulses) is

0.06, implying that a 1 per cent higher price increases food diversity by 0.06 per cent, on average. On the other hand, the elasticity with respect to price of milk/meat and eggs is −0.03, implying that a 1 per cent higher price resulted in a lowering of food diversity by 0.03 per cent. If price of fruits and vegetables rose by 1 per cent, food diversity was higher by 0.065 per cent. But a 1 per cent higher price of vanaspati oil had a negligible effect on food diversity (as the elasticity was 0.0005 per cent). The elasticity with respect to price of sugar (0.05 per cent) was larger.

Why these food price elasticities differ in sign is difficult to explain as we do not know what the cross-price effects are – or, in other words, the extent of substitution between different food commodities as price of one changes. Despite this limitation, it is evident that food price changes resulted in diet diversity.

Somewhat surprising is the low elasticity with respect to expenditure (0.006). But it cannot be ruled out that part of the effect of (relative) affluence is subsumed in the middle class variable with an elasticity of 0.037.

Over and above the time effects in interactions with food price and expenditure variables, food diversity rose over the period 1993–2009, pointing to the effects of life-style changes, growth of supermarkets and popularity of convenience foods.

Let us examine the impact of these variables on calorie intake. Using food diversity *instead* of FDI (with a sign reversal), calorie intake reduced with greater food diversity. Somewhat surprisingly, the price of cereals (including pulses) did not have a significant effect on calorie intake. Nor were interactions with time dummies significant. The higher the price of milk/meat/eggs, the higher was calorie intake but with a weakening of this effect between 1993–2004. As it turns out, the overall effect was negative. The higher the price of fruits and vegetables, the lower was the calorie intake, with a weakening in 1993–2004 and strengthening in 2004–09. The overall effect was positive. The price of vanaspati oil lowered calorie intake and more so over time. A higher price of sugar increased calorie intake with a weakening of this effect over time.

Higher expenditure resulted in larger calorie intake but this effect weakened over time. The effect, however, was positive.

Household size was inversely related to calorie consumption given proportion of adults and dependency burden. So size lowered calorie intake without change in household composition. Proportion of adults had a significant positive effect on calorie intake but dependency burden reduced it. Education of both adult males and females enhanced calorie intake.

While STs had lower calorie intake, Others had higher calorie intake, relative to the SCs (the omitted group).

Locational characteristics also influenced calorie intake. Urban areas (relative to the rural) consumed fewer calories. BIMARU states had lower calorie intakes and Coastal had higher intakes, relative to other states.

After accounting for interaction effects of time dummies with food prices and expenditure, residual time effects were positive in both time periods (1993–2004 and 2004–09).

In order to get a better sense of the magnitudes involved, elasticities of calorie intake with respect to food prices and expenditure were computed. These are given in Table 8A2.4.

It is significant – especially in the context of evidence offered in support of improvement in nutritional outcomes consequent upon growing food diversity – that it is associated with a large reduction in calorie intake. As the elasticity is −0.322, it follows that a 1 per cent higher diversity results in 0.32 per cent reduction in calorie intake.

Subject to the caveat that cross-price effects on food commodity demands cannot be captured and thus their implications for calorie demand/intake are unclear, the food price elasticities reveal a contrast.[24]

As noted earlier, it is surprising that cereal price did not have a significant effect on calorie intake, as also its interactions with time dummies. Higher milk/meat/egg prices reduced calorie intake but the elasticity was small (−0.028). Higher price of fruits and vegetables increased calorie intake but by a small amount (the elasticity being 0.009). Higher vegetable oil price, however, had a moderate negative effect on calorie intake (the elasticity being −0.06). In sharp contrast, the price of sugar had a large positive effect on calories (with an elasticity of 0.13). So, food prices played a role in explaining changes in calorie intake.

Expenditure had a moderate positive effect on calories (the elasticity being 0.08).

Protein

Our comments are based on Table 8A2.2. We will first comment on the marginal effects and then on selected elasticities.

As the results on FDI index (or food diversity) are identical to those in Table 8A2.1, it is unnecessary to comment on them.

In contrast to the results on calories, food/diet diversity increases protein intake (given the sign reversal of a negative coefficient of instrumented FDI). This is consistent with extant evidence but with a methodological caveat (i.e. failure to correct for endogeneity of food diversity).

Price of cereals (including pulses) reduced protein intake, with positive effects of the two time dummies (for 2004 and 2009, respectively). However, the overall effect was positive. Price of milk/meat/eggs was negative but with a positive coefficient of the 2004 dummy variable and a negative coefficient of the 2009 dummy. Altogether the effect was negative. Price of fruits/vegetables had a negative effect but with a large positive effect of the 2009 dummy variable. The overall effect on protein intake was positive. A higher price of vanaspati oil reduced protein intake with non-significant coefficients of the two dummy variables. A higher price of sugar reduced protein intake and the coefficients of the time dummies were non-significant.

Higher expenditure increased protein intake but with considerable weakening during the period 2004–09. The overall effect, however, was positive.

Household size reduced protein intake, as also dependency burden. A higher proportion of adults was, however, associated with larger protein intake. Higher education of adult males increased protein intake while that of adult females did not have a significant effect.

STs had lower protein intake while Others had larger protein intake, relative to the SCs.

Locational characteristics mattered too, with urban households recording lower protein intake. Somewhat surprising is the contrast with BIMARU states consuming more protein and coastal ones consuming lower amounts than the rest.

Brief comments on selected elasticities (Table 8A2.4) are given below.

A higher price of cereals (including pulses) induced higher protein intake but by a

188 *Handbook on food*

small amount (the elasticity being 0.02). The price of milk/meat/eggs resulted in lower protein effect with a slightly higher (absolute) elasticity (−0.031). A higher price of fruits and vegetables is associated with slightly larger protein intake (the elasticity being 0.005). A higher sugar price induces higher protein intake (0.05). So food prices influenced protein intake with small or moderate effects.

Elasticity with respect to expenditure or (relative) affluence was moderate (0.09).

Fat

Our comments are based on the results in Table 8A2.3. As in the case of protein, we will confine our comments to the determinants of fat intake.

As expected, food diversity results in a higher intake of fast (recall that food diversity and FDI are inversely related and there is a sign reversal).

Prices have significant effects too. Higher cereal price resulted in larger fat intake with a weakening of this effect over time. The price of milk/meat/eggs lowered fat intake with the first time dummy weakening this effect and the second strengthening it. The overall effect, however, was negative. A higher price of fruits and vegetables lowered fat intake with the two time dummies weakening this effect – especially the second. The overall effect, however, was negative but small. The price of vanaspati oil lowered fat intake with a strengthening of this effect over the period 1993–2004. So the overall effect was negative. The price of sugar was inversely related to fat intake with positive coefficients of the time dummies. As a result, the overall effect of higher sugar prices was positive.

The effect of expenditure or (relative) affluence was positive with a weakening during 2004–09. The overall effect was positive.

Household size lowered fat intake but higher proportions of adults and dependency burden increased it. Higher education of adult males was associated with increased fat intake.

Only Others consumed more fat than the omitted SCs.

Among locational characteristics, only coastal states possessed a significant but negative coefficient.

Let us now consider the elasticities in Table 8A2.4. The price of cereals (and pulses) had a moderate elasticity (about 0.12). The price of milk/meat/eggs had a negative but moderate elasticity of −0.074. A higher fruit/vegetable price lowered fat intake, but by a small amount (the elasticity being −0.03). A higher vanaspati oil price substantially reduced fat intake with an elasticity of −0.36. A higher sugar price increased fat intake, but moderately (the elasticity being 0.06). Affluence (relative) increased fat intake more than moderately as the elasticity was 0.14. The largest effect is associated with greater food diversity (the elasticity being 0.44).[25]

Slowing down of dietary transition

To understand better the slowing down of the dietary shift over the period 2004–09, let us first briefly consider an important argument of Behrman and Deolalikar (1989). They examine the conjecture that food variety per se is valued so that people value more variety in food consumption as their incomes rise while calorie intakes change slightly. They focus on two characteristics of consumer preferences over different foods: the degree of curvature and centrality (relative to the axes) of the location of food indifference curves which represent the consumer preference over two kinds of food, e.g. staple foods, a cheaper source of calories, and non-staple foods, such as meat or vegetables, the expensive source of calories. If obtaining calories with low costs dominates a household's food choices at very low incomes, the food indifference curves are likely to be relatively flat and located closer to the axis for the staple foods. As household income and food budgets increase, food indifference curves may be more sharply curved and centred far away from the staple foods' axis towards the non-staple foods axis. In sum, Behrman and Deolalikar (1989) characterise 'a taste for food variety' by greater curvature and locational centrality of food indifference curves.

Our results show that the dietary shift was associated with a more than moderate reduction in calorie intake. So the taste for food variety lowered calorie intake. Hence the Behrman–Deolalikar indifference curve analysis framework could be applied. The two building blocks of the taste for variety argument – centrality of indifference curves and their curvature – are relevant. Our analysis shows that a few food price effects weakened (e.g. fruits and vegetables, sugar in the food diversity equation) or strengthened (e.g. cereals and pulses) over time, implying lower or higher substitutions between different sources of calories (or, change in the curvature of indifference curves between cereals and other more expensive sources of calories). The effect of (relative) affluence also weakened over time.[26] With higher expenditure (as a ratio of the poverty cut-off point) and a shift of the food budget constraint – the latter also determined by changes in relative food prices – the food indifference curve moved away from the cheapest source of calories.

But a more definitive explanation requires a panel data analysis that is not feasible with the data used in the present analysis.

In sum, our analysis confirms first that the methodological refinement of adjustment of food/diet diversity for its endogeneity makes a difference. The nutritional outcomes are mixed with a lowering of calorie intake and higher intakes of protein and fats. Although average intakes of protein and fats are well below the desired levels, sizable segments of the rural and urban populations consume fat in excess of the recommended level. So the implications of dietary shifts for the rising burden of obesity and risk of NCDs ought not to be overlooked. A related contribution is the elaboration of the important roles of food prices and growing affluence in explaining both the dietary shift and nutritional outcomes. Finally, a conjecture is offered to explain the slowing down of the dietary shift – especially during 2004–09.

8.7 CONCLUDING OBSERVATIONS

The main findings are summarised from a broad policy perspective.

Dietary shifts – a switch away from traditional staples towards food products including milk/meat/eggs, oil, and fruits and vegetables with some variation – is confirmed over the period 1993–2009. Changes in consumption baskets of the poor and non-poor between rural and urban areas and sub-periods, 1993–2004 and 2004–2009, differed. Our analysis points to the important roles of food prices, expenditure, demographic characteristics and life-style changes in diet diversification and nutritional outcomes.

Two results are somewhat surprising: one is the slowing down of dietary transition in both rural and urban areas – especially in the former – over the period 2004–09.

Another is that the slowing down was faster among the poor than among the non-poor – especially in rural areas. In urban areas, among the non-poor, diet diversification diminished slightly in more recent years. Our econometric analysis offers a conjecture on the slowing down at all-India level. The clues relate to weaker or stronger food price, expenditure and life-style effects over time-especially during 2004–09. How these are linked to changes in food preferences and taste for variety calls for a more detailed analysis than attempted here.

Contrary to extant literature and dominant explanations of the calorie intake reduction over the last three decades, our analysis confirms that dietary shift has a mixed effect on nutritional outcomes. While calorie intake reduced, protein and fat intakes increased with diet diversification. Although opinions differ on calorie cut-offs, more than 35 per cent of the rural households had calorie intakes of below 1800 in 2009, pointing to pervasive calorie deprivation. Lowering of calorie intake in this context is thus not desirable. By contrast, both protein and fat intakes rose in association with diet diversification. As their averages are well below the desired intakes, increases in their intakes are desirable. However, given excess fat intakes among moderate to large segments of the population (21 per cent of the population consumed more than 50 g of fat), dietary shift has the potential for aggravating the risk of NCDs.

While concerns for poverty and hunger must dominate the policy agenda, the options for dealing with obesity and the upsurge in non-communicable diseases can only be neglected at the peril of millions of lives that may suffer their worst consequences. Although shifts in diet and physical activities are desirable in many ways – arguably varied and pleasurable – it will be a mistake to overlook the onerous nutritional and health effects and the tragic but avoidable loss of well-being.

A challenge is to raise awareness of the health implications of the dietary transition *despite* its slowing down in more recent years. As growing affluence, life-style changes and urbanisation are *irreversible*, the focus must shift to provision of public goods (e.g. rural infrastructure) to facilitate participation of smallholders in high-value chains, regulation of food safety standards, nutrition labelling, food and nutrition supplementation, stringent restrictions on tobacco and alcohol consumption, nutritional education – especially of women – and active involvement of the private sector in adhering to regulatory standards and nutritional norms. The latter is largely a question of designing appropriate incentives for the private sector to collaborate better with the public sector. Whether these regulatory measures and norms alone will suffice is unclear as food preferences are shaped in complex ways by some irreversible changes taking place.

NOTES

* The authors are grateful to Thomas Elhaut for encouragement, support and guidance, and Anil Deolalikar, Raghbendra Jha and C. Peter Timmer for valuable suggestions, and Raj Bhatia for competent econometric analysis. We are also grateful to B.M. Popkin for sharing his recent research and detailed suggestions. The first author would also like to record his appreciation of the support of and guidance by Bish Sanyal, Department of Urban Studies and Planning, MIT. An earlier version was presented at the 13th International Economic Association of World Congress in Beijing in July, 2012 and the present version has benefited from the comments of the participants. Although this study was funded by Asia and the Pacific Division of IFAD, the views expressed are those of the authors' alone.

1. This is broadly defined by high intakes of refined carbohydrates, added sugars, fats, and animal-source

food. In low- and middle-income countries, these changes are typical of urban areas but, more recently, increasingly visible in rural areas too. Diets rich in legumes, other vegetables, and coarse grains are declining in importance in all regions and countries (Popkin et al., 2012).
2. As observed by Popkin et al. (2012), on the global level, new access to technologies (e.g. cheap edible oils, foods with excessive 'empty calories', modern supermarkets, and food distribution and marketing) and the regulatory environments (the World Trade Organization and freer flow of goods, services and technologies) are changing diets.
3. In a perceptive comment, Timmer (2010) addresses the following questions: impact of supermarkets on poor consumers, supply of staples, price stability, linkages with global markets and health of consumers. While supermarkets offer greater consumer choice and lower prices, they consolidate the supply chain to only a few producers who are increasingly responsible for compliance with the cost, quality and safety standards. Although supermarkets are increasingly driving the food policy agenda, the state has to play a proactive role in laying down food safety standards, their compliance and in ensuring greater awareness of healthy food habits.
4. Ruel (2002) observes that in spite of the variety in measurement approaches and in environmental conditions, the results are highly consistent in showing a positive association between dietary diversity and growth in young children. One of the main weaknesses of most studies, however, is the lack of appropriate control for socioeconomic factors. It may be that the association between diversity and growth is largely confounded by socioeconomic factors, since dietary diversity is also found to be strongly associated with household socioeconomic characteristics. Thus, it may be that dietary diversity is a good proxy for socioeconomic status and that children with higher dietary diversity are also children from wealthier households whose better growth is due to a combination of favourable conditions, including higher maternal education, household income, or greater availability of health and sanitation services, to name a few.
5. These estimates cannot be accepted at face value as dietary shifts and nutritional outcomes are based on food/nutrient availability. For illustrative evidence pointing to not just greater prevalence of calorie deprivation but also reversal of a declining trend in proportion of undernourished in India over the period 1993–2009, see Gaiha and Kulkarni (2012).
6. For recent analyses, see Mahal et al. (2009) and Popkin et al. (2001, 2012).
7. For a rigorous and innovative analysis of the overall effect of health on income, labour productivity, savings and population effects, see Bloom et al. (2009).
8. This analysis builds on Kaicker et al. (2011).
9. With three data points, a robust trend cannot be established. However, some useful insights are obtained into changing consumer behaviour over a period of two decades.
10. For details, see Gaiha et al. (2010).
11. We use a Heckman model in which two steps are involved: first, the probability of eating out is determined and then, conditional on it, the amounts spent on eating out. For details, see Gaiha et al. (2010).
12. It is well documented that sugar content of beverages is underestimated. See, for example, Popkin et al. (2012).
13. For an earlier and influential analysis over the period 1983–2004, see Deaton and Dreze (2009).
14. For a rich and insightful analysis of dietary changes in India – specifically, higher fat consumption by the bottom six per capita expenditure deciles over the period 1993–2004 – see Deolalikar (2010).
15. Single food or food group counts have been frequently used as measures of food/ dietary diversity in developing countries, probably because of their simplicity. The number of servings based on dietary guidelines was not considered in any of the developing country studies reviewed in Ruel (2002). In a refinement, Hoddinott and Yohannes (2002) used a weighting system, which scored foods and food groups according to their nutrient density, the bioavailability of the nutrients they contain, and typical portion sizes. For example, foods that were usually consumed in small amounts (e.g. condensed milk) were given a lower score than foods with similar nutrient content that were consumed in larger amounts (e.g. fluid milk). While this is a considerable improvement on food or food group counts, the precise weights seem arbitrary. This is, of course, an improvement over various indices of diet diversity or food variety used in the extant literature as it allows for differences in shares of food commodity groups consumed. Our index is justified on the grounds that the food group shares are *actual*.
16. For an algebraic exposition, see Appendix 2.
17. For a rich and comprehensive exposition, see Behrman and Deolalikar (1988). For early important contributions to price induced food commodities' substitutions, and empirical verification of taste for food variety, see Timmer (1981) and Behrman and Deolalikar (1989). For an extension of the latter with India's data, see Jha et al. (2009).
18. For an elaboration and validation of the instrument variable designed to correct the endogeneity of FDI, see Appendix 2.
19. Hoddinott and Yohannes (2002), in their multi-country analysis of data from ten countries, tested

whether household dietary diversity was associated with household per capita consumption (a proxy for household income) and energy availability (a proxy for food security). Dietary diversity was measured as the sum of individual foods consumed in the previous seven days. The authors also tested the findings with a food group diversity indicator, which included twelve food groups (using the food groups from the FAO food balance sheets). Household per capita consumption was measured by a consumption/expenditure instrument, which estimates the value of consumption of food and non-food goods during the previous seven days. Household energy consumption was calculated from the information on *food consumption/expenditures* in the same interval. Their results show that a 1 per cent increase in dietary diversity is associated with an average 1 per cent increase in per capita consumption/expenditure and a 0.7 per cent increase in total per capita energy availability. When separating energy from staples and non-staples, the authors show that a 1 per cent increase in household dietary diversity is associated with a 0.5 per cent increase in household energy availability from staples and a 1.4 per cent increase in energy availability from non-staples. There are, however, three problems: whether income is an appropriate instrument, omission of food prices, and endogeneity of energy availability. So whatever the plausibility of their findings, their lack of bias and robustness are *suspect*.

20. Recall that this is a methodological improvement on extant studies reviewed in Ruel (2002), which do not correct dietary diversity for its endogeneity.
21. To avoid confusion, comparison of elasticities is in *absolute* terms if the values are negative.
22. Recall that FDI and food diversity are inversely related: higher value of FDI implies lower food diversity and *vice versa*.
23. To make the results more intuitive, our comments focus on food diversity and not on FDI. So the signs are opposite of those in the regression results.
24. Note that, since calorie, protein and fat demands are obtained from intake data, we use the two interchangeably.
25. Recall that since food diversity and FDI are inversely related, the sign of the elasticity is reversed.
26. For a useful exposition of the distinction between observed (or Cournot) food price elasticities and Slutsky elasticities and how the latter vary with income, see Timmer (1981). As computation of Slutsky elasticities is an exercise in itself, we have confined our comments to observed food price elasticities. This is a convenient but not necessarily a reliable approximation.
27. For a rich and comprehensive exposition, see Behrman and Deolalikar (1988).
28. Following Ruel (2002), dietary quality has traditionally been used to reflect nutrient adequacy. Thus, commonly used measures of dietary quality have been the nutrient adequacy ratio (NAR) and the mean nutrient adequacy ratio (MAR). The NAR is defined as the ratio of intake of a particular nutrient to its recommended dietary intake (RDA). The MAR is the average of the NARs, computed by summing the NARs and dividing by the number of nutrients. We prefer the first but with the difference that we use the quantity of a nutrient. The average is hard to interpret as each nutrient has its own role in determining the nutrition status.
29. Recall that this is a methodological improvement on extant studies reviewed in Ruel (2002) which do not correct dietary diversity for its endogeneity.

REFERENCES

Behrman, J. and A. Deolalikar (1988), Health and nutrition. In H. Chenery and T.N. Srinivasan (eds), *Handbook of Economic Development*, Vol. 1. Amsterdam: North Holland Publishing Company, pp. 631–711.
Behrman, J. and A. Deolalikar (1989), Is variety the spice of life? Implications for calorie intake. *Review of Economics and Statistics*, **71**(4), 666–72.
Bloom, D., D. Canning and G. Fink (2009), Disease and development revisited. Cambridge: MA: NBER Working Paper 15137.
Bloom, D. and E.T. Cafiero (2012), Not in the pink of health. *The Hindustan Times*, 8 November.
Deaton, A. and J. Dreze (2009), Food and nutrition in India: facts and interpretations. *Economic and Political Weekly*, **XLIV**(7), 42–65.
Deolalikar, A. (2010), The middle class in Asia: emerging trends and patterns and their implications. A paper presented at a workshop on the Asian middle class, Asian Development Bank, 27–28 May.
FAO (Food and Agriculture Organisation) (2012), *The State of Food Insecurity in the World* (SOFI, 2012). Rome: Food and Agriculture Organisation.
Gaiha, R., R. Jha and V.S. Kulkarni (2010), How pervasive is eating out in India? Working Paper, Australia South Asia Research Centre, Australian National University.
Gaiha, R. and V.S. Kulkarni (2012), A decline in hunger? Comparison of SOFI 12 estimates with those of NSS

reveals a glaring contrast. *The Economic Times*, 31 December 2012. Available at: http://articles.economictimes.indiatimes.com/2012-12-31/news/36079441_1_world-food-day-estimates-hunger.

Hoddinott, J. and Y. Yohannes (2002), *Dietary Diversity as a Food Security Indicator*. Food and Nutrition Technical Assistance, Academy for Educational Development.No. 2010/16, Washington DC.

India Human Development Survey (2005), University of Maryland and NCAER. Available at: http://ihds.umd.edu/index.html.

Jha, R., R. Gaiha and A. Sharma (2009), Modelling variety in consumption expenditure on food in India. *International Review of Applied Economics*, **23**(4), 503–519.

Kaicker, N., Vani S. Kulkarni and R. Gaiha (2011), Dietary transition in India: an analysis based on NSS data for 1993 and 2004. A paper given at the 13th IEA World Congress, Beijing, July.

Kennedy, E., P. Webb, P. Walker, E. Saltzman, D. Maxwell, M. Nelson and S. Booth (2011), The evolving food and nutrition agenda: policy and research priorities for the coming decade. *Food and Nutrition Policy*, **32**(1), 60–68.

Kulkarni, V.S. and R. Gaiha (2010), India in transition: dietary transition in India. Philadelphia, PA: CASI, University of Pennsylvania, March. Available at: http://casi.sas.upenn.edu/iit/kulkarnigaiha.

Mahal, A., A. Karan and M. Engelan (2009), *The Economic Implications of Non-Communicable Diseases for India*. Washington DC: World Bank.

Pingali, P. (2004), Westernisation of Asian diets and the transformation of food systems: implications for research and policy. ESA Working Paper No. 04-17, FAO, Rome.

Pingali, P. (2006), Westernisation of Asian diets and the transformation of food systems: implications for research and policy. *Food Policy*, **32**, 281–298.

Popkin, B., S. Horton, S. Kim, A. Mahal and J. Shuigao (2001), Trends in diet, nutritional status, and diet-related non-communicable diseases in China and India: the economic costs of the nutrition transition. *Nutrition Reviews*, **59**(12), 379–390.

Popkin, B.M., L.S. Adair and S.W. Ng (2012), Global nutrition and the pandemic of obesity in developing countries. *Nutrition Review*, **70**, 3–21.

Rashid, D.A., L.C. Smith and T. Rahman (2011), Determinants of dietary quality: evidence from Bangladesh. *World Development*, **39**(12), 2221–2231.

Ruel, M. (2002), Is dietary diversity an indicator of food security or dietary quality? Do the determinants of diet quantity and quality differ? Mimeo, International Food Policy Research Institute, Washington DC.

Timmer, C.P. (1981), Is there curvature in the Slutsky matrix? *The Review of Economics and Statistics*, **63**(3), 395–402.

Timmer, C.P. (2010), Reflections on food crises past. *Food Policy*, **35**(1), 1–11.

APPENDIX 1

Table 8A1.1 Per capita consumption of food commodities (g), 1993, 2004 and 2010

Year	Cereals	Milk Products Ghee/Butter	Vanaspati oil	Sugar	Eggs	Meat/ Fish/Poultry	Pulses/ Nuts/Dry Fruits	Fruits	Vegetables
				Rural India					
1993–94	446.8	113.4	12.4	26.2	1.2	10.5	368.6	16.4	158.0
2004–05	404.0	111.7	16.2	24.7	1.9	11.3	203.4	19.6	167.7
2009–10	378.2	117.3	18.7	23.5	1.8	10.7	255.7	16.5	157.8
Growth									
(1993–94 to 2004–05)	–10%	–1%	31%	–6%	58%	8%	–45%	20%	6%
(2004–05 to 2009–10)	–6%	5%	16%	–5%	–4%	–5%	26%	–16%	–6%
(1993–94 to 2009–10)	–15%	3%	51%	–10%	53%	2%	–31%	1%	0%
				Urban India					
1993–94	354.7	143.0	18.7	32.4	2.9	13.9	520.8	32.4	167.4
2004–05	331.4	149.0	22.1	29.0	3.3	14.1	327.0	33.1	182.4
2009–10	312.9	157.9	24.1	27.7	3.1	13.2	290.6	45.3	167.7
Growth									
(1993–94 to 2004–05)	–7%	4%	18%	–10%	14%	1%	–37%	2%	9%
(2004–05 to 2009–10)	–6%	6%	9%	–4%	–7%	–7%	–11%	37%	–8%
(1993–94 to 2009–10)	–12%	10%	29%	–15%	6%	–5%	–44%	40%	0%

Source: Authors' calculations based on various rounds of the NSS.

Table 8A1.2 Per capita consumption of food commodities (g), 2009–10 by deciles of monthly per capita expenditure

Deciles of MPCE	Cereals	Milk Products Ghee/Butter	Vanaspati-Oil	Sugar	Eggs	Meat/Fish/Poultry	Pulses/Nuts/Dry Fruits	Fruits	Vegetables
Rural India									
1	339.1	25.4	11.2	10.9	0.7	4.0	14.4	4.5	110.6
2	354.1	41.4	14.0	15.0	1.1	5.9	17.9	7.6	132.4
3	368.4	62.4	15.2	17.3	1.3	7.0	19.4	9.2	139.3
4	371.2	78.3	16.6	19.1	1.5	8.3	19.9	10.7	148.5
5	382.2	93.9	18.3	21.4	1.6	8.7	22.1	12.5	156.5
6	380.5	111.9	19.1	23.5	1.8	10.1	23.2	15.3	159.9
7	390.7	131.1	20.6	25.7	2.1	11.7	24.6	17.0	167.5
8	391.7	159.5	21.7	28.3	2.3	12.6	27.7	21.5	171.4
9	401.8	194.5	23.6	32.6	2.4	15.3	29.8	25.1	185.6
10	402.4	275.0	27.1	40.9	3.5	23.6	36.8	41.6	205.9
Urban India									
1	314.5	50.9	14.5	16.6	1.2	5.9	17.3	7.3	115.7
2	318.3	77.7	18.1	21.2	2.0	9.7	20.9	12.4	134.8
3	315.7	100.9	20.4	23.4	2.2	10.2	22.3	15.6	141.6
4	320.3	121.1	22.4	25.4	2.6	11.2	25.3	19.9	155.2
5	322.9	136.8	23.9	27.6	2.9	12.1	28.0	22.6	158.3
6	317.2	164.6	25.2	29.6	3.1	14.0	30.2	27.4	171.8
7	315.1	183.3	27.0	30.8	3.7	14.8	33.2	33.0	176.3
8	311.7	210.6	28.6	32.6	3.5	14.7	35.7	38.8	189.7
9	307.6	241.5	29.5	33.5	4.0	17.8	37.7	48.5	203.6
10	285.6	292.2	31.6	36.8	5.6	21.1	43.1	77.8	230.5

Source: Authors' calculations based on various rounds of the NSS.

APPENDIX 2

IV Estimation

A demand-theory-based explanation is used to throw new light on the dietary shift and its nutritional outcomes. An instrumental variable regression estimation (IV) is employed. First, a reduced form demand relation is used in which the dependent variable is the Food Diversity Index (FDI), as defined earlier, and the right side/explanatory variables include prices of food commodities, income, household characteristics, location, and the general environment (e.g. life-style changes, health environment) captured through time dummies.[27]

$$FDI_{ijt} = \alpha + P_{jt}\beta + \gamma E_{it} + X_{it}\delta + \partial CD_{it} + \lambda_1 D_t^1 + \lambda_2 D_t^2 + \theta RD^1 + \theta RD^2 + \varepsilon_{ijt}$$

where the dependent variable is the food diversity index for ith household in time t, P_{jt} is a vector of food prices (for selected commodity groups) computed from the NSS at the village level (j) and time t, E_{it} is household per capita expenditure as a ratio of the poverty cut-off point of ith household in time t, X_{it} is a vector of household characteristics (e.g. proportion of adults, household size, whether adult males and females possessed middle or higher level of education) and a few others specified as dummy variables (caste and education), D_t^1 is a dummy variable that takes the value 1 for 2004 and 0 otherwise, and another time dummy D_t^2 that takes the value 1 for 2009 and 0 otherwise (to allow for changes in factors other than food prices and expenditure over time), two regional dummies, RD^1 and RD^2, denoting BIMARU and coastal states, respectively, and whether a household belongs to the middle class or not, denoted by CD_{it} based on whether it owns consumer durables (e.g. TV), and ε_{ijt} is the error term.

As dietary transition is closely linked to the emergence of the middle class (Pingali, 2004, 2006; Deolalikar, 2010; Popkin et al., 2012), the latter serves as an instrument for the diet/food diversity equation. It must be emphasized here that our choice of the instrument is guided by the consideration that this variable directly influences diet composition (through, for example, more frequent eating out) and, through changes in diet composition, nutrient intakes. As shown later, validity of this instrument is corroborated.

In the second stage, calories consumed per capita per day, calories$_{it}$, and two other nutrients, protein and fat, are successively regressed on all exogenous variables in the reduced form except the instrument, CD_{it}, as shown below:[28]

$$Calories_{ijt} = \alpha + P_{jt}\beta + \gamma E_{it} + X_{it}\delta + \pi \widehat{FDI}_{ijt} + \lambda_1 D_t^1 + \lambda_2 D_t^2 + \theta RD^1 + \theta RD^1 + u_{ijt}$$

As may be noted, all right side variables are the same as in the previous equation, except that the instrument is omitted while an instrumented value of FDI is inserted, $\widehat{FDI}_{it}$. Standard errors are corrected for heteroscedasticity.[29]

The regression results are given in Tables 8A2.1 to 8A2.4. The definition of variables used is given in Table 8A2.5.

As we have already commented on these results, we will confine our comments to tests of the validity of the instrument and identification.

As the dependent variable is FDI, the instrument (whether affiliated to the middle class) has a significant negative coefficient (with a t-value of -43.59). This is further corroborated by the F test of excluded instrument (F (1, 308891) = 1899.87 which is significant at the < 0.0001 level. The null of underidentification is rejected by the Kleibergen–Paap rk LM statistic=1671.4, chi^2 (1) P-value=0.0000. The null of weak identification is rejected by Kleibergen–Paap rk Wald F statistic =1899.87, given the critical value of 8.96 (for 15 per cent maximal IV size).

Table 8A2.1 Instrumental variables regression estimates (calorie)

	FIRST STAGE (Dependent Variable: Food Diversity Index)			SECOND STAGE (Dependent Variable: Calorie Intake)		
	F(31, 308891) = 1907.94 Prob > F = 0.0000			F(31, 308891) = 885.41 Prob > F = 0.0000		
Predicted value of FDI from 1st Stage				2092.6	(4.87)	***
Time Dummy 1 (2004=1)	−0.150	(−54.84)	***	245.659	(3.44)	***
Time Dummy 2 (2009 = 1)	−0.174	(−62.89)	***	216.523	(2.6)	***
Price of Cereals and Pulses	−0.001	(−14.07)	***	0.209	(0.13)	−
Interaction (Price of Cereals and Pulses*Time Dummy1)	−0.001	(−9.68)	***	3.582	(1.22)	−
Interaction (Price of Cereals and Pulses*Time Dummy2)	−0.000	(−4.37)	***	2.283	(1.11)	−
Price of Milk and Milk Products	0.000	(12.83)	***	−2.381	(−8.85)	***
Interaction (Price of Milk and Milk Products*Time Dummy1)	−0.000	(−3.49)	***	1.855	(5.61)	***
Interaction (Price of Milk and Milk Products*Time Dummy2)	0.000	(2.32)	**	0.026	(0.12)	−
Price of Fruits and Vegetables	−0.002	(−50.28)	***	2.614	(2.13)	**
Interaction (Price of Fruits and Vegetables*Time Dummy1)	0.000	(8.07)	***	−5.117	(−2.67)	***
Interaction (Price of Fruits and Vegetables*Time Dummy2)	0.002	(21.78)	***	3.359	(2.39)	**
Price of vanaspati oil	−0.001	(−20.83)	***	−1.010	(−2.36)	**
Interaction (Price of Vanaspati Oil*Time Dummy1)	0.001	(20.24)	***	−3.052	(−3.22)	***
Interaction (Price of Vanaspati Oil*Time Dummy2)	0.001	(22.31)	***	−1.221	(−1.88)	*
Price of Sugar	−0.003	(−37.56)	***	12.361	(8.19)	***
Interaction (Sugar*Time Dummy1)	0.004	(30.9)	***	−6.842	(−3.15)	***
Interaction (Sugar*Time Dummy2)	0.004	(42.2)	***	−14.854	(−7.86)	***
Ratio of MPCE to the Poverty Line	−0.002	(−4.48)	***	127.901	(4.44)	***
Interaction (Ratio of MPCE to Poverty Line*Time Dummy1)	0.002	(3.16)	***	−30.033	(−0.89)	−
Interaction (Ratio of MPCE to Poverty Line*Time Dummy2)	0.003	(4.89)	***	−70.919	(−2.42)	**
Household Size	0.003	(49.06)	***	−56.413	(−29.97)	***
Proportion of Adults in the household	−0.000	(−0.27)	−	616.295	(42.73)	***

Table 8A2.1 (continued)

	FIRST STAGE (Dependent Variable: Food Diversity Index)			SECOND STAGE (Dependent Variable: Calorie Intake)		
	$F(31, 308891) = 1907.94$ Prob > F = 0.0000			$F(31, 308891) = 885.41$ Prob > F = 0.0000		
Education Dummy Males (Above Middle education =1)	−0.009	(−28.94)	***	111.346	(15.39)	***
Education Dummy Females (Above Middle education =1)	−0.006	(−22.33)	***	21.543	(3.68)	***
Dependency Ratio (People aged below 15 and above 55 as a ratio of people in the age group 15–54)	0.000	(1.11)	–	−20.503	(−7.88)	***
Caste Dummy (ST =1, Ref Category = SC)	−0.005	(−7.17)	***	−30.949	(−2.68)	***
Caste Dummy (Others =1, Ref Category = SC)	−0.009	(−13.28)	***	70.933	(7.22)	***
Sector Dummy (Urban = 1)	−0.002	(−6.77)	***	−91.458	(−11.04)	***
State Dummy (Bimaru = 1)	−0.014	(−22.27)	***	92.248	(13.84)	***
State Dummy (Coastal States = 1)	−0.001	(−2.56)	**	−176.64	(−27.21)	***
Ownership of consumer durables (Instrument)	−0.029	(−43.59)	***			
Constant	0.518	(186.62)	***	1031.1	(4.7)	***

Notes:
Number of observations = 308923.
***, ** and * refer to 1%, 5% and 10% significance levels, respectively.

Table 8A2.2 Instrumental Variables Regression Estimates (Protein)

	FIRST STAGE (Dependent Variable: Food Diversity Index)			SECOND STAGE (Dependent Variable: Protein Intake)		
	F(31, 308891) = 1907.94 Prob > F = 0.0000			F(31, 308891) = 1502.46 Prob > F = 0.0000		
Predicted value of FDI from 1st Stage				−15.687	(−1.38)	−
Time Dummy 1 (2004=1)	−0.150	(−54.84)	***	−7.056	(−3.78)	***
Time Dummy 2 (2009 = 1)	−0.174	(−62.89)	***	−11.404	(−5.05)	***
Price of Cereals and Pulses	−0.001	(−14.07)	***	−0.086	(−1.89)	*
Interaction (Price of Cereals and Pulses*Time Dummy1)	−0.001	(−9.68)	***	0.292	(3.67)	***
Interaction (Price of Cereals and Pulses*Time Dummy2)	−0.000	(−4.37)	***	0.207	(3.59)	***
Price of Milk and Milk Products	0.000	(12.83)	***	−0.062	(−8.55)	***
Interaction (Price of Milk and Milk Products*Time Dummy1)	−0.000	(−3.49)	***	0.042	(3.9)	***
Interaction (Price of Milk and Milk Products*Time Dummy2)	0.000	(2.32)	**	−0.012	(−1.95)	*
Price of Fruits and Vegetables	−0.002	(−50.28)	***	−0.064	(−1.67)	*
Interaction (Price of Fruits and Vegetables*Time Dummy1)	0.000	(8.07)	***	−0.052	(−0.98)	−
Interaction (Price of Fruits and Vegetables*Time Dummy2)	0.002	(21.78)	***	0.366	(8.02)	***
Price of Vanaspati Oil	−0.001	(−20.83)	***	−0.074	(−5.91)	***
Interaction (Price of Vanaspati Oil*Time Dummy1)	0.001	(20.24)	***	0.003	(0.15)	−
Interaction (Price of Vanaspati Oil*Time Dummy2)	0.001	(22.31)	***	−0.021	(−1.15)	−
Price of Sugar	−0.003	(−37.56)	***	0.193	(4.6)	***
Interaction (Sugar*Time Dummy1)	0.004	(30.9)	***	−0.080	(−1.3)	−
Interaction (Sugar*Time Dummy2)	0.004	(42.2)	***	−0.071	(−1.35)	−
Ratio of MPCE to the Poverty Line	−0.002	(−4.48)	***	3.442	(4.49)	***
Interaction (Ratio of MPCE to Poverty Line*Time Dummy1)	0.002	(3.16)	***	−0.840	(−0.95)	−
Interaction (Ratio of MPCE to Poverty Line*Time Dummy2)	0.003	(4.89)	***	−1.929	(−2.42)	**
Household Size	0.003	(49.06)	***	−1.251	(−24.46)	***
Proportion of Adults in the household	−0.000	(−0.27)	−	17.404	(43.5)	***
Education Dummy Males (Above Middle education =1)	−0.009	(−28.94)	***	2.222	(11.6)	***
Education Dummy Females (Above Middle education =1)	−0.006	(−22.33)	***	0.069	(0.36)	−
Dependency Ratio (People aged below 15 and above 55 as a ratio of people in the age group 15–54)	0.000	(1.11)	−	−0.361	(−4.97)	***
Caste Dummy (ST =1, Ref Category = SC)	−0.005	(−7.17)	***	−0.616	(−2.19)	**

Table 8A2.2 (continued)

	FIRST STAGE (Dependent Variable: Food Diversity Index)			SECOND STAGE (Dependent Variable: Protein Intake)		
	$F(31, 308891) = 1907.94$ Prob $> F = 0.0000$			$F(31, 308891) = 1502.46$ Prob $> F = 0.0000$		
Caste Dummy (Others =1, Ref Category = SC)	−0.009	(−13.28)	***	1.606	(6.59)	***
Sector Dummy (Urban = 1)	−0.002	(−6.77)	***	−3.252	(−14.14)	***
State Dummy (Bimaru = 1)	−0.014	(−22.27)	***	6.365	(32.62)	***
State Dummy (Coastal States = 1)	−0.001	(−2.56)	**	−8.457	(−48.32)	***
Ownership of consumer durables (Instrument)	−0.029	(−43.59)	***			
Constant	0.518	(186.62)	***	63.553	(11.09)	***

Notes:
Number of observations = 308923.
***, ** and * refer to 1%, 5% and 10% significance levels, respectively.

Table 8A2.3 Instrumental variables regression estimates (fats)

	FIRST STAGE (Dependent Variable: Food Diversity Index)			SECOND STAGE (Dependent Variable: Fat Intake)		
	F(31, 308891) = 1907.94 Prob > F = 0.0000			F(31, 308891) = 1365.87 Prob > F = 0.0000		
Predicted value of FDI from 1st Stage				−290.38	(−9.65)	***
Time Dummy 1 (2004=1)	−0.150	(−54.84)	***	−21.952	(−3.98)	***
Time Dummy 2 (2009 = 1)	−0.174	(−62.89)	***	−32.215	(−5.64)	***
Price of Cereals and Pulses	−0.001	(−14.07)	***	0.479	(7.62)	***
Interaction (Price of Cereals and Pulses*Time Dummy1)	−0.001	(−9.68)	***	−0.124	(−1.06)	−
Interaction (Price of Cereals and Pulses*Time Dummy2)	−0.000	(−4.37)	***	−0.175	(−2.56)	**
Price of Milk and Milk Products	0.000	(12.83)	***	−0.061	(−4.24)	***
Interaction (Price of Milk and Milk Products*Time Dummy1)	−0.000	(−3.49)	***	0.037	(2.3)	**
Interaction (Price of Milk and Milk Products*Time Dummy2)	0.000	(2.32)	**	−0.131	(−16.95)	***
Price of Fruits and Vegetables	−0.002	(−50.28)	***	−0.310	(−4.02)	***
Interaction (Price of Fruits and Vegetables*Time Dummy1)	0.000	(8.07)	***	0.065	(0.74)	−
Interaction (Price of Fruits and Vegetables*Time Dummy2)	0.002	(21.78)	***	0.587	(9.46)	***
Price of Vanaspati Oil	−0.001	(−20.83)	***	−0.227	(−8.89)	***
Interaction (Price of Vanaspati Oil*Time Dummy1)	0.001	(20.24)	***	−0.195	(−2.36)	**
Interaction (Price of Vanaspati Oil*Time Dummy2)	0.001	(22.31)	***	0.051	(1.15)	−
Price of Sugar	−0.003	(−37.56)	***	−0.646	(−6.37)	***
Interaction (Sugar*Time Dummy1)	0.004	(30.9)	***	1.273	(8.5)	***
Interaction (Sugar*Time Dummy2)	0.004	(42.2)	***	0.998	(7.89)	***
Ratio of MPCE to the Poverty Line	−0.002	(−4.48)	***	3.559	(4.42)	***
Interaction (Ratio of MPCE to Poverty Line*Time Dummy1)	0.002	(3.16)	***	−0.092	(−0.09)	−
Interaction (Ratio of MPCE to Poverty Line*Time Dummy2)	0.003	(4.89)	***	−1.400	(−1.64)	−
Household Size	0.003	(49.06)	***	−0.992	(−6.86)	***
Proportion of Adults in the household	−0.000	(−0.27)	−	14.536	(18.17)	***
Education Dummy Males (Above Middle education =1)	−0.009	(−28.94)	***	2.268	(4.03)	***
Education Dummy Females (Above Middle education =1)	−0.006	(−22.33)	***	0.386	(1.06)	−
Dependency Ratio (People aged below 15 and above 55 as a ratio of people in the age group 15–54)	0.000	(1.11)	−	0.365	(2.26)	**
Caste Dummy (ST =1, Ref Category = SC)	−0.005	(−7.17)	***	−0.975	(−1.17)	−

Table 8A2.3 (continued)

	FIRST STAGE (Dependent Variable: Food Diversity Index)			SECOND STAGE (Dependent Variable: Fat Intake)		
	F(31, 308891) = 1907.94 Prob > F = 0.0000			F(31, 308891) = 1365.87 Prob > F = 0.0000		
Caste Dummy (Others = 1, Ref Category = SC)	−0.009	(−13.28)	***	2.188	(3.26)	***
Sector Dummy (Urban = 1)	−0.002	(−6.77)	***	−0.323	(−0.63)	−
State Dummy (Bimaru = 1)	−0.014	(−22.27)	***	0.086	(0.2)	−
State Dummy (Coastal States = 1)	−0.001	(−2.56)	**	−6.376	(−14.07)	***
Ownership of consumer durables (Instrument)	−0.029	(−43.59)	***			
Constant	0.518	(186.62)	***	160.881	(10.64)	***

Notes:
Number of observations = 308923.
***, ** and * refer to 1%, 5% and 10% significance levels, respectively.

Table 8A2.4 Elasticities

	FIRST STAGE	SECOND STAGE		
DEPENDENT VARIABLE	FDI	Calorie Intake	Protein Intake	Fat Intake
Price of Cereals and Pulses	−0.0673	−	0.0188	0.1185
Price of Milk and Milk Products	0.0336	−0.0284	−0.0312	−0.0738
Price of Fruits and Vegetables	−0.0644	0.0094	0.0053	−0.0302
Price of Vanaspati Oil	−0.0048	−0.0623	−0.0723	−0.3591
Price of Sugar	−0.0490	0.1288	0.0473	0.0555
Ratio of MPCE to the Poverty Line	−0.0058	0.0876	0.0860	0.1445
Ownership of consumer durables (Instrument)	−0.0373			
Predicted Value of FDI		0.3224	−0.0024	−0.0447

Note: The elasticities referred to in the text are with respect to food diversity which is inversely related to FDI.

Table 8A2.5 Variable definition

Food Diversity Index (FDI)	Sum of squares of the shares of various food items in the consumption basket. The various categories of food are: (1) Cereals and Pulses (2) Milk, Meat and Eggs (3) Fruits and Vegetables (4) Vanaspati-Oil and (5) Sugar. The FDI ranges between 0 and 1, a higher value implying a more concentrated food basket
Calorie Intake	Calorie consumption per capita per day
Protein Intake	Protein consumption per capita per day
Fat Intake	Fat consumption per capita per day
Time Dummy 1	The time dummy gives a value 1 to the year 2004 (reference category: 1993)
Time Dummy 2	The time dummy gives a value 1 to the year 2009 (reference category: 1993)
Price of Cereals and Pulses	Price index of Cereals and Pulses (weighted by value) at the village level
Price of Milk and Milk Products	Price index of Milk and Milk Products, Meat and Eggs (weighted by value) at the village level
Price of Fruits and Vegetables	Price index of Fruits and Vegetables (weighted by value) at the village level
Price of Vanaspati Oil	Price index of Vanaspati Oil at the village level
Price of Sugar	Price index of Sugar at the village level
Ratio of MPCE to the Poverty Line	The Monthly per capita Expenditure (at 2004 prices) divided by the poverty line
Household Size	No. of people in a household
Proportion of Adults in the household	No. of adults in a household divided by the total no. of people in a household
Education Dummy Males	The highest level of education of male members in a household. Takes the value 0 if less than middle level of education, and 1 if more than middle level of education
Education Dummy Females	The highest level of education of female members in a household. Takes the value 0 if less than middle level of education, and 1 if more than middle level of education
Dependency Ratio	People aged below 15 and above 55 in a household as a ratio of people in the age group 15–54 in a household
Caste Dummy 1	The caste dummy takes the value 1 for the category Scheduled Tribes (Reference category: Scheduled Castes)
Caste Dummy 2	The caste dummy takes the value 1 for the category Others (Reference category: Scheduled Castes)
Sector Dummy	The sector dummy takes the value 0 for rural areas, and 1 for urban areas
State Dummy 1	The State dummy takes the value 1 for BIMARU states, i.e. Bihar, Madhya Pradesh, Rajasthan and Uttar Pradesh (Reference Category: Other States)
State Dummy 2	The State dummy takes the value 1 for all the states along the Coastline (Reference Category: Other States)
Ownership of consumer durables (Instrument)	This variable determines whether a household belongs to the middle class or not based on whether it owns consumer durables or not. It is measured as the proportion of households at the village level with at least one of the following (1) Air conditioner (2) Television (3) Refrigerator

9. Dietary change, nutrient transition and food security in fast-growing China
Jing You

9.1 INTRODUCTION

China is perhaps one of the most viable developing countries around the world. The economy has witnessed a miracle of consistent and fast growth at an annual rate of 10 per cent for more than three decades. Large population, lagging rural areas and prosperous coastal cities are all distinguishing marks of the country. Along with its socioeconomic transformation, China has also been undergoing a marked transition in its diet and nutritional status.

In the Chinese context, there have been gradual institutional changes in agricultural and food industries since the early 1980s, which have led to subsequent shifts in food consumption. In particular, the Household Responsibility System established between 1981 and 1984, released agricultural productivity, which in turn contributed to 49 per cent (Lin, 1992) of the annual income growth of 7.5 per cent during that period (Ravallion, 2009). Meanwhile, the state procurement covered fewer products (from 113 in 1981 to 60 in 1984; Zhang, 2001) and food prices increased by 8.1 per cent per annum (Fan et al., 1995) because of the lifted price control. However, the agricultural procurement price remained about half the market price (Brandt and Holz, 2006) and staple foods were rationed until 1993. Between 1993 and 1995, the central government introduced further relaxation of price controls in order to increase farmers' incomes. With the abolition of agricultural taxes in 2004, there have been successive increases in grain yields since 2003. That said, China's grain imports also soared to feed people's growing and diversified appetite. The country's grain imports have grown by more than 50 per cent per annum in recent years and hit new records in the first 11 months of 2012: rice imports skyrocketed by more than 21 times compared to the same period in 2011, followed by a four-fold increase for wheat and three-fold for corn.[1] China has also become the biggest pork producer and consumer in the world, and is expected to hold this rank in the future.

The importance of issues of food security transcends the current debate in China. How have the Chinese changed their taste in food during rapid economic growth and structural changes in the country? What are the consequences of their changing food consumption behaviour for nutrition and health? This chapter aims to answer these questions by using the most recent available data and by providing an up-to-date review of literature. The remainder of the chapter is structured as follows: section 9.2 identifies individual dietary changes. Their impact on nutritional outcomes is scrutinised in section 9.3. Section 9.4 describes the macro picture of food security in China and discusses any possible influence of China's expanded food consumption on other countries who are trade partners or competitors with China. Based on both micro and macro evidence, section 9.5 summarises China's current agricultural policy interventions and suggest possible improvement in the future.

9.2 DIETARY CHANGE

This section first reviews the general patterns of dietary shift for both rural and urban China. In the remaining subsections, it elaborates on selected issues that have emerged during this shift, including the impact of rising inequality on food demand, the choice between quantity and quality, the role of participation in urban job markets and of urbanisation in changing people's diets, and the higher frequency of eating out as people become wealthier.

9.2.1 Patterns and Structural Changes in Food Consumption

China's economy has expanded fast since the open-door reform of 1978. As shown in Figure 9.1, the per capita net income for rural households has increased nearly four times, from 1489.7 yuan in 1978 to 6977 yuan in 2011.[2] Urban households' per capita disposable income has increased 9.5 times over the same period, from 2083.8 yuan to 21810 yuan. Similarly, households' per capita total consumption has grown by 6.7 times in rural areas (from 730 yuan to 5633 yuan) and seven times in urban areas (from 2350 yuan to 18750 yuan). As expected, the Engel's coefficient[3] has declined from 0.677 to 0.404 for rural residents and from 0.575 to 0.363 for urban residents. Along with a decreasing share of food consumption, both rural and urban households spend more on education, entertainment, communication, medicine and health (Figure 9.2).

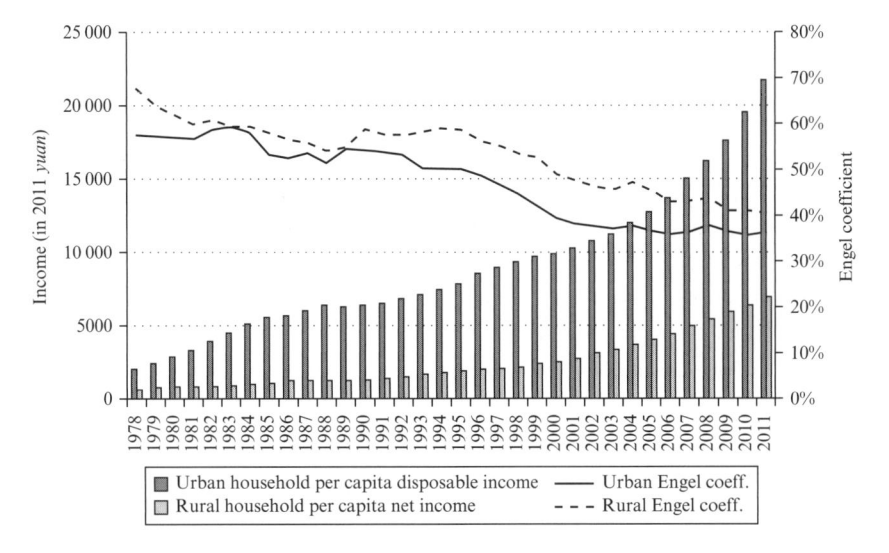

Source: Author's calculation and compilation based on data from China Statistical Yearbooks published by the NBS and the China Macroeconomy Database provided by GTA.

Figure 9.1 Pattern of income and food consumption in China, 1978–2011

206 *Handbook on food*

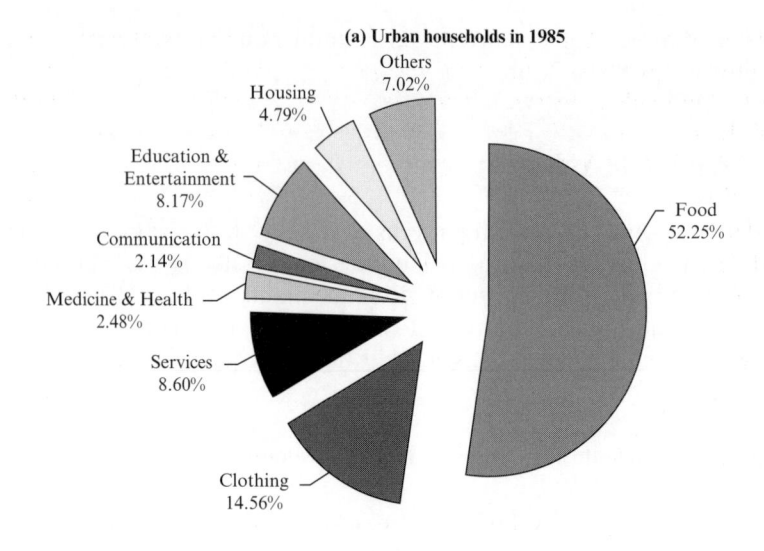

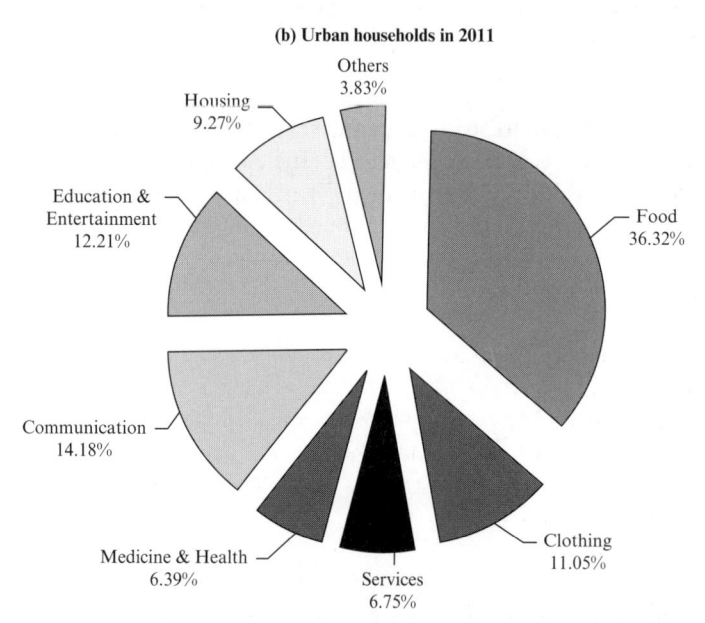

(a) Urban households in 1985

- Others 7.02%
- Housing 4.79%
- Education & Entertainment 8.17%
- Communication 2.14%
- Medicine & Health 2.48%
- Services 8.60%
- Clothing 14.56%
- Food 52.25%

(b) Urban households in 2011

- Others 3.83%
- Housing 9.27%
- Education & Entertainment 12.21%
- Communication 14.18%
- Medicine & Health 6.39%
- Services 6.75%
- Clothing 11.05%
- Food 36.32%

Source: Author's calculation based on data from China Statistical Yearbooks published by the NBS. The initial household consumption data come from annual Rural Household Survey which is conducted by the NBS in almost every province.

Figure 9.2 Decomposition of household per capita consumption expenditure

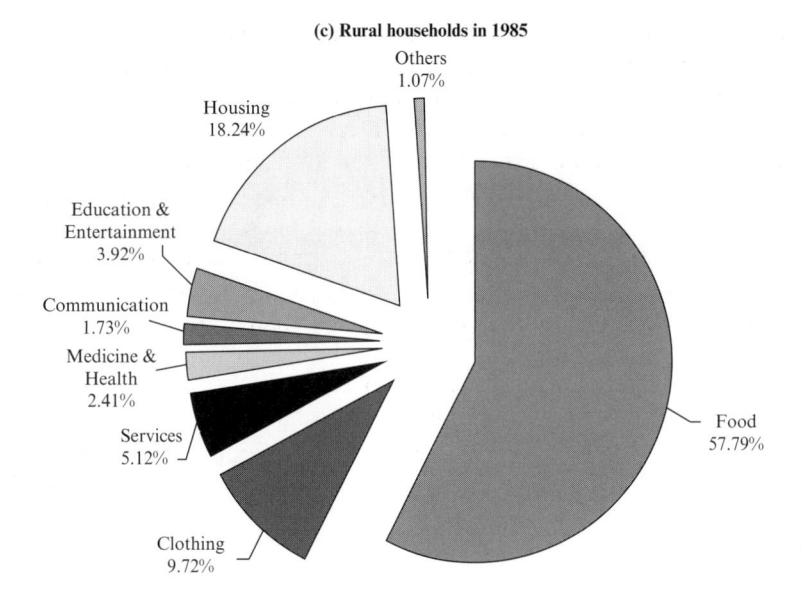

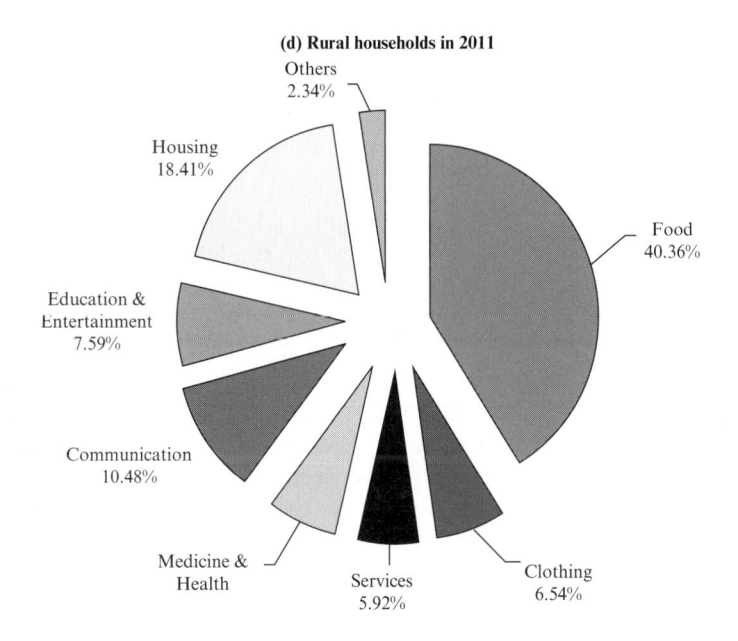

Dietary change, nutrient transition and food security in China 207

(c) Rural households in 1985

- Others 1.07%
- Housing 18.24%
- Education & Entertainment 3.92%
- Communication 1.73%
- Medicine & Health 2.41%
- Services 5.12%
- Clothing 9.72%
- Food 57.79%

(d) Rural households in 2011

- Others 2.34%
- Housing 18.41%
- Education & Entertainment 7.59%
- Communication 10.48%
- Medicine & Health
- Services 5.92%
- Clothing 6.54%
- Food 40.36%

Figure 9.2 (continued)

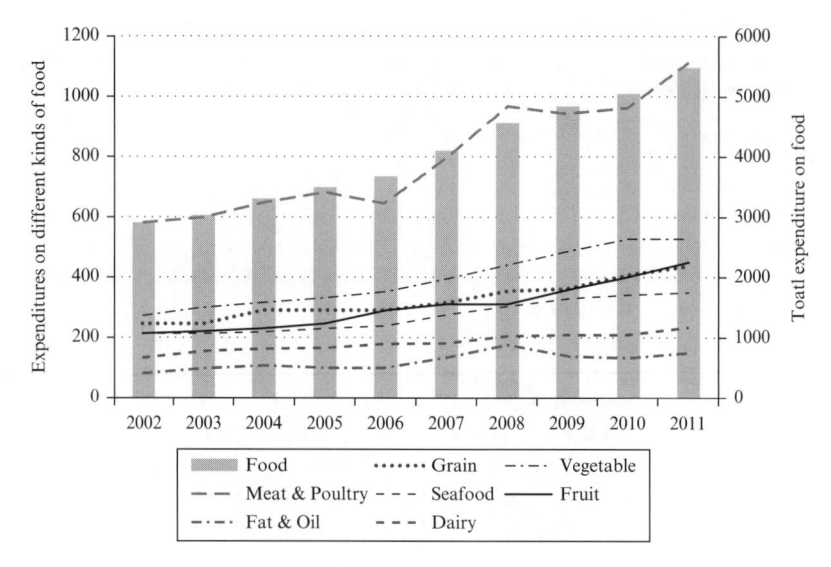

Note: Meat includes pork, beef and mutton.

Source: Author's calculation based on data from various issues of China Statistical Yearbooks published by the NBS. The urban consumer price index used to obtain real values in 2011 yuan comes from the same source.

Figure 9.3 Urban households' per capita food consumption expenditure, 2011 yuan

The diet has changed concurrently. As shown in Table 9.1, people's food demand favours fewer staples (grain) and vegetables in 2011 than in 1978, while more fruits, meat, poultry, seafood and fat and oil. Take urban residents, for instance. The top line in Figure 9.3 suggests that meat and poultry had the most significant rise: about 11–36 per cent of the increased total expenditure on food went on meat and poultry. Among various kinds of meat, Ortega et al. (2009) find the largest share of these increases was due to pork, which has become a necessity, while poultry, beef, mutton and fish are considered luxuries. The pressure stemming from households' added demand for animal products and fine grains will be transmitted and aggregated to the whole country's food security. This issue will be discussed further in section 9.4.

By comparing rural and urban residents over the period 1978–2011, we can see from Table 9.1 that decreases in grain consumption are less in rural households (31 per cent) than in urban households (46 per cent). On the other hand, per capita vegetable consumption in rural households (37 per cent) dropped more than in urban households (24 per cent). Per capita seafood, meat consumption and fat and oil in rural households increased by 5.75, 1.8 and 2.75 times in turn, while 37 per cent, 73 per cent and 7.42 times in urban households. Both groups of people shift towards more diversified diets, while rural households have experienced more dramatic changes. Similar patterns can also be found in the household-level data. Using two cross-sections between 1995 and 2003 covering 11 commodities in urban China, Hovhannisyan and Gould (2011) conclude that an average Chinese household has switched to items of western diet (fine grains) and a majority of food staples have changed. For rural households, Carter

Table 9.1 Household per capita food consumption, 1978–2011 (kg)

Year	Rural[a]							Urban[b]						
	Grain	Vegetable	Meat[c]	Poultry	Seafood	Fruit	Fat & oil	Grain	Vegetable	Meat[c]	Poultry	Seafood	Fruit	Fat & oil
1978	247.80	141.50	5.80	0.30	0.80	–	2.00	148.4	150.1	14.2	0.30	–	–	2.20
1979	256.70	131.20	6.50	0.30	0.70	–	2.40	152.3	157	18	0.40	–	–	2.70
1980	257.20	127.20	7.70	0.70	1.10	–	2.50	154.6	154.2	19.6	0.40	–	–	2.90
1981	256.10	124.00	8.70	0.70	1.30	–	3.10	145.40	152.30	18.60	1.90	7.30	–	4.80
1982	260.00	132.00	9.00	0.80	1.30	–	3.40	144.60	159.10	18.70	2.30	7.70	–	5.80
1983	259.90	131.00	10.00	0.80	1.60	–	3.50	144.50	165.00	19.90	2.60	8.10	–	6.50
1984	266.50	140.00	10.60	0.90	1.70	–	4.00	142.10	149.00	19.90	2.90	7.80	–	7.10
1985	257.40	131.10	11.00	1.00	1.60	–	4.00	131.20	147.70	20.20	2.90	7.80	–	6.40
1986	259.30	133.60	11.80	1.10	1.90	–	4.20	137.90	148.30	21.60	3.80	7.80	–	6.20
1987	259.40	130.40	11.60	1.20	2.00	–	4.70	133.90	142.60	22.00	3.70	8.20	–	6.40
1988	259.50	130.10	10.70	1.20	1.90	–	4.80	137.20	147.00	19.70	3.40	7.90	–	7.00
1989	262.30	133.40	11.00	1.30	2.10	–	4.80	133.90	144.60	20.20	4.00	7.10	–	6.20
1990	262.10	134.00	11.30	1.20	2.10	–	5.20	130.70	138.70	21.80	3.70	7.60	–	6.40
1991	255.60	127.00	12.20	1.30	2.20	–	5.60	127.90	132.20	22.20	3.40	7.70	41.10	6.90
1992	250.50	129.10	11.80	1.50	2.30	–	5.80	111.50	124.90	21.40	4.40	8.00	–	6.70
1993	251.80	107.40	11.70	1.60	2.80	–	5.70	97.80	120.60	20.80	5.10	8.20	47.40	7.10
1994	257.60	107.90	11.00	1.60	3.00	–	5.70	101.70	120.70	20.20	3.70	8.00	38.90	7.50
1995	256.10	104.60	11.30	1.80	3.40	–	5.80	97.00	116.47	19.68	4.10	8.50	40.00	7.11
1996	256.20	106.30	12.90	1.90	3.70	–	6.10	94.68	118.51	20.37	3.97	9.20	36.56	7.13
1997	250.70	107.20	12.70	2.40	3.80	–	6.20	88.59	113.34	19.04	3.97	–	40.72	7.20
1998	248.90	109.00	13.20	2.30	3.70	–	6.10	86.72	113.76	19.22	4.94	–	45.48	7.55
1999	247.40	108.90	13.90	2.50	3.80	–	6.20	84.91	114.94	20.00	4.65	10.30	47.86	7.78
2000	250.20	106.70	14.40	2.80	3.90	–	7.10	82.31	114.74	20.06	4.92	11.74	46.07	8.16
2001	238.60	109.30	14.50	2.90	4.10	–	7.00	79.69	115.86	19.12	5.44	–	49.13	8.08
2002	236.50	110.60	14.90	2.90	4.40	–	7.50	78.48	116.52	23.28	5.30	10.92	50.88	9.00
											9.24		56.52	

Table 9.1 (continued)

Year	Rural[a]								Urban[b]					
	Grain	Vegetable	Meat[c]	Poultry	Seafood	Fruit	Fat & oil	Grain	Vegetable	Meat[c]	Poultry	Seafood	Fruit	Fat & oil
2003	222.40	107.40	15.00	3.20	4.70	17.50	6.30	79.52	118.34	23.74	9.20	11.12	56.57	9.59
2004	218.30	106.60	14.80	3.10	4.50	17.00	5.30	78.18	122.32	22.85	8.41	10.45	56.45	9.61
2005	208.80	102.30	17.10	3.70	4.90	17.20	6.00	76.98	118.58	23.86	8.97	10.58	56.69	9.61
2006	205.60	100.50	17.00	3.50	5.00	19.10	5.80	75.92	117.56	23.78	8.34	10.90	60.17	9.68
2007	199.50	99.00	14.90	3.90	5.40	19.40	6.00	77.60	117.80	22.14	9.66	10.24	59.54	19.26
2008	199.10	99.70	13.90	4.40	5.20	19.40	6.30	–	123.15	22.70	–	10.44	54.48	20.54
2009	189.30	98.40	15.30	4.30	5.30	20.50	6.30	81.33	120.45	24.20	10.47	10.58	56.55	19.34
2010	181.40	93.30	15.80	4.20	5.20	19.60	6.30	81.53	116.11	24.51	10.21	10.21	54.23	17.68
2011	170.70	89.40	16.30	4.50	5.40	21.30	7.50	80.71	114.56	24.58	10.59	10.02	52.02	18.52

Notes:
a. Rural household per capita food consumption includes self-production and purchased food.
b. Urban household per capita food consumption is purchased food.
c. Meat includes pork, beef and mutton.
'–' means no data.

Source: Author's compilation of data from China Statistical Yearbooks and China Urban Life and Price Yearbooks from 2007 to 2012, and Great Changes of China's Economy in 60 Years (1947–2007). All are published by the NBS.

and Zhong (1999) also find that people in Heilongjiang province prefer rice to coarse grains.

Chinese food consumption and preferences have been undergoing structural changes (Dong and Fuller, 2010, for 1981–2004; Hovhannisyan and Gould, 2013, for 2002–10). Structural change in food consumption, which is broadly defined as changing parameters underlying consumers' food consumption decisions, can be evoked by various factors, such as information on nutrition and health, changing tastes, consumers' socioeconomic status, policy reforms, market structure and openness, etc. This chapter focuses on two: income and price. Tables 9.2 and 9.3 summarise the demand elasticities of income/consumption expenditure and price for various foods in rural and urban China, respectively. For the whole country, Zhuang and Abbott (2007) estimate the rural and urban population weighted average per capita income elasticities of demand for agricultural products over the period 1978–2001.[4] The own-price elasticities for grains vary from −0.244 for wheat to −0.445 for rice and are −0.339 and −0.13 for pork and poultry, respectively. The income elasticities are the highest for wheat (0.768) and the lowest for corn (0.079) in the category of grains, while are 0.136 for pork and 0.225 for poultry. Overall, we can observe positive income elasticities and negative own-price elasticities in Chinese diets, indicating that these foods are normal goods in Chinese diets.[5] Many estimators of expenditure elasticities are greater than 1, especially in urban areas. This implies that food consumption is an important aspect of Chinese daily life. In 2011, food consumption accounted for 29.4 per cent of urban household per capita consumption and 37.4 per cent of rural household per capita consumption.[6]

By comparing the magnitude of elasticities across rural and urban areas in Tables 9.2 and 9.3, we can see that rural households' food demand is less responsive to both income and price than urban households'. This may be because 83 per cent of grain, half of meat and poultry, 39 per cent of fruits and a third of edible oil are self-produced by rural households rather than being purchased from markets (Gale et al., 2005).

It is worth mentioning that those elasticities are distinct across areas. Local geographic conditions and dietary tradition affect households' behaviour. As shown in Table 9.4, both rural and urban households in the west (central and western regions) consume more grain than in the east (eastern and northeastern regions). Rice is the main staple, especially in the northeast where the consumption of rice is 2.5 times as high as that of wheat. People increasingly prefer rice to wheat: the ratio of consumption increased from 1.9 in 2005 to 2.3 in 2011 in the central region. Even in the west where wheat production dominates, the ratio rose from 1.4 to 1.5 in the same period. With regard to different kinds of meat, eastern and western regions have higher pork consumption and the majority of beef and mutton is consumed in the west. This is consistent with the household-level data that nearly half of additional animal product expenditure in the west is on beef and mutton, and between 55 per cent and 60 per cent of that in coastal and southern regions is on aquatic products (Ma et al., 2004). Most poultry consumption goes to the east. Ma et al. (2004) also find that the central and the coastal regions could increase their chicken expenditure shares from 2001 (13.6 per cent and 8.4 per cent, respectively), while there could be a decline in the south. They also speculated the increasing share of dairy products in animal-product spending in the coastal region and the south but fall in the central and western regions.

Along with this changing taste, people's food consumption also varies substantially

Table 9.2 Demand elasticity of diet in rural China

	Study Period	Study Areas	Data	Income/Expenditure	Own-price
Grain					
Carter and Zhong (1999)	1993, 1994	Heilongjiang and Jiangsu provinces	Household	0.03 in Heilongjiang, −0.37 in Jiangsu	−0.18 in Heilongjiang, −0.26 in Jiangsu
Huang and Rozelle (1998)	1993	Hebei province	Household	0.510	−0.570
Jiang and Davis (2007)	1991–1995	Jilin province	Household	0.640	–
Yu and Abler (2009)	1994–2003	26 provinces	Provincial	0.310	–
Zhang et al. (2001)	1986–1995	Guangdong province	Household	0.200[a]	−0.307
Vegetables					
Huang and Rozelle (1998)	1993	Hebei province	Household	1.400	−0.820
Jiang and Davis (2007)	1991–1995	Jilin province	Household	0.440	–
Yu and Abler (2009)	1994–2003	26 provinces	Provincial	0.350	–
Zhang et al. (2001)	1986–1995	Guangdong province	Household	0.381[a]	−0.156
Seafood					
Ma et al. (2004)	1999–2001	28 provinces	Provincial	1.280[a]	−0.521
Yu and Abler (2009)	1994–2003	26 provinces	Provincial	0.170	–
Zhang et al. (2001)	1986–1995	Guangdong province	Household	0.850[a]	−0.844
Fats and oil					
Yu and Abler (2009)	1994–2003	26 provinces	Provincial	0.190	–
Meats and poultry					
Jiang and Davis (2007)	1991–1995	Jilin province	Household	0.760[c]	–
Ma et al. (2004)	1999–2001	28 provinces	Provincial	1.419[a,b]	−1.004[b]
Zhang et al. (2001)	1986–1995	Guangdong province	Household	0.672[a]	−0.282
Dairy products					
Yu and Abler (2009)	1994–2003	26 provinces	Provincial	0.180	–
Other					
Zhang et al. (2001)[d]	1986–1995	Guangdong province	Household	1.197[a]	−1.066

Notes:
a. Expenditure elasticity.
b. The average value across pork, chicken, beef and mutton.
c. All animal products.
d. 'Other' category includes alcohol and tobacco.
'–' means no data.

Source: Author's compilation.

Table 9.3 Demand elasticity of diet in urban China

	Study Period	Study Areas	Data	Income/Expenditure	Own-price
Grain					
Gould and Villarreal (2006)	2001	Shandong, Jiangsu, Heilongjiang, Henan and Guangdong provinces	Household	1.163[a] for rice; 0.752[a] for other grains	−0.636 for rice; −1.027 for other grains
Hovhannisyan and Gould (2011) (rice only)	1995, 2003	Jiangsu, Shandong, and Guangdong provinces	Household	0.040 and 0.200[a] in 1995; 0.112 and 0.404[a] in 2003	−1.458 in 1995; −1.160 in 2003
Wang et al. (2011)	2007	Beijing	Household	1.237[a]	−1.839
Yen et al. (2004)	2000	30 cities in 29 provinces	Household	0.820[a]	−0.900
Zheng and Henneberry (2009)	2004	Jiangsu province	Household	0.795[a]	−1.221
Vegetables					
Gould and Villarreal (2006)	2001	Shandong, Jiangsu, Heilongjiang, Henan and Guangdong provinces	Household	0.948[a]	−0.664
Hovhannisyan and Gould (2011)	1995, 2003	Jiangsu, Shandong, and Guangdong provinces	Household	0.179 and 0.895[a] in 1995; 0.166 and 0.601[a] in 2003	−0.520 in 1995; −0.457 in 2003
Wang et al. (2011)	2007	Beijing	Household	1.396[a]	−0.800
Yen et al. (2004)	2000	30 cities in 29 provinces	Household	0.830[a]	−0.720
Zheng and Henneberry (2009)	2004	Jiangsu province	Household	0.814[a]	−0.067
Seafood					
Gould and Villarreal (2006)	2001	Shandong, Jiangsu, Heilongjiang, Henan and Guangdong provinces	Household	1.404[a]	−0.570
Hovhannisyan and Gould (2011)	1995, 2003	Jiangsu, Shandong, and Guangdong provinces	Household	0.398 and 1.986[a] in 1995; 0.406 and 1.469[a] in 2003	−0.709 in 1995; −0.546 in 2003
Ma et al. (2004)	1999–2001	28 provinces	Provincial	1.812[a,b]	−1.403[b]
Wang et al. (2011)	2007	Beijing	Household	1.651[a]	−0.490
Yen et al. (2004)	2000	30 cities in 29 provinces	Household	1.410[a]	−0.370
Zheng and Henneberry (2009)	2004	Jiangsu province	Household	1.198[a]	−0.100

Table 9.3 (continued)

	Study Period	Study Areas	Data	Income/Expenditure	Own-price
Fats & Oil					
Gould and Villarreal (2006)	2001	Shandong, Jiangsu, Heilongjiang, Henan and Guangdong provinces	Household	1.335[a]	−0.747
Hovhannisyan and Gould (2011)	1995, 2003	Jiangsu, Shandong, and Guangdong provinces	Household	−0.030 and −0.151[a]	−0.587
Ma et al. (2004)	1999–2001	28 provinces	Provincial	0.832[a,b]	−0.704[b]
Yen et al. (2004)	2000	30 cities in 29 provinces	Household	0.980[a]	−0.550
Zheng and Henneberry (2009)	2004	Jiangsu province	Household	0.717[a]	−1.312
Meat and poultry					
Gould and Villarreal (2006)	2001	Shandong, Jiangsu, Heilongjiang, Henan and Guangdong provinces	Household	1.188[a] for meat incl. beef and pork; 1.202[a] for poultry	−0.816 for meat incl. beef and pork; −0.885 for poultry
Hovhannisyan and Gould (2011)	1995, 2003	Jiangsu, Shandong, and Guangdong provinces	Household	0.145 and 0.721[a] for pork, 0.315 and 1.572[a] for beef, 0.491 and 2.447[a] for poultry	−0.550 for pork, −0.961 for beef, −0.883 for poultry
Wang et al. (2011)	2007	Beijing	Household	1.300[a]	−1.618
Yen et al. (2004)	2000	30 cities in 29 provinces	Household	1.22 for meat incl. beef, pork and other meat; 1.26 for poultry	−0.723 for meat incl. beef, pork and other meat; −0.75 for poultry
Zheng and Henneberry (2009)	2004	Jiangsu province	Household	1.040[a] for meat; 1.001[a] for poultry	−0.853 for meat; −0.348 for poultry

Dairy products				
Gould and Villarreal (2006)	2001	Shandong, Jiangsu, Heilongjiang, Henan and Guangdong provinces	Household	1.004[a]	−0.391
Hovhannisyan and Gould (2011)	1995, 2003	Jiangsu, Shandong, and Guangdong provinces	Household	0.430 and 2.146[a] in 1995; 0.481 and 1.742[a] in 2003	−1.163 in 1995; −1.037 in 2003
Ma et al. (2004)	1999–2001	28 provinces	Provincial	1.144[a]	−1.191
Wang et al. (2011)[c]	2007	Beijing	Household	0.496[a]	−1.509
Yen et al. (2004)	2000	30 cities in 29 provinces	Household	1.400[a]	−1.400
Zheng and Henneberry (2009)	2004	Jiangsu province	Household	1.372[a]	−1.209
Other				
Gould and Villarreal (2006)	2001	Shandong, Jiangsu, Heilongjiang, Henan and Guangdong provinces	Household	0.615[a]	−0.346
Hovhannisyan and Gould (2011)	1995, 2003	Jiangsu, Shandong, and Guangdong provinces	Household	0.332 and 1.655[a] in 1995; 0.373 and 1.351[a] in 2003	−0.923 in 1995; −0.699 in 2003
Wang et al. (2011)[e]	2007	Beijing	Household	1.269[a]	−0.274
Zheng and Henneberry (2009)[f]	2004	Jiangsu province	Household	1.180[a]	−1.609

Notes:
a. Expenditure elasticity.
b. The average value across pork, chicken, beef and mutton.
c. Includes eggs only.
d. Includes fruits.
e. Includes beans.
f. Includes starch and tubers, alcohol beverage, beverages and cakes.

Source: Author's compilation.

Table 9.4 Household per capita food consumption in 2011, by region (kg)

Item	Rural[a]				Urban[b]			
	Eastern	Central	Western	Northeastern	Eastern	Central	Western	Northeastern
Grain:	157.21	172.86	181.68	163.36	77.42	86.57	78.24	85.69
Wheat	54.09	48.84	62.69	40.52	–	–	–	–
Rice	89.18	110.91	92.37	99.66	–	–	–	–
Soybeans	0.68	1.82	1.17	3.57	–	–	–	–
Fresh vegetables	85.21	99.26	82.54	102.31	108	116.61	118.06	129.84
Edible vegetable oil	7.49	6.79	5.07	9.89	8.1	10.25	9.83	10.57
Pork	14.43	12.18	16.69	11.75	20.95	19.93	23.4	15.28
Beef and mutton	1.11	0.60	3.73	0.96	3.52	3.18	5.22	4.88
Poultry	6.11	3.97	3.96	3.16	12.65	8.95	10.48	6.07
Eggs and processed products	7.07	5.99	3.12	7.61	10.81	10.45	7.62	11.57
Milk and processed products	5.63	2.91	6.77	3.90	14.94	10.81	15.15	12.37
Fruits	24.58	22.50	15.89	30.24	52.29	52.05	47.79	59.37

Notes:
a. Rural household per capita food consumption includes self-production and purchased food.
b. Urban household per capita food consumption is purchased food.
'–' means no data.

Source: Author's compilation and calculation based on data from China Statistical Yearbook 2012.

across provinces. Carter and Zhong (1999) find that the own-price elasticity for wheat in Jiangsu is 50 per cent higher than in Heilongjiang (Table 9.2) as rural households in Jiangsu province increasingly substitute rice for wheat. In general, as suggested in Tables 9.2 and 9.3, household food consumption in southern and eastern provinces like Guangdong and Jiangsu tends to respond less to income and price than in northern provinces like Jilin. However, as income keeps growing, urbanisation is likely to narrow the differences in taste between northern and southern China. In large cities, the pattern that the north region traditionally prefers wheat to rice while the south region sees the opposite would be less significant possibly because of the increasingly diversified population (Zhang and Wang, 2003). People in northern provinces traditionally prefer wheat to rice, while those in south have the opposite taste. Urbanisation and the associated growing number of interprovincial migrants result in the population in large cities becoming a mixture of both northern and southern people. Therefore, it becomes less apparent that wheat (rice) is consumed more than rice (wheat) in the North (South) (Zhang and Wang, 2003).

Over time, the individual-level data from China Health and Nutrition Surveys (CHNS) show that income effects on low-fat and high-fibre food such as wheat-flour products and coarse grains fell from 1989 to 1993, proportionally more among richer households, while income elasticities of pork, edible oil and eggs increased significantly (Guo et al., 2000). Ma et al. (2004) and Hovhannisyan and Gould (2011) also find that expenditure elasticities become smaller and stabilised over the period 1995–2003. The consequences of these shifts on nutrition will be discussed in section 9.3.

When comparing the price and income effects, existing literature suggests that structural change in food consumption is more attributable to price than to income growth. Based on the annual urban household survey conducted by the NBS, Dong and Fuller (2010) recognised the structural change period over 1982–90 by looking at institutional changes in pricing agricultural products and by checking empirically that the estimated coefficients for time path variables in food demand equations are significantly different from zero. Price elasticities were negative prior to it except grain and all foods became price inelastic from 1990 to 2004. Using updated data to 2010, Hovhannisyan and Gould (2013) further demonstrate decreasing own-price uncompensated elasticities, with the exception of eggs.

9.2.2 Quantity Versus Quality

It is worth noting that quantity of food consumption does not necessarily increase with demand for better quality in China. The correlation between households' per capita calorie intake and per capita income is only 0.04 in the CHNS (Shimokawa, 2013). Higher income did not improve nutrient intakes in rural India (Behrman and Deolalikar, 1987), either. However, this revisionist view was rejected later by Subramanian and Deaton (1996) who found moderate nutrient elasticities of consumption expenditure (0.3–0.5) in rural Maharashtran state of India and suggested that policy makers promote economic development proxied by consumption rather than by income.

It also can be seen from Table 9.1 that household per capita consumption of fat and oil grew at an average of 2.7 per cent in rural areas and 11.6 per cent in urban areas between 2003 and 2011, while lower amounts of vegetables and fruits were consumed over time. Fine grains and rice become increasingly popular instead of coarse grains (Carter and Zhong, 1999). The Chinese diet has been shifting away from traditional style with coarse grains as the staple to the westernised one full of high-carbohydrate foods. Using the CHNS 2000 wave, Capacci et al. (2008) identify a negative relation between household wealth and quality of diet. More wealth results in worsening diet structure in terms of higher energy intake from fats but proportionately less from fruits and vegetables. Higher fruit and vegetable intake only compensate partly for the worsening diet. Shimokawa (2013) draws upon Guenther et al.'s (2008) healthy-eating index (HEI) for developing countries and calculates Chinese HEI containing eight categories and ranging between 0 and 90.[7] Data in his study is CHNS 2000–06. The scores vary from 16.2 to 79.9 in different waves with the mean of 49.5. The negative association between income growth and dietary quality is particularly pronounced for the poor as their food demand elasticities of income and price are higher than those of the rich (Du et al., 2004).

One may suspect that with more health information and knowledge, people may be more willing and likely to adopt healthy diets. However, using CHNS from 2000 to 2006, Shimokawa (2013) also finds that when expectation of food availability increases, dietary knowledge affects mainly the quantity and only marginally improves quality (i.e. 2.6 per cent higher vegetable intake). When expectation of food availability decreases, a one standard deviation increase in dietary knowledge can lead to 1 per cent lower calorie intake from fat and sugar only. Moreover, dietary education significantly affects quality in terms of consumption of grains, meat and beans for non-overweight adults compared with overweight ones under decreasing expectation of food availability. Based on the same dataset, Zhao et al. (2013) find that when receiving hypertension diagnosis, richer individuals reduce more fat intake than poorer ones and again, among the rich, lower education is associated with a greater reduction in fat consumption.

Although in general there is a limited role of education for better food quality, there appears to be a gender-differentiated phenomenon. Based on CHNS in 1991, Bhandari and Smith (2000) document a positive impact of female education on nutritious food, while the impact of male education is closely tied to income levels as better-educated males could secure off-farm employment raising household income and thus afford more 'westernised' foods. The problem of over-consumption for high-energy high-fat foods and over-nutrition might be harnessed by educating females.

9.2.3 Income Inequality and Pattern of Food Consumption

As discussed in section 9.2.1, price effects dominate income effects in the shift of household food consumption. Although richer households are more able to afford the increased purchase of grains, meat, seafood and fruits in the presence of rising prices, the income elasticities diminish as income keeps rising, especially for staple foods like grains, edible oil and eggs (Table 9.5). The emerging middle class in Asia, in general, favours more processed and fried food (ADB, 2010). Poor rural households tend to increase grain consumption as higher income is available, while urban households would rather consume less grain as they become rich. The poor in rural areas see the highest income elasticity for edible oil, vegetables and eggs (also found by Popkin, 2007), and the absolute increase in oil consumption is also the largest across different income groups in rural and urban areas (Guo et al., 2000). Although the general demand for meat rises

Table 9.5 Income elasticities by food item and income level, 2002–03

	Rural household per capita income (yuan)			Urban household per capita income (yuan)			
Food category	900	2500	6000	2500	7500	10000	22000
Grains	0.18	0.06	0.02	0.01	−0.09	−0.10	−0.11
Edible oil	0.51	0.23	0.14	0.17	−0.08	−0.11	−0.16
Vegetables	0.60	0.16	0.03	0.20	0.09	0.08	0.05
Eggs	0.72	0.46	0.38	0.50	0.10	0.05	−0.03
Pork	0.25	0.24	0.23	0.44	0.13	0.09	0.03
Beef	−0.76[a]	0.39[a]	0.71[a]	0.93	0.19	0.10	−0.06
Mutton				1.14	0.18	0.06	−0.14
Dairy products	−1.50	0.70	1.30	1.74	0.64	0.50	0.28
Poultry	0.74	0.66	0.63	0.78	0.38	0.33	0.25
Aquatic products	0.91	0.93	0.94	0.72	0.52	0.49	0.45
Fruit	0.38[b]	0.48[b]	0.50[b]	0.95	0.35	0.27	0.15
Melons				0.85	0.32	0.25	0.15
Alcohol	–	–	–	0.88	0.16	0.08	−0.07
Other beverages	–	–	–	1.69	1.03	0.94	0.81

Notes:
a. Estimators are for beef and mutton.
b. Estimators are for fruit and melons.
'–' means no data.

Source: Adapted from Table 2 of Gale and Huang (2007: 14). Estimation is based on the Rural Household Survey and the Urban Household Survey that are representative of China and are conducted annually by the NBS.

along with higher income, people's preferences for different kinds of meat vary and the demand for meat varies substantially across income distribution as well as between rural and urban areas. As listed in Table 9.5, richer rural households' demand for beef quickly expands as their income rises, while the demand for pork is stable. Richer urban households may not consume more beef and mutton, but may substitute dairy products, poultry and aquatic products for them. Using the Urban Household Survey collected by the NBS in Jiangsu in 2004, Zheng and Henneberry (2010) find similar trends of income elasticities across five income strata. However, negative income elasticities of beef and mutton and the positive, albeit small, ones of pork for the richest group in urban areas imply that pork is still the primary choice for the richest urban consumers. This is consistent with Guo et al.'s (2000) calculation that absolute quantity of pork consumed by urban population is still the highest among all varieties of meat. There seems to be satiation for food consumption for wealthy households at the top of income distribution, especially for items with lower unit values (Huang and Gale, 2009). By contrast, there seems to be ample room for future increases in pork (Guo et al., 2000), milk and dairy products (Fuller et al., 2006). As discussed in section 9.2.2, the dietary transition in China follows an unhealthy pattern in terms of more energy intake from fat and oil. The description here further indicates a more detrimental trend for the poor in rural China. Alarmingly, rising income inequality accompanies more unequal distribution of calories and protein – the estimates of their Gini coefficients based on CHNS between 1991 and 2004 have increased by 15.7 per cent and 47.7 per cent in rural and urban areas, respectively (Bishop et al., 2010). In contrast, as the poor consume proportionately more fat than the rich, the Gini coefficient of fat intake decreased by 24 per cent in rural areas and remained the same in urban areas over the same time period.

9.2.4 Labour Participation and Urbanisation

Positive effects of migration on households' economic situation have been widely identified in the literature. A recent review by Zezza et al. (2011) suggests that migration also helps improve food and nutrition security in many developing countries such as Vietnam, Tajikistan, Guatemala and El Salvador. China has the largest migration flow in the developing world. The total out-migration in 2012 was registered at 160 million. Migration has proved to be an important means to earn more income (Du et al., 2005) and to loosen financial constraints on agricultural production (Rozelle et al., 1999b; Taylor et al., 2003). Consequently this stimulates agricultural productivity (Rozelle et al., 1999a), adds to rural households' consumption expenditure (de Brauw and Giles, 2008) and increases investment in housing and consumer durables (de Brauw and Rozelle, 2008). Alarmingly, an improved economic situation may not assist rural households in improving children's nutritional status. De Brauw and Mu (2011) find that children in older rural families with out-migrating family members (typically parents) have to take on more household chores, household production and take care of the elderly, and remaining adults spend less time in preparing meals. They actually experience declined nutritional intake. By contrast, younger children aged 7–12 years are less likely to be overweight. Exploiting the household panel data in Gansu province between 2000 and 2004, You (2013) also documents a negative estimated coefficient of migration on left children's nutrition. Older children (aged between 12 and 18 years) living in households with migrating members spent 38.3 per cent more time per week (10.97 hours) on household agricultural production, business and housework than those in families without out-migration (7.93 hour per week). Migration is unlikely to affect nutrition.

9.2.5 Meals Away From Home

As income grows, food preparation and shopping behaviour also change. The annual growth rate of cash purchases of food by rural Chinese households was 7.4 per cent from 1994 to 2003 (Gale et al., 2005), which has benefited from commercialisation of food markets (Huang and Rozelle, 2006).

In urban China, households are increasingly fascinated by eating out, which also emerges in other fast growing economies such as India (e.g. Gaiha et al., 2013). The supply side also prospers: from 2007 to 2011, the number of catering enterprises registered formally with local Commercial Administration Departments rose by 60 per cent (from 14 000 to 22 500); total area of catering services doubled; and the gross revenue in constant prices increased by 74.5 per cent.[8] The household per capita expenditure on food away from home (FAFH) rose from 2002 to 2011 (Figure 9.4) with an average annual growth rate of 9.5 per cent. The share of this expenditure in total food con-

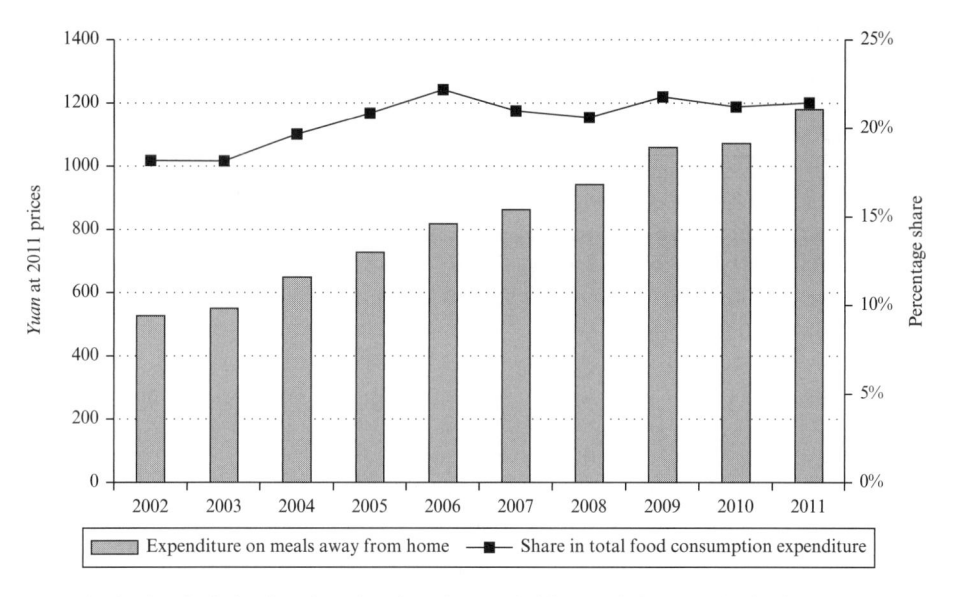

Dietary change, nutrient transition and food security in China 221

Source: Author's calculation based on data from issues of China Statistical Yearbooks from 2003 to 2012 published by the NBS.

Figure 9.4 Urban household per capita expenditure on meals away from home, 2002–11

sumption expenditure also rose from 18.2 per cent to 21.5 per cent at the same time (Figure 9.4). About 4.3 per cent of household income has been spent on dining out, with significant differences across provinces and income distribution (Gould and Villarreal, 2006). For example, in Gould and Villarreal's (2006) study, households in Guangdong in 2001 spent 26.2 per cent of total food expenditure in FAFH, while those in Henan spent only 9.5 per cent. The share of FAFH in total food consumption was 29.7 per cent in the highest income decile as opposed to 6 per cent in the lowest group. If accounting for hosted meals, the estimates of expenditure on dining out would increase further by a half according to Bai et al. (2010). The household survey in Bejing in 2007 from Wang et al. (2011) documents more than a doubling in meat consumption and drink as well as a more than a three-fold decrease in fruit consumption when households eat away from home rather than at home. On observing the outcomes of changing taste and preferences of food processing, Wang et al. (2011) further find that raw foods are more income elastic than the semi- and fully-processed ones: the elasticities of raw grain and meat are 363 per cent and 61 per cent higher than semi-processed ones, respectively, and 284 per cent and 27.8 per cent higher than those of ready ones.

Bai et al. (2010) and Ma et al. (2006) also identify determinants of households' decisions on eating out. The likelihood of dining out is positively associated with higher household income, lower levels of expenditure on food away from home, higher time opportunity costs and the value of received hosted meals, and some demographics such as fewer children and seniors. More importantly, the neglected rapid rise of FAFH demand in national statistics of household aggregate meat demand may explain partly the gap between (overstated) output of livestock and (understated) meat demand in China (Ma et al., 2006).

9.3 NUTRITION TRANSITION AND EMERGING CHALLENGES

9.3.1 The Paradox of Increased Income and Decreased Nutrient Intake

Many studies of developed countries suggest a positive impact of wealth on health, while there is no conclusive evidence for developing countries. Recent literature reviews from Alderman (2012) and Ecker et al. (2012) finds no warrant for positive impact of economic growth on better health and nutritional outcomes in the developing world. Income growth is neither a sufficient or necessary condition for better nutrition (Fan and Brzeska, 2012), while low incomes may be conducive to poverty nutrition traps. Dasgupta and Ray (1986) formulate a two-way causality between low incomes/wages and nutrition, which was confirmed empirically in India by Jha et al. (2009): low wages lower people's ability to afford nutrition-rich food and this further undermines people's productivity and results in low wages in a vicious circle.

In the Chinese context, as reviewed in section 9.2, there have been dramatic behavioural changes in food consumption patterns along with income growth. Even a small decline in diet quality might trigger substantial adverse effects on nutritional attainment. Rising commodity prices also impose a heavier burden on households' food consumption and thus deter nutrient intake, while at the same time higher income might endow people with more feasible food consumption plans. It is therefore necessary to unravel directly the nutritional outcomes of economic prosperity.

Studies based on the CHNS suggest higher income does not lead to a smaller number of undernourished population measured against a certain daily calorie or protein threshold. There are nearly zero income elasticities of calories and protein intake (Bishop et al., 2010) regardless of households' situation: 0.08 and 0.09 for non-agricultural and agricultural households at median income, respectively (Lu and Luhrmann, 2013). Tian and Yu's (2012) estimation of households' income elasticities of various micronutrients as listed in Table 9.6 also demonstrate that people's nutritional intake is less responsive to income growth, especially among the rich. However, whether economic growth can eliminate malnutrition in the developing world is still controversial. For example, by using consumption as a proxy of individual welfare, Subramanian and Deaton (1996) find clearly non-zero consumption elasticities of nutrient intake (0.3–0.5) in rural India. It would be interesting to investigate how the estimates of Chinese elasticities of nutrient intake would respond to different welfare measures (income or consumption) and estimation strategies which have been contended as the reasons for these contrary views.

There exists an inverted U-shaped relationship between household income and calorie intake (Lu and Luhrmann, 2013). Using another dataset, Urban Household Income and Expenditure Surveys conducted annually by the NBS from 1986 to 2000, Meng et al. (2009) also find overall non-increasing trend in calorie intake, and the low- and middle-income groups even experienced lower calorie and protein consumption. The short-run significant drop in calorie and protein levels between 1993 and 1995 can be explained by sharp increases in food prices as part of the government agricultural policy.[9] In the mid- and late-1990s, however, the main reason for reduction in nutrient intake has been income uncertainty and large expenditure on health, medicine and education incurred by economic reforms on state-owned enterprises (i.e. forced layoff) and large-scale but

Table 9.6 Income elasticities of micronutrients

Micronutrient	Full sample	Poor	Rich
Energy	0.122***	0.322***	0.064
Protein	0.127***	0.246**	0.098
Fat	0.149***	0.210	0.084
Carbohydrate	0.107***	0.308**	0.073
Fibre	0.131***	0.441***	0.057
Cholesterol	0.293***	0.309	0.433**
Vitamin A	0.140	0.306	0.194
Thiamin-B1	0.155***	0.118	0.154
Riboflavin-B2	0.126***	0.325**	0.067
Niacin-B3	0.154***	0.225*	0.149
Vitamin C	0.135**	0.086	0.167
Vitamin E	0.147**	0.215	0.026
Calcium	0.061	0.240	−0.057
Phosphorus	0.132***	0.225**	0.116
Potassium	0.103***	0.111	0.082
Magnesium	0.105***	0.311**	0.066
Sodium	0.012	−0.060	−0.107
Iron	0.135***	0.241**	0.166*
Zinc	0.130***	0.219**	0.113
Selenium	0.166***	0.306**	0.155
Copper	0.119***	0.245**	0.008
Manganese	0.088	0.213*	0.030

Notes:
***, ** and * denote 1%, 5% and 10% significance levels, respectively.

Source: Adapted from Tian and Yu's (2012) estimation.

ununified social welfare reform between rural and urban areas and across different sectors. Since China's accession to the World Trade Organization (WTO), rising grain prices impose the largest adverse effects on calorie and protein consumption (Zheng and Henneberry, 2012).

In contrast to calories and protein, the income elasticity of fat is relatively high, indicating that fat is a normal good for Chinese consumers (Du et al., 2004; Bishop et al., 2010). Moreover, Engel curves for households' fat converge in the rich cohort in the CHNS, suggesting that households have the same taste for fat when their income reaches 35 000 yuan at 2009 levels (Lu and Luhrmann, 2013). Increased weight and obesity as consequences of increasing fat intake will be discussed in the next subsection.

Among various groups of the population, the vulnerable in the society, such as females and children, seem to suffer more from malnourishment. In CHNS, the income elasticity of calories for females is 146–266 per cent (39–104 per cent) higher than that for males in agricultural (non-agricultural) households (Lu and Luhrmann, 2013). Qiu and Qiu (2013) do not find statistically significant impact of household income on either rural or urban children's nutritional outcomes measured by height-for-age z-scores (i.e. stunting) but they do find indirect effects of income: higher community-level income improves children's nutrition as they could access better health facilities, clean water and sanitation. This is not surprising given the positive role of income growth on chronic undernutrition identified in the developing world (e.g. cross-country analyses by Haddad et al., 2003, and Headey, 2013). In rural Gansu, where per capita GDP has always been in the bottom 3 out of 30 provinces in China, a quarter of sample mothers in a household panel dataset covering 100 villages in 2000 (Gansu Survey of Children and Families, GSCF; see Hannum and Frongillo, 2012) reported not having enough food for the family in the past year. This share dropped quickly to 8.7 per cent in 2004, but food insecurity for children was aggravated. Of families with children under 16 years old, 22.6 per cent deliberately reduced the amount of food for children because of insufficient food or money to buy enough food; 6.45 per cent said this had happened in almost every month; and 48.4 per cent reported quite a few months. A total of 5.8 per cent of children had sometimes gone without food for a whole day.

Worsened nutritional status among the poor might trigger nutritional poverty traps which have been found in other developing countries such as India (Jha et al., 2009). As found by Jha et al. (2009), there is a two-way causality between low incomes/wages and malnutrition in India. Undernutrition also dampens children's formation of human capital in the long term. Based on GSCF 2000–04, Hannum et al.'s (2012) study warns that long-term undernourishment significantly undermines children's academic performance by one third of a standard deviation lower literacy score and food insecurity strikes the poorest disproportionately.

9.3.2 Non-communicable Diseases

Sections 9.1 and 9.2 have demonstrated the shift towards palatable food with fine processed ingredients and high energy. A problem that the Chinese government has to contend with is high weight and obesity. As a result of increasing intake of fat and oil, the proportion of overweight adults rose from 9.7 per cent in 1982 to 14.9 per cent in 1992 according to national surveys including over 80 000 urban respondents (Guo et al., 2000) and recently approached a quarter (Popkin, 2007). For adolescents, Zhang and Wang (2013) calculate the BMI of students aged 7–18 years in Shandong province from 1985 to 2010. The rate of those overweight plus obesity increased considerably from 3.6 per cent (urban male), 3 per cent (urban female), 0.77 per cent (rural male) and 1.47 per cent (rural female) in 1985 to 36.6 per cent, 19.4 per cent, 29.6 per cent and 18.8 per cent in 2010, respectively. Similar to previous calculations, the poor also bear the brunt of the high weight and poor diets compared with the rich. The poor suffer from larger increases in incidences of hypertension, stroke, and adult-onset diabetes (Popkin, 2008).

Such non-commutable diseases are likely to impose a financial burden on individuals and on public medical expenditure. The New Cooperative Medical Scheme piloted in rural China in 2003 and radical reforms of the health care system in urban China have been criticised for requiring large out-of-pocket health expenditure and even financial risk for the poor due to the tendency of overprescribing, overuse of higher-level medical devices and inefficiency of hospitals (see Wagstaff et al., 2009, for a review). Nutrition-related non-communicable diseases will add further to China's health-care costs, which have recently risen quickly. The related costs represent 4–8 per cent of the economy and 'public investments are needed to head off a huge increase in the morbidity, disability,

Dietary change, nutrient transition and food security in China 225

absenteeism and medical care costs linked with this nutritional shift' (Popkin, 2008: 1064).

9.4　FOOD SECURITY IN CHINA

9.4.1　Expanding Food Demand and Supply in China and its Impact on the Rest of the World

As reviewed in section 9.2.1, the average food consumption in China has undergone structural change with fewer staple foods and more animal products being consumed. This is also reflected at the macro level. As shown in Figure 9.5, the share of households' grain consumption[10] in total grain demand declined by 15.88 percentage points from 1995 (58.67 per cent) to 2009 (42.79 per cent), while the demand for industrial processing uses witnessed a growth rate of 9.04 per cent per annum (Tang and Li, 2012). Figure 9.6 suggests that most grain demand goes to soybean crush which relates to edible oil. This is consistent with the individual analysis in section 9.2.1 that Chinese people use more edible oil than before. The second largest destination of industrial grain demand lies in alcohol. This is unsurprising as the output of liquor tripled between 2003 and 2011 and the output of beer doubled. China's total output of alcohol currently ranks first in the world.

China faces a huge challenge to feed its large population with changing appetite as well as growing production and demand for agricultural product-based industrial goods. Figure 9.7 depicts food production in China over the period 1985–2011. After some variable harvest in the 1990s and early 2000s, grain production has grown continuously by 30 per cent over the period 2003–11. As shown in Figure 9.7b, both the level and growth rate of pork production are larger compared to those of beef and mutton. China

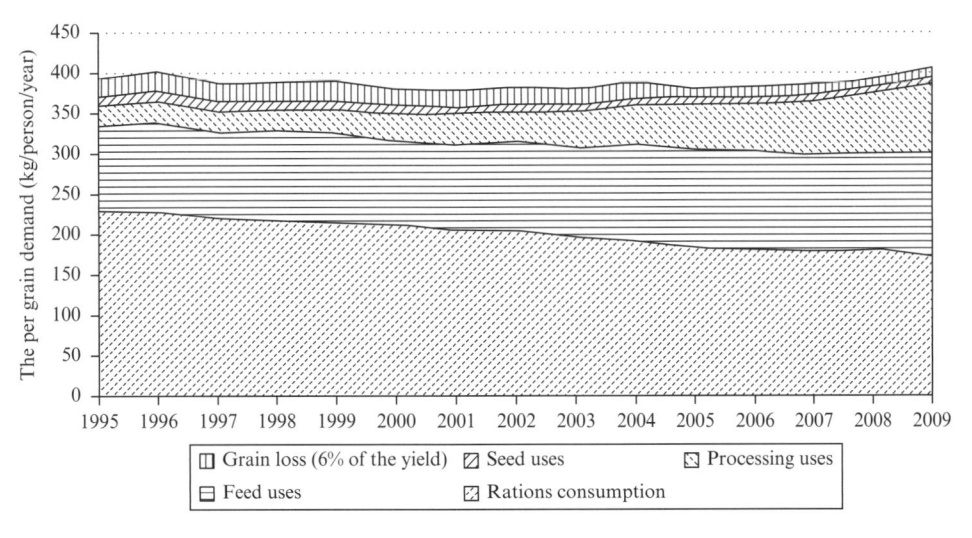

Source: Adapted from Figure 4 in Tang and Li (2012).

Figure 9.5 The changing structure of per capita grain demand

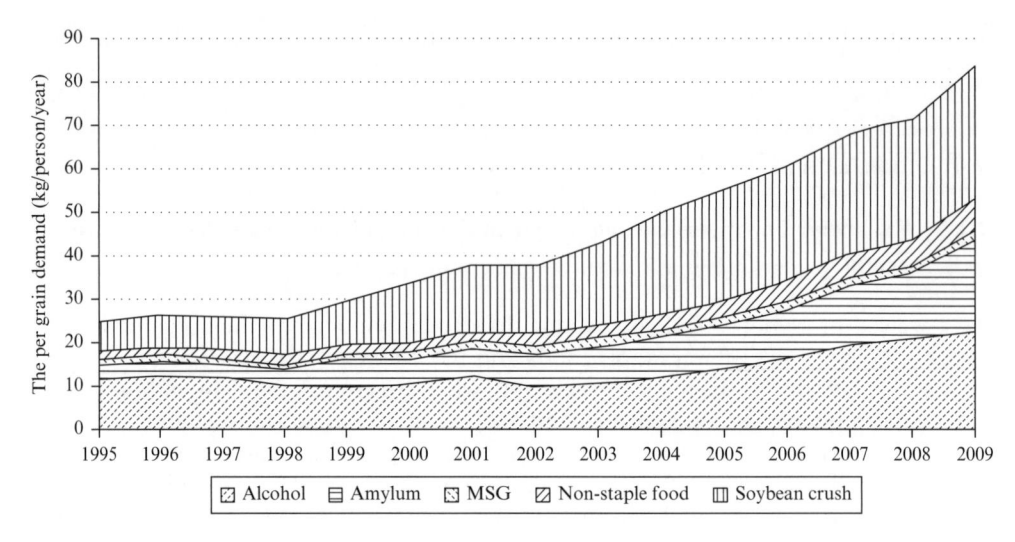

Source: Adapted from Figure 5 in Tang and Li (2012).

Figure 9.6 The changing structure of per capita grain demand for industrial use

is currently not only the largest pork consumer around the world, but also the largest producer. The most dramatic increase lies in milk production with an average annual growth rate of 14.3 per cent since 2000. Nevertheless, behind this are a large number of backyard and small-scale dairy farms using low-yield breeds, which result in increasing productivity inequality compared to large-scale dairy farms and possibly explains the melamine scandal of milk powder in 2008 (Yu, 2012). It is also worth noting that aquatic production has surpassed pork since 2006. China has embarked on international fishing and the State Council has mapped out a subsidy plan for it since the its first 2012 Policy Document, known as the No. 1 Central Document, issued at the beginning of every year on China's agricultural policy.

Harvests since 2003 have also resulted in increased per capita food production, except for oil crops (Figure 9.8). Per capita grain production has remained above 400 kg since 2010, which is deemed the food security threshold in China. Despite expanded domestic food supply, China needs increasingly more food with its population and income growth. As listed in Table 9.7, China has become consistently a net importer of total grain since 2003, which has been driven by wheat import, and of soybeans since 1996. The import growth rate of rice hit its recent peak at 54 per cent in 2011 after its historical records of 220 per cent in 1995 and 196 per cent in 2004. Wheat import in 2009 was 21.6 times as much as that in 2008 and corn import in 2010 was 17.7 times as in 2009. Although China achieved 18 million tons higher grain output for the ninth consecutive year in 2012 compared to 2011, setting a new record of nearly 600 million tons, grain imports also kept rising to 77 million tons. This means that 19 million Chinese people (1.4 per cent of total population) are consuming imported, rather than home-grown grain.

Despite expanded need for grain, some studies suggest that the self-sufficiency rate of grain ratio is still higher than 97 per cent as a result of a recent 8-year successive increase in harvest, while this drops below 90 per cent if taking soybeans into account.[11]

(a) Grain

Figure 9.7 Food production, 1985–2011 (10000 tons)

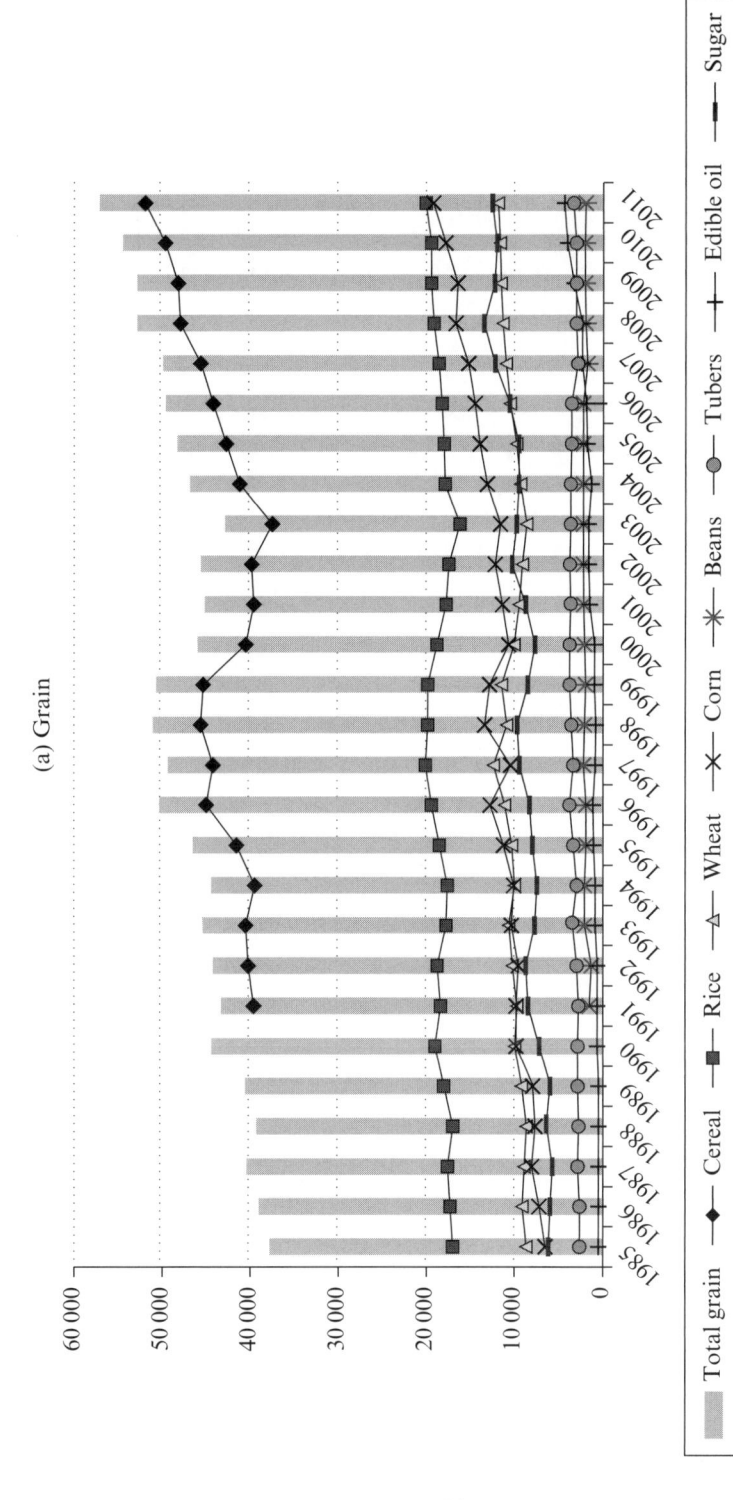

Source: Author's compilation of data from China Statistical Yearbook 2012 published by the NBS, the China Macroeconomy Database provided by GTA and China Rural Statistical Yearbook 2012 published by the Ministry of Agriculture.

(b) Meat, dairy and aquatic products

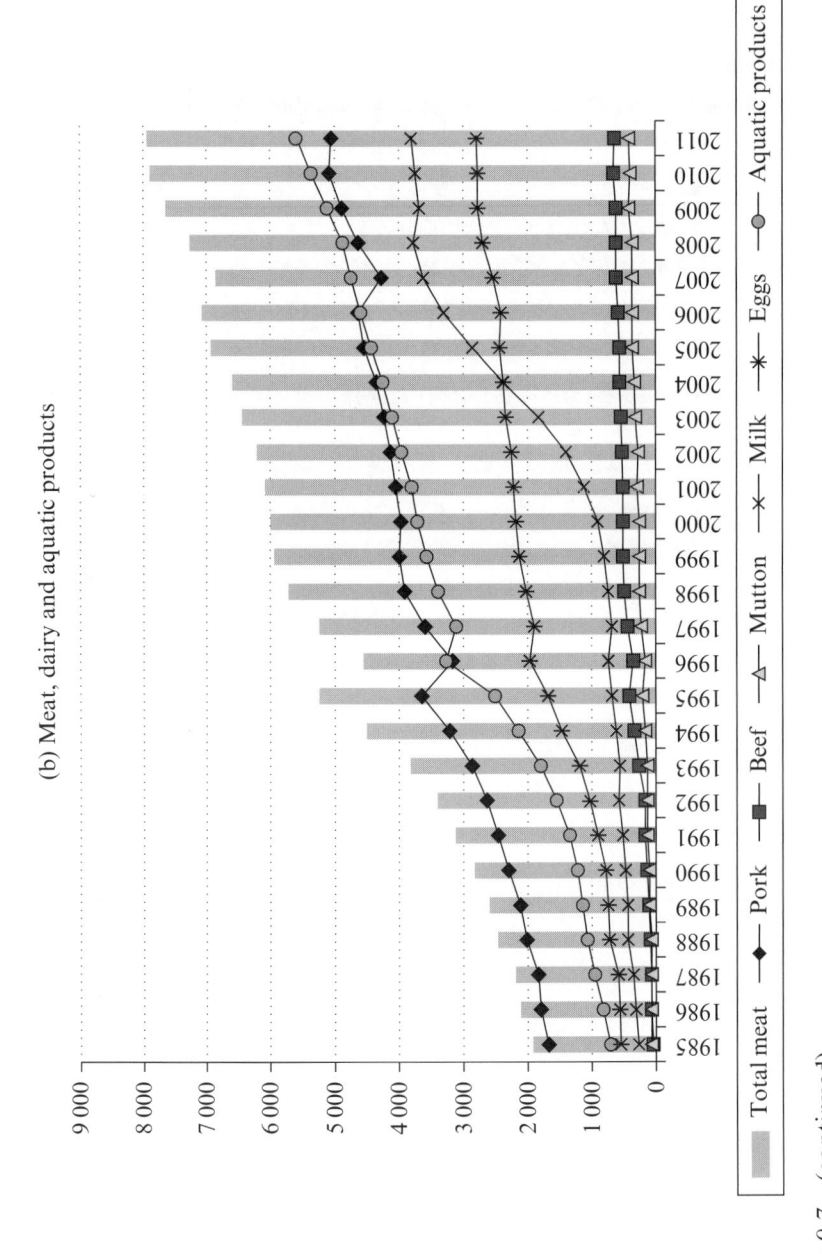

Figure 9.7 (continued)

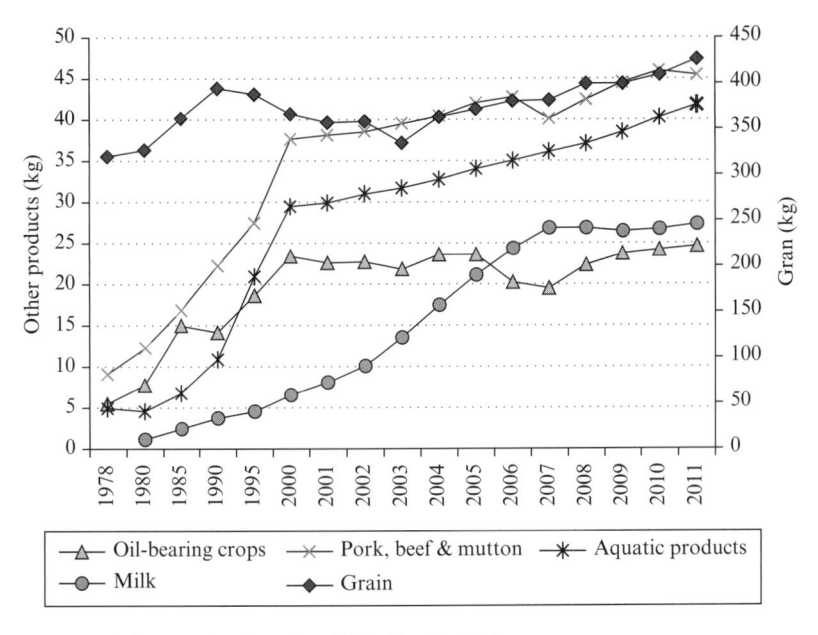

Dietary change, nutrient transition and food security in China 229

Source: China Statistical Yearbook 2012 published by the NBS.

Figure 9.8 Per capita food production, 1978–2011

According to the World Bank (Figure 9.9), China is at the margin of balancing between self-production and imports with slightly negative share of net cereal imports as a share of consumption, while African and some Latin American developing countries rely heavily on cereal imports. Huang et al.'s (2010) simulation suggests an even more positive prospect for China. The self-sufficiency rates of many products are higher than 90 per cent, except for sugar (71–72 per cent) and milk (80-81 per cent). For example, the self-sufficient level of rice will be 103 per cent at the baseline of GDP per capita growth rate (6.7 per cent during 2011–15 and 5.9 per cent during 2016–20) and 102 per cent at a higher scenario (7.4 per cent and 7.5 per cent in two periods respectively). Around 95 per cent of wheat demand under the baseline scenario would be met by domestic production and 92 per cent under the high-growth scenario. However, by looking at key grain varieties, we have to recognise potentially huge challenges.

Alarmingly, China turned from a net exporter of rice to a net importer in 2011, with the volume of net import of 78 000 tons. In 2012 the net import skyrocketed to 2.09 million tons.[12] China has become the largest buyer of American agricultural products since 2010 – its import registered at US$17.5 billion which accounted for 15.1 per cent of the US total agricultural export. Up to 2011, China's grain import has accounted for 5.7 per cent of the world total grain import and 19.5 per cent of that of low- and middle-income countries.[13] Suppose China could continue its good appetite with a moderately higher increase rate, i.e. assuming the share of its grain import in the world's total grain import could increase in accordance with its most recent annual growth rate in 2011 (3.4 per cent). China's share of grain import in the world would be 36.4 per cent by 2030, which is almost the limit of a country's import in international trade. This undoubtedly

Table 9.7 Food import, 1985–2011 (10000 tons)

	Total grain	Rice	Wheat	Corn	Soybeans	Edible oil	Sugar	Pork
1985	600.00	–	541.00	9.10	0.10	3.50	191.00	–
1986	773.00	–	611.00	58.80	29.10	19.80	118.00	–
1987	1628.00	–	1320.00	154.20	27.30	51.10	183.00	–
1988	1533.00	31.00	1455.00	10.90	15.20	21.40	371.00	–
1989	1658.00	–	1488.00	6.80	0.10	105.60	158.00	–
1990	1372.00	6.00	1253.00	36.90	0.10	112.00	113.00	–
1991	1345.00	14.00	1237.00	0.10	0.10	61.00	101.00	–
1992	1175.00	1.00	1058.00	–	12.10	42.00	110.00	–
1993	752.00	–	642.00	–	9.90	24.00	45.00	14.09
1994	925.00	51.40	730.00	0.20	5.20	163.00	155.20	18.62
1995	2081.00	164.50	1159.00	526.20	29.40	353.00	295.00	23.33
1996	1200.00	77.40	825.00	44.70	111.40	264.00	125.00	18.55
1997	705.00	35.90	186.00	0.30	280.10	285.00	78.30	15.68
1998	708.00	26.00	149.00	25.20	319.70	205.00	50.80	15.82
1999	772.00	19.10	45.00	7.90	431.70	208.00	42.00	13.25
2000	1357.00	24.90	88.00	0.30	1041.60	179.00	64.10	23.79
2001	1738.00	29.30	69.00	3.90	1394.00	165.00	120.00	20.40
2002	1417.00	23.80	63.00	0.80	1132.00	319.00	118.30	21.95
2003	2283.00	25.90	45.00	0.10	2074.00	514.00	78.00	31.20
2004	2298.00	76.60	726.00	0.20	2023.00	676.00	121.00	29.11
2005	3286.00	52.20	354.00	0.40	2659.00	621.00	139.00	19.98
2006	3189.00	73.00	61.00	6.50	2827.00	671.00	137.00	21.88
2007	3237.00	48.70	10.00	3.50	3082.00	838.00	119.00	47.31
2008	4131.00	33.00	4.00	5.00	3744.00	817.00	78.00	91.39
2009	5223.00	35.70	90.41	8.40	4255.00	816.00	106.00	52.80
2010	6695.00	38.80	123.00	157.30	5480.00	687.00	177.00	90.21
2011	6390.00	59.80	125.81	175.40	5264.00	657.00	292.00	135.04

Note: '–' means no data.

Source: Author's compilation of data from China Rural Statistical Yearbook 2012 and China Agricultural Development Report 2012.

will present a huge challenge for the Chinese government to feed its population and also impact the rest of the world, especially China's trade partners. For example, the new exporter of rice Myanmar, which has seen tripled increases in rice exports over the last 3 years. It sold 1.5 million tons of rice to the world in the 2012–13 fiscal year, an estimated 53 per cent of which was transported to China (Dapice, 2013). One reason for the quickly expanding trade of rice between China and Myanmar could be attributed to rising demand and price of rice in China – the Chinese government raised the domestic rice price from US$272 per ton in 2010 to US$421 in 2013, in contrast to US$200 per ton in Myanmar (Dapice, 2013), partly because of its lower quality compared to that from Thailand and Pakistan. According to the Myanmar Farmer Association, the export volume of rice could soar to 4.3 million tons in the 2019–20 fiscal year.[14] Without bilateral agreements and in the presence of China's price control policy, more rice is pre-

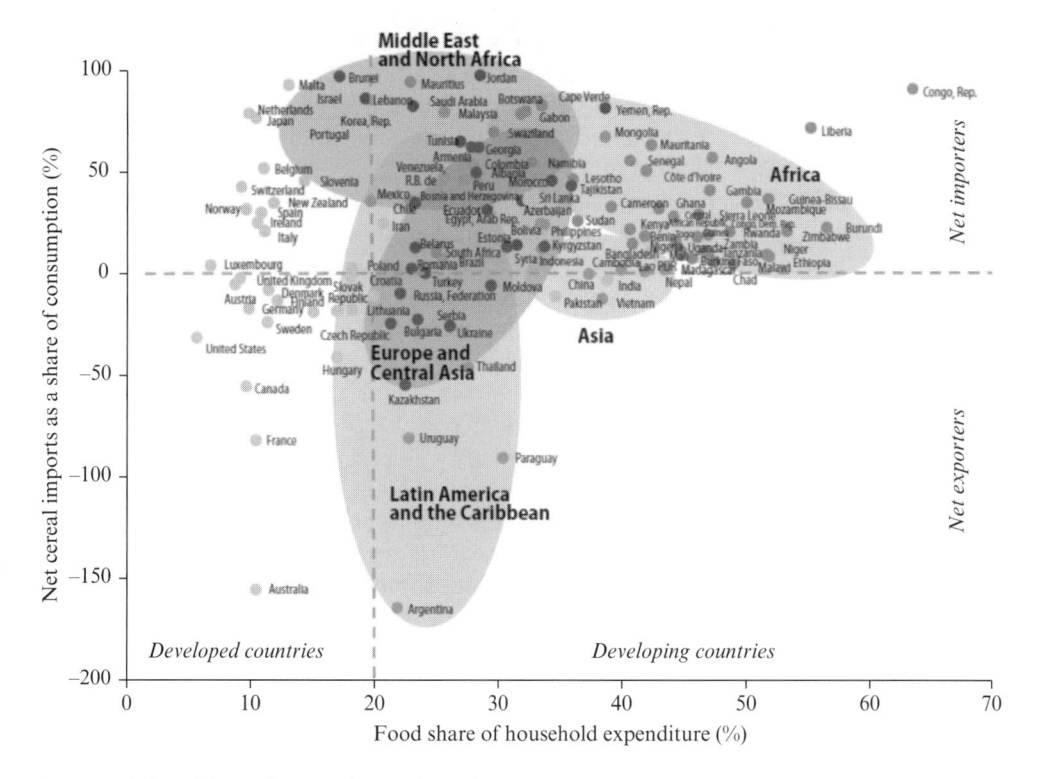

Dietary change, nutrient transition and food security in China 231

Source: Adapted from Figure 1.3 in World Bank (2012).

Figure 9.9 Share of cereal imports in domestic consumption

dicted to be shipped to China in at least the near future (Dapice, 2013). That said, some uncertainties may undermine this speculation. The selling price from Myanmar to China appears to be increasing with a recent record of US$360/ton for 25 per cent broken rice[15] and there would be uncertain import policy for the Yunnan government when faced with more volatile world markets. However, it is unlikely that Myanmar will quickly supersede Vietnam, Pakistan and Thailand, for China because of their advantages of price, quality and convenient and cheap transportation.

It is still unclear to what extent China's rising food consumption can affect the world price and markets. Given the above rough calculations, it could be predicted that China will push forward the world price of agricultural products. However, recent simulations in Huang et al. (2010) show that a 10 per cent increase in China's annual growth rate of GDP would increase its food and feed net import by US$3 billion in 2020, which would lift world prices, and China's trade share of food and feed crops in the world would be 10.3 per cent under the high GDP growth scenario. Other countries, especially exporters, would benefit from higher world prices and from adjusting their production structure as a response to China's growth, e.g. increasing their agricultural production by 0.1–0.5 per cent. However, countries such as India with similar export structures to China would be hurt slightly. The authors also argue that cereal demand will not be able to keep its increasing momentum as 'all cereal grains will have negative income elasticities' (Huang et al., 2010: 52). However, we may not be so positive because households' food consumption is still sensitive to both own-prices, as listed in Tables 9.2 and 9.3 in section 9.2, and relative prices (Zhong et al., 2012). We also have to take into account the remaining 157 million poor people in rural areas holding relatively high food-demand elasticities of income.[16]

Given the difficulties of making significant scientific breakthroughs in agricultural technology, it is of paramount importance to maintain sufficient cultivated land for food production. The current arable land per capita in China appears to be insufficient to support a diet satisfying basic nutrient requirements. For example, according to Zhen et al.'s (2010) estimate for Guyuan district in Gansu province, per capita rural arable land needed to meet the basic requirement of various nutrients is 1520 m², while the average for rural China was only 392 m². Moreover, along with the huge challenge of food security, the total sown land allocated to grain crops keeps shrinking year by year. As illustrated by Figure 9.10, 73 per cent of sown land was used to plant various grain crops, mainly rice and wheat, while roughly 50 per cent of total sown land was left to plant grain crops. In contrast, the areas for vegetables were doubled. There are also changing structures within grain crop planting. Over time more corn but less rice and wheat were planted, which might also explain China's expanded import of rice and wheat from the supply side. More alarmingly, farming land is giving way to fast urbanisation promoted by the Chinese government. The rate of urbanisation measured by the share of population permanently living in urban areas in the total population rose consistently from to 29 per cent in 1995 to 51.27 per cent in 2011.[17] More farmland has been transferred and developed for the purpose of urban construction. Together with soil erosion, land contamination, natural disasters and, after 2000, large-scale ecological restoration, the total areas of arable land in China have shrunk by 8.6 per cent, from 122.1 million hectares in 1995 to 111.6 million in 2011.[18] The arable land per capita dropped by 18 per cent, from 0.101 hectares per person in 1995 to 0.083 in 2011 which was only 41.5 per cent of the world average. The total cultivated land used for rice and wheat declined by 2.2 per cent and 16 per cent, respectively, over the same period.[19]

9.4.2 Food Market Interventions in China

Price regulations

The Chinese government has utilised price regulations as an instrument to manage food supply and markets. Complete price control was not abandoned until 1993. The government had kept the purchasing price at no more than 50 per cent of the market price (Brandt and Holz, 2006), which led to low income and high poverty incidence for rural households. Since the mid-1990s, the government has attempted to reconcile purchasing and market prices for agricultural products. The government's purchasing prices were lifted quickly. Take rice, for instance. The real purchasing price was 274.6 yuan per ton (at 1978 price levels) in 1995, which was less than half of the real market price 472.7 yuan, but rose quickly to 334.9 yuan in 1997 and was higher than the market price of 309.8.[20] Consequently, rural households' per capita income increased and the poverty incidence experienced the fastest reduction (Chen and Ravallion, 2010).

Price regulation, import protection and limiting exports of major grains have helped China maintain stable domestic food prices when faced with rising and volatile global

(a) 1995

- Others 5.41%
- Vegetables 6.35%
- Tobacco 0.98%
- Sugar crops 1.21%
- Fiber crops 0.25%
- Cotton 3.62%
- Oil-bearing crops 8.74%
- Grain crops 73.43%

- Rice 20.51%
- Wheat 19.26%
- Corn 15.20%
- Soybeans 7.49%
- Tubers 6.35%
- Other crops 4.62%

(b) 2011

- Others 5.95%
- Vegetables 12.10%
- Tobacco 0.90%
- Sugar crops 1.20%
- Fiber crops 0.07%
- Cotton 3.10%
- Oil-bearing crops 8.54%
- Grain crops 49.61%

- Rice 18.52%
- Wheat 14.96%
- Corn 20.67%
- Soybeans 6.56%
- Tubers 5.49%
- Other crops 1.94%

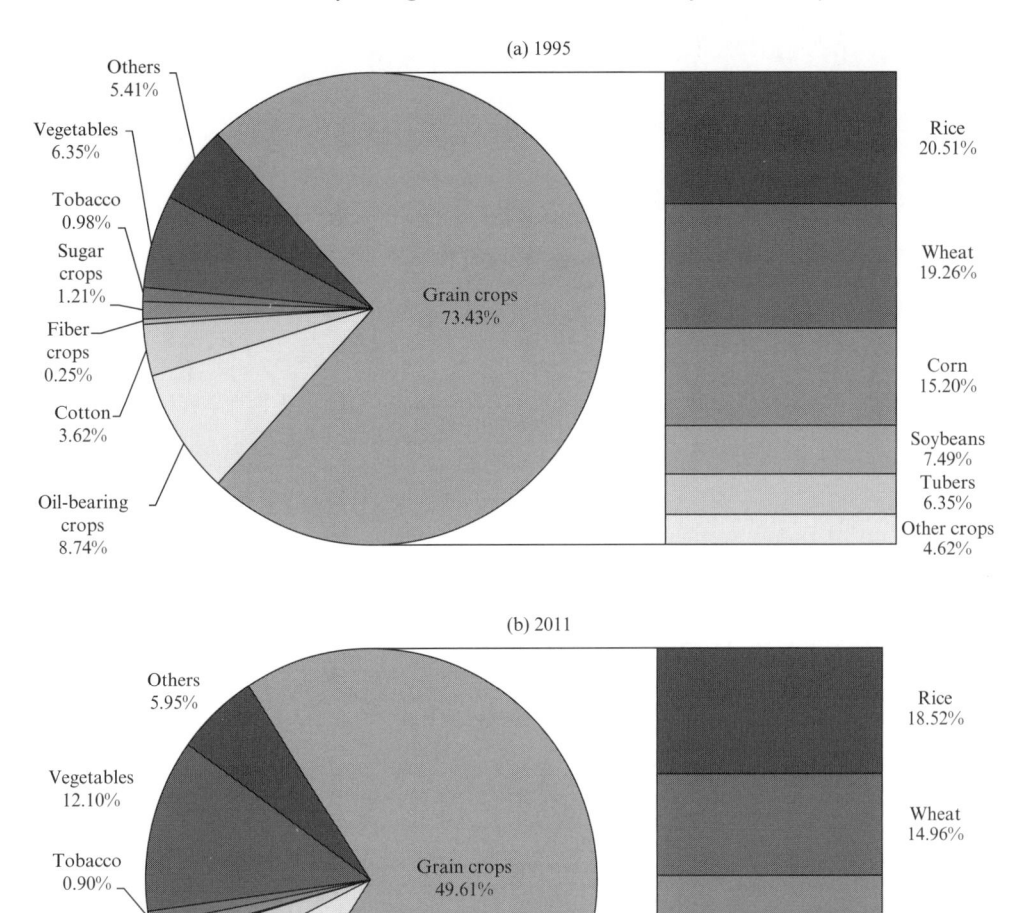

Source: China Statistical Yearbook 2012 published by the NBS.

Figure 9.10 Farming structures of major crops, 1995–2011

food prices (Yang et al., 2008; Yu and Abler, 2009; World Bank, 2012). It can be seen from Figure 9.11 that domestic prices of major grain products like rice, wheat and corn seemed to be less responsive to global prices. During the food price spike from the 2nd quarter of 2007 to the 2nd quarter of 2008, only 22 per cent of international rice price was passed through to China's domestic market prices as opposed to 25 per cent in India,

234 *Handbook on food*

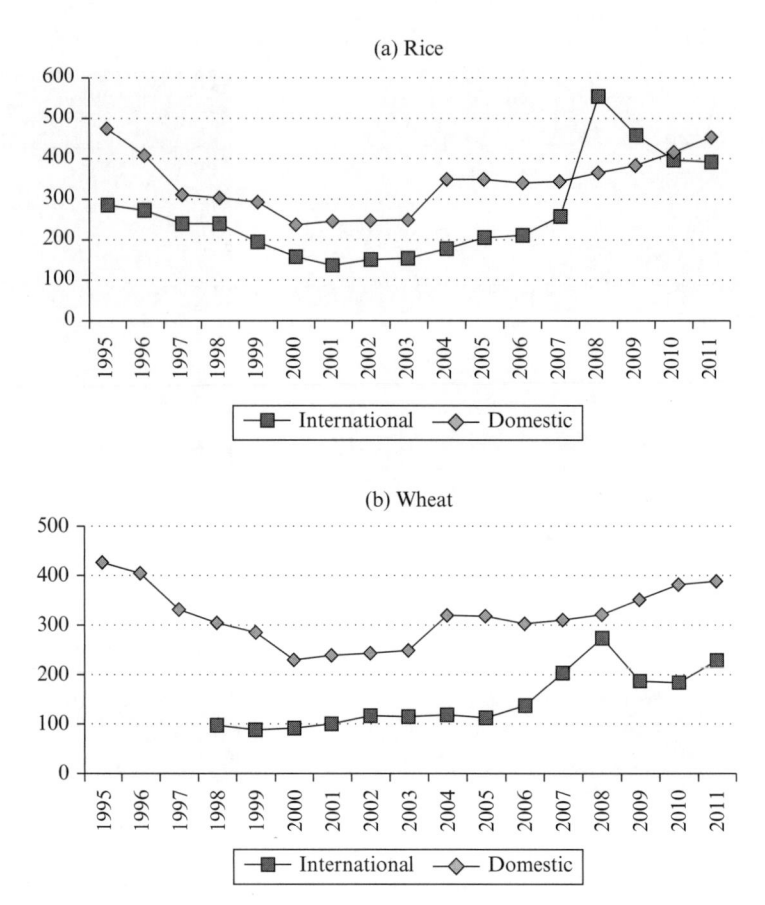

(a) Rice

(b) Wheat

Notes:
Price of rice is the average of early-, middle-, late-season and japonica rice. Price of other goods is for their mediumquality. All domestic prices are the average of 160 counties whose prices are monitored by the Ministry of Agriculture and are issued in the China Agricultural Development Report 2012. International prices are all free on board (FOB) ones. The goods taken as the international reference price are the FOB prices of 100% B-level rice at Bangkok, No. 2 hard red winter wheat, No. 2 yellow corn, and No. 1 yellow beans. Purchasing power parity (PPP)used to exchange the US dollars to yuan and then, used the national Consumer Price Index (CPI) to translate nominal yuan to the real values at the 1978 constant price level. Data on PPP conversion ratio and the official market exchange rate are from World Bank World Development Indicators. The domestic national CPI (1978 = 100) is drawn from China Statistical Yearbook 2012.

Source: Author's calculation.

Figure 9.11 Market prices of food, 1995–2011 (yuan/ton, yuan at 1978 price)

55 per cent in Bangladesh, 63 per cent in the Philippines and 98 per cent in Cambodia (World Bank, 2012). China's low vulnerability to global food price shocks may benefit from its zero dependence on imports when the food crisis hit, as shown previously in Figure 9.9. The only exception is soybeans for which the above policy instruments are not available (Yang et al., 2008). The domestic price of soybeans has closely followed the international price since 2004 (Figure 9.11d).

(c) Corn

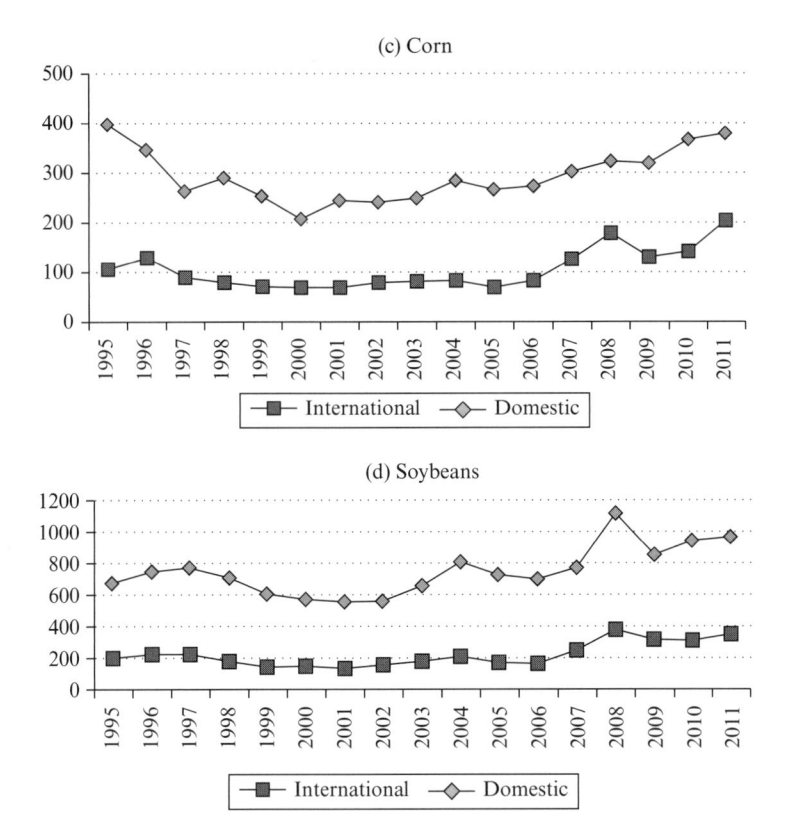

(d) Soybeans

Figure 9.11 (continued)

Notwithstanding, food prices in China are not immune to the rising trend of food prices around the world. The prices of agricultural products have risen fast since the early 2000s (Figure 9.12). The prices of grain and forestry products rose more than 10-fold between 1978 and 2011. Figure 9.13 shows that the driving forces of rising prices of agricultural products appear to be the supply side, including higher oil price which rose nearly 12-fold since 1978, and more costly labour and chemical fertilisers. According to the forecasts from CASS (2013), the prices of inputs will continue to grow in 2013 at a rate of 8 per cent and so will food consumption – their forecast of the annual growth rate is 7 per cent driven mainly by vegetables (10 per cent) and grain (8 per cent). Moreover, as mentioned earlier, the Chinese government began to raise the purchasing prices of agricultural products in the mid-1990s in order to increase farmers' income. This could also contribute to increased prices.

Relatively high and stable grain prices do help promote production. Yu et al.'s (2012) estimation of farmers' yields elasticity of own-price is 0.27 in the short term and 0.81 in the long term.[21] The policy aimed at raising agricultural prices since 2004 does provide incentives for farmers to increase grain production. The average amount of grain sold by a rural household nearly doubled between 2004 (287.2 kg) and 2011 (481.5 kg).[22]

236   *Handbook on food*

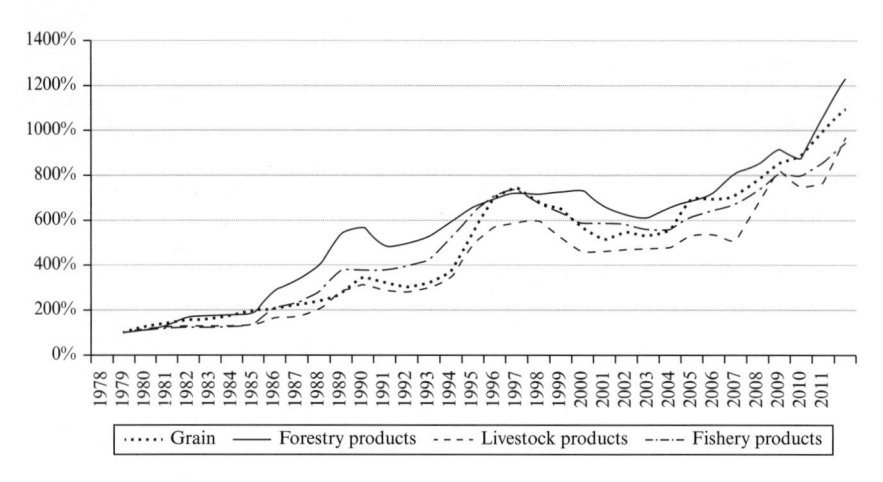

Source: China Agricultural Products Statistical Yearbook 2012 published by the NBS.

Figure 9.12   Price indices of agricultural products (1978 = 100%)

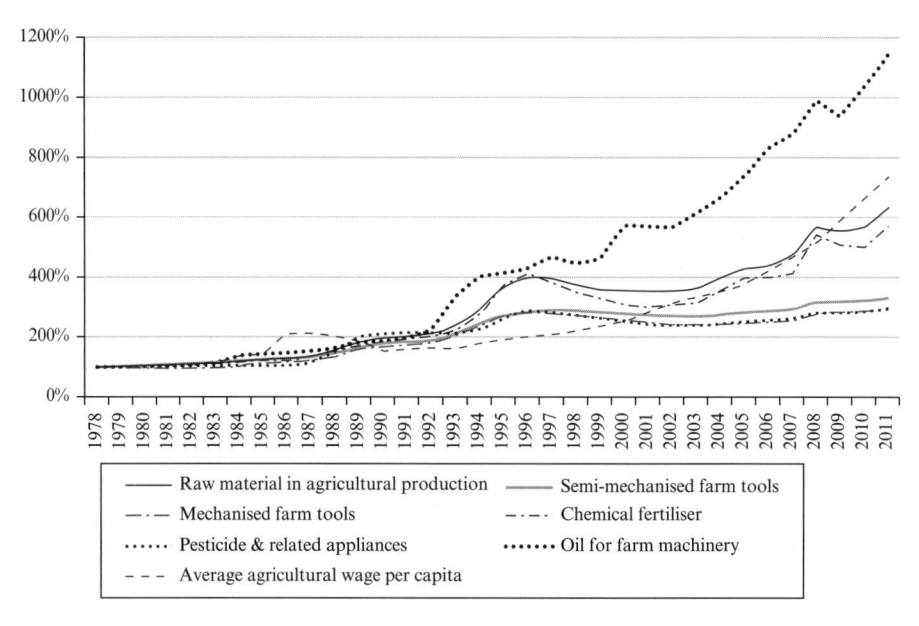

Source: Author's calculation based on data from various issues of China Statistical Yearbooks published by the NBS.

Figure 9.13   Price indices of inputs in agricultural production, 1978–2011 (1978 = 100%)

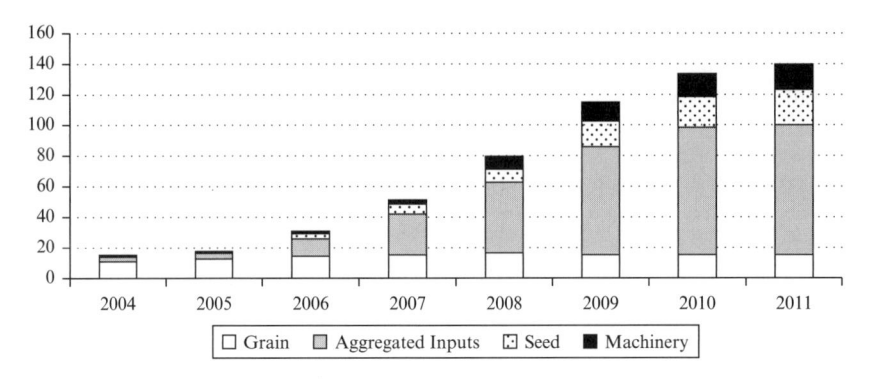

Source: National Bureau of Statistics, adopted Figure 1 in Huang et al. (2013).

Figure 9.14 Agricultural subsidies (billion yuan)

Agricultural subsidies

The national guided agricultural tax was initially set at 15.5 per cent of the monetary value of the annual yield and the local governments were enabled to adjust it no higher than 25 per cent. The average agricultural tax rate declined gradually to 8 per cent for grain and 8–10 per cent for vegetables and fruits in the early 2000s. In 2004, China began to transform its longstanding agricultural policy from taxing farmers to subsidising them, for the purpose of enhancing national grain self-sufficiency and raising farmers' income, and abolished agricultural taxes throughout the country in 2006. There were nearly zero subsidies before 2002, while a sharp increase from US$12.1 million in 2002 to US$22.3 billion in 2011 (Figure 9.14), constituting at least 2.9 per cent of agricultural GDP.

A national representative dataset suggests that about 87 per cent of farm households in rural China received subsidies in 2008 (Huang et al., 2013). On the per acre cultivated land basis, China is arguably the major subsidiser in the world. Huang et al.'s (2013) dataset shows that the sum of subsidies actually received by farmers was US$34.4 per acre in 2008, which is equivalent to agricultural subsidies received by a typical farmer in Illinois (US$30–50 per acre) at the same time. However, given that land holdings and farming in China is fragmented among smallholders, the total amount of subsidies received by Chinese farmers is still far below that of American farmers. An average Chinese farm household in 2008 had 8.4 mu of contract land (approximately 1.4 acre) and the typical grain and input subsidies for a farm household was 327 yuan.[23] This means that subsidies contribute 1.7 per cent of household income for an average farming household with four members and this proportion is 7.6–10.4 per cent for the poor and the ultra-poor measured by the national poverty lines. Over the period 2003–08, subsidies for grain production increased from US$4–10 per acre to US$36–48 per acre. Rice received the highest subsidies, while the lowest were applied to maize. Seed and machinery subsidies began to expand quickly in 2008 (Figure 9.13) and the No. 1 Central Document 2012 further planned to extend subsidies programmes to non-grain production such as livestock and fishery industries in the near future. Although subsidies are high, grain and input subsidies do not appear to distort farmers' production decisions in terms of sown areas and input use (Huang et al., 2011) and cereal price subsidies helped the poor increase calories intake from fat and protein by enhancing their purchasing power (Shimokawa, 2010).

9.5 HOW TO ADDRESS CHALLENGES OF NUTRIENT SHIFT, FOOD SUSTAINABILITY AND SECURITY IN CHINA

At the individual level, Ruel and Alderman (2013) summarise the attributes of nutritional status from the perspectives of agriculture, social safety nets, early child development and schooling. In China, where agricultural production still dominates rural households' livelihood, agriculture should receive the greatest attention from policy makers. Boosting agricultural production, especially targeted agricultural programmes, keeping (real) food prices low and affordable for the poor, and increasing income are all undisputable paradigms for nutrition-sensitive programmes – they have been justified by the changes of Chinese dietary pattern and the estimation of the demand and supply elasticities of income and price. Moreover, farmers are better connected to markets in the process of economic reforms which creates not only opportunities, but also intensified transmission from retail prices of grain to farmgate prices. The price transmission elasticities of rice vary from 0.542 in Sichuan to 0.868 in Jiangsu which is the main production area; wheat and maize have similar estimation; apple, citrus and pork experience the highest transmission elasticities, higher than 1 (Liu et al., 2012). Nutrition-sensitive programmes by means of agriculture will need to be complemented by safety nets policies to cushion intensified risk and shocks transmitted to farmers.

Given severe child malnutrition in poor rural China, the current policy interventions include provincial governments providing one egg a day per child in Shaanxi and Ningxia provinces from 2009–10. The local leaders began to recognise the importance of treating micronutrient deficiencies after the publication of a series of reports (e.g. Lou et al., 2005). However, Kleiman-Weiner et al. (2013) find that giving children chewable vitamins rather than the 'one-egg-a-day' policy has significant impact on child nutrition, but local governments are reluctant to hand out vitamins. Food fortification programmes may suffer from lack of sustainable financial support from local governments. There is still debate and trials are investigating which method would improve child nutritional status in the long term. There are also issues surrounding persuading the government to take actions in the long term which have been proved to be effective by recent empirical research rather than imaginary policy intervention like the 'one-egg' campaign.

At the macro-level, agriculture may also hold the key to understanding and addressing issues relating to food sustainability and security. The role of agriculture in development has recently regained attention. Cross-country empirical studies and literature review show that agriculture is an effective means to lift people's living standard, especially in an early stage of development. The marginal impact of growth in agricultural sector on reducing the poverty gap measured against US$1/day is more than five-times bigger than that of growth in other sectors (Christaensen et al., 2011; Imai et al., 2012). As the economy develops, expanded non-agricultural sectors along with industrialisation and urbanisation would contribute more to income growth than the relatively small-sized agricultural sector (Christaensen et al., 2011), especially the skilled non-farm employment as found by Imai et al. (2013) in rural India and Vietnam, while the rcent food crisis keeps agriculture in a broadened development agenda (de Janvry, 2010).

In the Chinese context, a 1 per cent increase in agricultural growth would bring about 0.45 per cent more aggregate growth, as opposed to 0.2 per cent if additional increase takes place in non-agricultural sectors (de Janvry and Sadoulet, 2009). Agricultural growth also contributes most to poverty reduction compared to industry and services sectors and unbalanced growth across three sectors deters the speed of poverty reduction (Ravallion and Chen, 2007; Montalvo and Ravallion, 2010). By means of agricultural growth, households can escape poverty and therefore be more able to afford food consumption and cope with various risks and shocks that stem from food price volatility, less developed insurance arrangements and market failures (Dethier and Effenberger, 2013).

Agriculture also plays a role in directly addressing food security as the supply side of food. As reviewed in sections 9.2 and 9.3, Chinese diets are changing towards more animal products, oil and sugar, while reduced cereal consumption leads to lower calorie intake. The shifting preference towards animal products in food consumption requires more agricultural products and land to feed the livestock than those under the traditional diets relying more on coarse grains. This pattern requires more agricultural output than the traditional diets. The government should pay attention to ensure growth of agricultural output in order to maintain high self-sufficiency in food. Then, the question boils down to how to achieve a sustained food supply. Based on China's situation presented in previous sections and the Central Government's policy, there are three major ways adopted or planned in China.

First, the No. 1 Central Document 2012 announced the government's major efforts were to push agricultural technological innovation, and this year's document further puts food security at the top of the agenda. According to Mr Xiwen Chen, the Deputy Head of Central Rural Work Group of the State Council, 53.5 per cent of yield increases in 2011 were attributable to agricultural technological innovation, while this share still fell far behind developed countries, and the harvest of half of cultivated land still depended entirely on the weather.[24] The Document stated more funds allocated to research on agricultural technology. The goal of agricultural capacity building set by the No. 1 Central Document 2012 is to achieve 50 million tons of annual increases in grain output. Furthermore, the 2013 Document explicitly emphasises the first priority of food security for China's agricultural policy and commits to continuing support for agricultural technological innovation. Yu et al.'s (2012) simulation based on the county-level data from 1998 to 2007 also justifies this policy by identifying a positive impact of agricultural research on grain yields.

Second, given difficulties in technological breakthrough in the short-term, more agricultural output requires more arable land. Considering this, in a recent report in 2012, the State Council set up a minimum threshold of cultivated land at 1.8 billion mu (approximately equivalent to 120 million hectares) to secure by 2020, in order to assure the volume of agricultural production in the future.

It is worth noting two matters relating to this policy of farmland protection. In addition to securing the total area of arable land, the government should pay attention to the use and transfer of land in China's fast urbanisation process. Additionally, loss of soil quality caused by pollution and environmental degradation is more severe than that caused by expanded cities. The arable land converted to urban use in the last two decades is less than 2.8 million hectares, as opposed to 20 million hectares under heavy metal contamination alone (Stage et al., 2010). The latter 'loss' of arable land is more detrimental to food security not only in quantity but also in quality.

Third, the government will continue to practise price and subsidies policy. The No. 1 Central Document 2012 planned to expand the price monitor and regulation from grain to fresh agricultural products such as vegetables, fruits and pigs. The 2013 Document announces further increases in subsidies direct to farmers, especially machinery subsidies and subsidies and tax exemption for overseas fisheries, and increase bonuses for counties with higher grain, edible oil and livestock (especially pigs) output.

While these policies seem appropriate given China's situation, there appears to emerge an inevitable conflict between food security and environmental conservation that is worth mentioning. The Grain for Green programmes in China aimed at restoring forests and grass-lands. The pilot programmes took place in 1999 and were extended to 20 provinces in 2001. This campaign is one of the main reasons for decreased areas of cultivated land.[25] By using the household survey conducted in the first 3 years after implementation, Xu et al. (2006) do not find significant threat of Grain for Green programmes to grain yields: they only accounted for 4.5 per cent and 4.6 per cent) of decreases in wheat and maize production, respectively, and no effect on rice. By contrast, Uchida et al.'s (2009) study documents significant shift of labour allocation from on- to off-farm work based on a survey conducted after 5 years. It could be conjectured that, as the programmes spread, participants would have sufficient time to find off-farm jobs and quit agricultural production. The government is expected to play a role in this process to utilise properly the farmland that would be contracted out or transferred by those households.

A more viable solution to ensure food supply would be a package of agricultural policies rather than a simple list of goals and policy interventions. For example, although price or subsidies per se can encourage farm households, they continue to suffer from various external shocks such as weather and potential price spikes transmitted from the international markets (e.g. Yu et al., 2012). Policy instruments such as price, regulation and subsidies would be better complemented by other policy instruments such as better rural construction (to facilitate integration of agricultural markets and farmers' response to prices) and insurance arrangements (to help farmers cope with weather shocks). As another example, when the government embarks on securing arable land, environmental protection should also be emphasised.

More importantly, as an important aspect of 'package agricultural policy', we should recognise the role of agricultural interventions in improving nutrition health (e.g. Fan and Brzeska, 2011; Hawkes et al., 2012). There are three pathways through which agriculture affects nutrition and health outcomes: development, own-production and market pathways (Dorward, 2013). Agricultural growth would increase farmers' income, i.e. building their development capacity, which in turn would lead to better individual education, health, sanitation and other investment that would lead to improved food utilisation.[26] The own-production pathway emphasises the impact of farmers' increased income from food or non-food sales on their consumption of own-produced foods. Changes of food supply in the market will affect prices and consumers' food demand behaviour, i.e. the market pathway. Both of the pathways attempt to link the individual basket (*cai lan zi*) to agriculture in a broader context, which would allow the government to maintain food security and to improve people's nutrition and health simultaneously.

Admittedly, there are still many details that need ironing out, and operating the agriculture–nutrition link requires more empirical analyses. For example, when introducing support for agriculture, the government should be aware of and deal with the possible rise of obesity and other non-communicable diseases (Webb and Block, 2011); more research would clarify the relation between the composition of agricultural production and the composition of diets (Headey et al., 2012).

NOTES

1. Data from the monthly Statistical Bulletin from the General Administration of Customs of P.R. China.
2. The figures in this paragraph are real terms in 2011 yuan and are author's calculations based on data from *China Statistical Yearbook 1996* and *2012* published by the National Bureau of Statistics (NBS).
3. The Engel coefficient is defined as the proportion of income spent in food consumption.
4. Their model allows for correlated errors across food items as consumers' behavioural representation and across equations of a single commodity system as the market effects, but the constant correlation by assumption does not consider a shift of demand curve over time.
5. The only exception is the income elasticity of wheat in rural Jiangsu in Carter and Zhong (1999) (the first row of Table 9.2). The authors find that high income households tend to substitute away from wheat toward rice and meat and ascribe this phenomenon to the preference towards a more diversified diet for households in rural Jiangsu who had formerly consumed much wheat (68 kg per capita).
6. Author's calculation based on data from *China Statistical Yearbook 2012* published by the NBS and China Macroeconomy Database at GTA.
7. A complete HEI consists of 12 nutrients which are collected by using 24-hour recalls of dietary intake in national surveys in the United States. It should be noted that HEI-2005 and HEI-2010 incorporate different kinds of nutrients, although there are 12 nutrients in total. Each component is assigned some points from 5 to 20 if its intake meets certain standards which can be found at http://riskfactor.cancer.gov/tools/hei/comparing.html (accessed 11 August 2013). The Chinese HEI in Shimokawa (2013) contains eight components due to data limitation in the CHNS. They are total fruits (10 points), total vegetables (10 points), total grains (10 points), milk and milk products (10 points), meat and beans (10 points), oils (10 points), share of calories from total fat (10 points) and share of calories from solid fat, alcoholic beverages and sugars (20 points).
8. Author's calculation based on data from *China Statistical Yearbook 2012* published by the NBS.
9. The prices of grain rose by 16.7–46.6 per cent per annum from 1993 to 1995. There was a similar upward trend for the prices of livestock products with an annual growth rate of 14.2–44.6 per cent over the same period. The prices of fruits and vegetables increased by 13.7–35 per cent per annum, which was only marginally lower than those of grain and livestock products. Substitutions among them might be limited. Data come from *China Statistical Yearbook 1997* published by the NBS.
10. Tang and Li (2012) calculate households' grain consumption as the population weighted sum of urban and rural households' grain consumption. Urban households' grain consumption includes those purchased from the markets and those converted from their expenditure on eating out. Rural households' grain consumption includes self-produced and purchased grain. Relevant data come from various issues of *China Statistical Yearbook* and *China Yearbook of Household Survey* published by the NBS, and China Agricultural Development Report published by the Ministry of Agriculture.
11. From the interview for Mr Xiwen Chen, the Deputy Head of Central Rural Work Group of the State Council. Available at http://china.caixin.com/2013-02-01/100488841.html [in Chinese, accessed 25 July 2013].
12. Author's calculation based on data from Statistical Bulletin of China's Economy, March 2013, China Data Centre, University of Michigan.
13. Author's calculation based on data from World Bank World Development Indicators.
14. http://myanmarfarmer.org/?q=node/39 [accessed 31 July 2013].
15. http://www.mmtimes.com/index.php/business/4247-myanmar-s-paddy-rice-price-keeps-up-with-china-rise.html [accessed 31 July, 2013].

16. The World Development Indicators at the World Bank suggest that 11.8 per cent of population lived below US$1.25/day in 2009. Here the number of the poor is the product of this poverty rate and the total population in 2009 reported in *China Statistical Yearbook 2012*.
17. Data from *China Statistical Yearbook 2012*.
18. Author's calculation based on data from World Bank World Development Indicators.
19. Author's calculation based on data from *China Statistical Yearbook 2012*.
20. Data source and calculations are the same as the note of Figure 9.8.
21. The elasticity of relative price is also positive, indicating that increasing agricultural prices relative to other non-agricultural goods can also encourage farmers to expand production.
22. Data from *China Statistical Yearbook 2012* and *2005*.
23. It varies substantially across provinces. In Huang et al. (2013), Sichuan saw the lowest average grain subsidies of 50 yuan but the highest input subsidies of 229 yuan, while the input subsidies were the lowest in Zhejiang, 30 yuan.
24. His interview can be found at http://english.cntv.cn/program/newsupdate/20120202/121588.shtml [accessed 25 July 2013].
25. For example, about 30 per cent (39 per cent) of reduction of sown land of wheat (maize) between 1999 and 2003 were because of the implementation of Grain for Green programmes. However, the sown areas of rice were by and large unaffected.
26. It is noticeable that income alone cannot improve directly nutritional intake. As shown in Table 9.6, income elasticities of micronutrients are small and even statistically insignificant for the poor. Here the development path should be better understood as the 'indirect' impact of income on nutrition through capacity building.

REFERENCES

ADB (2010), *Key indicators for Asia and the Pacific: The Rise of Asia's Middle Class*. Manila, Philippines: Asian Development Bank.
Alderman, H. (2012), The response of child nutrition to changes in income: linking biology with economics. *CESifo Economic Studies*, **58**, 256–73.
Bai, J., T.I. Wahl, B.T. Lohmar and J. Huang (2010), Food away from home in Beijing: effects of wealth, time and 'free' meals. *China Economic Review*, **21**, 432–41.
Behrman, J.R. and A.B. Deolalikar (1987), Will developing country nutrition improve with income? A case study for rural south India. *Journal of Political Economy*, **95**, 108–138.
Bhandari, R. and F.J. Smith (2000), Education and food consumption patterns in China: household analysis and policy implications. *Journal of Nutrition Education*, **32**, 214–24.
Bishop, J.A., H. Liu and B. Zheng (2010), Rising incomes and nutritional inequality in China. In J.A. Bishop (ed.), *Research on Economic Inequality*. Bingley, UK: Emerald Group Publishing Limited, pp. 257–66.
Brandt, L. and C.A. Holz (2006), Spatial price differences in China: estimates and implications. *Economic Development and Cultural Change*, **55**, 43–86.
Capacci, S., M. Mazzocchi and Y. Liu (2008), Diet quality and income in rural and urban China: evidence from the health and nutrition survey. Paper presented at the European Association of Agricultural Economists 2008 International Congress, 26–29 August 2008, Ghent, Belgium.
Carter, C.A. and F. Zhong (1999), Rural wheat consumption in China. *American Journal of Agricultural Economics*, **81**, 582–92.
CASS (2013), *Green Book of Rural Area: Analysis and Forecast on China's Rural Economy (2012–2013)*. Beijing: Chinese Academy of Social Sciences (CASS) and the Department of Rural Social and Economic Survey at National Bureau of Statistics.
Chen, S. and M. Ravallion (2010), China is poorer than we thought, but no less successful in the fight against poverty. In S. Anand, P. Segal and J.E. Stiglitz (eds), *Debates on the Measurement of Global Poverty*. Oxford: Oxford University Press, Chapter 13.
Christaensen, L., L. Demery and J. Kuhl (2011), The (evolving) role of agriculture in poverty reduction: an empirical perspective. *Journal of Development Economics*, **96**, 239–54.
Dapice, D. (2013), Rice policy in Myanmar: it's getting complicated. Occasional Papers, ASH Center, Harvard University. Available at: http://www.ash.harvard.edu/extension/ash/docs/RicePolicy.pdf (accessed 31 July 2013).
Dasgupta, P. and D. Ray (1986), Inequality as a determinant of malnutrition and unemployment: theory. *The Economic Journal*, **96**, 1011–1034.
de Brauw, A. and J. Giles (2008), Migrant labor markets and the welfare of rural households in the develop-

ing world: evidence from China. The World Bank Policy Research Working Paper, No. 4585, World Bank, Washington DC.
de Brauw, A. and R. Mu (2011), Migration and the overweight and underweight status of children in rural China. *Food Policy*, **36**, 88–100.
de Brauw, A. and S. Rozelle (2008), Migration and household investment in rural China. *China Economic Review*, **19**, 320–35.
de Janvry, A. (2010), Agriculture for development: new paradigm and options for success. *Agricultural Economics*, **41**(s1), 17–36.
de Janvry, A. and A. Sadoulet (2009), Agricultural growth and poverty reduction: additional evidence. *World Bank Research Observer*, **25**, 1–20.
Dethier, J. and A. Effenberger (2013), Agriculture and development: a brief review of the literature. *Economic Systems*, **36**, 175–205.
Dong, F. and F. Fuller (2010), Dietary structural change in China's cities: empirical fact or urban legend. *Canadian Journal of Agricultural Economics*, **58**, 73–91.
Dorward, A. (2013), How can agricultural interventions contribute in improving nutrition health and achieving the MDGs in least developed countries? CeDEP (Centre for Development, Environment and Policy) Working Paper. Available at: http://www.lcirah.ac.uk/sites/default/files/Dorward%202013%20Agri%20Nutrition%20Working%20Paper.pdf (accessed 23 July 2013).
Du, S., T.A. Mroz, F. Zhai and B.M. Popkin (2004), Rapid income growth adversely affects diet quality in China: particularly for the poor! *Social Science & Medicine*, **59**, 1505–1515.
Du, Y., A. Park, and S. Wang (2005), Migration and rural poverty in China. *Journal of Comparative Economics*, **33**, 688–709.
Ecker, O., C. Breisinger and K. Pauw (2012), Growth is good, but is not enough to improve nutrition. In S. Fan and R. Pandya-Lorch (eds.), *Reshaping Agriculture for Nutrition and Health*. Washington DC: IFPRI, pp. 47–54. Available at: www.ifpri.org/sites/default/files/publications/oc69.pdf.
Fan, S. and J. Brzeska (2011), The nexus between agriculture and nutrition: do growth patterns and conditional factors matter? In S. Fan and R. Pandya-Lorch (eds), *Reshaping Agriculture for Nutrition and Health*. Washington DC: IFPRI, pp. 31–38. Available at: www.ifpri.org/sites/default/files/publications/oc69.pdf.
Fan, S., E. Wailes and G. Cramer (1995), Household demand in rural China: a two-state LES–AIDS model. *American Journal of Agricultural Economics*, **77**, 54–62.
Fuller, F., J. Huang, H. Ma and S. Rozelle (2006), Got milk? The rapid rise of China's dairy sector and its future prospects. *Food Policy*, **31**, 201–215.
Gaiha, R., Jha, R. and V.S. Kulkarni (2013), How pervasive is eating out in India? *Journal of Asian and African Studies*, **48**, 370–86.
Gale, F., P. Tang, X. Bai and H. Xu (2005), Commercialization of food consumption in rural China. Research Report Number 8, United States Department of Agriculture Economic Research Service, Washington DC.
Gale, H. and K. Huang (2007), Demand for Food Quantity and Quality in China. USDA Economic Research Report, No. 32.
Gould, B.W. and H.J. Villarreal (2006), An assessment of the current structure of food demand in urban China. *Agricultural Economics*, **34**, 1–6.
Guenther, P.M., J. Reedy, S.M. Krebs-Smith, B.B. Reeve and P.P. Basiotis (2008), *Development and Evaluation of the Healthy Eating Index, 2005*. Washington DC: Center for Nutrition Policy and Promotion, US Department of Agriculture.
Guo, X., T.A. Mroz, B.M. Popkin and F. Zhai (2000), Structural change in the impact of income on food consumption in China, 1989–1993. *Economic Development and Cultural Change*, **48**, 737–60.
Haddad, L., H. Alderman, S. Appleton, L. Song and Y. Yohannes (2003), Reducing child malnutrition: how far does income growth take us? *World Bank Economic Review*, **17**, 107–131.
Hannum, E., J. Liu and E.A. Frongillo (2012), Poverty, food insecurity and nutritional deprivation in rural China: implications for children's literacy achievement. *International Journal of Educational Development*. DOI: http://dx.doi.org/10.1016/j.ijedudev.2012.07.003. First published online on 3 July 2012.
Hawkes, C., R. Turner and J. Waage (2012), Current and planned research on agriculture for improved nutrition: a mapping and a gap analysis. Report for DFID, London.
Headey, D. (2013), Developmental drivers of nutritional change: a cross-country analysis. *World Development*, **42**, 76–88.
Headey, D., A. Chiu and S. Kadiyala (2012), Agriculture's role in the Indian enigma: help or hindrance to the crisis of undernutrition? *Food Security*, **4**, 87–102.
Hovhannisyan, V. and B.W. Gould (2011), Quantifying the structure of food demand in China: an econometric approach. *Agricultural Economics*, **42**, 1–17.
Hovhannisyan, V. and B.W. Gould (2013), Structural change in urban Chinese food preferences. *Agricultural Economics*. First published online on 27 June 2013. DOI: 10.1111/agec.12038.

Huang, J. and S. Rozelle (1998), Market Development and Food Consumption in Rural China. *China Economic Review* **9**, 25–45.

Huang, J. and S. Rozelle (2006), The emergence of agricultural commodity markets in China. *China Economic Review*, **17**, 266–80.

Huang, J., J. Yang and S. Rozelle, (2010), China's agriculture: drivers of change and implications for China and the rest of world. *Agricultural Economics*, **41**, 47–55.

Huang, J., X. Wang, H. Zhi and S. Rozelle (2011), Subsidies and distortions in China's agriculture: evidence from producer-level data. *Australian Journal of Agricultural and Resource Economics*, **55**, 53–71.

Huang, J., X. Wang and S. Rozelle (2013), The subsidization of farming households in China's agriculture. *Food Policy*, **41**, 124–32.

Huang, K.S. and F. Gale (2009), Food demand in China: income, quality, and nutrient effects. *China Agricultural Economics Review*, **1**, 395–409.

Imai, K., R. Gaiha and G. Thapa (2012), Role of agriculture in achieving MDG1 in the Asia and the Pacific region. Occasional Papers 14, IFAD, Rome.

Imai, K., R. Gaiha and G. Thapa (2013), Does non-farm sector employment reduce rural poverty and vulnerability? Evidence from Vietnam and India. RIEB Discussion Paper Series DP2012-25, Kobe University.

Jha, R., R. Gaiha and A. Sharma (2009), Calorie and micronutrient deprivation and poverty nutrition traps in rural India. *World Development*, 37, 982–91.

Jiang, B. and J. Davis (2007), Household food demand in rural China. *Applied Economics*, **39**(3), 373–380.

Kleiman-Weiner, M., R. Luo, L. Zhang, Y. Shi, A. Medina and S. Rozelle (2013), Eggs versus chewable vitamins: which intervention can increase nutrition and test scores in rural China? *China Economic Review*, **24**, 166–76.

Lin, J.Y. (1992), Rural reforms and agricultural growth in China. *American Economic Review*, **82**, 34–51.

Liu, B., M. Keyzer, B. Van den Boom and P. Zikhali (2012), How connected are Chinese farmers to retail markets? New evidence of price transmission. *China Economic Review*, **23**, 34–46.

Lou, D.Q., Lesbordes, J.C., Nicolas, G., Viatte, L., Bennoun, M., Van Rooijen, N., Kahn, A., L. Renia and S. Vaulont (2005), Iron- and inflammation-induced hepcidin gene expression in mice is not mediated by Kupffer cells in vivo. *Hepatology* **41**, 1056–1064.

Lu, L. and M. Luhrmann (2013), The impact of Chinese income growth on nutritional outcomes. Paper presented in the Royal Economics Society Annual Conference held at University of London, Royal Holloway, April 2013.

Ma, H., A. Rae, J. Huang and S. Rozelle (2004), Chinese animal product consumption in 1990s. *Australian Journal of Agricultural and Resources Economics*, **48**, 569–90.

Ma, H., J. Huang, F. Fuller and S. Rozelle (2006), Getting rich and eating out: consumption of food away from home in urban China. *Canadian Journal of Agricultural Economics*, **54**, 101–19.

Meng, X., X. Gong and Y. Wang (2009), Impact of income growth and economic reform on nutrition availability in urban China: 1986–2000. *Economic Development and Cultural Change*, **57**, 261–95.

Montalvo, J.G. and M. Ravallion (2010), The pattern of growth and poverty reduction in China. *Journal of Comparative Economics*, **38**, 2–16.

Ortega, D.L., H.H. Wang and J.S. Eales (2009), Meat demand in China. *China Agricultural Economic Review*, **1**, 410–19.

Popkin, B. (2007), The world is fat. *Scientific American*, **297**, 88–95.

Popkin, B. (2008), Will China's nutrition transition overwhelm its health care system and slow economic growth? *Health Affairs*, **27**, 1064–1076.

Qiu, H. and Y. Qiu (2013), The effect of income on child nutrition in China. *Research Journal of Applied Sciences, Engineering and Technology*, **5**, 1144–1148.

Ravallion, M. (2009), Are there lessons for Africa from China's success against poverty. *World Development*, 37, 303–313.

Ravallion, M. and Chen, S. (2007), China's (uneven) progress against poverty. *Journal of Development Economics*, **82**, 1–42.

Rozelle, S., L. Guo, M. Shen, A. Hughart and J. Giles (1999a), Leaving China's farms: survey results of new paths and remaining hurdles to rural migration. *The China Quarterly*, **158**, 367–93.

Rozelle, S., E. Taylor, and A. de Brauw (1999b), Migration, remittances, and agricultural productivity in China. *American Economic Review*, **89**, 287–91.

Ruel, M.T. and H. Alderman, (2013), Nutrition-sensitive interventions and programmes: how can they help to accelerate progress in improving maternal and child nutrition? *Lancet*, **382**, 536–51.

Shimokawa, S. (2010), Nutrient intake of the poor and its implications for the nutritional effect of cereal price subsidies: evidence from China. *World Development*, **38**, 1001–1011.

Shimokawa, S. (2013), When does dietary knowledge matter to obesity and overweight prevention? *Food Policy*, **38**, 35–46.

Stage, J., J. Stage and G. Mcgranahan (2010), Is urbanization contributing to higher food prices? *Environment and Urbanization*, **22**, 199–215.

Subramanian, S. and A. Deaton, (1996), The demand for food and calories. *Journal of Political Economy*, **104**, 133–62.
Tang, H. and Z. Li, (2012), Study on per capita grain demand based on Chinese reasonable dietary pattern. *Scientia Agriculture Sinica*, **45**, 2315–2327 [in Chinese].
Taylor, J. E., S. Rozelle and A. de Brauw (2003), Migration and incomes in source communities: a new economics of migration perspective from China. *Economic Development and Cultural Change*, **52**, 75–101.
Tian, X. and X. Yu (2012), The Enigma of TFP in China: A meta-analysis. *China Economic Review*, **23**(2), 396–414.
Uchida, E., S. Rozelle, and J. Xu (2009), Conservation payments, liquidity constraints, and off-farm labor: impact of the Grain-for-Green program on rural households in China. *American Journal of Agricultural Economics*, **91**(1), 70–86.
Wagstaff, A., W. Yip, M. Lindelow and W.C. Hsiao (2009), China's health system and its reform: a review of recent studies. *Health Economics*, **18**, S7–S23.
Wang, H., R. Mittelhammer, J. McCluskey and J. Bai (2011), Food processing degrees: evidence from Beijing household survey. Paper presented at AAEA & NAREA Joint Annual Meeting, 24–26 July 2011, Pittsburgh, PA.
Webb, P. and S. Block (2011), Support for agriculture during economic transformation: impacts on poverty and undernutrition. *PNAS*, **109**, 12309–12314.
World Bank (2012), *Global Monitoring Report 2012: Food Prices, Nutrition and the MDG*. Washington DC: World Bank.
Xu, Z., J. Xu, X. Deng, J. Huang, E. Uchida and S. Rozelle (2006), Grain for green versus grain: conflict between food security and conservation set-aside in China. *World Development*, **34**, 130–148.
Yang, J., H. Qiu, J. Huang and S. Rozelle (2008), Fighting global food price rises in the developing world: the response of China and its effect on domestic and world markets. *Agricultural Economics*, **39**, 453–64.
Yen, S.T., Fang, C. and S. Su (2004), Household food demand in urban China: a censored system approach. *Journal of Comparative Economics*, **32**(3), 564–585.
You, J. (2013), The role of microcredit in child nutrition: quasi-experimental evidence from rural China. Memo.
Yu, B., F. Liu and L. You (2012), Dynamic agricultural supply response under economic transformation: a case study of Henan, China. *American Journal of Agricultural Economics*, **94**, 370–376.
Yu, X. (2012), Productivity, efficiency and structural problems in Chinese dairy farms. *China Agricultural Economic Review*, **4**, 168–75.
Yu, X. and D. Abler (2009), The demand for food quality in rural China. *American Journal of Agricultural Economics*, **91**, 57–69.
Zezza, A., C. Carletto, B. Davis and P. Winters (2011), Assessing the impact of migration on food and nutrition security. *Food Policy*, **36**, 1–6.
Zhang, S. (2001), Liberalization of grain price and cancelation of food stamps: research of Changes in China's grain purchase and sale policy. Available at: http://www.china-review.com/gao.asp?id=9897 (accessed July 13, 2013) [in Chinese].
Zhang, W. and Q. Wang (2003), Changes in China's urban food consumption and implications for trade. Paper presented at American Agricultural Economics Association Annual Meeting, 27–30 July 2003, Montreal, Canada.
Zhang, X. and R. Kanbur (2001), What Difference Do Polarisation Measures Make? An Application to China. *Journal of Development Studies*, **37**(3), 85–98.
Zhang, Y. and S. Wang (2013), Rural–urban comparison in prevalence of overweight and obesity among adolescents in Shandong, China. *Annals of Human Biology*, **40**, 294–97.
Zhao, M., Y. Konishi, and P. Glewwe (2013), Does information on health status lead to a healthier lifestyle? Evidence from China on the effect of hypertension diagnosis on food consumption. *Journal of Health Economics*, **32**, 367–85.
Zhen, L., S. Cao, S. Cheng, G. Xie, Y. Wei, X. Liu and F. Li (2010), Arable land requirements based on food consumption patterns: case study in rural Guyuan district, western China. *Ecological Economics*, **69**, 1443–1453.
Zheng, Z. and S.R. Henneberry (2010), The impact of changes in income distribution on current and future food demand in urban China. *Journal of Agricultural and Resource Economics*, **35**, 51–71.
Zheng, Z. and S.R. Henneberry (2012), Estimating the impacts of rising food prices on nutrient intake in urban China. *China Economic Review*, **23**, 1090–1103.
Zhong, F., J. Xiang, and J. Zhu (2012), Impact of demographic dynamics on food consumption: a case study of energy intake of China. *China Economic Review*, **23**, 1011–1019.
Zhuang, R. and P. Abbott (2007), Price elasticities of key agricultural commodities in China. *China Economic Review*, **18**, 155–69.

10. Poverty nutrition traps
Raghbendra Jha, Katsushi S. Imai and Raghav Gaiha

> President Obama, seeking to put the prosperity and promise of the middle class at the heart of his second-term agenda, called on Congress on Tuesday night to raise the federal minimum wage to $9 an hour, saying that would lift millions out of poverty and energize the economy.
> *International Herald Tribune*, 12 February 2013 reporting on President Obama's State of the Union Speech.

10.1 INTRODUCTION

Undernutrition or undernourishment refers to an outcome that results from insufficient food intake and tends to cause infectious diseases in developing countries. The broader notion of 'hunger' for the population as a whole is, however, multidimensional. Thus, the International Food Policy Research Institute's (IFPRI's) Global Hunger Index (GHI) has three components: (1) Undernourishment, i.e. the proportion of people with inadequate intake of calories, (2) Child underweight, i.e. the proportion of children below 5 years who are underweight, and (3) Child mortality, i.e. the mortality rate of children under the age of 5 years. IFPRI's Global Hunger Index is a simple unweighted sum of these three magnitudes. Table 10.1 gives figures on these magnitudes for select developing countries.

That said, quantifying undernutrition, itself, is a challenging task with the extent of undernutrition varying according to age, occupation and gender. The United Nations Children's Fund (UNICEF), with its emphasis on child nutrition, uses the following multidimensional approach for children aged 0–59 months: (1) underweight for one's age including being dangerously thin (wasted), (2) too short for one's age (stunted), and (3) deficient in macro (calorie and/or protein) or micro (vitamins and minerals) nutrients. Thus, in 2012, 146 million children in the world were underweight of which 57 million lived in India, 8 million each in Bangladesh and Pakistan, 7 million in China, 6 million each in Nigeria, Ethiopia and Indonesia, 3 million each in Democratic Republic of Congo and Philippines, 2 million in Viet Nam and another 40 million in other developing countries. Similar figures are available for the other two criteria.[1]

There is extensive literature on the implications of undernutrition on health, education and other key outcomes. In this chapter we are concerned about a particular form of spillover from undernutrition to labour market outcomes, while the broader and related literature of poverty traps is also reviewed. Commonly known as the 'poverty nutrition trap' (henceforth PNT), it refers to a situation in which undernutrition leads to low productivity in the labour market and hence lower labour market earnings, which then perpetuate undernutrition. This phenomenon is integral to food security and requires special policy attention.

This chapter is organized as follows. In section 10.2 we provide an overview of the

Table 10.1 Global Hunger Index and its components in select developing countries

	Proportion of population undernourished (%)		Prevalence of underweight children under 5 (%)		Under 5 mortality rate (%)		GHI	
	2000–02	2006–08	1999–03	2005–10	2001	2010	2001 (data from 1999–03)	2012 (data from 2005–10)
Cambodia	29	25	39.5	28.8	9.6	5.1	26.0	19.6
China	10	10	7.1	3.4	3.1	1.8	6.7	5.1
Ghana	9	5	19.6	14.3	9.7	7.4	12.8	8.9
India	20	19	44.4	43.5	8.3	6.3	24.2	22.9
Kenya	33	33	17.5	16.4	10.8	8.5	20.4	19.3
Lao, PDR	26	22	36.4	31.6	8.4	5.4	23.6	19.7
Pakistan	24	25	31.3	25.4	9.9	8.7	21.7	19.7
Philippines	18	13	20.7	20.7	3.9	2.9	14.2	12.2
Sri Lanka	20	20	23.3	21.6	2.2	1.7	15.2	14.4
Uganda	19	22	19.0	16.4	13.9	9.9	17.3	16.1
Zambia	43	44	23.3	14.9	15.3	11.1	27.2	23.3

Source: IFPRI (2012).

concept and prevalence of PNT. Section 10.3 briefly discusses some other aspects of poverty traps that have been discussed in the literature. Section 10.4 gives some illustrative evidence of the existence of PNT in India. Section 10.5 concludes.

10.2 AN OVERVIEW OF THE POVERTY NUTRITION TRAP

While economic growth has been associated with poverty reduction, it has often been observed that such poverty reduction has largely benefited people living just below the poverty line and not those who are well below it and severely deprived (e.g. Imai and You, 2013), particularly in terms of nutrition (e.g. Imai et al., 2012a). In particular, socially deprived sections of society (e.g. Scheduled Castes (SC) and Scheduled Tribes (ST) in India) and/or people living in remote areas are overly represented in this severely deprived group. Further, members of this group have very few assets, apart from their labour. Hence, such workers may work even under conditions of nutritional stress. If a PNT exists for these workers, a decision to enter the labour market, while rational in the short run, may have a negative impact on their long-term welfare. Particularly at low levels of nutrition, workers are physically incapable of doing hard manual labour. Their productivity tends to be low, which then implies that they get low wages, have low purchasing power and, therefore, low levels of nutrition, completing a vicious cycle of deprivation. These workers are unable to save very much and so their assets – both physical and human – are minimal, i.e. they are obliged to work to maintain the minimum living standard for their survival. This sequence of events reduces their chances of escaping the PNT.[2]

It should be emphasized that while 'nutritional deprivation' often implicitly refers to 'calorie deprivation' in the extant literature on the PNT, it captures only a part of the broader phenomenon of hunger. First, one has to be clear about the particular nutrient with respect to which a worker is deficient. While the literature on the PNT has primarily focused on calorie deprivation, deprivations in terms of the other macronutrient, protein, and various micronutrients are also important in analysing the PNT. Hence, a PNT may potentially exist across a range of nutrient categories and may affect workers in different ways. In addition, the PNT for various nutrients may exist for different types of work and for different types of workers. For instance, a PNT may exist for calories for men engaged in harvesting or for iron for women engaged in sowing, but not for other nutrients or for other types of work/workers. Further, hunger may be associated with loss of energy, apathy, increased susceptibility to disease and premature death. But, in line with the extant literature on PNT, this chapter will focus mainly on nutritional deprivation. In particular, we will work with calorie deprivation, although micronutrient deprivation will also be considered in some cases. The effect of nutritional intake on labour productivity and wage rates has been an important area of research for health economists and nutritionists for some time. Early expression of this concern was articulated in the form of the efficiency wage hypothesis developed by Leibenstein (1957), Mazumdar (1959) and Myrdal (1968), and formalized and extended by Mirrlees (1975), Dasgupta and Ray (1986, 1987) and Dasgupta (1993, 1997), among others. Early surveys include Bliss and Stern (1978a, b) and Binswanger and Rosenzweig (1984). Thus, Bliss and Stern (1978a, b) argued that poor quantity and quality of consumption were the main causes of low productivity of labour in many developing countries while low productivity was the principal reason for low wages. Bliss and Stern (1978a) provided a theoretical rationale for this argument, whereas a companion piece (Bliss and Stern, 1978b) provided some empirical evidence. The related efficiency wage hypothesis postulated that workers need to be paid a premium over the market wage (an efficiency wage) so that they consume more and their productivity rises. Their productivity rises as a consequence of this strategy, which assures higher returns to both employers and employees.

In developing countries, there is a substantial literature on empirically testing for the existence of PNT.[3] Thomas and Strauss (1997), for example, investigate the impact of four indicators of health (height, body mass index, per capita calorie intake and per capita protein intake) on wages of workers in urban Brazil. They discover that, even after accounting for endogeneity issues and controlling for education and other dimensions of health, these four indicators have significant positive effects on wages. The effect of the nutritional variables – per capita calorie intake and per capita protein intake – on wages was higher at low levels of nutrition.[4] In contrast, using the fixed-effects panel model jointly estimating wage and farm production, Deolalikar (1988) finds that in rural South India calorie intake does not affect either wages or productivity, but a measure of weight-for-height does. He concludes that calorie intake does not affect wages or productivity, indicating that the human body can adapt to short-run shortfalls in calorie intake. However, the fact that weight-for-height affects both wages and productivity indicates that undernutrition is an important determinant of productivity and wages. Swamy (1997), however, argues that in the Indian case a cut in the wage rate would lower the efficiency cost of labour without reducing productivity. However, a limitation of this study should be noted: the analysis is based on a very small sample and it does not involve a formal test of the efficiency wage hypotheses, being confined to computation of the cost per efficiency unit labour.

Furthermore, the PNT argument has often been motivated in terms of calorie deficiency. It has been argued that, to the extent that deficiencies of other nutrients are correlated with calorie deficiency, it may not be necessary to model the PNT in terms of nutrients other than calories. However, deprivation in terms of other nutrients may be higher than that for calories. Also, workers in a wide range of nutritional status are likely to be affected by both calorie and other nutrient deprivation. In such cases a modelling of the PNT in terms of other nutrients is still relevant. Furthermore, micronutrient deficiency has independent deleterious effects on health and productivity. For instance, Barrett (2002) indicates that micronutrient deficiency directly reduces the intensity of cognitive and physical activity and, hence, labour productivity. Besides, such deficiency indirectly reduces labour productivity by increasing susceptibility to diseases and infections. Horton and Ross (2003) show that iron deficiency in developing countries is related to a variety of functional consequences with economic implications, such as mental impairment in children and low work productivity in adults. Hence, it is important to examine the effects of micronutrient as well as calorie deficiency on productivity and/or PNT, as most of the previous works did.[5] Dasgupta and Ray (1986, 1987), Dasgupta (1997, 2009) and Svedberg (2000) have examined the reasons for the persistence of poverty and undernutrition in developing countries.

Let us first consider intuitively the model proposed by Dasgupta (1997, 2009). Two assumptions are invoked: (1) the maintenance requirement is a large fraction of total energy expenditure (60–75 per cent goes towards maintenance and the remaining 25–40 per cent is spent on 'discretionary' activities – work and leisure); and (2) at levels of energy intake exceeding maintenance requirement, there are diminishing gains in productivity from further increases in consumption. Of the two, the first assumption is crucial for understanding why a society's poverty causes stark inequality in striking contrast to a common presumption that inequality causes poverty.

Consider a private-ownership-based agrarian economy with a relatively larger number of assetless people than expected by the aggregate wealth of the economy. It is further assumed that (1) the economy in the aggregate is poor; and (2) the distribution of assets is unequal. For simplicity, all are identical in nutritional status. The agricultural market is characterized by long-term contracts. The only alternative to agricultural employment is to live off common property resources (e.g. forest products) – an inferior option.

A person either works in agriculture or lives off the commons. Imagine that the efficient productivity level of a landless agricultural worker is achieved at an energy intake that is greater than the amount available from the commons. Living off the commons thus results in a steady deterioration in nutritional status. Under these assumptions, the agricultural labour market does not clear, or, there is no wage rate at which demand for labour equals its supply. So there is rationing, and a fraction of the landless find employment in agriculture, while the remaining live off the commons. Those employed receive a wage rate equal to the wage at which efficient productivity is attained (efficient wage hypothesis). The unemployed cannot undercut the employed as it would make them less attractive as workers. Thus, different classes emerge from a homogeneous group.[6]

Various critiques rely on related evidence and their implications. These argue that: (1) No more than 15–20 per cent of a casual agricultural labourer's wage is needed to break out of the PNT; (2) There is a wide range of calorie intake responses to higher expenditure (Behrman and Deolalikar, 1990; Subramanian and Deaton, 1996) but in no case is it unity; and (3) The implication that there is budgetary slack among the poor is then used to reject the PNT model (Srinivasan, 1994; Strauss and Thomas, 1995). Dasgupta (1997), however, refutes this contentious view on the grounds that the poor have other priorities too – support for other family members, contingencies and other nutrients' requirements.

Another interesting model but with a somewhat broader objective is formulated in Svedberg (2000). It focuses on the behaviour of nutritionally constrained individuals who face given prices at which they can choose their workload. A distinction is made between the biological production function that converts the energy in food into muscular activity and the economical production function that turns this muscular activity into work which earns an income. Job-specific wages are exogenously determined by aggregate demand and supply in which the individual works (being unrelated to the nutritional status of the individual). The central issue is not unemployment, but how a poor individual's economic and biological behaviour is affected by energy entering as an input in the labour production function.

For an individual engaged in a given work activity, an exogenous increase in his wage (or price of the product) makes him increase his work activity and body weight and thus his calorie intake/expenditure. Or, the association between calorie intake and income is *positive*. Alternatively, income or food in kind support could also reduce calorie intake if he has disutility of effort. Because of inter-individual differences in the work activities (more or less physically demanding) and in biological characteristics, higher incomes are associated with lower calorie intake (or body weight). A reason is that well-paid jobs are often less physically demanding than low-paid manual jobs. But there is no causality as both income and nutrition are *endogenous*.[7]

While both Dasgupta's and Svedberg's models seek to throw light on the persistence of undernutrition and poverty, there are some striking differences in the determination of agricultural wage rate, labour market equilibrium and dynamics of nutrition–poverty linkages. The latter, for example, is static, and does not illuminate the dynamic pathways through which the individual adjusts his work effort, calorie intake and body weight in the face of exogenous shocks. Nor does it offer insights into intra-household inequality.

A significant gap in the extant literature on India is the neglect of the impact of micronutrient deprivation on labour productivity – including the possibility of the existence of a PNT with respect to micronutrients. In an important contribution, Weinberger (2003) discusses the impact of iron deficiency on labour productivity in rural India but does not model the impact of micronutrient deficiency on PNT. In fact, Jha et al. (2009) provide the first systematic basis for testing of the PNT hypothesis for calorie and micronutrient deficiency for male and female workers, and for different types of work in the case of rural India.[8] Given the advantages of Dasgupta's approach and despite its somewhat narrow focus, Jha et al. (2009) chose it for their empirical analysis.

10.3 OTHER FORMS OF POVERTY TRAPS

Bonds et al. (2010) consider the possibility that the incidence of infectious diseases may trigger a poverty nutrition trap. They argue that diseases, particularly epidemics, represent complex ecological phenomena. As such they are likely to behave in a highly erratic nonlinear fashion. When such diseases and epidemics attack poor people who are typically least able to get treated and have incomplete, if any, health insurance, descent into a poverty trap may ensue. Critical determinants of the possibility of falling into such a poverty trap are the levels of economic productivity and public health. If these are high enough then the probability of falling into a poverty trap is low. With imperfect insurance medical treatment is often unsatisfactory. In some cases this kind of phenomenon can become chronic. Consequently, antidotes to a disease induced poverty trap include enhancing labour productivity, providing wider and inexpensive health insurance and enhancing public health delivery. Both these are possible only in the medium to long term. It follows that in the short run, disease-induced poverty traps may persist and may indeed become chronic.

Some other forms of poverty traps also exist in the literature (Dercon, 2003), although these should not be called PNT in the sense that we have used it. More specifically, a poverty trap could be linked to the presence of chronic market failure. All of these involve the paucity of assets other than labour. Under these conditions extreme poverty has its own dynamics. People deprived of assets try to ensure survival through marketing the only asset they have, their labour, and in so doing, make future income and consumption growth less likely.

At the heart of this argument is severe market failure. Three types of market failures have been discussed in the literature. The first is credit market failure. With perfect markets with no problems of adverse section, moral hazard or imperfect information credit would be available at the going market interest rate without the need for any collateral. With credit market failure, however, collateral becomes necessary. Collateral serves as a means to get around the many problems that beset credit markets, such as, asymmetric information – namely, adverse selection and moral hazard – and contract enforcement. In particular, borrowers may not be able to decipher which products are more risky than others among a whole portfolio of such projects. In many such situations, as shown by Eswaran and Kotwal (1986), the rural poor have to provide land as collateral, whereas wealthy farmers do not. Wealthy farmers have the resources to acquire all the inputs for cultivation, whereas poor farmers would probably have to rent out their land or use it as collateral for a loan. Given this liquidity constraint the poor farmer will use less of other key inputs, such as irrigation and fertilizer, and will, therefore, have lower yields and be caught in a poverty trap. Binswanger et al. (1995) provide a lucid summary of the empirical evidence.

The argument above, although drawing upon agriculture, is not confined to it. In general, whenever full participation in profitable activities is stymied because of low assets, the resulting shortfall in incomes can lead to a poverty trap.

Another commonly cited reason for the existence of a poverty trap in the literature is the presence of external effects. Bourguignon (2001) suggests that rampant poverty and inequality might cause violent crime triggering drops in efficiency. Since the poor are given the least amount of security their efficiency is the most adversely affected and this could lead to their being caught in a poverty trap, whereby poverty leads to reduced security which leads to further poverty. World Bank (2001) made similar arguments as did Collier (2008). Another source of externality often discussed in the literature in the present context is the effect of neighbourhoods. Poor people often tend to congregate in areas poorly serviced by hygiene, water and other services, which increases the vulnerability of residents to disease and reduces their productivity. Further, 'remoteness' of an area is often associated with its high poverty status. The remoteness of an area is typically associated with lack of roads, electricity, communication and other essential infrastructure. This reduces employment opportunities and access to growing markets. Thus, residents in such remote areas could be susceptible to the onset of a poverty trap. For instance, poverty incidence varies a great deal according to geographical locations in both Laos and Cambodia (Gaiha et al., 2013).

Banerjee and Mullainathan (2008) drew their attention to the fact that the mutual relationship between nutrition and productivity is empirically weak and proposed an analytical model of how home life and work life interact based on the idea that attention is a scarce resource that is important for productivity. In their analytical model, 'people may not be able to fully attend to their jobs if they are also worrying about problems at home, and being distracted in this way reduces productivity' (p. 489). That is, psychological factors as well as lack of services to avoid such a distraction (e.g. baby sitter services, steady/secure piped water or power or electricity supplies) are likely to be the reason for workers' low productivity. Their model will thus provide an alternative explanation for poverty traps. That is, poor access to home services or infrastructure will reduce the productivity or the quality of work of poor workers in the labour market. It is also likely that the nutritional factor and the psychological factor will complement each other given the complex causality of poverty (Dasgupta, 2010).

Final reasons for the existence of a poverty trap are the disproportionate incidence of risk on the poor and the differential ability to undertake risky and profitable activities between the poor and the non-poor due to a different degree of insurance for unexpected risks. Many poor households in developing countries face incomplete or nonexistent insurance markets for mitigating or avoiding risk. These strategies include entering into low-risk (low profit) activities, growing more drought-resistant crops, entering into very low value-added activities such as firewood collection or recycling material. The disproportionate incidence of risk may, therefore, induce the poor to take up low value-added, low paying jobs which perpetuate their poverty. Dercon and Christiaensen (2011) modelled the different ability of households to undertake riskier production technologies and applied the model to Ethiopian household data. They showed that the households without insurance or alternative means of consumption smoothing tend to be trapped into the low return and lower risk production and poverty over time. Using the Kenyan household data, Imai (2003) also finds that households without liquidity assets (e.g. livestock) tend to be trapped into low return/risk crops and thus poverty.

Although many poor households devise elaborate mechanisms for risk management and risk coping, their efforts are nowhere near adequate. As a consequence their efficiency is disproportionately reduced. Thus, Rosenzweig and Binswanger (1993) show that in the case of India the loss in efficiency between the top and the bottom quantile of the population differed by nearly 25 per cent. Similar evidence for China was reported by Jalan and Ravallion (2003). Elbers et al. (2003) develop an econometric growth model that accounts for risk and responses in the case of rural Zimbabwe and find that risk substantially reduces growth. This would imply that the incomes of those on whom the incidence of risk is greatest, i.e. the poor, would fall the most. This would perpetuate a poverty trap.

Several authors have empirically tested for the presence of a poverty trap (e.g. Barrett et al., 2006). Because of non-availability of long panel data this analysis is usually conducted with short panels, even cross-sectional data, although the very notion of a poverty trap is dynamic. Recently, however, Antman and McKenzie (2007) have argued that long pseudo-panels can be constructed for groups of individuals which allow for nonlinear income dynamics and can be used for testing for the presence of a poverty trap, although it is another matter that they do not find any evidence of a poverty trap in urban Mexico.

10.4 POVERTY NUTRITION TRAPS IN INDIA

Jha et al. (2009) present an empirical approach to estimate the PNT in the context of rural India. The analysis is based on the NCAER rural household survey data in 1993–94. To our knowledge, this is the first paper to model PNT with respect to several micronutrients, for male and female workers separately as well as for different types of occupations, e.g. sowing and harvesting.[9]

Any empirical strategy to estimate the PNT must deal with the mutual endogeneity of wage and nutrition. In the literature, two standard approaches to this have been followed: (1) the Tobit (Tobin, 1958) involving a Maximum Likelihood Multinomial Logistic Regression, and (2) The Heckman self-selection procedure. Jha et al. (2009) use the Heckman approach in view of its well-known advantages (Greene, 2003; Smith and Brame, 2003) over the Tobit specification.

Heckman-type sample selection models have the advantage that a different set of variables and coefficients determine the probability of censoring and the value of the dependent variable given that it is observed, unlike in the Tobit model. These variables may *overlap*, to a point, or may be *completely* different. Second, sample selection models allow for greater theoretical development because the observations are said to be censored by some other variable, which we call Z. This permits us to take into account the censoring process since selection and outcome are not independent, leading to consistent estimates of the individual parameters.

The problem of sample selection arises when the data in the survey is incidentally truncated or non-randomly selected. The model employed by Jha et al. (2009) to determine the wage nutrition relationship contains the following main regression equation:

$$Y_i = \beta' X_i + \varepsilon_i$$

where Y_i is the wage rate and X_i is a vector comprising the nutrition and other household characteristics. While Y_i in the model refers to a wage rate for all the individuals, we observe it only for those who are actually employed. That is, the model is truncated as the sample is selected on the basis of wages (in the agricultural sector).

Formally, the wages are observed only if:

$$Z_i^* = \gamma' W_i + u_i$$

where W_i are independent variables that contribute to the employment probability of an individual. W_i may or may not overlap with the X_i.

This is called the selection equation. The sample rule thus becomes that Y_i^* (the wage rate) is observed only when $Z_i^* > 0$ (or the person under consideration is employed in agricultural sector). The choice of variables for the two stages of the estimation needs to be justified. Ideally, in the selection equation, higher rainfall needs to be included since it increases the intensity of agricultural activity and, hence, employment. Further, a number of household characteristics that are commonly used in the literature, e.g. age of household head and its square, gender of household head, number of adult males and females in the household, land possessed by the household and its square, and the social group to which the household belongs (e.g. SC or ST in the case of India) need to be incorporated in the selection equation. In addition, Jha et al. (2009) control for state-level effects such as economic backwardness or whether they are coastal through dummy variables. The inclusion of these variables is motivated by the fact that these variables have implications for job searching (e.g. the job search is less costly with better infrastructure, and easier access to labour markets), and farm and non-farm employment opportunities.

The second stage estimation is designed to explain the wage rate. These wage rates are modelled as a function of predicted nutrient intake and its square (separately for each regression), rainfall and all other household characteristics used in the first stage. The inclusion of the predicted nutrient and its square are motivated by the PNT analysis, rainfall will affect agricultural output and hence agricultural wages, and household characteristics are included because these might independently affect the wage earned (for example, reservation wage would vary with the amount of land possessed, and inversely with SC/ST affiliation). Dummy variables for the traditionally less well-off states, Bihar, Madhya Pradesh and Rajasthan (BIMARU) and coastal states are included because these may have state level effects on the agricultural wage. In addition, prices for four food groups, pulses, gur/sugar, edible oil and milk, are included. Data on prices of other food groups is not available for the whole sample. In any case these food items cover the most important categories of foods: pulses are consumed as a major food item, gur/sugar and edible oil are intermediates and milk is a relative luxury for the poor. The extant literature places emphasis on both direct and indirect effects of food prices on agricultural wages. The indirect effect is through the nutrient intake (Pitt and Rosenzweig, 1986; Behrman and Deolaikar, 1990; Lakdawalla et al. 2005), whereas the direct effect is through labour market responses emanating from changes in the food market (Bardhan, 1984; Stiglitz, 1987; Ravallion, 1990; Barrett and Dorosh, 1996; Datt and Olmsted, 2004). Jha et al. (2009) include the nutritional status and food prices in the wage equation to capture both types of effects.

Jha et al. (2009) use this approach to model PNT in 30 cases. Five nutrients were considered: calories, iron, carotene, thiamine and riboflavin for male and female workers and for three types of occupations, viz. sowing, harvesting, and others. The PNT exists in one-third (i.e. ten) of the 30 cases considered. These are: female harvest wage and female sowing wage for calories; male workers engaged in harvesting in the case of carotene, both male and female workers engaged in harvesting in the case of iron, female workers engaged in harvesting and sowing and male workers engaged in harvesting in the case of riboflavin, and female workers engaged in harvesting and sowing in the case of thiamine.

Since harvesting is more physically demanding than sowing there is higher incidence of PNT in harvesting.

It is worth noting that the traditional calorie-based PNT holds only for female sowing and female harvesting wages in the Indian context (Jha et al., 2009). The calorie PNT does not hold for male workers in any of the occupations. PNT with respect to micronutrients is important for both male and female workers. It holds for males in the case of male harvesting wages (carotene, iron and riboflavin). For female workers, the PNT holds for harvest and sowing wages for thiamine and riboflavin. There is no PNT with respect to carotene and one exists only for female workers engaged in harvesting in the case of iron. Two points follow from Jha et al. (2009). First, exclusive attention to calories can give misleading picture about the extent of nutritional deprivation (in particular PNT). Second, women workers are more likely to be prone to PNT than their male counterparts. Hence, there is a specific gender, apart from an occupation, characteristic of PNT.

Related to the empirical literature of testing the PNT hypothesis, researchers have debated the empirical 'puzzle': why per capita calorie consumption has declined across all households with different income levels in both rural and urban areas despite high rates of income and consumption growth in recent India (e.g. Palmer-Jones and Sen, 2001; Patnaik, 2004, 2007; Deaton and Drèze, 2009; Gaiha et al., 2014b). For instance, Deaton and Drèze (2009) argue that 'the calorie Engel curve', which plots per capita total calories or cereal calories and household per capita expenditure, has shifted consistently downwards during 1983–2005, based on National Sample Survey (NSS) data. However, if we focus on the rural wage earners, the possibility of PNT exists, that is, the labour productivity and wage rates are affected by nutritional intakes as predicted by the efficiency wage hypothesis and thus those undernourished tend to be trapped in poverty. As an extension of Jha et al. (2009), Imai et al. (2012a) have tested the two hypotheses, that is, (1) the poverty nutrition trap hypothesis that wages affect nutritional status and (2) the activity hypothesis that activity intensity affects adult nutrition as measured by BMI in the context of India. The analyses draw upon quantile regressions and three rounds of National Family Health Survey (NFHS) data in 1992, 1998 and 2005 and NCAER data in 2005. Imai et al. (2012a) find strong support for both hypotheses in India. They found that physically intensive activity tends to worsen the nutritional conditions and there is evidence for a poverty nutrition trap associated with labour market participation. In other words, the PNT was found to exist even after talking account of the activity hypothesis.

With a focus on the demand-side explanation for 'the puzzle', Gaiha et al. (2014b) investigated in detail the dietary changes, their nutritional implications, and the policy response to alleviate nutritional deprivation using National Sample Survey (NSS) data in India in the period 1994–2005. They found that the downward shifts in the calorie intakes over the period 1993–2004 were associated with changes in diets. Higher food prices and near stagnant expenditure/income in rural India were found to play significant roles, while lower calorie 'requirements' due to less strenuous activity patterns, life-style changes and improvements in the epidemiological environment are allowed. Despite the dietary changes, they concluded that manifestations of undernutrition imply serious welfare implications not just in the present but also in the longer-term PNT and suggested the important role of Public Distribution System (PDS) and National Rural

Employment Guarantee Scheme (NREGS) in improving nutritional status of the poor and breaking PNT.

Another important approach for PNT is to incorporate inter-generational aspects or personal histories which may lead an individual to be trapped into poverty in the long run. The long-term malnutrition of infants tends to be associated with lower cognitive development and the undernourishment of pregnant women tends to cause that of their children (Dasgupta, 2010). Using the household dataset on Rajasthan for the period 1977–2010, Krishna (2012) has shown that poverty was transmitted over generations and the poverty status was made worse by adverse shocks. Given the persistency of undernourishment over the generations, the high prevalence of malnutrition of children in India, which has been confirmed by Imai et al. (2012b) using NFHS data in 1993–2006, is a significant concern for policy makers in reducing poverty in the long run. More importantly, children's malnutrition is found to be associated with women's autonomy or empowerment in India (Imai et al., 2012b),[10] the mechanism of PNT should also be interpreted in the intergenerational context as well as in the broader social context.

10.5 CONCLUSIONS AND POLICY IMPLICATIONS

A principal reason for the existence of poverty traps and the particular problem of PNT is the fact that workers have very few assets apart from their labour. Consequently, they are obliged to work under circumstances which perpetuate their poverty/hunger. Any long-term solution to the problem of poverty traps must, therefore, involves augmentation of worker assets so that they are not obliged to work under unfavourable conditions. These conditions require both positive and negative public policy initiatives. On the positive side all-out efforts must be made to create an environment that permits income and, particularly, asset growth of the poor. In operational terms this will necessitate investment into productivity augmentation for poor workers. In the long run, this alone will provide the basis for fruitful work in the labour market without the risk of falling into a poverty trap. This, then, is an efficiency-based argument in favour of pro-poor growth. In the short run, however, urgent steps are needed to augment worker's productivity by improving their nutrition. This could be done through provision of subsidized nutritious food, particularly to the most vulnerable sections of the population, e.g. pregnant and lactating women and infants and children. It is also important to reduce vulnerability and risks faced by the poor who tend to be not only undernourished but also poor in asset-holdings. This is because they tend to be less insured and less productive and thus unable to undertake profitable and risky production whereby they can escape from poverty traps. Furthermore, certain sections of the population may be particularly prone to falling into poverty traps, e.g. those living in remote areas or, in the case of some countries like India, socially disadvantaged groups such as SCs and STs.

NOTES

1. See UNICEF (2006). Gaiha et al. (2014a) provide a consolidated index of child undernutrition in India.
2. In this chapter, we use the terms efficiency wage hypothesis and PNT interchangeably.

3. For a comprehensive review, see Strauss and Thomas (1998).
4. The literature of nutritional science generally supports the positive relationship between workers' productivity and their nutritional status. For instance, in his work on Colombian sugarcane cutters and loaders, Spurr (2009, cited by Dasgupta, 2010) estimated the relationship between productivity (W) of workers in units of tons per day and (i) their maximal oxygen uptake in litres per minute (V or $VO_2\,max$), the percentage of body weight in fat (F) and height in cms (H) as $W = 0.81V - 01.4F + 0.03H - 1.962$.
5. Lakdawala et al. (2005) found that micronutrient deficiency needed to be considered in addition to calorie deficiency in the case of the United States and conjectured that this was probably also true of developing countries.
6. The prediction of inequality generalizes to informal markets, and nonmarket institutions (e.g. the household). For an extension in which time and history result in horizontal inequity, see Dasgupta (1997, 2009).
7. In a meticulous review of empirical evidence on demand elasticities for calories and also the reverse impact of nutrition on productivity, Svedberg (2000) offers a different perspective. Noting data shortcomings and use of different econometric techniques, he argues that the diversity reflects the actual situation: there is no general systematic relationship between calorie intake (or body size) and income across households in different directions (p. 54).
8. Dasgupta (2009, 2010) emphasized that each factor, such as macro or micronutrient, may serve as complement of one another, that is, it is not sufficient to investigate the deficiency in one component. Jha et al. (2009) thus analysed the impact of deficiency in several macro and micronutrients in one model.
9. To our knowledge, there have been few empirical studies on PNT on Asian countries outside India. China is no exception. However, Imai and You (2013) have applied duration models to the long household panel data to China for the period 1989–2009 and analysed poverty dynamics in household consumption. Consistent with the PNT hypothesis, poverty is persistent and the poor cannot easily escape from poverty unless they find the employment in the agricultural sector or have access to migration opportunities. However, they did not use the nutritional measures in analysing poverty dynamics and future study should investigate the link between workers' productivity and their nutritional status in China.
10. See similar empirical evidence for Nepal (Eklund et al., 2007) and Papua New Guinea (Imai and Eklund 2008).

REFERENCES

Antman, F. and D. McKenzie (2007), Poverty traps and non-linear income dynamics with measurement error and individual heterogeneity. *Journal of Development Studies*, **43**(6), 1057–1083.
Banerjee, A. and S. Mullainathan (2008), Limited attention and income distribution. *American Economic Review: Papers and Proceedings*, **98**(2), 489–93.
Bardhan, P. (1984), *Land, Labour and Poverty*. New York: Columbia University Press.
Barrett, C. (2002), Food security and food assistance programmes. In B. Gardner and G. Rausser (eds), *Handbook of Agricultural Economics*. Amsterdam: Elsevier Science, pp. 2103–2190.
Barrett C. and P. Dorosh (1996), Farmers welfare and changing food prices: nonparametric evidence from Madagascar. *American Journal of Agricultural Economics*, **78**, 656–69.
Barrett, C., P. Marenya, J. McPeak, B. Minten, F. Murithi, W. Oluoch Kosura, F. Place, J.C. Randrianarisoa, J. Rasambainarivo and J. Wangila (2006), Welfare dynamics in rural Kenya and Madagascar. *Journal of Development Studies*, **42**(2), 248–77.
Behrman J. and A. Deolalikar (1990), The intrahousehold demand for nutrients in rural south India: individual estimates, fixed estimates and permanent income. *Journal of Human Resources*, **24**, 665–97.
Binswanger J. and M. Rosenzweig (1984), Contractual arrangements, employment and wages in rural labour markets: a critical review. In J. Binswanger and M. Rosenzweig (eds), *Contractual Arrangements Employment and Wages in Rural Labour Markets in Asia*, New Haven, CT: Yale University Press, pp. 1–40.
Binswanger, H., K. Deininger and G. Feder (1995), Power, distortions, revolt and reform in agricultural and land relations. In J. Behrman and T.N. Srinivasan (eds), *Handbook of Development Economics*, Vol. 3. Amsterdam: North Holland, pp. 2659–2772.
Bliss, C. and N. Stern (1978a), Productivity, wages and nutrition. Part I: the theory. *Journal of Development Economics*, **5**, 331–62.
Bliss, C. and N. Stern (1978b), Productivity, wages and nutrition. Part II: some observations. *Journal of Development Economics*, **5**, 363–98.
Bonds, M., D. Keenan, P. Rohani and J. Sachs (2010), Poverty trap formed by the ecology of infectious diseases. *Proceedings of the Royal Economic Society*, **277**, 1185–1192.

Bourguigon, F. (2001), Crime as a social cost of poverty and inequality: a review focusing on developing countries. In S. Yusuf, S. Evenett and W. Wu (eds), *Facets of Globalization*. Washington DC: The World Bank.
Collier, P. (2008), *The Bottom Billion: Why the Poorest Countries are Failing and What Can Be Done About It*. New York: Oxford University Press.
Dasgupta, P. (1993), *An Inquiry into Well-Being and Destitution*. Oxford: Oxford University Press.
Dasgupta, P. (1997), Nutritional status, the capacity for work, and poverty traps. *Journal of Econometrics*, **77**, 5–37.
Dasgupta, P. (2009), Poverty traps: exploring the complexity of causation. In J. von Braun, R.V. Hill, and R. Pandya-Lorch (eds), *The Poorest and the Hungry: Assessments, Analyses, and Actions*. Washington DC: IFPRI, pp. 129–46.
Dasgupta, P. (2010), Personal histories and poverty traps. In J. Lin and V. Plescovik (eds), *Proceedings of the Annual World Bank Conference on Development Economics*. Washington DC: World Bank, pp. 87–144.
Dasgupta, P. and D. Ray (1986), Inequality as a determinant of malnutrition and unemployment: theory. *Economic Journal*, **96**, 1011–1034.
Dasgupta, P. and D. Ray (1987), Inequality as a determinant of malnutrition and unemployment: policy. *Economic Journal*, **97**, 177–88.
Datt G. and J. Olmsted (2004), Induced wage effects of changes in food prices in Egypt. *The Journal of Development Studies*, **40**, 137–66.
Deaton, A. and J. Drèze (2009), Food and nutrition in India: facts and interpretations. *Economic and Political Weekly*, **XLIV**(7), 42–65.
Deolalikar, A. (1988), Nutrition and labour productivity in agriculture: estimates for rural south India. *Review of Economics and Statistics*, **70**, 406–13.
Dercon, S. (2003), Poverty traps and development: the equity–efficiency tradeoff. Paper presented at the Conference on Growth, Inequality and Poverty, organized by the Agence francaise de development and the European Development Research Network (EUDN).
Dercon, S. and L. Christiaensen (2011), Consumption risk, technology adoption and poverty traps: evidence from Ethiopia. *Journal of Development Economics*, **96**(2), 159–73.
Eklund, P., K. Imai and F. Felloni (2007), Women's organisations, maternal knowledge, and social capital to reduce prevalence of stunted children: evidence from rural Nepal. *Journal of Development Studies*, **43**(3), 456–89.
Elbers, C., J. Lanjouw and P. Lanjpouw (2003) Micro-level estimation of poverty and inequality. *Econometrica*, **71**(1), 355–64.
Eswaran, M. and A. Kotwal (1986), Access to capital and agrarian production organisation. *Economic Journal*, **96**, 482–98.
Gaiha, R., M.S. Azam, S. Annim and K. Imai (2013), Agriculture, markets and poverty: a comparative analysis of Laos and Cambodia. *Asian Journal of Agriculture and Development*, **9**(1), 97–111.
Gaiha, R., R. Jha and V. Kulkarni (2014a), *Diets, Malnutrition and Disease: The Indian Experience*. New Delhi: Oxford University Press.
Gaiha, R., R. Jha, V. Kulkarni and N. Kaicker (2014b), Diets, nutrition and poverty: the Indian experience. in Herring (ed.), *Handbook on Food, Politics and Society*, New York: Oxford University Press (forthcoming).
Greene W. (2003), *Econometric Analysis* (5th edn). Upper Saddle River, NJ: Prentice Hall.
Horton, S. and J. Ross (2003), The economics of iron deficiency. *Food Policy*, **28**, 51–75.
Imai, K. (2003), Is livestock important for risk behaviour of rural households? Evidence from Kenya. *Journal of African Economies*, **12**(2), 271–95.
Imai, K. and P. Eklund (2008), Women's organisations and social capital to reduce prevalence of stunted children: evidence from Papua New Guinea. *Oxford Development Studies*, **36**(2), 209–33.
Imai, K. and J. You (2013), Poverty dynamics of households in rural China. DP2013–16, RIEB, Kobe University.
Imai, K., S.K. Annim, R. Gaiha and V.S. Kulkarni (2012a), Nutrition, activity intensity and wage linkages: evidence from India. RIEB DP2012-10, Kobe University.
Imai, K., S.K. Annim, R. Gaiha and V.S. Kulkarni (2012b), Does women's empowerment reduce prevalence of stunted and underweight children in rural India? DP2012–11, RIEB, Kobe University.
International Food Policy Research Institute (IFPRI) (2012), *Global Hunger Index: The Challenges of Hunger, Ensuring Sustainable Food Security Under Land, Water and Energy Stresses*. Bonn, Washington DC, Dublin: IFPRI, October.
Jalan, J. and M. Ravallion (2003), Household income dynamics in rural China. In S. Dercon (ed.), *Insurance against Poverty*. Oxford: Oxford University Press, pp. 107–24.
Jha, R., R. Gaiha and A. Sharma (2009), Calorie and micronutrient deprivation and poverty nutrition traps in rural India. *World Development*, **37**, 982–91.
Krishna, A. (2012), Characteristics and patterns of intergenerational poverty traps and escapes in rural north India. *Development Policy Review*, **30**(5), 617–40.

Lakdawalla, D., T. Philipson and J. Bhattacharya (2005), Welfare enhancing technological change and the growth of obesity. *American Economic Review*, **95**(2005), 253–57.
Leibenstein, H. (1957), *Economic Backwardness and Economic Growth*. New York: John Wiley.
Mazumdar, D. (1959), The marginal productivity theory of wages and disguised unemployment. *Review of Economic Studies*, **26**, 190-197.
Mirrlees, J. (1975a), A pure theory of underdeveloped economies. In L. Reynolds (ed.), *Agriculture in Development Theory*. New Haven: Yale University Press, pp. 84–108.
Myrdal, G. (1968), *Asian Drama: An Inquiry into the Poverty of Nations*. Middlesex, UK: Allen Lane.
Palmer-Jones, R. and K. Sen (2001), On Indian poverty puzzles and statistics of poverty. *Economic & Political Weekly*, **36**(3) (January 20), 211–17.
Patnaik, U. (2004), The Republic of Hunger. *Social Scientist*, **32**(9–10), 9–35.
Patnaik, U. (2007), Neoliberalism and rural poverty in India. *Economic & Political Weekly*, **42**(30), 3132–3150.
Pitt, M. and M. Rosenzweig (1986), Agricultural prices, food consumption and the health and productivity of Indonesian farmers. In I. Singh, L. Squire and J. Strauss (eds), *Agricultural Household Models: Extensions, Applications and Policy*. Baltimore, MD: Johns Hopkins University Press, pp. 153–82.
Ravallion, M. (1990a), Rural welfare effects of food price changes under induced wage responses: theory and evidence for Bangladesh. *Oxford Economic Papers*, **42**(2), 574–85.
Rosenzweig, M. and H. Binswanger (1993), Wealth, weather risk and the composition and profitability of agricultural investment. *Economic Journal*, **103**(1), 56–78.
Smith, D. and R. Brame (2003), Tobit models in social science research: some limitations and a more general alternative. *Sociological Methods and Research*, **31**, 364–88.
Spurr, G.B. (2009), The impact of chronic undernutrition on physical work capacity and daily energy expenditure. In G.A. Harrison and J.C. Waterlow (eds), *Diet and Disease in Traditional and Developing Countries*. Cambridge: Cambridge University Press, pp. 24–61.
Srinivasan, T. (1994), Destitution: a discourse. *Journal of Economic Literature*, **32**(4), 1842–1855.
Stiglitz, J. (1987), The causes and consequences of the dependence of quality on price. *Journal of Economic Literature*, **25**(1), 1–48.
Strauss, J. and D. Thomas (1995a), Human resources: empirical modeling of household and family decisions. In J. Behrman and T.N. Srinivasan (eds), *Handbook of Development Economics*, Edition 1, Vol. 3, Number 3. Amsterdam: Elsevier, pp. 3–34.
Subramanian, S. and A. Deaton (1996), The demand for food and calories. *Journal of Political Economy*, **104**(1), 133–62.
Svedberg, P. (2000a), *Poverty and Undernutrition*. Oxford and New York: Oxford University Press.
Svedberg, P. (2004), Has the relationship changed between malnutrition and income changed?, Comment on Behrman, Alderman and Hoddinott *Hunger and malnutrition*. Copenhagen consensus opponents note, May.
Swamy, A. (1997), A simple test of the nutrition-based efficiency wage model. *Journal of Development Economics*, **53**, 85–98.
Thomas, D. and J. Strauss (1997), Health and wages: evidence from men and women in Urban Brazil. *Journal of Econometrics*, **77**(1), 159–85.
Tobin J. (1958), Estimation of relationships for limited dependent variables. *Econometrica*, **26**, 24–36.
United Nations International Children's Emergency Fund (UNICEF) (2006), Progress for Children: A Report Card on Nutrition. Number 4, May, Geneva.
Weinberger, K. (2003), The impact of micronutrients on labour productivity: evidence from rural India. Paper presented at the 25th International Conference of Agricultural Economists (16 August), Durban, South Africa.
World Bank (2001), *World Development Report 2000/1: Attacking Poverty*. New York: Oxford University Press.

11. The political economy of dietary allowances
C. Sathyamala*

There is an assumption that dietary recommendations, including norms for nutritional requirements, have been arrived at through impartial inquiry. This chapter examines the proposition that, to the contrary, they are very much shaped by the socio-political contexts in which they are formulated. Based on a review of literature, key shifts in the development of nutrition are analysed to support this assertion.

11.1 EMERGENCE OF NUTRITIONAL SCIENCE

The science of nutrition began in the mid-nineteenth century with the explicit linking of food chemistry and animal physiology (Kamminga and Cunningham, 1995: 5). Along the lines of the Cartesian notion, the body was visualised as a self-regulating steam engine needing a constant supply of fuel in the form of food to maintain its temperature and carry out work. The use of calorimeter[1] in studying food metabolism led to the adoption of the unit of heat measurement, the calorie,[2] in quantifying energy studies in physiology (Hargrove, 2006). The German scientist Max Rubner (1854–1932) successfully verified his law of isodynamic equivalence, that 'in accordance with their heat-producing value' (as quoted in Chambers, 1952: 4), the three macronutrients (carbohydrates, proteins and fats) could replace each other in the body and calculated their 'standard values' with 1 g of protein being equivalent to 4.1 calories, 1 g fat to 9.3 calories and 1 g carbohydrate to 4.1 calories.[3] This was a turning point in nutrition as the complexity of food culture could now be deciphered, reduced and compared in terms of the ubiquitous, unifying calorie.

Developing as it did, in the context of the Industrial Revolution, with the flow of people from the countryside to urban areas in a situation of destitution, scientific knowledge of the nutritional needs of the population became an important consideration (Lusk, 1909: 223). Thus, in the pre-war period, subject to the prevalent socio-political realties and preoccupation of the emerging nation states, the question – what should be considered an adequate dietary need for these populations – was addressed differently in Europe, Britain (and its colonies) and the United States.

11.2 PRE-WAR PERIOD

11.2.1 Dietary Studies in Europe: Labour and War

In an economically competitive world, which relied on the output from physical labour and was politically at war, the need in Western Europe at that time was to work out the most appropriate diet for the industrial worker and the soldier. Based on animal studies and observations on human population, the German physiologist Carl Voit (1831–1908), recommended for a labourer performing moderate work, a daily consumption of 118 g. protein, 500 g carbohydrate and 56 g fat equivalent to a total of 3055 calories (Lusk, 1909: 211). For heavy work, he increased protein intake to 150 g and fat to 200 g daily (Mitchell, 1937: 9). For sedentary workers, the recommendation was 85 g of protein, 56 g of fat and 400 g of carbohydrates amounting to 2400 calories per day (Milles, 1995: 78). Rubner estimated energy requirements for men with varying body weights ranging from 80 kg (2864 calories) to 40 kg (1810 calories) (Lusk, 1909: 210).

Although in 1878 the German government had passed the *Sozialistengesetz* (Socialist law)[4] to suppress all democratic organisations including trade unions, German employers wanted their workers to be productive and healthy (Milles, 1995: 80). Thus, for instance, in the 1889 'International Work Protection' Conference in Berlin, one section of the German General Exhibition on the Prevention of Accidents was on nutrition. In 1890, the French physiologist Gautier, arrived at 2604 calories for a worker at rest, 3556 calories at hard work, 3800 calories for fatiguing work and 5000 calories for 'exceptionally severe work' (Rabinbach, 1990: 130–131).

11.2.2 Dietary Studies in Britain: Prisoners and the Working Class

Unlike Europe, which was grappling over the question of how best to increase productivity by feeding its workers and prepare for war, '[i]t was controversy over the feeding of prisoners that forced the British Government in the middle of the 19th century' to examine the question of 'nutritional requirements of humans' (Carpenter, 2006: 1). Reports that prisoners in Millbank prison were being fed an 'extravagant' (p. 1) diet that 'no honest hard-working laborer [sic] could afford' (p. 3)[5] had created serious outrage and the prisoners' rations were reduced drastically. Within a year of this, sickness (dysentery and scurvy) and debilitation increased among the prisoners.

Edward Smith (1818–74), a prison doctor, opposed the logic of starving the prisoners on a meagre diet which in combination with the hard labour they, as part of punishment, were put through in treadmills, 'induce[d] disease and a premature death [with] so much human flesh and life wasted' (as quoted in Chapman 1967: 12). Smith's recommendation that changes in body weight be used as an indicator of food adequacy, was refuted by William Guy, the spokesperson of the prison medical officers, who advised that the quantity of food for the prisoners could be reduced with 'safety and economy' (Guy, 1863: 280). In 1864, a Scientific Commission set up by the Inspectors of Prisons to review prison diets, with Guy as the chair, not surprisingly, concluded, 'gain or loss of weight is not to be trusted as an indication of health, or as a test of the sufficiency of our [prison] dietaries'(as quoted in Carpenter, 2006: 6).

But Smith's work with the prisoners had been noted, and, in 1863, he was sent by the Privy Council to investigate the famine situation in Lancashire following the closure of the British Cotton mills (Carpenter 1991) and to recommend, 'the least cost per head per week for which food can be bought in such quantity and in such quality as will avert starvation disease from the unemployed population' (as quoted in Oddy, 1983: 76–77). Smith's data showed that in 57 per cent of the single women households and in 33–37 per cent of families, there was a reduction in food expenditure (Scola, 1992: 276). While all of them had reduced their meat and potato consumption, the diet of the single women households were worse, consisting of just tea, bread and a bit of butter or treacle. Though conscious of the limitations imposed by cost, Smith recommended that men should receive food equivalent to 2800 calories with 80 g of protein and that women should receive similar amounts but because of their body weights, would need 10 per cent less than men, but nursing mothers, children and infants needed more food, particularly protein, per body weight (Carpenter, 1991: 1518). His recommendation included fresh vegetables, at least 1 pint of non-fat milk, since the preferred full cream milk was too expensive, and some fresh meat or herrings, the latter being more suitable for older people with poorer digestion. According to Chapman (1967: 15), 'Smith's survey, and those that followed over the next two years, rank as monumental advances in public health research ... his was the first scientifically oriented nutrition survey and ... the first sensible dietary standards of any kind set up for Britain.'

It is not surprising that a latter day reviewer includes Edward Smith in the list of doctors in the Industrial Revolution in Britain who applied their 'professional skills and knowledge to the problems of an industrializing and urbanizing society' (Rose, 1971: 22). Yet, his work was marginalised in his own lifetime.

Chapman (1967) is at a loss to understand why Smith's exemplary work, 'plowing [sic] new ground' (p. 22) in the physiology of nutrition, was acknowledged by his European contemporaries, but ignored in Britain, thereby delaying the progress of physiology both in Britain and in the United States and wonders at the 'failure of Smith's innovations ... to influence health legislation in Britain within reasonable time' (p. 23). While Chapman puts it down to Smith's alleged quarrelsome and disagreeable personality as perceived by his peers, the more likely explanation could be the political implications of his work which posed a challenge to the then prevailing orthodoxy in nutritional science, and to the policies of the state; that he was apparently not a person who 'contrive[d] to conciliate the affection of his colleagues' (Anonymous, 1874: 653) made it convenient for his British colleagues to find a justifiable reason to marginalise him.

11.2.3 Dietary Surveys in the United States: Nutrition and Labour Reform

The American story too revolves around the diet of the people from the working class but from a diametrically opposite point of view as the baton of scientific research in nutrition shifted from Germany to the United States in the late nineteenth century.

Wilbur O. Atwater (1844–1907), instrumental in putting the United States on the nutritional science map, was a second generation American agricultural chemist exposed to the scientific developments on nutrition in Germany (Carpenter, 1994). Atwater argued that it was possible, scientifically speaking, to eat well for less money. Combining economics with nutritional chemistry, he showed that 25 cents spent on cheese provided 240 g of protein, which was three times as much that available in 25 cents worth of a sirloin of beef. This was the perfect answer that Edward Atkinson, a Boston financier and a laissez-faire liberal, had been searching for his question: how to get the workers to eat better without having to resort to an increase in wages (Aronson, 1982).

In the United States, this question had become particularly urgent in the late nineteenth century, with the escalation of labour unrest, marked by a series of strikes and violent confrontations between the workers, the employers and the state.[6] The average annual income of an urban worker was only about US$400 to US$500, a sum insufficient to support a family and had to be supplemented by the labour of his wife and children (National Humanities Center, 2010).

Referring dismissively to the 'so-called "iron law of wages" developed by Lasalle [sic] and Carl [sic] Marx', Atkinson (1889 [1973]: 162) propounded a solution for the 'Remedies for Social Ills':

> With respect to food, . . . [e]ach adult person requires substantially the same quantity of food, varying *a little* with the work done; the man who is engaged at hard labor [sic] requires and can digest a greater quantity than the rich man. In quantity rightly consumed, therefore, little economy or saving may be expected or desired; the saving is to be made by right selection of the materials. (Atkinson, 1889: 242) (emphasis added)

The coming together of Atwater and Atkinson was a defining moment as, '[t]he alliance between nutrition science and labor [sic] . . . gave birth to the definition of nutrition as a social problem inextricably tied to labor [sic] reform' (Aronson, 1982: 476) with its central query, what is the nutritional requirement of human subsistence, the point where questions of 'political economy and nutrition research coincided' (p. 477).

With the backing of the state and finance capital, by late 1880s, Atwater and his colleagues had completed over 4000 analysis of dietaries (Maynard, 1962) on populations from diverse geographical, ethnic, occupational and socioeconomic backgrounds and the data was used to formulate dietary standards (Darby, 1994).

'Atwater met frank hunger for the first time' writes Dirks (2003: 84), who has reviewed the data from these studies, but it seems to have left him unmoved. The primary foods among more than half the households were cornmeal, wheat flour, bacon, lard and granulated sugar. There was severe seasonal deprivation and the tenant farmers and plantation labourers experienced a steep fall in food intake during winter, due to the mortgage system that forced them to plant cash crops with little money left over to purchase sufficient food through the year. Among the railway and factory workers, while there was more variety in the foods consumed as compared to the rural households, nearly half of the households were unable to feed their family members resulting in many underweight children. Dirks (p. 95) observes that while it was known that the African Americans living in Black belt communities were poorly nourished, the dietaries revealed its magnitude and concludes that hunger was class based, worsening from the onset of winter through early spring and present in both rural and urban areas.

In contrast, the working class immigrants from Europe and Quebec consumed substantially more protein, fat and energy. It was then this group of migrant households that fitted Atwater's and Atkinson's notion of wasteful calories needing reform (Levenstein, 1980). For the population that was native born, poor, of American and/or African descent, the levels of nutritional intake they were surviving under was so low that the solutions proposed by Atwater and Atkinson would have had no place in their lives as they could not have eaten more cheaply than they were doing.

In contrast, the diets of the better off were looked upon indulgently, as can be seen from the comment on two female missionaries in New York City who weighed 200 and 175 pounds respectively:

> Their weight was . . . due . . . to solid muscle on large, well-knit frames. In their work among the poor . . . climbing long flights of stairs gave ample exercise . . . [They] were working hard in a

very wearing occupation . . . and . . . their table [was] attractive without being extravagant. (As quoted in Aronson, 1982: 482)

In effect, the nutritional theories were applied 'in a class-stratified fashion, dividing foods into two categories – those for workers and the poor and those for the middle and upper classes. The moral imperative of nutrition was: do not aspire to things that are above one's station in life' (Aronson, 1982: 483).[7]

11.3 INTER-WAR PERIOD

11.3.1 Public Health and Commerce[8]

It was in the inter-war period, that nutrition gained 'widespread recognition [as] a factor of primary importance to public health and to the economic and social welfare of nations' (Eliot and Heseltine, 1937: 331), and the first attempt made to arrive at an international consensus on dietary requirements. In June 1935, the delegates at the Nineteenth Session of the International Labour Conference had to deal with a paradoxical situation of falling food consumption among the poor even while there was enormous surplus of agricultural produce. To keep prices up, the western food-producing countries were restricting food production or destroying it; grains were burnt or ploughed under, cattle were slaughtered, fish were dumped back into the sea and 'in the midst of this feverish destruction of food, it [was] estimated that more than 25 000 000 were unemployed in Europe and America and the majority of these were suffering from . . . undernourishment and malnutrition' (Gangulee, 1934: 21). In the context of plentiful production, there was a need for a solution to hunger which would leave profit margins untouched. Thus, it was that the Labour Conference, while advocating for an adequate living wage, laid the foundation for economic considerations as a basis for setting nutritional standards. The Report of the Director, International Labour Office, noted that,

> [t]his question of consumption is not only national but international in its scope. If it is agreed that *the only real solution of the problem of economic balance is not through scaling down production but in levelling up consumption* . . . The cares of the American, Argentine, Australian, Canadian or Eastern European farmer would be conjured away if the urban population of Europe and America could eat even a little more bread, butter and meat per head.' (as quoted in Aykroyd, 1936: 639–40; emphasis added)

In September 1935, the Sixteenth Session of the Assembly of the League of Nations added nutrition and health, and their bearing on world agricultural problems to their agenda, agreeing that increased consumption of agricultural products and the purchasing power of the agriculturalists must rise, to the benefit of industry and world trade in general as captured by the phrase of an Australian delegate, 'marry health and agriculture' (Aykroyd, 1936: 640). A 'Mixed Committee' comprising nutritionists, economists and agricultural and financial experts was set up to formulate the first international dietary standard; but first, nutrition had to be established as a social problem:

> The economic interests of the community as a whole are bound up in maintaining the standard of physical efficiency among the people and laying the foundations of the health and well-being

of future generations. Moreover, there is a definite social and political interest in the accomplishment of this task, owing to the well-ascertained relationship between the deficiency of food and especially of protective foods and social unrest. (League of Nations, 1936a: 26–27)

Therefore, the state had to recognise that one of its collective duties was to 'exercise general supervision over the nutrition of the people as a whole' (League of Nations, 1936a: 29–30) and in order to do that, each country had to formulate a centralised national policy 'bringing nutrition and economic policy into harmony' (p. 27); this could then form the basis for international collaboration at a later stage (p. 30). As to the nature of the problem, '[l]eaving the more backward countries out of account for the time being', it was not so much the lack of 'energy giving foods (proteins, fats and carbohydrates)' as the lack of 'protective foods (foods rich in minerals and vitamins)', (League of Nations, 1936a: 15) that needed to be addressed; which,

would mean, even in a comparatively well-fed country like England, a very great increase in the demand for dairy products, eggs, fruit, vegetable etc., and ... such a demand would enormously stimulate the agricultural industry. The ideas of our 'over-production' in agriculture, and of restricted production as a way out of the economic depression, seem to be finally defunct. (Aykroyd, 1936: 640–41)

The other means of creating demand was to widen the constituency of recipients to include children, the rationale being that national investment in the health of young children would be richly rewarded by the 'improved vigour and physique of the adult population' (League of Nations, 1936a: 21); the older children, on the other hand, were 'damaged goods' (p. 21) unworthy of national spending. Pregnant and lactating women were added to the group needing state attention because the health of the child, while *in utero* and when breast-fed, was dependent on the mother's nutritional status.[9]

Reiterating the 'modern' scientific basis of the recommendations, the report laid down the concept of 'sound nutrition' (p. 79) as a mixed diet containing adequate amounts of protective foods, and 'good' protein, at least 50 per cent of which was to be from animal sources (p. 32). Instead of settling for a 'minimum' diet, the policy makers were urged to strive for an 'optimum' diet intended to provide 'an adequate supply of nutritive elements for all the physiological requirements of the human body'(p. 17) and 'for the full development of the individual for efficiency without exhaustion and for his [sic] resistance to disease' (p. 53). Since protective foods were expensive,

[i]t may be increased indirectly by public assistance, whether that be [sic] afforded in cash or in kind or in such a combination of these two as is constituted by rendering essential foodstuffs available to the poor at especially low prices. (League of Nations, 1936a: 81).

Regarding energy requirements, the recommendation was, 'after deducting waste in cooking and at table', 2400 calories per day, for an 'average adult ... living an ordinary everyday life in a temperate climate and not engaged in manual work' as, 'conditions and age being equal, no difference [is] made between the sexes' (p. 56); supplementary requirements were to be added, depending on the muscular effort involved in specific occupations, categorised as light, moderate, hard and very hard work, and the number of hours of work thus engaged. A table of coefficients was provided for calculation of dietary needs for children at different ages and pregnant/nursing women. Protein requirements were calculated separately with minimum of 1 g per kg body weight for adults, and higher allowances for children up to the age of 21 years and pregnant/nursing mothers (League of Nations, 1936b: 13–15). It is noteworthy that body weight was not taken into consideration while calculating energy needs.

The League of Nations' proposal to increase nutritional requirements, particularly of more expensive foods, was greeted with enthusiasm by the industry. The national governments, on the other hand, were unhappy as these new standards, higher than their own advisory groups' recommendations, would force member governments to raise the minimum standards for calculating unemployment and maternity benefits for their populations (Borowy, 2008). But more importantly, the scaling up of standards resulted in amplifying the proportion of malnourished even in countries in the west, for instance, Great Britain (Weindling, 1995). Thus, these standards, set to provide universal measuring yardsticks for assessing the nutritional status of nations, were not necessarily linked to the actual health experiences of a population; nor had they been reached through purely scientific reasoning.

11.3.2 Nutritional Standards for the Colonised: A Dual Policy

The international dietary standard was however considered too high for the subjugated people in the colonies. The Sub-Committee on Colonial Territories (1938), while agreeing that the population in tropical countries were not different from the western populations, suggested reducing it to 'some attainable goal for the purposes of practical nutrition work' (as quoted in Raymond, 1940: 118). For instance, for an adult male from southern India, the estimate was 2600 calories (with 5 per cent added for wastage in cooking, i.e. a total of 2730 calories), and for the adult woman who would require less than the adult male, a factor of 0.85 was to be used for conversion (Raymond, 1940). Similar reduction in calorie requirement was made for populations in other colonies as well; for instance, administrators in East Africa felt that same dietary requirements as suggested by the League of Nations Health Organisation (LNHO) could not be applied for the native populations because of economics, and this unwillingness to apply equal standards was attributed to racism (Little, 1991).

In India, the nutritional requirement was accepted, at 2590 calories (Gangulee, 1934: 69), 10 calories less than that recommended for a male sedentary worker by the LNHO. Even with this lowered norm, at the retail prices prevailing then in South India, a well-balanced diet was out of reach for the poor:

> [I]f a coolie has to support himself, his wife, his father, and three children on 16 rupees a month, the diet of the family will *inevitably* be ill-balanced and probably insufficient in quantity as well. It will, in fact, be waste of time to attempt to persuade him of the advantages of the well-balanced diet, which is quite beyond his means. (Aykroyd as quoted in Gangulee, 1934: 233) (emphasis as in original)

Within the Indian National Movement disagreement regarding nutritional standards was apparent. The Sub-Committee on National Health headed by Col. S.S. Sokhey set up by the National Planning Committee (NPC) in 1938 was unambiguous in its statement:

Indians require as much food of different types as is required in other parts of the world, to permit of [sic] growth and to maintain health. This Sub-Committee cannot do better than suggest to the Planning Committee that they should adopt the standard fixed by the Technical Commission of the Health Committee of the League of Nations, both as regards caloric needs and the provision of proteins, fats and other dietary requirements. (National Planning Committee 1948: 39)

However, the introduction to this report, authored by K.T. Shah, contained a contradictory recommendation, reflecting the compulsions of the newly independent country:

For our purpose, it is enough if, *as recommended by the National Planning Committee in its Instructions for the Guidance of its Sub-Committees*, an average dietary of 2400 to 2800 calories per day per head were aimed at and achieved as amongst the first objectives of a successful National Plan. (National Planning Committee, 1948: 34) (emphasis added)

The Bhore Committee, that had been set up in 1943 by the British government, as was to be expected, recommended a diet yielding 2600 calories (Health Survey and Development Committee, 1946: 56).

11.4 POST-WAR PERIOD

11.4.1 Whittling Away at the Norms

'The construction of post-war international order began with food' (Cullather, 2007: 362) when, at the behest of the US Government, 44 governments meeting in Hot Springs, Virginia, United States, committed themselves to founding a permanent organisation for food and agriculture[10] with an implicit goal of balancing mass production with mass consumption (Cullather, 2007). From the time of its inception, the Nutrition Division of the Food and Agricultural Organization (FAO) was assigned with the task of determining the 'calorie and nutrients' requirements of humans (Weisell, 2002: 15). While, on the face of it, there was to be no binding on the member states, the implicit message was that revisions in the successive meetings were to be viewed as outcomes of scientific deliberations and therefore above partisan interests.

The following table from Payne (1990: 15) (Table 11.1) summarises the shifts in recommended calorie requirements from late 1950s to the 1980s, with specific focus on India.

A close reading of Payne's table shows that the title, 'Energy requirements of a male adult with a nominal body weight of 55 kg (BMI 22.4)', is misleading, for, within the body of the table, estimates shift to a 44 kg man (line 7). Payne chooses 44 kg because 'this is about the lowest body weight consistent with survival and economic activity for a person of average height' (p. 16) and because the 'actual body sizes of many poor but active Indian men are lower than [55 kg]' (p. 15). This shift is in keeping with the changing position of the FAO with regards to calorie recommendations.

From 1950 until 1985, the FAO norms on calorie requirements, based on western populations, were formulated for planning food supplies at the population level and not as a 'yardstick for the detection of undernutrition' (Payne, 1990: 15). But from 1985 onwards, FAO introduced a notion of calorie requirements for prescriptive purposes, i.e.

Table 11.1 Energy requirements of a male adult with a nominal body weight of 55 kg (BMI 22.4)

Basis of calculation	kcal/day
FAO 1957 Moderate activity	2830
FAO 1973 Moderate activity	2530
WHO/FAO/UNU 1985 Moderate activity	2710
ICMR 1982 Moderate activity	2700
FAO 1985 Corrected for overestimation of BMR[a]	2450
As above, without 'discretionary' activity[b]	2200
As above, with body weight adjusted to 44 kg (BMI 18)	1960
80% of ICMR Lipton (1983) 'ultra poor'	2100
FAO 1985 'survival' requirement (1.27 × BMR)[c]	1550
As above, with BMR adjusted by 15% (1.2 BMR)	1470

Notes:
a. BMR calculated using the equation of Quenouille et al. (1951).
b. Discretionary activities are described in the 1985 UN report as those connected with social and recreational pursuits. They amount to about 250 kcals per day for a man of 55kg.
c. Allows for minimal activities such as washing, dressing, standing, etc. No discretionary or occupational activities.

Source: Payne et al. (1990); Payne (1990: 15).

'recommend[ed] intakes which *should* be anticipated in populations with adequate levels of income, social welfare and health provision' as distinct from diagnostic purposes, 'levels below which individuals would be likely to experience some detrimental effects' (p. 15; emphasis as in original); in other words, minimal survival levels below which negative effects can be expected. In addition, the Body Mass Index (BMI),[11] was introduced as a more appropriate indicator because, 'individuals are no longer automatically classed as undernourished simply because they are smaller: indeed some people are prepared to concede that there may even be advantages to being small' (Payne, 1990: 15).

The use of BMI and Payne's rationale for reducing the FAO recommendations from 2450 calories (line 5) to 1960 calories for a 44 kg man with a BMI of 18 (line 7)[12] are based on a problematic notion of adaptation, a notion I would term 'Indian exceptionalism', which has its origin in the protein-calorie debate of the 1960s, spearheaded by Indian scientists, leading to a proposition of the 'small but healthy' hypothesis.

11.4.2 Protein Versus Calorie or Protein and Calorie

In the early 1930s, in Gold Coast, an illness, kwashiorkor, was described in young children being weaned early with a probable cause of dietary deficiency of some amino acids (McLaren, 1974: 93). Soon, this disease, primarily localised in some communities, mostly in Africa, was cast as a world problem by the FAO and the World Health Organization (WHO) and its cure by skimmed milk came at an opportune moment to resolve the situation of domestic surplus of milk in the United States (McLaren, 1974).

In the mid-1960s, Gopalan, the then Director of the Nutritional Research Laboratories, Hyderabad, India, one among those who opposed the generalisation of the 'protein problem' (Newman, 1995), challenged the dichotomisation of kwashiorkor and marasmus[13] in children as being two distinct clinical entities, the former said to be due to sufficient calories but inadequate protein and the latter due to insufficiency of both calories and protein. Drawing upon the concept of adaptation, he explained marasmus and the stunting which went with it, as adaptations to low food intake which protected physiological functioning, whereas, in the case of kwashiorkor, there was 'dysadaptation' or failure to adapt, the body being overwhelmed by either an acute or chronic insufficiency (Gopalan, 1968: 57). Sukhatme, the then Director of the Statistics division, FAO, picked up the concept of adaptation proposed by Gopalan and argued,

> [f]or the vast . . . majority who adapt themselves to available diet, low in calories and low in protein but with protein value about adequate for health, and who eventually establish some sort of equilibrium between body-weight, development and physical activity on the one hand and low intake of food on the other, the need is for more food of the type they are eating today. (Sukhatme, 1970: 182–83)

By the mid-1970s, Gopalan's proposition that the protein gap was part of a food gap (Jaya Rao and Kamala, 1976) and a cereal based diet, if adequate in calories, contained within it adequate quantity of proteins, was largely accepted (Wagstaff, 1976). While the turn of opinion, that inadequacy due to deprivation was the cause of nutritional deficiency rather than inappropriateness due to eating wrong foods, was welcome, there was now a shift to a singular preoccupation with calories, with Gopalan declaring 'the major deficiency in the diets of preschool children in India is calorie deficiency' (Gopalan, 1970: 37); the pendulum now swung to the other extreme of minimising the role of protein and protein-rich foods, particularly of animal origin.

11.4.3 The Indian Exceptionalism: The Small but Healthy Hypothesis

The die was cast when two Indian economists, Dandekar and Rath decided, in 1971, to incorporate calorie requirement in their poverty line for identifying and quantifying the poor. Using a mean per capita daily consumption of food, providing 2250 calories,[14] on the assumption that a household that could not afford even this amount should be considered poor, they arrived at an estimate of poverty – that in 1960–61, one third of the rural population and half of the urban population 'lived on diets inadequate even in respect of calories' (Dandekar and Rath, 1971: 29–30).

> People not familiar with these sections of the population . . . have wondered how men [sic] at all subsist at these levels. Therefore, when somebody occasionally brings these facts to public notice, some of them are shocked and are righteously indignant; others simply do not believe. Nevertheless, such are the facts of poverty in this country. (Dandekar and Rath, 1971: 27)

Sukhatme, one such disbeliever, in 1978, a few years after the publication of Dandekar and Rath's report, challenged their estimates as greatly exaggerated, by questioning the use of mean intakes as minimum requirements, because energy needs varied between individuals and, through autoregulation, within individuals as well.[15] In 1981, introducing a new dimension into the debate, Sukhatme averred that, in fact, lowered calorie intake led to better efficiency because,

[w]hen the total calorie intake is less, the body wastes less, thus using the intake with greater efficiency. As the intake increases the wastage also increases and the energy is used with decreased efficiency. However, a point is reached in the intake of food below which BMR gets depressed and the body is forced into parting with its fat in favour of a more vital need to maintain body heat. That is the point of undernutrition. Likewise a point is reached in the intake of food above which the body gets too hot and is forced into storing the energy as fat. This is the point of overnutrition [sic]. (Sukhatme, 1981: 1319)

This explanation on food metabolism by a statistician reflected a lack of understanding of physiology of food, but since it was to an audience of predominantly economists and political scientists it went unchallenged. The explanation was also looked upon favourably because it appeared scientific enough to support a hypothesis which an American economist, had put forward as the outcome of his 'intellectual odyssey' while traveling through India:

[w]hile one does not see a great deal of visible malnutrition in India, one does see a lot of extremely small people – and the poorer people are, the smaller they tend to be . . . if the poor weigh less than the weight assumed in the calculation of nutrient requirements, their real nutrient requirements will be less than their assumed requirements at any given point in time . . . most of the people of the world who are considered malnourished are simply 'Small but Healthy' people. (Seckler, 1980: 223)

Had Seckler travelled through Britain in the late nineteenth century, he would have come across equally small people:

The British army recruiting for the Boer war . . . found around 50% of young working class recruits to be so malnourished as to be unfit for service . . . Twenty years later . . . the infantry were forced to lower the minimum height for recruits from 5' 4" . . . to 5'. (Clayton and Rowbotham, 2008: 285)

Seckler's proposition about Indians was a circular one: poor people adapt to their low intake by becoming small (short and thin) and because they are short and thin, they require reduced intake. Sukhatme added to Seckler's hypothesis, that smallness was in fact superior because small bodies were more efficient, by illustrating with the real-life experience of women in a community kitchen, rolling 400 to 600 chapatis[16] in an 8-hour shift, whose efficiency increased by over 60 per cent as their intake decreased: 'for any given level of activity, output per unit of calorie intake [was] highest at the lower range of habitual intake as low as 1500 and . . . decrease[d] as intake increase[d] to 2400 calories.' (Sukhatme, 1982: 2014).

What manner of bodies were these that performed more efficiently when the fuel was reduced?

Before joining the kitchen, the women [in this study] were poor, in that, they had hardly any home or shelter worth the description, little clothing, no hygiene and sanitation worth the name and no education. Many of these women were behind bars for petty thefts when they were recruited for the kitchen. Their poverty was such that they were hardly living as human beings; and the food they ate was what they managed somehow to beg, borrow or steal, living much the way animals live. (Sukhatme, 1982: 2014).

Some of them probably looked thin, perhaps emaciated, but their bodies were 'efficient' enough to roll, chapaties at the rate of one a [sic] minute for eight hours, of four hours shift each, [which] calls for hard muscular work and high concentration to ensure that the chapaties are rolled to size, to weigh uniformly and to bake properly. (Sukhatme, 1982: 2013)

The description seems reminiscent of the treadmill in the Victorian prisons with similar compulsions; but, were these women healthy is a question that Sukhatme does not answer as he is consumed with the notion of efficiency. If weight is taken as a measure of nutritional sufficiency (heights were not provided), at recruitment, the women were in the range of 34 kg to 51 kg; two-thirds of them weighed less than 45 kg, and among them one third weighed less than 40 kg. Though it was expected that the women would gain body weight to develop the strength needed for this muscular work, at the end of one year of observation, one third of them lost weight (no information on the range of loss), and one quarter remained at the same level; data on individual changes was, however, not presented.

During the earlier protein debate, Gopalan (1968) had evoked the concept of adaptation to explain the stunting seen in children with reduced food intake as a negative pathological process. He responded to Sukhatme that while the notion of intra-individual variation in calorie intake was unexceptional, what was unacceptable was that people who are 'permanently obliged to subsist on ... the lower limits of their normal intra-individual variation, can *permanently* adapt their requirement to this low intake without any functional impairment' and that 'it may represent a pathological rather than a physiological equilibrium' (Gopalan, 1983: 593; emphasis as in original). Jaya Rao and Kamala (1985) explains why the response from nutritionists was muted,

[Sukhatme] was quicker than the nutritionists, who for some reason kept quiet for a long time. Either we were overwhelmed by the statistical language, or the whole debate was considered to pertain only to statistics ... It was an opportunity lost for the nutritionists and a tactical gain for Sukhatme. (Jaya Rao and Kamala, 1985: unnumbered)

The end result was that the image of an under-fed, thin, small body of an Indian from the working class as an extraordinary efficient machine became fixated in the minds of the policy makers.[17]

The late nineteenth century Atwater's and Atkinson's proposition in the United States that poor people should consume cheaper foods and live within their means was recast anew as policies to be adopted by poor nations but with a singular difference: unlike the poor in rich nations, the poor in poor nations should economise not just by reducing quality but also the quantity of their food intakes because the western dietary allowances were wasted on their small (wasted) bodies.

11.4.4 Defining Away the Poor

The timing of Sukhatme's proposition coincided with the changing paradigm initiated in the World Food Conference of 1974 in Rome where malnutrition was cast as a development problem, 'both a contributor to and consequence of underdevelopment' (Berg and Austin, 1984: 304). Sukhatme's prescription, that the basic cause of malnutrition was due to lack of water and that, '[a] nutrition intervention programme will at best help to treat the symptoms – not the cause of hunger and malnutrition' (Sukhatme, 1982: 2015), changed the focus, 'to the question of technological needs of the poor (such as water and environmental hygiene and sanitation)', taking away the attention 'from the central issue, the distribution of economic power and therefore food' (Zurbrigg, 1983: 2084). It also fitted with the Indian state's need, post emergency,[18] to define away the poor.

Contestation over nutritional threshold continues in the contemporary period, and this need has become acute, particularly after countries structurally adjusted their economies. Lately, there is an added urgency to resolve the puzzle of stagnating nutritional level, in the context of 'unprecedented' economic growth and falling cereal consumption in India (Deaton and Drèze, 2009: 42). Increasingly, the use of calorie intake as a nutrition indicator at the population level (Deaton and Drèze, 2009: 63) and at the individual level (Svedberg, 2000: 24) is being questioned. To do away with the problematic minimum calorie thresholds, Jensen and Miller (2010) recommend the use of a new measure, 'staple calorie share' (SCS) on the assumption that those 'who consume 80 per cent or more of their calories from the staple are likely to be undernourished, while those who receive less than 80 per cent from the staple reveal through their behavior that they have passed subsistence' (p. 20). Their assumption is based on a controlled experimental study on the urban poor in two provinces in China, with mean calorie intake of 1710 in the poorer province and 1800 in the slightly better off province, where they observed that when given an opportunity to buy more food, if the poor households opt for the more expensive food (fish) to add flavor to their diet instead of increasing consumption of the cheaper staple, it would indicate that they are above subsistence level (Jensen and Miller, 2008). They explain the rationale in a less dense article in the American popular press:

> Imagine you are a poor consumer in a developing country. You have very little money in your pocket, not enough to afford all the calories you need. And suppose you have only two foods to choose from, rice and meat. Rice is cheap and has a lot of calories, but you prefer the taste of meat. If you spent all your money on meat, you would get too few calories . . . when faced with true hunger, taste is a luxury you can't [sic] afford. (Jensen and Miller, 2011)

While we do not hear the voices of the people in the study to know why they did what they did, Oddy (1970) comments on a similar situation in the late nineteenth century when the Inter-Departmental Committee on Physical Deterioration disapproved the behaviour of the working class spending money on pickles and vinegar to add flavor to their food: 'However, this [Committee's] attitude fails to take account of the need for food to be palatable. In a diet high in carbohydrate foods such as these families in the 1890s ate, palatability was probably the overwhelming consideration in expenditure on food.' (Oddy, 1970: 322).

Should the poor not be allowed to have 'discretionary foods? . . . permitted to have palates and preferences? A sweet tooth perhaps?' (Saith, 2005: 4604).

The use of SCS has been criticised both on theoretical grounds and policy implications (Kaicker and Gaiha, 2011), yet it could appeal to policy makers precisely because of that, as it 'yields an estimate of undernourishment or hunger that is half of that estimated by the traditional method using a minimum threshold' (Jensen and Miller, 2010: 4). From a nutritional point of view, Jensen and Miller's 'minimum-cost' constructed diets that require a person to consume daily, anything from 500 g to 1000 g cereal to meet energy needs, could increase morbidities and mortalities in such populations because high carbohydrate diet is indicted as a risk factor in cardio vascular disease (Merchant et al., 2007).

11.4.5 Dietary Allowances: A Contested Territory

While, converting the three macronutrients in food into calories has become an accepted way to provide a balance sheet for accounting inputs, it makes little physiological sense in terms of output. Though technically, the body can utilise proteins as energy, it does so only in times of starvation for its primary function is to provide amino acids for building body proteins; and fats, a concentrated source of energy, not only acts as a buffer during periods of starvation or excess energy needs (as in breast feeding), but provides essential fatty acids which have a vitamin-like function in the body (Gopalan et al., 2012: 2). The critical role of vegetables and fruits to provide essential vitamins and minerals has been known for more than a century. Moreover, the requirements would vary according to age, gender, work and physiological status as in pregnancy and lactation.

The dissonance between the economic and public health reasoning in the choice of dietary recommendations seems to be linked to their differing objectives as the former is preoccupied with defining poverty and the latter with health.

Thus, in India, in 2009, an expert group reviewing the methodology for estimation of poverty utilised FAO's revised calorie norm of 1770 per capita per day in its calculations (Government of India, 2009) for no reason other than that it was closer to the actual observed intake of 1776 calories (p. 2). In contrast to this, around the same time, the recommendations arrived at by the Indian Council of Medical Research (ICMR) based on studies on Indian populations was far higher, with, for instance, a male (55 kg) engaged in moderately heavy work requires 2560 calories and a female (50 kg.) engaged in moderately heavy work requires2050 calories (Indian Council of Medical Research, 2010: 50).[19] Table 11.2 gives the recommended energy, protein and fat intake for adult males and females in India as per the National Institute of Nutrition.[20]

11.5 CONCLUDING REMARKS

While revising of dietary norms is to be expected as advances are made in nutritional science, recommendations of dietary allowances become a contested territory. Depending on particular socio-political contexts, recommendations have been scaled up or scaled down to suit the needs of the state and capital. Use of calorie counts in poverty calculations has taken the focus off from the need to provide for a diet with all the necessary, equally important nutrients in appropriate quantities for optimal health, irrespective of costs. As pointed out by Gopalan (1983) reliance on only calories is unwarranted from the point of view of nutrition, as '*[a]ll nutrient deficiencies* represent undernutrition' (Gopalan, 1983: 591; emphasis as in original).

Table 11.2 Nutrient Requirements for Indians (adults)

	Category	Body weight (kg)	Energy			Protein	Visible fat
			kcal/d[a]	kcal/kg/day	g/kg/d	Total	g/d
Men	Sedentary work	60	2320	39	1.0	60	25
	Moderate work	60	2730	46	1.0	60	30
	Heavy work	60	3490	58	1.0	60	40
Women	Sedentary work	55	1900	35	1.0	55	20
	Moderate work	55	2230	41	1.0	55	25
	Heavy work	55	2850	52	1.0	55	30
	Pregnant	55 + GWG[b]	+350			55 + 23	30
	Lactating	55 + WG[c]	+600 +520			55 + 19 (first six months) 55 + 13 (next six months)	30

Notes:
a. Rounded off to the nearest 10kcal/d.
b. GWG – Gestational weight gain.
c. WG – Gestational weight gain remaining after delivery.

Source: Indian Council of Medical Research (2010: 50, 82 and 103).

NOTES

* I wish to thank Ashwani Saith, Amrita Chhachhi and the editors of this volume for their valuable feedback.
1. Calorimeter – an apparatus used for measuring heat (*calor* – heat in Latin) in the study of thermo-chemistry.
2. Calorie – defined as the amount of energy required to raise the temperature of one kilogramme of water by one degree Celsius at one atmosphere of pressure (Hargrove, 2006). Energy in food is quantified as kilocalories (kcal).
3. This was later refined by Atwater to 4, 8.9 and 4 calories, respectively (Maynard, 1962: 8), the conversion factors currently in use.
4. The 'law against the dangerous activities of social democracy', an emergency law extended till 1890. Source: http://translate.google.com/translate?hl=en&sl=de&u=http://www.uni-giessen.de/~g41007/sozialis.html&ei=wOmIS9PFCsLr-AaOy4TkDQ&sa=X&oi=translate&ct=result&resnum=2&ved=0CA0Q7gEwAQ&prev=/search%3Fq%3DSozialistengesetz%26hl%3Den%26sa%3DG. Accessed 27 February 2010.
5. The prisoners' accounts were very different from the popular perception. The food was so inadequate that, 'The first part visibly affected was the neck. The flesh shrinks, disappears and leaves what look like two artificial props to support the head . . .' (as quoted in Priestley 1985: 158).
6. http://www.digitalhistory.uh.edu/database/article_display.cfm?HHID=224(till234). Accessed 25 February 2010.
7. Strangely though, while focusing on eating cheaply to reduce costs, Atwater refused to lower his dietary standards for intake of protein which were higher than that of Voit's, and despite his own studies showing lower requirements (Maynard, 1962: 6). This was probably linked to the emerging beef industry.

8. Part of this section and the next one on colonial diet was published earlier as a working paper (see Sathyamala, 2010).
9. This recommendation was controversial then, because even as late as 1946, the medical advice to pregnant women in many parts of the western world was to refrain from gaining weight during pregnancy to facilitate easy delivery, particularly in the context of contracted pelvises and destructive surgeries with adverse maternal and child outcomes (Luke and Johnson, 1991).
10. Source: A short history of FAO, http://www.fao.org/UNFAO/histo-e.htm. Accessed 25 May 2010.
11. Body Mass Index is a proportion of weight for height in squares with a normal range said to be from 18.5 to 24.99.
12. This is also misleading because the lower range of normal BMI is 18.5. The height for this man works out to be 156 cm and if he had a BMI of 18.5, the lower cutoff point, with the same weight, he will have to drop 2 cm from his height.
13. Another clinical manifestation in young children due to food deprivation.
14. This was considered 'adequate under conditions of climate etc.' (Dandekar and Rath, 1971: 129).
15. The paper by Sukhatme and Margen (1982) was published after this; for a critique, see Dasgupta and Ray (1990).
16. Indian unleavened flatbread.
17. In 1929, the passing of the Bombay Maternity Act also saw a similar debate, with opponents to the bill stressing that 'coolie women had a different body and capacity for physical endurance that could do continue working up to practically a few days before confinement' (Chhachhi, 2004: 73).
18. In India, the period from 26 June 1975 to 21 March 1977 was declared as a period of emergency with the suspension of civil liberties.
19. Although the ICMR report was published in 2010, the first meeting took place in April 2009, 7 months before the publication of the report of the Expert Group on Poverty Estimation.
20. See the report of the expert committee on nutrient requirements (Indian Council of Medical Research, 2010) for dietary allowances of other nutrients for Indians.

REFERENCES

Anonymous (1874), The Late Dr. Edward Smith, F.R.S. *British Medical Journal*, **2**(725), 653–654.
Aronson, N. (1982), Nutrition as a social problem: a case study of entrepreneurial strategy in science. *Social Problems*, **29**(5), 474–87.
Atkinson, E. (1889), *The Industrial Progress of the Nation: Consumption Limited, Production Unlimited*. Reprinted edition, 1973. New York: Arno Press.
Aykroyd, W.R. (1936), Nutrition, international and national. *Current Science*, **4**, 639–42.
Berg, A. and J. Austin (1984), Nutrition policies and programmes: a decade of redirection. *Food Policy*, **9**(4), 304–12.
Borowy, I. (2008), Crisis as opportunity: international health work during the economic depression. *Dynamis*, **28**, 29–51.
Carpenter, K.J. (1991), Edward Smith (1819–1874). *The Journal of Nutrition*, **121**, 1515–1521.
Carpenter, K.J. (1994),The life and times of W.O. Atwater (1844–1907). *The Journal of Nutrition*, **124**, 1707S–1714S.
Carpenter, K.J. (2006), Nutritional studies in Victorian prisons. *The Journal of Nutrition*, **136**, 1–8.
Chambers, W.H. (1952), Max Rubner (1854–1932). *The Journal of Nutrition*, **48**(1), 3–12.
Chapman, Carleton B. (1967), Edward Smith (?1818–1874): physiologist, human ecologist, reformer. *Journal of the History of Medicine and Allied Sciences*, **XXII**(1), 1–26. Available at: http://jhmas.oxfordjournals.org/cgi/reprint/XXII/1/1.pdf .
Chhacchi, A. (2004), Eroding citizenship: gender and labour in contemporary India. PhD dissertation, University of Amsterdam, Amsterdam.
Clayton, P. and J. Rowbotham (2008), An unsuitable and degraded diet? Part one: public health lessons from the mid-Victorian working class diet. *Journal of the Royal Society of Medicine*, **101**, 282–89.
Cullather, N. (2007), The foreign policy of the calorie. *American Historical Review*, **112**(2), 337–64.
Dandekar, V.M. and N. Rath (1971), Poverty in India I: dimensions and trends. *Economic and Political Weekly*, **6**(1), 25–48.
Darby, W.J. (1994), Contributions of Atwater and USDA to knowledge of nutrient requirements. *The Journal of Nutrition*, **24**, 1733S–1737S.
Dasgupta, Partha and Debraj Ray (1990), Adapting to undernourishment: the biological evidence and its implications. In J. Drèze and A. Sen (eds), *The Political Economy of Hunger*, Vol. I, Oxford: Clarendon.

Deaton, A. and J. Drèze (2009), Nutrition in India: facts and interpretations. *Economic and Political Weekly*, **44**(7), 42–65.
Dirks, R. (2003), Diet and nutrition in poor and minority communities in the United States 100 years ago. *Annual Review of Nutrition*, **23**, 81–100.
Eliot, M.M. and M.M. Heseltine (1937), Review: nutrition studies of the League of Nations and the International Labour Office, Geneva, 1936. *The Social Service Review*, **11**(2), 331–34.
Gangulee, N. (1934), *Health and Nutrition in India*. London: Faber & Faber.
Gopalan, C. (1968), Kwashiorkor and marasmus: evolution and distinguishing features. In R.A. McCance and E. Widdowson (eds), *Calorie Deficiencies and Protein Deficiencies: Proceedings of a Colloquium held in Cambridge, April 1967*. London: J. & A. Churchill Ltd., pp. 49–58.
Gopalan, C. (1970), Some recent studies in the nutrition research laboratories, Hyderabad *American Journal of Clinical Nutrition*, **23**(1), 35–51.
Gopalan, C. (1983), Measurement of undernutrition: biological considerations. *Economic and Political Weekly*, **18**(15), 591–95.
Gopalan, C., B.V. Rama Sastri and S.C. Balasubramanian (2012), *Nutritive Value of Indian Foods*. Hyderabad: National Institute of Nutrition.
Government of India (2009), *Report of the Expert Group to Review the Methodology for Estimation of Poverty*, New Delhi: Planning Commission.
Guy, W.A. (1863), On sufficient and insufficient dietaries, with special reference to the dietaries of prisoners. *Journal of the Statistical Society of London*, **26**(3), 239–80.
Hargrove, J.L. (2006), History of the calorie in nutrition. *The Journal of Nutrition*, **136**, 2957–2961.
Health Survey and Development Committee (1946), *Report of the Health Survey and Development Committee*, Vol. I, Survey. Delhi: Government of India.
Indian Council of Medical Research (ICMR) (2010), *Nutrient Requirements and Recommended Dietary Allowances for Indians*. A Report of the Expert Group of the Indian Council of Medical Research. Hyderabad: National Institute of Nutrition.
Jaya Rao and S. Kamala (1976), The myth of the protein gap. Medico Friend Circle Bulletin 4. Available at: http://www.mfcindia.org/mfcpdfs/MFC004.pdf (accessed 12 June 2010).
Jaya Rao and S. Kamala (1985), Blessed are the small in size – if they are Indians. *Medico Friend Circle Bulletin*. Available at: http://www.mfcindia.org/mfcpdfs/MFC115.pdf (accessed 2 June 2010).
Jensen, R.T. and N.H. Miller (2008), Giffen behavior and subsistence consumption. *American Economic Review*, **98**(4), 1553–1577.
Jensen, R.T. and N.H. Miller (2010), A revealed preference approach to measuring hunger and undernutrition. NBER Working Paper Series: 16555, National Bureau of Economic Research, Cambridge MA.
Jensen, R.T. and N.H. Miller (2011), A taste test for hunger. *The New York Times*, 9 July 2011. Available at: http://www.nytimes.com/2011/07/10/opinion/sunday/10gray.html?_r=0 (accessed 14 May 2013).
Kaicker, N. and R. Gaiha (2011), Calorie thresholds and undernutrition in India, 1993–2004. *Journal of Policy Modeling*, **35**(2013), 271–88.
Kamminga, H. and A. Cunningham (1995), Introduction. In H. Kamminga and A. Cunningham (eds), *The Science and Culture of Nutrition, 1840–1940*. Amsterdam: G.A. Rodopi B.V, pp. 1–14.
League of Nations (1936a), *The Problem of Nutrition; Volume I: Interim Report of the Mixed Committee on the Problem of Nutrition*. Geneva: League of Nations.
League of Nations (1936b), *The Problem of Nutrition; Volume II: Report on the Physiological Basis of Nutrition* Geneva: League of Nations.
Levenstein, H. (1980), The New England kitchen and the origins of modern American eating habits. *American Quarterly*, **32**(4), 369–86.
Little, M. (1991), Imperialism, colonialism and the new science of nutrition: the Tanganyika experience, 1925–1945. *Social Science & Medicine*, **32**(1), 11–14.
Luke, B. and T.R.B. Johnson (1991), Nutrition and pregnancy: a historical perspective and update. *Women's Health Issues*, **1**(4), 177–86.
Lusk, G. (1909), The elements of the science of nutrition (2nd edn). London: W.B. Saunders.
Maynard, L.A. (1962), Wilbur O. Atwater: a biographical sketch (3 May 1844–6 October 1907). *The Journal of Nutrition*, **78**(1), 62–69.
McLaren, D.S. (1974), The great protein fiasco. *The Lancet*, **304**(7872), 93–96.
Merchant, A.T. and others (2007), Carbohydrate intake and HDL in a multi ethnic population. *American Journal of Clinical Nutrition*, **85**, 225–30.
Milles, D.(1995), Working capacity and calorie consumption: the history of rational physical economy. In H. Kamminga and A. Cunningham (eds), *The Science and Culture of Nutrition, 1840–1940*. Amsterdam: Rodopi B.V., pp.75–96.
Mitchell, H.H. (1937), Carl von Voit. *Journal of Nutrition*, **13**(1), 2–13.

National Humanities Center (2010), The gilded and the gritty – timeline America: 1865–1913. Available at: http://nationalhumanitiescenter.org/pds/gilded/timeline.pdf (accessed 25 February 2010).
National Planning Committee (1948), *National Health. Report of the Sub-Committee*: National Planning Committee Series. Bombay: Vora & Co., Publishers Ltd.
Newman, J.L (1995), From definition, to geography, to action, to reaction: the case of protein–energy malnutrition. *Annals of the Association of American Geographers*, **85**(2), 233–45.
Oddy, D.J. (1970), Working-class diets in late nineteenth-century Britain. *The Economic History Review*, New Series, **23**(2), 314–323.
Oddy, D.J. (1983), Urban famine in nineteenth century Britain: the effect of the Lancashire cotton famine on working-class diet and health. *The Economic History Review*, **36**(1), 68–86.
Payne, P.R. (1990), Measuring malnutrition. *IDS Bulletin*, **21**(3), 14–30.
Payne, P., Lipton, M., Longhurst, R., J. North and S. Treagust (1990), How Third World Rural Households Adapt to Dietary Energy Stress. International Food Policy Research Institute, Washington, DC, mimeo.
Priestley, Philip (1985), *Victorian Prison Lives: English Prison Biography: 1830–1914*. London and New York: Methuen.
Quenouille, M.H., Boyne, A.W., W.B. Fisher and I. Leitch (1951), *Statistical studies of recorded energy expenditure of man*. Technical Communication No. 17. Commonwealth Bureau of Animal Nutrition, Aberdeen.
Rabinbach, A. (1990), *The Human Motor: Energy, Fatigue and the Origins of Modernity*. New York: Basic Books, A Division of Harper Collins Publishers.
Raymond, W.D. (1940), Tanganyika territory: minimum standards for East African natives. *East African Medical Journal*, **17**, 249. Available at: http://lib3.dss.go.th/fulltext/Journal/analyst/Analyst1941/1941v66p118-121.pdf.
Rose, Michael E. (1971), The doctor in the Industrial Revolution. *British Journal of Industrial Medicine*, **28**, 22–26.
Saith, Ashwani (2005), Poverty lines versus the poor: method versus meaning. *Economic and Political Weekly*, **40**(43), 4601–4610.
Sathyamala, C. (2010), Nutrition as a public health problem (1900–1947). ISS Working Paper No. 510. The Hague: International Institute of Social Studies. Available at: http://repub.eur.nl/res/pub/21788/wp510.pdf (accessed 15 May 2013).
Scola, R. (1992), *Feeding the Victorian City: The Food Supply of Manchester 1770–1870*. Manchester: Manchester University Press.
Seckler, D. (1980), 'Malnutrition': an intellectual odyssey. *Western Journal of Agricultural Economics*, **5**(2), 219–27.
Sukhatme, P.V. (1970), Protein deficiency in urban and rural areas: its measurement, size and nature. *Proceedings of the Nutrition Society*, **29**, 176–83.
Sukhatme, P.V. (1981), On measurement of poverty. *Economic and Political Weekly*, **16**(32), 1318–1324.
Sukhatme, P.V. (1982), Measurement of undernutrition. *Economic and Political Weekly*, **17**(50), 2000–2016.
Sukhatme P.V. and S. Margen (1982), Autoregulatory homeostatic nature of energy balance. *The American Journal of Clinical Nutrition*, **35**, 355–65.
Svedberg, Peter (2000), *Poverty and Undernutrition*. Oxford: Oxford University Press.
Wagstaff, H.R. (1976), Protein consumption or food consumption? Comment. *European Review of Agricultural Economics*, **3**(4), 549–51.
Weindling, Paul (1995), The role of international organizations in setting nutritional standards in the 1920s and 1930s. In H. Kamminga and A. Cunningham (eds), *The Science and Culture of Nutrition, 1840–1940*. Amsterdam: G.A Rodopi B.V., pp. 319–32.
Weisell, Robert (2002), The process of determining nutritional requirements. Available at: ftp://ftp.fao.org/docrep/fao/005/y3800m/y3800m01.pdf (accessed 25 May 2010).
Zurbrigg, S.(1983), Ideology and the poverty line debate. *Economic and Political Weekly*, **18**(49), 2083–2084.

12. Economic prosperity and non-communicable disease: understanding the linkages
Ajay Mahal and Lainie Sutton

12.1 INTRODUCTION

The period since the end of World War II has been characterised by major gains in the economic well-being of the world's population. Global Gross Domestic Product (GDP) per capita rose from roughly $4430 to $16905 (2005 international $) between 1950 and 2010, and with the notable exception of sub-Saharan Africa, all regions of the world experienced substantial economic gains during this period (see Figure 12.1). The postwar period has also been characterised by large improvements in population health. The average Frenchman could expect, at the time of birth, to live for 64 years in 1950. In 2010, his life expectancy at birth was almost 78 years. The gains in life expectancy have been even more dramatic in low- and middle-income countries. In India, life expectancy at birth increased from 39 years in 1950 to 65 years in 2010, an increase of almost 67 per

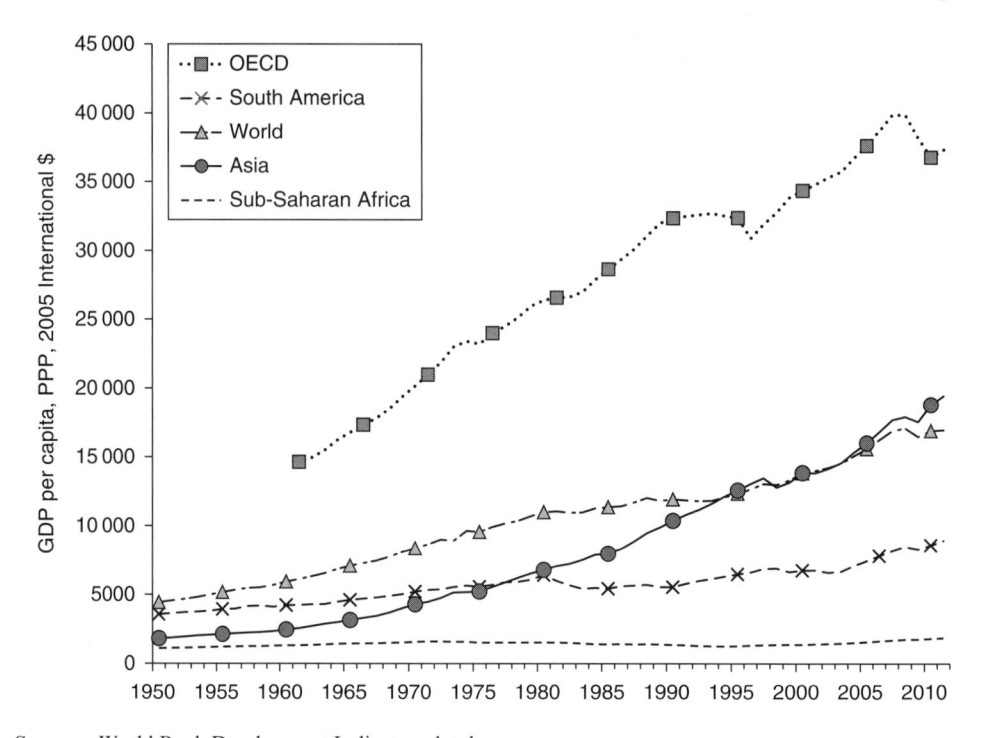

Source: World Bank Development Indicators database.

Figure 12.1 Long term trends in GDP per capita in the world

cent; and Uganda, which was severely affected by an HIV/AIDS epidemic during the 1980s and 1990s, saw its life expectancy at birth increase from 38 years in 1950 to 54 years in 2010, more than a 40 per cent increase. Overall, the gains in life expectancy worldwide since the early 1900s have been sufficiently large to exceed the cumulative improvement in life expectancy in the preceding 200 000 years of human history (Fogel, 1986).

Even as these health and economic gains are being experienced, health policy makers around the world are faced with the growing challenge of non-communicable chronic diseases (NCDs) (Lopez et al., 2006; Daar et al., 2007). According to the most recent estimates available, heart disease, cancers, diabetes and mental health account for 25.5 million deaths annually, or about 48.2 per cent of all-cause mortality worldwide, with 80 per cent of these deaths occurring in low- and middle-income countries (Lozano et al., 2012; World Health Organization (WHO), 2010). The annual death toll from NCDs is projected to be 52 million in 2030, five times the number of projected deaths due to communicable diseases, maternal, perinatal and nutritional conditions combined. NCDs accounted for 51.4 per cent of DALYs (disability adjusted life years) lost globally in 2008, and are projected to account for three times as many DALYs lost due to communicable diseases, maternal, perinatal and nutritional conditions combined by 2030 (Mathers and Loncar, 2005; WHO, 2010). To highlight just one condition, the estimated incidence of cancer diagnoses is predicted to rise from 12.7 million globally in 2008 to 21.4 million by 2030, with two thirds of diagnosed cases occurring in low- and middle-income countries (WHO, 2010).

Health outcomes apart, there are also serious concerns about the impacts of NCDs on the level and distribution of economic well-being. One perspective has been to consider NCDs as a collateral damage of affluence (Trowell and Burkitt, 1981). This essentially suggests that losses of earnings, treatment expenses and the associated risk of impoverishment among NCD-affected households need to be better accounted for against the economic gains of the now richer populations; and moreover that these conditions occur at levels of material outcomes that can be labelled 'affluent'. If there is a policy implication it is that market failures related to preventive actions (e.g. inadequate physical activity or second-hand smoking) and financial risk protection (insurance) may be needed.

Another perspective, however, is that low economic status itself disproportionately increases the risk of acquiring NCDs, a position best exemplified in the recent 'Marmot Review' (Marmot, 2010). From this latter standpoint and quite apart from the position that any associated socioeconomic 'gradient' in NCDs is deemed unfair, the economic and health impacts of NCDs will fall disproportionately upon the economically disadvantaged. This has led to policy suggestions targeting broad areas of social policy to interventions focused on the health of the needy (Marmot, 2010; Canning and Bowser, 2010). How NCDs influence economic gains and how they are influenced by economic status is, therefore, of considerable significance from a policy perspective. There is a large empirical literature that seeks to shed light on these ideas, although it has tended to be repetitive and is often unclear in the basis for its policy suggestions, especially on the causal linkages running from income to health (Chandra and Vogl, 2010).

The primary goal of this chapter is to discuss the key findings of the existing empirical literature and available data in a way as to disentangle the links between incomes (and associated indicators such as education and wealth) and NCDs, focusing in particular on how incomes influence NCDs. Because much of the focus in the existing literature

280 *Handbook on food*

is on developed countries, a related goal of the chapter is to highlight the main conclusions thus far of the emerging literature on the economic status–NCD relationship in developing countries. For reasons of space and data availability we focus primarily on cardiovascular disease and cancers although investigation of the economic status–NCD relationship for conditions such as diabetes, mental health, chronic obstructive pulmonary disease and oral health is obviously warranted in future work.

12.2 NATIONAL, REGIONAL AND MICRO-LEVEL ASSOCIATIONS BETWEEN ECONOMIC OUTCOMES AND NCD: SOME STYLISED FACTS

Here we highlight key stylised facts about the global NCD epidemic. At the national level, a strong quadratic association exists between NCD and economic outcomes (see also Ezzati et al., 2005). This can be seen in cross-country relationships between GDP per capita and indicators of NCDs, such as the share of population deaths due to NCDs, or the share of DALYs accounted for by NCDs. The latter is a composite indicator that is intended to capture both mortality and morbidity due to a health condition (Murray, 1994).

The central observation, as illustrated in Figure 12.2a and b, is that GDP per capita is positively correlated with the share of deaths or DALYs accounted for by cancers and cardiovascular disease (CVD) up to about US$35 000 (purchasing power parity (PPP) adjusted at 2005 International Dollars) and declining thereafter. The basic associations do not change even if we consider cancer and CVD individually against income per capita, whether in terms of shares in total DALYs lost, or as a share of deaths from all causes.

High rates of CVD incidence and associated mortality in middle-income countries that

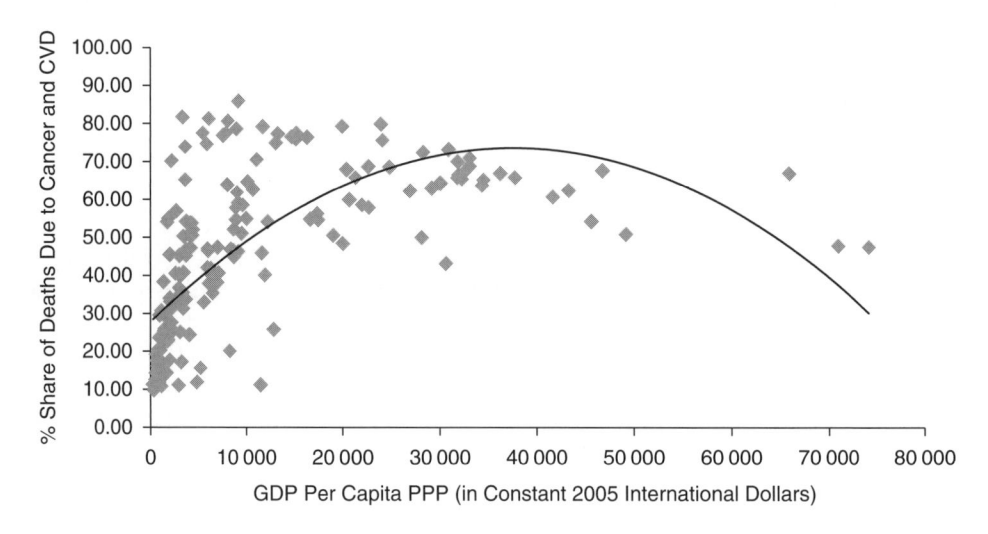

Figure 12.2a *Cross-country relationship between GDP per capita and share of deaths due to cancers and CVD, 2004*

Figure 12.2b   Cross-country relationship between income per capita and share of DALYs lost due to cancers and CVDs 2004

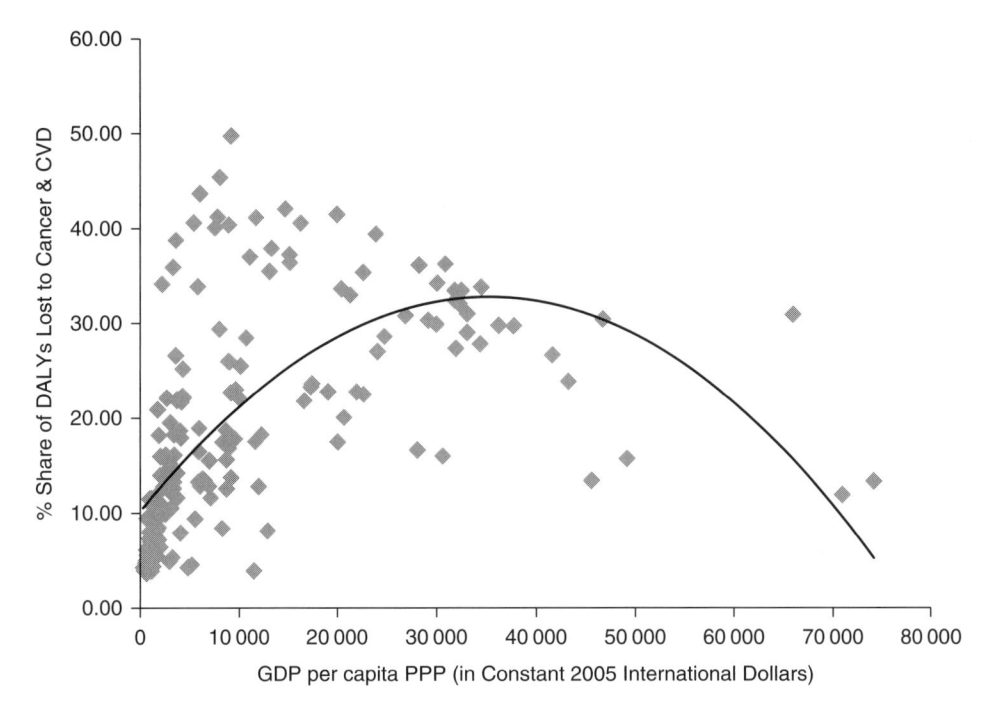

were once part of the former Soviet Union explain a large part of the noise around the trend lines. Excluding these countries makes the fit much tighter. The first conclusion from these charts that although the share of NCDs rises with income per capita, it is not strictly monotonic and, in fact, it may fall with income per capita beyond a point. We prefer to interpret the data as indicating that a stable share of NCDs in all-cause deaths and DALYs lost arises beyond a certain level of GDP per capita, given the very few data points beyond the threshold of $35 000.

Because age distributions across poor and rich countries are likely to be different, and because different age-groups are likely to be more prone to different causes of death, it is useful to assess whether the association between income per capita and the shares of deaths due to cancers and CVD would change if age-distributions in each country were restricted to be the same (that is, after 'age-adjustment' of mortality rates). Figure 12.2c indicates that the association between the share of deaths due to cancers, CVD and diabetes and income per capita essentially remain unaltered even after using a standardised population used to construct age-adjusted mortality by the WHO. That is, the relationship holds even if we suppress the changing age-distribution of population that usually accompanies economic development.

One might also suspect that similar relationships to exist across regions within countries, especially if there is adequate inter-regional variation in economic performance. Unfortunately, mortality or DALY data appropriate for measuring the associations

282 *Handbook on food*

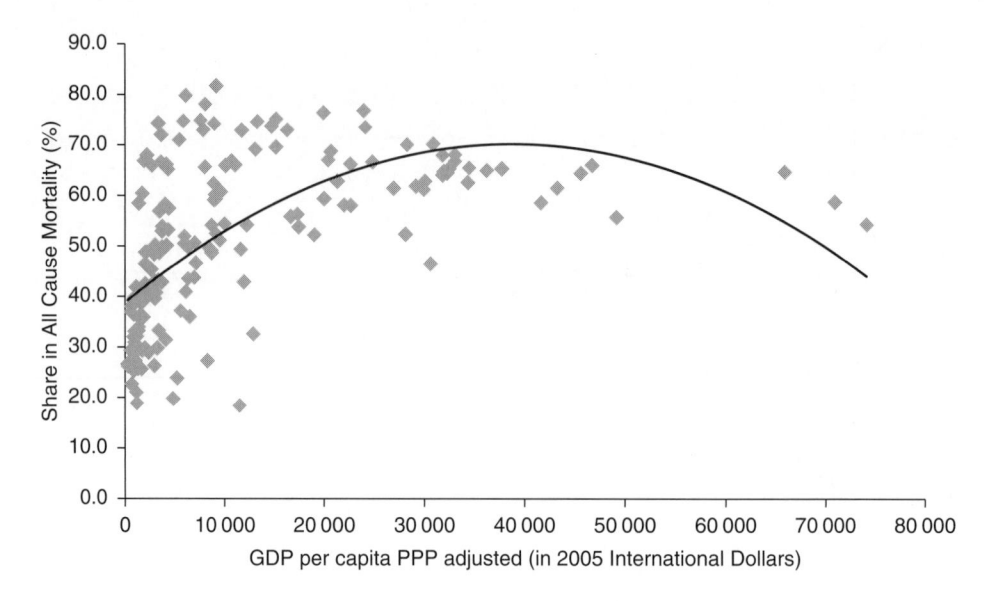

Source: Author estimates, using data from the World Bank and WHO.

Figure 12.2c Cross-country relationship between income per capita and age-adjusted share of cancer and CVD in all cause deaths, 2004

between the share of deaths by specific cause(s) and income per capita are more limited across regions and when available, are confined to developed countries. One country for which corresponding data on mortality by cause and income per capita are readily available and for a sufficiently large number of regions is the United States. Moreover, differentials in income per capita are also significant, with Connecticut enjoying a per capita income of US$36 775 in 2010, more than 80 per cent higher than per capita income in Mississippi, the poorest state in the United States.

Figure 12.3 indicates that although income per capita is still positively correlated with the share of deaths due to heart disease and cancers across states in the United States, although the fit is somewhat poor and the slope coefficient is small in magnitude, relative to cross-country data. Yet the small coefficient of the log of income per capita in Figure 12.3 is consistent with the cross-country associations in Figure 12.2a and b, given that the US income per capita broadly falls around the stationary point.

12.2.1 Are Populations Becoming Sicker from Cancers and CVD Before Becoming Richer?

The seminal work of Preston suggests that despite the strong cross-sectional association between country GDP per capita and life expectancy at birth, much of the worldwide gains in life expectancy in the twentieth century are associated not so much to movements along a curve such as in Figure 12.2a, but to public health interventions (water, sanitation and vaccines), drugs (penicillin) and new treatments for cardiovascular disease bringing about sharp mortality reductions (Preston, 1975; Cutler et al., 2004). That is,

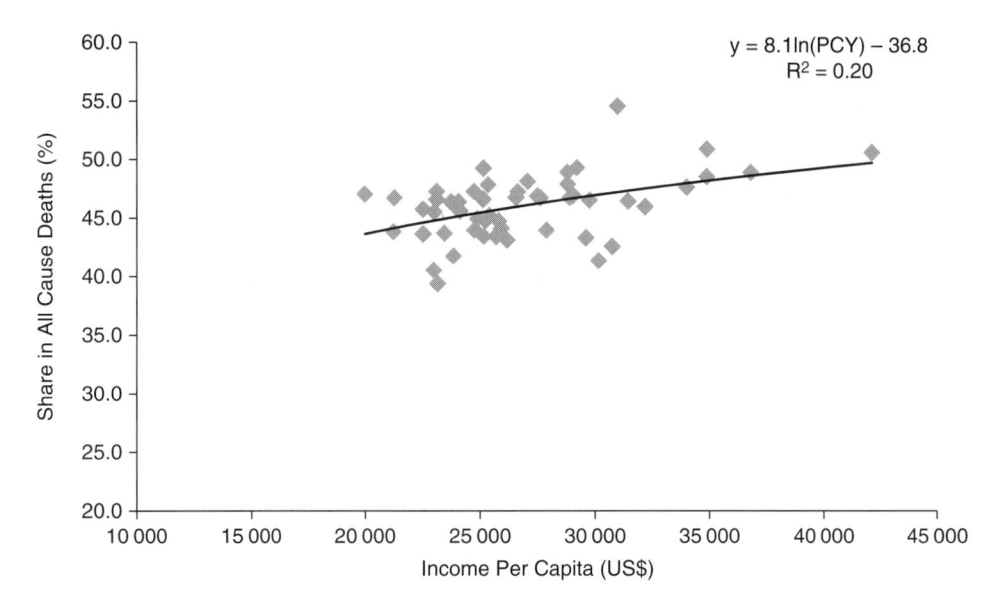

Economic prosperity and non-communicable disease 283

Source: Centers for Disease Control and US Bureau of the Census.

Figure 12.3 Income per capita and deaths from cancers and CVD (as share of all cause deaths) in the United States, 2010

the cross-sectional income–mortality relationship simply shifted over time. Irrespective of the argument that knowledge about public health interventions and their implementation may itself be a function of economic progress, is such a shift occurring in the relationship between income per capita and the share of cancers and CVD in mortality?

Until recently, data were not available for a large number of countries and over time. The recently completed Global Burden of Disease 2010 Study (Lozano et al., 2012; Institute of Health Metrics and Evaluation, 2013) put together country-specific information on the share of years of life (YLL) lost 'prematurely' due to death by cause for 1990 and 2010. Here YLL is the difference between a pre-specified 'ideal' age and the actual age at death, and is best thought of as an indicator of mortality weighted appropriately by the age distribution of deaths. Although information is currently available only for the top 25 causes of YLL in each country, we were able to construct the shares of YLL lost due to ischaemic heart disease and stroke for nearly 170 countries for two points in time – 1990 and 2010. Figure 12.4 describes the association between the proportion of all-cause YLL lost due to CVD and cancers in 1990 and 2010 (expressed as an odds ratio) and corresponding PPP adjusted per capita income levels. We also estimated simple quadratic specifications for the odds ratio of YLL lost due to CVD and cancers and GDP per capita in the 2 years (also shown in Figure 12.4; for 2010, we use the continuous line and for 1990 the dotted line).

Although the only data points we have are no more than 20 years apart, there are two features of the data in Figure 12.4 that are of interest. First, the estimated relationship between the share of YLL (as an odds ratio) lost due to ischaemic heart disease and stroke and per capita income, albeit noisy, has become flatter over time (the 1990

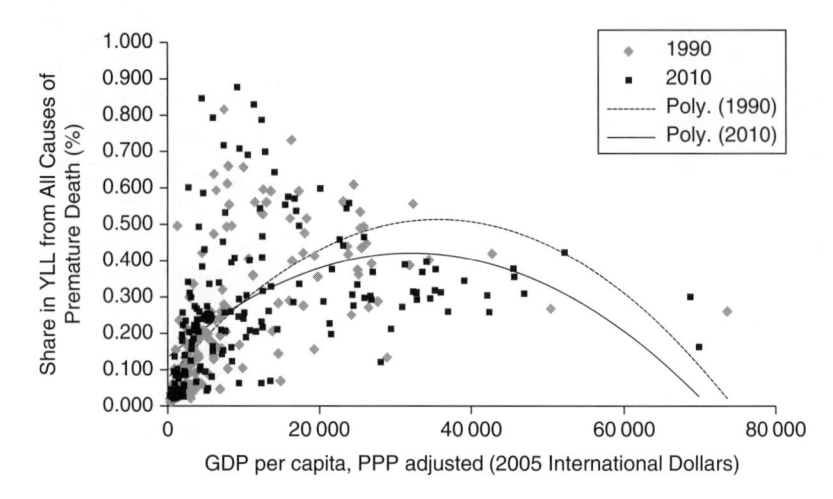

Source: Institute of Health Metrics and Evaluation (2013).

Figure 12.4 The changing association between income per capita and share of years of life lost due to premature death from stroke and IHD

relationship is the dotted line and the 2010 is the continuous line). The second is that in 2010, the share of YLL lost to stroke and ischaemic heart disease equals that in 1990 at levels of income per capita that are lower than in 1990 for countries below a certain threshold (approximately $9000, PPP adjusted, in this case). On average, the latter set of countries could then be said to have become more susceptible to CVD mortality at lower levels of income than in 1990. However, the opposite holds true on average for countries above the threshold (PPP adjusted). Evidence that death rates among individuals aged 60 years and younger due to CVD are much higher in developing countries than their counterparts in developed countries lends some support to this point (WHO, 2010).

12.2.2 Age-Specific Mortality from Cancers and CVD

Figures 12.2–12.4 highlight that as incomes increase, beyond some income threshold the share of deaths due to cancers and CVD increases very slowly. Given that developing and middle-income countries have a greater share of younger populations who are likely to have a lower incidence of cancers and heart disease (all else the same), the flattening out of the relationship between income and the share of CVD and cancer in all cause premature deaths, suggests that in fact mortality rates from cancer and CVD are lower in richer countries in older age groups. Figure 12.5 illustrates this point with data on age-adjusted mortality rates from cancers and CVD for countries at different levels of income per capita. Indeed, the inverse relationship between age-specific mortality and income per capita can be seen even in cross-state data in the United States.

Cross-sectional data capture a snapshot at a point in time and may suppress variation in mortality trends that exists across countries occurring independently of the pattern of economic growth (Bloom and Canning, 2007). Mirzaei et al. (2009) present time trends for varying periods for mortality from CVD for 55 primarily middle- and high-income

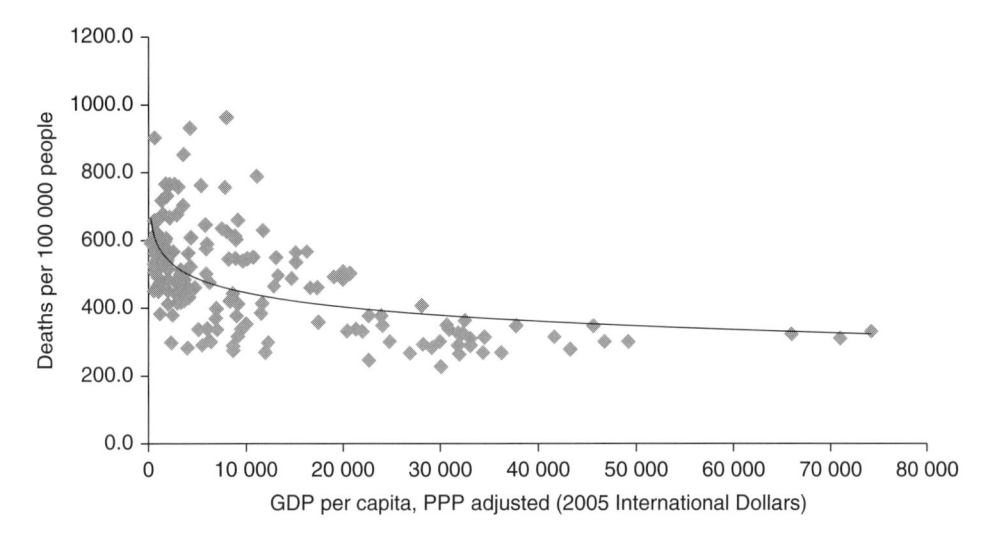

Figure 12.5 *Age-adjusted mortality rates from cancer and CVD by income per capita in a cross-section of countries, 2004*

countries. Trends vary significantly across countries and regions. Thus, CVD epidemics in Western Europe, the United States, the United Kingdom and Australia peaked in the late 1960s and early 1970s and age-adjusted CVD mortality has been declining ever since (Ford and Capewell, 2007; Australian Institute of Health and Welfare, 2010; Rosamond et al., 2012). East European countries (e.g. the Czech Republic and Poland) saw peak age-specific mortality due to CVD in the late 1980s, after which declines have been observed. CVD mortality rates have remained stable (starting from low initial rates) in Southern Europe, in countries such as Greece, Portugal and Spain. Japan has amongst the lowest rates of ischaemic heart disease deaths, and has also experienced continuous declines for over 60 years (Mirzaei et al., 2009).

Cancer mortality rates have also declined over time in developed countries and these declines have been slower and of more recent origin than those for CVD mortality. Figure 12.6 reports age-specific mortality rates for colorectal cancer among men in five developed countries (the trends for women are similar) suggesting a slow but steady decline, at least since the 1980s. However, as Honore and Lleras-Muney (2007) note, the declines in cancer-mortality over time are likely even greater than observed because in a competing-risks framework, large decreases in CVD mortality will have pushed cancer incidence (and hence deaths from cancer) upwards. Indeed, the slowdown in innovations in CVD treatments likely explain at least some of the recent observed declines in cancer mortality. In contrast to colorectal cancer, age-specific mortality from lung cancer has been declining among men since the mid-1990s, whereas among women it has remained stable in recent years, at rates significantly higher than half a century ago.

Less clear is the situation in developing and middle-income countries, which are also plagued by limited trend information on mortality by cause. In Brazil, one study found that colorectal mortality rates are increasing over time across most regions in

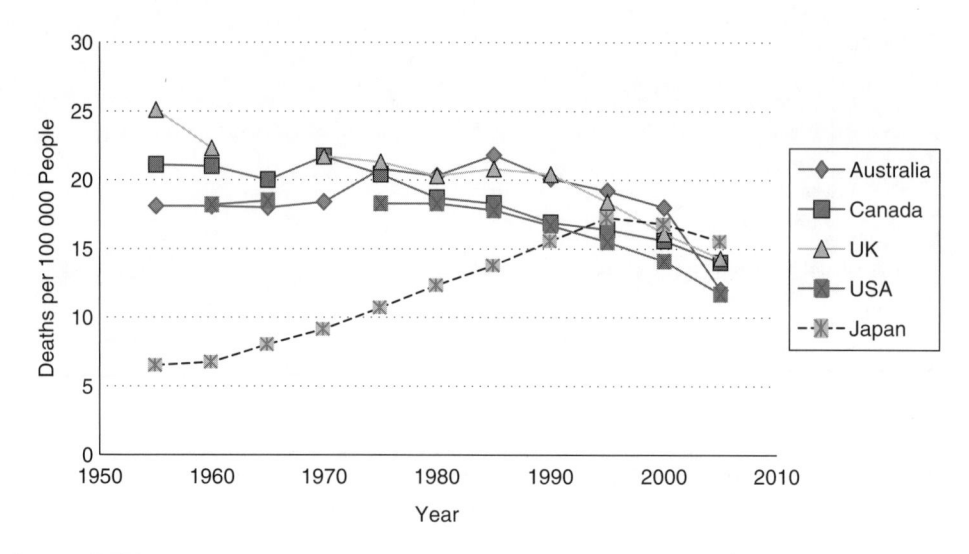

Source: WHO.

Figure 12.6 Age-adjusted mortality rates for colorectal cancer in five developed countries, 1955–2005

the country, although no age-adjusted estimates were reported (das Neves et al., 2005). Breast cancer rates on the other hand, have remained stable, increasing in regions of low socioeconomic status, and declining in better-off regions (Freitas Junior et al., 2012). Overall, age-adjusted cancer mortality rates have declined over the last two decades in the Republic of Korea; but lung cancer mortality rates among women and colorectal cancer mortality rates have risen over the same period (Jung et al., 2011).

Broadly, trends in cancer and CVD mortality suggest the curve in Figure 12.5 is shifting downwards, at least for incomes above a certain level. However, countries that were formerly part of the Soviet Union have experienced dramatic increases in age-specific mortality from CVD since the mid-1980s. Finally, the literature also highlights concerns about rising mortality from CVD among younger age groups in developing countries (O'Flaherty et al., 2008), which, together with declining age-adjusted mortality for CVD in richer countries, seems consistent with the pattern in Figure 12.4.

12.2.3 Association between Socioeconomic Status, Incidence and Mortality from Cancers and CVD in Micro-Level Data

Information at the level of households and small-area populations performs a useful role in understanding the relationship between economic outcomes, cancers and CVD for at least two reasons. First, data on cancer and CVD incidence and mortality for smaller population sub-groups are more commonly available, even for developing countries. Second, longitudinal studies are often feasible, three prominent examples being the Framingham Study in the United States, the Nurses' Health Study, also in the United States, and the Whitehall Study in the United Kingdom (Marmot, 2010). The availability of information over time and extensive information on covariates at the household and individual level can better account for the relationship between various indicators of economic status, cancers and CVD, including any 'confounding' information. Here we focus on the broad associations between economic status and cancer and CVD incidence and mortality, leaving a discussion on causal directions to the following sections (see Table 12.1 for selected examples from a vast literature).

For developed countries, there are three main conclusions reached by this literature, some of which run parallel to the conclusions reached on the basis of cross-country data. First, after controlling for age, economic status is inversely correlated with incidence and mortality rates of cancers and heart disease. Second, when longitudinal data are available, the evidence suggests that age-specific mortality rates are declining across socioeconomic groups, whether for cancer or for CVD. However, the decline in mortality rates is often slower for poorer groups. Third, there are disease- and region-specific differences in the relationship between economic status and cancer and CVD incidence that are noteworthy. Of specific note is the finding that breast cancer incidence is positively correlated with economic status.

For developing and middle-income countries, stronger conclusions may need to await further information (see Table 12.1 again for some relevant studies). A recent review of stroke outcomes suggests that mortality rates for cancer and CVD are higher among groups with low economic status. An analysis for Pakistan suggests that the 5-year survival rate for breast cancer mortality is negligible for poor women; and a study for Nepal points to greater lung cancer risk among poorer Nepalese men. However, there are also studies that suggest otherwise. Thus, Kurkure and Yeole (2006) found higher breast cancer mortality among women of higher economic status in their study of Mumbai women, compared to the less well off. A recent review of 53 studies from India argues for higher incidence of CVD among better off individuals (Subramanian et al., 2013). Another study of Korean civil servants found that the risk of myocardial infarction (non-fatal) was positively associated with economic status (Song et al., 2006). In addition, there are multiple studies (as seen in the next section) indicating that risk factors for CVD (although not mortality) may be higher among people with high economic status.

12.2.4 Main Conclusions

The available cross-sectional and times series evidence at the national and regional levels suggest the following 'stylised' features of the epidemic of cancers and CVD worldwide:

> **Fact 1**: Higher incomes per capita are usually positively associated with increased numbers of cases of cancers and CVD and in their share in total mortality (deaths and premature YLL) and/or morbidity (DALYs), but the relationship flattens or even changes direction after a certain income threshold. The association between economic outcomes and shares of cancers and CVD appears relatively flat across regions within a developed country (for US data).
> **Fact 2**: The existing share of CVD in mortality/YLL in poor countries is occurring at levels of income per capita that is lower than their richer counterparts, than when the latter were at a similar stage of the NCD epidemic in 1990.
> **Fact 3**: Age-adjusted mortality for CVD and cancer is lower among richer countries and regions, relative to their poorer counterparts.

Table 12.1 The association of CVD and cancer incidence and mortality with socioeconomic status (SES): a summary of selected studies from developed and developing countries

Study	Country	Condition/Data	Indicators	Findings
Developing and middle-income countries				
Yusuf et al. (2004)	52 Developed and Developing Countries	Heart disease 29 972 individuals (INTERHEART study)	Myocardial Infarction	Smoking, hypertension, diabetes, abdominal obesity, psychosocial factors, lack of consumption of fruits and vegetables, regular alcohol consumption, lack of regular physical activity linked to myocardial infarction – across gender, age groups and regions
Aziz et al. (2008)	Pakistan	Breast cancer	Tumor size, stage, 5-year survival	Poorer patients presented with more advanced stage of the disease; negligible 5-year survival rates
Kurkure and Yeole (2006)	India	Cancer (study in Mumbai, India)	Cancer incidence and mortality	Increased incidence of cancer mortality in women with higher educational attainment; higher risk of cervical cancer among less well educated women
Zhou et al. (2006)	China	Stroke (n = 806 patients with stroke, 1999–2005)	3-year all-cause mortality	Income and house size and non-manual work were significantly negatively associated with stroke mortality
M. Hashibe et al. (2010)	Nepal	Lung cancer (n = 522)	Lungcancer 'risk'	Inversely linked with educational status; Late stage cancers were common among women, elderly and individuals with less education
Samuel et al. (2012)	India	Risk Factors for CVD (n = 2218 aged 26–32 years)	Obesity, diabetes, IGT, total cholesterol to HDL ratio, triglyceride, tobacco use	Risk factors higher in urban than in rural areas and educational attainment
Subramanian et al. (2013)	India	CVD and risk factors (systematic review, 53 studies)	SES–CVD link	CVD and CVD risk factors more prevalent among the high SES groups (with the exception of hypertension and tobacco); CVD-related mortality higher among low SES, the share of CVD deaths is higher among high SES
Xu et al. (2008)	China	Stroke (Cross-sectional study, n = 29 340, 45 administrative villages in 2000–01)	Stroke prevalence	SES was positively correlated with stroke prevalence. White collar workers had higher stroke prevalence than blue collar workers

Study	Country	Disease	Measure	Findings
Addo et al. (2012)	Developed and developing countries	Stroke (Review of studies between 2006–2011)	Stroke incidence and mortality	Mortality rates for stroke significantly higher in developing countries compared to developed countries; high rates of stroke incidence and mortality in low SES populations. Poor people may also receive less effective care
Developed countries				
Avendano et al. (2006)	(Finland, Norway, Denmark, UK, Belgium, Switzerland, Austria, Italy and Spain)	Longitudinal data on ischaemic heart disease mortality from registries	Age-standardised rates and Rate ratios for IHD mortality (by educational status), populations aged 30–59 years and 60+ years	IHD mortality was higher among populations with lower educational status; disparities higher in Northern Europe; smaller SES variations in IHD mortality among elderly women
Sacerdote et al. (2012)	Europe	Diabetes (8 Western European Countries, n = 16 835)	Incidence of diabetes cases (using hazard ratios)	Individuals with lower educational attainment had higher risk of acquiring type II diabetes. BMI positively associated with type II diabetes, and explains some of the education–diabetes link
Dalstra et al. (2005)	Europe	Cancer, heart disease, stroke, diabetes 8 West European countries (National Health Surveys)	Self-reported prevalence rates	*Stroke and diabetes prevalence* negatively correlated with socioeconomic status; cancer prevalence in 20–59 age-group was higher in low-educated groups; but higher in higher educated groups in the 60–79 category; socioeconomic differences were greater among women than for men in diabetes, hypertension and heart disease prevalence; socioeconomic inequalities in heart disease prevalence higher in north European countries compared to their Southern counterparts
Rathmann et al. (2006)	Germany	Diabetes (1476 individuals aged 55–74 years)	Diabetes status, C-reactive protein (CRP) – inflammatory marker	While diabetes was (inversely) associated with SES, controlling for CRP status did not influence the SES–diabetes relationship. Moreover, the SES–CRP relationship among women vanished once BMI and waist circumference were controlled for (there was no relationship among men)

Table 12.1 (continued)

Study	Country	Condition/Data	Indicators	Findings
Developed countries				
Davey Smith et al. (1998)	Scotland	(Stroke, cancers, heart disease) 5645 men aged 35–64 years	Mortality from different causes	Men whose fathers had higher ranking professions saw lower rates of *mortality from coronary heart disease, some types of cancers and stroke.* Controlling for current socioeconomic status and various risk factors tended to lower the inverse relationship, but not eliminate it
Whyte (2006)	Scotland	(Stroke, cancers, heart disease)	Mortality from different causes	Mortality from CVD declined for both males and females (15–74 year age group) over a 50-year period from 1950 to 2000; Areas with lower SES in Scotland saw higher rates of CVD mortality than their richer counterparts
Chaturvedi et al. (1998)	United Kingdom	(Heart disease, diabetes) 17 264 male civil servants examined in 1967–69; and another 300 diabetics examined in 1975–77	Mortality from all causes and heart disease	*Risk factors:* 50% of the increased risk of mortality among lower socioeconomic groups was due to risk factors such as smoking and hypertension (more prevalent among lower socioeconomic groups) *Prevalence of heart disease* higher among lower socioeconomic groups (diabetics and non-diabetics separately); *mortality from heart disease* was also greater in lower socioeconomic groups, irrespective of diabetic status
Van Rossum et al. (2000)	United Kingdom	(Heart disease, stroke, cancers) 18 001 male civil servants, 40–69 years old during 1967–69 followed up 25 years later (Whitehall Study)	All-cause mortality rate differentials, and mortality rate differentials by individual causes of death	Mortality rate differentials in heart disease, cancer and other causes persist even after 25 years of follow-up, with senior officials at lower risk of death compared to the junior-most categories. However, differences across occupational categories did decline as the population became older following retirement; Risk factors such as smoking, high blood pressure and cholesterol cannot explain more than one third of this differential
Aarts et al. (2010)	Europe, United States and Canada	Colorectal cancer (Review)	Incidence, treatment, survival	*Incidence:* SES and incidence inversely related in United States and Canada; positively associated with SES in Europe *Treatment, survival and mortality rates inversely related to SES*

Study	Country	Cancer type/data	Outcome	Findings
Forrest et al. (2013)	Developed countries	Lung cancer (review: longitudinal studies only)	Whether treatment received following diagnosis	SES was inversely related to the likelihood of receiving treatment, conditional on a given diagnosis/stage of cancer
Sidorchuk et al. (2009)	Developed countries	Lung cancer (review: 64 studies)	Incidence	SES inversely related to lung cancer incidence, even after controlling for smoking
Menvielle et al. (2009)	Europe (10 countries)	Lung cancer (European Prospective Investigation Study into Cancer and Nutrition) n = 391 251	Lung cancer incidence	In north Europe and in Germany, SES (educational attainment) was *inversely related* to lung cancer incidence; In southern Europe, incidence was *positively associated* with educational attainment. *Smoking* explained about half of these socioeconomic differences in lung cancer incidence
Menvielle et al. (2010)	Europe (10 countries)	Lung cancer (European Prospective Investigation Study into Cancer and Nutrition)	Lung cancer incidence	*Occupational exposures to asbestos, heavy metals and PAH* explains some of the socioeconomic (educational attainment) differences in lung cancer incidence
Coleman et al. (2004)	United Kingdom	Cancer (2.2 million patients diagnosed with cancer between 1986 and 1999 and followed up)	Survival rates	*Survival rates are increasing over time, and across genders.* However, survival among richer groups is increasing at a faster than their poorer counterparts
Lejeune et al. (2010)	United Kingdom	Colorectal cancer (71 917 patients)	Survival rates, treatment	*Low SES patients had lower survival and lower likelihood of receiving timely treatment, or any treatment.* Indeed the stage at which cancer was diagnosed and speed of treatment explained much of the socioeconomic difference in survival
de Kok et al. (2008)	Netherlands	Cancers (n = 12 978, longitudinal GLOBE study)	Cancer incidence	Low SES of respondents associated with increased risk of various cancers – lung, colorectal, breast

Table 12.1 (continued)

Study	Country	Condition/Data	Indicators	Findings
Developed countries				
Diez-Roux et al. (2001)	United States	Heart disease (n = 13 009, cohort study) Atherosclerosis Risk in Communities Study, 45–64 years at baseline	Risk of acquiring Coronary heart disease	People living in disadvantaged areas had a greater risk of heart disease than those living in more advantaged areas and this held even if one controlled for race, incomes and other risk factors for coronary heart disease. Possibly effect of neighbourhoods works via risk factors; Personal income was also negatively correlated with the risk of coronary heart disease
Malik et al. (2010)	Multiple developed and developing countries	CVD (Literature review)	CVD incidence	*Impact CVD*: large cohort studies show a link between sugar sweetened beverage (SSB) intake and heart disease, and the effect remains even after accounting for the BMI increasing effect of SSB
Pudrovska and Anikputa (2012)	United States	Breast cancer (Wisconsin Longitudinal Study, n = 10 317)	Age at breast cancer diagnosis; age at breast cancer death	Higher SES of parents increases risk of acquiring breast cancer, but lowers the risk of mortality from breast cancer
Vona-Davis and Rose (2009)	United States	Breast cancer (Literature review and population level statistics on mortality and cancer epidemiology)	Stage of breast cancer at first diagnosis	SES and breast cancer mortality rates are positively correlated; low economic status likely explains poor breast cancer prognosis among African Americans and Hispanic women. Obesity was correlated with advanced breast cancer at first diagnosis
Alter et al. (2004)	Canada	Myocardial Infarction (n = 2256) discharged from Canadian hospitals between 1999 and 2002	Use of services, satisfaction with care received, mortality	Better educated patients received more intensive treatment. Although no differences in mortality were observed in 1 year after discharge
Loucks et al. (2012)	United States	Coronary heart disease (Framingham Study)	10-year CHD incidence	Education status is inversely associated with CHD risk
Song et al. (2006)	Republic of Korea	CVD (n = 578 576, Korean male civil servant cohorts, 1990–2001)	Myocardial infarction and stroke incidence, fatality outcomes	SES and mortality risk from CVD were inversely related; non-fatal myocardial infarction was positively correlated with socioeconomic status. Case fatality was inversely related to SES after hospitalization

Fact 4: Cross-sectional associations mask significant country and regional variations in trends in age-adjusted mortality for CVD. While CVD mortality rates are declining over time for developed countries, they are increasing in countries formerly part of the Soviet Union, with information for poorer countries not yet sufficient to allow for sharp conclusions.

Fact 5: Reliable trends in age-specific cancer mortality are available primarily for developed countries and suggest that age-specific mortality is declining over time for multiple cancers, although the levels and rates of decline vary across countries. Lung cancer mortality rates among women are either slowly rising or are stable at levels much higher than in the past.

Fact 6: Individual- and household-level information in developed countries concludes that economic status is inversely related to age-specific mortality and incidence rates. Less clear is the relationship in developing countries, where evidence of an inverse relationship has been found but the current literature also supports findings of an opposite association.

12.3 THE ECONOMIC ROOTS OF CANCERS AND CVD

The strong association between incomes and cancer and CVD in cross-country and micro-level data raises the question of whether income and socioeconomic status more generally, is a major *causal* factor in driving CVD and cancers. This section of the chapter assesses the evidence on the causality running from income (and related measures of socioeconomic status) to NCD.

Short of carefully designed experiments establishing causality running directly from income and/or other measures of economic status to cancers and CVD, there are two natural ways to think about any causal linkages running from economic outcomes to the incidence of cancers and CVD and their share in all-cause mortality. The first link rests on the idea that rising income and associated improvements in public health lower the risks of illness and death from infectious disease. The lowering of infectious disease risks and the increased longevity that implies simultaneously increases the risk of illness and mortality from NCDs, such as cancers and CVD at older ages, reflecting the competing nature of disease and mortality risks. The second causal explanation relies on the relationship between economic advancement and various risk factors that increase the likelihood of acquiring cancers and CVD. Of course the two channels can occur simultaneously.

12.3.1 Competing Risks, Longevity and the Demographic Dividend

In general, a lower risk of dying from infectious conditions or maternal and child health conditions more broadly will raise the risk of dying at older ages from NCDs such as cancer as CVD, even as all-cause mortality rates decline.

Figure 12.7 presents a simple linear plot of life expectancy at birth against the share of cancers and CVD in all-cause deaths, indicating that longevity differences (mainly, but not solely, explained by differences in infant and child mortality rates) have strong predictive power for the observed higher share of cancers and CVD in developed countries

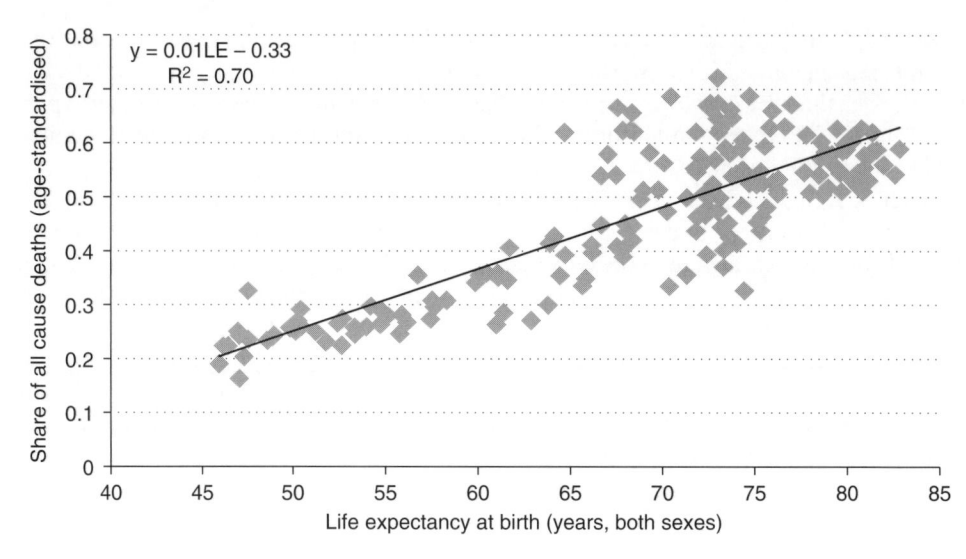

Figure 12.7 Share of all-cause deaths and life expectancy at birth in a cross-section of countries, 2008

relative to their poorer counterparts. This fits in well with the competing risks explanation, but what about the relationship between economic advancement and longevity?

Bloom and Canning (2007) note at least three separate explanations to support a causal impact of income on longevity. Their first explanation relied on Fogel (1986) and was based on the impact of rising incomes on improved nutrition. This could take the form of healthier children being born to better off and healthier parents who would then be at less risk of dying from infectious diseases and other causes of death traditionally associated with early ages. For instance, maternal nutrition (which influences the likelihood of child survival) could improve on account of incomes, as suggested by Case's (2004) study of the impact of South African pensions for the elderly on meals consumed by adults. Moreover, there could be direct impacts on the health of children: Aguero et al. (2006) showed that unconditional cash transfers to South African households in the form a 'child support grant' led to improved child health outcomes. However, economic growth could also increase public resources for health. Glewwe et al. (2003) investigated the impact of household income growth and public investments in health in Vietnam during its phase of rapid growth in the 1990s, concluding that while household income increases mattered for child nutrition, public sector investments for child health appeared to be even more important.

A second set of explanations rely on the impact of income on public health activities such as clean water, improved sanitation and immunisation (Deaton, 2006). Cutler and Meara (2004) assess that nearly half of the longevity gains in the United States in the twentieth century could be accounted for by public health interventions. The impact of income could take the form of enhanced public sector investments in public health on the supply side, and it may also involve increased use of clean water and sanitation or vaccination by economically better off households. Thus, Case (2004) analysing the causal impact of pensions on South African households found that getting a pension was positively associated with flush toilets being available in the household and negatively associated with reliance on sources of water outside the home. As another example, Robertson et al. (2013) assessed the impacts of an unconditional cash transfer in Zimbabwe and found that it led to an increase in the share of children with up-to-date immunisations. A third channel of the impact of income could be considered an offshoot of the broader process of technological change underlying economic growth: namely, innovations in health care, such as the emergence of sulfa drugs and penicillin and new heart disease treatments (Cutler and Meara, 2004).

Other actions of higher-income parents may reinforce the above linkages. For instance, higher income parents may also invest more in schooling children, and higher educated individuals will then grow up to be healthier adults, a sort of accumulated benefit over time (e.g. Case et al., 2002; Case, 2004). Indeed many careful studies in different European countries and the United States suggest a causal link running from improvements in child education to their subsequent longevity (Arendt, 2005; Lleras-Muney, 2005; van Kippersluis et al., 2011).

There are multiple complications to the income to longevity channels described above which limit the precision by which we can assign cancers and CVD as a collateral damage of longevity introduced by economic growth. First, as Cutler and Meara (2004) and Preston (1975) point out, much of the gains in longevity in the twentieth century have occurred due to public health and technological advances, but these gains are not well correlated with periods of economic growth. For instance, Deaton and Paxson (2004) studied long-term trends in mortality in the UK and United States, which they found remained very similar even when rates of change in GDP per capita. Easterly (1999) reached similar conclusions for a much larger set of countries. To be sure, higher incomes may well facilitate the diffusion of various public health interventions, modern treatment methods and vaccination coverage, but as these studies suggest, formulating a clear understanding of the income-related determinants of improved health is difficult, and likely involves a mix of lagged income effects, educational attainments, foreign intervention (including aid) and pure chance. Second, declining child mortality is likely to have set in motion incentives to have fewer children, a key element of demographic transition. The 'baby boom' that results ends up raising incomes per capita when boomers reach working ages, all else the same, a phenomenon popularly referred to as the demographic dividend (Bloom and Williamson, 1998). Then longevity and current income per capita might end up being positively correlated even though it is the income that is being influenced by health gains.

12.3.2 An Alternative Channel: Economic Status to Risk Factors for Cancers and CVD

The other mechanism whereby economic progress can affect cancers and CVD is via increasing the risks for individuals to acquire these conditions. There is now a good understanding of the proximate causes of cardiovascular disease – primarily coronary heart disease (CHD) and stroke. The former entails a thickening of coronary arteries by accumulation of plaque involving lipids such as cholesterol and triglycerides. The thickening process itself is regulated by molecules such as C-reactive protein (Steptoe and Marmot, 2005). By reducing the supply of blood to the heart – either by the narrowing process itself, or through formation of blood clots that often occur due to the rupture of accumulated plaque – outcomes such as chest pain (angina) and myocardial infraction result. A stroke is said to occur when the blood supply to the brain is affected. The most common type of stroke (ischaemic stroke), is caused by blockages of blood supply to the brain. In addition, the rupture of arteries inside the brain result in what are referred to as haemorrhagic strokes.

An extensive literature provides the biological links between 'proximate' risk factors such as obesity, diabetes, hypertension, physical inactivity, diet, smoking and alcohol use, and CHD and strokes. Studies, many based in the United States, have found an association between obesity and diabetes prevalence over the last 20 years. Intra-abdominal fat, common in obesity, is a particular risk factor for insulin resistance due to the hyper-expression of adipokine secretion genes when compared to subcutaneous fat. As Dokken (2008) notes, diabetes patients tend to have 'bad' cholesterol particles that are longer lived and stick more easily to walls of arteries increasing the risk of CHD and stroke. Lower insulin sensitivity characteristic of diabetics, also raises triglycerides in the blood and can cause heart damage. Obese individuals are also at heightened risk of ischaemic heart disease, mediated in part through obesity-induced hypertension.

There is a close link between obesity, physical activity, diets and hypertension. In their review of evidence on the role of diets, Reddy and Katan (2004) conclude that certain kinds of dietary fats (saturated fats) worsen the lipid profile (e.g. raise total cholesterol); others, such as dietary fibre and a variety of nutrients found in fruits and vegetables, lowered the risk of CHD; and carbohydrates were associated with CHD primarily via weight and central obesity. Higher levels of salt consumption are linked to increased blood pressure. Physical activity lowers the risk of CHD and stroke by reducing blood pressure for periods following exercise, lowering levels of C-reactive protein and a lowering of inflammation process that underlies the development of plaque formation for CHD. It also lowers weight with its attendant benefits, which include lowering diabetes risk (Leon and Bronas, 2009). Hypertension can damage arteries, which could then become a repository for plaque, in addition to making the plaque less stable. It also increases the workload of the heart, resulting in changes that lower its ability to pump blood to the body and an increased risk of heart attack (Escobar, 2002). Separately, it can impact plaque formation increasing the risk of ischaemic stroke; and increase the likelihood of a haemorrhagic stroke by causing arteries to rupture in the brain.

Smoking is a major risk factor for CHD and according to the American Heart Foundation, elevates blood pressure, increases the risks of blood clotting and lowers the ability to undertake physical exercise. Many of these elements also imply that smoking increases the risk of stroke. However, the association of increased alcohol intake with CHD is less unidirectional with factors both raising and lowering risk for CHD as it raises the triglycerides and blood pressure, but also increases 'good cholesterol' and lowers the risk of blood clots (Mukamal and Rimm, 2013).

Many of the above risk factors are relevant for cancers as well. According to a recent review, nearly one third of all cancer-related deaths in the United States were accounted for by tobacco-related causes and another one third by diet and physical inactivity. Physical activity may lower cancer risk both by reducing weight, as well as by direct influence on hormone metabolism and insulin production. There is some evidence that greater consumption of vegetables and fruits in diets lowers and the use of red meats and processed foods increases cancer risk and alcohol consumption is also associated with increased risk of colorectal cancer among men (Kushi et al., 2012). It has also been determined that people who are overweight or obese are at an increased risk of developing several cancer types including endometrial, kidney, breast (in postmenopausal women) and colon cancer. Insulin resistance, in addition to leading to Type 2 Diabetes Mellitus (DMII), is thought to contribute to several cancers including colon cancer and endometrial cancer. Heightened levels of circulating oestrogen hormones, also strongly related to obesity, mediate breast and endometrial cancers in women (Calle and Kaaks, 2004).

The economic underpinnings of risk factors for CVD and cancers: cross-country evidence
Cross-country evidence on the association between incomes and various risk factors for cancers and CVDs also suggests linkages in the same direction as that for income per capita and share of cancers and CVDs in mortality and DALYs.

Consider, for instance, the association between income per capita and obesity across countries (Figure 12.8). Although the fit is generally poor, it does suggest a sharp rise of population level obesity at low levels of income per capita. Separately, current trends and recent studies suggest that although obesity is developed countries is continuously rising, it is increasing more sharply in developing countries (Prentice, 2006; Balarajan and Villamor, 2009; Xi et al., 2012).

Data from the World Health Surveys show that physical inactivity is also positively (although weakly) associated with income per capita (WHO, 2010), but trend data are instructive. Although leisure-time physical activity is rising worldwide, this has been accompanied by a declining contribution of occupations, commuting and housework to physical activity. In developed countries this has resulted in (mostly) stable but in some

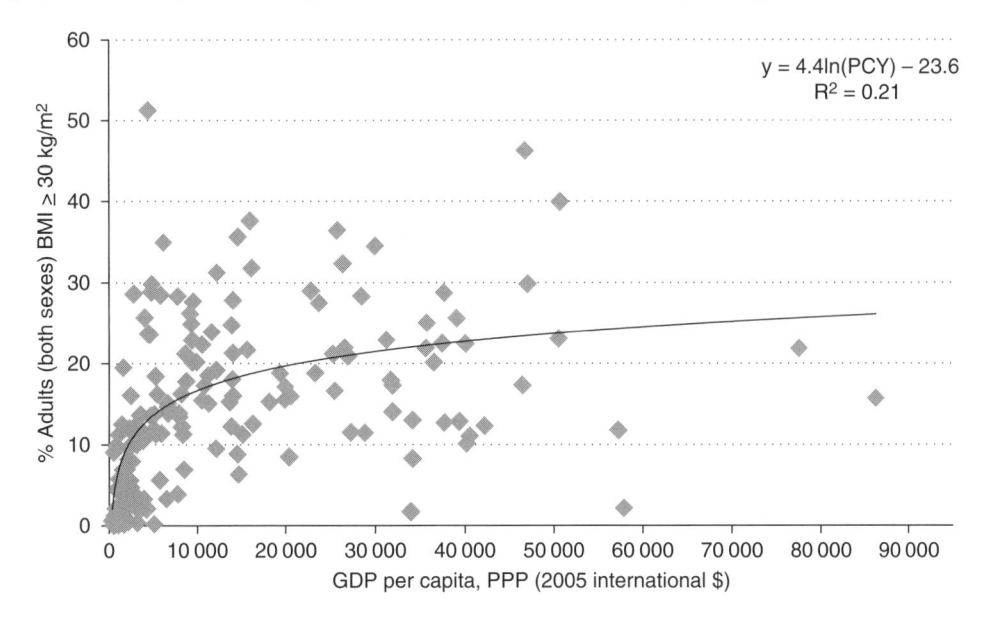

Source: WHO (2010).

Figure 12.8 Income per capita and obesity prevalence, around the world, both sexes, aged 15+ years, 2010

cases, a slow decline in the overall level of physical activity (Brownson et al., 2005; Cavill et al., 2006; Borodulin et al., 2007; Samdal et al., 2007; Petersen et al., 2010). In developing countries increases in leisure-time physical activity have also fallen short of declining physical activity in other categories, but the lowering of overall physical activity may be greater. Ng et al. (2009a) tracked physical activities in China over multiple rounds of the China Health and Nutrition Survey between 1991 and 2006, concluding that overall levels of physical activity declined sharply, primarily due to declines in occupation-related activities among men, as leisure time activities remained stable or even increased somewhat. For Chinese women, reduction in house-related work also contributed to declines in levels of physical activity. Declines in physical activity levels have also been noted in some parts of Brazil (Knuth et al., 2010).

Dietary patterns are also differentiated by income per capita. Although not directly indicative of actual intake, 'food balance sheets' produced by the Food and Agricultural Organization (FAO) suggest that the per capita availability of calories and the level of saturated fats (as a proportion of energy intake) is higher among populations in developed countries (FAO, 2002; Fresco and Baudoin, 2002). In developed countries, some studies indicate stable dietary habits over the last two decades (Hulshof et al., 2003; OECD, 2012). Popkin (2006) though, notes that even in developed countries portion sizes have become larger, there is more eating out, snacking and consumption of sugar-sweetened beverages. For India, Gaiha et al. (2012) use consumption expenditure data from the National Sample Survey Organization to show a sharp increase in the share of edible oils, sugar and processed food in food expenditures of Indian households over the period from 1992 to 2009; and for China, Du et al. (2004) used longitudinal data from the China Health and Nutrition Survey to show that dietary habits moved rapidly from carbohydrates to diets high in fat and energy dense foods over a short period of time in the 1990s. These dietary patterns have also been noted in other developing countries (Popkin, 2006; Kearney, 2010).

Smoking and alcohol consumption rates are higher in the more developed countries and among both men and women, relative to their developing country counterparts (WHO, 2010, 2011). But, among men who smoke much more than women, cross-country differences in prevalence rates are low (WHO, 2010). Smoking, a major risk factor for cancers and CVD, has seen declining prevalence in Latin America and developed countries since the mid-1970s. However, smoking prevalence rates have been relatively unchanging in Asia and in developing countries outside of Africa; the latter has actually experienced increased prevalence since the mid-1990s (Guindon and Boisclair, 2003). In a recent article based on major nationally representative surveys in 14 low- and middle-income countries, Giovino et al. (2012) conclude that high rates of smoking continue.

Available cross-country data on age-adjusted hypertension (systolic BP > 140 or diastolic BP > 90) prevalence among individuals aged 25 years and over indicates rates typically much lower among developed country populations, especially women (WHO, 2010). However, trends in systolic blood pressure (SBP) – a key determinant of the diagnosis of hypertension – suggest that SBP has been falling in developed countries over the last three decades. By contrast, it rose in countries in Eastern Africa, South and Southeast Asia during the same period, indicating competing risks for CVD. Overall, male SBP was amongst the highest in countries in the Baltic region, which are at high risk for CVD mortality (Danaei et al., 2011).

The economic underpinnings of risk factors for cancer and CVD: cross-sectional evidence from individual- and household-level data

A key question is: what is the role of income in driving the pattern of CVD and cancer risks thus far? The extensive cross-sectional associations based on studies reported in Table 12.2 provide us with some insight, which will be used to construct plausible stories of causation in the next section.

One key conclusion is that the evidence points to an inverse association between socioeconomic status (education even more so than income and wealth) and risk factors for cancers and CVD in developed countries. A second conclusion is that in developing countries, there is a positive association between risk factors and indicators of economic status, with the possible exception of hypertension, and smoking prevalence among men. Finally, recent analyses for developing countries appear to show that the socioeconomic gradient for physical activity is becoming similar to the pattern observed in middle-income countries, particularly when education is used as an indicator of socioeconomic status.

12.3.3 Evidence on Causality from Economic Status to Risk factors for Cancers and CVD

The cross-sectional associations and trends in risk factors do not, at least not directly, establish a causal link between economic advancement, cancers and CVDs. They do, however, permit at least two plausible stories for why the changes that accompany economic development *cause* some of the increased cancer and CVD risks.

Lakdawalla and Philipson (2009) offer one such framework. Their argument relies on technological changes that underpin economic growth, two of which interest them in particular. The first are technological changes that cause agricultural productivity to increase, characteristic of many influential theories of modern economic development (Nurkse, 1953; Timmer, 1988). Related is the emergence of advances (including economies of scale and scope) in the processed food industry, which sharply reduced the costs of getting food inputs ready for consumption. The second characteristic of models of economic growth is a modern sector with high levels of labour productivity, such as the well-known 'Lewis model' and its modern counterparts that emphasise increasing returns (e.g. Romer, 1986). In the Lakdawalla and Philipson framework, one interprets the expanding modern sector as being characterised by work becoming less physically demanding (or 'sedentary'), while being more remunerative per unit of time spent. For instance, increased productivity in the industrial and services sector – underpinned by the emergence of trains, airplanes, robots, computers and the organisation of the modern corporation – while raising incomes, is consistent with lower physical effort involved in work.

Lakdawalla and Philipson argue that the above technological and organisational changes will result in rising obesity among populations, primarily owing to a decline in physical activity from work. Specifically, increased agricultural and food processing productivity would lead to a downward pressure on prices on the one hand, and increased sedentary work would lower food demand on the other, further causing prices to fall. They show that one would observe lower food prices, ambiguous trends in calorie consumption and increased weight because physical activity declines. In addition, rising

Table 12.2   Economic correlates of risk factors for CVD and cancers: a selected list of studies

	Country	Condition/Data	Indicators	Findings
Developing and middle-income countries				
Agardh et al. (2011)	Low-, middle- and high-income countries	Diabetes (Case-cohort and cohort studies published between 1966 and 2010)	Diabetes Incidence	Risk of diabetes was negatively correlated with educational level and income in the three sets of countries (high-, middle- and low-income). Few studies from low- and middle-income countries
Dinsa et al. (2012)	Low- and middle-income countries	Obesity (literature review)	Weight	In poorer countries, obesity and socioeconomic status (SES) are positively correlated; In middle-income countries (inverse relationship between SES and obesity for women and unclear relationship for men). Obesity among children highly positively correlated with economic status
Mendez et al. (2005)	36 developing countries	Demographic and Health Surveys from 1992–2000, 148,579 women aged 20–49 years	BMI >= 25 (overweight) and BMI <= 18.5 (underweight)	Ratio of overweight to underweight = 5.8 (urban) and 2.1 (rural). These ratios were positively correlated to the degree of urbanization and income per capita of a country, and held even among women of low SES
Subramanian et al. (2011)	Developing countries	Overweight and obesity (538 140 women in 54 DHS surveys between 1994 and 2008)	BMI (among women)	Rising wealth associated with increased weight – one quartile increase in wealth associated with a 0.54 increase in BMI. This also held true for rural and urban areas, although more so for urban areas
Ma et al. (2013)	China (urban)	Hypertension Systematic Review of Studies in Urban China (27 studies with 195 027 individuals)	Blood Pressure	Hypertension prevalence of 21% among adults in urban areas. Urban areas had higher rates of hypertension than the national average (and rural areas)
Mendez et al. (2003)	Jamaica	Hypertension (2082 adults in a peri-urban area of Jamaica)	Blood Pressure	BP was positively correlated with SES for women; results for men were less clear. Men with low SES were also less likely to receive treatment for hypertension

Author	Country	Study	Measure	Findings
Erem et al. (2009)	Turkey	Hypertension (4809 adults in one region of Turkey)	Blood Pressure	Hypertension positively correlated with age, being male, BMI, smoking and family history. Negatively linked to educational status and physical activity
Ismail et al. (1997)	Developing Countries	Sugar consumption trends Literature review	Sugar consumption	Evidence of rising sugar consumption and sugar-sweetened drinks in South Asia, Southeast Asia, China; and of higher levels of sugar consumption in Latin America and the Middle East
M. Hashibe et al. (2010)	Nepal	Lung cancer (n = 522)	Lung-cancer 'risk'	Inversely linked with educational status; Late stage cancers were common among women, elderly and individuals with less education
Samuel et al. (2012)	India	Risk factors for CVD (n = 2218 aged 26–32 years)	Obesity, diabetes, IGT, total cholesterol to HDL ratio, triglyceride, tobacco use, alcohol use	Risk factors higher in urban than in rural areas; indicators of economic status were positively associated with all risk factors (abdominal obesity, cholesterol) in both rural and urban areas and among men and women, with the exception of tobacco intake (where the relationship was inverse). Use of own and parental education as SES led to associations for which no discernible pattern could be detected
Subramanian et al. (2013)	India	CVD and risk factors (Systematic review, 53 studies)	SES-CVD link	CVD and CVD risk factors more prevalent among the high SES groups (with the exception of hypertension and tobacco); CVD-related mortality higher among low SES, the share of CVD deaths is higher among high SES
Kinra et al. (2011)	India	Cardio-metabolic risk (4221 study participants, matched sibling comparison – rural versus urban residents, migrant factory workers), 2005–077	Body fat, systolic blood pressure, fasting insulin	Body fat increases rapidly upon move from rural to urban areas and especially for individuals with low SES; slower increase for other cardio-metabolic risk factors
Reddy et al. (2007)	India	Risk factors for CHD (n = 19 973; cross-sectional study of workers and family members in ten industries in India)	Tobacco use, hypertension, dyslipidaemia, diabetes, overweight	Tobacco use and hypertension prevalence inversely linked to SES; dyslipidaemia prevalence higher in higher SES groups; in highly urbanized areas, SES was inversely linked to tobacco use, hypertension, diabetes prevalence and overweight

Table 12.2 (continued)

	Country	Condition/Data	Indicators	Findings
Developing and middle-income countries				
Hosseinpoor et al. (2012)	48 low- and middle-income countries	Smoking World Health Survey data	Self-reported smoking	Smoking prevalence disproportionately higher among poor men relative to richer counterparts; however, mixed results for women – in 20 countries smoking prevalence higher among poor women; and in 9 countries, higher among richer women
Barguera et al. (2008)	Mexico	Beverage consumption (1999 Mexican Nutrition Survey; 2006 Mexican Health and Nutrition Survey)	Beverage intake	Trends: large increase in beverages (whole milk, sugar sweetened beverages, soda, fruit juices). High income elasticities of demand
Smith and Goldman (2007)	Mexico	Obesity, alcohol use and smoking (Mexican Health and Aging Study)	Indicators of weight, smoking, alcohol use and problematic alcohol use	Income positively associated with smoking, obesity and risky alcohol consumption; education inversely associated with obesity in urban areas – opposite in rural areas
Grittner et al. (2013)	33 low- and high-income countries	Alcohol use (cross-sectional surveys in 33 countries; n = 101 525)	Alcohol use, indicators of risky drinking	Individual SES was positively associated with alcohol use in all countries; lower SES was associated with risky drinking in developed countries; in low-income countries, higher SES was associated with risky drinking among women (not men)
Yadav and Krishnan (2008)	India	Physical activity, Obesity (Cross-sectional survey; n = 7981)	BMI, indicators of physical activity	Obesity prevalence in urban areas greater than in rural areas; physical activity much higher among rural populations; female obesity significantly higher than male obesity in both rural and urban areas
Hallal et al. (2006)	Brazil	Physical activity (4452 adolescents aged 10–12 years in cohort study)	Less than 300 minutes of physical activity per week, physical activity score	Income, maternal education and being female positively associated with physical sedentary lifestyle and physical activity scores. Early habits (at age 4 years) seemed to predict later activity

Monteiro et al. (2003)	Brazil	Physical activity (Living Standards Measurement Survey, 1996–97) 11 033 individuals, aged 20 years or older	Measures of leisure time physical activity (>30 minutes daily)	Only 3.3% reported doing the minimum for 5 days a week; physical activity was increasing in age and socioeconomic status (education or economic status); and higher among men relative to women
Hallal et al. (2003)	Brazil	Physical activity (Cross-sectional survey, physical activity among adults 20 years and older)	Physical activity measure based on 150 mins or less per week in course of leisure, work, transportation and housework	Physical 'inactivity' positively associated with SES indicates that studies on physical activity in developing countries may be seriously biased if they do not include activities other than those in leisure time
Knuth et al. (2010)	Brazil	Physical activity (Cross-sectional surveys in 2002, 2007; urban population), n = 6168, 20 years or older)	Physical activity	Prevalence of physical inactivity increased over time and primarily due to increased inactivity among poorer individuals; changing SES-gradient – no association between SES gradient and physical inactivity in 2007 – positive in 2002; physical inactivity inversely associated with schooling
Ebrahim et al. (2010)	India	CVD risk factors (obesity, diabetes) (cross-sectional study, n = 6510)	Measures of obesity, insulin resistance, diabetes status	Overall, urban origin factory workers and rural migrants (working in factories) had greater diabetes and obesity prevalence than comparable rural populations. BP rates and lipid levels were lower among rural men relative to urban/migrant counterparts (but not among women)
Dahly et al. (2009)	Philippines	Obesity (CEBU study, cross-sectional, young adults, n = 1806)	BMI, measures of central adiposity	Indicators of asset holding and being married correlated with obesity among males and among rural women; but not among rural women

Table 12.2 (continued)

	Country	Condition/Data	Indicators	Findings
Developing and middle-income countries				
Bauman et al. (2010)	Australia, China, Malaysia, Philippines, Fiji, Nauru	Physical activity (cross-sectional surveys between 2002–06, n = 173 206)	Measures of physical activity in leisure time and during work	*China, Fiji, Malaysia*: individuals with higher income and education and urban-based were more active during leisure time, but less so during work time, compared to individuals in rural areas and with less education/income
Trinh et al. (2008)	Vietnam	Physical activity among adults (Cross-sectional survey, n = 1906, 25–64 years, urban population)	Time spent on physical activity during work, commuting and leisure time (<150 mins)	High levels of physical inactivity (44%) main source of physical activity was from work and active commuting; physical inactivity *among men* inversely associated with income and wealth
Ng et al. (2009a)	Bangladesh, India, Indonesia, Thailand, Vietnam	Physical activity (nine demographic surveillance sites, rural populations)	Physical activity during work, leisure time and travel included	Men more physically active than women; more educated less physically active than less educated; age inversely associated with physical inactivity
Shi et al. (2006)	China	Physical activity (Adolescents in school in China; n = 824, 12–14 years)	Indicators of physical activity	Males more physically active than females; SES (parental education and income) and vigorous physical activity uncorrelated; but high SES inversely correlated with walking to school
Du et al. (2004)	China	Diet (Longitudinal survey, 3129 households)	Measures of diet composition; longitudinal regressions	Income positively associated with moving from a diet of carbohydrates to diets that were energy-dense rich in fats. Effects particularly significant for poorer groups
Monteiro et al. (2004)	Developing countries	Obesity (Literature review between 1989 and 2003)	Obesity measures	The slope of the socioeconomic gradient of obesity varies across countries at different levels of income per capita; with rising incomes associated with lower obesity as countries become richer (above $2500 GDP per capita)
Neuman et al. (2013)	38 low- and middle-income countries	Urbanization and BMI (DHS data)	BMI indicators	Found that BMI in urban areas is higher than in rural areas but that this effect vanishes when socioeconomic status is controlled for

Author	Region	Study/Sample	Measures	Findings
Boissonnet et al. (2011)	7 capital cities in Latin America	Obesity and metabolic syndrome (cross sectional study, n = 11 550; men and women aged 25–64 years)	Waist circumference, BMI, metabolic syndrome	Among women, SES was inversely related to BMI and waist circumference, except in two cities; no relationship observed for men
Balarajan and Villamor (2009)	India, Bangladesh, Nepal	Obesity and overweight (repeated cross-sections. DHS data; women only, 1996–2006)	Measures of obesity and overweight	Found that in all three countries, obesity and overweight was rising among women aged 15–49 years; positively correlated with SES (wealth); and higher in urban areas
Developed Countries				
McLaren (2007)	Developed and developing countries	Literature Review Between 1988–2004	Measures of obesity	Concluded that (a) In developed countries: most indicators of SES were negatively associated with obesity among women; among men the findings were often of statistical insignificance, but sometimes of negative association; (b) In developing countries, the findings among women were of a positive association with SES; and among men either of statistical insignificance or a positive relationship
Sacerdote et al. (2012)	Europe	Diabetes (8 Western European Countries, n = 16 835)	Incidence of diabetes cases (using Hazard Ratios)	Individuals with lower educational attainment had higher risk of acquiring type II diabetes. BMI positively associated with type II diabetes, and explains some of the education-diabetes link
Tanaka et al. (2012)	United Kingdom	Diabetes (9053 individuals, aged greater than 50 years)	Prevalence and incidence of diabetes	*Diabetes*: Negative association between wealth status and diabetes prevalence among men and women; negative association between diabetes incidence over a 4-year period and wealth; BMI attenuated this relationship *Obesity*: obesity prevalence and wealth are negatively associated in women
Dalstra et al. (2005)	Europe	Cancer, heart disease, stroke, diabetes 8 West European countries (National Health Surveys)	Self-reported prevalence rates	*Stroke and diabetes prevalence* negatively correlated with socioeconomic status; cancer prevalence in 20–59 age-group was higher in low-educated groups; but higher in higher educated groups in the 60–79 category; socioeconomic differences were greater among women than for men in diabetes, hypertension and heart disease

Table 12.2 (continued)

	Country	Condition/Data	Indicators	Findings
Developed Countries				
Rathmann et al. (2004)	Germany	Diabetes (1354 individuals 55–74 years)	Oral Glucose Tolerance Test (for undiagnosed diabetes or impaired glucose tolerance)	prevalence; socioeconomic inequalities in heart disease prevalence higher in north European countries compared to their Southern counterparts Among women, low occupational status was negatively correlated with *undiagnosed diabetes*; among men, occupational status was positively correlated with IGT but not diabetes; educational status was uncorrelated with IGT or diabetes
Rathmann et al. (2006)	Germany	Diabetes (1476 individuals aged 55–74 years)	Diabetes status, C-reactive protein (CRP) – inflammatory marker	While diabetes was (inversely) associated with SES, controlling for CRP status did not influence the SES-diabetes relationship. Moreover, the SES-CRP relationship among women vanished once BMI and waist circumference were controlled for (there was no relationship among men)
van Rossum et al. (2000)	United Kingdom	(CVD and Cancers) 18 001 male civil servants, 40–69 years old during 1967–69 followed up 25 years later (Whitehall Study)	All-cause mortality rate differentials, and mortality rate differentials by individual causes of death	Mortality rate differentials in heart disease, cancer and other causes persist even after 25-years of follow-up, with senior officials at lower risk of death compared to the junior-most categories. However, differences across occupational categories did decline as the population became older following retirement; Risk factors such as smoking, high blood pressure and cholesterol cannot explain more than one third of this differential
de Irala-Estevez et al. (2000)	15 European Countries	Fruit/vegetable consumption (Systematic review of surveys of food habits, 1985–1999)	Daily consumption per capita	Educational level/Occupational status positively associated with consumption of fruits and vegetables per capita daily. True for both men and women
Hulshof et al. (2003)	Netherlands	Fruits, vegetables and fibre intake (Repeated cross-sections of Food Consumption	Daily consumption per capita	Vegetable and fruit consumption inversely related to SES and stable pattern over time

Study	Country	Data/Sample	Measure	Findings
Smith (2007)	United States	Diabetes National Health and Nutrition Examination Surveys (NHANES), 1976–2002; limited to men. Surveys, 1987–88 to 1997–98	HbA1C test > 6.5% as indicator of clinical diabetes; Oral glucose tolerance tests >140mg/dL; self-reports of diagnosed diabetes	*Gradient*: Self-reported diagnosed diabetes prevalence higher among Hispanics and African-Americans; However, these groups are also underdiagnosed – so 'overall' diabetes differentials are even greater (Negative Education and Income) gradient in prevalence of 'overall' diabetes. Ageing and ethnicity accounts for 50% of SES gradient. Gradient has worsened over time. *Education*: predicts a lower prevalence of diabetes *Obesity*: male obesity rates doubled over the period of the study esp. fast among non-Hispanic Whites. *Under-Diagnosis*: Undiagnosed diabetes declining over time, but fastest decline among better off and more educated. *Better self-management (controlled diabetes)*: correlated with indicators of good behaviour (low smoking and low obesity), income, education
Goldman & Smith (2002)	United States	Diabetes (Diabetes Control and Complications Trial)	Indicators of good diabetes management – blood tests, insulin regimens, exercise, etc.; also level of glycosolated hemoglobin	Showed that rigorously enforced treatment regimen improved outcomes for less educated. But less educated are less able to adhere to treatment regimens. Education influenced adherence by enabling individuals to better evaluate the future consequences of current behaviour
Tang et al. (2003)	Canada	Diabetes Data from National Survey, 39 021 individuals > 40 years	Self-reported diabetes status	Higher educational achievement and incomes were associated with lower risk of self-reported diabetes; adjusting for age, residence, physical activity and BMI eliminated the SES-diabetes link for men (not women)
Diez-Roux et al. (2001)	United States	Heart disease (n = 13 009, cohort study) 45–64 years at baseline	Risk of acquiring coronary heart disease	People living in poor areas had greater risk of heart disease. Possibly effect of neighbourhoods works via increased risk factors; income was also negatively correlated with the risk of coronary heart disease

Table 12.2 (continued)

	Country	Condition/Data	Indicators	Findings
Developed Countries				
Malik et al. (2010)	Developed and developing countries	Weight gain, diabetes, CVD (Literature review)	SSB, diabetes outcomes, metabolic syndrome, CVD	Great increase in global consumption of sugar sweetened beverages (SSB), especially for Mexico and United States (data in the paper); SSB linked to weight gain and increased risk of diabetes and of metabolic syndrome. *Impact CVD*: large cohort studies show a link between SSB intake and heart disease, and the effect remains even after accounting for the BMI increasing effect of SSB.
Hiscock et al. (2011)	Developed/developing countries	Smoking (Literature review)	Smoking prevalence	Smoking rates are inversely correlated with SES (education, income, non-manual versus manual work, neighbourhoods)
Han and Powell (2013)	United States	SSB, fruit drinks/soda (NHANES survey)	Consumption of beverages	*Trends*: consumption of SSB increased among children and decreased among adults and adolescents; low SES was associated with greater consumption of SSB, soda and fruit drinks across all ages
Giles-Corti and Donovan (2002)	United States	Leisure physical activity (Cross sectional survey of 1803 individuals)	Vigorous physical activity	Residents living in poorer areas undertook 36% less vigorous physical activity even after controlling for amenities (parks, pavements, etc.). Residents of poorer areas perceived that their environment had more traffic and generally less amenable for physical activity
Tucker-Seeley et al. (2009)	United States	Leisure Physical Activity (Cross-sectional 2004 Health and Retirement Survey, > 50 years)	Indicators of leisure time physical activity	Education, household income and wealth were all inversely associated with leisure-time physical activity; perception of neighbourhood safety adversely affected physical activity
Williams et al. (2012)	Australia	Diabetes 4572 individuals aged 25 years and over; AusDiab Study	Abnormal Glucose Metabolism, using oral glucose tolerance tests (fasting plasma glucose, 2-h plasma glucose)	Individuals living in socioeconomically deprived areas more at risk of developing abnormal glucose metabolism; focus is on local environments where people live. The relationship between the two may be partly working via levels of physical activity and central adiposity

Study	Location	Sample	Outcome	Findings
Grimes et al. (2013)	Australia	Salt and Sugar Intake (2283 children aged 2–16 years)	Salt intake and intake of SSB	Salt consumption positively correlated with age and SSB consumption; both salt and SSB intake were negatively correlated with SES
Matshushima et al. (1996)	Japan	All-cause mortality among diabetics 180 matched-cases (90 dead, 90 alive)	Death	Patients with greater educational achievement, and exhibited better management (attended clinic on diabetes, kept the same doctor, more frequent clinic attendance, etc.) experienced lower mortality
Ostbye et al. (2013)	Singapore	Overweight/Obesity (National Survey, n = 4371 > 60 years)	BMI, Abdominal obesity	Education lowered risks of obesity among women only; Malays and Indian ethnicity at greater risk; overall women had higher rates of overweight/obesity than men
Ball and Crawford (2005)	Developed countries	Review of literature on SES and 'changes in weight' over time	Measures of weight	Among studies using data from non-black populations, individuals from low occupations/educational status saw faster weight gains than their counterparts from higher-level occupations and educational status; among black populations, the relationship was unclear
Colhoun et al. (1998)	Developed and developing countries	Hypertension Literature review from 1966–96	Blood pressure	Inverse relationship between SES and Blood Pressure in developed countries. Mainly due to differences in BMI and alcohol use across SES (not treatment differences). In less developed countries SES and BP are positively correlated, mainly due to higher alcohol and salt intake and BMI among those with higher SES
Stalsberg and Pedersen (2010)	Developed countries	Physical Activity (Literature review focused on adolescents – 13–18 years and SES)	Indicators of physical activity	Positive association between SES and physical activity among adolescents, but there are plenty of articles that report no effect or an opposite conclusion. Multiple measures of SES complicate conclusions

opportunity costs of housework (owing to higher labour market returns) would lead to increased female participation in the workforce and this may lead to less 'monitoring' of foods consumed at home, more snacking, eating out, etc. (Chou et al., 2001). Although the Lakdawalla–Philipson analysis was directed primarily to the US experience it can be readily extended to observed developing country experience by allowing for rising demand for variety in food (including processed food) as incomes rise. Then food prices, calorie intake as well as physical inactivity can all simultaneously increase as noted in the evidence on trends in the previous sub-section.

Lakdawalla and Philipson (2009) also use their framework to reconcile the differences between cross-country findings of rising weight and physical inactivity with income per capita, and within country findings (in developed countries) of an inverse relationship between the two. Their explanation rests on the idea that weight gains due to unearned income were likely to be less than weight gains from equivalent earned income (that is, from more sedentary work which replaces leisure time physical activity or housework). Then, noting that differences in income across countries primarily reflect technological differences in income earned from sedentary work (populations in richer countries being more technologically advanced, do more sedentary work) and that differences within countries reflect primarily differences in unearned income (with richer individuals having more unearned income in a setting with similar work technology), they could explain the observed empirical regularities. A tweak to this basic approach – highlighting that earned income may well explain income differences within developing countries – could also explain the positive association that one finds between income and risk factors there. Empirical analyses, using data from the National Longitudinal Survey among Youth in the United States provides some justification for this framework (Lakdawalla and Philipson, 2009). Ruhm (2007) provides further empirical support, showing a strong association between economic booms and deaths from CHD, with one potential channel being the impact of rising employment in booms (and presumably sedentary work) on physical activity and weight.

Another explanation rests on rising income inequality that typically accompanies rapid economic growth of the kind observed in the now developing countries. Specifically, Steptoe and Marmot (2005) argue, based on analysis of the Whitehall longitudinal study of British civil servants, that an inferior position on the socioeconomic scale has biological effects that translate into increased risks for CVD. Their analysis is based primarily on experimental and other work assessing how biological responses of individuals at different points on the economic (social status) scale respond to stimuli that increase stress and analyses of how repeated stress responses increase the cumulative wear and tear on the body, often referred to as the 'allostatic load'. In particular, they suggest that in response to equivalent external stressors (1) individuals of low socioeconomic status tend to have larger responses on blood pressure, heart rate variability, C-reactive proteins, etc. and (2) recovery to original, pre-stimuli, levels of the biological indicators of such individuals is slower. In the literature on 'social determinants of health', this perspective gives rise to the idea that inequalities are bad for health.

Predictions based on a Steptoe–Marmot type argument are consistent with cross-sectional data on risk factor prevalence at the micro-level, especially in developed countries and also on some of the new evidence emerging from developing countries. They are also consistent with the growing burden of CVD observed in many rapidly growing developing economies that are also simultaneously experiencing rising levels of inequality. However, to interpret their findings in this manner raises some obvious methodological and empirical issues. For instance, giving a role to economic development in the rise in CVD in this framework would depend on how different individuals assess who their comparators are for ranking purposes; and it is not clear that income or material possessions are the sole criterion. In addition, recent work by Deaton and others suggests that the link between income inequality and health outcomes cannot be seen in the data, either in cross-country data, or within-country analyses (Deaton, 2003; Deaton and Lubotsky, 2003). In particular, Deaton and Lubotsky (2003) found that although income inequalities and mortality rates were positively associated in a large cross-section of US cities and states, these effects vanished once racial composition was included in the analytical mix. This occurred because white incomes tended to be positively associated with the share of black population (increasing between-group income inequality), but white mortality rates were positively associated with the share of black population. They conjectured that the positive association of white mortality with the share of black population may have a basis in lower levels of social capital.

It is also not obvious that the laboratory-based findings related to stress response in the work of Marmot hold up in real-life settings. Recently, Stringhini et al. (2010) concluded that much of the differential observed in CVD incidence and mortality risk among the civil servants studied by Marmot could be explained by differences in behaviours at risk for CVD – diet, physical activity and alcohol consumption – so that the impact of inequality directly on the allostatic load sounds less convincing. To be sure, social inequality could well explain differences in cancers and CVD across groups, but this may need additional evidence.

Methodological challenges
Even if the Lakdawalla and Philipson story is plausible, it faces at least three main methodological bottlenecks in empirical verification. The first, as they themselves note, is the issue of selection. For example, unhealthy individuals (at risk for CVD or cancer) may end up in lower ranking positions and with lower earnings rather than the other way round (Baum and Ford, 2004). As another example, individuals who discount the future more may end up undertaking both more unhealthy practices as well as investing less in their education and presumably earnings (Munasinghe and Sicherman, 2006). Second, there may also be direct two-way causality in the sense that households containing individuals at high risk for CVD and cancers and related mortality are likely to spend more on health services and suffer earnings losses due to illness and foregone work time due to caregiving (e.g. Mahal et al., 2010), well established in the literature on health and economic outcomes at the household level (Gertler and Gruber, 2002). Thus households affected by cancers and CVD may end up with inferior economic outcomes and not the other way round. At the national level, countries with large numbers of sick individuals may well end up incurring higher healthcare costs and losses in human capital formation so that lower national income may result (Bloom and Canning, 2000; Abegunde et al., 2007). Finally, there are standard measurement error problems, with income, wealth and consumption self-responses to survey questions being potentially susceptible to reporting error.

The consequence of the above concerns has been research efforts directed towards approaches that can more credibly address identifying the direction of causality from economic outcomes to risk factors for cancers and CVD using (mostly) micro-level data. Analyses have moved from simple associations to experimental and quasi-experimental methods to assess causality, to relying on longitudinal datasets and variables that are more plausibly exogenous (e.g. parental income and education) than measures of contemporaneous income, wealth and own education.

Empirical literature on causality running from economic status to risk factors
A striking feature of some of the recent work on the link between economic status and risk factors has been the use of natural experiments and quasi-experimental techniques to get around the challenge of endogeneity in the risk factors and economic outcomes. With few exceptions, approaches relying on natural experiments focus on identifying appropriate instruments for the economic status indicator of interest, whether, education, wealth or income. Among the most popular instruments for education in recent research have been changes in regulations related to schooling such as compulsory schooling laws, schooling reforms at the secondary school and college levels that were differentially introduced over time or space. Another popular instrument (for college education) is the Vietnam War era draft lottery. Instruments for income have included shocks in the stock market and earned income tax credit rules (for the United States). Inheritances have been used to instrument for wealth and immigration lotteries for migration. Quasi-experimental approaches have relied on multiple methods, including studying twins (in Australia) to analyse the effects of education and matching methods (to assess the impacts of education and rural–urban migration). Data limitations have meant that much of this work has concentrated on developed countries, with a few notable developing country exceptions. However, there are multiple studies for developing countries that use longitudinal data and indicators of parental economic outcomes.

Obesity and physical activity
Although there are exceptions, available studies broadly conclude that education (whether secondary schooling, or college education, or years of schooling) lowers BMI (body mass index) and increases physical activity, particularly among women (Arendt, 2005; Grabner, 2008; Braga and Bratti, 2012; Buckles et al., 2012; Brunello et al., 2013). In a study of Australian twins, Webbink et al. (2010) concluded that higher education lowers weight among male twins but not female twins. A recent review for developed countries also concluded that parental socioeconomic status is generally inversely associated with physical inactivity among adolescents (Stalsberg and Pederson, 2010). However, wealth has no effect on physical activity among adults (Kim and Ruhm, 2012). The situation for developing countries is the opposite. In China, studies of school-going children suggest that there was no link between parental educational status and vigorous physical activity among children aged 12–14 years attending school. However, children of parents with lower education were more likely to walk to school (Shi et al., 2006). Hallal et al. (2006) found that maternal education positively associated with physical inactivity among children 12–14 years old in Brazil. These findings are reflected in Dinsa et al (2012) whose review of the literature concluded that parental economic status (wealth and education) was usually positively associated with childhood obesity in developing countries.

Another branch of work that can shed light on the link between income and CVD risk is the experience of children born with low birth weight, presumably reflecting some combination of poor parental health and low economic status (Conley and Bennett, 2001); or those born in times of extreme resource constraints such as famines. Using data from the Panel Study of Income Dynamics in the United States, Johnson and Schoeni (2011) showed that babies with low birth weight were at greater risk for diabetes and heart disease during adulthood. The precise channel for this outcome is less clear, and Morley et al. (2006) showed that low birth weight need not be directly linked to increased CVD risk based on their study of nineteenth-century Melbourne residents. An alternative mechanism was suggested by Barker relying on a combination with energy-rich western diets leading to rapid weight gain in childhood following an originally low birth weight (Barker, 2006). This mechanism potentially allows for a role for income, both through low birth weight as well through rapid weight gain among children born with low weight in a regime with cheap and energy-dense western diets. It may also explain rising childhood obesity among children of better off individuals in developing countries who consume similar diets. Related is the study of children born during famines. The future health outcomes of children born during such periods is usually taken as a confirmation the well-known 'Barker's hypothesis' (Barker, 1998) that argues that adaptation by the foetus to nutrient shortages increases disease risks later in life. However, it can also be taken to reflect a period of extreme resource scarcity experienced by the parents, with the foetal or child physiological adaption being the mechanism through with the income works its effect. Multiple studies – from Netherlands, China and elsewhere – indicate that children born during times of food scarcity have higher risks of diabetes, higher BMI and an inferior lipid profile to counterparts born at other times (Roseboom et al., 2001; Yang et al., 2008; Huang et al., 2010).

Diets
In developing countries, improved economic status tends to result in diets that lower risk for cancers and CVDs. Adda et al. (2009) show that higher income raised expenditures on fruits and vegetables in the United Kingdom. This pattern is also reflected in studies for the United States and Australia, where parental economic status was inversely correlated with childhood consumption of sugar-sweetened beverages and salt (Grimes et al., 2013; Han and Powell, 2013). However, the impact of income on dietary patterns is different in developing countries. Du et al. (2004) use longitudinal data from the China Health and Nutrition Survey to estimate income elasticities for different types of food between 1989 and 1997, and conclude that income elasticities for foods that are high in fat content and foods based on animal products are positive and especially large for poorer groups. The relatively high income elasticities for various food groups linked to cancer and CVD risk – sugar, milk and meat – have also been seen previously in a longitudinal study in a poor Indian rural population (Bhargava, 1991).

Smoking and alcohol use
In general, educational attainment was associated with lower smoking rates (particularly college education) among adults, including smoking by women during pregnancy (Currie and Moretti, 2003; Arendt, 2005; de Walque, 2007; Grimard and Parent, 2007; Buckles et al., 2012). However, Reinhold and Jurges (2010) who used the abolition of

secondary school fees as an instrument for secondary schooling did not find an impact on smoking. In the only study based on a randomised experiment reported here, for the Dominican Republic, Lleras-Muney and Jensen (2012) found that staying longer at school lowers smoking and drinking among school-age children, presumably through a mix of lower earning opportunities and peer-group effects. Kenkel et al. (2012) used changes in earned income credit rules as an instrument to assess the impact of income on smoking in low-income households in the United States and found that smoking rises with income. Adda et al. (2009), using stock market shocks as instruments for income in a study in the UK, also concluded that both smoking and alcohol use rise with income. Finally, Kim and Ruhm (2012) find that increases in wealth raise (heavy) alcohol use but not smoking. Indeed, cross-state panel-data analyses for the United States by Ruhm (2000, 2005) suggest that recessions improve individual health because they are associated with individuals exercising more and smoking less, which he links partly to the opportunity cost of time during booms.

Blood pressure
For the two developed countries where we could locate experimental studies, no clear conclusion can be drawn about the link between household resources and blood pressure. Adda et al. (2009) did not find any effect of higher incomes on blood pressure in the United Kingdom, but Schwandt (2011), using US health and retirement survey data found that increased wealth leads to higher blood pressure. In developing countries, available analyses have focused on the impact of migration and urbanisation on blood pressure. One study of Tongan participants in a New Zealand immigration lottery concluded that immigration (and presumably higher incomes) raised blood pressure; and a study of Indian migrant factory workers in urban areas concluded that longer stays in urban settings are associated with increased blood pressure and weight (Kinra et al., 2011). Others suggest that this is not a consequence of urbanisation per se, but of increased wealth associated with the move from rural to urban areas (Neuman et al., 2013).

Key conclusions
In general, the conclusion of this literature supports the contention that education is inversely related to risk factors for cancers and CVD, whereas the effects of income are typically unclear in developed countries. In developing countries, both seem to raise the prevalence of risk factors for cancers and CVDs. Why might this be so? Cutler et al. (2011) suggest that the most likely explanation is that education affects the ability to process information and cognition and this may influence the ability to process information on healthy behaviours. More educated individuals seem to use more medicines recently approved by the FDA, especially if the medicines are for longer-term use – chronic conditions, allowing for a role for learning and self-management (Lleras-Muney and Lichtenberg, 2005). Similar findings have been noted in Glied and Lleras-Muney (2008). In developing countries though, these beneficial effects of education may be overwhelmed by the underlying technological changes and a closer relationship of education to earned income effects of the Lakdawalla–Philipson variety, and by the rising demand for variety in food with income, noted by Du et al. (2004).

One area where the effect of education may not conflict with the implications of rising levels of earned income in developing countries is in the context of health service use. It is well known that increased access to healthcare coverage is associated with increased health service use in developed countries (van Doorslaer et al., 2006). Recently, Baicker et al. (2013) compared the outcomes of Medicaid expansion program for adults drawn randomly from a list to those who were not. They concluded that diagnosis and medications for diabetes increased in the treated group. Interestingly, Ruhm (2007) noted that elderly mortality from CHD increases sharply during booms in the United States, conjecturing that it is linked to lower access to services and caregiving attention diverted way from the relatively less well-off elderly during such times. Given limited coverage in developing countries, higher household incomes will likely translate into increased health service access for cancers and CVD as seen in Mahal et al. (2010). More generally, as the now developing countries get wealthier, they may be able to finance expansions in publicly funded healthcare coverage, which can lead to increased health service use (Yip and Mahal, 2008). The findings on the inverse relationship between socioeconomic status and hypertension and mortality risk from cancers and CVD even in developing countries suggests that health service use may be countering the impacts of the rising incidence risks of these conditions.

12.4 CONCLUSIONS

As can be seen the relationship between income, education and other indicators of economic status and indicators of NCD is a complex one. This chapter has sought to lend some clarity to the inter-linkages involved, but clearly there is a need for substantial additional work.

Our assessment first, is that there are at least two major causal pathways through which economic advancement is linked to the growing burden of NCD worldwide. These are essentially (1) a competing risks mechanism whereby individuals living longer end up becoming at greater risk for acquiring an NCD; and (2) impacts via risk factors for NCD.

Second, the complex inter-linkages between income, education and NCD outcomes imply that it is difficult to assign a precise role to the different causal mechanisms and the impact of economic outcomes. The literature suggests that not only can income, education and the processes underlying economic growth influence NCD through both of the above channels, but also that there are multiple confounders whose impacts are not properly understood at this time. These are further complicated by long-term impacts of economic circumstances during pregnancy and childhood. Moreover, there are feedback effects of health outcomes on economic outcomes, which suggest the need for more careful studies of the causal impacts of interest.

Third, recent work has begun to disentangle some of the causal ties running from economic outcomes to risk factors for NCD. The key finding here is that education may work differently than income in developed countries – one lowers risks for cancers and CVD, the other leaders to unclear conclusions – with the possible exception of healthcare. In developing countries both effects work in the same direction. This has led Cutler et al. (2011) to argue that education needs to be treated separately from income. But should it be? There is a strong correlation between income and education, as illustrated by the well-known Mincer equation that focuses on earnings and schooling and experience. Moreover, many of the effects of income may be working through education and indeed, rising levels of income per capita and opportunities for earnings may enable countries (and households) to invest more in education.

There are other channels through which economic progress can be felt on cancers and CVD that we did not discuss adequately in this chapter. Differential economic performance can promote migration between countries and across regions. In two quasi-experimental studies we accessed, urbanisation and international migration were linked to increased levels of hypertension and risks for CVD (Gibson et al., 2010; Ebrahim et al., 2010). But it is unclear whether the effect is through rising incomes or the move itself. Another risk factor is that of pollution, particularly during the early stages of economic growth when regulations cannot keep pace with manufacturing. For example, while some cancers are hereditary, some others are driven by infectious agents, and exposure to radiation (sun, CT-scans, X-rays, etc.) has also been associated with cancer, as has been exposure to carcinogens such as asbestos, cobalt, quartz, etc.

We also did not explore adequately the issue of 'neighbourhood effects' where it is not the individual's income or education but neighbourhood characteristics that are important. Multiple studies indicate the association of neighbourhood economic characteristics to NCD outcomes and risk factors (some are indicated in Tables 12.1 and 12.2). The major methodological issue here is that of endogeneity in locational decisions, so that poor and less-educated people live together, have less influence on public resource allocation decisions and have poor NCD outcomes and related high risk behaviours. Finally, further work may also be needed on the relationship between economic development, political systems and health outcomes related to NCD. One strand of the literature focuses on 'welfare state' regimes that focus on lowering inequalities (e.g., Chung and Muntaner, 2007). These studies generally tend to find that health outcomes are better in states that have a more redistributive economic system. This raises the subject of population preferences for redistribution and associated allocations to health services as a potential driver of NCD risks on the one hand and the implications of economic change as an influence on political structures on the other.

REFERENCES

Aarts, M., V. Lemmens, M. Louwman, A. Kunst and J. Coebergh (2010), Socioeconomic status and changing inequalities in colorectal cancer? A review of the associations with risk, treatment and outcome. *European Journal of Cancer*, **46**(15), 2681–2695.

Abegunde, D., C. Mathers, T. Adam, M. Ortegon and K. Strong (2007), The burden and costs of chronic diseases in low-income and middle-income countries. *The Lancet*, **370**, 1929–38.

Adda, J., J. Banks and H. von Gaudecker (2009), The impact of income shocks on health: evidence from cohort data. *Journal of the European Economic Association*, **7**(6), 1361–1399.

Addo, J., L. Ayerbe, K. Mohan, S, Crichton, A. Sheldenkar, R. Chen et al. (2012), Socioeconomic status and stroke: an updated review. *Stroke*, **43**(4), 1186–1191.

Agardh, E., P. Allebeck, J. Hallqvist, T. Moradi and A. Sidorchuk (2011), Type 2 diabetes incidence and socioeconomic position: a systematic review and meta-analysis. *International Journal of Epidemiology*, **40**(3), 804–818.

Aguero, J., M. Carter and I. Woolard (2006), The impact of unconditional cash transfers on nutrition: the South African Child Support Grant. Unpublished, Department of Economics, University of California.

Alter, D., K. Iron, P. Austin, C. Naylor and SESAMI Study Group (2004), Socioeconomic status, service patterns, and perceptions of care among survivors of acute myocardial infraction in Canada. *Journal of the American Medical Association*, **291**(9), 1100–1107.

Arendt, J. (2005), Does education cause better health? A panel data analysis using school reforms for identification. *Economics of Education Review*, **24**(2), 149–60.

Australian Institute of Health and Welfare (2010), Cardiovascular disease mortality: trends at different ages. Cardiovascular series no. 31, category no. 47, AIHW, Canberra.

Avendano, M., A. Kunst, M. Huisman, F. Lenthe, M. Bopp, E. Regidor et al. (2006), Socioeconomic status and ischaemic heart disease mortality in 10 western European populations during the 1990s. *Heart*, **92**(4), 461–67.

Aziz, Z., J. Iqbal and M. Akram (2008), Effect of social class disparities on disease stage, quality of treatment and survival outcomes in breast cancer patients from developing countries. *The Breast Journal*, **14**(4), 372–75.

Baicker, K., S. Taubman, H. Allen, M. Bernstein, J. Gruber, J. Newhouse et al. (2013), The Oregon experiment: effects of Medicaid on clinical outcomes. *New England Journal of Medicine*, **368**, 1713–1722.

Balarajan, Y. and E. Villamor (2009), Nationally representative surveys show recent increases in the prevalence of overweight and obesity among women of reproductive age in Bangladesh, Nepal and India. *Journal of Nutrition*, **139**(11), 2139–2144.

Ball, K. and D. Crawford (2005), Socioeconomic status and weight change in adults: a review. *Social Science and Medicine*, **60**(9), 1987–2010.

Barguera, S., L. Hernandez-Barrera, M. Tolentino, J. Espinosa, S. Ng, J. Rivera et al. (2008), Energy intake from beverages is increasing among Mexican adolescents and adults. *Journal of Nutrition*, **138**(12), 2454–2461.

Barker, D. (1998), *Mothers, Babies and Health in Later Life*. Edinburgh: Charles Livingstone.

Barker, D. (2006), Commentary: birthweight and coronary heart disease in a historical context. *International Journal of Epidemiology*, **35**(4), 886–87.

Baum, C. and W. Ford (2004), The wage effects of obesity: a longitudinal study. *Health Economics*, **13**(9), 885–89.

Bauman, A., G. Ma, F. Cuevas, Z. Omar, T. Waqanivalu, P. Phongsavan et al. (2010), Cross-national comparisons of socioeconomic differences in the prevalence of leisure time and occupational physical activity, and active commuting in six Asia-Pacific countries. *Journal of Epidemiology and Community Health*, **65**(1), 35–43.

Bhargava, A. (1991), Estimating short and long run income elasticities of foods and nutrients for rural South India. *Journal of the Royal Statistical Society Series A*, **154**(1), 157–74.

Bloom, D. and D. Canning (2000), The health and wealth of nations. *Science*, **287**(5456), 1207–1209.

Bloom, D. and D. Canning (2007), The Preston curve 30 years on: still sparking fires. *International Journal of Epidemiology*, **36**(3), 498–99.

Bloom, D. and J. Williamson (1998), Demographic transitions and economic miracles in emerging Asia. *World Bank Economic Review*, **12**(3), 419–55.

Boissonnet, C., H. Schargrodsky, F. Pellegrini, A. Macchia, B. Champagne, E. Wilson et al. (2011), Educational inequalities in obesity, abdominal obesity and metabolic syndrome in seven Latin American cities: the CARMELA study. *European Journal of Preventive Cardiology*, **18**(4), 550–56

Borodulin, K., T. Laatikainen, A. Juolevi and P. Jousilahti (2007), Thirty-year trends of physical activity in relation to age, calendar time and birth cohort in Finnish adults. *European Journal of Public Health*, **18**(3), 339–44.

Braga, M. and M. Bratti (2012), The causal effect of education on health and health-related behaviour: evidence from a compulsory schooling reform Unpublished. Department of Economics, Milan, Italy.

Brownson, R., T. Boehmer and D. Luke (2005), Declining rates of physical activity in the United States: what are the contributors? *Annual Review of Public Health*, **26**, 421–43.

Brunello, G., D. Fabbri and M. Fort (2013), The causal effect of education on body mass: evidence from Europe. *Journal of Labor Economics*, **31**(1), 195–223.

Buckles, K., O. Malamud, M. Morrill and A. Wozniak (2012), The effect of college education on health Discussion paper no. 6659, Bonn, Germany: Institute for the Study of Labour (IZA)

Calle, E. and R. Kaaks (2004), Overweight, obesity and cancer: epidemiological evidence and proposed mechanisms. *Nature reviews. Cancer*, **4**(8), 579–91.

Canning, D. and D. Bowser (2010), Investing in health to improve the well being of the disadvantaged: reversing the argument of Fair Society, Healthy Lives (The Marmot Review). *Social Science and Medicine*, **71**, 1223–1226.

Case, A. (2004), Does money protect health status? Evidence from South African pensions. In D. Wise (ed.) *Perspectives in the Economics of Aging*. Cambridge, MA: National Bureau of Economic Research, pp. 287–312.

Case, A., D. Lubotsky and C. Paxson (2002), Economic status and health in childhood: the origins of the gradient. *American Economic Review*, **92**(5), 1308–1334.

Cavill, N., S. Kahlmeier and F. Racioppi (2006), *Physical Activity and Health in Europe: Evidence for Action*. Copenhagen, Denmark: World Health Organization.

Chandra, A. and T. Vogl (2010), Rising up with shoe leather? A comment on Fair Society, Healthy Lives (The Marmot Review). *Social Science and Medicine*, **71**(7), 1227–1230.

Chaturvedi, N., J. Jarrett, M. Shipley and J. Fuller (1998), Socioeconomic gradient in morbidity and mortality in people with diabetes: cohort study findings from the Whitehall study and the WHO multinational study of vascular disease in diabetes. *British Medical Journal*, **316**, 100–106.

Chou, Y., M. Grossman and H. Saffer (2001), An economic analysis of adult obesity: results from the Behavioral Risk Factor Surveillance System Unpublished. Department of Economics, City University of New York, New York.

Chung, H. and C. Muntaner (2007), Welfare state matters: a typological multilevel analysis of wealthy countries. *Health Policy*, **80**(2), 328–39.

Coleman, M., B. Rachet, L. Woods, E. Mitry, M. Riga, N. Cooper et al. (2004), Trends and socioeconomic inequalities in cancer survival in England and Wales until 2001. *British Journal of Cancer*, **90**(7), 1367–1373.

Colhoun, H., H. Hemingway and N. Poulter (1998), Socioeconomic status and blood pressure: an overview analysis. *Journal of Human Hypertension*, **12**(2), 91–110.

Conley, D. and N. Bennett (2001), Birthweight and income: interactions across generations. *Journal of Health and Social Behaviour*, **42**, 450–65.

Currie, J. and E. Moretti (2003), Mother's education and the intergenerational transmission of human capital: evidence from college openings. *Quarterly Journal of Economics*, **118**(4), 1495–1532.

Cutler, D., A. Deaton and A. Lleras-Muney (2004), The determinants of mortality. Draft, Department of Economics, Princeton University, Princeton NJ.

Cutler, D., A. Lleras-Muney and T. Vogl (2011), Socioeconomic status and health: dimensions and mechanisms. In S. Glied and P. Smith (eds), *Oxford Handbook of Health Economics*. New York: Oxford University Press.

Cutler, D. and E. Meara (2004), Changes in the age distribution of mortality over the 20th century. In D. Wise (ed.), *Perspectives in the Economics of Aging*. Cambridge, MA: National Bureau of Economic Research, pp. 333–66.

Daar, A.S., P.A. Singer, D.L. Persad, S.K. Pramming, D. Matthews, R. Beaglehole, A. Bernstein et al. (2007), Grand challenges in chronic non-communicable diseases. *Nature*, **450** (November), 20–22.

Dahly, D., P. Gordon-Larsen, B. Popkin, J. Kaufman and L. Adair (2009), Associations between multiple indicators of socioeconomic status and obesity in young adult Filipinos vary by gender, urbanicity and indicator used. *Journal of Nutrition*, **140**(2), 366–70.

Dalstra, J., A. Kunst, C. Borrell, E. Breeze, E. Cambois, G. Costa et al. (2005), Socioeconomic differences in the prevalence of common chronic diseases: an overview of 8 European countries. *International Journal of Epidemiology*, **34**(2), 316–26.

Danaei, G., M. Finucane, J. Lin, G. Singh, C. Paciorek, M. Cowan et al. (2011), National, regional and global trends in systolic blood pressure since 1980: systematic analysis of health examination surveys and epidemiological studies with 786 country-years and 5.4 million participants. *The Lancet*, **377**(9765), 568–77.

das Neves, F., I. Mattos and R. Koifman (2005), Colon and rectal cancer mortality in Brazilian capitals, 1980–97. *Arquivos de Gastroenterologia*, **42**(1), 63–70.

Davey Smith, G., C. Hart, D. Blane and D. Hole (1998), Adverse socioeconomic conditions in childhood and cause-specific adult mortality: prospective observational study. *British Medical Journal*, **316**, 1631–1635.

de Walque, D. (2007), Does education affect smoking behaviours? Evidence using the Vietnam draft as an instrument for college education. *Journal of Health Economics*, **26**, 877–95.

Deaton, A. (2003), Health, inequality and economic development. *Journal of Economic Literature*, **41**, 113–58.

Deaton, A. (2006), The great escape: a review of Robert Fogel's *The Escape from Hunger and Premature Death, 1700–2100*. *Journal of Economic Literature*, **44**, 106–114.

Deaton, A. and D. Lubotsky (2003), Mortality, inequality and race in American cities and states. *Social Science and Medicine*, **56**, 1139–53.

Deaton, A. and C. Paxson (2004), Mortality, income and income inequality over time in Britain and the United States. In D. Wise (ed.), *Perspectives on the Economics of Ageing*, Cambridge, MA: National Bureau of Economic Research, pp. 247–286.

Diez-Roux, A., S. Stein Merkin, D. Arnett, L. Chambless, M. Massing, F. Javier Nieto et al. (2001), Neighborhood of residence and incidence of coronary heart disease. *The New England Journal of Medicine*, **345**(2), 99–106.

Dinsa, G., Y. Goryakin, E. Fumagalli and M. Suhrcke (2012), Obesity and socioeconomic status in developing countries: a systematic review. *Obesity Reviews*, **13**(11), 1067–1079.

Dokken, B. (2008), The pathophysiology of cardiovascular disease and diabetes: beyond blood pressure and lipids. *Diabetes Spectrum*, **21**(3), 160–65.

Du, S., T. Mroz, F. Zhai and B. Popkin (2004), Rapd income growth adversely affects diet quality in China – particularly for the poor! *Social Science and Medicine*, **59**(7), 1505–1515.

Easterly, W. (1999), Life during growth. *Journal of Economic Growth*, **4**(3), 239–75.

Ebrahim, S., S. Kinra, L. Bowen, E. Andersen, Y. Ben-Shlomo, T. Lyngdoh et al. (2010), The effect of rural-to-urban migration on obesity and diabetes in India. *PLOS Medicine*, **7**(4), e1000268 doi:10.1371/journal.pmed.1000268.

Erem, C., A. Hacihasanoglu, M. Kocak, O. Deger and M. Topbas (2009), Prevalence of pre-hypertension and hypertension and associated risk factors among Turkish adults: Trabzon Hypertension Study. *Journal of Public Health*, **31**(1), 47–58.

Escobar, E. (2002), Hypertension and coronary heart disease. *Journal of Human Hypertension*, **16**(S1), S61–S63.

Ezzati, M., S. Vander Hoorn, C. Lawes, R. Leach, W. James, A. Lopez et al. (2005), Rethinking the 'diseases of affluence' paradigm: global patterns of nutritional risks in relation to economic development. *PLOS Medicine*, **2**(5)e133, doi:10.1371/journal.pmed.0020133.

Fogel, R. (1986), *Nutrition and the Decline in Mortality since 1700: Some Preliminary Findings*. Cambridge, MA: National Bureau of Economic Research.

Food and Agricultural Organization (FAO) (2002), *World Agriculture: Towards 2015/2030*. Rome: FAO.

Ford, E. and S. Capewell (2007), Coronary heart disease mortality among young adults in the U.S. from 1980 to 2002: concealed levelling of mortality rates. *Journal of the American College of Cardiology*, **50**(22), 2128–2132.

Forrest, L., J. Adams, H. Wareham, G. Rubin and M. White (2013), Socioeconomic inequalities in lung cancer treatment: a systematic review and meta-analysis. *PLOS Medicine*, **10**(2), e1001376.

Freitas-Junior, R., C. Gonzaga, N. Freitas, E. Martins and R. Dardes (2012), Disparities in female breast cancer mortality rates in Brazil between 1980 and 2009. *Clinics*, **67**(7), 731–37.

Fresco, L. and W. Baudoin (2002), Food and nutrition security towards human security. In *Proceedings of the International Conference on Vegetables*, 11–14 November 2002, Bangalore India Prem Nath Agricultural Science Foundation.

Gaiha, R., N. Kaicker, K. Imai, V. Kulkarni and G. Thapa (2012), Diet diversification and diet quality in India: an analysis. Discussion paper DP 2012-30, Kobe University, Research Institute for Economics and Business Administration, Kobe, Japan.

Gertler, P. and J. Gruber (2002), Insuring consumption against illness. *American Economic Review*, **92**(1), 51–70.

Gibson, J., S. Stillman, D. McKenzie and H. Rohorua (2010), Natural experiment evidence on the effect of migration on blood pressure and hypertension. Working paper, University College, Department of Economics and Center for Research Analysis of Migration, London, UK.

Giles-Corti, B. and R. Donovan (2002), Socioeconomic status differences in recreational physical activity levels and real and perceived access to a supportive physical environment. *Preventive Medicine*, **35**(6), 601–11.

Giovino, G., S. Mirza, J. Samet, P. Gupta, M. Jarvis, N. Bhala et al. (2012), Tobacco use in 3 billion individuals from 16 countries: an analysis of nationally-representative cross-sectional surveys. *The Lancet*, **380**(9842), 668–79.

Glewwe, P., S. Koch and B. Nguyen (2003), *The Impact of Income Growth and Provision of Healthcare Services on Child Nutrition in Vietnam*. Washington DC: The World Bank.

Glied, S. and A. Lleras-Muney (2008), Technological innovation and inequality in health. *Demography*, **45**, 741–61.

Goldman, D. and J. Smith (2002), Can patient self-management help explain the SES health gradient? *Proceedings of the National Academy of Sciences*, **99**(16), 10929–10934.

Grabner, M. (2008), The causal effect of education on obesity: evidence from compulsory schooling laws. Unpublished. Department of Economics, University of California, Davis, CA.

Grimard, F. and D. Parent (2007), Education and smoking: were Vietnam war draft avoiders also more likely to avoid smoking? *Journal of Health Economics*, **26**(5), 896–926.

Grimes, C., L. Riddell, K. Campbell and C. Nowson (2013), Dietary salt intake, sugar-sweetened beverage consumption and obesity risk. *Pediatrics*, **131**(1), 14–21.

Grimm, K., H. Blanck, K. Scanlon, L. Moore and L. Grummer-Strawn (2010), State-specific trends in fruit and vegetable consumption among adults: United States, 2000–2009. *Morbidity and Mortality Weekly Report*, **59**(35), 1127–1130.

Grittner, U., S. Kuntsche, G. Gmel and K. Bloomfield (2013), Alcohol consumption and social inequality at the individual and country levels: results from an international study. *European Journal of Public Health*, **23**(2), 332–39.

Guindon, E. and D. Boisclair (2003), Past, current and future trends in tobacco use Unpublished. Center for Tobacco Control Research and Education, University of California.

Hallal, P., C. Victora, J. Wells, and R. Lima (2003), Physical inactivity: prevalence and associated variables in Brazilian adults. *Medicine and Science in Sports and Exercise*, **38**, 1894–1900.

Hallal, P., J. Wells, F. Reichart, L. Anselmi and C. Victora (2006), Early determinants of physical activity in adolescence: a prospective cohort study. *British Medical Journal*, **332**, 1002.

Han, E. and L. Powell (2013), Consumption patterns of sugar-sweetened beverages in the United States. *Journal of the Academy of Nutrition and Dietitics*, **3**(1), 43–53.

Hashibe, M., B. Siwakoti, M. Wei, B. Thakur, C. Pun, B. Shreshtha et al. (2010), Socioeconomic status and lung cancer risk in Nepal. *Asia-Pacific Journal of Cancer Prevention*, **12**, 1083–1088.

Hiscock, R., L. Bauld, A. Amos, J. Fidler and M. Munafo (2011), Socioeconomic status and smoking: a review. *Annals of the New York Academy of Sciences*, **1248**(1), 107–23.

Honore, B. and A. Lleras-Muney (2007), Bounds in competing risks models and the war on cancer. *Econometrica*, **74**(6), 1675–1698.

Hosseinpoor, A., L. Parker, E. Tursan d'Espaignet and S. Chatterji (2012), Socioeconomic inequality in smoking in low-income and middle-income countries: results from the World Health Survey. *PLoS ONE*, **7**(8), e42843.

Huang, C., Z. Li, M. Wang and R. Martorell (2010), Early life exposure to the 1959–61 Chinese Famine has long-term health consequences. *Journal of Nutrition*, **140**(10), 1874–1878.

Hulshof, K., J. Brussard, A. Kruizinga, J. Telman and M. Lowik (2003), Socioeconomic status, dietary intake and 10 year trends: the Dutch National Food Consumption Survey. *European Journal of Clinical Nutrition*, **57**, 128–37.

Institute of Health Metrics and Evaluation (2013), *Global Burden of Disease Protocol*. Available at http://www.healthmetricsandevaluation.org/gbd/2013/protocol (accessed 20 January 2014).

de Irala-Estevez, J., M. Groth, L. Johansson, U. Oltersdorf, R. Prattala and M. Martinez-Gonzalez (2000), A systematic review of socioeconomic differences in food habits in Europe: consumption of fruits and vegetables. *European Journal of Clinical Nutrition*, **54**, 706–14.

Ismail, A., J. Tanzer and J. Dingle (1997), Current trends in sugar consumption in developing societies. *Community Dental Oral Epidemiology*, **25**(6), 438–43.

Johnson, R. and R. Schoeni (2011), Early-life origins of adult disease: national longitudinal population-based study of the United States. *American Journal of Public Health*, **101**(12), 2317–2324.

Jung, K., S. Park, H. Kong, Y. Won, J. Lee, E. Park et al. (2011), Cancer statistics in Korea: incidental, survival, mortality and prevalence in 2008. *Cancer Research and Treatment*, **43**(1), 1–11.

Kearney, J. (2010), Food consumption trends and drivers. *Philosophical Transactions of the Royal Society B: Biological Sciences*, **365**(1554), 2793–2807.

Kenkel, D., M. Schmeiser and C. Urban (2012), Is smoking inferior? Evidence from variation in earned income credit. Unpublished. Department of Economics Cornell University, Cornell, NY.

Kim, B. and C. Ruhm (2012), Inheritances, health and death. *Health Economics*, **21**(2), 127–44.

Kinra, S., E. Andersen, Y. Ben Shlomo, L. Bowen, T. Lyngdoh, D. Prabhakaran et al. (2011), Association between urban life-years and cardio-mtabolic risk: the Indian Migration Study. *American Journal of Epidemiology*, **174**(2), 154–64.

van Kippersluis, H., O. O'Donnell and E. van Doorslaer (2011), Long-run returns to education: does schooling lead to an extended old age? *Journal of Human Resources*, **46**(4), 695–721.

Knuth, A., G. Bacchieri, C. Victora and P. Hallal (2010), Changes in physical activity among Brazilian adults over a 5-year period. *Journal of Epidemiology and Community Health*, **64**(7), 591–95.

de Kok, I., F. van Lenthe, M. Avendano, M. Louwman, J. Coebergh and J. Mackenbach (2008), Childhood social class and cancer incidence: results of the GLOBE study. *Social Science and Medicine*, **66**(5), 1131–1139.

Kurkure, A. and B. Yeole (2006), Social inequalities in cancer with special reference to South Asian countries. *Asia-Pacific Journal of Cancer Prevention*, **7**(1), 36–40.

Kushi, L., C. Doyle, M. McCollough, C. Rock, W. Demark-Wahnefried, E. Bandera et al. (2012), American Cancer Society Guidelines on nutrition and physical activity for cancer prevention: reducing the risk of cancer with healthy food choices and physical activity. *CA: A Cancer Journal for Clinicians*, **61**(1), 30–67.

Lakdawalla, D. and T. Philipson (2009), The growth of obesity and technological change. *Economics and Human Biology*, **7**(3), 283–93.

Lejeune, C., F. Sassi, L. Ellis, S. Godward, V. Mak, M. Day et al. (2010), Socioeconomic disparities in access to treatment and their impact on colorectal cancer survival. *International Journal of Epidemiology*, **39**(3), 710–17.

Leon, A. and U. Bronas (2009), Pathophysiology of coronary heart disease and biological mechanisms for the cardioprotective effects of regular aerobic exercise. *American Journal of Lifestyle Medicine*, **3**, 379.

Lleras-Muney, A. (2005), The relationship between education and adult mortality in the United States. *Review of Economic Studies*, **72**, 189–221.

Lleras-Muney, A. and R. Jensen (2012), Does staying in school (and not working) prevent teen drinking and smoking? *Journal of Health Economics*, **31**(4), 644–75.

Lleras-Muney, A. and F. Lichtenberg (2005), Are the more educated more likely to use new drugs *Annales d'Economie et de Statistique*, **79–80**, 671–96.

Lopez, A.D., C. Mathers, M. Ezzati, D. Jamison and C.L. Murray (2006), Global and regional burden of disease and risk factors, 2001: systematic analysis of population health data. *Lancet*, **367**(9524), 1747–57. Available at: http://dx.doi.org/10.1016/S0140-6736(06)68770-9 [Accessed July 16, 2012].

Loucks, E., S. Buka, M. Rogers, T. Liu, I. Kawachi, L. Kubzansky et al. (2012), Education and coronary heart disease risk associations may be affected by early-life common causes: a propensity matching analysis. *Annals of Epidemiology*, **22**(4), 221–32.

Lozano, R., N. Naghavi, K. Foreman, S. Lim, K. Shibuya, V. Aboyans et al. (2012), Global and regional mortality from 235 causes of death for 20 age groups in 1990 and 2010: a systematic analysis for the Global Burden of Disease Study 2010. *The Lancet*, **380**(9859), 2095–2128.

Ma, Y., W. Mei, P. Yin, X. Yang, S. Rastegar and J. Yan (2013), Prevalence of hypertension in Chinese cities: a meta-analysis of published studies. *PLOS ONE*, **8**(3), e58302.

Mahal, A., A. Karan and M. Engelgau (2010), Economic implications of noncommunicable disease for India. Discussion paper, The World Bank, Health Nutrition and Population Washington DC.

Malik, V., B. Popkin, G. Bray, J. Despres and F. Hu (2010), Sugar sweetened beverages, obesity, Type 2 Diabetes and cardiovascular disease risk. *Circulation*, **121**(11), 1356–1364.

Marmot, M. (2010), *Fair Society, Healthy Lives*. London: The Marmot Review.

Mathers, C. and D. Loncar (2005), Updated projections of global mortality and burden of disease, 2002–2030: data sources, methods and results. Evidence and Information for Policy Working Paper. Available at: www.who.int/healthinfo/statistics/bodprojectionspaper.pdf.

Matsushima, M., K. Shimizu, M. Maruyama, R. Nishimura, R. LaPorte and N. Tajima (1996), Socioeconomic and behavioural risk factors for mortality of individuals with IDDM in Japan: population-based case-control study. *Diabetologia*, **39**(6), 710–16.

McLaren, L. (2007), Socioeconomic status and obesity. *Epidemiologic Reviews*, **29**, 29–48.

Mendez, M.A., Cooper, R., Wilks, R., A. Luke and T. Forrester (2003), Income, education, and blood pressure in adults in Jamaica, a middle-income developing country. *International Journal of Epidemiology*, **32**, 399–407.

Mendez, M., C. Monteiro and B. Popkin (2005), Overweight exceeds underweight among women in most developing countries. *American Journal of Clinical Nutrition* **81**(3), 714–21.

Menvielle, G., H. Boshuizen, A. Kunst, S. Dalton, P. Vineis, M. Bergmann et al. (2009), The role of smoking and diet in explaining educational inequalities in lung cancer incidence. *Journal of the National Cancer Institute*, **101**(5), 321–30.

Menvielle, G., H. Boshuizen, A. Kunst, P. Vineis, S. Dalton, M. Bergmann et al. (2010), Occupational exposures contribute to educational inequalities in lung cancer incidence among men: evidence from the EPIC prospective cohort study. *International Journal of Cancer*, **126**(8), 1928–1935.

Mirzaei, M., A. Truswell, R. Taylor and S. Leeder (2009), Coronary heart disease epidemics: not all the same. *Heart*, **95**, 740–46.

Monteiro, C., W. Conde, S. Matsudo, V. Matsudo, I. Bonsenor and P. Lotufo (2003), A descriptive epidemiology of leisure time physical activity in Brail 1996–97. *Revista Panamericana de Salud Publica*, **14**(4), 246–54.

Monteiro C.A., W.L. Conde and B.M. Popkin (2004), Obesity and Inequities in Health in the Developing World. *International Journal of Obesity*, **28**, 1181–86.

Morley, R., J. McCalman and J. Carlin (2006), Birthweight and coronary heart disease in a cohort born 1857–1900 in Melbourne, Australia. *International Journal of Epidemiology*, **35**(4), 880–85.

Mukamal, K. and E. Rimm (2013), Alcohol's effects on the risk for coronary heart disease. National Institutes for Health, United States. Available at: http://pubs.niaaa.nih.gov/publications/arh25-4/255-261.htm (accessed 26 May 2013).

Munasinghe, L. and N. Sicherman (2006), Why do dancers smoke? Smoking, time preference and wage dynamics. *Eastern Economic Journal*, **32**(4), 595–616.

Murray, C. (1994), Quantifying the burden of disease: the technical basis for disability-adjusted life years. *Bulletin of the Worl Health Organization*, **72**(3), 429–45.

Neuman, M., I. Kawachi, S. Gortmaker and S. Subramanian (2013), Urban–rural differences in low- and middle-income countries: the role of socioeconomic status. *American Journal of Clinical Nutrition*, **97**(2), 428–36.

das Neves, F., I. Mattos and R. Koifman (2005), Colon and rectal cancer mortality in Brazilian capitals, 1980-97. *Arquivos de Gastroenterologia*, **42**(1), 63–70.

Ng, N., M. Hakimi, H. Minh, S. Juvekar, A. Razzaque, A. Ashraf et al. (2009a), Prevalence of physical inactivity in nine rural INDEPTH health and demographic surveillance systems in five Asian countries. *Global Health Action*, 2, 10.

Ng, S., E. Norton and B. Popkin (2009b), Why have physical activity levels declined among Chinese adults? Findings from the 1991-2006 China health and nutrition surveys. *Social Science and Medicine*, **68**(7), 1305–1314.

Nurkse, R. (1953), *Problems of Capital Formation in Underdeveloped Countries*. New York: Oxford University Press.

O'Flaherty, M., E. Ford, S. Allender, P. Scarborough and S. Capewell (2008), Coronary heart disease trends in England and Wales from 1984 to 2004: concealed levelling of mortality rates among young adults. *Heart*, **94**, 178–81.

Organisation for Economic Cooperation and Development (OECD) (2012), *Health at a Glance: Europe 2012*. Paris: OECD.

Ostbye, T., R. Malhotra and A. Chan (2013), Variations in and correlations of body mass status of older Singaporean men and women: results from a National Survey. *Asia-Pacific Journal of Public Heath*, **25**(1), 48–62.

Petersen, C., L. Thygesen, J. Helge, M. Gronbaek and J. Tolstrup (2010), Time trends in physical activity in leisure time in the Danish population from 1987 to 2005. *Scandinavian Journal of Public Health*, **38**(2), 121–28.

Popkin, B., K. Duffey and P. Gordon-Laren (2005), Environmental influences on food choice, physical activity and energy balance. *Physiology and Behavior*, **86**, 603–13.

Prentice, A. (2006), The emerging epidemic of obesity in developing countries. *International Journal of Epidemiology*, **35**(1), 93–99.

Preston, S. (1975), The changing relationship between mortality and the level of economic development. *Population Studies*, **29**(2), 231–48.

Pudrovska, T. and B. Anikputa (2012), The role of early life socioeconomic status in breast cancer incidence and mortality: unravelling life course mechanisms. *Journal of Ageing and Health*, **24**(2), 323–434.

Rathmann, W., B. Haastert, A. Icks, G. Giani, R. Holle and C. Meisinger (2004), Sex differences in the associations of socioeconomic status with undiagnosed diabetes mellitus and impaired glucose tolerance in the elderly population: the KORA survey 2000. *European Journal of Public Health*, **15**(6), 627–33.

Rathmann, W., B. Haastert, G. Giani, W. Koening, A. Imhof, C. Herder et al. (2006), Is inflammation a causal chain between low socioeconomic status and type 2 diabetes? Results from the KORA survey. *European Journal of Epidemiology*, **21**(1), 55–60.

Reddy, K. and M. Katan (2004), Diet, nutrition and the prevention of hypertension and cardiovascular diseases. *Public Health Nutrition*, **7**(1A), 167–86.

Reddy, K., D. Prabhakaran, P. Jeemon, K. Thankappan, P. Joshi, V. Chaturvedi et al. (2007), Educational status and cardiovascular risk profile of Indians. *Proceedings of the National Academy of Sciences*, **104**(41), 16363–16368.

Reinhold, S. and H. Jurges (2010), Secondary school fees and the causal effect of schooling on health behaviour. *Health Economics*, **19**(8), 994–1001.

Robertson, L., P. Mushati, J. Eaton, L. Dumba, G. Mavise, J. Makoni et al. (2013), Effects of unconditional and conditional cash transfers on child health and development in Zimbabwe: a cluster-randomized trial. *The Lancet*, **381**(9874), 1332–1347.

Romer, P. (1986), Increasing returns and long-run growth. *Journal of Political Economy*, **94**, 1002–1037.

Rosamond, W., L. Chambless, G. Heiss, T. Mosley, J. Coresh, E. Whitsel, L. Wagenknecht, H. Ni and A. Folsom (2012), Twenty-two-year trends in incidence of myocardial infraction, coronary heart disease mortality and case fatality in 4 US communities 1987–2008. *Circulation*, **125**, 1848–1857.

Roseboom, T., J. van der Meulen, A. Ravelli, C. Osmond, D. Barker and O. Bleker (2001), Effects of prenatal exposure to the Dutch Famine on adult disease in later life: an overview. *Twins Research*, **4**(5), 293–98.

van Rossum, C., M. Shipley, H. van de Mheen, D. Grobbee and M. Marmot (2000), Employment grade differences in cause-specific mortality: a 25-year follow up of civil servants from the first Whitehall study. *Journal of Epidemiology and Community Health*, **54**, 178–84.

Ruhm, C. (2000), Are recessions good for your health. *Quarterly Journal of Economics*, **115**(2), 617–50.

Ruhm, C. (2005), Healthy living in hard times. *Journal of Health Economics*, **24**(2), 341–63.

Ruhm, C. (2007), A healthy economy can break your heart. *Demography*, **44**(4), 829–48.

Sacerdote, C., F. Ricceri, O. Rolandsson, I. Baldi, M. Chirlaque, E. Feskens et al. (2012), Lower educational level is a predictor of incident type II diabetes in European countries: the EPIC-Interact Study. *International Journal of Epidemiology*, **41**(4), 1162–1173.

Samdal, O., J. Tynjala, C. Roberts, J. Sallis, J. Villberg and B. Wold (2007), Trends in vigorous physical activity and TV watching of adolescents from 1986 to 2002 in seven European countries. *European Journal of Public Health*, **17**(3), 242–48.

Samuel, P., B. Antonisamy, P. Raghupathy, J. Richard and C. Hall (2012), Socioeconomic status and cardiovascular risk factors in rural and urban areas of Vellore, Tamil Nadu, South India. *International Journal of Epidemiology*, **41**(5), 1315–1327.

Schwandt, H. (2011), Is wealth causing health? Evidence from stock market induced health shocks. Unpublished. Department of Economics, Universitat Pompeu Fabra, Barcelona, Spain.

Shi, Z., N. Lien, B. Kumar and G. Holmboe-Ottesen (2006), Physical activity and associated sociodemographic factors among school adolescents in Jiangsu province, China. *Preventive Medicine*, **43**(3), 218–21.

Sidorchuk, A., E. Agardh, O. Aremu, J. Hallqvist, P. Allebeck and T. Moradi (2009), Socioeconomic differences in lung cancer incidence: a systematic review and meta-analysis. *Cancer Causes Control*, **20**(4), 459–71.

Smith, J. (2007), Diabetes and the rise of the SES health gradient. Working paper no. 12905, National Bureau of Economic Research, Cambridge MA.

Smith, K. and N. Goldman (2007), Socioeconomic differences in health among older adults in Mexico. *Social Science and Medicine*, **65**(7), 1372–1385.

Song, Y., R. Ferrer, S. Cho, J. Sung, S. Ebrahim and G. Davey Smith (2006), Socioeconomic status and cardiovascular disease among men: the Korean National Health Service propsective cohort study. *American Journal of Public Health*, **96**(1), 152–59.

Stalsberg, R. and A. Pedersen (2010), Effects of socioeconomic status on the physical activity in adolescents: a systematic review of the evidence. *Medicine and Science in Sports*, **20**(3), 368–83.

Steptoe, A. and M. Marmot (2005), Socioeconomic status and coronary heart disease: a psychobiological perspective. *Population and Development Review*, **30**, 133–50.

Stringhini, S., S. Sabia, M. Shipley, E. Brunner, H. Nabi, M. Kivimaki and A. Singh-Manoux (2010), Association of socioeconomic position with health behaviours and mortality. *Journal of the American Medical Asssociation*, **303**(12), 1159–1166.

Subramanian, S., D. Corsi, M. Subramanyam and G. Davey Smith (2013), Jumping the gun: the problematic discourse on socioeconomic status and cardiovascular disease in India. *International Journal of Epidemiology*, doi:10.1093/ije/dyt1017.

Subramanian, S., J. Perkins, E. Ozaltin and G. Davey Smith (2011), Weight of nations: a socioeconomic analysis of women in low- to middle-income countries. *American Journal of Clinical Nutrition*, **93**(2), 913–21.

Tanaka, T., E. Gjonca and M. Gulliford (2012), Income, wealth and risk of diabetes among older adults: cohort study using the English Longitudinal Study of Ageing. *European Journal of Public Health*, **22**(3), 310–17.

Tang, M., Y. Chen and D. Krewski (2003), Gender-related differences in the association between socioeconomic status and self-reported diabetes. *International Journal of Epidemiology*, **32**(3), 381–85.

Timmer, C. (1988), The agricultural transformation. In H. Chenery and T. Srinivasan (eds), *Handbook of Development Economics I*. Amsterdam: North Holland, pp. 275–331.

Trinh, O., N. Nguyen, M. Dibley, P. Phongsavan and A. Bauman (2008), The prevalence and correlates of physical inactivity among adults in Ho Chi Min City. *BMC Public Health*, **8**, 204.

Trowell, H. and D. Burkitt (eds) (1981), *Western Diseases, Their Emergence and Prevention*. Cambridge, MA: Harvard University Press.

Tucker-Seeley, R., S. Subramanian, Y. Li and G. Sorensen (2009), Neighborhood safety, socioeconomic status and physical activity among older adults. *American Journal of Preventive Medicine*, **37**(3), 207–13.

van Doorslaer, E., C. Masseria and X. Koolman (2006), Inequalities in access to medical care by income in developed countries. *Canadian Medical Association Journal*, **174**(2), 177–83.

Vona-Davis, L. and D. Rose (2009), The influence of socioeconomic disparities on breast cancer tumor biology and prognosis: a review. *Journal of Women's Health*, **18**(6), 883–93.

Webbink, D., N. Martin and P. Visscher (2010), Does education reduce the probability of being overweight? *Journal of Health Economics*, **29**, 29–38.

Whyte, B. (2006), *Scottish Mortality in a European Context 1950–2000: An Analysis of Comparative Mortality Trends*. Edinburgh: Scottish Public Health Observatory.

Williams, E., D. Magliano, P. Zimmet, A. Kavanagh, C. Stevenson, B. Oldenburg and J. Shaw (2012), Area-level socioeconomic status and incidence of abnormal glucose metabolism: the Australian Diabetes, Obesity and Lifestyle (AusDiab) Study. *Diabetes Care*, **35**(7), 1455–1461.

World Health Organization (2010), *Global Status Report on Noncommunicable Diseases 2010: Description of the Global Burden of NCDs, Their Risk Factors and Determinants*. Geneva: World Health Organization.

World Health Organization (2011), *Global Status Report on Alcohol and Health*. Geneva World Health Organization.

Xi, B., Y. Liang, T. He, K. Reilly, Y. Hu, Q. Wang et al. (2012), Secular trends in the prevlence of general and abdominal obesity among Chinese adults, 1993–2009. *Obesity Reviews*, **13**(3), 287–96.

Xu, H., Tang, Y., Liu, D.Z., Ran, R., Ander, B.P., Apperson, M., Liu, X.S., Khoury, J.C., Gregg, J.P., Pancioli, A., Jauch, E.C., Wagner, K.R., Verro, P., J.P. Broderick and F.R. Sharp (2008), Gene expression in peripheral blood differs after cardioembolic compared with large-vessel atherosclerotic stroke: biomarkers for the etiology of ischemic stroke. *Journal of Cerebral Blood Flow and Metabolism*, **28**, 1320–1328.

Yadav, K. and A. Krishnan (2008), Changing patterns of diet, physical activity and obesity among urban, rural and slum populations in north India. *Obesity Reviews*, **9**(5), 400–408.

Yang, Z., W. Zhao, X. Zhang, R. Mu, Y. Zhai, L. Kong et al. (2008), Impact of famine during pregnancy and infancy on health in adulthood. *Obesity Reviews*, **9**(S1), 95–99.

Yip, W. and A. Mahal (2008), The healthcare systems of China and India: performance and future challenges. *Health Affairs*, **27**(4), 921–32.

Yusuf, S., S. Hawken, S. Ounpuu, T. Dans, A. Avezum, F. Lanas et al. (2004), Effect of potentially modifiable risk factors associated with myocardial infarction in 52 countries (the INTERHEART study): case-control study. *The Lancet*, **364**(9438), 937–52.

Zhou, G., X. Liu, G. Xu, R. Zhang and W. Zhu (2006), The effect of socioeconomic status on three-year mortality after first-ever ischaemic stroke in Nanjing, China. *BMC Public Health*, **11**(6), 227.

13. Trade, food and welfare
Alexandros Sarris

13.1 INTRODUCTION

What is the influence of trade and trade policy on food security? Are open economies more likely to achieve food security, or is it that trade openness creates problems for the most food insecure? Can one trust global food markets to deliver food commodities when needed and at reasonable cost? These are the main questions that are relevant when one thinks about international trade in the context of food security. The marked increases in the world prices of many basic food commodities in 2007–08, which were followed by new price increases in 2010–11, led to many short-term policy reactions, both trade- and domestic-policy related, which may have exacerbated the negative impacts of the price rises, and also renewed concerns about the role of international agricultural trade in achieving food security. The purpose of this chapter is to discuss how agricultural trade and trade policy affect food security.

According to the most complete accepted (by governments) definition, that has undergone considerable modifications over the past decades (for a brief history of the evolution of the concept, see Pieters et al., 2012) *'Food security exists when all people, at all times, have physical and economic access to sufficient, safe and nutritious food that meets their dietary needs and food preferences for an active and healthy life.'* This definition includes four key dimensions – availability, access, utilization and stability – which need to be satisfied simultaneously in order to achieve food security. Trade affects all four of the above aspects. Food availability is affected by trade to the extent that sufficient quantities of food can be provided through production, stock levels, net trade and food aid. Food access is affected to the extent that trade affects the incomes that individuals need to obtain appropriate food for a safe and nutritious diet. Food utilization is achieved through a nutritious and safe diet, the availability of clean water, adequate sanitation and proper health care. These are affected indirectly by trade through incomes. Finally, food stability refers to the temporal dimension of the above, and is directly affected by trade. In this respect, a key distinction is between temporary shocks and cyclical events that give rise respectively to transitory or chronic food insecurity.

Sudden global staple food commodity price spikes create considerable food security concerns, especially among those individuals or governments of countries who are staple food dependent and net buyers. These concerns range from possible inability to afford increased costs of basic food consumption requirements, to concerns about adequate supplies, irrespective of price. Such concerns can lead to trade policy reactions that may actually lead to higher food commodity prices. For instance excessive concerns about adequate supplies of staple food in exporting countries' domestic markets may induce concerned governments to take measures to curtail or ban exports, thus inducing further shortages in world markets and higher international prices. The latter in turn may induce permanent shifts in production and/or consumption of the staple in net importing countries, with the result that subsequent global supplies may increase and import demands may decline permanently altering the fundamentals of the market.

The recent food price spikes had their origin primarily in international markets, which are well linked to the markets of large producing and trading countries, but for most countries the attendant shock was exogenous to their economies. However, there are several occasions where countries are affected by domestic food related shocks. The most prevalent among these are production related negative shocks. In most of these cases trade is an inevitable component of the adjustment to the shock, but the way in which trade is organized and conducted, particularly as it pertains to the private versus public nature of the institutions involved, can affect considerably the food security outcome of any one shock. Related to this, the policy context as well as policy interventions and distortions can influence a lot the impact of any specific food shock.

The recent food market spike occurred in the midst of another important longer-term trade development. Over the last two decades there has been the shift of developing countries from the position of net agricultural exporters – up to the early 1990s – to that of net agricultural importers (Bruinsma, 2003; Alexandratos, 2011). Projections to 2030 indicate a deepening of this trend (ibid.), which is due to the projected decline in the exports of traditional agricultural products, such as tropical beverages and bananas, combined with a projected large and growing deficit of basic foods, such as cereals, meat, dairy products, and oil crops. According to the latest FAO figures (FAO, 2012) in 2011–12 global imports of all cereals were 292.9 million tons, 227.3 million tons of which were imports of developing countries. Within developing countries, those classified as Least Developed Countries (LDCs) have witnessed a fast worsening of their agricultural trade balance in the last 15 years. Since 1990, the food import bills of LDCs have not only increased in size, but also in importance, as they constituted more than 50 per cent of the total merchandise exports in all years. In contrast, the food import bills of other developing countries (ODCs) have been stable or declined as shares of their merchandise exports (FAO, 2004; Konandreas, 2012).

This trend has been particularly pronounced for Africa, while it is less pronounced for Asia and Latin America. This suggests that the issue of growing food imports with inability to pay is mostly an African LDC country problem. The conclusion is that many developing countries and especially LDC countries in Africa, have become more food import dependent, without becoming more productive in their own agricultural food producing sectors, or without expanding other export sectors to be able to counteract that import dependency. This implies that they may have become more exposed to international market instability and hence more vulnerable.

A recent analysis by Ng and Aksoy (2008) supports the above observations. It reveals that of 184 countries analysed with data for 2004–05, 123 were net food importers, of which 20 were developed countries, 62 middle-income countries and 41 low-income countries. From 2000 to 2004–05, more low-income countries have become net food importers. The 20 middle-income oil-exporting countries are the largest food importers, and that their net food imports have increased significantly. This is the group that is most concerned about reliability of supplies rather than cost of imports. They also revealed that several small island states (which are generally middle-income countries) and low-income countries (mostly in Africa) are most vulnerable to food price spikes. Analysis of recent data indicates that among the non-grain exporting oil exporters the average share of cereal imports to total domestic supply is 56 per cent. Among small island developing states, the same average is 68 per cent.

Another problem that surfaced during the recent food price spike was the one of reliability of import supplies. Several net food importing developing countries (NFIDCs) that could afford the cost of higher food import bills, such as some of the middle-income oil exporting countries and small island states mentioned above, faced problems of not only unreliable import supplies but also the likelihood of unavailability of sufficient food import quantities to cover their domestic food consumption needs. This raises a different problem for these countries, namely the one of assurance of import supplies. Several of these countries, e.g. those surrounding the Arab Peninsula and the Persian Gulf, have unfavourable domestic production conditions and rely on imports for a substantial share of their domestic consumption. Unavailability of supplies creates large food security concerns for these countries.

Demeke et al. (2011) reviewed policies adopted in response to the recent food price spike and they indicate that trade-related measures constituted about half of all the total policy responses to the crisis. The responses of developing countries to the food security crisis appear to have been in contrast to the policy orientation most of them had pursued over the last decades as a result of the implementation of the Washington consensus supported by the Bretton Woods Institutions. This period had been characterized by an increased reliance on the market – both domestic and international – on the ground that this reliance would increase efficiency of resource allocation, and by taking world prices as a reference for measuring economic efficiency. The availability of cheap food on the international market was one of the factors that contributed to reduced investment and support to agriculture by developing countries (and their development partners), which is generally put forward as one of the reasons for the recent crisis. This increased reliance on markets was also concomitant to a progressive withdrawal of the state from the food and agriculture sector, on the ground that the private sector was more efficient from an economic point of view.

The food crisis revealed some drawbacks of this approach. Countries depending on the world market have seen their food import bills surge, while their purchasing capacity decreased, particularly in the case of those countries that also had to face higher energy import prices. This situation was further aggravated when some important export countries, under intense domestic political pressure, applied export taxes or bans in order to protect their consumers and isolate their prices from world prices.

As a result, several countries changed their approach through measures ranging from policies to isolate domestic prices from world prices; moving from food security based strategies to food self-sufficiency-based strategies; by trying to acquire land abroad for securing food and fodder procurement; by trying to engage in regional trade agreements or; by interfering with the private markets through price controls, anti-hoarding laws, government intervention in output and input markets, etc. Clearly trade policies were an integral part of many of these strategies.

There are already several analyses of the relationships between trade and trade policy reforms on the one hand and poverty (see for instance Winters, 2002; UNDP, 2003; Winters et al., 2004; UNCTAD, 2004; FAO, 2005; among others). This chapter will not cover the extensive discussion of all the various issues covered in those reports. It will rather focus on conceptual issues relevant to trade and trade reforms and food security on the one hand, as well as on some policy aspects that have become more relevant in the context of the recent crisis. Section 13.2 discusses the relationship between trade and food security. Section 13.3 reviews the nature of global agricultural markets. Section 13.4 examines how trade contributes to the reliability and stability of domestic food availability. Section 13.5 discusses the role of trade policy in ensuring food security. Section 13.6 concludes.

13.2 HOW ARE AGRICULTURAL TRADE AND FOOD SECURITY RELATED?

Food security is a state of affairs that is conditioned and influenced by a variety of factors. Food security has to do with levels and variability of consumption of adequate amounts of food by households, so the first question is what determines these. Clearly consumption of food is determined by household real income, by the availability and prices of basic foods in the economy, and by the stability of the above. Food insecure households are those who have both inadequate real income to acquire the required food (lack of accessibility) or those who may have adequate real income but may find that food is not available for some reason. Instability of the above also conditions food insecurity. The dependence of food security on real incomes, suggests that poverty is a major determinant of food insecurity. In fact, one of the most popular methods to measure poverty is by designating a food poverty line, namely a minimum food basket that is deemed as essential and costing this, along with some additional income for other essentials.

There are many factors that link trade and food security. As shown in Winters (2002) and Winters et al. (2004) trade and household welfare are linked via prices, factor markets, especially labour markets, and consumer preferences. The first linkage occurs at the border. When a country trades a food product, international market prices affect domestic prices, and traded quantities affect the domestic supplies of the product. In such a setting, when a country liberalizes its own trade policies by, for instance, lowering tariffs, this will result in lower market prices for imports at the country's border. When other countries change their trade policies, this will alter international prices, and consequently affect border prices of the first country's imports and exports.

The second linkage concerns how prices are transmitted from the border to local markets within the country. This is conditioned by the nature of markets (monopolistic, oligopolistic, competitive), but also by the type of government interventions and policies that are in effect. A major factor also affecting the degree to which producers, consumers and households experience border price changes is the quality of transport infrastructure and the behaviour of domestic marketing margins, which in turn are affected by not only transport costs, but also by market structure. The empirical literature suggests that the degree of price transmission from the border to the local market can vary considerably across different markets, even within a single country. There are countries and markets where transmission of international food product market prices is almost nil, while in others transmission is perfect.

The initial impact of a trade-related change on households occurs through local market price changes. Not surprisingly, households that are net sellers of products whose prices rise, in relative terms, benefit in this first round. Net purchasers of such goods lose. However, these first-round effects are altered significantly because of developments in other markets, for both traded products but also non-traded ones, and attendant household adjustments in consumption and production. In response to changing relative prices, households modify their consumption choices, adjust their supply of labour and adjust the allocation of their time to other activities and occupations. Changes in relative prices can even affect a household's long-term investment in human capital. As households change, their spending levels and employment patterns and as landowners and firms adjust their production and hiring patterns, a wide range of effects flows through the economy. For example, trade effects that stimulate agricultural production often lead to a general increase in wages for unskilled labour. This, in turn, benefits households that are net suppliers of unskilled labour, which normally includes many of the food insecure households. Finally, the long-run growth effects associated with trade openness and liberalization need to be considered, including increases in firm productivity due to access to new inputs and technologies as well as potential gains due to the disciplining effect of foreign competition on domestic mark-ups.

Exactly how trade affects poverty and food security depends upon each country's specific structural conditions, including the structure of production and consumption of those deemed as food insecure, and the degree to which trade affects the various markets and factors that are involved in these structures. Understanding these relationships requires country-specific research and analysis.

The recent episode of high food commodity prices provided an opportunity to estimate how trade affected the food insecure. Ivanic and Martin (2008), for instance, used household survey data for several countries and applied a framework due to Deaton (1989) and estimated the poverty impact of global price changes for seven key staples between 2005 and 2007. They also used a Computable General Equilibrium (CGE) model to simulate the increase in wages for unskilled agricultural labour that would follow from the food price increase under various assumptions. Their results show that the effects of rising world commodity prices on poverty differ considerably between countries and commodities, but that poverty increases are considerably more frequent and larger than poverty reductions. Urban households are typically hit harder than rural households, though many in rural areas are also net consumers of food and therefore adversely affected by price rises. Their results depend significantly on assumptions of the extent to which global prices are passed through to domestic markets, and hence on trade openness. Similarly, FAO in the 2011 report on the State of Food Insecurity in the World (FAO, 2011), showed that the trade exposure of the country was a major factor in the differential impact of the high food prices on the poor.

Two broad strategies relating to trade have generally been followed by countries attempting to achieve adequate levels of food security: food self-sufficiency and food self-reliance.

- Food self-sufficiency implies that the provision of the required amounts of most basis food commodities is from national resources. Generally these amounts will be larger than what is implied by free trade under certain international prices. While this approach implies the provision of sufficient domestic production to meet a substantial part of consumption requirements, it does not necessarily imply

that all households in the country have access to all the food they require. This is because albeit food maybe available domestically, the income to have access to it, may not be available for several households. In fact there are several countries which are not only self sufficient, but net food exporters, where a large number of households suffer from malnutrition.
- A strategy of food self-reliance reflects a set of policies where the supplies of food products are determined by international trade patterns and markets. This implies that staple food products that are produced in adequate amounts domestically, maybe exported instead of consumed domestically, if better prices are fetched by international markets, leaving domestic supplies smaller and more expensive than what may be necessary for the poor to ensure adequate diets. This strategy has become more common as global trade has become more liberal. However, it was seriously tested during the recent crisis, when many countries introduced export controls, in order to assure that domestic supplies of basic staples would be available and at affordable prices. Advocates of this strategy argue that improved food security, as well as higher incomes may be achieved more satisfactorily, even in countries where agriculture remains a major contributor to GDP, by shifting resources into the production of non-food export products and importing staple food requirements.

The above debate is influenced by prevailing trade theories. On general grounds, standard comparative advantage theory, of the Ricardian or Heckscher–Ohlin variety, argues that differences in productivity and opportunity costs of production between countries form the underlying reasons why it is advantageous for countries to engage in trade. Many reasons explain why such differences occur, of which climate, availability of arable land, and availability of water supply, are of obvious importance for agriculture, along with differential access to productive technologies.

A non-technical exposition of comparative advantage is that countries concentrate or gain the most by producing those products that use relatively intensively the factors with which the country is relatively well endowed. This implies that, other things being equal, the labour-abundant countries would export labour-intensive goods, the capital-abundant country exports capital-intensive goods. This process could play an important role in poverty reduction in labour-abundant developing countries, by bidding up the price of labour and thus raising workers' incomes.

Advocates of free trade argue that, under competitive market conditions, free trade maximizes potential economic welfare internationally by creating a situation where no country can be made better off without another being made worse off. It is a situation where those that gain from trade could fully compensate those that lose and still be better off: the total gain will be greater than the total loss. With free trade a point would be reached where more of each traded good is produced, such that everyone will gain if suitable redistribution is made.

There are a number of important qualifications to these predictions of the model, however, that must be held in mind. First, the consequences described are dependent on the assumption of competitive markets. In the absence of these, countries may be better off intervening to restrict free trade. Second, countries will not necessarily gain equally from trade: the individual gains will depend on relative prices or the terms of trade. Third, there are no mechanisms in place to ensure that losers in the world market will be compensated by those that benefit, so the gains remain potential. Fourth, the issue of redistribution also applies within countries, where there will also be gainers and losers from trade. Finally, any comparative static solution described by the conventional theory assumes that all external costs are internalized, including environmental externalities, a subject of much contemporary debate. Although this theory is the basis of modern 'orthodox' trade economics, this does not mean that it is accepted without questioning.

A large number of empirical studies have considered the extent to which the hypotheses of conventional trade theory are supported by empirical observation. These have usually tested the 'factor proportion' prediction of the model by comparing the factor intensities of imports and exports. While empirical observations suggest that factor proportions alone cannot explain the pattern of international trade, the theory does seem to provide a partial explanation of trade flows. In addition, a variety of extensions to the model have been developed to take account of any empirical shortcomings, and to cater for such factors as externalities and the absence of perfect competition.

In sum, the conventional theory has proven to have considerable analytical power, and to produce clear, testable predictions. For these reasons, it remains the dominant framework of analysis for the policy decisions of governments and international organizations. The theoretical approach outlined above underpins the policy advice concerning trade liberalization given to governments by international institutions, as well as the approach adopted by the World Trade Organization (WTO) Agreement on Agriculture. Advocates of food sovereignty and food self-sufficiency, however, tend to question the hypothesis that markets are free and perfect, and therefore consider it overly risky to fully rely on global markets for the fulfilment of basic needs.

A topic that has received relatively little attention, but is relevant in the context of food security, is whether unstable and unpredictable international markets change the general conclusions of static trade theory under certainty. Theoretical work on this topic suggests that comparative advantage can be altered by production uncertainty or price uncertainty of the trade products and in fact the optimal production pattern could shift against what would be predicted by comparative advantage under certain prices (for early expositions, see Anderson and Riley, 1976; Helpman and Razin, 1978). This is easy to see, as under uncertainty, an optimal production structure would dictate some degree of diversification, rather than specialization.

The implication of this for food security, is that the existence of uncertain domestic production and international prices, coupled with risk aversion to food insecurity may suggest that a country maybe better off with a production pattern closer to self sufficiency, rather than what would be dictated by free trade certainty. This, of course, depends on the specific production conditions of a country, coupled with the structure of food insecurity. Empirical analyses suggest that if a country wants to maintain food consumption at levels compatible with food security objectives, and is faced with domestic production uncertainty and international market variability, it should not opt for complete self sufficiency, but rather a modified version of self reliance (for relevant analyses, see Jabara and Thompson, 1980, and Sarris, 1985).

The detrimental effects of market uncertainty or unpredictability on both private agents, as well as governments are not hard to understand, and have been the object of both discussion as well as research for a long time. For instance, Keynes (1942) argued that commodity price fluctuations led to unnecessary waste of resources, and, by creating fluctuations in export earnings, had a detrimental effect on investment in new productive capacity, and tended to perpetuate a cycle of dependence on commodities, what we may call in modern growth terminology a 'commodity development trap'.

While Keynes viewed the issues largely from a macro perspective, in recent years his argument has been refined and applied to the microeconomics of households facing risks, but the concepts can easily be adapted to the problems of commodity dependent developing countries. The basic insight of all the recent literature is that the presence of uncertainty when there is inability to borrow to smooth negative income shocks, leads agents to accumulate liquid precautionary reserves in the form of money or other easy to liquidate assets, like food stocks. On average the level of buffer stocks that must be carried is positive, even if the probability distribution of future outcomes is known with certainty. Second, in poor country environments, these reserves must be liquid enough, in order to be readily accessible in times of need. This positive and liquid level of reserves implies that the resources devoted to buffer stocks cannot be used for productive but illiquid investments, and it is this that leads to the negative impact on overall growth (Dercon and Christiaensen, 2011).

The responses of credit constrained low income households to unexpected high food commodity prices may include effects such as reducing the diversity of diets, reducing calories consumed, reducing non-food consumption expenditures or reducing investment expenditures, such as children's education, health outlays or expenditures on fertilizers of farm machinery. Some of these adjustment responses may have permanent effects, and it is these that may reduce subsequent income opportunities. There has been some evidence of these adjustments in the recent food crisis (Rapsomanikis, 2009).

Similar effects can occur at the macro level as liquidity and foreign exchange constrained governments of countries that have large food import bills may limit food commodity imports, or reduce imports of other essential expenditures in response to high costs of essential food imports. This can reduce growth. The issue has been examined empirically by Dehn (2000), who constructed an index of price instability that distinguishes between negative and positive shocks, and found, as expected theoretically, that negative commodity price shocks have a significant negative effect on overall economic growth. Recently, Cavalcanti et al. (2011) also estimated that negative terms of trade shocks (which include high food import costs) have stronger negative growth impacts than positive terms of trade shocks for developing countries.

Considerable literature has been devoted to understanding the costs of market volatility and uncertainty. The articles in Prakash (2011) offer a thorough survey. While some literature (Lucas, 2003) suggested that the cost of market volatility is quite small in developed countries with efficient capital markets, other literature, that took into account credit constraints and imperfect transmission from international to domestic markets, showed that the cost of market volatility can be substantial for low income developing countries exposed to commodity shocks (Guillaumont et al., 1999; Prasad and Crucini, 2000; Rapsomanikis and Sarris, 2008; Subervie, 2008; Bellemare et al., 2010).

An important question emerges from this brief review, however. If free trade could potentially raise economic welfare in the world as a whole and even in all trading nations, why are border policies so commonly used by governments to restrict free trade? This holds both for agricultural trade as well as non-agricultural trade, but clearly it is agricultural trade that is of concern here. Trade theory literature provides three main explanations for this apparent anomaly. First, the case of the 'optimum tariff' shows that in certain circumstances a country can gain more from imposing a tariff than from free trade (assuming other countries do not retaliate). Such gains are at the expense of losses by trading partners (a zero-sum game, in other words). However, the optimum tariff argument mainly applies to large countries, which can use tariffs to influence their terms of trade in world markets. It does not generally inform developing countries' portfolios of potential policies, unless they are part of a larger trading bloc.

A more interesting reason for protection in the context of this study is the infant industry perspective. Where an industry has large economies of scale, firms may need protection to allow them time to grow before competing with more established firms overseas. This assumes that an underlying comparative advantage in the particular product exists. This remains an important justification of protectionism in developing countries, especially for manufacturing industries. While generally agriculture is not regarded as being characterized by economies of scale, the issue may be applied to primary processing industries, in the context of a development strategy involving an export shift from raw materials to processed products.

A final explanation concerns political imperatives, including the influence of groups which gain from protection, and the importance of revenue from border measures for developing country governments, where other tax bases are not strong. While the latter may be something that could be difficult, in some cases, to substitute for without reducing government spending or increasing borrowing, the importance of non-trade concerns such as food security and rural viability are often put forward as powerful imperatives for protecting domestic agriculture. The Common Agricultural Policy of the European Union, which included significant trade restrictions, was motivated by food security concerns. The political economy of trade policy, suggests that the glaring gap between theory (of gains from free trade) and reality (of widespread protectionism) can be largely explained by the political and economic forces that come into play when the assumptions of perfect competition and frictionless exchange do not hold.

Many researchers and analysts suggest that a positive correlation and even causation exists between more open trade regimes and economic growth. Although the evidence for this may be questionable (for instance see Rodriguez and Rodrik, 1999), it can be argued that a production structure based on current comparative advantage is more likely to be efficient in terms of resource allocation. The case is less clear-cut with regard to the distributional consequences of this form of economic strategy, however. For example, positive employment outcomes and consequences for the poorer and more food-insecure strata of society may not be guaranteed by this type of economic structure.

More open trade implies a change in the structure of production. This implies factor movements across sectors. If there are rigidities in such adjustments, as would be for instance the case when labour is not easily adaptable or trainable to skills required by new sectors, then permanent poverty pockets may develop. If trade openness leads to a contraction of the agricultural sector, it may be neither easy nor quick for investment and employment opportunities to be created elsewhere in the economy, thus exacerbating any prior food insecurity problems. It is such adjustment fears that have motivated the substantially protective structures for agriculture in most developed economies.

It has also been argued that a more open trade regime reduces the supply variability of staple foods. This is certainly likely in the context of stable and predictable international markets, where reliance on domestic stocks to stabilize domestic consumer (and producer) prices may be an expensive alternative. If, however, the open trade context is less stable and predictable than under protection, then supply variability may increase.

A further advantage of more open agricultural trade, it is argued, stems from the possibility of lower domestic food prices, when there is no protection. If this does not occur, there would be no reason for protection in the first place. Lower food prices, however, are not necessarily good for food security. This is because the impacts of lower prices depend on the location and income sources of the food insecure. If, for instance many of the poorest households are dependent directly or indirectly on agricultural production for their main income, the overall effect of lower prices on food security may be negative.

The logic of free trade which has dominated conventional wisdom as well as policy advice in recent years as far as trade policy is concerned, makes an implicit assumption that liberalization will engender economic growth which will in turn lead to enhanced economic welfare. This subsumes any argument regarding who is made better off by the growth which ensues, it being assumed that in the long-term no-one will be made worse off. Once this assumption is accepted (as it is within most structural adjustment strategies) it becomes straightforward to model economic policy around a growth strategy, with distributional issues relegated to the role of short-term ameliorative measures, such as the provision of a social and economic safety net.

To summarize, in terms of the links between trade and food security, the direct links involve changes in the markets of products that are produced and consumed by the food insecure. These are normally markets for basic staple foods, such as wheat, maize, rice, etc. The indirect links involve changes in the labour markets that are relevant for the food insecure, and these invariably are the unskilled labour markets. They also involve changes in the demand for non-farm goods produced by the poor and food insecure.

The basic arguments in favour of a more open trade regime, suggest first that positive impacts on food security will arise from faster growth, which in turn will come about from efficiency gains, due to the resource allocations induced by the 'right prices'. Furthermore, more open trade will lead to lower food prices, which will increase consumption. Other arguments emphasize the lower variability of domestic food supplies because of the ease of securing imports in times of shortage, and the enhanced ability to import food, that comes about from the increased foreign exchange that is expected from a more open and export oriented economy.

On the opposite side, opponents of a more open food trade regime argue that the induced changes in production structure may damage the average incomes of the food insecure, and increase their income risks. Lower food prices induced by a more liberal trade regime could damage the incomes of those who depend on food production and sales. More open trade may also lead to adjustment pressures, especially for many of the food insecure. Finally, a more open regime may make supply of food more unstable, if foreign markets are more unstable than the domestic markets.

13.3 THE NATURE OF GLOBAL AGRICULTURAL COMMODITY MARKETS AND THE DETERMINANTS OF GLOBAL MARKET UNCERTAINTY

Proper assessment of the role of trade in food security depends on adequate assessment of the nature of global agricultural markets, and the type of shocks experienced. Agricultural markets are by their very nature unstable, as they are characterized by many producers and consumers, uncertain market supplies, and fluctuating demands. However, what causes most concern is large and sudden departure from 'normal' market fluctuations, namely changes that are not foreseeable and lie much outside the realm of past experience. It is in this sense that the recent 2007–11 market upheavals have raised concerns about the structure of international markets.

The causes and nature of the recent food commodity market crisis have been analysed in a series of papers and monographs (e.g. Abbott et al., 2008, 2009; Headey and Fan, 2010). While no one factor has emerged as the main fundamental cause of the price shock, causes that have received prominence and have some empirical support include, sustained demand growth in emerging economies, demand for some agricultural products such as maize and vegetable oils for biofuel production, the weak US dollar, low interest rates, high petroleum prices, low commodity stocks, climate change induced supply shocks, increased speculative activity on commodity exchanges and the rise of commodity funds, and government destabilizing policies. Most of these factors were also prominent in the previous big food shock of 1973–75.

It has already been indicated above that there seems to be a negative link between unanticipated shocks and economic growth by developing economies, implying first that unpredictable negative shocks are detrimental to growth and, moreover, that past unpredictability has been dealt with inadequately by the governments of affected countries. The point has to do with the policy responses to a negative shock. If the shock is permanent, then a policy response that is based on the assumption that the shock is temporary is clearly inadequate. Similarly, a policy response that is based on an assumption that a shock is permanent, is clearly wrong, if in fact the shock is temporary. There has been a series of such inadequate policy responses to wrongly perceived shocks in many developing countries in the past that have proven very costly (see for instance Bevan et al., 1990; Collier and Gunning, 1999; Deaton, 1999).

There are several issues that concern agricultural commodity markets, and especially prices, that are crucial in this respect. The first is whether commodity prices have trends. The second concerns the degree to which commodity price shocks are temporary or permanent. The third has to do with the persistence of commodity booms and busts. The fourth involves the co-movement of commodity prices. The fifth concerns the changing nature of unanticipated shocks. A brief review of what is known on these issues is given below, largely based on the more extensive reviews of Cashin and McDermott (2006), Gilbert (2006) and Stigler (2011).

There is a long history of attempts to discern negative long-term deterministic trends in real commodity prices, spurred by the Prebisch–Singer finding of declining terms of trade for commodity exporting developing countries (see Singer 1950). Grilli and Yang (1988) confirmed that there exist downward trends that in fact accelerated after 1921. Further work by Ardeni and Wright (1992), Leon and Soto (1995) and Cashin and

McDermott (2001) have strengthened these findings, and suggested that there indeed seem to be negative overall real commodity price trends, but which are quite small compared to the overall price variability. In other words the so-called signal to noise ratio in commodity prices is too small to be able to make firm empirical assessments of trends. The empirical resolution of the issue seems to depend on the period that is utilized, and the type of data (aggregate or individual commodity data), but overall most studies point out that there is a weak long-term negative trend.

The issue of permanent or temporary shocks is very important for the adoption of trade and production strategies. If a shock results, for instance, in a permanent price decline for a food commodity, then a policy of increasing the domestic supply of the commodity in order to reduce imports is not appropriate. Irrespective, however, of whether shocks are permanent or temporary, most studies consistently point out to another fact about commodity prices. They exhibit irregular booms and slumps, each of which lasts a long time. In other words there is considerable persistence in commodity shocks. This is of particular policy concern as it is related to the duration of policies designed to deal with commodity booms and slumps.

The final issue concerns the changing nature of commodity price volatility. Given that the variability of commodity prices is much larger than any underlying trend, it is interesting to understand the changing nature of this volatility. In other words do commodity markets exhibit constant or changing patterns of price instability around their underlying trends? This issue has not been researched very much. Early analyses by Cashin and McDermott (2001) found that over a long period (from before 1900 to the 1990s), aggregate commodity price indices seem to exhibit rising variability. This has not, however, been the case in the analysis of Sarris (2000), who utilized individual cereal world prices, and concluded that empirically it was impossible to reject the hypothesis of unchanging price variability.

More recently Gilbert and Morgan (2010) examined the price volatility of 19 internationally traded agricultural commodities over the period 1970–2009, and when they compared the two 20-year periods in this range, they found that volatility had statistically significantly increased in only three of these (rice, sorghum and bananas), while it had significantly fallen for nine commodities (cocoa, sugar, soybeans, groundnut oil, palm oil, soybean oil, beef, lamb, fishmeal) and had insignificant changes one way or the other in the others. Balcombe (2011) also found that there is conflicting evidence on the trend of volatility of agricultural commodities.

A topic that has gained considerable prominence during the recent crisis is whether speculative activity in organized exchanges has increased general global market volatility. There are conflicting views on this. Gilbert (2010), for instance, argues that speculative activity has exaggerated price changes of food commodity prices, and the same has been argued by Masters and White (2008). On the other hand Irwin et al. (2009), argue that speculation in organized exchanges accounts for a small part of market volatility. In this context it is important to distinguish between speculation in organized exchanges and speculation in the actual markets. Both of them are important, and needed for proper operation of the markets. As prices in organized markets are related to prices in physical markets, because of various types of hedging and other risk-management-related operations of physical market participants, the main issue is whether 'excessive speculation' has led to a breakdown of the traditional relations between futures and physical markets, thus distorting price signals and disorienting market participants. This, however, is difficult to assess, and has not been investigated conclusively to date.

Many analysts argue that the world has entered a new era characterized by much more unstable food prices on the international markets due to new factors, most of which (biofuels and oil prices, exchange rates, speculation, macroeconomic factors) are external to the food economy (Masters and White, 2008; Sarris, 2009, 2010). A high level of food price instability in developing countries may, then, have serious consequences on food security both in the short term (consumer access to food) and in the long term (incentive for producers to invest and increase production). Food market instability can also lead to various undesirable short- and long-term impacts, especially for vulnerable households, as several studies have documented (Ivanic and Martin, 2008, and several other studies in the same special issue of the Journal *Agricultural Economics*).

13.4 HOW DOES TRADE INFLUENCE THE RELIABILITY OF SUPPLIES

Trade openness affects considerably the reliability of total imports and hence domestic supplies. It is important in this context to ascertain the types of risks that are relevant to food importers. Food imports take place under a variety of institutional arrangements in developing countries. A study by FAO (2003) contains an extensive discussion of the state of food import trade by developing countries. It notes that while in some low-income food-deficit countries (LIFDCs) state institutions still play a very important role in the exports and imports of some basic foods, food imports have been mostly privatized in recent years, although with some exceptions, and in some countries, state agencies operate alongside with private importers.

A public sector food importer, namely a manager of a food importing or a relevant food regulatory agency each year faces the problem of determining the requirements that the country will have to satisfy the various domestic policy objectives. Such objectives may include domestic price stability, satisfaction of minimum amount of supplies, demands to keep prices at high levels to satisfy farmers, or low to satisfy consumers and many others relevant to various aspects of domestic welfare. For instance if the government of the country needs to keep domestic consumer prices of a staple food commodity stable at some level p_c then an estimate of domestic requirements in a year t could be given by a simple formula such as

$$R_t = D(p_{ct}) - Q_t$$

Where R denotes the yearly requirements, $D(.)$ the total domestic demand of the commodity (which will, of course, depend on other variables than just price), and Q denotes the domestic production. Private stockholding behaviour would be part of the demand estimates.

The problem of the manager of the food agency is four-fold. First there needs to be a good estimate of the requirements. This is not easy for several reasons. First estimates of domestic production are not always easy, and more so the earlier one needs to know them. While richer countries have developed over time sophisticated systems of production monitoring, this is not the case for developing countries, especially those that are large and obtain supplies from a large geographical area. Another problem in assessing requirements concerns the estimates of domestic demand, which are also subject to considerable uncertainties. These uncertainties involve the other variables that enter the demand of the staple, such as disposable incomes, the prices of substitute staples, the behaviour of private stocks, and many other variables. Clearly these errors are larger the longer in advance one tries to make an estimate of domestic requirements, and the less publicly available information exists about the variables that determine demand.

The second problem of the public sector food agency manager, once the domestic requirements have been estimated, is to decide how to fulfil them, namely through imports, or by reductions in publicly held stocks, if stock holding is part of the agency's activities. A related problem is the risk of non-fulfilment of the estimated requirements which may cost domestic social problems and food insecurity. The third problem of such an agent is how to minimize the overall cost of fulfilling these requirements, given uncertainties in international prices and international freight rates, and to manage the risks of unanticipated cost overruns. For instance, if the agency imports more than is needed, as estimated by *ex-post* assessment of the domestic market situation, then the excess imports will have to be stored or re-exported and these entail costs. Finally, but not least, and related to the overall cost of fulfilling the requirements, the agent must finance the transaction, either through own resources, or through a variety of financing mechanisms.

In many countries the state has withdrawn from domestic food markets, and it is private agents who make decisions on imports. The problem, however, of private agents, is not much different or easier than that of public agents. A private importer must assess with a significant time lag, the domestic production situation, as well as the potential demand just like a public agent, and must plan to order import supplies so as to make a profit by selling in the domestic market. Clearly, the private importer faces risks similar to those of the public agent, as far as unpredictability of domestic production, international prices and domestic demand are concerned, and in addition faces an added risk, namely that of unpredictable government policies that may change the conditions faced when the product must be sold domestically. During the recent food price crisis, surveys by FAO documented the adoption of many short-term policies in response to high global staple food prices, which created considerable added risks for private sector agents. Furthermore, the private agent may be more credit and finance constrained than the public agent. In fact the study by FAO (2003) indicated that the most important problem of private traders in LIFDCs is the availability of import trade finance.

The above discussion pertains to risks faced by food importers, whether public or private, in determining their appropriate trade strategies, whether these involve imports only or imports and stock management. However, once the level of imports needed is determined, there are two additional risks faced by import agents, apart from the price risk. The first is the financing risk, namely the possibility that import finance may not be obtainable from domestic of international sources. This is the risk identified as most crucial by the FAO (2003) study for agents in LIFDCs. The second risk is counterparty performance risk, namely the risk that a counterparty in an import purchase contact will default and fail to deliver. This latter risk is one that came to the fore during the recent price spike, and is can be due to both commercial and non-commercial factors. Commercial factors may include the inability for the supplier to secure the staple grain at the amount and prices contracted because of sudden adverse movements in prices. Non-commercial factors includes things such as export bans, natural disasters or civil strife, in the sourcing country that may render it impossible to export an agreed upon amount of the staple.

It is clear from the above that trade, namely increased reliance on international markets to satisfy domestic food need, entails risks that may affect the supplies of basic food commodities in a country and hence domestic food security. On the other hand, trade assures a country of a diverse set of sources of supply, something that diminishes the risk of non-availability of import quantities.

13.5 TRADE POLICY AND FOOD SECURITY

Agriculture the world over is characterized by many policy-induced distortions, and trade policies are only few of the many policies that affect it. Trade policy can affect domestic markets and household welfare, through its impact on prices, as well as domestic supplies of food commodities.

Research on agricultural distortions by the World Bank (Anderson, 2009) has revealed an interesting pattern of agricultural protection, in the sense that less developed countries seem to utilize policies to basically tax their agricultural sectors, while developed ones utilize policies to support them. Figure 13.1 indicates this pattern in a comprehensive manner. The figure plots the yearly averages and ranges of what Anderson (2009) has termed the Nominal Rate of Assistance (NRA), defined as the percentage by

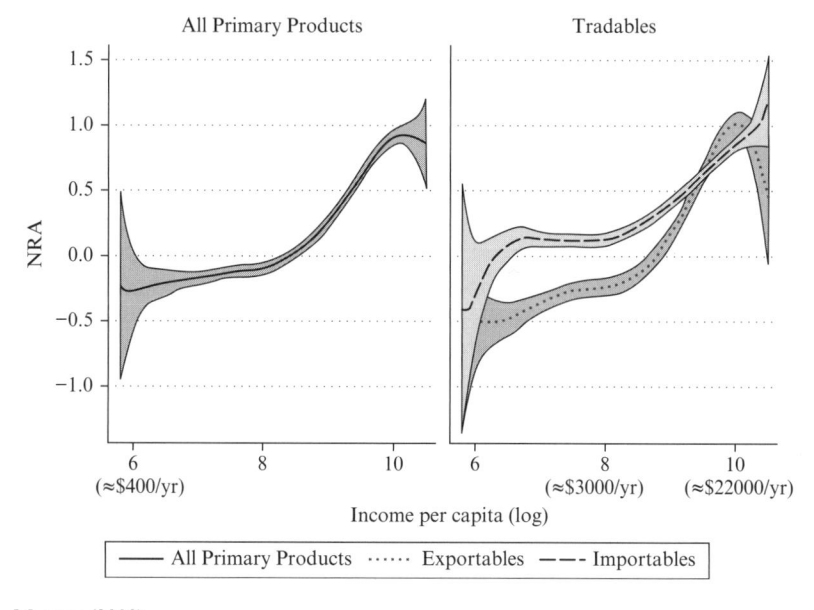

Source: Masters (2009).

Figure 13.1 Average Nominal Rate of Assistance (NRA) to agricultural producers as a function of country per capita income

which government policies have raised gross returns to farmers above what they would be without the government's intervention. For each country, agricultural and non-food products were separated between importables, exportables and non-tradables, and an NRA coefficient was estimated for each. A value smaller than zero indicates that agriculture is taxed, while a value larger than zero that it is subsidized.

In developing countries, farm policies have been driven largely by the need to accelerate a transition from low income agrarian structures to more developed industrialized and service-oriented economies. The overall effect of such policies, as measured by NRAs, has been largely to tax producers (namely negative NRAs). In the process, the agricultural sectors in many countries have faced negative policy biases and low growth, while inducing increasing import dependence. However, when average incomes grow (typically at a per capita income level of US$8000 or more), the type of farmer support in developing countries seems to turn positive and seems to follow a pattern similar to that of now developed countries, namely NRAs increase as the share of agriculture in the economy declines and average agricultural and total incomes increase. The results from the World Bank study bore this out by showing that developing countries broadly taxed agriculture via price and trade policies from the early 1960s to the late 1970s/early 1980s before gradually reducing the taxation and, by the mid-1990s, switching to slightly positive assistance to agriculture in aggregate.

By contrast, high-income countries supported agriculture and that support rose steadily from the 1950s to the late 1980s before declining slightly over the 15 years to 2004. Within countries, farm support and resulting distortions were more pronounced for importables than for exportables or non-tradables. Commodities that received the highest form of support included rice, sugar, dairy, beef, poultry and cotton. Trade measures at the border (export and import taxes or subsidies and their equivalent from quantitative trade restrictions and multiple exchange rates) accounted for 75 per cent of the total NRA for developing countries and over 90 per cent for high-income countries.

Figure 13.2 exhibits the average rate of tariff for all countries by type of agricultural product. The main observation is that products produced and exported by temperate zone developed countries, such as dairy, meats and sugar have the highest rates of protection. Table 13.1 indicates the average rate of tariff by different countries for the various types of agricultural products. The main observation is that import protection for basic products such as cereals and rice is highest in developed countries, and relatively low in developing countries. In several developing countries, trade measures are justified on the grounds of counteracting other domestic distortions. However, it is well known from trade theory that the best way to tackle a domestic distortion is by a policy that affects it directly, and not indirectly as is the case with trade policy.

Apart from the average border protection, which affects average prices, of considerable importance in the context of food security is transmission of world prices to domestic markets. It is well known that many countries insulate their domestic food markets from international market variations through a variety of trade and other policy interventions. This has the tendency to make global markets more unstable (Tyers and Anderson, 1992). There is substantial literature on the topic (for two very recent additions relevant to the recent food crisis, see Gilbert, 2011, and Rapsomanikis, 2011). Most of the literature finds that there is imperfect price transmission, with international prices taking some time before being reflected in domestic market prices, and

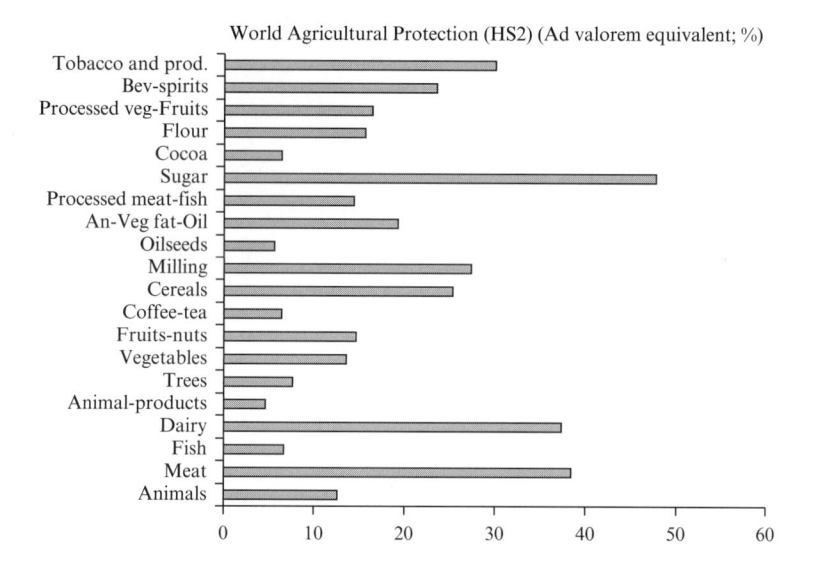

World Agricultural Protection (HS2) (Ad valorem equivalent; %)

Source: Bouët and Laborde (2009).

Figure 13.2 World agricultural protection at the HS2 level

this depends a lot on the specific country policies pursued. This is especially true for developing countries.

Policy makers in their efforts to try to lessen the impacts of sudden high international prices, employ a variety of short-term trade policy measures. Such measures include temporary decreases in tariffs, custom fees and other restrictions on imports of staple food products, bans or extra taxes on exports of food products, import subsidies and others. Such measures are usually adopted in order to protect specific groups deemed as food insecure from sudden welfare losses. Apart from the issue of a collective action problem, in the sense that if many countries adopt a restrictive policy the overall effect on international markets may be detrimental to all (Rutten et al., 2011; Martin and Anderson, 2012), the issue is whether such measures, *ceteris paribus*, are effective in accomplishing their objective of safeguarding food security. Changing the fundamentals of a domestic food commodity market by trade policy will affect all who produce and consume the relevant commodity, and not only the food insecure. If the latter are a minority of those who are affected by the specific market, the trade measure is bound to create a lot of unintended consequences for the non-food insecure. Hence trade policy for a commodity is less effective as a food security policy, as the share of the commodity produced and consumed domestically by food insecure households is smaller.

The standard theoretical arguments for free trade have been extended by applying the principle of targeting as the basis for interventions in the presence of a variety of distortions.[1] The principle of targeting states that when markets operate imperfectly, the first best solution to achieving a Pareto efficient equilibrium is to combine free trade with an appropriate tax or subsidy that directly offsets the source of market failure.[2] This principle, however, depends on a variety of assumptions that may not hold in practice. Buffie (2001) has reviewed these assumptions and has indicated a variety of circumstances

Table 13.1 Average tariffs of agricultural products by different groups of countries (circa 2004)

	Rest of OECD	Australia/ New Zealand	North America	China/ India	Argentina/ Brazil	Rest of Latin America and Caribbean	EU 27	Russia and Former USSR	Middle East	North Africa	Rest of Asia	Sub-Saharan Africa LDC	Sub-Saharan Africa non-LDC	Rest of the World
Cereals	38.5	0.2	2.4	9.5	5.8	7.5	7.9	6.2	17.4	16.8	10.0	11.2	5.2	17.9
Rice	284.5	0.0	1.5	5.2	5.3	8.4	44.6	4.4	24.2	4.7	19.1	9.7	29.6	9.5
Oilseeds	34.3	0.3	13.4	13.9	3.3	3.6	0.1	16.5	8.7	15.0	12.7	7.3	6.3	24.8
Fruits and vegetables	27.1	0.4	1.9	12.3	6.6	12.5	8.6	11.0	36.5	26.0	11.6	18.9	11.8	33.2
Sugar	79.9	0.1	38.8	29.4	4.7	6.9	74.4	12.4	48.1	12.8	18.0	10.1	10.4	27.6
Plan based fibers	0.8	0.0	0.3	6.8	3.5	2.5	0.1	2.2	0.9	1.3	6.2	5.3	1.7	0.4
Meats and live animals	22.2	0.3	2.1	6.6	4.0	7.3	14.8	10.1	28.4	23.4	7.9	14.1	9.2	85.1
Dairy products	64.5	3.2	43.4	7.4	7.6	12.6	36.0	9.0	45.2	18.8	11.1	18.7	29.9	29.9
Vegetable oils and fats	8.3	0.8	2.7	18.8	7.3	12.1	10.7	10.3	16.0	12.7	8.2	14.6	14.1	30.6

Source: Computed from the GTAP database.

under which a free trade policy is suboptimal from a welfare point of view. These include the presence of administrative costs and the presence of underinvestment and underemployment, problems of greatest concern to LDCs.

Buffie also discusses extensively the issue of simultaneous import protection in combination with export promotion, a general policy approach that seems to have produced positive results in the late industrializing economies of East and South-East Asia. He shows theoretically, as well as empirically through simulations, that such policies can produce more favourable growth results, compared to free trade.

Buffie (2001) has not cast his analysis in terms of agriculture versus non-agriculture, but rather in terms of exportable, importable or import competing, and non-tradable sectors. However, for many LDCs and especially commodity dependent ones, this distinction is closely related to an agriculture–non-agriculture distinction, and to an exportable import competing distinction within agriculture, as many of them rely considerably on agricultural exports for foreign exchange, while also producing substantial amounts of import competing agricultural products, such as basic foods, in which they have seen their imports rise considerably in recent years. It must be realized that agricultural export promotion for many agriculture dependent economies may run up against the low inelasticity of world demand for agricultural exportables produced by LDCs, especially undifferentiated ones.

In a more recent article Buffie (2010) considers an archetypal low-income developing country that depends on agriculture for the bulk of its merchandise exports. In this country agriculture also constitutes a large share of the economy. The bulk of agricultural production, apart from exportable products, consists of either basic foods, or non-tradable agricultural products. The non-agricultural sector produces semi-tradable products, in the sense that they are imperfectly or non-competitive with imports. Under these and some other structural assumptions concerning employment, underinvestment and underemployment, Buffie shows that the optimal trade policies for aggregate growth involve a moderate level of protection of importables (of the order of 10–25 per cent under some reasonable empirical assumptions), some degree of export subsidization, and an escalated pattern of import protection with tariffs on intermediates and investment goods lower than tariffs on imported consumer goods. These results also hold under assumptions that are meant to emphasize poverty reduction in addition to growth. Buffie obtains his results not having differentiated between agriculture and non-agriculture, and assumes that the bulk of the imported consumer goods are manufactured ones. While this seems appropriate for many developing countries, it appears that many LDCs currently are experiencing a substantial growth in their imports of basic foods, and hence the basic food sector must be considered as one of the competing importable sectors in the above model. Whether the results of Buffie's analysis will extend to this case is not clear, but his model provides a reasonable basis on which to build an analysis of trade policy in agricultural products.

A number of arguments have been given by both sides of the debate as to whether intervention through trade policy provides an appropriate way of promoting agriculture's contribution to food security and economic growth via improvements in food staples productivity, or whether such policies actually suppress growth and poverty reduction efforts both through their impact on food prices and by constraining appropriate resource reallocation. Such arguments relate to issues such as optimal tariff (tax) policy, the infant industry argument, the unpredictability of policy interventions, the relationship between tariffs and food prices, the relationship between food staples prices and the production and consumption behaviour of poor households.

A starting point often taken is that market failure rarely justifies trade restrictions (Masters, 2007) and therefore that failures in domestic markets and trade policy are essentially unrelated. Masters contends that second best policies may be optimal where first best policies are constrained, but stresses that as they don't solve the root problem, the optimal second best intervention is likely to be small. However, he does acknowledge that where trade taxes play a significant role in the generation of government revenue, the optimal trade policy intervention could be greater.

Such insights draw on Corden (1974), who demonstrates that under generally assumed conditions, there is a hierarchy of interventions associated with a distortion in a factor market that is causing marginal private costs to exceed marginal social costs. In this hierarchy, a direct subsidy to the factor such as labour or credit, ranks higher than a direct subsidy to the sector in terms of a subsidized product price. This in turn is preferred to a combination of tariff and export subsidy, which is itself preferred to imposing a tariff alone. The tariff ranks fourth best in this example because of its suppressing effect on factor use intensity, the fact that it creates a consumption distortion and that it creates a bias towards production for the domestic market. Corden argues that going down the hierarchy of policy interventions requires justification. In particular, where an intervention is to address a marginal divergence, the form of intervention needs to balance the benefit of higher output with any potential consumption costs.

Corden concedes however, that where subsidy disbursement costs are allowed for, the ranking can change. In many rural economies, it is costly to intervene at the point of marginal divergence, whereas tariffs have no disbursement costs and may therefore become first best. This argument is reiterated by Buffie (2010) who cites the principle of targeting whereby a first best policy would maintain free trade and subsidize or tax at source if, and only if, this does not involve high administrative costs.

Advice to developing countries on trade policy has tended to focus on promoting opportunities for increased exports to international markets (be they traditional or non-traditional), while playing down the potential role that trade policy could play in enhanced competitiveness of import substitutes and in supporting the development of market opportunities in domestic and regional markets.

But if poorer countries have found it difficult to stimulate agriculture led growth through the promotion of more favourable conditions for the production of exportables, is there a case for a greater focus on policies, including trade policies, conducive to growth and food security based on the production of import competing staple food commodities? The issue can be examined by reference to the following considerations: (1) Where do the real market opportunities for poorer developing countries' agriculture lie? (2) Are the potential multiplier effects greater in expansion of import competing agricultural products than with export crop expansion?

On market opportunities, one argument for a greater focus on the role of import competing crops is that the market conditions and opportunities for domestically or regionally produced staples are potentially more favourable to poorer developing countries than opportunities for expanding exports to the global market.

Many poorer countries are not yet at the stage where domestic markets for high value products are growing. In India, 50 per cent of the value of agricultural production is now high value, but in Africa it is only 5 per cent. Hazell (2006) cites an IFPRI analysis which projects that in sub-Saharan Africa (SSA)

> even with a regional annual growth rate of 6 per cent per year for non-traditional exports, per capita agricultural real income would grow by only 0.2 to 0.3 per cent per year more than in a baseline scenario. Because of the small initial value of these exports, even rapid growth would not translate into significant economic leverage within the next 10 to 15 years.

By contrast, the current value of Africa's domestic demand for food staples is about US$50 billion per year, and this figure is projected to almost double by 2015, a $50 billion increase in market opportunity by 2015 (Hazell, 2006). Only part of this output is currently sold (the rest is consumed on farm), but it still represents a large and growing market. Diao et al. (2010) further argue that Africa currently imports 25 per cent of grain products such as maize, rice and wheat, and that domestic production could potentially displace some of these imports. There is in principle, therefore, very large scope for expansion of cereals production, including by small farmers, especially in SSA merely by import substitution.

Concerning multipliers of food staples versus export crops, in contrast to export commodities, where improved market conditions generally imply increased producer prices and incomes, basic food commodities, such as cereals, are on the whole, imported by poor developing countries. Hence, there is a greater degree of conflict between price increases faced by consumers and those received by producers because of the importance of the commodities in the consumption baskets of poor households in these countries. However, for this reason, cereal-based intensification can generate significant potential multipliers (see for example Haggblade and Hazell, 1989).

While urban households are expected to be net food consumers, the same is true of many rural households, including, especially poorer, agricultural households. For instance, a typical rural African population may include segments of food insecure households affected in different ways by price changes in major food crops. Poulton et al. (2005) identify four such categories of households:

- poor consumers whose income is not directly dependent on agricultural activities;
- net deficit producers who need to cover consumption needs from the market in the run up to harvest and whose consumption and production decisions will be affected by food staple prices;
- net deficit sellers, who may need to sell staples production for cash immediately post-harvest even though they have insufficient food production to satisfy their consumption needs and which include some of the poorest;
- surplus producers whose biggest problem is a price reduction in surplus years.

Clearly the impacts of price changes induced by trade policy on different types of net consumers will differ from those on different types of net producers. If, for instance, the majority of the food insecure are in farm households which are surplus producers of food, then price increases will help them, and the same will be the case for net food buyers, who are primarily workers, if the real incomes of labourers increased sufficiently to offset the price increases.

A study by Jayne et al. (2000), for example, addresses the question as to whether Kenyan farmers really want higher maize prices. They conclude that 'dealing with the agriculture sector as if farmers are a homogenous group with similar characteristics is misleading'. They reach this conclusion on the empirical fact that maize accounts for only 14 per cent of household income on average (including consumption out of own production) and does not exceed 25 per cent even in maize bread-basket areas. Small-scale farmers obtain 25 to 75 per cent of their income from non-farm sources. They calculate that most maize (74 per cent) marketed comes from 10 per cent of smallholder farms.

Further questioning the appropriateness of liberal agricultural trade policies comes from evidence from studies on the impact of trade policy reforms on reductions in levels of poverty and food insecurity. Such studies suggest that greater openness to international markets has had limited positive effects on food security (FAO, 2006; Sarris and Morrison, 2010).

As already indicated, in many contemporary developing countries, the taxation of agriculture (whether direct through export taxes, or perhaps inadvertently through misaligned exchange rates) had been a common feature in the past. A dramatic illustration of the conditions under which developing country producers operated in the period preceding the widespread implementation of structural adjustment programs of the 1980s is provided in the Krueger et al. (1991) study. The aggregate result of direct and indirect intervention of all selected products was to tax agriculture in all regions. Total net taxation of agriculture was greater than 25 per cent of the value of production in all regions, and exceeded 50 per cent in the SSA countries. As a result, domestic prices of imported food in the studied countries were significantly higher than prices at countries' borders, whereas domestic prices for key export items were held below international levels.

However, the extent and sources of distortions in developing countries' agriculture have changed significantly since the early 1980s as unilateral reforms implemented during the 1980s and 1990s in many developing countries reduced this quantifiable anti-agricultural bias in domestic policy, particularly that associated with indirect taxation. Given fiscal constraints on the use of subsidies, trade policy is now the primary tool used to protect agriculture in developing countries, but, partly as a result of the adjustment programs, this form of protection has decreased. As a result, domestic producers have become more exposed to world market conditions and it would follow that incentives for tradables as opposed to non-tradables must have become more favourable.

Given the major change in the overall direction of agricultural total protection/taxation since the 1980s it is interesting to examine the degree to which structures of agricultural economies have changed with greater openness. Theory, and the rationale for liberalization and structural adjustment, is that opening local markets to trade will cause a shift from the production of non-tradables to the production of tradables as prices adjust. Given that liberalization and structural adjustment policies have been implemented over the last 20 years, this is a long enough time period over which one would expect to see substantial changes in production patterns.

Table 13.2 makes an attempt to explore this for agricultural commodity dependent LDCs (defined as those with a share of agricultural products in total merchandise exports larger than 30 per cent in late 1990s). The table shows the shares of exportables

Table 13.2 Evolving production structure in commodity dependent developing countries

	Ratio of the value of production of exportables to the total value of agricultural production (%)			Ratio of the value of production of importables to the total value of agricultural production (%)		
	1980–82	1989–91	2001–03	1980–82	1989–91	2001–03
Africa (24 countries)	23.1	22.1	21.8	24.7	25.7	25.0
Latin America (11 countries)	48.1	52.8	48.0	45.0	43.8	41.8
Oceania (3 countries)	45.8	39.3	37.1	8.4	9.5	12.6

Source: Authors'calculations from FAO data.

and importables in the value of total agricultural production. The exportables and importables include all products which cumulatively accounted for 90 per cent of total agricultural exports and imports respectively in the period 2000–02.

Although the policy regimes in the commodity dependent countries have changed significantly over the past two decades (see FAO, 2006, for case study experiences), in general, the structure of importables, exportables and non-tradables (calculated as a residual) has remained relatively constant in the majority of countries.[3] Of the individual African countries included, in only five cases did the values of importables as a percentage of the total value of production increase by more than 3 percentage points and in only three cases did the value of exportables as a percentage of the total value of agricultural production increase. Similarly in only a handful of countries (four in the case of importables and three in the case of exportables) did the relevant shares decrease.

One explanation that may be provided for this limited structural change is that incentives have been counter to the development of the tradables sector. However, evidence does not bear this out. FAO (2006) provides trends in agricultural terms of trade in 15 case study countries. For many of the reported countries, there has been an upward (or at least not decreasing) trend in the agricultural terms of trade and there appeared to be

> a positive, if not strong, correlation between changes in the agricultural terms of trade and the growth rate of the value of production of the agricultural sector (in constant local currency units), although this correlation appears much weaker in the last decade or so, raising questions about the determinants of agricultural output.

To a large extent, this positive movement in the face of declining global primary commodity prices over the period is explained by favourable exchange rate movements as previously overvalued exchange rates were devalued (or allowed to depreciate). These 'corrections' tended to occur in the 1980s/early 1990s and domestic agricultural prices often increased as a result.

It is thus difficult to argue that in general, the changes in price incentives for production of tradables (as reflected in border prices) have been overly negative in recent decades. Therefore, it is all the more puzzling why there have not been larger structural changes within the agricultural sector of poorer developing countries.

From the above it appears that the issue of trade policy for food staples, if it is to be responsive to food security concerns, must be conditioned by a variety of factors, most of which relate to the structure of markets, as well as the income/consumption structure of the food insecure. Trade and market policy must be seen as integral to the support of food staples development. However, there is no 'one size fits all' approach to trade policy design and implementation. The specific context in terms of the role of the sector in the wider economy, the extent to which smallholders participate as sellers in markets, and the functionality of these markets needs to be integrated into policy analyses.

While theory and evidence may lend some insights as to how trade policy might best be structured to promote longer term development of the sector, the design of recent policy interventions has clearly been driven more by the practicalities of intervention, essentially to meet short-term interests. No matter what the insights from theoretical or empirical investigation, there are a number of categories of practical factors that will continue to make intervention through trade policy problematic.

Amongst the key constraints to the adoption of the most appropriate policy from a food security perspective, is the political economy of decision making. Indeed, many commentators acknowledge that political economy arguments can shed more light on actual policy decisions than can economic theory and generally provide a richer explanation than the market failure story.

13.6 CONCLUDING COMMENTS

This chapter started with some questions regarding the role of trade in ensuring food security. What are the key messages from the exposition? First we asked what is the influence of trade and trade policy on food security and whether open economies are more likely to achieve food security. The answer to this is that it depends on how trade and trade policy interact with the domestic markets that affect those that are food insecure. Trade generally is expected to play a positive role in both supplying domestic markets in times of deficits, and in relieving domestic markets of occasional surpluses. A closed economy while insulated from external shocks, is more vulnerable to domestic shocks. So whether trade openness makes domestic markets more stable and reliable depends on the relative size of domestic and external food shocks. The more the domestic food sector is affected by domestic shocks, the more appropriate is to have an open trade regime.

On the issue of whether a country can trust global food markets to deliver food commodities when needed and at reasonable cost, the answer is in general yes. However, there are occasions, such as the events of 2006–08, when international markets become excessively unstable and unreliable. How frequent are such events? History suggests that such occurrences are not frequent, perhaps once every 30 years or so. Similarly food commodity markets are characterized by infrequent spikes. What can a country that faces food security problems do? The review above suggests that a drive towards complete self sufficiency is almost never the answer, but on the other hand some degree of adequate domestic productive food capacity is wise.

The design of appropriate trade policies to deal with food security must start with a thorough description of the structure and problems faced by those deemed as food insecure. The next step is to outline policies that are likely to affect directly the livelihoods and food access of the food insecure. It is most likely that the bulk of relevant policies will involve domestic measures. However, trade policies are crucial in assisting domestic policies to achieve their objectives. In this context trade policy must be regarded as auxiliary to other more direct food security strategies. Whether the best relevant trade policies are protective or not will depend on a variety of structural conditions specific to each country, as well as the relevant policy objectives.

Governments have multiple objectives concerning domestic food security. These may involve among others, stable prices, adequate supplies, and low prices for consumers. Trade policy can affect all these objectives, and must be designed in ways that are flexible to accommodate both changing domestic market structures, as well as changing international conditions.

NOTES

1. The following exposition draws from Morrison and Sarris (2010).
2. For an early review of this literature, see Corden's (1974) classic book.
3. There have been exceptions to the general stickiness of these activities, for example Côte d'Ivoire has seen a significant shift towards both importables and exportables, but Malawi has seen a fall in the share value of production of both importables and exportables.

REFERENCES

Abbott, P.C., C. Hurt and W.E. Tyner (2008), *What's Driving Food Prices?* Oak Brook IL: Farm Foundation.
Abbott, P.C., C. Hurt and W.E. Tyner (2009), *What's Driving Food Prices? March 2009 Update*. Oak Brook, IL: Farm Foundation.
Alexandratos, N. (2011), World food and agriculture to 2030/50 revisited. Highlights and views four years later, in P. Conforti (ed.), *Looking Ahead in World Food and Agriculture: Perspectives to 2050*. Rome: FAO, pp. 11–56.
Anderson, J. and T.G. Riley (1976), International trade with fluctuating prices. *International Economic Review*, **17**, 79–97.
Anderson, K. (ed.) (2009), *Distortions to Agricultural Incentives: A Global Perspective, 1955–2007*, London: Palgrave Macmillan.
Ardeni, P.G. and B. Wright (1992), 'The Prebisch–Singer Hypothesis: a reappraisal independent of stationarity hypotheses. *Economic Journal*, **102**(413): 803–12.
Balcombe, K. (2011), 'The nature and determinants of volatility in agricultural prices: an empirical study. in Prakash (ed.), *Safeguarding food security in volatile global markets*, Rome: FAO, pp. 89–110.
Bellemare, M.F., C.B. Barrett and D.R. Just (2010), 'The welfare impacts of commodity price fluctuations: evidence from rural Ethiopia. MPRA Paper 24457, Germany: University Library of Munich.
Bevan, D.L., P. Collier, and J.W. Gunning with A. Bigsten and P. Horsnell (1990), *Controlled Open Economies: A Neoclassical Approach to Structuralism*. Oxford: Clarendon Press.
Bouët A. and D. Laborde (2009), Market access versus domestic support: assessing the relative impacts on developing countries agriculture. Paper prepared for FAO.
Bruinsma, J. (ed.) (2003), *World Agriculture: Towards 2015/30: An FAO Perspective*. Rome: FAO.
Buffie, E.F. (2001), *Trade Policy in Developing Countries*, Cambridge: Cambridge University Press.
Buffie, E.F. (2010), Trade, agriculture and optimal commercial policy in Eastern and Southern Africa. In A. Sarris and J. Morrison (eds), *Food Security in Africa: Market and Trade Policy for Staple Foods in Eastern and Southern Africa*. Cheltenham, UK, and Northampton, MA, USA: Edward Elgar, pp. 8–40.
Cashin, P. and C.J. McDermott (2001), The long run behavior of commodity prices: small trends and big variability. Working Paper WP/01/68, International Monetary Fund Research Department.
Cashin P. and C.J. McDermott (2006), 'Properties of international commodity prices: identifying trends, cycles and shocks. In A. Sarris and D. Hallam (eds), *Agricultural Commodity Markets and Trade: New Approaches*

to *Analyzing Market Structure and Instability*. Cheltenham, UK, and Northampton, MA, USA: Edward Elgar, pp. 16–30.
Cavalcanti, T., V. de V., K. Mohaddes and M. Raissi (2011), Commodity price volatility and the sources of growth. Cambridge working papers in economics, Cambridge University.
Collier, P. and J.W. Gunning and Associates (1999), *Trade Shocks: Theory and Evidence*. Oxford: Clarendon Press.
Corden, W.M. (1974), *Trade Policy and Economic Welfare*. Oxford: Clarendon Press.
Deaton, A. (1989), Rice prices and income distribution in Thailand: a nonparametric analysis. *Economic Journal*, **99** (Conference), 1–37.
Deaton, A. (1999), Commodity prices and growth in Africa. *Journal of Economic Perspectives*, **13**(3), 23–40.
Dehn, J. (2000), The effects on growth of commodity price uncertainty and shocks. World Bank, Policy Research Working Paper No. 2455, Washington DC.
Demeke, M., G. Pangrazio and M. Maetz (2011), Country responses to turmoil in global food markets: the nature and preliminary implications of the policies pursued in the 2006–08 episode. In A. Prakash (ed.), *Safeguarding Food Security in Volatile Global Markets*. Rome: FAO, pp. 183–209.
Dercon, S. and L. Christiaensen (2011), Consumption risk, technology adoption and poverty traps: evidence from Ethiopia. *Journal of Development Economics*, **96**(2), 317–41.
Diao, X., P. Hazell and J. Thurlow (2010), The role of agriculture in African development. *World Development*, **38**(10), 1375–1383.
FAO (2003), Financing normal levels of commercial imports of basic foodstuffs in the context of the Marrakesh Decision on least-developed (LDC) and net food importing developing countries (NFIDC). FAO, Commodities, and Trade Division Rome.
FAO (2004), *The State of Agricultural Commodity Markets*. Rome: FAO.
FAO (2006), *Trade Reforms and Food Security: Case Studies*. Rome: FAO.
FAO (2011), *State of Food Insecurity in the World*. Rome: FAO.
FAO (2012), *Food Outlook*. Rome: FAO, May 2012.
Gilbert, C.L. (2006), Trends and volatility in agricultural commodity prices. In A. Sarris and B. Hallam (eds), *Agricultural Commodity Markets and Trade: New approaches to Analyzing Market Structure and Instability*. Cheltenham, UK, and Northampton, MA, USA: Edward Elgar, pp. 31–60.
Gilbert, C.L. (2010), How to understand high food prices. *Journal of Agricultural Economics*, **61**, 398–425.
Gilbert, C.L. (2011), Grains price pass-through, 2005–09. In A. Prakash (ed.), *Safeguarding Food Security in Volatile Global Markets*. Rome: FAO, pp. 127–48.
Gilbert, C.L. and C.W. Morgan (2010), Food price volatility. *Philosophical Transactions of the Royal Society of London, Series B: Biological Sciences*, **365**(1554), 3023–3034, available at http://rstb.royalsocietypublishing.org/content/365/1554/3023.abstract.
Grilli, E.R. and M.C. Yang (1988), Primary commodity prices, manufactured goods prices, and the terms of trade of developing countries: what the long run shows. *The World Bank Economic Review*, **2**(1), January.
Guillaumont, P.S., S. Guillaumont-Jeannenee and J.F. Brun (1999), How instability lowers economic growth. *Journal of African Economies*, **8**(1), 87–102.
Haggblade, S. and P. Hazell (1989), Agricultural technology and farm–non-farm growth linkages. *Agricultural Economics*, **3**, 345–64.
Hazell, P. (2006), Transformations in agriculture and the impacts on rural development. Paper prepared for a conference on Beyond Agriculture: The Promise of the Rural Economy for Growth and Poverty Reduction. 16–18 January 2006. Rome: FAO.
Headey, D. and S. Fan (2010), Reflections on the global food crisis. Research Report No 165. International Food Policy Research Institute, Washington DC.
Helpman, E. and A. Razin (1978), *A Theory of International Trade Under Uncertainty*. New York and London: Academic Press.
Irwin, S.H., D.R. Sanders and R.P. Merrin (2009), Devil or angel: the role of speculation in the recent commodity price boom (and bust). *Journal of Agricultural and Applied Economics*, **41**(2), 377–91.
Ivanic, M. and W. Martin (2008), Implications of higher global food prices for poverty in low-income countries. *Agricultural Economics*, **39** (supplement), 405–16.
Jabara, C.L. and R.L. Thompson (1980), Comparative advantage under uncertainty: the case of Senegal. *American Journal of Agricultural Economics*, **62**(2), 188–98, May.
Jayne, T., Y. Yamano, J. Nyoro and T. Awour (2000), *Do Farmers Really Benefit From High Food Prices? Balancing Rural Interests in Kenya's Maize Pricing and Marketing Policy*. Kenya: Tegemeo Institute for Agricultural Policy and Development.
Keynes, J.M. (1942), *The International Control of Raw Materials*. UK Treasury Memorandum, reprinted in *Journal of International Economics*, **4** (1974), 299–315.
Konandreas, P. (2012), Trade policy responses to food price volatility in poor net food-importing countries. International Centre for Trade and Sustainable Development, Issue paper No. 42.

Krueger, A., M. Schiff and A. Valdes (eds) (1991), *The Political Economy of Agricultural Pricing Policy*. The World Bank and Johns Hopkins University Press: Washington DC.

Leon, J. and R. Soto (1995), Structural breaks and long-run trends in commodity prices. Policy Research Working Paper 1406. World Bank, Washington DC.

Lucas, R.E. (2003), Macroeconomic priorities. *American Economic Review*, **93**, 1–14.

Martin, W. and K. Anderson (2012), Export restrictions and price insulation during commodity price booms. *American Journal of Agricultural Economics*, **94**(2) (1 January), 422–7.

Masters, M.W. and A.K. White (2008), The Accidental Hunt Brothers. how institutional investors are driving up food and energy prices. Special Report, 31 July. Available at www.accidentalhuntbrothers.com.

Masters, W. (2007), Trade policy for food and agriculture in East and Southern Africa. Paper presented at an FAO workshop on Staple Food Trade and Market Policy Options for Promoting Development in Eastern and Southern Africa. Rome: FAO. Available at: http://www.fao.org/es/esc/common/ecg/17/en/MASTERS_FAO_1Mar07.ppt.

Masters, W. (2009), Trends in Agricultural protection: how might agricultural protection evolve in the coming decades? Paper prepared for FAO.

Morrison, J. and A. Sarris (2010), Determining the appropriate level of import protection consistent with agriculture led development in the advancement of poverty reduction and improved food security. In A. Sarris and J. Morrison (eds), *Food Security in Africa: Market and Trade Policy for Staple Foods in Eastern and Southern Africa*. Cheltenham, UK, and Northampton, MA, USA: Edward Elgar.

Ng, F. and M.A. Aksoy (2008), Food price increases and net food importing countries: lessons from the recent past. *Agricultural Economics*, **39**, 443–52.

Pieters, H., A. Vandeplas, A. Guariso, N. Francken, A. Sarris, J. Swinnen, N. Gerber, J. von Braun, and M. Torero (2012), Perspectives on relevant concepts related to food and nutrition security. Working paper. Food secure project, University of Leuven.

Poulton, C., J. Kydd, S. Wiggins and A. Dorward (2005), State intervention for food price stabilisation in Africa: can it work? Paper prepared for World Bank-DFID workshop Managing Food Price Risks and Instability. 28 February–1 March, Washington DC.

Prakash, A. (ed.) (2011), *Safeguarding Food Security in Volatile Global Markets*. Rome: FAO.

Prasad, B. and M. Crucini (2000), Commodity prices and the terms of trade. *Review of International Economics*, **8**, 647–66.

Prebish, R. (1950a), *The Economic Development of Latin America and its Principal Problems*. New York: United Nations Department of Economic Affairs.

Rapsomanikis, G. (2009), The 2007–2008 food price swing: impact and policies in Eastern and Southern Africa. FAO Commodities and Trade Technical paper No 12, Trade and Markets Division, FAO, Rome.

Rapsomanikis, G. (2011), Price transmission and volatility spillovers in food markets. In A. Prakash (ed.), *Safeguarding Food Security in Volatile Global Markets*. Rome: FAO, pp. 149–68.

Rapsomanikis, G. and A. Sarris (2008), Market integration and uncertainty: the impact of domestic and international commodity price variability on rural household income and welfare in Ghana and Peru. *Journal of Development Studies*, **44**(9), 1354–1381.

Rodriquez, F. and D. Rodrik (1999), Trade policy and economic growth: a skeptic's guide to the cross-national evidence. CEPR Discussion Paper No. 2143, May.

Rutten, M.M., L.J. Chant and G.W. Meijerink (2011), Sit down at the ball game: how trade barriers make the world less food secure. MPRA Paper. University Library of Munich, Germany.

Sarris, A.H. (1985), Food security and agricultural production strategies under risk in Egypt. *Journal of Development Economics*, **19**(1/2), September–October.

Sarris, A. (2000), Has word cereal market instability increased? *Food Policy*, **25**, 337–50.

Sarris, A. (2009), Factors affecting recent and future price volatility of food commodities. *Schriften der Gessellschaft fur Wirtschafts- und Sozialwissenschaften des Landbaues*, e.V., Bd. **44**, 29–48.

Sarris, A. (2010), Evolving structure of world agricultural market instability and requirements for new world trade rules. In A. Sarris and J. Morrison (eds), *The Evolving Structure of World Agricultural Trade: Implications for Trade Policy and Trade Agreements*. Rome: FAO, pp. 9–38.

Sarris, A., and J. Morrison (eds) (2010), *Food Security in Africa: Market and Trade Policy for Staple Foods in Eastern and Southern Africa*. Cheltenham, UK, and Northampton, MA, USA: Edward Elgar.

Singer, H. (1950), The distribution of gains between investing and borrowing countries. *American Economic Review*, **49** (Papers and proceedings), 251–73.

Stigler, M. (2011), Commodity prices: theoretical and empirical properties. In A. Prakash (ed.), *Safeguarding Food Security in Volatile Global Markets*. Rome: FAO, pp. 27–44.

Subervie, J. (2008), The variable response of agricultural supply to world price instability in developing countries. *Journal of Agricultural Economics*, **59**(1), 72–92.

Tyers, R. and K. Anderson (1992), *Disarray in World Food Markets: A Quantitative Assessment*. Cambridge and New York: Cambridge University Press.

UNCTAD (United Nations Conference on Trade and Development) (2004), *The Least Developed Countries Report: Linking International Trade with Poverty Reduction*. Geneva: UNCTAD.
UNDP (United Nations Development Program) (2003), *Making Global Trade Work for People*. Earthscan: London.
Winters, L.A. (2002), Trade liberalization and poverty: what are the links?. *World Economy*, **25**(9), 1339–1367.
Winters, L.A., N. McCulloch and A. McKay (2004), Trade liberalization and poverty: the evidence so far. *Journal of Economic Literature*, **XLII**(1), 72–115.

14. Enhancing food security: agricultural productivity, international trade and poverty reduction
Peter Warr

14.1 INTRODUCTION

Food security is back on the global agenda. Over the three decades following the mid-1970s, falling international food prices signaled abundant global food supplies, resulting in widespread overconfidence about the prospects for continued reductions in global hunger. But dramatic international food price increases in 2007 and 2008 and subsequent price surges in 2010 and 2011 ended this complacency. Between 2006 and 2008 the international price of rice tripled, with wheat and maize not far behind. Between them, these three cereals are the staple foods of the majority of the world's poorest people and expenditure on them accounts for a large proportion of household budgets. Among the poor, net purchasers of these commodities typically outnumber net sellers, such as small farmers. Poor people are consequently those most vulnerable to an increase in food prices. For those poor people who are net purchasers of food and for the governments and other institutions concerned with their welfare, highly volatile food prices are deeply worrying.

Figure 14.1 shows long-term data on the international prices of rice, wheat and maize, relative to manufactured commodities, covering more than a century. Three features of the behaviour of these prices are revealed by the data:

1. all three real prices have declined markedly over the long term;
2. all three have been highly volatile; and
3. all three increased significantly in recent years.

At the end of the twentieth century the real price of food was well below half of its level a century before. Even at the very height of the price increases of 2007–08, the relative price of food was still well below its level throughout the first two decades of the twentieth century. Advances in agricultural productivity were the central source of this achievement, confounding the eighteenth century prediction of Thomas Malthus that mass starvation was (and remains) inevitable. This long-term trend of cheaper food explains the recent complacency regarding agriculture and food discussed above. But the price surges of the last decade have shown the folly of ignoring food security (Timmer, 2010).

Although food and agriculture are now receiving greater attention, decades of neglect have not helped (Headey and Fan, 2008; Timmer, 2008). Between 1980 and 2005 total annual foreign assistance to less-developed countries that was designated for agricultural development declined from US$8 billion to US$3.4 billion, a reduction from 17

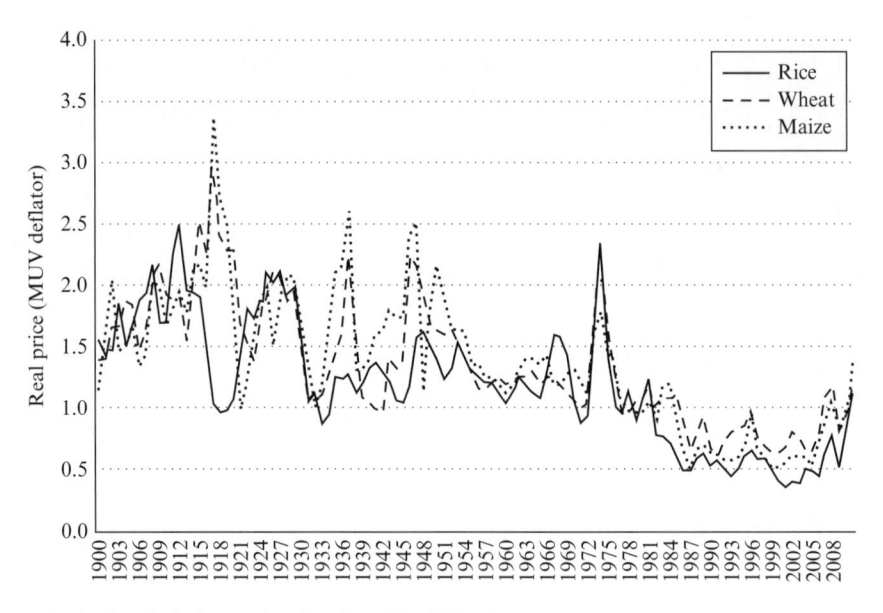

Source: Author's calculations, using data from World Bank.

Figure 14.1 International real prices of rice, wheat and maize, 1900 to 2012

to 3 percent of total foreign assistance to these countries. In the 1980s, 25 percent of US foreign aid went to agriculture. In the 1990s, it was 6 percent and, in 2011, it was 1 percent. The share of World Bank lending going to agriculture was 30 percent in 1978, 16 percent in 1988 and 8 percent in 2006. In many developing countries themselves, public commitment to investment in agriculture has also waned, as other development priorities have seemed more promising.

Human well-being requires a continuous and reliable supply of nutritious and safe food, in adequate quantities. Obviously, the concern for food security derives from the reality of food *in*security, the social and political consequences of which are potentially dire. But what does food security or its opposite mean, and what determines it? Are there degrees of food insecurity? The definition of food security is discussed in Section 14.2, including the possibility of developing quantitative measures for it.

The theme of the chapter is that enhancing food security has three major components:

1. reducing the relative price of food;
2. reducing poverty; and
3. providing special food-related assistance to disadvantaged groups and to the wider population in emergency circumstances.

Point (1) is about reducing the cost of producing and delivering food domestically or purchasing it on international markets, and hence the price at which food is available to households. Point (2) relates to households' capacity to purchase food, along with other essential commodities. Point (3) recognises the necessity to care for individuals and groups who are missed by the drivers of poverty reduction and for whom even reduced real prices of food do not ensure dietary adequacy. It also relates to the broader public provision of emergency food supplies during natural and anthropogenic disasters.

Subsumed in the definition of 'food' in this discussion is a nutritional and safety issue, meaning food which meets human nutritional requirements and which is hygienic. These three themes of poverty reduction, reducing the relative price of food, and the provision of social food safety nets, are pursued in the remainder of this chapter.

Reducing the relative price of food (point (1)) means lowering the price at which households can obtain food with the nutritional and safety characteristics they require. Two distinct sets of policy-related issues are involved in the determination of food prices: the productivity and competitiveness of the domestic food production and marketing system; and the role of international trade. These two sets of issues are discussed in Sections 14.3 and 14.4 of this chapter, respectively. Globally, the levels of productivity in agriculture and in off-farm food processing and distribution systems are the principal long-term determinants of food prices, though trade can also play a cost-reducing role by making the global food system more efficient. But for individual countries trade policy with respect to food can be a critical determinant of domestic food prices (Warr, 2005, 2008). Following the food price shocks of 2007–08 the issue is how the long-term cost-reducing benefits of international trade can be achieved without exposure to huge short-term price spikes in food prices, induced by volatile international markets.

Poverty reduction (point (2)) is central because for most people, for most of the time, food security is a matter of purchasing power. The rich are never food insecure, except in the most extreme circumstances of wars or natural disasters, and even then the poor are more severely affected. Sustainable poverty reduction is central to enhancing food security, long-term, because by definition poverty reduction entails increasing the capacity of poor households to purchase essential commodities, including food. Fortunately, quite a lot is known about what it takes to achieve a sustainable reduction in poverty. But food is different in some important respects, especially in the short-term. Section 14.5 of this chapter examines the relationship between poverty reduction and food security.

Special food-related assistance (point (3)) relates to the role of social food safety nets, including whether special assistance is best provided in-kind, in the form of food itself, or in cash. It can generally be expected that poverty reduction will coincide with improved food security, but exceptions can occur. Recent research on India illustrates the possibility that although poverty incidence declines, food security may not improve. This is especially likely when food prices rise significantly relative to other prices. Although poverty reduction can be expected to reduce the proportion of the population that is food insecure, there will always be groups requiring special assistance, or periods when food prices rise unexpectedly, causing more widespread food insecurity.

Competing demands for agricultural output, coming from feed and fuel demands, in addition to food for a rising population, mean increased pressure on Asian food markets. In most of Asia, there is very limited scope for increasing the supply of agricultural land, but agricultural yields have barely kept up with population growth. As the demand for agricultural output rises, land will become even more scarce. Overuse of fertilizers, pesticides and herbicides will become an increasing danger, with serious environmental consequences. The development of pesticide resistance within major insect pest populations is a particular danger, given the widespread overuse of a limited number of major pesticides in monocrop rice agriculture.

International food markets can play a constructive role at the margin, but in almost all Asian countries the challenge of rising demands for food must be met overwhelmingly by expansion of domestic output. Moreover, this must be achieved with no more, and possibly less, land allocated to agriculture than at present and with a diminishing proportion of the total workforce. If this is to occur without substantial increases in food prices there is only one mechanism available – increased productivity. This must occur especially within agriculture itself but also throughout the food supply and input supply chains. Improved agricultural technology makes it possible to achieve expanded food production without raising domestic prices, thereby injuring the poor, and without necessarily drawing large areas of additional land into agricultural production, promoting the destruction of remaining forests and other ecologically important habitats.

Raising productivity requires investing in rural infrastructure and promoting research and development activities that facilitate food production. The agricultural sectors of the developing countries of Asia and the Pacific have great potential for increased productivity. But adaptive research at the individual country level is required to achieve that potential. Greatly enhanced long-term public investment in agricultural research and development is required. But agricultural research has been neglected in many countries of the Asia-Pacific region.

Against this lies the specter of climate change, which promises to make the maintenance of food security even more challenging. Rising temperatures are likely to have a greater effect on wheat production than on rice or maize, but changes in the location of production, in response to climatic change, would be enormously costly for rice-producing Asia. Research is required to find means to cope most effectively with the consequences for agricultural production of significant increases in temperature, which now seem unavoidable.

14.2 THE MEANING OF FOOD SECURITY

14.2.1 Why Food is Different

Food is not a 'normal' commodity. It has no substitutes. If we are unable to obtain adequate food we suffer, and soon die, regardless of how much we possess of other things. Moreover, because our bodies lack the capacity to store large amounts of energy and other essential nutrients, we must have adequate food intake almost continuously. This applies most especially to children, whose development may be impaired irreversibly by prolonged dietary inadequacy. But for large numbers of poor people, the reliability of food supplies cannot be assumed. The prospect of food insufficiency, even if the probability is small and even if the expected duration of inadequate intake is short, is frightening for anyone. For these reasons, it makes sense to speak of 'food security' in a way that we do not speak of, say, 'clothing security' or 'entertainment security'. We can survive for a long time without a reliable supply of these things.

Food is different, but not *uniquely* so. Other things are also essential for well-being, including clean drinking water, shelter, access to basic medical care and basic education for children. None have substitutes. If any one of them is lacking, no amount of the others can make up for it. The cruel nature of poverty is that it compels households to make choices among these items, *all* of which are essential for a minimally adequate standard of living. It is therefore important to recognize that a focus on food security and nutritional adequacy does not mean that other requirements for a decent life can be ignored or that they can necessarily be sacrificed in the interest of greater food security.

14.2.2 Defining Food Security

At the 1996 World Food Summit food security was defined as existing 'when all people at all times have access to sufficient, safe, nutritious food to maintain a healthy and active life.' The World Health Organization (WHO) adds to this definition a description that is widely cited and drawn upon in subsequent studies. It says that food security rests on three pillars:

- food availability (sufficient quantities existing);
- food access (households are able to obtain the quantities required); and
- food use (appropriate nutrition and hygiene).

Both definitions are useful. Because the WHO decomposition is so widely adopted, it is helpful to consider its relationship to the three principal themes of this chapter – that improved food security rests on poverty reduction, reductions in the price of food and the existence of social safety nets.

The first two components of the WHO definition, food availability and food access, are generally understood to relate to the national level (aggregate supplies) and the household level (capacity to purchase). But there is another way of interpreting these two categories. Food availability may be thought of in terms, not of aggregate quantities of food, but of the prices at which food is available. This in turn depends on productivity in the production and distribution of food within the domestic economy, the capacity of international trade to augment domestic food supplies and supplementary measures to provide food to households otherwise unable to purchase it. *Improving food availability is about reducing the supply price of food.*

Food access, the capacity of households to obtain the food they require, depends on the level of household incomes relative to the price of food. In the case of economically disadvantaged households and in emergencies, it also depends on the existence of food social safety nets. But as noted above, food is not the only requirement for a decent life. The poverty line is a measure of the amount of income required to purchase the goods and services needed for a minimally adequate standard of living, and because food accounts for such a large share of the household budgets of the poorest households it necessarily forms a large component of the poverty line. Poverty incidence measures the proportion of households whose incomes fall below this poverty line. Food access is therefore inversely related to poverty incidence. A lower level of poverty incidence means a higher proportion of households with adequate access to food. But reducing poverty incidence is not enough. Some households will continue to be food-deficient even though poverty incidence falls, and unexpected disasters can also lead to temporary but widespread hunger. *Improving food access is about reducing poverty and creating food social safety nets.*

Viewed in this way, the WHO decomposition of food security maps directly into the three-part framework: price of food/poverty reduction/food social safety nets. But a remaining problem with both the WHO and World Food Summit definitions is that they are non-quantitative. Our interest in the subject of food security derives from the fact that the stated conditions for food security do *not* always exist, as defined. But the degree of departure from these conditions varies. The focus on food security is motivated by the possibility of food insecurity, but there are clearly degrees of food insecurity, some more severe than others (United States Department of Agriculture, 2000). It is not obvious how varying degrees of departure from full food security could be quantified, based on the World Food Summit or WHO definitions. An operational definition would make quantification meaningful.

It is not enough to know merely whether food security does or does not exist. We need to be able to quantify the degree of departure from full food security. In contrast, for example, the concept of poverty incidence has been precisely defined quantitatively, making it possible to study scientifically the causes of changes in poverty incidence over time and across environments.

It is helpful to distinguish between three levels of food security.

1. *Household level* food security refers to having access to adequate food at all times, roughly along the lines of the above definition. At the household level, food 'security' relates to more than just the adequacy of food intake today. It implies something forward-looking, involving *expectations* of future circumstances and not simply present conditions. In particular, it relates to the expected availability of sufficient food in the future, which inherently involves uncertainty.

Oversimplifying, suppose there are just two time periods, 'today' and 'tomorrow'. Food security relates to the household's expectations about the availability of food tomorrow, relative to the amount required. The household may have adequate food today, and may always have done so in the past, but there is nevertheless some possibility of not having adequate food available in the future, and this is the basis for a measure of the degree of the household's food insecurity.

2. *National level* food security must surely be founded on food security at the household level. If households are not food secure, it is hard to see how the nation could be. But national food security is often taken to mean something quite different – *food self-sufficiency* – meaning that sufficient food is present within the country to make imports unnecessary. The basis for the focus on eliminating imports is mistrust of international markets as sources for a nation's food requirements. But this concept does not coincide with food security at the household level and can be in conflict with it.

For example, consider a country that normally imports food. One way to eliminate imports is to prohibit them (disregarding the possibility of smuggling). This will raise the price of food within the country, stimulating additional supplies and reducing demand. The domestic price will rise sufficiently to eliminate the difference between total domestic demand and supply. But the increase in the price means that household food consumption will be lower than the level in the presence of imports and may be below that required by the World Food Summit definition. That is, food self-sufficiency may be in conflict with food security (Warr, 2005, 2011).

3. *Global level* food security means whether global supplies are sufficient to meet aggregate global requirements. Reportedly, there are around 1 billion hungry people in the world and also 1 billion obese people. The amount of food currently produced is

seemingly enough for everyone, leaving only a problem of distribution among individuals. But while arithmetically correct, this simplistic description of the problem does not necessarily provide a practical means of reducing hunger in poor countries. Increasing food production in the poorest parts of the world may often be the most effective means of reducing global hunger.

14.2.3 More Than Calories

Nutritionists emphasize that food security is about more than just caloric intake. Protein intake is important as well, along with essential fats and micronutrients. Moreover, data relating to average, population-wide nutrient intakes miss the special importance of adequate nutrition for the development of children. Malnutrition in childhood contributes to mortality, mental and physical impairment and chronic disease risk across the life cycle in a way that cannot always be remedied by improved diets later in life. In economic terms, malnutrition in childhood impedes the formation of human capital through investment in education, with subsequent implications for economic growth. Survey-based data summarized by Neufeld et al. (2012) show high levels of stunting in children under 5 years of age in South and Central Asia and parts of Southeast Asia. In South Asia childhood stunting has been reported in 40 percent of children and severe wasting in over 5 percent. But in addition the data show high levels of both anemia (low levels of blood hemoglobin, arising from dietary iron deficiency) and vitamin A deficiency in India, Pakistan, Nepal, Cambodia and Myanmar. Not far behind are Bangladesh, Vietnam, Indonesia and the Philippines.

Data assembled by WHO confirm that as real GDP per capita rises, the incidence of childhood stunting declines, on average, but the incidence of adult and childhood obesity rises. A reflection of the latter is the rising incidence of diabetes in Asia. In India and China the incidence of diabetes is already far higher than in Japan and even exceeds that in Western countries like the United States and Italy. Caloric adequacy is a necessary but not sufficient condition for food security. *Nutritional security* is about meeting (but not overly exceeding) dietary requirements across a range of essential nutrients. Clearly, nutritional insecurity can exist for some groups even in the presence of food abundance.

14.2.4 Quantifying Food Security

The expectations-based concept of household-level food security is illustrated in Figures 14.2 and 14.3. Consider a household that is uncertain about future food availability. Figure 14.2 depicts a probability density function (PDF) describing that household's expectations about future food availability, relative to the amount required, R. The probability, p, that food consumption will be inadequate is given by the shaded area under the PDF, as indicated. Figure 14.3 now converts this same information to a cumulative distribution function (CDF) showing, on the vertical axis, the cumulative probability that available consumption will be less than or equal to the amount indicated by the horizontal axis. The probability that consumption will be less than or equal to R is now the intersection between R and the CDF, shown as p. This probability provides one possible measure of food insecurity and $1 - p$ is a measure of food security.

Figure 14.3 makes it possible to add something not readily inferred from Figure 14.2.

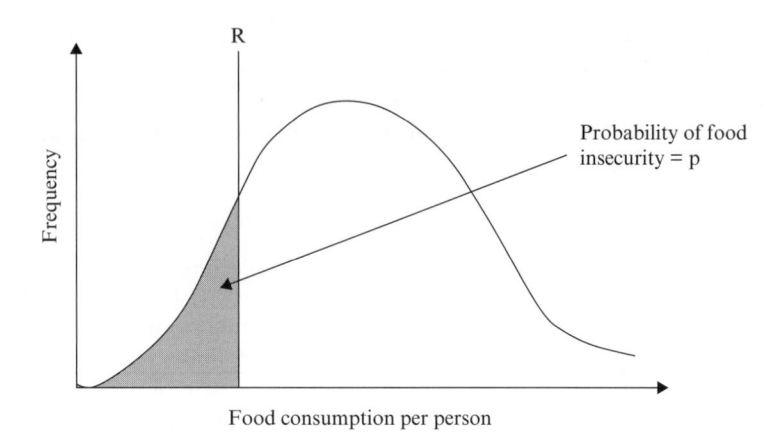

Figure 14.2   Expected food intake for a household: probability density function (PDF)

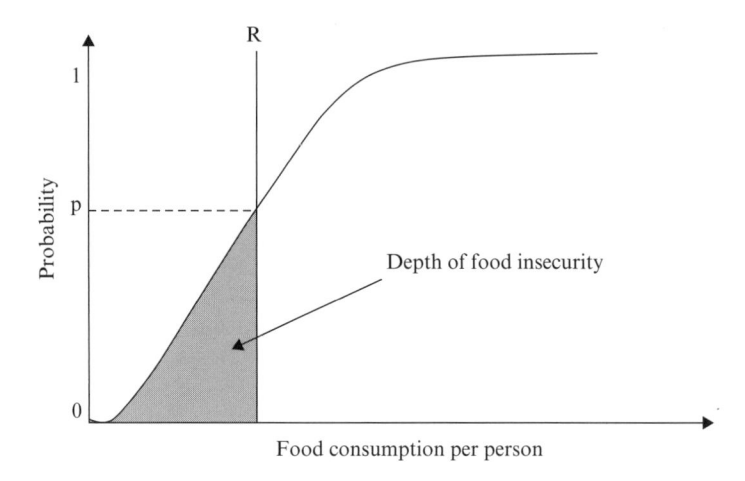

Figure 14.3   Expected food intake for a household: cumulative distribution function (CDF)

We can measure not just the probability that consumption will be inadequate, but also the expected magnitude of the inadequacy. The area under the curve, shown by the shaded area, represents the expected (probability-weighted) gap between the amount of food required, R, and the amount that will actually be available. For the better off, this expected gap may negligible, but this is far from the case for poor households. Conceptually, this gap measure provides a better indicator of the magnitude of food insecurity than just p, the probability of food insecurity. Measuring it empirically is another matter.

At the national level, Figure 14.4 now draws upon the above concepts to show a cumulative distribution function of expected food consumption per person. The population of size N is ordered from lowest food consumption per person (left hand side of the horizontal axis) to the highest (right hand side). If food requirement per person is again

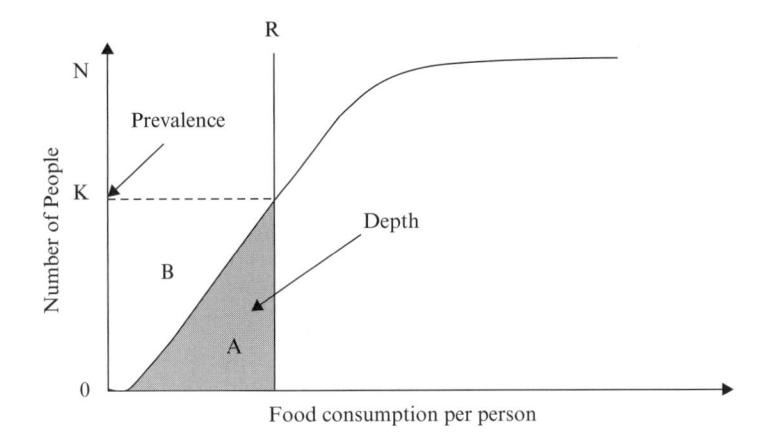

Figure 14.4   Expected food insecurity for the nation: cumulative distribution function (CDF)

R, the number of persons with intake less than or equal to R, the *prevalence of food insecurity*, is given by K. The proportion of the population whose intake is expected to be inadequate is therefore K/N. The total amount of food that would need to be consumed by these K persons for their intake to be adequate is given by the rectangle KR. Their actual consumption is the area B. Area A is therefore a measure of the degree to which actual consumption falls below the requirement. It indicates the *depth of food insecurity*, or alternatively the magnitude of the food security gap. A measure of the depth of food insecurity that might be compared across countries is its magnitude relative to either total consumption or the total consumption that would occur if all persons consumed exactly R, given by RN.

The concept of food security that makes most sense relates to forward-looking expectations of what food intake may be in the future, both at the individual and national levels. But these expectations are not readily observed empirically. Data about current levels of food intake are useful as indicators of what these expectations may be.

14.2.5   Empirical Estimates of Food Security

Several measures of food security are available, all based at the national level. The International Food Policy Research Institute (IFPRI) publishes a Global Hunger Index (GHI) and various Food Security Vulnerability Indices (FCVI). The Economist Intelligence Unit in association with Dupont publishes a Food Security Index (FSI). In addition the Food and Agriculture Organization (FAO) of the United Nations, in association with the World Bank publishes a widely used Food Price Index (FPI).

It is important that the calculation of the FPI uses as commodity weights the values of *international trade* in the commodities concerned, rather than *global consumption*. This means that commodities such as sugar, that are highly traded, receive high weights relative to commodities such as rice, where international trade is small, even though rice is a much more important commodity in terms of global consumption. This has been important in interpreting recent price surges because sugar prices have been increasing dramatically, but not those of staples such as rice. The FPI has increased as a result of the sugar price increases, reflecting their large weight in the index, but staple food prices were much more stable, a fact not reflected in the behavior of the index. While the spikes in the level of the FPI in 2007–08 did indeed reflect increased prices of staples, more recent price surges did not.

Considerable progress in the quantification of food security was made in a recent joint report of the FAO, the International Fund for Agricultural Development (IFAD) and the World Food Program (WFP), *The State of Food Insecurity in the World, 2012* (FAO/IFAD/WFP, 2012). The report presents improved estimates, for most countries of the world, of average availability of dietary energy supplies and average protein supplies. It also provides data on access to food, measured as physical access in the form of paved roads relative to total roads, road density and the density of rail lines, and economic access in the form of food prices, though these prices are not related in the report to incomes, as is done in measures of poverty incidence. The report contains important information on nutritional outcomes, including the prevalence of undernourishment and the 'depth of the food deficit', corresponding closely to the concepts discussed in relation to Figure 14.4, above.

Over the two decades from 1990–02 to 2010–02 the total number of undernourished people in the world declined from 1 billion to 868 million and the number in the Asia-Pacific region declined from 739 to 563 million. Figure 14.5 and Table 14.1 summarize these newly available data. While in 2010–12 the proportion of the population that was undernourished was lower in the Asia-Pacific region than in sub-Saharan Africa (at 26.8 percent), the population of Asia and the Pacific was so much larger that the absolute number of undernourished people in Asia and the Pacific was still more than double (at 563 million) the number in sub-Saharan Africa (at 234 million). In South Asia alone the number of undernourished people (327 million) exceeds the total number in sub-Saharan Africa.

The most striking feature of the data is the variation in the rates at which undernourishment has declined in different parts of the world. In Asia as a whole the rate of decline far exceeds the global rate. In sub-Saharan Africa the absolute number of undernourished people increased over these two decades by 38 percent, but within Asia the total declined by 24 percent. The rate of improvement also varied widely within Asia. In Southeast Asia the absolute number of undernourished people declined by more than 50 percent and East Asia was not far behind, at 36 percent. But the rate of decline was much lower in South Asia, at 7 percent. There may be many reasons for the variation but the differences seemingly correlate with differences in rates of poverty reduction, themselves correlating with differences in rates of economic growth.

The relationship between undernourishment and poverty incidence is explored further in Figure 14.6. For the developing countries as a whole, progress towards achieving the Millennium Development Goal target of halving by 2015 the 1990 rate of undernourishment is slightly behind schedule (shown by the dashed line), whereas for Asia and the Pacific as a whole the target has already been reached. The chart suggests that movements in undernourishment and poverty incidence are correlated, but that the relationship is far from a perfect one-to-one connection.

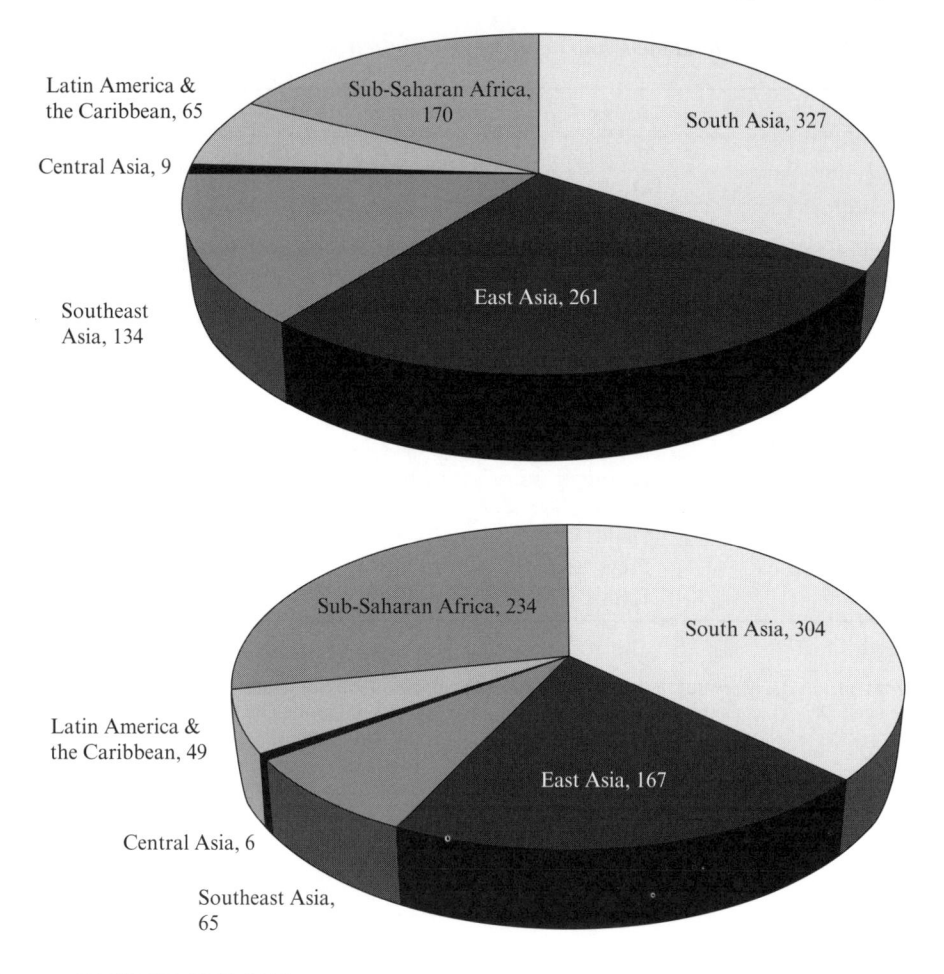

Source: FAO/IFAD/WFP (2012).

Figure 14.5 Numbers of undernourished people, 1990–92 and 2010–12

14.3 ENHANCING FOOD SECURITY THROUGH PRODUCTIVITY IMPROVEMENT

What caused the long-term decline in real food prices shown in Figure 14.1? The main answer is clear: improvements in farm-level productivity, combined with post-harvest productivity gains (Alston et al., 2010). Both agricultural productivity and post-harvest productivity are discussed in this section.

14.3.1 Raising Agricultural Productivity

Agricultural productivity determines the cost of producing food at the farm level. Sombilla et al. (2012) study the long-term rates and determinants of productivity growth

Table 14.1 Undernourishment and depth of food deficit

Region		1990–92	2000–02	2010–12
World	Prevalence	18.6	14.9	12.5
	Depth	130	106	94
Asia	Prevalence	23.7	17.6	13.9
	Depth	165	125	104
Central Asia	Prevalence	12.8	14.5	7.4
	Depth	NA	98	51
East Asia	Prevalence	20.8	14.3	11.5
	Depth	151	98	77
South Asia	Prevalence	26.8	21.3	17.6
	Depth	175	150	127
South East Asia	Prevalence	29.6	19.2	10.9
	Depth	214	132	77
Oceania	Prevalence	13.6	15.9	12.1
	Depth	82	98	74
Sub-Saharan Africa	Prevalence	32.8	29.7	26.8
	Depth	235	219	205

Notes:
Prevalence means the percentage of the population with caloric intake less than the minimum daily requirement. *Depth* means the mean difference between intake and minimum daily caloric requirement, in kcal per person per day, among those whose intake is below the minimum daily requirement.

Source: Data from FAO *Food Security Indicators*, 2012.

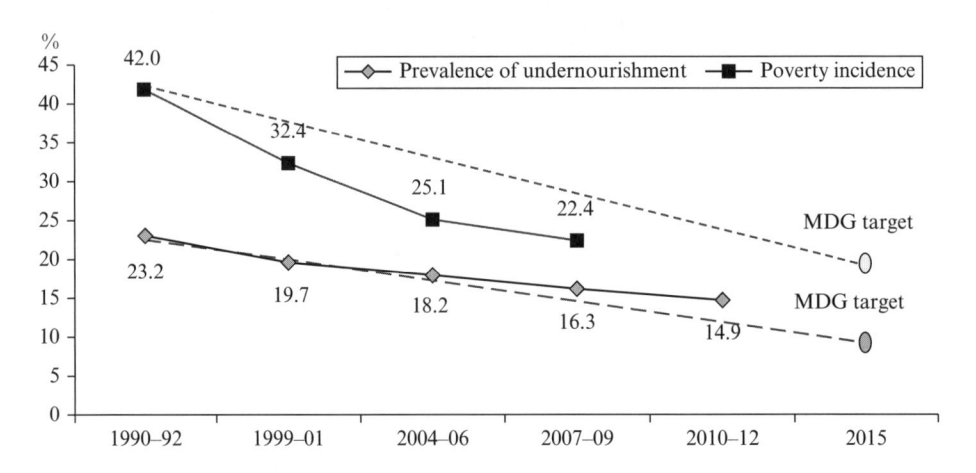

Note: Poverty incidence data are not yet available for 2010–12.

Source: Data from FAO *Food Security Indicators*, 2012 and World Bank, PovcalNet database (http://iresearch.worldbank.org/PovcalNet/index.htm).

Figure 14.6 Undernourishment and poverty in the developing countries

in Asian agriculture. Their study focuses on rice and wheat, which together account for half of total caloric intake in Asia (rice, 34 percent; wheat, 16 percent). Their data show that within Asia as a whole, expansion of the area planted to rice and wheat (allowing for multiple cropping) has declined since the 1960s from about 1.4 percent per annum to zero in the decade 2000–10. Yield growth also declined over the same period from about 5 percent per annum (wheat) and 3 percent (rice) to 1 percent for both crops. Production growth for both crops is therefore currently 1 percent per annum, and declining, barely keeping pace with population growth.

Sombilla et al. (2012) present preliminary evidence on rates of total factor productivity growth (TFPG) that are more encouraging. Their data run from the decade of the 1980s to the decade of the 2000s. In the case of rice, these data show that TFPG increased in the Asia-Pacific region as a whole from 1.27 percent per annum (1980s) to 2.7 percent (2000s). According to these results, TFPG in rice production in the decade of the 2000s was 2.22 percent per annum in East Asia, 3.52 percent in south Asia and 3.1 percent in Southeast Asia. Combining this with the information on declining yield growth, the productivity of factors of production other than land must have been increasing rapidly, more rapidly than the reported rate of TFPG, which is a cost-share weighted average of the growth rates of productivity of the individual factors. This must mean, in particular, that labor productivity was increased by mechanization. In the case of wheat the data indicate a moderate decline in TFPG from 4.94 percent per annum (1980s) to 3.15 percent (2000s).

Constraints on sustaining the growth of productivity include the exhaustion of the potential of the Green Revolution technology, the problem of maintaining soil health in the presence of multiple cropping and the threats posed by new strains of pests and diseases, some with resistance to existing chemical methods of control. Soil erosion and salinization, water pollution and excessive water withdrawal from underground sources also threaten continued TFPG at the rates measured. Small farm sizes are a constraint to raising productivity through mechanization, despite the emergence of machinery rental markets in some areas.

Tenure arrangements affect rights to land and this in turn affects incentives of farmers to invest in productivity-enhancing improvements. Improvements in legal rights to land have not been rapid enough in many Asian countries. Credit markets remain insufficiently developed, partly as a result of ill-defined rights to land, limiting its capacity to serve as collateral. Public investment in infrastructure, especially roads, reduces transport costs and thus simultaneously raises prices received from sale of output and reduces prices paid for purchased inputs, again raising incentives for farmers to invest in productivity enhancement (Menon and Warr, 2008).

By far the most important constraint on productivity improvement is the supply of knowledge, determined by investment in research and extension. This is taken up the following section, drawing upon evidence for Indonesia.

14.3.2 Does Agricultural Research Contribute to Productivity Growth?

Growth of total factor productivity (TFPG) has contributed significantly to output growth in Asian agriculture. There has apparently been a TFPG slowdown in recent years, especially for Asian countries other than China. Refocusing attention on what determines

TFPG in agriculture is thus important for understanding and sustaining long-term agricultural growth and thereby maintaining its contribution to reduction of real food prices.

This section looks at these issues within the context of Indonesia. It examines the extent to which agricultural research within Indonesia contributes to the enhancement of productivity growth, while controlling for other possible determinants of agricultural productivity growth, including international agricultural research, infrastructure investments, extension, weather changes and epidemics. The data used relate to the years 1974–2006. The results show that the expenditure on agricultural research had a significant effect on total factor productivity in Indonesian agriculture. The impact elasticity (percent change in total factor productivity from a 1 percent increase in research expenditure) is estimated at 0.0774.

Based on these econometric results a projection is made of the impact on total factor productivity within Indonesian agriculture of a 1 billion Rupiah increase in agricultural research occurring in the year 1975. The impact that this expenditure change has on the value of Indonesian agricultural output is estimated from the analysis, extending over the three decades following the initial investment. The results are depicted in Figure 14.7 below. The figure shows the initial investment cost of 1 billion Rupiah and the value of the subsequent stream of additional output that this investment makes possible, all measured at constant prices. From this it is possible to estimate the real rate of return (at constant prices) from a marginal increase in investment in Indonesian agricultural research. The estimated annual real rate of return is 27 percent, well above rates normally required for public investments. It is concluded that Indonesia has vastly under-invested in this form of public expenditure and an increase is warranted. If means could be found to raise the efficiency of publicly funded agricultural research this would further enhance the case for increased public investment.

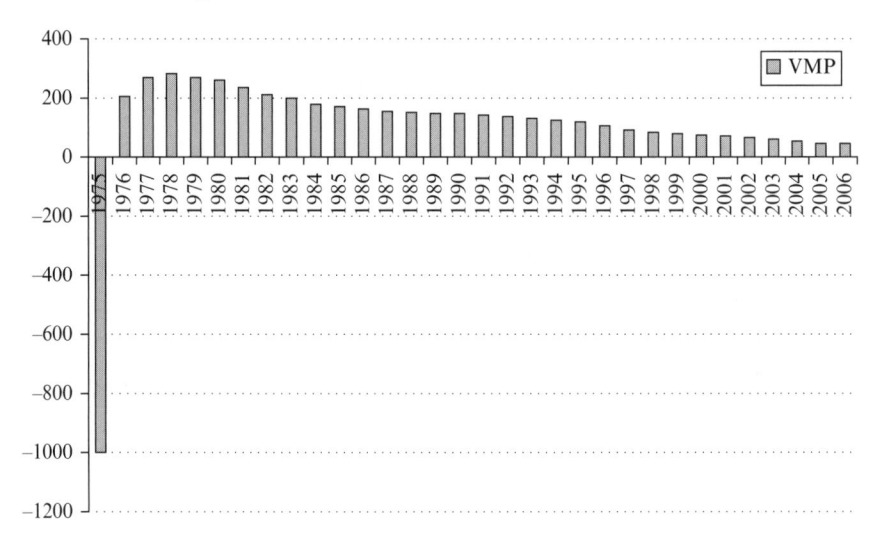

Source: Author's calculations.

Figure 14.7 Estimated stream of effects, 1 billion Rupiah investment in agricultural research in 1975 (millions of Indonesian Rupiah, constant 1975 prices)

14.3.3 Declining Research and Extension Expenditures

In several countries, public investment in agricultural productivity has declined markedly. This is shown in the case of Thailand, in Figure 14.8 below. The figure shows research and extension intensities, which means expenditure on research and extension, respectively, expressed as a ratio of the level of crops' contribution to GDP, or the level of value-added generated in crop agriculture.

The decline since 2001 is especially notable. A significant policy story lies behind these data. Since 2001, successive Thai governments have not neglected rural people but have instead sought to benefit them, and win their electoral support, through transfers of public revenue that benefit rural people in the short-term rather than through investments in agricultural productivity that benefit rural people in the long-term.

The flow of new agricultural technologies emerging from the CGIAR agricultural research system has slowed. Renewed international commitment is urgently required. Investment is also needed in agricultural research within the developing countries themselves and in training the next generation of agricultural researchers, needed to maintain the momentum of productivity growth in agriculture over the coming decades. The kind of research that is most needed is adaptive, taking the outputs of the international research establishments and modifying them to suit local circumstances. While fundamental agricultural research involves long lags before it produces benefits in the form of enhanced productivity, the adaptive research needed in developing countries pays off much more quickly. But commitment to it has declined alarmingly in many countries.

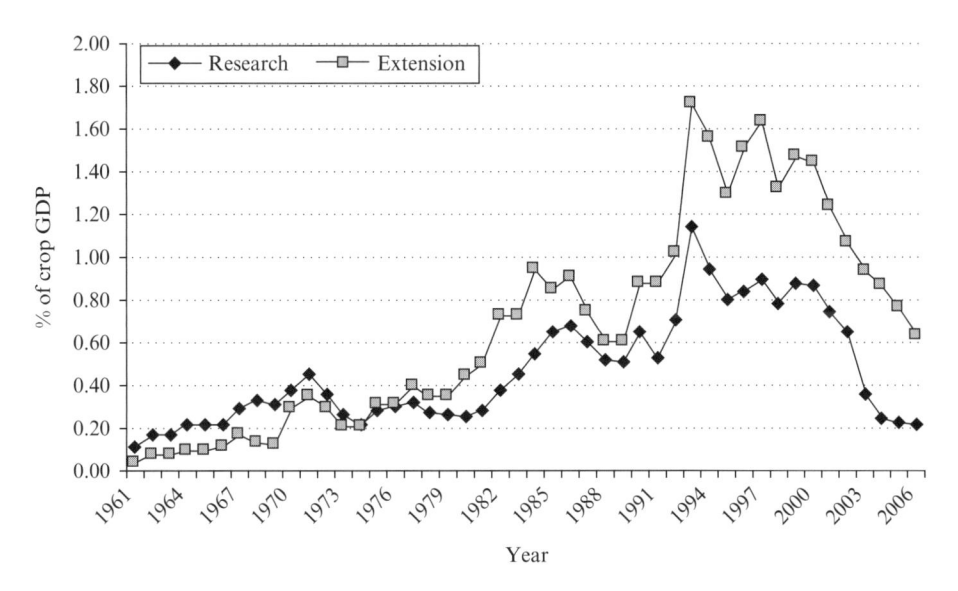

Source: Public research and extension budget from the Bureau of the Budget and agricultural GDP from the National Economic and Social Development Board, Bangkok.

Figure 14.8 *Research and extension intensities in crops in Thailand, 1961 to 2006*

14.3.4 Raising Post-harvest Productivity

Although international trade has an important role to play in the enhancement of food security, domestic trade is far more important. For example, in the extreme case of rice, only 2 percent of Asia's total consumption is traded internationally. The economic shape of the other 98 percent is changing rapidly, especially in the way food is marketed. Reardon et al. (2012) point out that a transformation is occurring in all three segments of the overall food value chain: upstream (farming and input supply), midstream (processing and wholesale) and downstream (retail). As a rough average, about half of the final price of food to the Asian consumer is estimated to arise at the farm level and the other half is accounted for by post-farm costs. Of course, these proportions vary considerably across localities and across commodities. The important point is that productivity is relevant at both farm and off-farm levels. Both affect food security by driving access to food because they determine the cost of food to the final consumer. Off-farm productivity is approximately as important for food security as farm level productivity, but receives far less attention.

Overall, the food supply chain revolution is capable of delivering benefits to both farmers and consumers, by lowering off-farm costs. The process is driven primarily by the private sector, but public policy has an important role to play. First, monopolistic practices must be prevented, through the maintenance of competition. Reduction of barriers to entry of new firms is an effective means of preventing the development of exploitative monopolies. Second, much of the private sector activity is dependent on the provision of public infrastructure. Reliable electricity supplies are necessary for cold storage. Road construction and maintenance opens new farming areas to possible participation in the supply chain revolution by reducing transport costs. Liberalization of foreign direct investment (FDI) restrictions facilitates the development of cost-efficient supermarkets and processing facilities.

14.3.5 Adapting to Climate Change

The 2007 report of the IPCC projects rising temperatures throughout the twenty-first century. The range of projected temperature increases is wide, reflecting scientific uncertainty and the dependence of the outcome on future human decisions. Nelson et al. (2009), Rosegrant et al. (2010), Knox et al. (2011) and several other studies, present evidence that Asian crop yields will decline, despite the beneficial plant growth effects of an increase in carbon dioxide concentration in the atmosphere. In South Asia, for example, the effect is projected as a substantial reduction in crop production by the end of the century. The effect will be larger on wheat yields than on rice yields, but rice yields are also projected to decline. Water run-off from upstream glacial sources will increase, but this will occur primarily during the monsoonal season, rather than the dry season, when the water is required. The effect will be increased risk of flooding. Overall, the climate is likely to become more volatile and less readily predictable. These worrying effects are superimposed on increasing demand for land from non-agricultural sources and the effects of land degradation.

Rosegrant (2012) reports the results of biophysical crop modeling studies that provide quantitative estimates of yield effects of expected climate change by 2050, compared with a no-change scenario. For irrigated rice the effect is a reduction of 14 to 20 percent, for irrigated wheat 32 to 44 percent, irrigated maize 2 to 4 percent, irrigated soybean 9 to 18 percent. The spread in expected yield effects is wider for rainfed crops, with the possibility of some positive effects, especially in more temperate regions. In Pacific island countries, significant yield reductions are expected in traditional staple crops, including sweet potato, taro and cassava.

Combining these results with economic modeling, Rosegrant projects an increase in food prices of about 20–70 percent by 2050. Compared with the no-change scenario, these price increases imply an average reduction in caloric intake in Asia of 13–15 percent. Childhood malnutrition levels, which are directly linked to caloric intake, are projected to increase from the 65 million in 2050, projected under the no-change scenario, to around 75 million with projected rates of climate change. Rosegrant concludes that aggressive investments in agricultural research, rural roads and irrigation facilities could eliminate about three fourths of the increase in childhood malnutrition that climate change will otherwise produce.

Timmer (2012) emphasizes that the effects of climate change will be highly variable, but may be largest in tropical and equatorial regions, with some increases in productivity in temperate regions. The effects are likely to include a net global loss of agricultural land, changing crop suitability, increased frequency of natural disasters, and greater temporal and geographic variance in production. Given the geographical heterogeneity of expected effects and the scientific uncertainty surrounding them, Timmer emphasizes the importance of flexibility in the policy adaptation to climate change.

14.4 ENHANCING FOOD SECURITY THROUGH INTERNATIONAL TRADE

International trade plays an important role in promoting the food security of importing countries and, through earnings of foreign exchange, in promoting the economic development of exporting countries. But international markets can also be sources of instability in access to food, provoking policy responses that can accentuate the very volatility of international prices that motivated these interventions. How can the volatility of international food prices be reduced?

In the absence of international trade, the costs of producing food would differ between countries. In those countries where food production costs are lower, international trade encourages expanded food production. In countries where food production costs are higher, production shifts away from food and towards other commodities. The former countries become exporters of food and the latter importers. The result is a global lowering of the costs of delivering food. But as the events of 2007–08 illustrate, these gains carry with them a vulnerability to short-term international price increases.

The international food price increases of 2007–08 had significant effects on the way food security is perceived. In Asia, the overwhelmingly important staple is rice, although wheat is also important in some areas, especially in parts of South Asia. The thinness of the international rice market exacerbates its volatility and limits the capacity of the international market to buffer the effects of periodic disruptions to supply in individual countries (Gilbert, 2011).

370 *Handbook on food*

Unfortunately, the responses of individual countries to fluctuations in food prices have in some cases accentuated the volatility of the international market. When the international price of rice increased in 2007–08 both exporting and importing countries attempted to shield their domestic consumers from the high international prices. Some exporters restricted the quantities that could be exported and some importers reduced tariffs and increased public sector purchases. Although the aim in both cases was to stabilize domestic prices Martin and Anderson (2011) have shown that the effects were at least partly offsetting. Both sets of policies reduced domestic prices relative to international prices but they had reinforcing effects on the international price itself – raising it well above the level it would have reached in the absence of these protectionist responses. For the international rice market to play its important stabilizing role, means must be found to discourage these beggar-thy-neighbor protectionist responses.

The discussion that follows focuses on the role of stocks. Price spikes tend to occur when the level of stocks is unusually low. The discussion asks whether action to raise the level of stocks could play a constructive role in stabilizing international food prices. Following Galtier (2012), Figures 14.9, 14.10 and 14.11 combine information on the international prices of rice, wheat and maize since 1960 with data on stocks for these three commodities, respectively. A striking point emerges. Consider the periods when prices spiked for each of these three commodities. These periods are marked with circles. There were three such periods for rice and five each for wheat and maize. Now consider the periods when stocks were lowest. They coincide. Prices spiked when stocks were lowest and only then.

The level of private stocks is determined by the business decisions of people who hold these stocks for the purpose of making profits (Williams and Wright, 1991; Wright,

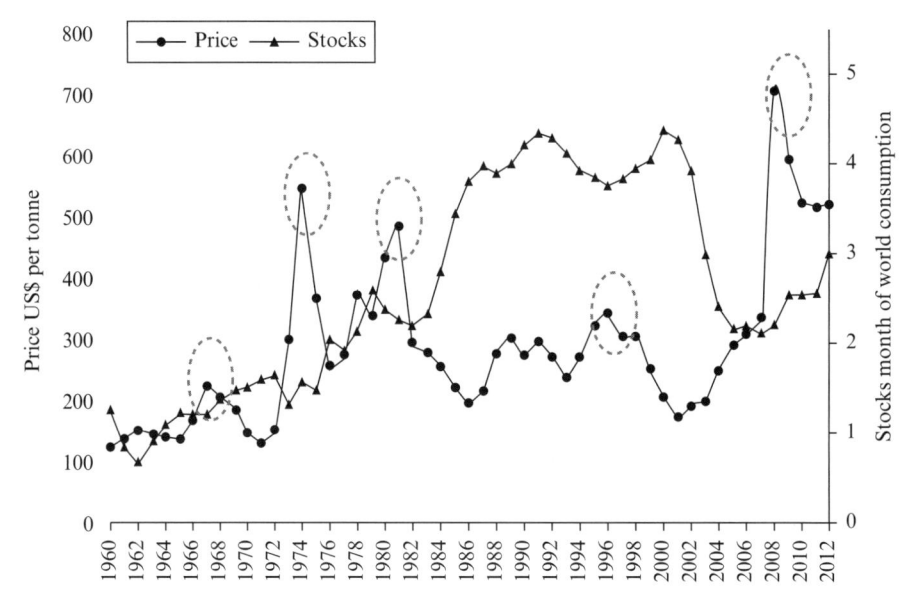

Source: Stocks, US Dept of Agriculture; prices, International Monetary Fund.

Figure 14.9 Rice: international prices and stocks, 1960 to 2008

Enhancing food security 371

Source: Stocks, US Dept of Agriculture; prices, International Monetary Fund.

Figure 14.10   Wheat: international prices and stocks, 1960 to 2008

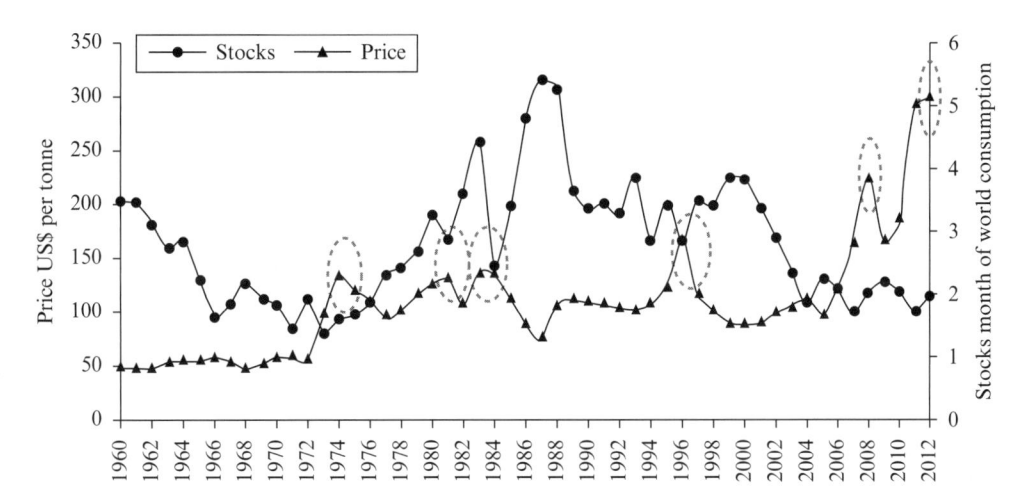

Source: Stocks, US Dept of Agriculture; prices, International Monetary Fund.

Figure 14.11   Maize: international prices and stocks, 1960 to 2008

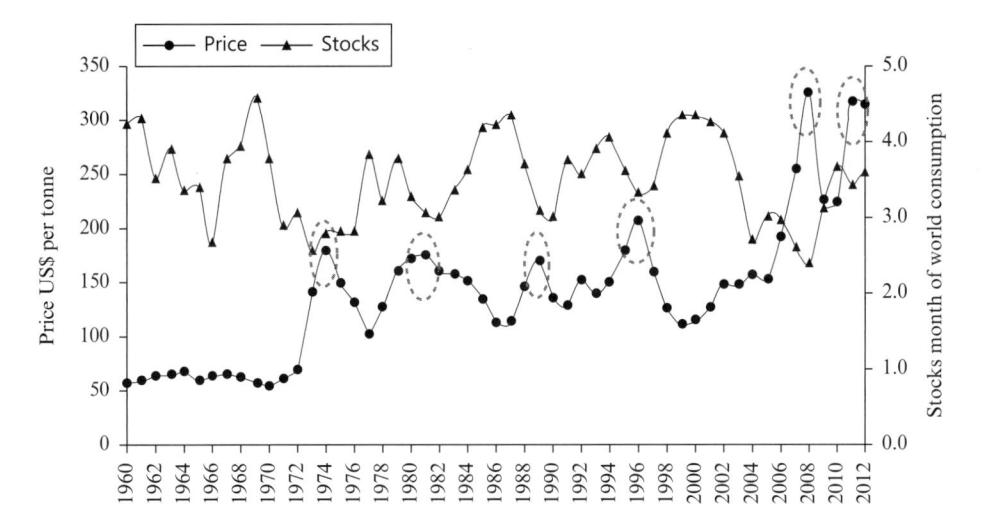

2011). But at times the level of stocks that emerges from this market-driven process is too low, from a social standpoint, because it increases the likelihood of price spikes that have harmful consequences. That is, there is a market failure in relation to the level of privately held stocks. The harmful consequences are not only that poor people suffer from food insecurity induced by the spike in prices. But the responses of individual national governments can magnify the problem. This can happen in both exporting and importing countries.

It can be rational for individual exporting countries to introduce export bans in these circumstances. This is exactly what happened during the 2007–08 crisis, when Russia introduced export bans on wheat and India and Vietnam did the same for rice. These export bans were motivated by the desire to protect domestic consumers from high international prices. Although there was a great deal of international criticism of these decisions, the reasoning behind the introduction of the bans is easily recognized and rational. Governments must protect their own consumers. But the bans themselves exacerbated the international price instability. It has been estimated (Headey, 2011) that export bans were responsible for almost half of the international price increase of rice.

The response of some importing countries also contributed to the price increase. Fearful of being unable to obtain the rice that was needed for domestic consumption the Philippines (then the world's largest importer of rice) sharply *increased* its demand for imported rice, for the purpose of replenishing the level of stocks held by the government's food agency, the National Food Administration. This further exacerbated the international price increases. Headey (2011) estimates that between them, the export bans and the panic buying by some importers almost fully explains the price increase for rice.

The point is that these government responses were not necessarily irrational from their own national points of view. But their global effect is to magnify the volatility of the international food prices concerned. Is it possible for public action to address this market failure?

14.4.1 Option 1: An Internationally Agreed Prohibition of Export Bans

Export bans are legal under existing WTO agreements. The proposal to introduce WTO prohibitions on export bans for food has been discussed at the G20 level and it is possible that some progress could be made on this proposal. These steps may be desirable, but it is not apparent that WTO action could be effective. If international prices spike, the very survival of governments can be at stake if they allow these prices to be transmitted to domestic markets. Will governments risk the loss of office because of the existence of WTO rules prohibiting them from insulating their own domestic markets? It is not clear that the proposal could be enforced in the presence of international price spikes. Furthermore, this proposal does nothing to prevent panic import buying. It is not clear that WTO action can solve the problem.

14.4.2 Option 2: International Cooperation to Stabilize Prices

Is it possible for international institutions to stabilize prices, to prevent these bubbles from occurring in the first instance? If prices were maintained within internationally agreed bands there would be no need for exporting countries to ban exports or for importing countries to engage in emergency buying. That is, food price panics could be averted.

Unfortunately, the history of International Commodity Agreements (ICAs), directed to just this objective, is sobering. Examples include agreements to stabilize the international prices of cocoa, natural rubber, coffee and sugar. They all collapsed. The central problem is that the institutions concerned have tended to become dominated by producer interests who see them as a means to *support* prices, by raising their mean levels, rather than just a means to *stabilize* prices, by reducing their variance. The result was over-production. High international prices could be maintained only by purchasing huge quantities of the commodity concerned, which was then stored at great cost. As this process continued, excessive amounts of money were eventually needed to purchase the huge stocks required for continued price support. When the funding became insufficient, the scheme collapsed. For international stabilization to work, the tendency to support prices, rather than simply to stabilize them, would have to be resisted.

There is a further problem. For panic responses to be averted (exporters and importers), governments must be able to trust the governance of the price-stabilizing institutions. Is this possible? The prospect for success could be greatest at the regional level, focusing only on regionally important commodities. For the Asia-Pacific region, this means rice. Southeast Asia contains both the world's largest importers or rice (the Philippines and Indonesia) and the largest exporters (Thailand and Vietnam). Their interests diverge. Would regional management of a rice price stabilization scheme be capable of avoiding the fate of ICAs elsewhere? The proposal is worthy of close study, but the cost of failure would be high and caution is essential.

14.4.3 Option 3: Higher Levels of Stocks Maintained by Individual Governments

When the government owns the stocks itself, there is no need to trust international agreements. The proposal is therefore that governments maintain stocks for emergency purposes. These would be released only in a transparent, pre-announced manner and only when prices are unusually high. This is a costly activity. Private storage of rice is generally done only between seasons within the year. Storage from one year to the next is costly and significant deterioration occurs after about two years.

Moreover, it must be recognized that domestic price stabilization can be achieved only in the presence of trade restrictions that prevent transmission of international prices to the domestic market. Suppose international prices of rice surge, as they did in 2007. An importing country might release stocks of rice onto to the domestic market to force the domestic price to levels below the international price, but this would be effective only if exports were prohibited. Otherwise, it would be profitable for private agents to buy rice domestically at the now lower domestic price and sell it internationally at the higher price. Similarly, an exporting country would need to restrict exports to stabilize domestic prices. But this is exactly the policy action that a WTO ban on export restrictions (Option 1 above) would prohibit.

14.4.4 Option 4: No Intervention in Domestic Prices Combined with Cash or In-kind Transfers

Because of the computerization of transfer systems using the bank accounts of potential recipients, it is now possible to make cash transfers in a targeted manner. Further progress can be expected. When the international price surges, emergency relief could be provided to the poorest consumers (at least, those with bank accounts) in this manner.[1] But does this resolve the political problem of the government concerned? Suppose that when the international price increases the poorest consumers are indeed protected in this manner. What about the urban middle class? They must bear the cost of both the higher

374 *Handbook on food*

international prices and the fiscal burden of insulating the poor from the price increases. But the urban middle class is perhaps the group most feared by governments. While this option has much to recommend it, for the majority of the population the basic problem of food insecurity is left unresolved.

14.5 ENHANCING FOOD SECURITY THROUGH POVERTY REDUCTION

The second of the three drivers of food security is poverty reduction. The concepts of food (in)security and poverty incidence are closely related, but differ in some important respects. First, poverty incidence refers to the adequacy of otherwise of consumption of a wide range of goods, of which food is the paramount example, but not the only one. Studies determining 'poverty lines' – the levels of expenditure per person below which an individual or household is deemed to be poor – focus in particular on the level of total expenditure that coincides with dietary adequacy. Still, the fact that food is only one component of the goods and services making up the poverty line means that it is possible in principle for a poor person to be food secure and for a non-poor person to be food insecure.

A second, and more subtle, difference is that poverty incidence refers to the circumstances observable in the present. At the time the household is surveyed, consumption levels of food and other essential goods either are or are not adequate. If they are not, the household is deemed to be poor. But as argued above, food security refers more particularly to expectations about the future than to the circumstances of today. Individuals or households may judge themselves to be food insecure to some degree, even if their present level of food consumption is sufficient. 'Vulnerability to poverty' is conceptually closer to food insecurity than 'poverty incidence'. But vulnerability to poverty is a statistical concept, based on objective circumstances observable in the present, whereas food security is inherently more subjective, because it involves expectations about the future.

Despite these differences, the concepts of food insecurity and poverty are closely related, and undoubtedly very highly correlated. Food security is overwhelmingly an issue of purchasing power. Poor people are the most likely to be hungry. Measures that reduce poverty are likely to improve food security and vice versa. The rich do not go hungry in any country, except during wars, politically caused famines or natural disasters. Even then, the poor suffer more. Hunger is mainly due to poverty. This general conclusion requires qualification. Despite the empirical and theoretical presumption that poverty reduction generally leads to improved nutrition, exceptions have been identified.

14.5.1 A Counter-example From India?

Between 2004–05 and 2009–10, a period of rapid economic growth in India, measured poverty incidence declined rapidly, but average caloric intake apparently declined. These observations seemingly depart from the generalization that poverty reduction leads to improved nutrition. Data on other nutritional indicators are not yet available for 2009–10, so it is not yet known whether other relevant indicators, including

Table 14.2   Poverty reduction and reduced caloric intake, India, 2004–05 to 2009–10

	Poverty incidence (headcount measure)		Average caloric intake (Calories per day)	
	Rural	Urban	Rural	Urban
2004–05	41.8	25.7	2047	2020
2009–10	33.8	20.9	2020	1946

Source: Himanshu (2012), based on data from National Statistical Organisation, Government of India, *National Statistical Survey.*

protein intake, also deteriorated. Himanshu (2012) reviews the evidence, summarised in Table 14.2, above, and discusses some possible explanations for this apparent paradox.

No single explanation has yet gained wide acceptance. Patnaik (2010) and Gaiha et al. (2010) point to possible explanations arising from deficiencies in the available data. Lower demand for calories may have been caused by declining real income levels caused by rising food prices, where the rising prices were not properly measured by the methods used in constructing the poverty line. Since 2005 the statistical basis for measuring poverty in India has changed from the previous Lakdawala method, developed in 1993, to the Tendulkar method, based on a review of poverty measurement in India completed in 2005. A major component of these changes relates to the measurement the poverty line, particularly the replacement of consumer price indices, based on market prices, with unit value indices, extracted directly from the consumer expenditure surveys used to measure household expenditures. This change occurred during a period in which consumer prices were rising. If the rate of food price inflation was understated by the use of unit value indices the increase in the nominal value of the poverty line would be understated and the rate of poverty reduction would be overstated, possibly resolving the paradox.

Use of unit value indices in place of market prices can provide a misleading indicator of changes in the cost of living. Suppose food prices are rising relative to other prices, as in this period in India. Poor consumers may respond by switching to lower quality, lower priced caloric sources. The use of unit values may wrongly record this switch as a decline in the price, or at least a smaller increase than the true increase in the price of food of a given quality. The rate of increase of the poverty line will then be lower than the true increase in the cost of living, meaning that the rate of poverty reduction will be overstated.

A second set of issues relates to the way India's system of public distribution of subsidized food is allowed for in the measurement of both poverty incidence and caloric consumption. Much of the statistical discussion in India has focused on this set of issues. Because use of the public distribution system has expanded over time, it is possible that imperfect allowance for its nutritional impact may have contributed to the apparent paradox of declining poverty incidence together with the absence of improved nutrition, at least among some groups.

A more worrying explanation is also possible, one that does not treat these findings for

India as statistical anomalies. Periods of rapid growth often lead simultaneously to both reductions in poverty incidence and increased inequality. This was apparently especially true of this recent period of rapid growth in India. The headcount measure of poverty incidence declines over time when the number of households whose real expenditures move from below to above the poverty line exceeds the number moving in the opposite direction. That is, it depends only on changes occurring in the neighborhood of the poverty line. This says nothing about what happens to the very poor (who remain below the poverty line) or the non-poor (who remain above it).

As shown by Deaton and Drèze (2009), among higher income groups in India the expenditure elasticity of demand for calories tends to be negative. That is, as their total expenditures rise their diets may improve, including higher intake of protein, partly from animal sources, but total caloric intake declines, due to a dietary switch away from staple foods. This partly reflects a change in the physical requirements of work and other dimensions of improved living standards. Among lower income groups, especially those with expenditures below the poverty line, this is not the case. As their incomes rise, their average caloric intake also rises, and vice versa; as their incomes decline, their average caloric intake declines.

Now suppose that increased inequality meant that higher real expenditures were enjoyed primarily by better-off income groups, who remain above the poverty line, with some gain to those in the neighborhood of the poverty line, causing the observed reduction in the headcount measure of poverty. But there may have been little or no gain in real expenditures among the poorest groups, who remained below the poverty line. There could even have been a reduction in the real expenditures of households well below the poverty line because their money incomes failed to keep pace with the rapid increase in food prices that occurred during this period. The reduction in the average caloric intake of the better-off, combined with little if any increase in the caloric intake of the poorest groups, could be sufficient to cause the observed reduction in the average caloric intake of the whole population. This could occur even though the average caloric intake of households in the neighborhood of the poverty line increased. That is, the finding of reduced poverty incidence coexisting with reduced average caloric intake may reflect an increase in inequality, especially among the poor.

14.6 ENHANCING FOOD SECURITY THROUGH SOCIAL FOOD SAFETY NETS

The efficiencies and dynamism that accompany market processes are demonstrated sources of economic progress. But impersonal markets leave some segments of the population outside the set of beneficiaries. This is especially true in an environment of highly unequal asset ownership and capacity to participate in the market economy. Social safety nets are mechanisms to assist people in need. Access to food is necessarily a central focus. Recent increases in the volatility of food prices make these schemes even more critical for the avoidance of unnecessary suffering. Most Asian countries employ safety nets of some kind, intended to shield poor and vulnerable groups from severe deprivation. But their effectiveness depends on their capacity to target the poor and in this respect existing schemes have major deficiencies.

As a percentage of GDP social protection expenditures vary among Asian developing countries from 1.3 (Lao PDR), 1.9 (Indonesia), 2.2 (Philippines), 4 (India) 5.3 (Bangladesh) and 9.8 (Mongolia). In 10 out of 32 Asian countries the share is 2 percent or less. On average, poorer countries allocate lower proportions of GDP to social protection expenditures. In the United States the share is 9 percent, in Japan 16 percent and in the European Union it is 19 percent.

Jha et al. (2012) review existing social safety net schemes in four of the above countries: Bangladesh, India, Indonesia and the Philippines. The major categories of safety net programs are consumer food price subsidies, food-for-work progams, feeding programs and cash transfers. The authors find major problems in existing targeting systems. Within the subsidized food programs, which exist in all four countries, they describe high rates of both exclusion error (omitting households who qualify for inclusion) and inclusion error (providing assistance to households who do not meet the criteria for inclusion).

In India, the Public Distribution System for subsidized access to grains is said to entail both exclusion and inclusion errors of 70 percent. Similar rates of inclusion error are reported for Indonesia's Raskin (food for the poor) program and the Philippines subsized food program under the National Food Authority, though exclusion errors are somewhat lower at 29 percent (Indonesia) and 52 percent (Philippines).

These data do not necessarily demonstrate that the existing programs are worse than nothing, because some of the benefits do reach the intended beneficiaries. Nevertheless, the wastage and corruption associated with them is a serious concern and raises the question of whether the objectives of the programs could be attained more efficiently in another way. The fiscal stimulus expenditure programs and reduced government revenues that followed the Global Financial Crisis of 2008–09 have reduced the fiscal space available to national governments throughout Asia and increased the urgency of finding better ways of using public money.

The evidence points to regional and ethnic biases in the existing allocation schemes and practical problems in identifying the qualifying households, along with simple corruption. Sale of subsidized grain is apparently widespread, but this is not necessarily a problem if the sellers are the poor recipients of the grain themselves, who sell it to obtain other commodities or food of higher quality. It is a serious problem if the sellers are the public officials charged with distributing the subsidized grain. Overall, the failure of targeting of the existing systems raises the question of whether the programs might not be replaced by something better.

Jha et al. (2012) ask whether a cash transfer system might not be used to replace these in-kind programs altogether. Practicalities aside, political resistance could be expected. There are beneficiaries from the existing corruption and inefficiency, and these beneficiaries can be expected to oppose change. The practical problems are vast, but new technological developments promise the possibility of solutions. The simplest systems use the existing banking and post office systems to distribute cash to targeted groups. A problem arises when these facilities are not readily accessible. Within Africa, mobile phone systems have been used widely for this purpose. Any retail outlet can then be used as a distribution center for cash. Conditionality relating to school attendance and participation in health centers is possible within a cash transfer system and these systems have been well developed in Latin America. New systems of biometric identification and smart cards can be used to reduce fraud and enable the programs to deliver benefits to the target population. Better ways to identify eligible households might be combined with these systems. The existing systems are not working. In the Philippines, half of the households eligible for food subsidies are not receiving them at all.

Indonesia has already demonstrated the possibility of implementing cash transfers to compensate for economic shocks. The world's largest unconditional cash transfer system was introduced in 2008 to compensate Indonesian households for the impact of reductions in petroleum product subsidies. With the assistance of the World Bank, Indonesia was able to develop a system that achieved its objectives in a transparent manner. There is scope to build on that well-documented experience.

Overall, it seems very possible that new information technology can be used to provide social safety net programs more efficiency and with less corruption. It may be possible to dispense altogether with the need to redistribute food in kind, replacing it entirely with cash-based systems. Reducing the corruption associated with social safety nets is important, not only because of the direct fiscal implications, but also because corruption is not invisible. It reduces public support for these programs, at the expense of those who genuinely need them.

14.7 CONCLUSIONS

This chapter has argued that food security is a meaningful and important concept because of the special characteristics of food as a commodity. It is argued that food security is enhanced by three things:

1. *Reductions in the real price of food.* The chapter discusses the role of agricultural productivity enhancement through research and extension and through investments in rural infrastructure. The role of international trade in determining domestic food prices is also discussed, along with means of averting domestic food price spikes due to international price increases.
2. *Reductions in poverty incidence.* Under most circumstances, only the poor suffer from food insecurity. By increasing the real purchasing power of the poor they can be self-insulated against food insecurity.
3. *Establishing effective food social safety nets.* Some groups lie outside the reach of the forces of economic growth and poverty reduction. They require special assistance, especially with regard to food. Emergency food safety nets are also required in case of natural or anthropogenic disasters.

NOTE

1. See the World Food Programme study (Gentilini, 2007) for a critical review of the issues involved.

REFERENCES

Alston, J.M., B.A. Babcock and P.G. Pardey (eds), (2010), *The Shifting Patterns of Agricultural Production and Productivity Worldwide*. Ames, IA: Center for Agricultural and Rural Development, Iowa State University.

Deaton, A. and J. Drèze (2009), Nutrition in India: facts and interpretations. *Economic and Political Weekly*, XLIV(7), 42–65, 14 February.

FAO/IFAD/WFP (2012), *The State of Food Insecurity in the World, 2012*. Rome: FAO/IFAD/WFP.

Gaiha, R., R. Jha and V. Kulkarni (2010), Prices, expenditure and nutrition in India. ASARC Working Paper 2010/15, Australian National University.

Galtier, F. (2012), Export bans and grain price instability on international markets. Paper presented to International Association of Agricultural Economists, Triennial Conference, Foz do Iguazu, Brazil, 18–24 August.

Gentilini, U. (2007), Cash and food transfers: a primer. Occasional Papers No. 18, World Food Programme.

Gilbert, C.L. (2011), Food reserves in developing countries: trade policy options for improved food security. Issues Paper No. 37, International Center for Trade and Sustainable Development, Geneva.

Headey, D. (2011), Was the international food crisis really a crisis? Discussion Paper 01087, International Food Policy Research Institute, Washington DC.

Headey, D. and S. Fan (2008), Anatomy of a crisis: the causes and consequences of surging food prices. *Agricultural Economics*, **39**(3), 375–391.

Himanshu (2012), Poverty and food security in India. Paper presented to Symposium on Food Security in Asia and the Pacific, University of British Columbia, Vancouver, September.

Jha, S., A. Kotwal and B. Ramaswami (2012), The role of social safety nets and food programs. Paper presented to Symposium on Food Security in Asia and the Pacific, University of British Columbia, Vancouver, September.

Knox, J.W. et al. (2011), What are the projected impacts of climate change on food crop productivity in Africa and south Asia? DFID Systematic Review, Final Report, Cranfield University.

Martin, W. and K. Anderson (2011), Export restrictions and price insulation during commodity price booms. *American Journal of Agricultural Economics*, **94**(2), 422–427.

Menon, J. and P. Warr (2008), Rural roads and poverty: a multi-sector, multi-household analysis for Lao PDR. In D.H. Brooks and J. Menon (eds), *Infrastructure and Trade in Asia*. Cheltenham, UK and Northamptom, MA, USA: Edward Elgar, pp. 115–142.

Nelson, G.C. et al. (2009), *Climate Change: Impact on Agriculture and Costs of Adaptation*. Washington DC: International Food Policy Research Institute.

Neufeld, L., J. Chowdhury and M.T. Ruel (2012), Strengthening nutrition within the food security agenda. Paper presented to Symposium on Food Security in Asia and the Pacific, University of British Columbia, Vancouver, September.

Patnaik, U. (2010), A critical look at some propositions on consumption and poverty. *Economic and Political Weekly*, **XLV**(6), 74–80, 6 February.

Reardon T., B. Minten and K. Chen (2012), Rice value chain transformation in India and Bangladesh: survey findings with implications for food security. Paper presented to Symposium on Food Security in Asia and the Pacific, University of British Columbia, Vancouver, September.

Rosegrant, M.W. (2012), Climate change and agriculture in the Asia-Pacific region: impacts and policy responses. Paper presented at Australian Agricultural and Resource Economics Society Annual Conference, Sydney, February 2013.

Rosegrant, M.W., et al (2010), *Food Security, Farming, and Climate Change to 2050*. Washington DC: International Food Policy Research Institute.

Sombilla, M., D. Mapa and S.F. Piza (2012), Overcoming critical constraints to sustaining agricultural productivity growth in Asia and Pacific. Paper presented to Symposium on Food Security in Asia and the Pacific, University of British Columbia, Vancouver, September.

Timmer, C.P. (2008), Causes of high food prices. ADB Economics Working Paper Series, No. 128, Asian Development Bank, Manila.

Timmer, C.P. (2010), Behavioral dimensions of food security. *Proceedings of the National Academy of Sciences (PNAS)*, Agricultural Development and Nutrition Security Special Feature, **109**(31), 12315–12320.

Timmer, C.P. (2012), Coping with climate change: a food policy approach. paper to be presented at Australian Agricultural and Resource Economics Society Annual Conference, Sydney, February 2013.

United States Department of Agriculture, *Guide to Measuring Household Food Security* (revised 2000). Available at: http://www.fns.usda.gov/fsec.files.fsguide.pdf.

Warr, P. (2005), Food policy and poverty in Indonesia: a general equilibrium analysis. *Australian Journal of Agricultural and Resource Economics*, **49**(4), 429–451.

Warr, P. (2008), World food prices and poverty incidence in a food exporting country: a multi-household general equilibrium analysis for Thailand. *Agricultural Economics*, **39**(1), 525–537.
Warr, P. (2011), Food security vs. food self-sufficiency: the Indonesian case. *The Indonesia Quarterly*, **39**(1) (First Quarter), 56–71.
Williams, J.C. and B.D. Wright (1991), *Storage and Commodity Markets*. Cambridge, UK: Cambridge University Press.
Wright, B.D. (2011), The economics of grain price volatility. *Applied Economic Perspectives and Policy*, **33**(2), 32–58.

15. Best-fit options of crop staples for food security: productivity, nutrition and sustainability
Jill E. Gready

15.1 INTRODUCTION

15.1.1 Definition of Problem and Approach of this Chapter

Provision of sufficient nutritious food to feed the world's growing population is the most important problem facing the world, more so than energy. Several authors argue history shows that primary causes of survival crises are food shortages (Brown, 2012). By 'sufficient' and 'nutritious' here we mean sufficient for caloric (energy) needs, and nutritious as the quality (essential amino acids and micronutrients) necessary for childhood development and maintenance of health.

In this chapter we analyse this broad statement from multiple angles, with the aim of placing possible food-crop options, and agricultural and biotechnological solutions in context. The approach taken is to sketch the scale of the food supply and security problem, and dissect the interconnectedness of factors impacting on it, focussing on those critical for efficient, reliable and sustainable crop production and yield, and nutritional quality. We then examine the options, limitations and risks of crop-choice and -improvement options, including application of biotechnological methods.

Our starting thesis is that existing analyses are too piecemeal to represent the complexity of the problem adequately; thus, they do not provide a basis for understanding the interdependencies of contributing factors. This mode is represented, for example, by a special issue on food security in *The Economist* (2011). It presents the major issues in a series of synopses: 'The 9 billion-people question' (SS3-5); 'How much is enough' (SS5-8); 'Plagued by politics' (SS6; biofuels); 'No easy fix' (SS8-11; resources – pessimistic); 'Waste not, want not' (SS10; waste, spoilage); 'Doing more with less' (SS11-14; resources, seeds – optimistic); 'Crisis prevention: future of food' (SS12; prices, research investment); 'Our daily bread' (SS13; UK wheat-research lobby); 'Not just calories' (SS15; nutrition); 'A prospect of plenty' (SS16; not easy to solve but possible – upbeat). However, it makes no attempt to integrate these disparate views. If this had been done then the inconsistencies of proffered solutions and the risks of pursuing, or not pursuing, some options would start to be apparent.

We argue that in the absence of this framework, it is not possible to 'see' the best possible solutions nor to assess the value of their success or the risks of their failure to assuring food security or reducing food insecurity. Solutions currently proffered are mainly evolutionary rather than revolutionary, and unlikely to meet the scale of the problem, while others are technically unrealistic, unnecessarily complex or require a level of international cooperation and national management that, to date, has proven difficult to achieve or sustain. To a large extent they represent the existing vested interests of scientists, industry or others in charge of decision making. Typical outcomes of such siloed thinking as applied to other major problems by expert 'think tanks' are exemplified in Lomborg (2013).

We highlight the risks of accepting suppositions from these incomplete analyses that technological and other improvements to existing agricultural paradigms can provide the increase in efficiency of food-crop production required in an increasingly uncertain (geopolitical, climate change) and resource-constrained (water, land, nutrients) world. In particular, we question the unexamined emphasis on increasing production of current major food staples – rather than alternative crops better suited to resource limitations and harsh and unreliable growing conditions – and on food quantity, i.e. calories, rather than nutritional quality. We also draw attention to the growing gap in strategic planning and investment in agricultural development representing the interests of commercial agriculture in a largely food-secure developed world and transition countries with that serving the interests of the poor and most food-insecure peoples.

In discussing options and possible solutions, we also draw attention to the puzzling lack of recognition of the likely impact of powerful new disruptive technologies on crop development and agriculture in the next decades. Given revolutions in other areas of science and technology there is a conspicuous lack of imagination in mainstream debates and blindness to the likelihood of black-swan events (Taleb, 2010). A contributing reason is the comparatively small global R&D workforce in plant science and agriculture compared with biomedical and other areas of life sciences and technology, as well as computing and information science and technology, the major drivers for innovation. This huge global under-investment in agriculture – which has worsened over the last 40 years – has been widely commented on (The Royal Society, 2009). For example, the disparity in research funding will be starkly apparent by comparison of current annual US funding of plant science and agriculture (National Science Foundation, NSF, + US Department of Agriculture, USDA) of less than $1 billion with the more than $30 billion spent on biomedical science (National Institutes of Health, NIH) (Brutnell and Frommer, 2012), and consideration of the scale of funding of 'grand challenge' projects, such as the $150 billion spent on sending men to the moon.

15.1.2 Urgency and Feasibiity of Solutions

Despite a general realization that the food supply and security problem needs critical attention, the points raised above suggest that the urgency is not yet in prime focus and that assessments of the *feasibility* of solutions are not defensible. Now-standard statements along the lines of 'feeding the 9 billion people to 2050' are likely misleading in suggesting a timeframe for solutions of up to 40 years is available. Events so far in the new millennium indicate this is too optimistic. On the other hand, on the scale of optimism to pessimism, there are fatalistic viewpoints as to whether the food-security problem can or will be solved, with some predicting that humankind or human civilization are headed for extinction in this century.

Athough analyses of 'non-agriculture' mechanisms, such as trade and marketing and waste reduction, addressed in this volume, may correctly diagnose why they have had mixed success in the past they also highlight the complexity of the politicoeconomic drivers involved. Given these difficulties and unpredictability there is little assurance that the global cooperation and improved national and local programs necessary for the level of effectiveness required will be realized in the future.

As an example, claims that there is already enough food produced globally to feed the current population but that the problem is with waste, including storage spoilage, and distribution are distracting in implying confidence that these problems can and will be solved. India's problems of grain losses from inadequate storage and rodent control are long standing and have been the target of numerous national and international initiatives, but are still not adequately addressed. It is sobering to contrast views of progress in food security in modern times with historical examples. For example, famine and malnutrition were unknown in the Inca empire up to the late 1400s with food stores sufficient to feed a population of ~15 million for 7 years, a result of well-organized and efficient agricultural production despite very poor climatic and agronomic conditions (National Academies Advisory Panel, 1989).

15.1.3 Global Connectedness and Rapidity of Events

One clear sign of a changed world is that the phenomenon of famine following war (or crop failure due to adverse weather conditions) has increasingly been replaced by food insecurity triggering civil distrurbance and war, and mass human displacement. Events in recent years from food-price hikes provide graphic examples of coordinated action by people who had enjoyed relative food security slipping back into poverty and food insecurity. The communal awareness and self-organizing ability behind this people power has been largely enabled by the recent step jump in global connectedness from information technology.

Increased systemic risks result from an interconnected and interdependent global society sharing finite physical resources and subject to climatic variability. These conditions present novel, potentially catastrophic and rapid threats to global security, especially disruption of food production and supply chains. That is, not merely the known incremental increasing risks from population growth, environmental degradation and natural-resources depletion, that, however serious, the world has progressively accepted and adapted to. A global food system operating at its limits, as most projections indicate, is inherently unstable to these systemic risks. If the risk materializes, consequences are unpredictable and options for recovery and survival uncertain. The crop solutions advanced herein attempt to increase the robustness of food systems, especially for the most disadvantaged, to reduce these systemic risks.

15.1.4 Food Quantity and Quality

Our initial statement introduced the problem as *both* sufficient and *nutritious* food. In our examination of the suitability of current food staples and the prospects of increasing – or even maintaining – current yields under projected climatic and resource constraints, we will develop this theme by assessing possible alternative crops which could simultaneously meet both food quantity and *quality* needs.

The main point here is that the dominance of the current major food staples in the global food supply is largely an accident of history arising from ancient domestications and distant or more recent migrations, conquests or colonization. Many of these introduced staples are nutritionally inferior and less-well adapted to the local growing conditions than the native crops they displaced (Denison, 2012). In previous times, adequate supplementary protein and other foods with essential amino acids, micronutients (vitamins and minerals) critical for childhood development may have been available. But in current times with about 1 billion people chronically hungry due to poverty and a further 2 billion intermittently food insecure due to poverty, war, famine or civil disturbance, inadequate dietary variety has led to widespread chronic and acute malnutrition. Two thirds of the world's population, mostly women and children, suffer from at least one micronutrient deficiency – 'hidden hunger': up to 3 billion for zinc, 2 billion for iodine, 2 billion people for iron, and about 150 million for vitamin A (Stein and Qaim, 2007). The net result is generations of developmentally impaired children less able to benefit from education and who will grow into adults less able to care for themselves and their families.

15.1.5 Food Security or Food Insecurity?

Food security is a public concept, a largely geopolitical or socioeconomic viewpoint. WHO defines three aspects: availability of sufficient quantities of food on a consistent basis; access to sufficient economic and physical resources to get suitable foods for a nutritious diet; and use of food appropriate for basic nutrition and care, requiring also adequate water and sanitation. FAO adds a fourth aspect, namely stability of these three over time. On the other hand, food *insecurity* may be defined more as the private concerns of the general populace, their confidence in their ability to obtain sufficient affordable, safe and nutritious food reliably. This is a minimum basis for people's ability to live their lives and make plans for the future, such as educating their children. Perceptions and anxieties about food insecurity of a general populace now globally informed and connected by the internet can have unpredictable consequences, as noted above.

Attitudes of people most concerned about food insecurity, i.e. the 3 billion people noted above, are understandably conservative and risk averse. These attitudes and cultural preferences may lead to resistance to changes in food systems and food production that could reduce food insecurity. Similarly, geopolitical mechanisms such as trade agreements, are unlikely to allay the concerns of the food insecure or those only recently lifted out of poverty. Examples of downward spiral are too prominent in public perceptions and the risk of 'undeveloping' countries real.

Food is a primal need and governments of all countries must be able to assure the provision of basic foodstuffs for their citizens to sustain life and health. This has included a mix of national production, quite often heavily subsidized, and adequate stores to manage *known* risks to extended supply chains from natural crises or political events. The common European agricultural policy is a persistent reminder of public and government memories of food shortages during World War II. More recently, China has recognized its long-term need to source a proportion (currently ~10 per cent) of its basic food needs externally and has taken an aggressive approach to securing this supply by direct investment in agriculture in other countries rather than rely on open-trade systems, as previously. Citizens' concerns about food safety are also growing, posing problems of public confidence for national governments from extended international food-supply chains over which they have limited control. This trend is likely to increase as better informed peoples demand more choice of foods and information about how they are grown and processed.

15.2 APPROPRIATE CROPS AND DEVELOPMENT OPTIONS FROM IMPROVED PHOTOSYNTHESIS

Together, the above factors indicate the limitations of planning global food supply based on geopolitical mechanisms, such as trade agreements, and question whether refinement of current agricultural paradigms will be sufficient for future needs.

In this section we outline how improvement of photosynthesis of crop plants could provide the step-jump increase in food production necessary to meet current and projected needs and the advantages of this strategy for achieving this within global constraints of climate instability, environmental sustainability and resource limitations. We start with assessment of the current state of crop productivity.

15.2.1 Declining Yield Growth of Crops and Need for Step Jump in Crop Efficiency

It is widely credited that the 'Green Revolution' of the mid-twentieth century, which delivered new high-yielding crop varieties, prevented the deaths by starvation of up to a billion people. Norman Borlaug was awarded the Nobel Peace Prize in 1970 for his contributions. In addition to breeding in of new traits such as dwarfing genes in wheat to produce short-stature plants with a higher ratio of productive ears to unproductive straw, this success derived from changes in farming practices, particularly high use of fertilizers and irrigation. However, the Green Revolution has not been without long-term costs with consequent problems of depletion of soil nutrients and increase in soil salinity due to lowering of the watertable. These have impacted especially severely on poor farmers, often leading to crippling indebtedness.

Refinements to 'Green Revolution' paradigm methods are failing to deliver the continuing improvements in yield necessary to feed the forecast increase in world population, and are increasingly cost-ineffective and environmentally unsustainable. This is apparent from consideration of the decline in the rate of increase in global productivity of all the major food crops (maize, wheat, rice, soybean and roots and tubers) over the last 50 years. As shown in Figure 15.1, this decline is particularly serious for rice and wheat which together with maize provide more than 50 per cent of the food calories for the developing world. The global average annual yield increase of wheat has declined from about 3 per cent in the period from 1960–1990 to less than 1.5 per cent since then, with the figures for rice being from over 2 per cent to less than 1 per cent.

These small, incremental gains in plant productivity have come from plant breeding to improve resistance to stress – drought, cold, high salinity, pests and diseases – and through improvements in water and fertilizer-use efficiency. However, further gains at similar rates of increase will be insufficient for future food needs.

A second step change in plant productivity similar to the Green Revolution – a new 'wave' in agricultural technology – is required. But the options for solutions in the current global context are more limited. They will need to be sought in the context of other now pressing and interconnected global issues, particularly climate variability

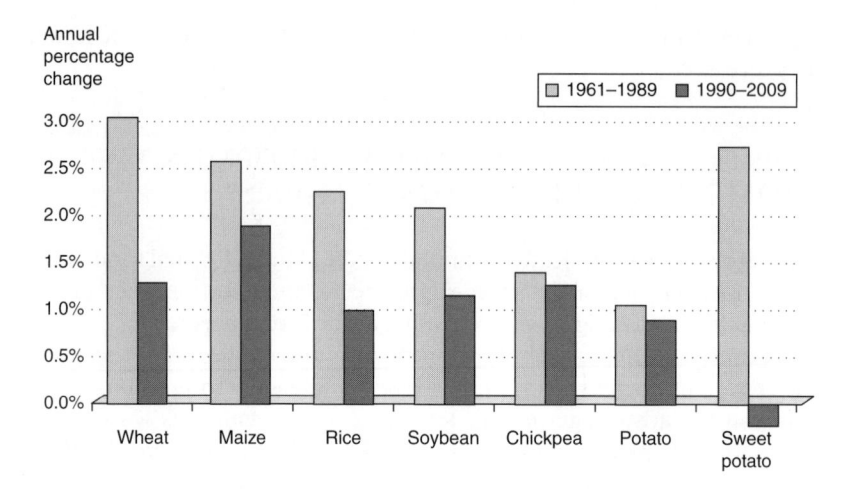

Note: Productivity is defined as yield or production per unit area of cultivated land, usually measured in tonnes per hectare.

Source: Data compiled from FAOSTAT.

Figure 15.1 Decline of average annual improvements in global productivity of major food crops averaged over two time periods, 1961–1989 and 1990–2009

and the increased risks from extreme weather events, environmental sustainability, and availability and cost of land, water, nutrient and energy resources. Indeed, there is a view that the Green Revolution signified a choice *not* to start developing better adapted crops, *not* to focus on improving traditional farming methods for increasing yields, such as mixed cropping, and *not* to support balanced traditional diets of grains and legumes (Kingsbury, 2009: 322). Viewed in this light, solving the tough problems has merely been postponed for 50 years or so to a time now when solutions are more urgently required and options more restricted.

15.2.2 Climate Change Projections and Plant Technology Options

International attention to – and planning for – possible scenarios within which solutions to declining yield increases need to be developed has been focussed by recent major studies predicting consequences of global climate change, especially increased uncertainty of temperature and precipitation. Analyses in the International Food Policy Research Institute (IFPRI) report of Nelson et al. (2009) suggest overall impacts of climate change on agriculture and human well-being will be negative, although there may be gains for some crops in some regions. Particularly severe adverse effects are predicted in sub-Saharan Africa and South Asia, the regions of the developing world expected to experience highest population growth in coming decades. It is predicted that irrigated food crops in South Asia will experience large yield declines, most seriously for wheat by 20–30 per cent, with maize yields in sub-Saharan Africa also much lower (Nelson et al., 2009). However, although alarming enough it should be noted that these estimates are derived from models based on incremental change. They do not provide guidance on realized rapid catastrophic risks on the food supply from unpredictable extreme weather events, regional or global.

As shown in Figure 15.1, possible gains from applying existing crop-development strategies have hit their limit. The recent report from The Royal Society of London (2009) argues for new solutions requiring technologies underpinned by good science, both building on existing knowledge and based on completely radical approaches. It recommends funding of long-term high-risk approaches to high-return targets in genetic improvement of crops, including genetically modified (GM) crops with improved photosynthetic efficiency or with nitrogen-fixation capability. Although the primary aim of agriculture is efficient conversion of solar energy into chemical energy stored in plant biomass of crops, knowledge accumulated over the last 50 years of this process of carbon fixation by photosynthesis in plants has not been a driver for increasing crop productivity. Hence, R&D to explore options for how the efficiency of photosynthesis of crops might be improved and how such strategies might be implemented in a variety of crops under different growing conditions to realize gains in crop yields is in its early stages.

In the following, we outline the processes of photosynthesis and options for improving it in crop plants using both GM and non-GM technologies, including two we have developed ourselves. We then discuss the impact of factors assisting and limiting photosynthesis and possible yield increases and other advantages of the photosynthetic-improvement option.

15.2.3 What is Photosynthesis?

Photosynthesis in plants converts the freely available resources of energy from sunlight and carbon from atmospheric carbon dioxide (CO_2) into energy-rich biological sugar compounds ('biomass') and oxygen (O_2). This process is the main route for assimilation of inorganic carbon into organic carbon in the biosphere. The resultant sugars and O_2 underpin all life, plant and animal. The overall process is summarized in Figure 15.2.

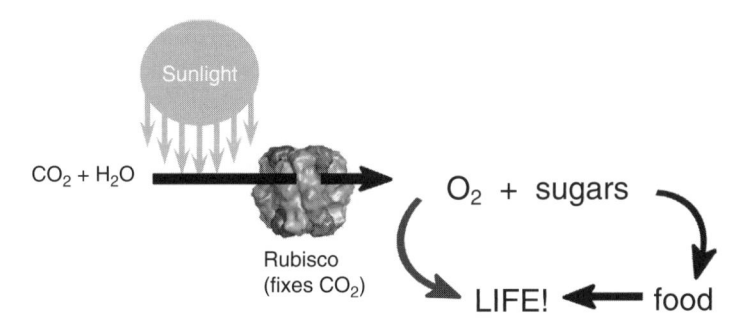

Figure 15.2 Summary of the process of photosynthesis in plants, the main route for assimilation of inorganic carbon into organic carbon in the biosphere and production of oxygen, which underpin life on earth. Primary inputs of atmospheric carbon dioxide (CO_2), water and energy from sunlight are incorporated into chemical energy of carbon-containing compounds (sugars) with fixation of CO_2 by the enzyme Rubisco and evolution of oxygen (O_2)

The capture ('fixation') of CO_2 into sugars is achieved by a complex series of chemical reactions catalyzed by the enzyme Rubisco. But despite this critical role Rubisco has the paradoxical distinction of being one of the slowest enzymes fixing only a few CO_2 molecules per second. It is also inefficient as it confuses CO_2 and O_2 and also fixes atmospheric O_2 into wasteful products that need to be recycled, costing energy and carbon and reducing the net productivity of photosynthesis by up to 50 per cent. These factors limit the potential yield of plant biomass over the plant growing season and, thus, of the yield potential of crops (vide infra). Also, to sustain sufficient rates of carbon assimilation, Nature's solution in most photosynthetic organisms is to synthesize large amounts of Rubisco, making it the most abundant protein in plants and, indeed, on earth – up to 50 per cent of leaf protein. This factor increases plants' need for nitrogen fertilizer, as nitrogen is required for synthesis of proteins (vide infra). However, in so-called 'C_4 plants' a mechanism has evolved to increase the concentration of CO_2 in specialized leaf cells containing the Rubisco allowing more efficient fixation of carbon in particular growing conditions, usually hot and dry. But this concentrating process requires expenditure of significant amounts of plant energy, placing a limit on its advantages over usual 'C_3 plant' photosynthesis (vide infra). Food crops with C_4 metabolism include maize, sugar cane, millet and sorghum.

The upside is that the amino acids of Rubisco, and other plant proteins, are remobilized (broken down and re-used), together with sugars and other compounds, during crop maturity and transformed into proteins, carbohydrates and oils in seeds or other storage bodies for the next generation, for example cereal grain, legume pods or roots and tubers, such as potatoes. This process determines the nutritional content and composition – proportions of protein, carbohydrate, oil, fibre, vitamins, etc. – of crops (vide infra).

Under optimal plant growing conditions, that is at optimum temperature (Sage, 2002) and with adequate sunlight, water and soil nutrients, the major factor limiting Rubisco efficiency is non-optimal concentration of CO_2 in the photosynthetic 'factories' (chloroplasts) in plant leaves where Rubisco is located. This deficiency is worse under drought conditions as the pores on the underside of leaves (stomata) close to reduce water loss, thus hindering entry of CO_2 into the internal leaf spaces and then into the chloroplasts of cells. Also, at temperatures higher than a plant's optimum – which varies for different plants, including crop plants, typically within the range of 20 to 30°C – Rubisco inefficiency due to fixation of O_2 progressively worsens, ultimately leading to shutdown of photosynthesis. Both these factors limit photosynthesis under hot and dry conditions (vide infra), with severity dependent on the natural conditions under which the plant evolved (vide infra).

These factors are critical for crop development, with increasing effort devoted to drought- and heat-tolerant varieties. In summary, introducing better Rubiscos into crops to improve photosynthetic capacity is expected to deliver multiple benefits:

- Greater plant biomass and crop yield;
- Improved nitrogen-use efficiency (NUE);
- Improved water-use efficiency (WUE);
- Increased resilience of crops under adverse growth conditions, such as heat and drought.

The inefficiency of Rubisco is a consequence of the large decrease in atmospheric CO_2 concentration (partial pressure, pCO_2), since Rubisco first appeared on earth in photosynthetic bacteria more than 3 billion years ago, compared with pO_2, which was negligible at that time. However, over geological time scales since then the absolute and relative (RO_2/CO_2) concentration of atmospheric CO_2 and O_2 have varied greatly with estimates of RO_2/CO_2 and $\%O_2$ since land plants arose 500–600 million years ago (MYA) ranging from 25 and 15 (550 MYA) to 14 and 18 (475 MYA) to <1 and 28 (300 MYA) to 6 and 12 (150 MYA) to <1 and 21 today (Berner, 2003). Viewed in this light, the robustness of Rubisco and photosynthesis and persistence of land plants (Igamberdiev and Lea, 2006) over geological time is very impressive. The advantages of current increases in atmospheric CO_2 for photosynthesis and crop productivity are discussed below.

15.2.4 Options and Possible Yield Increases from Photosynthesis

The Royal Society report (2009) identified improvement in photosynthetic capacity as the major trait remaining to target increases in yield potential of crops. An analysis of the maximum efficiency for conversion of solar energy into biomass (i.e. Figure 15.2) by photosynthesis produced estimates at 380 ppm atmospheric CO_2 concentration (now 400 ppm in 2013) of 4.6 and 6 per cent for C_3 and C_4 plants, respectively (Zhu et al., 2008). However, it is estimated that the C_4 advantage over C_3 photosynthesis will disappear as atmospheric CO_2 concentration nears 700 ppm (vide infra). Estimates of the potential radiation use efficiency (RUE) at each step from light capture to sugar synthesis shows energy loss of 63 per cent from the light reactions and a further 66 per cent (C_3) to 77 per cent (C_4) from the sugar synthesis reactions (net 87 per cent (C_3) to 91 per cent (C_4)) (Figure 2 of Zhu et al., 2008). As discussed below, Zhu et al. (2008) suggest opportunities for raising this low theoretical RUE to at best 8.8 per cent for a C_3 plant with a Rubisco that has no O_2-fixing activity; no such Rubisco has been identified and no suggestions for how one might be engineered proposed.

Analysis of the component processes of photosynthesis identifies a number of points at which improvements could increase photosynthetic capacity (Long et al., 2006; Murchie et al., 2009). These focus on interventions that increase efficiency of conversion of solar radiation (RUE) and include: Rubisco with decreased O_2-fixation activity (more efficient); Rubisco with higher CO_2-fixation rate (more effective); engineering of C_4 processes into C_3 plants (increase CO_2 concentration at Rubisco site); increased rate of recovery from photoprotection (plant mechanisms to limit damage from excess light); increased capacity to regenerate the Rubisco substrate, RuBP (under optimal conditions Rubisco activity may exhaust RuBP supply); and improved architecture of the plant canopy (leaf angle for light capture, etc.). Of possible interventions, those being considered for crop development focus on improving Rubisco activity – directly or indirectly, as above – rather than on improving the light-capture reactions that produce the biological energy needed to power the carbon-fixation reactions in the Rubisco cycle to produce biological sugars (Figure 15.2). Normally, the efficiency of the Rubisco-related reactions limits overall photosynthetic efficiency. Exceptions are under low-light conditions that produce less energy than could usefully be used by these reactions, or under conditions (high light, well-watered) where these reactions are running optimally and the rate of energy supply from the light reactions is insufficient.

Predicted levels of improvement in crop productivity from implementation of these different interventions (e.g. Long et al., 2006), or combinations of them, vary greatly with numbers from 0–100 per cent being published. The meaningfulness of these estimates is questionable, and they are misleading as drivers for making decisions of choices for R&D investment, as is currently happening. Scientifically, they are indefensible as the knowledge base for translating theoretical gains in basic photosynthetic processes in the chloroplast into predictions of increased yield in the field does not exist. Also, photosynthesis in different crop plants works optimally under different ranges of growing conditions that depend on their genetics, including Rubisco-activity profile, and evolutionary history, that is, conditions to which they are adapted; models that predict such performance are well established (von Caemmerer, 2000). Thus, there is no photosynthetic solution best for any given crop across the range of agroclimatic conditions under which it may be grown.

Finally, these estimates do not consider the relative advantage of increased resilience to seasonal variability or acute adverse growing conditions, such as heatwaves, compared with theoretical yield potential. We argue that these advantages are equally – and possibly more – important for food security and efficient use of resources, and should be major drivers for decision making on crop-development options (vide infra). The worth of these advantages differ among intervention types.

15.2.5 Two Complementary Approaches: GM and Direct Crop Breeding

Two major approaches to improving Rubisco performance in a crop plant are from re-engineering of the enzyme itself and introduction of the modified gene into the plant by genetic transformation, or by introducing naturally occurring 'better' variant Rubiscos into the plant by conventional or enhanced breeding (Tester and Langridge, 2010) methods. We have recently developed new unique, and complementary, technologies for both approaches.

For the former, a method for designing improved mutants of the Rubisco large subunit (LSU) that contains the Rubisco catalytic site required for fixation of CO_2 and implementing the modified *rbcL* gene into a test plant using chloroplast transformation has been developed, validated and patented since 2006 (Gready and Kannappan, 2013). Despite intensive efforts by others over the last three decades, these are the first Rubisco mutants produced with improved enzyme-kinetic activity; there is now a portfolio of mutants with variable kinetic profiles and suitability for crop-relevant growing conditions. Implementation into a crop plant would produce a GM variety of cisgenic type, i.e. the same *rbcL* gene as the crop species but with specific mutations (Holme et al., 2013).

The second strategy exploits natural diversity of Rubisco and selected co-evolving genes to identify variants more efficient and best adapted to specific growing conditions, especially heat and water stress and nitrogen limitation, from the tens or hundreds of thousands of seed samples of crops in international and national seedbanks. Seed varieties validated as containing superior Rubiscos and complementary genes can then be used directly in breeding new crop varieties for target growing conditions

(Gready et al., 2013). We have developed this methodology applied to wheat since 2009.

Both technologies exploit new capabilities for integrating sequence and functional knowledge in public databases and the literature, modern gene sequencing and molecular biology methods, the vast resources in seed banks and high-performance computing. Although both technologies have been developed with commercial or semi-commercial funding, agreements were negotiated which allow the IP to be used with no-cost licenses for development of crops for poor farmers in developing countries by international agriculture or other agencies (O'Rourkes, 2011). We note that perhaps the major contribution to food security from the GM method may come, at least initially, from improved WUE and increased yield from commercial implementation into materials crops (e.g. fibre or oil) resulting in less pressure on availability and cost of water and arable land for food production.

15.2.6 Factors Limiting or Assisting Photosynthesis

Following on from the preceding sections, we now review the implications of relevant current, projected or unpredictable global conditions that impact on photosynthesis, either assisting or limiting crop productivity.

Atmospheric pollution

Particulate matter, such as dust, pollutant gases, such as sulfur and nitrogen oxides, and ozone (O_3), which is produced by reactions of UV sunlight on air containing hydrocarbons or nitrogen oxides, all reduce the net effectiveness of photosynthesis by reducing light to the plant or from damage to the plant that requires plant energy to repair. In extreme cases volcanic eruptions such as that of Krakatoa in Indonesia in 1883 or most recently of Eyjafjallajökull in Iceland in 2010, distibute dust and, particularly, sulfur oxides globally. It has been suggested that the Krakatoa explosion produced a global cooling of about 1°C and chaotic weather patterns for several years, and a large global increase in sulfuric acid in high clouds, from ejection of large amounts of sulfur dioxide (SO_2) into the stratosphere, that fell as 'acid rain'. The effects of atmospheric pollutants and acid rain on European forests are well known, as are concerns of the atmospheric effects of large-scale nuclear explosion – 'nuclear winter'. Management of risks to the global food supply due to impairment of photosynthesis from unpredictable and unpreventable 'acts of nature', such as volcanic eruptions or meteor storms, requires attention for building a robust food security system. We note that stratospheric ozone depletion, ocean acidification and atmospheric aerosol loading are three of the nine 'planetary boundaries' identified by Rockström et al. (2009) (vide infra).

A recent review (Wilkinson et al., 2012) estimates that ozone pollution at ground level is currently decreasing global crop yields for maize, wheat and soybean by ~2.2–5.5 per cent, 3.9–15 per cent and 8.5–14 per cent, respectively, with different extents depending on genetic characteristics and growing conditions. It suggests this problem will increase. Thus, genetic resistance to oxidative damage from ozone represents a desirable criterion to consider in choosing crop types and developing crop varieties, as such damage represents a significant often-hidden loss to crop productivity in comparison with more obvious damage from pests and disease.

Increased atmospheric CO_2
The concentration of CO_2 ($[CO_2]$) in the atmosphere has increased from 280 ppm to 400 ppm (2013; 0.04 per cent) since the industrial revolution and may reach 550 ppm by 2050; it has been increasing at ~2 ppm/year over the last decade. Although possibly higher than at any time in the last 20 million years, the $[CO_2]$ is comparable with values about 300 million years ago and well below 10 per cent of its 500-million year peak (Berner, 2003). The discussion above (section 15.2.3) on Rubisco activity suggests that increasing $[CO_2]$ will be beneficial for photosynthesis and plant growth, and indeed free-air CO_2 enrichment (FACE) field experiments in which $[CO_2]$ is artificially increased ('CO_2 fertilization') to ~550 ppm show increases in plant biomass of 10–16 per cent compared with plants grown at ambient $[CO_2]$ (Long et al., 2006).

Experiments for wheat showed grain-yield increases of ~10 per cent at 550 ppm (Högy et al., 2009). For potato, similar studies at 360 (then ambient), 460, 560 and 660 ppm showed greater effects, with larger increases of ~10 per cent for each 100 ppm rise up to ~40 per cent at 660 ppm; these gains were translated into a higher number of tubers rather than greater mean tuber size (Miglietta et al., 1998). However, total wheat-grain protein concentration was decreased by ~7 per cent with changes also in protein and amino acid composition (Högy et al., 2009). A recent study evaluated effects on wheat productivity from *combined* impacts of increased CO_2 (700 ppm) *and* increases in temperature (2°C) above ambient, with and without terminal drought, to mimic conditions predicted from climate-change models. It showed biomass and grain yield were enhanced under elevated CO_2 at 2°C above ambient, regardless of watering regimen, and with reductions under terminal drought much less severe under elevated CO_2 (21–28 per cent) than ambient (45–50 per cent) (de Oliveira et al., 2012).

Analogous results to those for potato were obtained for sweet potato by Czeck et al. (2013) who showed major increases (doubling or more) in below-ground biomass (i.e. tubers) under CO_2 fertilization from ambient to 1515 ppm under greenhouse conditions. These results suggest that very high CO_2 levels could greatly improve crop production globally. Analogous studies at ambient and twice-ambient CO_2 and 28 to 40°C in rice and soybean aimed at determining whether elevated CO_2 could compensate for adverse effects of high growth temperatures on photosynthesis showed for both species that CO_2 enrichment more than compensated for the temperature-induced decline in photosynthesis at supraoptimal temperatures (Vu et al., 1997). This result suggests that projected adverse effects on rice yields, in particular, from global warming would not be realized if the $[CO_2]$ continues to increase.

These studies all show the beneficial effects of increased atmospheric CO_2 on photosynthesis of the major C_3 crops. However, a significant conclusion is that the scale of the response to increased CO_2 and temperature will depends on crop type, including cultivar, and growing conditions. Thus, in developing strategies for enhancing crop yields by improving photosynthesis under higher future atmospheric CO_2 and predicted warmer temperatures, thought should be given to which crops could maximize these benefits in given regions, taking account also of differential input costs, especially water and fertilizer.

There is also substantial evidence that increases in atmospheric CO_2 over the last 70 years or so from ~310 (1940) to 400 ppm today has had beneficial effects in increasing vegetation cover globally and reversing or slowing desertification in areas not detrimentally impacted by human activity. Of note is the recent study of Donohue et al. (2013) that has shown, from satellite observations from 1982–2010, an 11 per cent increase in global green foliage cover in warm, arid environments. Several authors have also suggested that the historically recent increase in CO_2 has produced substantial increases in crop productivity, i.e. more food has progressively been produced – up to 30 per cent now? – than would have been the case if there had been no increase and that this has had a major unrecognized impact on feeding the world. Also, as expected (section 15.2.3) increased photosynthetic capacity from increased atmospheric CO_2 has improved WUE, as now demonstrated for temperate and boreal forests of the northern hemisphere over the past two decades (Keenan et al., 2013).

Thus, we can expect that the effects on photosynthesis of projected increases in atmospheric CO_2 to 2050 and beyond will *enhance* both crop productivity and resilience to stresses such as heat and drought, and that, irrespective of the impact of carbon-emission mitigation attempts, will most likely have a net benefit on food production. For reference, we note that the boundary of 350 ppm on the atmospheric CO_2 concentration proposed by Rockström et al. (2009) in their nine-boundaries framework as necessary to prevent 'unacceptable' environmental change is *less than* the current value.

Natural climate range of crops

The major crops have been domesticated from wild species growing at specific sites (see section 15.3.2) and, thus, evolved for those agroclimatic conditions (Denison, 2012). This history has critical importance for their suitable range of growing conditions for photosynthesis, especially for temperature and water needs, despite most of these crops having been taken widely around the globe by humans. As noted in section 15.2.3, Rubisco has an optimum temperature range for different plants (Sage, 2002); this varies according to the climate in which it evolved. Thus, for example, wheat and barley are temperate-climate crops with optimal growing temperature about 25°C, whereas rice is a sub-tropical crop with an optimal growing temperature of about 30°C and C_4 crops such as maize and sorghum are adapted for hotter, drier cliamtes.

Indeed, a recent compehnsive analysis of the grass family Poaceae (aka Gramineae) found that the C_3-subfamily lineage Pooideae, which includes the cereals wheat, barley, oats and rye, had both the lowest mean annual temperature *and* precipitation range, whereas the C_3-subfamily Ehrhartoideae, which includes rice, had the equal highest mean annual temperature *and* highest mean annual precipitation range (Edwards and Smith, 2010, Figure 1). Thus, 'high temperature' corresponds to different values depending on crop. It is generally accepted that rice in South Asia is already being grown under conditions towards the upper limit of its temperature range (Redfern et al., 2012). Hence, the concern from climate-change predictions of an increase of 2°C as predicted from climate-change models (Nelson, 2009), although, as noted, this does not take into account a 'protective' effect from increased atmospheric CO_2. For the Panicoideae subfamily that includes both C_3 (including some millets) and C_4 (including maize, sorghum and some millets) species, the analysis showed, surprisingly, that although the C_4 species had a drier optimum than the C_3 species, there was little difference in the temperature optimums (both among highest; Edwards and Smith, 2010, Figure 1). Thus, C_4 evolution is not necessarily an adaptation for warmer environments, as had been assumed, but for drier environments.

Climate change and extreme weather events

As just discussed, apart from atmospheric CO_2 concentration, the plant growing conditions that most affect photosynthesis are temperature and water availability. Here we discuss the current different perspectives of possible impacts on crops from long-term climate change compared with risks from extreme weather events during the growing season.

The IRPRI report of Nelson et al. (2009) predicted the consequences of long-term climate change due to shifts in temperature and precipitation on crop productivity and human well-being, using data from two scenario models (CSIRO and MIROC). Despite significant variability between the models, predictions of regions most detrimentally affected were consistent – in developing countries, yield declines for the most important crops, with South Asia hardest hit and especially for irrigated crops (specifically rice). However, there are some predicted 'winners', particularly northern Europe. We can summarize these conclusions as 'climate change' acts as a threat multiplier to assuring sustainable food.

Knowledge of trends of weather unreliability, particularly whether the frequency of extreme weather events such as heatwaves or cold snaps might be increasing (Donat et al., 2013), is scant. The generally accepted most authoritative current source is the IPPC (2012) report. This uses 'calibrated uncertainty language' to convey the degree of certainty, and the terms 'exposure' and 'vulnerability' as determinants of disaster risk and likely impacts when risk is realized, recognizing also compounding of events (e.g. heat and drought).

Of relevance to our crop discussion, IPCC (2012) assesses that since 1950 an overall decrease in the number of cold days and nights, and an overall increase in the number of warm days and nights, for most land areas at the global scale is *very likely*. These changes are *likely* continent wide in North America, Europe, and Australia, with *medium confidence* in a warming trend in daily temperature extremes in much of Asia. Considering the determinants of exposure and vulnerability, it is apparent that if an event (e.g. heatwave) occurs at a critical time in crop plant growth in a crop vulnerable to a sudden variation in that determinant (e.g. already growing near its photosynthetic temperature limit; see Redfern et al., 2012, Table 2 for rice) then impact will likely be severe, and may lead to total crop failure.

In Australia, a recent Climate Commission report (Steffen et al., 2013) suggests record heat events are now happening three times more often than cold records (Steffen et al., 2013, Figure 8; CSIRO and BoM data) and may be five times more frequent by 2050 (Steffen et al., 2013, Table 1). The impacts of such events in October, as most recently in 2012, in the southern wheat-growing belt are, not surprisingly, severe.

Points raised in this and the previous section suggest more appropriate criteria for crop suitability to their prospective growing conditions now, and in the future, than the recent mantra of 'climate-ready' crops. These are that they should be naturally well adapted in the plant evolutionary sense (Denison, 2012) and more reliable and resilient, meaning better able to survive poor seasonal conditions, particularly hotter and/or drier, and survive and recover from extreme weather events, such as heat waves, to still produce a harvestable crop.

Summary: net benefits of increased photosynthetic capacity
To summarize the main conclusions from section 15.2.6, we can say that the net benefits of increasing photosynthetic capacity is that it widens the margins for plants to cope with both extreme short-term weather events and poor seasonal growing conditions and still produce a harvestable crop. Photosynthesis is the key trait to produce such benefits as it produces the plant's energy that can then be used by the plant to repair damage from heat, pollutants, disease, insect or other damage. Increasing photosynthetic capacity will provide reserve energy that can be transformed into grain etc. This is critical for reducing food insecurity for the poor and reducing economic risk for commercial farmers.

15.2.7   Resource Limitations: Phosphorus and Nitrogen

The sheer scale of disruption of major elemental cycles from global agriculture for all purposes, particularly of nitrogen (N) and phosphorus (P) but also other elements needed for plant growth, is well known. The interlinked nitrogen and phosphorus cycles are two of the nine 'planetary boundaries' identified as requiring limitation on changes from future human activities in order to prevent 'unacceptable' environmental change (Rockström et al., 2009).

The inevitable consequences of the high use of N and P fertilizers necessary in global agriculture systems to maintain current crop yields are obvious – not only large-scale redistribution but of loss from agricultural systems. To summarize this redistribution and loss: Crop growth uses soil nutrients. Farming systems that remove harvested crops and their waste products from the local environment prevent the natural recycling of nutrients from biological decay, leading to progressive depletion of soil nutrients. This depletion is of most concern for P as there are possibilities for partial replacement of N from legume crops. Nutrients end up as waste in landfill and incinerators, or in rivers and oceans via sewerage systems, removing them from the agricultural cycle and causing adverse effects on the environment from pollution. These trends are rapidly increasing with population shifts to cities and intercontinental redistributions resulting from food trade.

N and P fertilizers are costly to manufacture and transport, with these costs rising in line with energy-cost rises. However, as phosphorus is a scarce finite resource the cost, availability and possible even *access* for P (phosphate) fertilizer is more complex than for N fertilizer. The conference slide set of Rosemarin (2010) provides an excellent introduction to all the P-fertilizer issues.

Phosphorus for fertilizer is now almost entirely produced by mining of phosphate rock, as reserves of the P-rich and more easily extracted guano are now virtually exhausted. Questions about phosphate rock resources and their significance were recognized more than 20 years ago with the work of Herring and Fantel (1993) who noted a 'vital and indisputable link exists between phosphate rock and world food supply'. Lack of knowledge of world reserves of phosphate rock has led to uncertainty as to how long they will last with estimates of 50–100 years with peak production by about 2030 (Cordell et al., 2009) and a more recent assessment of hundreds of years (US Geological Survey, 2012). However, these figures depend on P-content (on average this is only 0.1 per cent by mass) and cost of extraction.

Of equal concern is the skewed global distribution of reserves and extraction capacity

(Gilbert, 2009; Vaccari, 2009). Of known phosphorus reserves, 90 per cent are in five countries (United States, China, South Africa, Jordan and Morocco and Western Sahara), with 40 per cent in Morocco and Western Sahara (US Geological Survey, 2012). Sulfuric acid, used to extract phosphate from rock, is also found in a limited number of countries (United States, Canada, China, Russia and eastern Europe and Saudi Arabia) mainly in the northern hemisphere. In contrast, two of the top four P-fertilizer consuming countries (India and Brazil) and other areas of the developing world in South Asia and Africa with large increasing populations and rapidly increasing usage have reserves of neither (Rosemarin, 2010). It has been recognized that this scenario 'makes phosphorus a geostrategic ticking time bomb' (Vaccari, 2009).

The seriousness for food security and environmental sustainability of the P-supply and P-waste problem has recently led to increased interest at both levels, such as discussion of opportunities for improving phosphorus-use efficiency (PUE) in crop plants (Veneklaas et al., 2012) and technologies to recover phosphorus from waste and sewerage (Cordell et al., 2009).

15.3 CURRENT FOOD CROPS – WHAT ARE THEY AND WHY?

A review of the history of domestication, breeding and introduction of crops to other areas by migration of peoples and more latterly conquest and colonization (Kingsbury, 2009), which underpins the current global distribution of food crops, is beyond our purpose here. A few points are noted in section 15.3.2. Here, in line with our main purpose of exploring options for increasing efficiency of crop production to produce sufficient nutritious food to assure food security and minimize food insecurity, we simply summarize the current position and point out the disadvantages of dependency on the current portfolio of staple crops.

15.3.1 Current Food Staples – Relative Importance and Nutritional Assessment

Although there are more than 50 000 edible plant species, only a few hundred are significant food sources and of these a mere 15 crops provide 90 per cent of the world's food energy intake (FAO, 1995). Just three – the cereals, rice, maize and wheat – make up two thirds of this, being staples for more than 4 billion people. Rice is eaten by almost half of humanity (vide infra). Roots and tubers – such as cassava, yams, potatoes and sweet potato – are important staples for more than 1 billion people in the developing world, accounting for about 40 per cent of food for half the population of sub-Saharan Africa. Their importance is increasing, and for our current purposes of identifying crop options with high potential for yield increases from improved photosynthesis they are especially attractive (vide infra). The remaining major food-staple type is pulses (legumes) – such as soybean, chickpea and other beans and peas. As noted above, pulses have the agronomic benefit of not requiring nitrogen fertilizer due to their nitrogen-fixing ability.

Remarkably, despite there being more than 10 000 species of the cereal family (Gramineae), few have been widely introduced into cultivation over the past 2000 years. This suggests that humans have long favoured crops for which domestication investment had shown continuous, satisfactory improvements and, thus, apparently have felt little need to explore other options. This point is important because, as discussed in section 15.2.1, this successful phase has now hit its limits.

Below we advance arguments as to whether the best option may be to 'cut losses' on further investment in some crops, at least for some growing areas, and consider developing crops better suited to current and projected agroclimatic conditions. Of particular note are concerns about the genetic bottlenecks resulting from intensive breeding of modern cultivars, and, for our immediate purposes, suggestions that it has not improved photosynthetic capacity (RUE) but may even unwittingly have led to decreased photosynthetic yield potential by selective breeding for other traits with concurrent loss of RUE genes. Modern Asian cultivated rice (*Oryza sativa*) has the lowest genetic diversity (only 10–20 per cent) of the major food crops (Zhu et al., 2007).

Nutritional content
The nutritional content of the four major cereals (maize, rice, wheat and sorghum), two tubers (potato and sweet potato) and a pulse (soybean) are shown in Table 15.1 together with data for quinoa, a pseudocereal native to Andean regions. Quinoa is being promoted for wider global cultivation because of its excellent nutritional and agronomic properties. The data were obtained from the USDA National Nutrient Database for Standard Reference (USDA, 2012) and scaled to dry-weight values for comparison. It will be apparent that although all have similar energy (calorific) content, they have quite different relative compositions of protein, fat, carbohydate and fibre. Soybean has the highest protein and fat content, whereas quinoa has the most balanced content overall. It will be apparent that the fat content is very variable ranging from low (rice, wheat, potato, sweet potato) to medium (maize, sorghum, quinoa) to high (soybean).

It is also apparent from Table 15.1 that amounts of key micronutrients (minerals and vitamins) also vary greatly among these typical staples, especially for those of concern for 'hidden malnutrition' (sections 15.1.1 and 15.1.4), iron, zinc and vitamin A, as well as vitamin C and folate. Only sweet potato has significant levels of vitamin A, and all staples are relatively poor in iron and zinc. However, as vitamin A is fat-soluble, it is desirable for its absorption that it be consumed with fat; sweet potato itself has minimal fat. Soybean and quinoa have the best overall spectrum.

In addition to overall protein content, other measures of nutritional quality are the major protein types, which affect digestibility, and amino-acid composition, especially essential amino acids (FAO/WHO/UNI, 2007). Essential amino acids were regarded as 'essential' not because they are more important components of proteins than the others, but because humans do not synthesize them *de novo*. It was thus considered that they needed to be acquired in the diet. Under this definition, 9 of the 20 amino acids are regarded as essential for humans – phenylalanine, valine, threonine, tryptophan, isoleucine, methionine, leucine, lysine and histidine – with cysteine, tyrosine and arginine required by infants and growing children. However, there are alternative definitions. For example, one that considers alternative human metabolic routes, divides amino acids into 'dispensable' and 'indispensable' groups, with the latter, comprising lysine, threonine and tryptophan, being absolute dietary necessities for maintenance of normal growth (Reeds, 2000). The nutritional-deficiency diseases pellagra (niacin/vitamin B_3, tryptophan, lysine) and beriberi (thiamine/vitamin B_1) can occur in people with dominant maize and (polished) rice diets.

The amino acid content of the selected staples and quinoa are shown in Table 15.2,

Table 15.1 Amounts (per 100 g dry weight[a]) of nutrients, minerals and vitamins in selected core staples

	Maize[b]	Rice[c]	Wheat[d]	Sorghum[e]	Potato[f]	Sweet potato[g]	Soybean[h]	Quinoa[i]
Water (g)	0	0	0	0	0	0	0	0
Energy (kJ)	1601	1716	1406	1480	1512	1460	**1757**	1692
Protein (g)	9.8	8.0	**12.9**	11.8	9.4	6.5	**37.1**	15.5
Fat (g)	5.0	0.7	1.6	3.4	0.4	0.2	**19.4**	6.6
Carbohydrates (g)	78	90	73	78	80	**81**	31	70
Fiber (g)	7.6	1.5	**12.5**	6.6	10.3	12.2	12.0	7.7
Calcium (mg)	7	31	30	29	56	122	**563**	51
Iron (mg)	2.8	4.8	3.3	4.6	3.7	2.5	**10.1**	5.0
Potassium (mg)	301	129	373	365	**1977**	1367	1771	616
Zinc (mg)	2.3	1.2	2.7	0.0	1.4	1.2	2.8	**3.4**
Vitamin C (mg)	–	–	–	–	**93**	10	83	–
Thiamin (mg)	0.40	**0.65**	0.39	0.25	0.38	0.32	**1.26**	0.39
Riboflavin (mg)	0.21	0.06	0.12	0.15	0.14	0.24	**0.51**	0.35
Niacin (mg)	3.8	**4.7**	5.6	3.1	4.9	2.3	**4.7**	1.7
Vitamin B6 (mg)	**0.65**	0.18	0.31	–	**1.41**	0.85	0.20	0.53
Folate Total (mcg)	20	**259**	39	–	75	45	**471**	201
Vitamin A (IU)	224	–	9	–	9	**57554**	514	15
Beta-carotene (mcg)	102	–	5	–	5	**34519**	–	–

Notes:
a. Dry weights have normalized against percentage wet weights: maize, 10; rice, 12; wheat, 13; sorghum, 9; potato, 79; sweet potato, 77; soybean, 68; quinoa, 13.
b. Maize, yellow.
c. Rice, white, long-grain, regular, raw.
d. Wheat, hard red winter.
e. Sorghum, raw.
f. Potato, flesh and skin, raw.
g. Sweet potato, raw, unprepared.
h. Soybean, green, raw.
i. Quinoa, uncooked.
'–' denotes no values provided.
Bold values are the highest nutrient densities amongst these staples.

Source: Data from USDA National Nutrient Database for Standard Reference USDA (2012).

again using USDA (2012) data and scaled to dry-weight values for comparison. This shows that soybean and quinoa have superior amounts of the indispensable and essential amino acids, with the cereals being relatively poorer, especially for lysine, although wheat and sorghum are better than maize and rice.

Table 15.2   Amounts (per 100g dry weight[a]) of amino acids in selected core staples

Amino Acid[b]	Maize[c]	Rice[d]	Wheat[e]	Sorghum[f]	Potato[g]	Sweet potato[h]	Soybean[i]	Quinoa[j]
Tryptophan (g)	0.06	0.08	**0.15**	0.12	0.02	0.03	0.15	0.16
Threonine (g)	0.37	0.29	0.37	0.36	0.31	0.34	**1.47**	0.46
Isoleucine (g)	0.35	0.35	0.47	0.45	0.31	0.22	**1.63**	0.55
Leucine (g)	**1.21**	0.66	0.88	**1.55**	0.45	0.37	**2.65**	0.92
Lysine (g)	0.28	0.29	0.34	0.24	**0.49**	0.27	**2.21**	0.84
Methionine (g)	0.21	0.19	0.21	0.18	0.15	0.12	**0.45**	0.34
<u>Cystine (g)</u>	0.18	0.16	**0.33**	0.13	0.11	0.09	**0.34**	0.22
Phenylalanine (g)	0.49	0.43	**0.61**	0.57	0.38	0.36	**1.67**	0.65
<u>Tyrosine (g)</u>	**0.40**	0.27	**0.40**	0.33	0.22	0.14	**1.33**	0.29
Valine (g)	**0.50**	0.49	0.57	0.58	0.47	0.35	**1.65**	0.65
<u>Arginine (g)</u>	0.49	0.67	0.61	0.37	0.47	0.22	**2.98**	1.19
Histidine (g)	0.30	0.19	0.29	0.26	0.16	0.13	**0.99**	0.45
Alanine (g)	0.74	0.46	0.46	1.08	0.29	0.31	1.66	0.64
Aspartic acid (g)	0.69	0.75	0.66	0.77	2.22	1.55	4.31	1.24
Glutamic acid (g)	1.85	1.56	4.11	2.54	1.62	0.63	6.95	2.04
Glycine (g)	0.40	0.36	0.54	0.36	0.26	0.26	1.54	0.76
Proline (g)	0.86	0.38	1.32	0.89	0.29	0.21	1.73	0.85
Serine (g)	0.47	0.42	0.60	0.48	0.34	0.36	2.06	0.62
Tryptophan (g)	0.06	0.08	0.15	0.12	0.02	0.03	0.15	0.16

Notes:
a. Dry weights normalized against percentage wet weights from USDA data: maize, 10; rice, 12; wheat, 13; sorghum, 9; potato, 79; sweet potato, 77; soybean, 68; quinoa, 13.
b. Bolded, indispensable; italics, essential; underlined, essential for infants and growing children. See definitions in section 15.3.1.
c. Maize, yellow.
d. Rice, white, long-grain, regular, raw.
e. Wheat, hard red winter.
f. Sorghum, raw.
g. Potato, flesh and skin, raw.
h. Sweet potato, raw, unprepared.
i. Soybean, green, raw.
j. Quinoa, uncooked.
Bold values denote high or highest nutrient densities amongst these staples.

Source: Data from USDA National Nutrient Database for Standard Reference USDA (2012).

In summary for our purposes, it is clear from Tables 15.1 and 15.2 that the major staples suffer to a greater or lesser extent from unbalanced overall nutritional composition or micronutrient levels, especially vitamin A (all but sweet potato). Note, however, that the USDA data reflect average values from major cultivars of these staples. As discussed for potato, native cultivars may have higher nutritional quality that has been lost in breeding of modern cultivars; nutritional value has not been a selection criterion in breeding. These deficiencies of crop staples are easily addressed by an adequate diet with food diversity, especially additional protein and fat sources, but this is often not the case in developing countries – and also increasingly in developed countries with calorie-rich diets and problems of obesity and malnutrition. This argues for increased consideration of alternative traditional 'native' foods, such as quinoa, with balanced and higher-quality nutritional composition (vide infra).

15.3.2 International Agriculture: CGIAR Programs

The Consultative Group on International Agricultural Research (CGIAR) describes itself as 'a global partnership that unites organizations engaged in research for a food secure future'. Structurally, CGIAR is a consortium of formerly independent centres or institutes that were brought into a network starting with 4 at its inception in 1971 and rising to 19 by the early 1990s. After some amalgamations there are now 15, dealing with the world's major food crops, livestock, fish, health and nutrition, climate change, soils, water, forests and biodiversity. CGIAR is funded by 36 Fund Donors – countries and some organizations, such as the World Bank.

CGIAR Centers focussed on major food staple crops, CIMMYT (International Maize and Wheat Improvement Center, 1971), IRRI (International Rice Research Institute, 1971), ICRISAT (International Crops Research Institute for the Semi-Arid Tropics, 1972), CIP (International Potato Center, 1973) and ICARDA (International Center for Agricultural Research in the Dry Areas, 1975), are early members and, of special relevance to the arguments proposed in this chapter, have entirely (CIMMYT, IRRI) or largely maintained their specific crop interests. In particular, activities for the three major staples are concentrated in just three centres – CIMMYT (wheat and maize), IRRI (rice) and ICARDA (wheat). This concentration represents a strength in terms of specific expertise but a major risk of vested interests in promoting and expanding uptake of their crop within international agriculture, i.e. 'finding new markets'. This is apparent from their now-global activities carried out at field stations or in partnership with national agriculture bodies, and introduction of maize into Asia and Africa.

As a result of dissatisfaction from several major donors in 2008 on effectiveness, efficiency and, indeed, continuing need for some Centers' activities, CGIAR underwent a restructure to an operational model of multidisciplinary thematic Research Programs (Özgediz, 2012) that aim to integrate research of the 15 Centers and their partners. The Programs of relevance here are briefly outlined below, using descriptions reflective of their summaries on the CGIAR website; the differences in emphases, approaches and language are quite telling. We also briefly summarize the native distribution of these crops and their domestication history and introduction to other regions in readiness for later discussion of adaptation and suitability for growing conditions (Denison, 2012).

> **The Research Program on Dryland Cereals**, a collaboration between ICARDA and ICRISAT, aims to assist the almost 1 billion poor people who live in the harsh dryland environments covering much of Africa and Asia by developing the hardy crops millets, sorghum and barley. *We note that these are crops native to these regions.*
>
> **The Research Program on Grain Legumes** (beans, pulses and oilseeds – often called 'poor people's meat'), is a collaboration between four main CGIAR Centers – CIAT (International Center for Tropical Agriculture), ICARDA, ICRISAT, and IITA (International Institute of Tropical Agriculture) – and seven other CGIAR, national agricultural research and USAID supported programs. It aims to benefit the nutri-

tion of 300 million poor people in Asia, Africa and Latin America by improving chickpea, common bean, cowpea, groundnut (or peanut), faba bean, lentil, pigeonpea and soybean crops grown by poor smallholder families. *We note that these are crops mostly native to the target regions. They also do not require N fertilizer.*

The Research Program on Roots, Tubers and Banana (RBT), is a collaboration initiated by four Centers, CIP, Bioversity International, CIAT and IITA, focussed on RBT crops including banana, plantain, cassava, potato, sweet potato, yams, and other roots and tubers. These crops are important globally in poor, rural areas and can grow in marginal conditions with relatively few inputs and simple techniques, are among the top ten most commonly consumed food staples, and provide one of the cheapest sources of energy and vital nutrients. However, they have been undervalued and suffered chronic underinvestment, problems the Program will address by creating critical mass, leveraging additional resources and exploiting commonalities across crops to create more diverse and robust food systems. It aims to work in consultation with stakeholders 'to identify the best bet research opportunities likely to give the highest return in terms of poverty reduction and improved food security'. *We note that the Program is introducing crops from their native areas into regions, globally, with agronomically suitable climates.*

The Research Program on Maize (MAIZE) led by CIMMYT and IIT will work with a large number of partners from other CGIAR Centers (CIAT, ICRISAT, IFPRI, ILRI, IRRI, World Agroforestry Centre), national, regional, international, private-sector and farmer organizations and institutes, NGOs (nongovernmental organizations) and universities 'who share MAIZE's commitment to reducing poverty and enhancing global food security and environmental sustainability'. It aims to use international agricultural research effectively to double productivity of maize-based farming systems, increasing their resilience and sustainability and increasing farmers' incomes and other opportunities, without using more land and increasing fertilizer, water and labour costs. MAIZE will respond to stakeholders' expressed needs by way of socioeconomic and agricultural policy Strategic Initiatives. *We note that maize was originally domesticated in Mesoamerica up to 10 000 years ago, spread within the Americas about 4500 years ago and was introduced to Europe, and then elsewhere, in the late fifteenth and early sixteenth centuries. It is now grown well outside its native agronomic range (hot and dry).*

The Research Program on Wheat (WHEAT) led by CIMMYT and ICARDA 'will be implemented with more than 200 partners' from other CGIAR Centers (Bioversity International, ICRISAT, IFPRI, ILRI, IRRI, IWMI), GIBS (Genomics and Integrated Breeding Service) and national, regional, international, private-sector and farmer organizations and institutes, NGOs and universities. It will build on this strength to 'catalyze and head an emergent, highly-distributed, virtual global wheat innovation network that will improve productivity and food security in wheat-based cropping areas of the developing world'. Its strategy is heavily focussed on cutting-edge research and technology to break the wheat yield barrier, including use of natural diversity of wheat and its wild relatives. *We note that wheat is an obligate temperate-climate crop native to the Levant region of the Near East and Ethiopian Highlands first domesticated about 10 000 years ago in the Fertile Crescent but now grown worldwide following early trade routes and later colonization.*

The Research Program on Rice, called the Global Rice Science Partnership (GRiSP), is a partnership between IRRI, The Arica Rice Center, CIAT, CIRAD (a French international agricultural R4D (research for development) institute) and JIRCAS (a Japanese international agricultural research centre) that will streamline current CGIAR rice R4D activities and align them with more than 900 rice R&D partners worldwide. GRiSP aims to 'increase rice productivity and value for the poor, foster more sustainable rice-based production and help rice farmers adapt to climate change'. It explains its program of 'Why rice' with four points: rice as the staple food for more than 3 billion people worldwide, including about 600 million living in extreme poverty; rice will remain the most important crop in Asia and will be increasingly important in Latin America and Africa; rice demand will outstrip supply; and rice price increases wreak havoc on the poor. GRiSP will deliver its program through six themes focussed on harnessing genetic diversity; accelerating development, delivery and adoption of new varieties; increasing sustainability; extracting more value from harvests; technology and other evaluations; and 'supporting the growth of the global rice sector'. These market-oriented assumptions and last objective are telling. *We note that although wild rice species are globally distributed, the two strains of the major domesticated rice, Oryza sativa, arose in China 8200–13 500 years ago and spread from East Asia to Southeast Asia and thence to Europe through Western Asia, and later to the Americas through European colonization. Independent domestication near the Niger River from a wild species native to sub-Saharan Africa about 2000–3000 years ago led to African rice, Oryza glaberrima. However, this is being largely replaced in Africa by O. sativa or its cross with O. glaberrima, NERICA* (Linares, 2002).

15.3.3 Crop Wild-relatives (CWR) Project

In late 2010 the Global Crop Diversity Trust (GCDT), with partners from national agricultural research institutes, the Royal Botanic Gardens, Kew and CGIAR, with initial funding of US$50 million from Norway, started a global program, the Crop Wild Relatives (CWR) campaign. Based on recognition that all these crops were originally domesticated from wild species under growing conditions, including climate, pest and disease, best suited to those times and places, its stated aims are to systematically find, collect, catalogue, use and store seeds of the wild relatives of 29 major food crops.

The current high rate of diversity loss makes this collection necessary protection for future global food supplies as it is realized that crop breeders need to go back to wild relatives to glean the required traits to develop new crop varieties adapted to the increasingly harsher and more variable present, and predicted future, growing conditions. The 29 targeted crops are: African rice (*O. glaberrima*), alfalfa (*Medicago sativa*), apple (*Malus domestica*), eggplant (*Solanum melongena*), bambara groundnut (*Vigna subterranea*), banana (*Musa acuminata*), barley (*Hordeum vulgare*), carrot (*Daucus carota*), chickpea (*Cicer arietinum*), common bean (*Phaseolus vulgaris*), cowpea (*Vigna unguiculata*), faba bean (*Vicia faba*), finger millet (*Eleusine coracana*), grasspea (*Lathyrus sativus*), lentil (*Lens culinaris*), lima bean (*Phaseolus lunatus*), oat (*Avena sativa*), pea (*Pisum sativum*), pearl millet (*Pennisetum glaucum*), pigeonpea (*Cajanus cajan*), plantain (*Musa balbisiana*), potato (*Solanum tuberosum*), rice (*O. sativa*), rye (*Secale cereale*), sorghum

(*Sorghum bicolor*), sunflower (*Helianthus annuus*), sweet potato (*Ipomoea batatas*), vetch (*Vicia sativa*) and wheat (*Triticum aestivum*). This list contains mostly *current* staple and major food crops, except for some so-called 'orphan crops' of sub-Saharan Africa (sorghum, millets, chickpea, cowpea, pigeonpea, grasspea, groundnut).

The importance of CWR and the imperative of an effective CWR-collection initiative is apparent from a financial analysis commissioned by Kew's Millennium Seed Bank for four crops (wheat, rice, potato and cassava). This considered FAO current and forecasted gross production values (GPV) and estimates of current value of commercial crops grown today, and in the future, containing improved productivity or stress resistance traits derived from CWR (CWR, 2013). Extrapolated to the 29 prioritized crops, values of $42 billion today, and potentially $120 billion in the future, were assigned. As the annual GPV of the 29 priority crops was $581 billion in 2010, this implies that CWR are already valued at about 7 per cent of annual production value. In this light, an initial budget of $50 million for the CWR Project may be seen as a gross underinvestment, especially given the benefits to the commercial agriculture sector which has enjoyed CWR resources virtually cost free.

But apart from inadequate budget for the job-in-hand, in the context of our current analysis the CWR strategy adopted has several major deficiencies, especially for the future. Although the budget will have placed limitations on its scope, the target list is notable both for its inclusions and omissions. It omits maize, soybean, cassava and yams, crops constituting current major food staples of large populations in Asia, Africa and other parts of the developing world, and is poorly representative of roots and tubers which are increasing in importance as more reliable crops under increasingly difficult growing conditions in Africa and Asia, especially (vide infra). In particular, it ignores ancient crops being promoted for the future for their superior nutritional qualities and hardiness under diverse growing conditions, such as the pseudocereals quinoa, amaranth and buckwheat, and other Inca tuber crops such as oca and ulluco, as well as analogous traditional crops of Africa (vide infra) (National Academies Advisory Panel, 1989, 1996). The strategy also follows from the assumption that 'many current crop varieties will need replacement to enable them to better suit the new and changing agro-environments' (Maxted et al., 2013) rather than that alternative and more suitable crops should be substituted (vide infra).

Also, the scoping ('gap analysis') studies being undertaken for each crop to identify high priority locations for collecting CWRs to fill gaps in current germplasm bank collections are based on a priori assumptions of a rather narrow genetic width (number of genera) for each crop (Ramírez-Villegas, 2010; Vincent et al., 2013). This is in accord with current breeding practices but ignores the much richer gene diversity present in more distant relatives, that can be introgressed with increased ease using modern wide-crossing methods (Sharma, 1995; Sharma et al., 1996). Furthermore, the limited informatic methodology of using panels of crop and taxonomic 'experts' to gather existing data from the world's herbaria and genebanks on the distribution of the chosen genera and species and comparing the results with locations from which seeds have already been collected has flaws; it assumes that the diversity is already known (not true) and that plant populations still exist in locations from which herbarium samples were collected up to 100 years or so ago (will often be untrue). Finally, the CWR collecting strategy is targeting traditional breeding traits, such as disease resistance, and heat, drought and salt tolerance. As noted, photosynthetic traits have not previously been targeted in crop breeding.

In summary, the CWR initiative will not provide, except unwittingly, the increased genetic resources required for the development of crops with improved photosynthetic capacity, nor for many attractive alternative native crops, such as quinoa now attracting wide attention (vide infra), for which germplasm resources are small, scattered and largely inaccessible to researchers and breeders.

15.3.4 Investment in Current Crops: Historical and Vested Interests

Our analysis so far has identified numerous instances where the power and momentum of existing vested interests both in national, international and commercial agriculture impedes an objective consideration of best options for nutritious and sustainable food crops for future food security.

Examples from the CGIAR international agriculture and CWR Project have been detailed above. Some of the new CGIAR crop Research Programs, with increased core funding from international-aid sources, have an operational R&D model akin to a multinational agbiotech company but without the ongoing mechanisms for fiscal accountability and restructure. Some also have an analogous 'marketing' dynamic to extending their influence, taking rice and maize to the world, for example. It is hardly surprising that an operation or country that 'does' rice, wheat or maize will see this as a 'solution' for the rest of the world.

We argue that an independent high-level strategic assessment and cost–benefit analysis needs to be undertaken on the wisdom of persevering with the existing portfolio of major staples, which are increasingly maladapted to their growing environments and for which further gains in efficient and *effective* productivity are modest or risky, rather than moving to a wider better-adapted more resilient and, thus, less risky basket of crops, including reintroduction of displaced native crops.

This assessment should include a comprehensive audit to define a preferred basket of staple crops against a number of technical 'robustness' or risk criteria: nutritional quality and balance; nutrient-use efficiency (especially NUE), WUE and RUE, and prospects for improvement; adaptability and resilience to abiotic stresses, especially extreme weather events and global climate shifts; environmental sustainability (ecological footprint); and suitability for small-scale farming and production.

An aim should be not only to minimize future use of resources (land, water, nutrients, etc.) while providing for the increased needs of the projected 9 billion people but to *reduce* the ecological footprint for human food production, a scenario that does not even seem to be contemplated.

15.3.5 Why Rice? – Fit-for-purpose?

As an illustration of broad questions that could be asked in the assessment proposed above, in this section we examine the CGIAR GRiSP four-point 'Why rice' justifications from section 15.3.2 from a different viewpoint – as a question. The domestication history of Asian (*O. sativa*) rice and its global spread, and of African (*O. glaberrima*) rice and its recent hybrid cross, NERICA rice (Linares, 2002), were noted in section 15.3.2. Rice is not native to the Americas but was introduced to Latin America, the Caribbean and Mexico during European colonization.

In line with our main aims, we will not deal with socioeconomic issues of inefficiencies in farming system technology, supply and marketing chains, and post-harvest losses, particularly in India. However, we note that the early hopes for NERICA rice have not been realized since its introduction in 1996, confounding effects being not only agronomic but from promotion of agribusiness in Africa that is threatening Africa's move to food soverignty by undermining small-scale farmers and growing of traditional rice varieties better adapted to local conditions (GRAIN, 2009).

Rice is central to food security for more than half the world population, with developing countries accounting for 95 per cent of global production. Average annual production over 2007–11 was 691 million tonnes, with seven Asian countries, China (195 million tonnes), India (146), Indonesia (63), Bangladesh (48), Vietnam (39), Thailand (33) and Myanmar (32) producing 81 per cent (FAO, 2011).

However, rice consumption has declined recently in many wealthier rice-consuming countries, such as Japan, Korea and Thailand, as rising incomes enable people to eat a more varied diet. As this pattern can be expected in the newly emergent middle-class of China, India and other Asian countries, the question can be asked who will be the potential major consumers of rice in the future (GriSP's expanding 'market') and is rice best for them? The answer is that it will continue to be the poorest people, most vulnerable to food insecurity and with lesser choices of a varied diet. The next question is whether rice is the best option for them or will it simply reduce their chances – and that of a significant proportion of the additional 2 billion people expected by 2050 – of escaping from poverty and malnutrition? The following arguments suggest it is a poor option.

First, rice cultivation has very high water needs and is labour-intensive. Without irrigated or rain-fed flooding of paddy fields, weed and pest control are more difficult and a different nitrogen fertilizer approach is necessary as, unusually, the rice plant absorbs N in the (reduced) ammonium – not nitrate – form, which is protected from oxidation in the anaerobic water-logged soil. Non-irrigated 'upland rice' is grown as a main staple in intertropical highlands with a high incidence of poverty, mostly inhabited by socially and politically disadvantaged ethnic minorities. However, these are low yielding.

In a recent FAO report on rice Redfern et al. (2012) summarize (with similar conclusions to Nelson et al., 2009) the *particular* agronomic deficiencies of rice-production systems in the context of global climate change. Thus, rice-growing areas are especially threatened due to their high water requirements and vulnerability to drought stress, as well as already experiencing temperatures close to those critically high for development of the rice plant at it different growth stages (Redfern et al., 2012, Table 2). We note that these conclusions do not take into account the results of Vu et al. (1997) which suggest that projected adverse effects on rice yields from global warming would not be realized – or not fully – if atmospheric CO_2 continues to increase.

Second, compared with other current food staples, rice's nutritional quality is, at best, modest and greatly inferior to alternative native or other crops (e.g. legumes) that might be more extensively grown instead of rice. Of note, is the 'Golden Rice' initiative started by German researchers in 1993 with funding from the Rockefeller Foundation, which aimed to produce a GM variety of *O. sativa* rice able to biosynthesize beta-carotene, a precursor of vitamin A (Enserink, 2008). Its objective was to produce a fortified food to be grown and consumed in areas, mostly by disadvantaged people in Asia, with a deficiency of dietary vitamin A, and, thus, prevent annual childhood deaths estimated at 670000. Although a biotechnology success (after two rounds), Golden Rice met sustained opposition from environmental and anti-globalization activists, and other uncertainty about who would use it and whether the beta-carotene would be absorbed. It has only recently (2013) been completing safety trials in the Philippines. In the context of the arguments in this chapter, the wisdom of this technological fix is questionable as the vitamin A problem could be readily addressed in other ways, including growing other crops, legume crops or carrots and some leafy vegetables.

Lastly, we consider prospects for improvement of photosynthetic capacity of rice. As already noted, modern Asian cultivated rice has the lowest genetic diversity (only 10–20 per cent) of the major food crops (Zhu et al., 2007). Such cultivars are, thus, not good starting points for photosynthetic improvement by either breeding or GM methods as RUE-trait genes and diversity will likely have been deleted and reduced.

Rice is the subject of a long-term and risky project, C_4 Rice, driven by a decade-long campaign by John Sheehy from IRRI before it was finally funded by the Bill and Melinda Gates Foundation and other donors and started in 2009. It aims to increase yield by re-engineering C_4 metabolism, and associated necessary changes to the cellular structure into rice, with the aim of producing more drought-resistant and temperature-tolerant rice. Whether it is technically feasible is unclear. Whether it is a best-bet option for photosynthetic improvement is dubious, especially given projections of negligible benefits of C_4 metabolism over C_3 metabolism with increasing atmospheric CO_2 (Zhu et al., 2008). Whether it is strategically defensible given the opportunity cost of distracting attention away from other breeding strategies to increase photosynthetic-yield potential is a major concern. Given the arguments in this chapter, it seems this decision was made without any analysis of the basic question 'Why rice?'

In summary, rice geopolitics could be considered as a major threat to global food security, but worse in aggravating food insecurity for the poor. If the risks of the 'rice industry' were considered against the ISO 31000:2009 risk management principles and guidelines (ISO, 2009) it might be well seen as not-fit-for-purpose as a global staple food!

15.4 BETTER ALTERNATIVES TO MAJOR STAPLE CROPS?

In previous sections we have discussed significant problems with the current portfolio of major staple crops from several angles. Points which we will develop further in this section are:

- their intrinsic unsuitability to growing conditions in some regions and climates in which they are cultivated – for example, wheat as an intrinsic temperate-climate plant – and, consequently, the increasing unreliability of harvests on a seasonal or long-term basis from adverse weather events or climate change;
- the usefulness of modern cultivars as starting points for further development, particularly for improvement of photosynthesis (RUE), due to loss of gene diversity from intensive breeding, for example, the severe 'domestication bottleneck' for rice (Zhu et al., 2007);

- their nutritional quality and balance (Tables 15.1 and 15.2), which are particularly poor for maize;
- persistence with the major staples and resistance to consider alternative crops due to the large existing investment and vested interests, not merely monetary, in current crops and agricultural systems;
- the high resource costs and threat to environmental sustainability from current agricultural paradigms.

15.4.1 Options for Meeting Increased Food Demand Sustainably

Tilman et al. (2011) considered environmental impacts for meeting increasing global food demand, estimated to be 100–110 per cent from 2005–50, depending on how global agriculture expanded to meet this demand. They compared impacts of continuing the current trend of greater agricultural intensification in richer nations and greater land clearing (extensification) in poorer nations with the alternative option of moderate intensification focused on existing croplands of underyielding nations, and adaptation and transfer of high-yielding technologies to these croplands, coupled with global technological improvements to reduce resource imnputs, e.g. nitrogen use. They concluded that 'attainment of high yields on existing croplands of underyielding nations is of great importance if global crop demand is to be met with minimal environmental impacts'. Foley et al. (2011) and Godfray et al. (2010) also addressed how to substantially grow food production while at the same time dramatically shrinking agriculture's environmental footprint. Although coming up with a similar to-do list as many other published analyses (e.g. *The Economist Special Issue*, 2011), including 'closing 'yield gaps' on underperforming lands', they did not prioritize elements as did Tilman et al. (2011).

15.4.2 Increased Risk of Disease and Monoculture of Global Food Staples

The huge economic cost of crop diseases is well known and, indeed, breeding in of disease-resistance traits, especially from crop wild relatives, has high focus. Within current agricultural thinking this costly never-ending co-evolutionary war with disease is accepted without question. The severity of this problem and the risks for global food security are linked to the global dominance of a small number of staple crops, especially wheat, rice and maize, grown in monoculture and often under stressed growing conditions (vide infra) that increase disease susceptibility. Thus, proposals below to expand the range and production of other staple crops would have benefits in reducing the risks of crop failure and production loss from disease.

As an example of the scale of current disease risk and cost, Ug99, a virulent strain of wheat stem rust, has been spreading globally since the initial outbreak in Uganda in 1998–99. Worst-case FAO predictions suggest it could reduce global wheat production by almost 10 per cent. Pardey et al. (2013) estimated 66 per cent of the world's wheat area was climatically suitable for development of stem-rust disease and suggest sustained investment of ~$50 million per year on stem-rust research was justified economically; this can be compared with recent investments of $67 million (2008–16) from the Bill and Melinda Gates Foundation (BMGF) and UK Department for International Development. These are large research expenditures compared with global annual investment in agriculture, especially for crops for poor farmers who cannot even afford commercial seed.

15.4.3 Cutting Losses of Investment in Current Crops?

The discussion so far leads us to address the question of whether a considered shift to a more balanced portfolio of crops and agricultural systems, focussed on increasing crop yield, reliability and nutritional value in underyielding nations or regions, is a better basis for future crop development for global food security and minimizing food insecurity. This would include efforts to increase yield potential from improvement in photosynthesis. That is, to recapitulate Kingsbury's (2009: 322) view, whether it is now time to start solving the tough problems that have been postponed for 50 years.

Apart from vested economic and other interests, the previous long timeframe for development of current crop varieties reinforces reluctance to abandon decades of work. However, crop development using recent technological advances, e.g. genomics and phenomics, can greatly decrease the time for phenotyping breeding crosses and introgressing target genes and producing new field-ready varieties, for both current (Feuillet et al., 2008; Tester and Langridge, 2010) and alternative crops (Varshney et al., 2012). Use of these methods, as well as those to assist in wide-crossing (Sharma, 1995), including embryo rescue (Sharma et al., 1996), would allow breeding efforts to make better use of wild varieties and landraces (farmers' varieties, native cultivars) to exploit the full range of natural diversity and adaptations to harsh and variable growing conditions, rather than continuing to breed from bottlenecked modern cultivars (e.g. rice; Zhu et al., 2007).

Perhaps, most importantly this would allow breeding *concurrently* for resistance to biotic stresses, e.g. plant diseases, *and* increased photosynthetic yield potential *and* nutritional composition starting from a rich gene pool. Designer crops fit-for-purpose assembled from natural and/or GM gene components!

15.4.4 Advantages of Native Crops as Alternative Staples

Although many plants have been domesticated or foraged for food, as discussed in section 15.3.1, few can be regarded as alternative *staple* crops, i.e. suitable to supply a significant proportion of energy needs in a diet.

Concerns going back now 20 years about the suitability of introduced staples, often of inferior nutritional value, for agronomic conditions (climatic and farming) in Africa compared with displaced native crops, led to a report by a US National Academies Advisory Panel (1996) which argued for reintroduction of these 'lost crops'. This three-volume (grains; vegetables, roots and legumes; and fruits) report has had some impact in Africa (see CGIAR Research Programs on Dryland Cereals, Grain Legumes and Roots, Tubers and Bananas in section 15.3.2). An earlier report by a National Academies Advisory Panel (1989), 'Lost Crops of the Incas', hoped to promote wider cultivation of native Andean crops in recognition of their exceptional agronomic and nutritional features. However, this hope has been little realized, despite promotion of two of these crops in FAO–UN International Year of the Potato (IYP in 2008; FAO, 2008; MacKenzie, 2008) and Quinoa (IYQ in 2013; FAO Regional Office, 2011).

At the time of the 1996 report, Africa was seen by many as a basket case, a vast region with seemingly poor prospects for being able to feed its growing population and no ready solutions. However, the reports recognized more than 2000 native grains, roots, fruits, and other food plants that had been feeding Africans for thousands of years but were now largely abandoned. These include the native cereals, African rice, millets, sorghum, tef and fonio which can thrive on relatively infertile soils with minimal land preparation and management, and grow well with other crops in mixed stands.

The 1989 Andean-crop report documented 'more than 30 promising Inca staples (that) remain largely restricted to their native lands and unappreciated elsewhere'. These include about a dozen root crops including potato and ulluco (Melloco), three pseudocereals, kaniwa and quinoa and kiwicha, three legumes, basul, nuñas and tarwi (chocho), and more than a dozen fruits and nuts. Although major staples such as maize and wheat have been widely introduced in mostly lowland regions of Andean countries (Peru, Bolivia, Ecuador and Colombia), since Spanish occupation in the fifteenth and sixteenth centuries, native crops have been continuously cultivated, especially in the highlands. Hence, native cultivars adapted to a very large range of, usually harsh, agronomic conditions have been preserved, for example more than 500 native Ecuadorian potato varieties (Monteros et al., 2011).

In summary, these native staple crops are generally more reliable, hardy (resilient) and resource-efficient than major staples and can be farmed simply with minimal land preparation. They thus well meet the criteria for suitability to their prospective growing conditions as well as the technical-assessment criteria suggested in section 15.3.4.

15.4.5 Advantages of Potato and Quinoa for Intensive Development

Continuing the discussion along the lines of 'Why rice?' in section 15.3.5, here we summarize why potato and quinoa are especially suitable for intensive development, using native Andean germplasm, and for introduction to regions globally with a wide range of agronomic and climatic conditions, particularly in the developing world.

Why potato?
Potato is the third most important food crop in the world after rice and wheat with average annual production over 2007–11 of 339 million tonnes (FAO, 2011). China is the largest producer (average 2007–11; 76 million tonnes/year), followed by India (35), Russia (30), Ukraine (20) and the United States (19). Potato is not a tradeable crop (~80 per cent water, Table 15.1), being grown in about 130 countries and consumed regionally. Over the last 40 years it has changed from a northern crop (85 per cent) to one with more than half production grown in less developed countries. Its growing importance was recognized by the UN declaring 2008 International Year of the Potato (IYP) (FAO, 2008; MacKenzie, 2008). More than 1 billion people eat potato.

Wild potato species (*Solanum tuberosum*) occur in a very wide ecogeographical range from latitude 40°N (SW USA) to 40°S (Chile) in 16 countries, from sea level to 4500 m, with average annual temperature from −1 and 26°C, and average annual precipitation < 250 mm (coastal desert of Peru) to > 3000 mm (Mesoamerica). This range covers habitats including high-altitude Andean grasslands, dry deciduous forests in Mexico, strand vegetation along beaches, and cool upland rain forests. Of the ~180 species, about

Figure 15.3 Photo showing variety of sizes, shapes and colours (yellow, orange, brown, red, purple, black and variegated) of tubers of native potato cultivars from Andean regions of South America. In indigenous agriculture up to 20 different cultivars may be grown in one field

90 per cent are in Peru, Bolivia, Colombia and Mexico and most occur between 2000 and 4000 m (Hijmans et al., 2002).

This wide adaptation of wild potato provides a rich resource for breeding for different agroclimatic conditions and natural resistance to pests and diseases, and indeed there are about 5000 different cultivars of potato, mostly grown regionally in the Andes. As noted in section 15.4.4, despite significant displacement of native Andean crops since Spanish occupation in the fifteenth and sixteenth centuries, potato has been continuously cultivated, especially in the highlands, preserving both the diversity of cultivars and farming systems. Up to 20 different varieties may be grown in one field (de Haan et al., 2010) providing risk management against failure of some varieties due to adverse weather conditions, pests or disease. Unfortunately, the varieties of potato introduced to Europe and then the rest of the world (see above for largest producers) represent only a small proportion of this diversity (white varieties preferred for cultural reasons by the Spanish?), with < 20 per cent of species used in pre-breeding and with most modern cultivars now bottlenecked.

CIP's brochures '50 potato facts' and 'Why potatoes' summarize the agronomic and nutritional advantages of potato. One hectare can yield two to four times the food value of grain crops, and potatoes produce more food per unit of water than any other major crop being up to seven times more efficient in using water than cereals. This has made the crop increasingly important in Asia's arid regions. Potatoes are a cheap source of carbohydrates but, as shown in Table 15.1, also contain significant amounts of protein (of same order as cereals), vitamins B and C, and minerals (iron, potassium and zinc).

However, these nutritional values for modern cultivars underrate the potential for breeding nutritionally better potato. A recent study of 100 Ecuadorian native cultivars showed varieties with significantly higher iron (up to 17 mg/100 g dry weight compared with 3.7 mg in Table 15.1) and zinc (5.1 mg compared with 1.4 mg), and up to 50 per cent and 100 per cent more vitamin C and beta-carotene than modern cultivars (Monteros et al., 2011).

Finally, we recapitulate the findings from earlier which showed that photosynthesis in potato was better able to take advantage of CO_2 fertilization than cereals, with gains being translated into a higher number of tubers rather than greater mean tuber size (Miglietta et al., 1998). Roots and tubers have the potential to adjust tuber development ('sink') more readily to amount of 'source' available (sugar, protein etc. that can be mobilized for storage in the tuber) than cereals, for which 'sink' is determined at flowering time (e.g. number of ears for wheat). Thus, biomass produced by photosynthesis – more or less depending on growing conditions – can be efficiently transformed into potatoes, to give more or less yield, thus, reducing risk of crop failure. Also, up to 85 per cent of the plant biomass can be stored as potatoes, i.e. edible human food, whereas for cereals with above-ground structure required to support ears with heavy grain the figure is around 50 per cent with significant non-food residue as straw.

Why quinoa?
As noted in section 15.4.4, quinoa was one of the highly recommended crops in the 1989 Report of the National Academies Advisory Panel on Lost Crops of the Incas, and 2013 is the FAO-UN International Year of Quinoa (IYQ; FAO Regional Office, 2011). UN support for IYQ-2013 was taken in recognition of 'the exceptional nutritional qualities of quinoa, its adaptability to different agro-ecological conditions and its potential contribution to the fight against hunger and malnutrition'. The technical report 'Quinoa: an ancient crop to contribute to world food security' (FAO, 2011) covers quinoa's nutritional qualities, genetic diversity, agronomic potential, products, industrial potential and other economic aspects, and its cultivation outside the Andean region. Facts and figures on quinoa are a peon of superlatives.

Quinoa (*Chenopodium quinoa* Willd) is one of the oldest crops in the Andean Region, with ~7000 years of cultivation, and was widely cultivated by pre-Columbian cultures. Average annual production over 2007–11 was only 70000 tonnes (FAO, 2011), with production recorded for only three countries, Peru (37000), Bolivia (32000) and Ecuador (700). In comparison, annual global rice production is ~700 million tonnes (section 15.3.5). However, production has increased 36 per cent from 2007 to 2011 due to increased export demand from developed countries. Tripling of prices in Bolivia has had the beneficial effect of increasing farmers' incomes and reducing poverty but negative effect of pricing it beyond ordinary Bolivian consumers for whom quinoa is now more expensive than rice.

Foremost in favour of expanded use of quinoa are its nutritional benefits and agricultural versatility. As indicated in Tables 15.1 and 15.2, it has an exceptional nutritional balance, contains high amounts of all the indispensable and essential amino acids, especially lysine, high vitamin and mineral content and is gluten-free (unlike wheat but as for rice). A key feature is that the grain, leaves and inflorescences (flowering parts) are all sources of high quality protein, mainly albumin and globulin types, with a balanced composition of amino acids similar to that of milk protein casein. This high quality protein is especially valuable for populations which rarely eat animal protein.

Quinoa's genetic variability has allowed it to adapt to a wide range of ecological environments (valleys, highlands, salt flats, etc.) with different relative humidity (from 40–88 per cent), altitudes (from sea level up to 4000 m), and temperatures (from −8°C to 38°C). It is highly water efficient and produces acceptable yields with rainfall as little as

100–200 mm. This adaptability to adverse climate and soil conditions allows it to grow where other crops cannot. Its production costs are also low as the crop requires little in the way of inputs, labour or soil preparation.

15.4.6 Agronomic Advantages from Native Crops: Mixed and Under-tree Cropping

Many problems of modern commercial agriculture, particularly weeds, pests and diseases derive from monoculture. Traditional landraces (farmers' varieties, native cultivars) were not pure lines but had significant diversity with inbuilt potential for assuring a harvestable crop if some variants did well and others poorly in a given growing season. Such harvests are perfectly suitable and equally nutritious as food sources for poor farmers and as locally marketed produce but are not 'marketable' more widely or tradeable. As noted, indigenous Andean farmers grow several different potato cultivars – as well as other tuber crops – in the same field, and such farming (effectively, 'gardening') systems are also still used worldwide in small-scale farming.

Cropping under trees can also protect from extreme heat and may also be useful to extend areas of arable land by regenerating degraded crop land or bringing marginal land into cultivation – stabilizing soil, increasing soil carbon and water retention. These crop conditions can be accommodated by appropriate tailoring of photosynthetic improvement under shaded or lower-light conditions by breeding from similarly adapted germplasm. However, such farming is also not commercially viable and there is currently little incentive to produce such varieties. Native legumes are also well suited to mixed farming.

15.5 CULTURAL AND OTHER ISSUES

For completeness, we briefly note cultural and other issues that are addessed fully by other authors, e.g. de Schutter and Cordes (2011).

15.5.1 Cultural Expectations and Culinary Preferences

Food is a major part of peoples' cultures and is often integral to cultural identity. However, recent history (e.g. rice-eaters; section 15.3.5) shows that these preferences are adaptable and, given choice and means, people readily accept alternative foods and prefer a more varied diet. Even switching to lower quality options from more expensive processed foods or alternative, including supposedly 'higher-status', foods introduced by relatively recent or more distant colonization or occupation! Cultural resistance to introduction of alternative staple crops, as proposed here, may thus be greater from people who could benefit most from the improved nutrition and food security they could provide.

15.5.2 Staple Foods as a 'Commodity'

Trade and other policy and economic systems treat staple foods that constitute a large proportion of calorie intake for billions of people as commodities, like other marketable and tradeable products. This has major implications for food security and food insecurity, as supply and demand or price manipulation have greater impact on the poor with limited other food options. This factor argues for the sustainable agriculture conclusion of Tilman et al. (2011) for focussing attention on increasing yields on existing croplands of underyielding nations to meet global crop demand with minimal environmental impacts as this strategy minimizes the commoditization of essential food for the food insecure.

15.5.3 Right to Food

It is accepted that food is a primal need and people have a right to food (de Schutter, 2011). In the context of 15.5.1 above, the interesting question arises as to whether this includes the right to *particular* staple foods, e.g. foods of cultural or culinary preference, if it becomes more difficult to grow them where they are needed than alternative, equally or more nutritious, crops that grow better and are more productive for given resources and more ecologically sustainable? Thus, given the low investment in global crop R&D for use by poor or small-scale farmers, how should these factors be weighed when making decisions on whether money should be spent on developing 'preferred' crops rather than more agronomically suitable and nutritious crops?

15.5.4 Urbanization and Agrarian Models

The dominant socioeconomic paradigm views progress as replacement of small-scale or 'subsistence agriculture' by larger 'more efficient' farming units using less labour and producing a marketable surplus to reduce rural poverty and feed the growing (displaced?) urban or non-farming rural population. The prosperous 'yeoman farmer' model is not generally in favour in the developing world, even though this is a renewed aspiration in developed countries with the option of supporting 'locally produced', 'know what we're eating' and 'transport miles' philosophies. These factors are the obverse of those of commoditization commented on in section 15.3.2, but supported by the same conclusions as Tilman et al. (2011).

It is also assumed that increased urbanization and larger farming units are a one-way move. However, the recent example of Russia after collapse of corporate (collectivized) agriculture and large decreases in food production in the early 1990s indicates otherwise. By 1999, 35 million small family plots produced 90 per cent of Russia's potatoes, 77 per cent of vegetables, 87 per cent of fruits, 59 per cent of meat, 49 per cent of milk, with this trend being maintained. The disparity in efficiency of food production between corporate farms (80 per cent of arable land, 41 per cent of agricultural production in 2005) and family plots (10 and 53 per cent) and peasant farms (10 and 6 per cent) is sobering (*Statistical Yearbook of the Russian Federation*, 2007). Parts of the developed or 'undeveloping' world may choose, similarly, for one reason or other to go backwards!

15.6 SUMMARY AND RECOMMENDATIONS FOR FUTURE STUDY

Ultimately the intrinsic *capacity* to produce sufficient nutritious food to sustain the world's population will be determined by several limiting factors:

- resource availability – land, water, nutrients and sunlight;
- growing conditions – climate and adverse seasonal or extreme weather events;
- choice of crops appropriate to these conditions to maximize yield and efficient use of resources, and with resilience to variable growing conditions;
- sufficient farmers to produce them *under these constraints*; and
- sustainable production to minimize environmental impact.

Simply stated, the challenge is to identify appropriate crop staples for further development and define appropriate farming systems that can: produce high yields efficiently in terms of resource inputs; provide reliable harvests and economic return for farm units of small to large scale; still produce enough nutrititious, affordable food for non-farming people, including the rural and urban poor; and protect the environment, and indeed reduce the ecological footprint.

Improvements in trade and market efficiency, and waste and storage-loss minimization cannot overcome an absolute deficiency in production. Although increasing photosynthetic efficiency is an excellent solution for increasing yield potential and production under these limiting factors, it cannot alone address production and access problems to assure food security and minimize food security.

This chapter argues for a rethink of of the problem of providing sufficient nutritious food from an integrated perspective that adequately represents the complexity of the problem, and, thus, provides a basis for understanding the interdependencies of contributing factors. Although some authors and larger consortia have enunciated the issues (e.g. Godfray et al., 2010; *The Economist Special Issue*, 2011; Foley et al., 2011) or attempted analyses from different perspectives, e.g. climate change (Nelson et al., 2009), sustainability (Keating et al., 2010; Tilman et al., 2011), planetary boundaries (Rockström et al., 2009) or human rights (de Schutter, 2011), we argue that no systematic framework capable of providing such an analysis has been proposed. We argue that this is necessary to allow a balanced objective assessment of options consistent with all the above needs and constraints, recognizing the vulnerabilties in the system and with appropraite weighting of risks.

15.6.1 Summary of Main Arguments and Conclusions

In the following we summarize our major conclusions from sub-sections of the analysis, continue with a technicai summary of opportunities from photosynthetic improvement of crops under uncertainties of future growing conditions, and conclude with suggestions for a comprehensive assessment that needs to be undertaken within the general framework proposed above.

Our analysis of predicted global and regional impacts on food production and threats to poor people in developing countries from global climate change (IFPRI report of Nelson et al., 2009) or unreliable or extreme weathee events (IPCC, 2012) suggested more appropriate criteria for crop suitability to their prospective growing conditions now, and in the future, than the recent mantra of 'climate-ready' crops. These are that they should be naturally well adapted in the plant evolutionary sense (Denison, 2012) and more reliable and resilient, meaning better able to survive poor seasonal conditions, particularly hotter and/or drier, and survive and recover from extreme weather events, such as heat waves, to still produce a harvestable crop.

Our analysis of the net benefits of increasing photosynthetic capacity is that it widens the margins for plants to cope with both extreme short-term weather events and poor seasonal growing conditions and still produce a harvestable crop. Photosynthesis is the key trait to produce such benefits as it produces the plant's energy that can then be used by the plant to repair damage from heat, pollutants, disease, insect or other damage. Increasing photosynthetic capacity can provide reserve energy for transformation into grain, tubers etc. This is critical for reducing food insecurity for the poor and reducing economic risk for commercial farmers.

There are particular concerns for regional and global redistribution of nutrients, especially phosphorus, and loss of nutrients from the agricultural cycle (into oceans and rivers) from current agricultural systems driven by trade-based production efficiency and urbanization. These losses are not costed as whole-of-lifetime food costs.

Our analysis of nutritional quality of the current major staple crops (Tables 15.1 and 15.2) indicate they suffer to a greater or lesser extent from unbalanced overall nutritional composition or micronutrient levels, especially vitamin A (all but sweet potato), a major problem for people (usually poor and disadvantaged) without dietary variety, including animal protein. This argues for increased consideration of alternative traditional 'native' foods, such as quinoa, with better balanced and quality of nutritional composition.

Our analysis of the CGIAR Research Program and Crop Wild Relatives (CWR) Project identified instances where the power and momentum of existing vested interests both in national, international and commercial agriculture impedes an objective consideration of best options for nutritious and sustainable food crops for future food security. Some of the new CGIAR Crop Research Programs, with increased core funding from international-aid sources, have an operational R&D model akin to a multinational agbiotech company but without the ongoing mechanisms for fiscal accountability and restructure. Some also have an analogous 'marketing' dynamic to extending their influence, taking rice and maize to the world, for example. We assess that the CWR initiative will not provide, except unwittingly, the increased genetic resources required for the development of crops with improved photosynthetic capacity, nor for many attractive alternative native crops, such as quinoa, for which germplasm resources are small, scattered and largely inaccessible to researchers and breeders.

Analysis of whether rice is suitable as a major staple crop, given its extreme vulnerabilty to climate-change threats, high resource and labour costs, and modest general nutritional spectrum and deficiency of vitamin A, we concluded negatively. Indeed, rice geopolitics can be considered as a major threat to global food security, especially for the poor. We concluded that, if the risks of the 'rice industry' were considered against the ISO 31000:2009 risk management principles and guidelines (ISO, 2009), it might be well seen as not-fit-for-purpose as a global staple food!

In considering options for meeting increased food demand sustainably, we noted the conclusion of Tilman et al. (2011) pursuing high yields on existing croplands of underyielding nations is the preferred option for meeting global crop demand with minimal environmental impacts compared with continuing the current trend of greater agricultural intensification in richer nations and greater land clearing (extensification) in poorer nations.

In our assessment of whether it would be better to cut losses of investment in some current crops as unsuitable for development for the future we agree with Kingsbury's

(2009) view that it is now time to start solving the tough problems that have been postponed for 50 years due to false confidence in the strategy and technologies of the Green Revolution of the 1960s which can no longer deliver in an increasingly resource-limited world. An major advantage of such a major shift in thinking is that it would allow use of modern breeding methods to *concurrently* develop crops for resistance to biotic stresses, e.g. plant diseases, *and* increased photosynthetic yield potential *and* nutritional composition starting from a rich gene pool. Designer crops fit-for-purpose assembled from natural and/or GM gene components!

Our analysis of advantages of native crops as alternative staples, recapitulated the conclusions of previous comprehensive studies of National Academies Advisory Panels (1989, 1996) who identified native staple crops that are more reliable, hardy (resilient) and resource-efficient than major staples and can be farmed simply with minimal land preparation. They thus well meet the criteria for suitability to their prospective current and future growing conditions in developing countries as well as the technical-assessment criteria under our suggested framework. Discussions of two of these crops, potato and quinoa highlight the advantages of these crops for the future uncertain world: agronomic versatility, hardiness and reliability, nutritional quality, low resource and labour inputs, and prospects for photosynthetic improvement.

15.6.2 Technical Factors Impacting on Prospects for Photosynthetic Improvement

Our analysis of the published technical literature has identified the following facts and figures, most of which are unknown in the general crop and climate-change literature and, thus, not considered in previous analyses.

- Increased atmospheric CO_2 has likely already had a major impact on food production, with suggestions that it is now ~30 per cent more than it would have been if [CO_2] had stayed at its 1930 level, a direct effect on increased photosynthesis (RUE). That is, if it had not increased the world would be hungrier than it is.
- Further increases in CO_2 to predicted 2050 levels will further increase food production by increased RUE.
- Thus, recommendations from the 'nine planetary boundaries' proposal (Rockström et al., 2009) to return to a [CO_2] level of 300 ppm, i.e. 100 ppm less than the current (2013) level, would be extremely detrimental for food production.
- Unknown to the climate-science community, photosynthesis research shows that the detrimental effects of projected increased temperatures on growth of major crops, such as rice, now growing at their limits in some regions are mitigated, or overcome with a net benefit, from projected increase in CO_2.
- Photosynthesis results show that the resilience of crops to adverse growing conditions, either from global shifts in water availablility or temperature or from extreme events from heatwaves or frosts, is increased by higher [CO_2] levels. This increases the margin for plants to survive and recover using the increased reservoir of plant energy for repair functions while still preserving enough energy to mobilize into grain, tubers etc. to produce a harvestable crop.
- The frequency of extreme temperature events is increasing (*high confidence*) in most regions of the world and possibly all major populated regions with high food

needs (*moderate confidence*) making the need to develop and/or deploy more resilient crops urgent (IPCC, 2012).
- Thus, we can expect that the effects on photosynthesis of projected increases in atmospheric CO_2 to 2050 and beyond will enhance both crop productivity and resilience to stresses such as heat and drought and extreme events, and that, irrespective of the impact of carbon-emission mitigation attempts, will most likely have a net benefit on food production.
- Although there are many options for how to improve photosynthesis of crop plants, some can be considered as preferred as they are more feasible and easy to implement in a broad range of crops as well as allowing co-development of appropriate varieties for a large, and flexible, range of growing conditions.
- Pursuit *and public promotion* of some very high-tech solutions for photosynthesis improvement with high risk of failure of coupled with a long timeline for assessment of likelihood of success (e.g. 25 years) as well as high research cost compared with general low investment levels in crop development, e.g. C_4 rice project, present a high-level risk to food security as they provide false confidence that the problem is being addressed and, by diverting funds, lead to lost opportunity for R&D with greater likelihood of success *and* impact.

15.6.3 Suggestion for an Independent High-level Strategic Assessment and Cost–Benefit Analysis

We suggest an audit of current and possible alternative crops, current and possible crop development methods, farming systems and investment mechanisms, against whole-of-food-system cost–benefit and risk analysis. Whole-of-lifetime cost issues encompass economic and social (health and nutrition) issues, rights and equity, environmental sustainability, biodiversity preservation, resource availability and costs (land, water, fertilizer), including geopolitical factors such as regional distribution of resources (access) and long-term availability (total reserves). Discussion focussed on sub-sets of these issues, i.e. eco-efficiency or climatic adapatability, are inadequate.

We argue that such as independent high-level strategic assessment and cost–benefit analysis needs to be undertaken as a basis for decision making on the wisdom of persevering with the existing portfolio of major staples, which are increasingly maladapted to their growing environments and for which further gains in efficient and *effective* productivity are modest or risky, rather than moving to a wider better-adapted more resilient and, thus, less risky basket of crops, including reintroduction of displaced native crops. Such a decision would necessarily require cutting losses in substantial investments in existing crops and provoke opposition from numerous vested interests.

This assessment would include a comprehensive audit to define a preferred basket of staple crops against a number of technical 'robustness' or risk criteria: nutritional quality and balance; nutrient efficiency (especially NUE), WUE and RUE, and prospects for improvement; adaptability and resilience to abiotic stresses, especially extreme weather events and global climate shifts; environmental sustainability (ecological footprint); and suitability for small-scale farming and production. The main aim is to define a set of preferred crops fit-for-purpose.

The aims of this exercise should be not only to minimize future use of resources while providing for the increased needs of the projected 9 billion people and assuring food security, minimizing food insecurity and reducing threats of global political instability and national security, but to *reduce* the ecological footprint for human food production, a scenario that does not even seem to be contemplated.

REFERENCES

Berner, R.A. (2003), The long-term carbon cycle, fossil fuels and atmospheric composition. *Nature*, **426**, 323–6.

Brown, L.R. (2012), *Full Planet, Empty Plates. The New Geopolitics of Food Scarcity*. New York: W.W. Norton.

Brutnell, T. and W.B. Frommer (2012), Food for thought. *The Scientist*, June 1. Available at http://www.the-scientist.com/?articles.view/articleNo/32151/title/Food-for-Thought/ (accessed 21 July 2013).

Cordell, D., J.-O. Drangert and S. White (2009), The story of phosphorus: global food security and food for thought. *Global Environmental Change*, **19**(2), 292–305.

CWR (2013), How much are CWR worth? Press release 30 July 2013 from the CWR Project website. Available at: http://www.cwrdiversity.org/how-much-are-cwr-worth/ (accessed 4 August 2013).

Czeck, B., A.H. Jahren, B. Schubert, S. Deenik, S. Crow and M. Stewart (2012), Growth, yield, and nutritional response of chamber-grown sweet potato to elevated carbon dioxide levels expected across the next 250 years. American Geophysical Union conference poster. Available at: http://fallmeeting.agu.org/2012/files/2012/12/AGU-Czeck-Sweet-Potato-FINAL-eposter.pdf (accessed 21 July 2013).

de Haan, S., J. Núñez, M. Bonierbale and M. Ghislain (2010), Multilevel agrobiodiversity and conservation of Andean potatoes in central Peru. *Mountain Research and Development*, **30**(3), 222–31.

Denison, R.F. (2012), *Darwinian Agriculture: How Understanding Evolution Can Improve Agriculture*. Princeton, NJ and Woodstock, UK: Princeton University Press.

de Oliveira, E.D., H. Bramley, K.H.M. Siddique, S. Henty, J. Berger and J.A. Palta (2012), Can elevated CO_2 combined with high temperature ameliorate the effect of terminal drought in wheat? *Functional Plant Biology*, **40**(2), 160–71.

de Schutter, O. (2011), Agroecology and the Right to Food. Report presented at 16th Session of UN Human Rights Council [A/HRC/16/49], Geneva, 8 March 2011. Available at: www.srfood.org/en/report-agroecology-and-the-right-to-food (accessed 4 August 2013).

de Schutter, O. and K.Y. Cordes (eds) (2011), *Accounting for Hunger: The Right to Food in the Era of Globalisation*. Oxford, UK and Portland, OR, USA: Hart Publishing.

Donat, M.G. and 28 other authors (2013), Updated analyses of temperature and precipitation extreme indices since the beginning of the twentieth century: the HadEX2 dataset. *Journal of Geophysical Research: Atmospheres*, **118**, 2098–2118.

Donohue, R.J., M.L. Roderick, T.R. McVicar and G.D. Farquhar (2013), Impact of CO_2 fertilization on maximum foliage cover across the globe's warm, arid environments. *Geophysical Research Letters*, **40**(12), 3031–3035.

Edwards, E.J. and S.A. Smith (2010), Phylogenetic analyses reveal the shady history of C_4 grasses. *Proceedings of the National Academies of Science of the USA*, **107**, 2532–2538.

Enserink, M. (2008).Tough lessons from golden rice. *Science*, **320**, 468–71.

FAO (1995), Dimensions of need: an atlas of food and agriculture. Available at: http://www.fao.org/docrep/u8480e/U8480E01.htm (accessed 21 July 2013).

FAO (2008), *International Year of the Potato 2008: New Light on a Hidden Treasure*, Rome, Italy: Food and Agriculture Organization of the United Nations, pp.144, Available at: http://www.potato2008.org/pdf/IYPbook-en.pdf (accessed 4 August 2013).

FAO (2011), FAOSTAT: Production-Crops, 2010 data. Available at: http://faostat3.fao.org/home/index.html (accessed 21 July 2013).

FAO Regional Office for Latin America and Caribbean (2011), *Quinoa: an Ancient Crop to Contribute to World Food Security*, El Paso, Bolivia: PROINPA (Fundación Promoción e Investigación de Productos Andinos).

FAO/WHO/UNI (2007), *Protein and Amino Acid Requirements in Human Nutrition*, Geneva, Switzerland: World Health Organization Press. Available at: http://whqlibdoc.who.int/trs/WHO_TRS_935_eng.pdf (accessed 22 July 2013).

Feuillet, C., P. Langridge and R. Waugh (2008), Cereal breeding takes a walk on the wild side. *Trends in Genetics*, **24**(1), 24–32.

Foley, J. A. and 20 other authors (2011), Solutions for a cultivated planet. *Nature*, **478**, 337–342.

Gilbert, N. (2009), The disappearing nutrient. *Nature*, **461**, 716–8.
Godfray H.C.J., J.R. Beddington, I.R. Crute, L. Haddad, D. Lawrence, J.F. Muir, J. Pretty, S. Robinson, S.M. Thomas and C. Toulmin (2010), Food security: the challenge of feeding 9 billion people. *Science* **327**, 812–8.
GRAIN (2009), Nerica: another trap for small farmers in Africa and Rice land grabs undermine food sovereignty in Africa. GRAIN briefings. Available at: www.grain.org/briefings/?id=215 and http://www.grain.org/article/entries/187-rice-land-grabs-undermine-food-sovereignty-in-africa (accessed 4 August 2013).
Gready, J.E. and B. Kannappan (2013), Process for generation of protein and uses thereof, Australian Patent 2007306926; US Patent Pending 12/422,190; European Patent Application No. 07815347.5; Chinese Patent 20078004511.6; Canadian Patent Application No. 2665766; Indian Patent Application No. 02498/CHENP/09; Argentinian Patent Application No. P070104488; Brazilian Patent Application No. P10717758.5.
Gready, J.E., B. Kannappan, A. Agrawal, K. Street, D.M. Stalker and S.M. Whitney (2013), Status of options for improving photosynthetic capacity through promotion of Rubisco performance: Rubisco natural diversity and re-engineering, and other parts of C_3 pathways. In J.E. Gready, S.A. Dwyer and J.R. Evans (eds), *Applying Photosynthesis Research to Improvement of Food Crops*. Canberra, Australia: Australian Centre for International Agricultural Research (ACIAR), in press.
Herring, J.R. and J. Fantel (1993), Phosphate rock demand into the next century: impact on world food supply. *Nonrenewable Resources* **2**(3), 226–6.
Hijmans, R.J., D.M. Spooner, A.R. Salas, L. Guarino and J. de la Cruz J. (2002), *Atlas of Wild Potatoes*. Systematic and Ecogeographic Studies on Crop Genepools 10, Rome: IPGRI (CGIAR). Available at: http://www.vcru.wisc.edu/spoonerlab/pdf/Potato per cent20Atlas per cent20Final.pdf (accessed 4 August 2013).
Högy, P., H. Wieser, P. Köhler, K. Schwadorf, J. Breuer, J. Franzaring, R. Muntifering and A. Fangmeier (2009), Effects of elevated CO_2 on grain yield and quality of wheat: results from a 3-year free-air CO_2 enrichment experiment. *Plant Biology*, **11** (Suppl. 1), 60–69.
Holme, I.B., T. Wendt and P.B. Holm (2013), Intragenesis and cisgenesis as alternatives to transgenic crop development. *Plant Biotechnology Journal*, **11**(4), 395–407.
Igamberdiev, A.U. and P J. Lea (2006), Land plants equilibrate O_2 and CO_2 concentrations in the atmosphere. *Photosynthesis Research*, **87**, 177–94.
IPCC (2012), *Managing the Risks of Extreme Events and Disasters to Advance Climate Change Adaptation*. A Special Report of Working Groups I and II of the Intergovernmental Panel on Climate Change, Field, C.B., V. Barros, T.F. Stocker, D. Qin, D.J. Dokken, K.L. Ebi, M.D. Mastrandrea, K.J. Mach, G.-K. Plattner, S.K. Allen, M. Tignor and P.M. Midgley (eds). Cambridge, UK and New York, NY: Cambridge University Press.
ISO (2009), ISO 31000:2009 – Risk management, Geneva, Switzerland: International Organization for Standardization. Available at: http://www.iso.org/iso/home/standards/iso31000.htm.
Keating, B.A., P.S. Carberry, P.S. Bindraban, S. Asseng, H. Meinke and J. Dixon (2010), Eco-efficient Agriculture: concepts, challenges, and opportunities. *Crop Science*, **50**, S109–S119.
Keenan, T.F., D.Y. Hollinger, G. Bohrer, D. Dragoni, J.W. Munger, H.P. Schmid and A.D. Richardson (2013), Increase in forest water-use efficiency as atmospheric carbon dioxide concentrations rise. *Nature*, **499**, 324–7.
Kingsbury, N. (2009), *Hybrid: the History and Science of Plant Breeding*. Chicago, IL, and London, UK: The University of Chicago Press.
Linares, O.F. (2002), African rice (*Oryza glaberrima*): history and future potential. *Proceedings of the National Academies of Science of the USA*, **99**(25), 16360–16365.
Lomborg, B. (2013), *How to Spend $75 Billion to Make the World a Better Place*. Washington DC: Copenhagen Consensus Center.
Long, S.P., X.-G. Zhu, S.L. Naidu and D.R. Ort (2006), Can improvement in photosynthesis increase crop yields? *Plant, Cell and Environment*, **29**, 315–330.
MacKenzie, D. (2008), Let them eat spuds. *New Scientist*, **191** (2667), 30–33.
Maxted, N., J. Magos Brehm and S. Kell (2013), *Resource Book for the Preparation of National Plans for Conservation and Use of Crop Wild Relatives and Landraces*, Rome: FAO Commission on Genetic Resources for Food and Agriculture. Available at: www.pgrsecure.bham.ac.uk/sites/default/files/documents/helpdesk/FAO_Toolkit_DRAFT_May_2013.pdf.
Miglietta, F., V. Magliulo, M. Bindi, L. Cerio, F.P. Vaccari, V. Loduca and A. Peressott (1998), Free air CO_2 enrichment of potato (*Solanum tuberosum* L.): development, growth and yield. *Global Change Biology*, **4**, 163–72.
Monteros, C., F. Yumisaca, J. Andrade-Piedra and I. Reinoso (2011), *Papas Nativas de la Sierra Centro y Norte del Ecuador: catálogo etnobotánico, morfológico, agronómico y de calidad*, Quito, Ecuador: Instituto Nacional Autónomo de Investigaciones Agropecuarias (INIAP). Available at: http://www.

scribd.com/doc/77440828/Papas-nativas-de-la-Sierra-Centro-y-Norte-del-Ecuador-Catalogo-etnobotanico-morfologico-agronomico-y-de-calidad (accessed 4 August 2013).

Murchie, E.H., M. Pinto and P. Horton (2009), Agriculture and the new challenges for photosynthesis research. *New Phytologist*, **181**, 532–52.

National Academies Advisory Panel (1989), *Lost Crops of the Incas: Little-Known Plants of the Andes with Promise for Worldwide Cultivation*, Washington DC: National Academies Press. Available at: http://www.nap.edu/catalog/1398.html.

National Academies Advisory Panel (1996), *Lost Crops of Africa: Volume I: Grains* (http://www.nap.edu/catalog/2305.html); *Volume II: Vegetables* (http://www.nap.edu/catalog/11763.html); *Volume III: Fruits* (http://www.nap.edu/catalog/11879.html). Washington DC: National Academies Press.

Nelson, G.C., M.W. Rosegrant, J. Koo, R. Robertson, T. Sulser, T. Zhu, C. Ringler, S. Msangi, A. Palazzo, M. Batka, M. Magalhaes, R. Valmonte-Santos, M. Ewing and D. Lee (2009), *Climate Change: Impact on Agriculture and Costs of Adaptation*, Washington DC: International Food Policy Research Institute (IFPRI).

O'Rourkes, L. (2011), Gains for grains. *ANU Reporter*, Summer issue, 28–9. Available at: http://issuu.com/anureporter/docs/anu_reporter_summer_2011 (accessed 21 July 2013).

Özgediz, S. (2012), *The CGIAR at 40: Institutional Evolution of the World's Premier Agricultural Research Network*. Washington DC: CGIAR. Available at: http://library.cgiar.org/bitstream/handle/10947/2761/cgiar40yrs_book_final_sept2012.pdf?sequence=1 (accessed 21 July 2013).

Pardey, P.G., J.M. Beddow, D.J. Kriticos, T.M. Hurley, R.F. Park, E. Duveiller, R.W. Sutherst, J.J. Burdon and D. Hodson (2013), Right-sizing stem-rust research. *Science*, **340**, 147–8.

Ramírez-Villegas, J., C. Khoury, A. Jarvis, D.G. Debouck and L. Guarino (2010), A gap analysis methodology for collecting crop genepools: a case study with *Phaseolus* beans. *PLoS ONE*, **5**(10), e13497.

Redfern, S.K., N. Azzu and J.S. Binamira (2012), Rice in Southeast Asia: facing risks and vulnerabilities to respond to climate change. In A. Meybeck, J. Lankoski, S. Redfern, N. Azzu and V. Gitz (eds), *Building Resilience for Adaptation to Climate Change in the Agriculture Sector*. Proceedings of a Joint FAO/OECD Workshop, Rome: FAO. Available at: www.fao.org/docrep/017/i3084e/i3084e18.pdf (accessed 4 August 2013).

Reeds, P.J. (2000), Dispensable and indispensable amino acids for humans. *Journal of Nutrition*, **130**(7), 1835S–1840S.

Rockström, J. and 29 other authors (2009), A safe operating space for humanity. *Nature*, **46**, 472–5.

Rosemarin, A. (2010). Peak phosphorus, the next inconvenient truth? 2nd International Lecture Series on Sustainable Sanitation, World Bank, Manila, 15 October. Available at: http://www.susana.org/docs_ccbk/susana_download/2-819-en-rosemarin-peak-phosphorus-manila-2010.pdf (accessed 21 July 2013).

Sage, R.F. (2002), Variation in the k_{cat} of Rubisco in C_3 and C_4 plants and some implications for photosynthetic performance at high and low temperature. *Journal of Experimental Botany*, **53**, 609–20.

Sharma, D.R., R. Kaur and K. Kumar (1996), Embryo rescue in plants – a review. *Euphytica*, **89**, 325–37.

Sharma, H.C. (1995), How wide can a wide cross be? *Euphytica*, **82**, 43–64.

Statistical Yearbook of the Russian Federation (2007), Rosstat – Federal State Statistical Service, Moscow (2008), Chapter 14, p.445 et seq. Available at: http://www.gks.ru/ Публикации > Электронные версии публикаций > Российский статистический ежегодник, 2007г.

Steffen, W., L. Hughes and D. Karoly (2013), *The Critical Decade: Extreme Weather*. Canberra, Australia: Climate Commission Secretariat (Australian Governmnet), pp.68. Available at: http://climatecommission.gov.au/wp-content/uploads/ExtremeWeatherReport_web.pdf (accessed 1 August 2013).

Stein, A.J. and M. Qaim (2007), The human and economic cost of hidden hunger. *Food and Nutrition Bulletin*, **28**, 125–34.

Taleb, N.N. (2010), *The Black Swan: the Impact of the Highly Improbable*. New York: Random House.

Tester, M. and P. Langridge (2010), Breeding technologies to increase crop production in a changing world. *Science*, **327**, 818–22.

The Economist Special Issue (2011), A special report on feeding the world. *The Economist*, **398** (8722), SS3–SS16.

The Royal Society Working Group (2009), REAPING the benefits: science and the sustainable intensification of global agriculture. Policy document 11/09. The Royal Society, London.

Tilman, D., C. Balzer, J. Hill and B.L. Befort (2011), Global food demand and the sustainable intensification of agriculture. *Proceedings of the National Academies of Science of the USA*, **108**(50), 20260–20264.

USDA (2012), Nutrient data laboratory. Available at: http://fnic.nal.usda.gov/ (accessed 21 July 2013).

US Geological Survey (2012) Phosphate rock. Available at: http://minerals.usgs.gov/minerals/pubs/commodity/phosphate_rock/mcs-2012-phosp.pdf (accessed 21 July 2013).

Vaccari, D.A. (2009), Phosphorus famine: the threat to our food supply. *Scientific American*, 3 June.

Varshney, R.K., J.-M. Ribaut, E.S. Buckler, R. Tuberosa, J.A. Rafalski and P. Langridge (2012), Can genomics boost productivity of orphan crops? *Nature Biotechnology*, **30**, 1172–1176.

Veneklaas, E.J., H. Lambers, J. Bragg, P.M. Finnegan, C.E. Lovelock, W.C. Plaxton, C.A. Price, W.-R.

Scheible, M.W. Shane, P.J. White and J.A. Raven (2012), Opportunities for improving phosphorus-use efficiency in crop plants. *New Phytologist*, **195**, 306–20.
Vincent, H., L. Wiersema, S.P. Kell, S. Dobbie, H. Fielder, N.P. Castañeda Alvarez, L. Guarino, R. Eastwood, B. Len and N. Maxted (2013), A prioritised crop wild relative inventory as a first step to help underpin global food security. *Biological Conservation*, submitted.
von Caemmerer, S. (2000), *Biochemical Models of Leaf Photosynthesis*. Collingwood, VIC, Australia: CSIRO Publishing.
Vu, J.C.V., L.H. Allen, K.J. Boote and G. Bowes (1997), Effects of elevated CO_2 and temperature on photosynthesis and Rubisco in rice and soybean. *Plant, Cell and Environment*, **20**, 68–76.
Wilkinson, S., G. Mills, R. Illidge and W.J. Davies (2012), How is ozone pollution reducing our food supply? *Journal of Experimental Botany*, **63**(2), 527–36.
Zhu, Q., X. Zheng, J. Luo, B.S. Gaut and S. Ge (2007), Multilocus analysis of nucleotide variation of *Oryza sativa* and its wild relatives: severe bottleneck during domestication of rice. *Molecular Biology and Evolution*, **24**(3), 875–88.
Zhu, X.-G., S.P. Long and D.R. Ort (2008), What is the maximum efficiency with which photosynthesis can convert solar energy into biomass?. *Current Opinion in Biotechnology*, **19**, 153–9.

16. Emissions of greenhouse gases from agriculture and their mitigation

Francesco N. Tubiello and Josef Schmidhuber

16.1 INTRODUCTION

As we move toward a global population of 9.5 billion people by 2050 (UNPD, 2013), land availability and natural resource use becomes an ever more critical issue. Even if the additional cropland needs for food production may remain limited, there are competing demands for non-food use, water, timber, energy, settlements, infrastructure, recreation and biodiversity (Alexandratos and Bruinsma, 2012). Previous assessments of greenhouse gas (GHG) emissions and mitigation potential in the agriculture, forestry and other land use (AFOLU) sectors have not accounted explicitly for the impacts of mitigation actions on the other services provided by land, especially food production and food security repercussions (Smith and Gregory, 2013).

Indeed, one of the greatest challenges facing humanity in coming decades is the need to feed a growing population while minimizing GHG emissions. The solution to both challenges must be met partly by changing the way we manage land. We also need to improve the resilience of food production to future environmental changes, protect biodiversity and freshwater resources, move to healthier diets and reduce the adverse impacts of food production on ecosystem functions (Easterling et al., 2007; FAO, 2011a). An additional challenge is represented by the increased demand for bio-energy from agricultural feed stocks. Recent higher energy prices and improved infrastructure have made a growing share of feed stocks competitive in the energy market. The huge size of the energy market (> 500 EJ yr^{-1})[1] compared to the small contribution of modern bio-fuels (~ 3 EJ yr^{-1}) suggests that higher energy prices and/or higher subsidies could siphon off large additional quantities of agricultural feed stocks into the energy market and thus hugely increase land needs for bio-fuel production (Schmidhuber, 2007, 2013).

Most studies to date have focussed on these challenges separately (e.g. GHG mitigation, food security, energy provision), without considering the multiple linkages that arise from the underlying use of the same land resources. In previous reports by the Intergovernmental Panel on Climate Change (IPCC), GHG mitigation potentials in the Agriculture, Forestry and Other Land Use (AFOLU) sector were assessed separately, and only using fixed, non-interacting, ex-ante prescribed changes in population, wealth, dietary preference (IPCC, 2001, 2007). By contrast, this work explores how GHG emissions from the AFOLU sector can be better quantified, so that improved analyses can be performed on how AFOLU contribute to GHG mitigation – and simultaneously how food supply capacity can be maintained, while using the same limited land resources. A special focus is given to examining how supply-side and consumption-side measures might usefully address the dual challenges of food security and climate change. This work is a synthesis review based largely on Tubiello et al.

(2013) for GHG emissions and Smith and Gregory (2013) for the associated mitigation analysis.

GHG emissions from fossil fuels increased by 3.3 per cent in 2010, reaching a record 31.6 Gt CO_2 eq yr^{-1} in 2011 – the highest level in history (IEA, 2011). At the same time, FAO estimates of GHG emissions from agriculture in 2010 were 5.3 Gt CO_2 eq yr^{-1}, with another 4.0–5.0 Gt CO_2 eq yr^{-1} from the forestry and other land use activities – the latter dominated by net deforestation, biomass fires and peat degradation (FAOSTAT, 2013; Tubiello et al., 2013). Compared to a total estimated GHG anthropogenic emissions of about 50 Gt CO_2 eq yr^{-1} in 2010, therefore, the AFOLU sector may have accounted for about 20 per cent of the total anthropogenic forcing.

Improved estimates of anthropogenic forcing and its trend evolution are needed to reliably predict medium to long-term climatic effects and determine realistic mitigation strategies (e.g. Houghton et al., 2012). Increased knowledge is fundamental, in particular, to support the ongoing dialogue on agriculture of the United Nations Convention on Climate Change (UNFCCC) Conference of the Parties/Meeting of the Parties (COP/MOP), which aims to identify new mechanisms that can usefully link climate change responses and rural development goals. To this end, AFOLU sectors may benefit from significant international funding in coming decades – for instance, up to US$100 billion annually under the Green Climate Fund or the United Nations Collaborative Programme on Reducing Emissions from Deforestation and Forest Degradation (UN-REDD) (FAO, 2011b).

16.2   MATERIALS AND METHODS

For national-level reporting of GHG emissions to the UNFCCC, IPCC guidelines (IPCC, 1996, 2000, 2003, 2006) endorse a range of methodological approaches, from simple bottom-up (i.e. Tier 1) to more complex methodologies, the latter often involving process modeling and rules for scaling-up in time and space (Tier 2 and Tier 3).

The FAOSTAT Emissions database (Tubiello et al., 2013; FAOSTAT, 2013) links basic agriculture, forestry and land use activity data (e.g. crop area, yield, livestock heads, land area changes, etc.) collected by member countries and reported to FAO, typically via National Agriculture Statistical Offices, with default IPCC guidelines. This process results in a coherent data platform covering key information on inputs, production, costs and socioeconomic indicators, trade and food balances, for a large range of agriculture and forestry products worldwide. The database is used widely in peer-reviewed literature as the basis for a range of AFOLU-related analyses, from global agriculture perspective studies to land-use change assessments of importance to carbon cycle studies (e.g. Friedlingstein et al., 2011).

The FAO Emission database applies IPCC default equations for assessing bottom-up, country level GHG emissions. Using IPCC guidelines and a Tier 1 approach (IPCC, 2006) it computes, for each sector in FAOSTAT:

$$GHG = EF*AD$$

Where: GHG = greenhouse gas emissions; EF = emission factor; and AD = activity data. Emissions are estimated for nearly 200 countries, for the reference period

1961–2010, covering emissions of non-CO_2 gases (CH_4 and N_2O) arising from enteric fermentation, manure management systems, synthetic fertilizers, manure applied to soils and left on pastures, crop residues and rice cultivation (Table 16.1). In addition, direct CO_2 emissions are estimated from net forest conversion, biomass burning and degradation of organic soils, based on FAOSTAT land-use statistics and the Forest Resource Assessment (FRA) (FAO, 2010).

16.3 RESULTS

This work focuses on analyses of temporal trends, regional dynamics and comparisons (Figure 16.1). An online version of the FAOSTAT Emission database, allowing for full country level analysis, was released in December 2012 and is available to users worldwide for further analyses and data downloads (Tubiello et al., 2013). It is noted that the FAOSTAT Emissions database is not a replacement for UNFCCC reporting of its member countries. Rather, it aims to support the international scientific community by providing continuous updates of emission trends from agriculture, and to support FAO member countries by means of a coherent framework for analyses of their emissions baselines and future trends, including the ability to perform comparisons across regions and over long time periods, consistently with their internationally reported activity data.

16.3.1 Global and Regional Trends in Agriculture Emissions

Global GHG annual agriculture emissions increased on average by 1.6 per cent per year from 1961 to 2010, reaching 5.3 Gt CO_2 eq yr^{-1} in 2010 (Table 16.2). Over the same period, crop, milk and meat production increased on average 2.2 per cent, 6.4 per cent annually (FAO, 2013), implying a significant reduction (up to three times better) in the carbon intensity of agricultural commodities. At the same time, carbon emissions from fossil fuel and cement manufacture increased at more than three times the rate of those from agriculture, on average 5.2 per cent annually (CDIAC, 2012).

In 2010, the largest contributors to agriculture emissions computed within the database were enteric fermentation (38 per cent), manure left on pasture (14 per cent), synthetic fertilizer (13 per cent), biomass burning (11 per cent), rice cultivation (9 per cent), manure management systems (7 per cent), N_2O emissions from organic soils (5 per cent), crop residues (3 per cent) and manure applied to cropland (2 per cent).

Under the UNFCCC reporting framework, N_2O emissions from agricultural soils, including emissions from synthetic fertilizers, manure and crop residues, are treated as a single reporting category. To this end, our estimates indicate a total contribution of 37 per cent in 2010, similar to that of enteric fermentation. A number of alternative aggregations to those indicated by IPCC are possible. For instance, a category 'manure', defined as the aggregate of emissions from manure left on pastures by grazing animals, manure applied to cropland as organic fertilizer, and manure treated in management systems, would represent 23 per cent of total emissions from agriculture. Importantly, a category 'livestock', defined as the sum of emissions from enteric fermentation and manure emissions, plus emissions from cropland related to feed,[2] would represent over 80 per cent of total agriculture emissions, in line with recent estimates (FAO, 2008; Leip et al., 2010),

Table 16.1 Activity data and emission factors used in the FAOSTAT Emission database

Emission category	Gas	Activity data	Emission factors (EF)[a]		EF unit	EF source[b]
Enteric fermentation	CH_4	Stocks (heads)	Dairy cattle	42–128	kg CH_4/head/yr	Tab.10.10
			Non-Dairy cattle	27–60		Tab.10.10
			Buffalo	55		Tab.10.11
			Sheep/Goats	5–8		Tab.10.11
			Camels	46		Tab.10.11
			Mules/Asses/Horses	10–18		Tab.10.11
			Pigs	1–1.5		Tab.10.11
			Llamas	8		Tab.10.11
Rice cultivation	CH_4	Area Harvested (ha)	Rice, paddy	10–27.5	g CH_4/m²/yr	Tab.4.13 (IPCC 1996)
Manure management	CH_4	Stocks (heads)	Dairy cattle	1–93	kg CH_4/head/yr	Tab.10.14
			Non-Dairy cattle	0–13		Tab.10.14
			Buffalo	1–9		Tab.10.14
			Sheep	0.10–0.37		Tab.10.15
			Goats	0.11–0.26		Tab.10.15
			Camels	1.28–3.17		Tab.10.15
			Mules/Asses	0.6–1.52		Tab.10.15
			Horses	1.09–3.13		Tab.10.15
			Market swine	0–45		Tab.10.14
			Breeding swine	0–37		Tab.10.14
			Poultry	0.01–0.09		Tab.10.15
	N_2O (direct)	Manure N (t N/year)	Manure	0–0.02	kg N_2O-N/kg N	Tab.10.21
	N_2O (indirect)		Volatilization	0.01	kg N_2O-N/kg N	Tab.11.3
			Leaching	0.0075	kg N_2O-N/kg N	Tab.11.3

Table 16.1 (continued)

Emission category	Gas	Activity data	Emission factors (EF)[a]		EF unit	EF source[b]
Synthetic fertilizers	N_2O (direct)	N Consumption (t N/year)	Soil	0.01	$kgN_2O\text{-}N/kg\ N$	Tab.11.1
	N_2O (indirect)		Volatilization	0.01	$kgN_2O\text{-}N/kg\ N$	Tab.11.3
			Leaching	0.0075	$kgN_2O\text{-}N/kg\ N$	Tab.11.3
Manure applied to soils	N_2O (direct)	Manure N (t N/year)	Soil	0.01	$kgN_2O\text{-}N/kg\ N$	Tab.11.1
	N_2O (indirect)		Volatilization	0.01	$kgN_2O\text{-}N/kg\ N$	Tab.11.3
			Leaching	0.0075	$kgN_2O\text{-}N/kg\ N$	Tab.11.3
Manure left on pasture	N_2O (direct)	Manure N (t N/year)	Dairy, non-dairy, buffalo, poultry and pigs	0.02	$kgN_2O\text{-}N/kg\ N$	Tab.11.1
			Sheep and "other animals"	0.01		
	N_2O (indirect)		Volatilization	0.01	$kgN_2O\text{-}N/kg\ N$	Tab.11.3
			Leaching	0.0075	$kgN_2O\text{-}N/kg\ N$	Tab.11.3
Crop residues	N_2O (direct)	Residues N content (t N/year)	Crops	0.01	$kgN_2O\text{-}N/kg\ N$	Tab.11.1
	N_2O (indirect)		Leaching	0.0075	$kgN_2O\text{-}N/kg\ N$	Tab.11.3
Cultivated organic soil						
Burning crop residues						
Land use, Land use change and Forestry (LULUCF)						
Forest land	CO_2	Area (1000 ha)	C stock in living forest biomass	3–318	(t C/ha)	FRA 2010

Notes:
a. The range is due to regional characteristics, developing/developed countries, temperature
b. All tables refer to IPCC guidelines 2006 if not specified.

Source: All activity data are derived or calculated by FAOSTAT database.

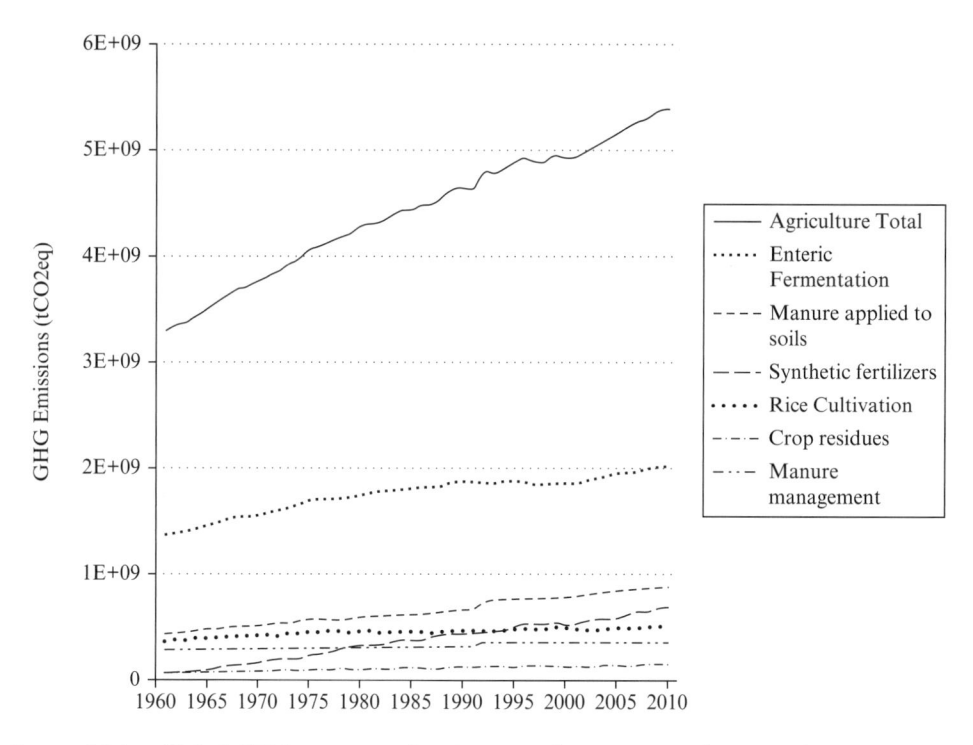

Figure 16.1 Global GHG emissions for the agriculture sector relative to the period 1961–90

and highlighting the fact that emissions related to food crops for direct human consumption contribute only 20 per cent to the agricultural total.

Enteric fermentation

Emissions in this category grew from 1.3 to 2.0 Gt CO_2 eq yr^{-1} during the period 1961–2010, with average annual growth rates of 0.95 per cent (Table 16.2). During the 1990s emission growth slowed down compared to the long-term average, but has picked up again since the year 2000. Over the period 2001–10, Brazil, Indonesia, Nigeria and the Democratic Republic of Congo had the largest net emission rates; China, the United States, Viet Nam and India had the largest absolute net sequestration rates. Suggestive evidence is provided in Figure 16.2. In 2010, over 1.5 Gt CO_2 eq yr^{-1} were emitted in developing countries, or 75 per cent of the total. Averaged over the period 2000–10, Asia and the Americas were the largest contributors (36 per cent and 34 per cent, respectively), followed by Africa (14 per cent) and Europe (12 per cent). Emissions growth rates were largest in Africa, on average[3] 2.4 per cent yr^{-1}. In both Asia and the Americas emissions grew at a slower pace (1–1.2 per cent yr^{-1}), while they decreased in Europe (−1.7 per cent yr^{-1}). Indeed, in 1990–2000 Europe's contribution to the total (17 per cent) was larger than Africa's (11 per cent). Over the period 2000–10, emissions were dominated by cattle, responsible for three quarters of the total (56 per cent non-dairy cattle; 19 per cent dairy cattle), followed by buffaloes (11 per cent), sheep (6.8 per cent) and goats (4.6 per cent).

Table 16.2 Agriculture GHG emissions (Mt CO2 eq yr-1) from agriculture in the FAOSTAT database by sector

Category	1961	1990	2000	2005	2010
Enteric Fermentation	1375	1875	1863	1947	2018
Manure left on Pasture	386	578	682	731	764
Synthetic Fertilizer	67	434	521	582	683
Rice Cultivation	366	466	490	493	499
Manure Management	284	319	348	348	353
Crop Residues	66	124	129	142	151
Manure on Cropland	59	88	103	111	116
Degraded Organic Soils	100	100	100	100	100
Biomass Burning	200	200	270	250	200
Agriculture Total	2903	4184	4506	4704	4884
Net Deforestation		4315	4296	3397	3374
Degraded Peatlands		1000	1000	1000	1000
Other Biomass Burning		500	500	500	500
Total		5815	5796	4897	4874
TOTAL AFOLU		9999	10302	9601	9758
Fossil Fuel and Cement	9460	22554	24750	29649	33509

Notes:
A combined total for 2005–10 is obtained by adding estimated emissions from biomass burning and degrading organic soils. The year 2005 is included for comparison to IPCC (2007). Emissions from net deforestation are also included, based on FAOSTAT and FRA data.

Manure
Emissions from manure N applied to cropland as organic fertilizer, left on pasture by grazing animals or processed in manure management systems, were computed mostly at Tier 1 level, using statistics of animal numbers reported to FAOSTAT for estimating both N_2O and CH_4 emission components. For N_2O emissions, a complex set of intermediate datasets was generated as per IPCC guidelines: manure N excretion rates; manure fractions disposed of to different manure management systems; manure fractions left on pasture; manure management system losses; and manure N application rates to cropland as organic fertilizer. The values of the intermediate datasets were animal and region specific. Indirect N_2O emissions related to volatilization and leaching processes of manure N management were also computed. For CH_4 emissions, IPCC required a Tier 2 approach to estimate methane production rates from specific manure management systems as a function of average annual temperatures by country. To this end, agro-meteorological output from the FAO global agro-ecological zone model (IIASA/FAO, 2012) was aggregated to obtain country-level mean annual temperature data. Global emissions from manure N applied to soils – organic fertilizer on cropland or left on pasture – grew during the period 1961–2010 from 0.44 to 0.88 Gt CO_2 eq yr^{-1}. Average annual growth rates were 2 per cent yr^{-1}, with a slow-down in recent decades. Emissions from manure left on pasture (Table 16.2) dominated this emission category, as they were far larger than those from manure used on cropland as organic fertilizer (87 per cent of

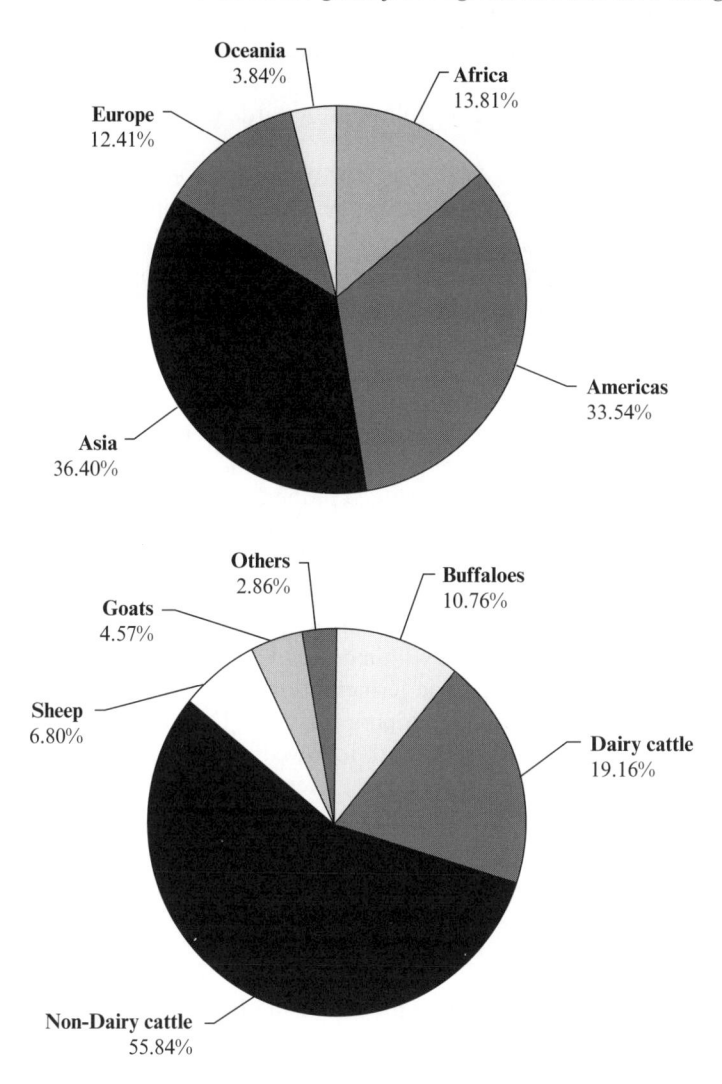

Figure 16.2 Sample analysis possible within the FAOSTAT emissions database. Break down of global emissions from enteric fermentation, by region and by animal type, averaged over the period 2000–10

the total in 2010; of which 80 per cent in developing countries). During the period 2000–10, the Americas (33 per cent), Asia (31 per cent) and Africa (25 per cent) dominated this emission category. Growth rates over the same period were largest in Africa, on average 2.4 per cent yr^{-1}. Emissions grew at a slower pace in both Asia and the Americas (1.2–1.7 per cent yr^{-1}), while they decreased in Europe (−1.4 per cent yr^{-1}). Grazing cattle were responsible for two thirds of the total (53 per cent non-dairy cattle; 11 per cent dairy cattle), followed by sheep (12 per cent) and goats (12 per cent). By contrast, emissions from manure applied to cropland as organic fertilizer were larger in developed compared to developing countries for the period 2000–10. The largest emitters were Europe (40 per cent), Asia and Americas (28 per cent each), while Africa represented a mere 3 per cent of the total, albeit with robust growth rates of 3.4 per cent yr⁻¹. Emissions from pigs were the largest contributors (53 per cent), followed by cattle (24 per cent dairy cattle, 18 per cent non-dairy cattle).

Compared to manure applied to soils, emissions from manure management grew more slowly, i.e. from 0.28 to 0.35 Gt CO_2 eq yr⁻¹ during the reference period 1961–2010, with average annual growth rates of only 0.5 per cent yr⁻¹ (Table 16.2). Over the period 2000–10, emissions were dominated by Asia (36 per cent), Europe (30 per cent) and the Americas (27 per cent). Africa and Oceania emitted each only 3–4 per cent of the total.

Synthetic fertilizer

Emissions from the use of synthetic fertilizers were computed using FAOSTAT fertilizer consumption statistics by country. Following IPCC guidelines, a single emission coefficient was used for all regions to estimate direct N_2O emissions. Indirect emissions due to volatilization and leaching were also included in the estimates. Emissions from synthetic fertilizers had the largest absolute growth rates in agriculture. They grew on average by 19 per cent yr⁻¹ during the reference period 1961–2010, specifically more than ten times, i.e. from 0.07 to 0.68 Gt CO_2 eq yr⁻¹ (Table 16.2). Growth slowed down in recent decades to about 2 per cent yr⁻¹. At the current pace, emissions from synthetic fertilizers will exceed those from manure N left on pasture within a decade. becoming the second largest agriculture emission category after enteric fermentation. In 2010, 70 per cent of emissions from synthetic fertilizer were from developing countries. During the period 2000–10, Asia was by far the largest emitter (63 per cent), followed by the Americas (20 per cent) and Europe (13 per cent). Emissions growth rates over the same period were robust in Asia (5.3 per cent yr⁻¹) and Europe (1.7 per cent yr⁻¹), but negative in Africa (−3.3 per cent yr⁻¹). Emissions and application of synthetic fertilizers had a year-on-year drop in 2008 in some regions, specifically −4.4 per cent (Europe) and −9.8 per cent (Americas) – although not statistically significant, the drop coincides with increased fertilizer costs that year.

Rice

Emissions from rice cultivation were computed using FAOSTAT statistics of harvested rice area and a regional-level distribution of rice management types and emission factors from the 1996 IPCC guidelines. Globally, during the reference period 1961–2010 GHG emissions grew slowly, from 0.37 to 0.49 Gt CO_2 eq yr⁻¹, with average annual growth rates of 0.7 per cent yr⁻¹ (Table 16.2). It should be noted that our emissions estimates are in line with recent assessments (Yan et al., 2009), which have revised down previously published data and databases (i.e. EDGAR, EPA).

Global emission growth slowed down in recent decades and likely reached a plateau in recent years – and even decreased on a year-on-year basis in several years during the period 2000–10. Slower growth in GHG emissions reflects lower growth in global rice demand with per capita consumption reaching satiation levels in many Asian countries; this in turn has already resulted in lower growth of input use and land expansion (paddy fields). Emissions from rice were dominated by developing countries, which contributed over 94 per cent of emissions during 2000–10. Asia was the largest contributor (89 per cent), followed by the Americas (5 per cent), Africa (4 per cent) and Europe (1 per cent). Emissions growth rates were nonetheless largest in Africa (1.8 per cent yr⁻¹), followed by

Europe (1.4 per cent). Growth rates in Asia and the Americas were lower (0.2 per cent yr^{-1}).

16.3.2 Global and Regional Trends in Emissions from Deforestation

GHG emissions from net forest conversion by country were computed at Tier 1, by using net forest land-use change – afforestation minus deforestation – by country, reported in FAOSTAT from FRA^4 data. This area was multiplied by country-level averages of C content in living forest biomass. The latter data is a Tier 2–3 assessment of biomass carbon stocks, provided by member countries to FAO (2010). Emissions from net source countries were then aggregated globally, to estimate a carbon loss from deforestation, while those from net sink countries were aggregated separately to estimate a carbon sink from afforestation. Losses and gains thus computed were considered to be instantaneous at the time of the reported land-use changes, as per IPCC guidelines (IPCC, 2006). It should be noted that carbon losses from deforestation as well as gains from afforestation are underestimated by using FAOSTAT and FRA data relative to net area change. Indeed, any afforestation activity in a net source country will imply greater deforestation rates than the net values derived herein; likewise, a net sink country may still have undergone some deforestation, resulting in actual larger afforestation rates than the net values imply. Using data from 2005 (FAO, 2010) that had a more detailed breakdown of deforestation and afforestation activities within most countries, we estimated that actual deforestation rates in 2005 were about 20 per cent larger than those estimated by using the net area changes used herein. The net global atmospheric signal derived by summing sinks and sources is, however, accurate – indeed such estimates are used routinely for global carbon balance assessments (e.g. Houghton et al., 2012).

Global carbon emissions from net deforestation during the period 2005–10 were estimated to be 3.4 Gt CO_2 eq yr^{-1}[11], in line with recent literature (see, e.g. Friedlingstein et al., 2011). These emissions have decreased steadily since 1990, with average growth rates of -1.1 per cent yr^{-1}, including a pronounced slow-down since the year 2000 (-2.2 per cent yr^{-1}). During the period 2000–10, carbon emissions from deforestation were largest in the Americas (60 per cent), followed by Africa (32 per cent), Oceania (4 per cent) and Asia (3 per cent). All regions exhibited a declining emission growth rate, with the largest in Asia (-18 per cent yr^{-1}). The Americas (-2.9 per cent yr^{-1}) and Africa (0.2 per cent yr^{-1}) showed smaller decreases, while emissions from deforestation grew only in Oceania, and significantly so (45 per cent yr^{-1}), largely due to the contribution of Papua New Guinea. As shown in Figure 16.2, over the period 2000–10, Brazil, Indonesia, Nigeria and the Democratic Republic of Congo had the largest net emission rates; China, the US, Viet Nam and India had the largest absolute net sequestration rates.

16.3.3 Land-Based Mitigation

Land is used for many purposes, e.g. production of goods and services through agriculture and forestry, housing and infrastructure, and absorption or deposition of wastes and emissions. Many of these functions limit the ability to deliver others, e.g. the area required for crops is not available for forestry or housing, leading to competition for land. In some cases, land use is related to the nature of land, e.g. forestry on steep, rocky slopes; in other cases land can be used for several purposes, illustrated in particular by small-farmers and indigenous groups in developing countries. Economic and population growth, changing consumption patterns and increased demand for bio-energy are expected to increase the competition for scarce land and water resources (Smith and Gregory, 2013).

Not all of the total land area of the planet (13.4 billion ha) is suitable for food production in fact, due to climatic, soil and topographic constraints. Specifically, the area of current cropland production is 1.56 billion ha, with an estimated additional 2.7 billion ha potentially available as prime or good land for the cultivation of conventional food and feed crops (FAO, 2011b). Cropland area may expand by about 70 million ha by 2050, which is the result of a 132 million ha expansion in the countries that are projected to increase land under crops (most of it in countries of sub-Saharan Africa and Latin America), and a 63 million ha decline in countries that are projected to reduce it (most of it in the developed countries but some also in developing ones) (Alexandratos and Bruinsma, 2012). Most of the increase in food supply will come from higher productivity, the lion's share of which is expected to stem from higher yields and a smaller contribution from increased cropping intensity.

Mitigation activities in agriculture and forestry can result from changes in land management practices and technology (i.e. supply-side measures), or changes in the consumption of land-based resources, including changes in diets (i.e. demand-side measures). Demand-side and supply-side measures may result in very different feedbacks on land use in terms of synergies and trade-offs.

Demand-side measures save GHG emissions by (1) reducing the production emissions of practices already established over land (e.g. CH_4 from enteric fermentation, N_2O from fertilizers or CO_2 from tractor fuels); and (2) by reducing land demand, i.e. making areas available for other uses, e.g. afforestation or bio-energy, through increases of system efficiencies (Erb et al., 2012a, b). Thus the ecological feedbacks of demand-side measures tend to reduce competition for land and water. Health impacts are also deemed positive, insofar as they may underlie a switch to healthier diets. By contrast, supply-side measures may require either more land and/or more inputs of other resources (e.g. fertilizers and irrigation water). Four main cases can be identified:

- **Reducing waste and optimization of biomass-flow** through use of residues and by-products, recycling and energetic use of wastes and residues (e.g. Haberl et al., 2003; WBGU, 2009). Such measures increase the efficiency of resource use, although trade-offs may exist, for example, using crop residues for bio-energy or roughage supply, which may adversely impact soil quality and the C balance of croplands.
- **Land-sparing measures** such as increases in crop yields (e.g. Tilman et al., 2011), grazing land or forestry, or increases in the efficiency of biomass conversion processes such as livestock feeding (Thornton and Herrero, 2010). Such options reduce demand for land, but there may be trade-offs with other ecological, social and economic costs (IAASTD, 2009). Increases in yields may also increase consumption, and thus potentially the GHG emissions, via the rebound effect, i.e., leading to local and regional land expansion, since technological improvements and productivity gains may increase profitability of specific agricultural activities (Rose et al., 2013).

Greenhouse gases from agriculture and their mitigation 433

- **Land-demand measures** for either C sequestration, maintenance of C stocks, or production of dedicated energy crops. These options increase demand for land (as well as water and biodiversity) and may have substantial social, economic and ecological effects that need to be managed (UNEP, 2009). Such measures may directly or indirectly result in higher land pressure and net C emissions.
- **Alternative uses of biomass** such as the use of grains for food, animal feed and as feedstock for bio-fuels, or the use of wood residues for chipboards, paper and bio-energy, offers opportunities for the agriculture and forestry sectors, by finding new markets for products and make profitable the use of biomass flows previously considered waste. Increased land demand may be linked to possible rebound effects described above.

16.3.4 Supply-side Estimates of Mitigation Potential

Supply-side mitigation measures act by reducing the net GHG emissions from agriculture and forestry by changes in management. There are six main ways that supply-side mitigation activities in the AFOLU sector can reduce climate forcing.

Reductions in direct N_2O or net CH_4 emissions from agriculture could result in emission reductions of around 600 Mt CO_2-eq. yr^{-1} in 2030, according to bottom-up estimates (Smith, 2008). Estimates from top-down models range from about 270–1900 Mt CO_2-eq. yr^{-1} (Smith et al., 2007). Reductions in N_2O largely arise through better management of soils and fertilizer applications, whereas reductions in CH_4 emissions arise from managing enteric fermentation emissions from livestock, emissions from rice paddies and emissions from manure management. More recent estimates suggest a higher mitigation potential for N_2O reduction from fertiliser use (Reay et al., 2012). Additives that modify the conversion processes affecting N in soil to decrease N_2O emission can be synthetic (e.g. nitrification inhibitors) or organic (e.g. biochar).

Potential reductions in GHG emissions from energy use in agriculture and forestry from direct (e.g. tractors) or indirect (e.g. production of fertilizers) uses, were estimated to be 770 Mt CO_2-eq. yr^{-1} in 2030 (Smith, 2008). Schneider and Smith (2009) suggested that energy emissions from global agriculture could be reduced by 500 Mt CO_2-eq. yr^{-1} if countries with below-average energy efficiency in agriculture increased their efficiency to the global average of the year 2000.

Reductions of carbon losses from biota and soils have the potential to reduce GHG emissions significantly through reductions of loss of large carbon stores such as those in soils and vegetation (particularly, peatlands and forests, respectively). These large carbon stores can be protected and sustainably managed by policies such as Reduced Emissions from Deforestation and Degradation (REDD), whereby the total elimination of deforestation by 2030 could theoretically deliver a mitigation potential ~2–3 Gt CO_2 eq yr^{-1} (UNFCCC, 2007; FAOSTAT, 2013). Peatland carbon stocks, amounting to 1–2 Gt CO_2 eq yr^{-1} (FAOSTAT, 2013), could be protected by similar policies. Leakage effects, i.e. increased land use in areas outside of large-scale protection programmes, may however reduce the effectiveness of these measures.

Enhancement of carbon sequestration in biota and soils has the potential to reduce GHG emissions by increasing carbon stocks in soils and vegetation. The potential for net sequestration of carbon through afforestation, reforestation, forest restoration and improved forest management (but excluding reduced deforestation – see above) was estimated to be 2.3–5.7 Gt CO_2 eq yr^{-1} (Nabuurs et al., 2007). Another possibility is to intercept and stabilize carbon cycling from plant to atmosphere through pyrolysis – producing both bio-energy in the form of combustible syngas and returning carbon to soil in the form of biochar, the solid product of pyrolysis. This process has an estimated technical potential to sequester 1.6 Gt CO_2 eq yr^{-1} (Berndes et al., 2011).

Change in albedo and evapotranspiration. Land-use changes may also influence climate by modifying physical properties of the surface, altering for instance evapo-transpiration rates and albedo, i.e. the extent to which the land surface reflects incoming sunlight. These impacts can be significant, but will not be discussed further here since they do not directly influence GHG fluxes.

Provision of biomass with low GHG emissions that can replace high-GHG materials and fossil fuels uses either dedicated energy crops (Havlík et al., 2011), or residues from agriculture and forestry (e.g. straw, dung, forest thinnings, slash). The estimates of the potential for GHG mitigation from bio-energy range widely, due to different assumptions about the underlying land available and the type of fossil fuels replaced. Estimates from global top-down energy models estimated the mitigation potential to be 0.7–1.3 Gt CO_2 eq yr^{-1} at carbon prices up to US\$20 t CO_2-eq.$^{-1}$ and ~2.7 Gt CO_2-eq. yr^{-1} at prices above US\$100 t CO_2-eq.$^{-1}$ (Smith et al., 2007).

16.3.5 Demand-side Mitigation Potentials

Food and fibre demand dynamics and patterns can strongly influence GHG emissions in the production chain. Two options exist to reduce GHG emissions through changes in food demand: (1) Reduction of losses and waste of food in the supply chain, processing, and in final consumption; and (2) Changes in diet, towards less resource-intensive food, i.e. shifts to less GHG-intensive animal food products or to appropriate plant-based food ensuring sufficient protein supply, as well as reduction of overconsumption (Smith and Gregory, 2013).

Reductions of losses in the food supply chain. Globally, it has been estimated that approximately 30–40 per cent of all food production is lost in the supply chain from harvest to final consumers (FAO, 2013). In developing countries, losses of up to 40 per cent occur on farms or during distribution as an effect of poor storage, distribution and conservation technologies and procedures. In developed countries, losses of food on farm or during distribution are smaller, but up to 40 per cent are lost in processing, distribution and at the consumer level (FAO, 2013). Parfitt et al. (2010) compared recent data for several industrialized countries and found food wastes at the household level of 150–300 kg food per household per year. Not all of these losses are avoidable however. In the UK, for instance, 18 per cent of the food waste was classified as 'unavoidable', the same amount as 'potentially avoidable' and 64 per cent as 'avoidable'.

A mass-flow modelling study based on FAO commodity balances that covered the whole food supply chain, but excluded non-edible fractions, found per-capita food loss values ranging from 120–170 kg cap^{-1} yr^{-1} in Sub-Saharan Africa, to 280–300 kg cap^{-1} yr^{-1} in Europe and North America. Despite substantial uncertainties, calculated losses ranged from 20 per cent in sub-Saharan Africa to > 30 per cent in the industrialized regions.

Most of these studies suggest a range of measures to reduce wastes throughout the food supply chain, including investments into harvesting, processing and storage technologies, as well as awareness raising, taxation or retail-sector measures. However, comprehensive bottom-up estimates of mitigation potentials do not exist, although FAO has recently estimated that waste corresponds to a significant one-third of all GHG emissions from agriculture, so that reducing waste by half could correspond to 1.0–2.0 Gt CO_2 eq yr^{-1}, including associated land use changes.

Changes in diets. Most plant-based food has lower GHG emissions than animal products, with the exception of vegetables grown in heated greenhouses or transported via airfreight. This also holds for GHG emissions per unit of protein, when animal-based and plant-based protein supply is compared (González et al., 2011). If land used for the production of different animal food products was instead assumed to sequester C corresponding to modelled natural vegetation growth, the resulting C sink would equate to 25–470 per cent of the GHG emissions associated with the food production – assuming the land was not subject to any other LUC during 30–100 years (Schmidinger and Stehfest, 2012).

Modelling studies show that changes in future diets can have a significant impact on GHG emissions from food production. Using the GLOBIOM model, Havlík et al. (2011) suggested that GHG mitigation potentials could be close to 2 Gt CO_2-eq. yr^{-1} under different future scenarios of crop and livestock production. Smith and Gregory (2013) report results from several published scenarios: In a 'constant diet' scenario, agricultural non-CO_2 emissions would rise from 5.3 Gt CO_2-eq. yr^{-1} in 1995 to 8.7 Gt CO_2-eq. yr^{-1} in 2055. With current dietary trends, emissions were projected to rise instead to 15.3 Gt CO_2-eq. yr^{-1}, while the GHG emissions of a 'decreased livestock product scenario' were estimated to be 4.3 Gt CO_2-eq. yr^{-1}. Popp et al. (2010) concluded that the potential to reduce GHG emissions through changes in consumption (i.e. demand-side measures) was substantially higher than that offered by supply-side, technical mitigation measures.

Demand-side options related to wood and forestry. Global carbon stocks in long-lived products were approximately 8.4 Gt CO_2 in 1900 and increased to 37.0 Gt CO_2 in 2008. The net amount of C sequestered annually (C inflows minus C outflows of socioeconomic C stocks) in long-lived wood products in recent decades ranged from ~180 to 290 Mt CO_2 yr^{-1} (Lauk et al., 2012). If inflows were to rise through increased use of long-lived wood products, C sequestration in wood-based products could be enhanced, thus contributing to GHG mitigation. Substitution of GHG-intensive construction materials (such as concrete) with wood may reduce emissions, but re-use of the wood for energy at the end of its life in buildings is critical as are the GHG reduction policies that would need to be implemented in the energy sector.

Improving traditional biomass use, which is mostly devoted to satisfying the cooking energy needs of the poor worldwide and involves large emissions of GHG gases and black carbon may also help to mitigate climate change. Improved cookstoves (ICS) and other advanced biomass systems for cooking are cost effective for achieving large benefits in energy use reduction and climate change mitigation (Berrueta et al., 2008). The global mitigation potential of advanced ICS, excluding black carbon emission reductions, was estimated to be between 0.6 and 2.4 Gt CO_2-eq yr^{-1}. Reduction in fuel wood and charcoal through adoption of advanced ICS may help reduce pressure on land and improve aboveground biomass stocks and soil and biodiversity conservation.

16.4 DISCUSSION

16.4.1 GHG Emission Data and Analyses

The FAOSTAT emission database presented herein allows for estimates of GHG emissions from all major agricultural activities, that are consistent with basic agriculture and land-use activity data reported at national level by FAO member countries. A number of limitations apply to the data. First, we followed IPCC guidelines developed for the period 1990–2010 to also derive GHG emissions for previous decades. A few key emission categories are largely unaffected by this choice, i.e. emissions from synthetic fertilizers and rice cultivation, which depend on physical processes and associated emission factors that do not change in time. By contrast, emission factors linked to specific livestock parameters – of importance to computing emissions from manure and enteric fermentation – were likely different in many regions in earlier decades compared to the period 1990–2010, due to the introduction of new breeds and more efficient production methods. Comparison of IPCC emission factors for developed and developing regions can be used as a proxy for such changes; they indicate that – while production efficiencies improve – GHG emissions per animal tend to increase when moving from traditional to market oriented production systems. This implies that our GHG estimates for categories linked to animal manure and enteric fermentation are likely overestimates prior to 1990, so that long-term historical growth rates in these categories may have been larger than estimated. Second, the database presented here is based on Tier 1 default IPCC methodology. While this approach is at the basis of building a coherent database – by contrast, UNFCCC GHG databases contains data from a range of Tiers, reducing comparability across countries – more refined computational methods could be used to reduce uncertainty of our estimates. We have to this end performed initial comparisons of the FAOSTAT GHG data (Tier 1) with the corresponding UNFCCC Annex I developed countries GHG data (largely Tier 2–3), finding only small, often statistically non-significant differences between the two datasets.

Within the limitations discussed above, the FAOSTAT emission data are an improvement over existing databases, offering a unified framework for coherent analyses of both activity data and emission estimates across time and space, at country level, within a unified data platform. The dataset can be updated annually from FAOSTAT data. As a first example of the database applications, FAO now estimates total GHG emissions from agriculture to be 5.3 $GtCO_2eq\ yr^{-1}$ in 2010, with a similar additional amount coming from net forest conversion and degraded organic soils, i.e., total AFOLU emissions of about 10–12 $GtCO_2eq\ yr^{-1}$ in 2010.

While it is tempting to also assess the share of emissions from agriculture and deforestation to the total anthropogenic forcing, we note that estimates of total anthropogenic GHG emissions are quite uncertain (see e.g. Montzka et al., 2011), because they depend on summing a fairly robust set of data – global carbon emissions from fossil fuel use and cement manufacture, plus non-CO_2 gases mostly from industrial production – to a highly uncertain one, related to agriculture, forestry and land-use changes. It is simpler and more accurate to compare total emissions from agriculture (without contributions from biomass burning and organic soils) and from deforestation to CO_2 global emissions from fossil fuel use and cement manufacture.

Over the reference period 1961–2010, agriculture GHG emissions grew at average annual increases of 1.6 per cent yr^{-1}, compared to 5.2 per cent yr^{-1} for fossil fuels and cement. As a result, the share of agricultural emissions to total anthropogenic fossil fuel emissions continuously decreased. Indeed, it roughly halved during the period 1961–2010, decreasing from 27.5 per cent to 13.7 per cent. For the more recent period, 1990–2010, agriculture GHG emissions declined from 17.2 per cent to 13.7 per cent, while emissions from deforestation declined from 19.1 per cent to 10.1 per cent of those from fossil fuels.

Finally, while emissions from agriculture were smaller than those from deforestation in 1990, from the year 2000 onwards GHG emissions from agriculture have become larger than those from deforestation. In the year 2010, emissions from agriculture were estimated to be about 40 per cent larger than those from deforestation, i.e. 5.3 GtCO$_2$eq yr^{-1} compared to 3.4 GtCO$_2$eq yr^{-1}.

16.4.2 Mitigation and Food Security

Food security is a multi-faceted challenge, involving much more than just food production, since it is to be analysed across the four dimensions of food supply, stability, access and utilization; we focused only on the linkages between food production and utilization that interface with GHG mitigation. Future increases in food supply will need to be met without large increases in agricultural area, i.e. more agricultural products will need to come from the same area (FAO, 2013).

The main means of intensifying crop production will be through increased yields per unit area together with a smaller contribution from an increased number of crops grown in a seasonal cycle. As cereal production (wheat, maize and rice) has increased from 877 Mt in 1961 to 2342 Mt in 2007, the world average cereal yield has increased from 1.35 t ha^{-1} in 1961 to 3.35 t ha^{-1} in 2007, and is projected to be about 4.8 t ha^{-1} in 2040. Simultaneously, per-capita arable land area has decreased from 0.415 ha in 1961 to 0.214 ha in 2007 (FAOSTAT, 2013). Put another way, had the increases in yield of the last 60–70 years not been achieved, almost three times more land would have been required to produce crops to sustain the present population; this would have meant to convert all of the remaining potential of 2.7 billion hectares of pasture and forest land into cropland.

Tilman et al. (2011) concluded that securing high yields on existing croplands of nations where yields are suboptimal is very important if global crop demand is to be met with minimal environmental impact. At the high-tech end are options such as the genetic modification of living organisms and the use of cloned livestock and nanotechnology (IAASTD, 2008; Foresight, 2011), whilst at low-tech options arise from closing yield gaps, for example by reallocating inputs such as nitrogen fertiliser from regions which over-fertilize to regions were nitrogen supply is limited and limiting, such as much of sub-Saharan Africa (Tilman et al., 2011).

Mueller et al. (2012) examined the closure of the yield gap as a mechanism of sustainable intensification by rebalancing the distribution of inputs to optimize production. Redistributing these imbalances could largely close the yield gap, showing that a reaching 75 per cent of the yield potential could add about 1 billion tonnes of added production. Other agronomic mechanisms for increasing crop productivity include better matching of nutrient supply to crop need (e.g. improved fertilizer management, precision farming), better recycling of nutrients and improved soil and water management (reduced erosion, increased fertility, improved nutrient status, improved irrigation efficiency). All of these efficiency improvements are possible now, but their impact on closing the yield gap has not been quantified.

By contrast to the quantifications made on the supply-side of production, prospects for demand side actions, i.e. efficiency improvements in the entire food-chain and dietary changes toward less land-demanding food have not been explored as extensively. Given that conversion efficiency of plant to animal matter is roughly 10 per cent, and that about a third of the world's cereal production is fed to animals, a reduction in the livestock product consumption could greatly reduce the need for more food. On average, the production of beef protein requires several times the amount of land and water than required by the production of vegetable proteins such as cereals. While meat currently represents only 15 per cent of the total global human diet, approximately 80 per cent of the agricultural land is used for animal grazing or the production of feed and fodder for animals. Much of the increasing demand for livestock products to 2050 is projected to occur in developing countries (Alexandratos and Bruinsma, 2012). Changes towards diets that include fewer livestock products may reduce food demand, increase food supply potential and dramatically decrease the demand for land (Smith and Gregory, 2013). In a reference scenario developed to represent FAO projections, global agricultural area expands, under business-as-usual assumptions, from the current 5.1 billion ha to 5.4 billion ha in 2030. Yet combining higher productivity growth with a substitution of pork and/or poultry for 20 per cent of ruminant meat, agricultural land use could drop to 4.4 billion ha.

16.4.3 Conclusions

AFOLU GHG emissions are increasing, but not as fast as the rate of emissions from fossil fuels, meaning that the total share of agricultural emissions in total anthropogenic GHG emissions is declining over time. Over the period 1961–2010, agricultural productivity has increased faster than have GHG emissions, suggesting an improvement in the GHG-intensity of agricultural products. This global trend masks different rates of progress in different regions. All categories of agricultural emissions are increasing, but some faster than others. For example, N_2O emissions from synthetic fertilizer application are growing faster than N_2O and CH_4 emissions from manure applied to soils, such that synthetic fertilizers will become a larger emission source over the next decade if increases continue at present rates. Deforestation emissions, however, are declining. In terms of difference between regions, agricultural GHG emissions in developing countries are increasing at a faster rate than those in developed countries, with some developed regions showing declines in GHG emissions.

The database and approach outlined in this chapter are more than an accounting exercise. The outputs provide important information on the key sources of GHG emissions from the AFOLU sector, the regions in which they occur and the rates of change. Wherever GHG emissions occur, there is potential to reduce emissions, so the outputs of this study can also be used to identify hotspots (in terms of regions and activities) for potential mitigation action. It is in defining the regionally appropriate mitigation actions that we can turn the problems identified in a spatial emissions database into solutions.

Supply-side mitigation measures have a mixed impact on food security. Some supply-side mitigation measures also enhance agricultural production, thereby helping to address food security issues. Improved timing of fertilization and nitrification inhibitors, for example, can increase crop production as can measures to improve carbon sequestration. Other supply-side measures aimed at GHG mitigation could potentially reduce production however, for example where the mitigation measure decreases crop yield (e.g. reduced fertilizer inputs). Demand-side measures, on the other hand, typically benefit both food security and GHG mitigation. Current literature indeed suggests that consumption-based measures offer a greater potential for GHG mitigation than do supply-side measures, yet demand-side measures have received far less attention than have supply-side measures so far (see, e.g., Smith et al., 2013).

Most technical supply-side measures considered in previous assessments of mitigation potential in the AFOLU sector are close to current practice and can be implemented by a relatively small number of land managers who can be incentivized to implement the measures. Demand-side measures, however, will require behavioural change towards dietary shifts, and require action from many more actors, requiring both policy and consumer action.

Clearly all available mitigation options, on both the supply and demand side, will need to be considered in a complementary fashion, if the enormous dual challenges of delivering food security and reducing climate forcing by 2050 are to be met. Supply-side measures should be implemented immediately, focusing on those that improve agricultural efficiency and allow the production of more agricultural product per unit of input. Demand-side measures need to be supported by strong policy measures, which should aim to co-deliver on other public goods and goals, such as improving environmental quality and dietary health.

ACKNOWLEDGEMENTS

We thank the Governments of Germany and Norway for their generous funding of 'Monitoring and Assessment of GHG Emissions and Mitigation Potential from Agriculture', FAO Trust Fund Projects GCP/GLO/GER/286 and GCP/GLO/NOR/325.

NOTES

1. 1 EJ = 1 Exajoule = 10^{18} Joule.
2. Computed as the ratio of feed to food for cereal production, or roughly 45 per cent over 2005–10 (FAOSTAT 2013).
3. Regional values are reported statistically as growth rates from appropriately specified ordinary least squares regressions.
4. Forest resource assessment, FAO.

REFERENCES

Alexandratos, N. and H. Bruinsma (2012), World Agriculture Towards 2030/2050, The 2012 Revision. Available at: http://typo3.fao.org/fileadmin/templates/esa/Global_perspectives/world_ag_2030_50_2012_rev.pdf.
Berndes, G., N. Bird and A. Cowie (2011), Bioenergy, land use change and climate change mitigation. Background Technical Report, International Energy Agency (IEA), Paris.
Berrueta, V.M., R.D. Edwards and O.R. Masera (2008), Energy performance of wood burning cook-stoves in Michoacan Mexico. *Renewable Energy*, **33**(5), 859–70.
Carbon Dioxide Information Analysis Center (CDIAC) (2012), Available at: http://cdiac.ornl.gov.
Easterling W., P. Aggarwal, P. Batima, K. Brander, L. Erda, M. Howden, A. Kirilenko, J. Morton and F.N. Tubiello (2007), Food, fibre and forest products. In M.L. Parry, O.F. Canziani, J.P. Palutikof, P.J. Van Der Linden and C.E. Hanson (eds), *Climate Change 2007: Impacts, Adaptation and Vulnerability. Contribution of Working Group II to the Fourth Assessment Report of the Intergovernmental Panel on Climate Change*. Cambridge, UK, Cambridge University Press.
Erb K.-H., H. Haberl and C. Plutzar (2012a), Dependency of global primary bioenergy crop potentials in 2050 on food systems, yields, biodiversity conservation and political stability. *Energy Policy*, **47**, 260–69.
Erb K.H., A. Mayer, F. Krausmann, C. Lauk, C. Plut, J. Steinberger and H. Haberl (2012b), The interrelations of future global bioenergy potentials, food demand and agricultural technology. In A. Gasparatos and P. Stromberg (eds), *Socioeconomic and Environmental Impacts of Biofuels: Evidence from Developing Nations*. Cambridge: Cambridge University Press, pp. 27–52.
FAO (2008), *Livestock's Long Shadow*. Rome: FAO.
FAO (2010), *Global Forest Resources Assessment*. Rome: FAO.
FAO (2011a), *The State of the World's Land and Water Resources for Food and Agriculture*. Rome: FAO.
FAO (2011b), *Linking Sustainability and Climate Financing: Implications for Agriculture*. Rome: FAO.
FAO (2013), *Statistical Yearbook 2013, World Food and Agriculture*. Rome: FAO.
FAOSTAT (2013), online database. Available at: http://faostat.fao.org/ (accessed 20 January 2014).
Foresight (2011), The future of food and farming. Final Project Report. London.
Friedlingstein P, S. Solomon, G.-K. Plattner, R. Knutti, and M. Raupach (2011), Long-term climate implications of twenty-first century options for carbon dioxide emission mitigation. *Nature Climate Change*, **1**, 4457–4461.
González A.D., B. Frostell and A. Carlsson-Kanyama (2011), Protein efficiency per unit energy and per unit greenhouse gas emissions: potential contribution of diet choices to climate change mitigation. *Food Policy*, **36**, 562–70.
Haberl, H., K.-H. Erb, F. Krausmann, H.B. Adensam and N. Schulz (2003), Land-use change and socio-economic metabolism in Austria, Part II: land-use scenarios for 2020. *Land Use Policy*, **20**, 21–39.
Havlík, P., U.A. Schneider, E. Schmid, H. Böttcher, S. Fritz, R. Skalský et al. (2011), Global land-use implications of first and second generation biofuel targets. *Energy Policy*, **39**(10), 5690–5702.
Houghton, R.A., G.R. van der Werf, R.S. DeFries, M.C. Hansen, J.I. House, C. Le Quéré, J. Pongratz and N. Ramankutty (2012), Chapter G2 Carbon emissions from land use and land-cover change. *Biogeosciences Discuss*, **9**, 835–78.
IAASTD (2009), Agriculture at a crossroads: global report. International Assessment of Agricultural Knowledge, Science and Technology for Development (IAASTD).
IEA (2011), *World Energy Outlook 2011*. Paris: IEA.
IIASA/FAO (2012), *Global Agro-ecological Zones (GAEZ v3.0)*, IIASA, Laxenburg, Austria, and Rome: FAO.
International Assessment of Agricultural Knowledge, Science and Technology for Development (2008), Agriculture at a crossroads. Synthesis Report, UNEP, New York.
IPCC (1996), *Guidelines for National Greenhouse Gas Inventories*. Paris: OECD.
IPCC (2000), IPCC special report, emission scenarios, summary for policymakers. Available at: https://www.ipcc.ch/pdf/special-reports/spm/sres-en.pdf.
IPCC (2001), Third assesment report: climate change 2001. Available at: http://www.grida.no/publications/other/ipcc_tar/ (accessed 12 November 2013).
IPCC (2003), Good practice guidance for land use, land-use change and forestry. Prepared by the IPCC National Greenhouse Gas Inventories Programme, J. Penman, M. Gytarsky, T. Hiraishi, T. Krug, D. Kruger, R. Pipatti, L. Buendia, K. Miwa, T. Ngara, K. Tanabe and F.Wagner (eds), IGES, Hayama, Japan.
IPCC (2006), *2006 IPCC Guidelines for National Greenhouse Gas Inventories*. Prepared by the National Greenhouse Gas Inventories Programme, H.S. Eggleston, L. Buendia, K. Miwa, T. Ngara and K. Tanabe (eds), Hayama, Japan: IGES.

IPCC (2007), Climate Change 2007: Mitigation. Contribution of Working Group III to the Fourth Assessment Report. Intergovernmental Panel on Climate Change, London.

Lauk, C., H. Haberl, K.-H. Erb, S. Gingrich and F. Krausmann (2012), Global socio-economic carbon stocks in long-lived products 1900–2008. *Environment Research Letters*, **7**, doi:10.1088/1748-9326/7/3/034023.

Leip A., F. Weiss, T. Wassenaar, I. Perez, T. Fellmann, P. Loudjani, F. Tubiello, D. Grandgirard, S. Monni and K. Biala (2010), Evaluation of the livestock sector's contribution to the EU greenhouse gas emissions (GGELS). Final report. European Commission, Joint Research Centre, Ispra, Italy.

Montzka, S.A., E.J. Dlugokencky and J.H.Butler (2011), Non-CO_2 greenhouse gases and climate change. *Nature*, **476**(7358), 43–50.

Mueller N.D., J.S. Gerber, M. Johnston, D.K. Ray, N. Ramankutty and J.A. Foley (2012), Closing yield gaps through nutrient and water management. *Nature*, **490**, 254–7.

Nabuurs, G.J., O. Masera, K. Andrasko, P. Benitez-Ponce, R. Boer, M. Dutschke, E. Elsiddig, J. Ford-Robertson, P. Frumhoff and T. Karjalainen (2007), Forestry. Climate Change 2007: Mitigation. Contribution of Working Group III to the Fourth Assessment Report of the Intergovernmental Panel on Climate Change. Cambridge University Press, Cambridge, pp. 543–84.

Parfitt J., M. Barthel and S. Macnaughton (2010), Food waste within food supply chains: quantification and potential for change to 2050. *Philosophical Transactions of the Royal Society B: Biological Sciences*, **365**, 3065–3081.

Popp, C., W. Dean, S. Feng, S.J. Cokus, S. Andrews, M. Pellegrini, S.E. Jacobsen and W. Reik (2010), Genome-wide erasure of DNA methylation in mouse primordial germ cells is affected by AID deficiency. *Nature*, **463**, 1101–1105.

Reay D.S., E.A. Davidson, K.A. Smith, P. Smith, J.M. Melillo, F. Dentener and P.J. Crutzen (2012), Global agriculture and nitrous oxide emissions. *Nature Climate Change*, **2**, 410–416.

Rose, S.K., A.A. Golub and B. Sohngen (2013), Total factor and relative agricultural productivity and deforestation. *American Journal of Agricultural Economics*, **1–9**; doi: 10.1093/ajae/aas113. (available online 14 December 2012).

Schmidhuber, J. (2007), Impact of an increased biomass use on agricultural markets, prices and food security: a longer-term perspective. Paper presented at the International symposium of Notre Europe. Paris, 27–29 November 2006. Available at: http://www.fao.org/fileadmin/templates/esa/Global_perspectives/Presentations/BiomassNotreEurope.pdf.

Schmidhuber, J. (2013), Sicherung der globalen Lebensmittel- und Energieversorgung, Ein Ausblick bis 2050 und darüber hinaus, ISSN 1611-4159 http://www.lfl.bayern.de/mam/cms07/publikationen/daten/schriftenreihe/agrarforschung_zukunft.pdf.

Schmidinger, K. and E. Stehfest (2012), Including CO_2 implications of land occupation in LCAs–method and example for livestock products. *The International Journal of Life Cycle Assessment*, doi: 10.1007/s11367-012-0434-7.

Schneider, U. and P. Smith (2009), Energy intensities and greenhouse gas emission mitigation in global agriculture. *Energy Efficiency*, **2**, 195–206.

Smith, P. (2008), Land use change and soil organic carbon dynamics. *Nutrient Cycling in Agroecosystems*, **81**, 169–78.

Smith, P. and P.J. Gregory (2013), Climate change and sustainable food production. *Proceedings of the Nutrition Society*, **72**, 21–8.

Smith, P., H. Haberl and A. Popp (2013), How much land based greenhouse gas mitigation can be achieved without compromising food security and environmental goals? *Global Change Biology*, **19**, 2285–2302.

Smith P., D. Martino, Z. Cai, D. Gwary, H.H. Janzen, P. Kumar, B. Mccarl, S. Ogle et al. (2007), Agriculture. In B. Metz, O.R. Davidson, P.R. Bosch, R. Dave and L.A. Meyer (eds), *Climate Change 2007: Mitigation. Contribution of Working group III to the Fourth Assessment Report of the Intergovernmental Panel on Climate Change*. Cambridge, UK and New York: Cambridge University Press, pp. 497–540.

Thornton P.K. and M. Herrero (2010), Potential for reduced methane and carbon dioxide emissions from livestock and pasture management in the tropics. *Proceedings of the National Academy of Sciences*, **107**, 19667–19672.

Tilman, D., C. Balzer, J. Hill and B.L. Befort (2011), Global food demand and the sustainable intensification of agriculture. *Proceedings of the National Academy of Sciences*, **108**, 20260–20264.

Tubiello, F., M. Salvatore, S. Rossi, A. Ferrara, N. Fitton and P. Smith (2013), The FAOSTAT database of greenhouse gas emissions from agriculture. *Environmental Research Letters*, **8**(015009), 10.

UNEP (2009), *Assessing Biofuels, Towards Sustainable Production and Use of Resources*, Paris: Division of Technology, Industry and Ecocnomics, United Nations Environment Programme (UNEP).

UNFCCC (2007), Investment and financial flows to address climate change. Bonn: United Nations Framework Convention on Climate Change.

UNFCCC, (2012), UNFCCC online GHG database. Available at: http://www.unfccc.int, (accessed September 2012).
United Nations Population Division (2013), World Population Prospects: The 2012 revision, UN Press release. Available at: http://esa.un.org/wpp/Documentation/pdf/WPP2012_Press_Release.pdf (accessed 12 November 2013).
WBGU (2009), *Future Bioenergy and Sustainable Land Use*. London: Earthscan.
Yan, X., H. Akiyama, K. Yagi and H. Akimoto (2009), Global estimations of the inventory and mitigation potential of methane emissions from rice cultivation conducted using the 2006 Intergovernmental Panel on Climate Change Guidelines. *Global Biogeochemical Cycles*, **23**, 1–15.

17. Land degradation, water scarcity and sustainability

Manab Das, Debashish Goswami,* Anshuman and Alok Adholeya

17.1 INTRODUCTION

Land degradation and water scarcity are factors that have direct negative consequences on the general status of ecosystems and their inhabitants. Excessive anthropogenic activities in agriculture, forestry and industrial sectors resulted in significant negative effect on soil health and water sustainability. Soil, a product of long natural processes that take thousands of years to produce its present form, is an overlooked limited natural resource. Land degradation affects more than 33 per cent of the planet's surface area, leading to negative consequences for 2.6 billion people in more than 100 countries.

The challenges of growing water scarcity are exacerbated by groundwater depletion, water pollution, degradation of water-related ecosystems, wasteful water use and land degradation. There are enough indications that water use exceeds sustainable levels. Producing food to feed everyone well, including the 2 billion additional people expected to inhabit the earth by mid-century, will place greater pressure on available water and land resources.

Extensive degradation and deepening scarcity of land and water resources have caused the food production system risk at the global and regional levels. Land degradation and water scarcity pose serious challenge to the task of feeding a world population projected to reach 9.1 billion people by the middle of this century. This chapter covers the issues related to land degradation and water scarcity at the global scale and in the context of the developing countries of the world, specifically India, and seeks possible solutions.

17.1.1 Definitions

Land degradation, a natural or anthropogenic process that refers to loss of land's ecosystem functioning or reduction of its productivity in terms of quality, quantity, goods and services (Oldeman et al., 1991). Some academicians define land degradation as a loss of the biological and/or economic resilience and adaptive capacity of the land system (Holling, 1986, 2001; Dean et al., 1995; Kasperson et al., 1995; IPCC, 2001). The United Nations Convention to Combat Desertification (UNCCD) defines land degradation as a:

> reduction or loss, in arid, semi-arid, and dry sub-humid areas, of the biological or economic productivity and complexity of rain-fed cropland, irrigated cropland, or range, pasture, forest, and woodlands resulting from land uses or from a process or combination of processes, including processes arising from human activities and habitation patterns, such as: (i) soil erosion caused by wind and/or water; (ii) deterioration of the physical, chemical, and biological or economic properties of soil; and (iii) long-term loss of natural vegetation. (WMO, 2005)

The GEF (Global Environment Facility) defines land degradation as any form of deterioration of the natural potential of land that affects ecosystem integrity either in terms of reducing its sustainable ecological productivity or in terms of its native biological richness and maintenance of resilience (GEF, 2009). Key components of all these definitions, depicts land degradation as (1) a human-induced phenomenon that cannot be caused by natural processes alone, and (2) decreases in the capacity of the land system to meet its user demands (Baartman et al., 2007). Land degradation threatens the long-term biological and/or economic resilience and adaptive capacity of the ecosystem.

Sustainability is based on the basic principle that everything that is needed for our survival and well-being depends on our natural environment. Sustainability maintains the conditions under which humans and nature can exist in productive harmony, that fulfils the social, economic and other requirements of present and future generations. Sustainability is important for ensuring that we have and will continue to have the water, materials, and resources to protect human health and the ecosystem (EPA, 2013). Gleick (1995) suggested a definition of sustainable water use as 'the use of water that supports the ability of human society to endure and flourish into the indefinite future without undermining the integrity of the hydrological cycle or the ecological systems that depend on it'. Water sustainability helps in maintaining the desired benefits to a particular group or place, undiminished over time, without reducing benefits to other users like the ecosystem, and without affecting the ability to provide comparable benefits into the future (Gleick, 1998). An area or region faces water stress when annual per capita water supply drops below 1700 m^3, and water scarcity when water supply drops below 1000 m^3 (Falkenmark and Widstrand, 1992; UN-Water, 2006b).

The 1996 World Food Summit adopted a definition of food security as the situation at the individual, household, national, regional and global levels when all people, at all times, have physical and economic access to sufficient, safe and nutritious food to meet their dietary needs and food preferences for an active and healthy life (FAO, 2003a).

17.1.2 Concerns Over Water Scarcity

Water is essential for agriculture, industries and household use, including drinking, cooking and washing, etc. It plays an important role in sustaining the earth's ecosystems (Rosegrant et al., 2002). Developmental and demographic growth coupled with inefficient use and overexploitation of water resources has posed serious challenges in water availability across many regions of the world. Water scarcity is already a serious problem in many parts of the world (Fedoroff et al., 2010). Water is essential for food production. The question of food security in interlinked with water security. Agricultural production accounted for about 90 per cent of global freshwater consumption during the past century (Shiklomanov, 2000). Today, we face the challenge of feeding 1 billion undernourished people out of the world's total population of 7 billion which is expected to reach 9 billion by 2050 (Jägerskog and Clausen, 2012). Table 17.1 shows the annual crop production growth (per cent) in different regions of the world. Projections have been made using a multitude of assumptions about the future. Aggregate crop production growth rate at the world level is projected to decrease from 2.1 per cent per year during the last 30 years of the twentieth century to 1.4 per cent during the 1997–2030

Table 17.1   Percentage annual crop production growth

Regions	1969–99	1979–99	1989–99	1997/99–2015	2015–30	1997/99–2030
All developing countries	3.1	3.1	3.2	1.7	1.4	1.6
South Asia	2.8	3.0	2.4	2.1	1.5	1.8
Industrial countries	1.4	1.1	1.6	0.9	0.9	0.9
World	2.1	2.0	2.1	1.5	1.3	1.4

Source: FAO (2003b).

period. For the developing countries as a group, the corresponding growth rates are 3.1 and 1.6 per cent per year, respectively (FAO, 2003b).

FAO predicts that food production needs to be increased by 70 per cent by the mid-century to feed the world's population. This will exert tremendous pressure on the already stressed water resources, that too at a time when additional water needs to be allocated to the energy sector to meet the increased energy demands (Jägerskog and Clausen, 2012). The solution to this problem lies in the sustainable use of water.

17.2   LAND DEGRADATION AND WATER SCARCITY: CURRENT STATE AND CHALLENGES

17.2.1   Global Scenario, Major Causes and Extent of Land Degradation

During 1991, GLASOD (Global Assessment of Soil Degradation) indicated that 15 per cent of the land surface was degraded; whereas their assessment study on 2008 identified 24 per cent of land as degrading but the areas hardly overlapped, which means that new areas were being affected (Bai et al., 2008). Poverty and undervaluing the natural resources are the critical factors responsible for land degradation and environmental mismanagement. People are more focused on immediate economic gain irrespective of damage to the same resources, they dependent on. More often, achievements in production have been associated with management practices that have degraded the land and water systems upon which the production depends (Figure 17.1).

The main causes of land degradation include biophysical causes and unsustainable land-management practices. Topography of land, which determines soil erosion hazard, and climatic conditions, such as rainfall, wind, and temperature, belong to biophysical causes (Nkonya et al., 2011). Unsustainable land management practices include (FAO, 1996):

1. Deforestation: Vast reserves of forests have been degraded by large-scale logging and clearance for farm and urban use. More than 220 million ha of tropical forests were destroyed during 1975–90, mainly for food production (FAO, 1996). In the past two centuries, about 70 per cent of the grassland, 50 per cent of the savannah, 45 per cent of the temperate deciduous forest, and 27 per cent of the tropical forest biome have been cleared or converted for agriculture (Foley et al., 2011).
2. Overgrazing: About 20 per cent of the world's pasture and rangelands have been damaged. Recent losses have been most severe in Africa and Asia.

446 *Handbook on food*

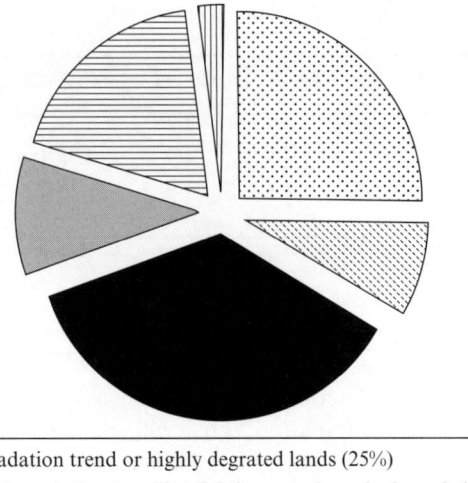

□ High degradation trend or highly degrated lands (25%)
▧ Moderate degradation trend in slightly or moderately degraded land (8%)
■ Stable land, slightly or moderately degraded (36%)
▢ Improving lands (10%)
☱ Bare lands (18%)
▥ Covered by inland water bodies (2%)

Source: Modified from FAO (2011).

Figure 17.1 Status and trends in global land degradation

3. Fuel wood consumption: About 1730 million m^3 of fuelwood are harvested annually from forests and plantations. Wood fuel is the primary source of energy in many developing regions.
4. Agricultural mismanagement: Water erosion causes soil loss, which is estimated at 25 000 million tons annually. Soil salinization and waterlogging affect about 40 million ha of land globally (FAO, 1996). During last 50 years, global fertilizer consumption increased by 500 per cent, resulting in contamination of water resources, increased energy use and widespread pollution (Foley et al., 2011). Current industrial agricultural practices use 1.5 times more pesticides than they did 40 years ago (UNCTAD, 2010).
5. Industry and urbanization: Urban growth, road construction, mining and industry are major factors in land degradation in different regions. Valuable agricultural land is often lost as a result of these.

Results of both biophysical and unsustainable land management practices include (FAO, 1996):

1. Decline in the chemical, physical and/or biological properties of soil, e.g. lower organic content and nutrient levels, salinization, pH changes in soil (acidification or alkalinization);
2. Reduced availability of potable water;

3. Lower volumes of surface water;
4. Depletion of aquifers due to lack of recharge;
5. Impacts on livestock and agriculture, e.g. loss of animals due to dehydration, reduced yields;
6. Water and food insecurity, famine;
7. Biodiversity loss;
8. General reduction of the ability for the community to depend on the natural environment for livelihood.
9. Decline in economic productivity and national development.
10. Conflict over access to resources;
11. Mass migration;
12. About 3–5 million cases of pesticide poisoning and more than 40 thousand deaths every year (UNEP, 2011).

Almost one fifth of global degrading land is cropland, an area equivalent to more than 20 per cent of all cultivated areas; 23 per cent is broadleaved forest, 19 per cent needle-leaved forests, and 20–25 per cent rangeland. The vast majority (78 per cent) of degrading lands are found in humid regions, which is contrary to the popular belief that most degradation occurs in dry lands; 8 per cent in the dry sub-humid, 9 per cent in the semi-arid, and 5 per cent in arid and hyper-arid regions (Bai et al., 2008).

17.2.2 Water Scarcity: Existing State and Major Challenges in Global and Indian Context

As already mentioned, water scarcity can result in reduced food production. Irrigation is a tool that enhances agricultural production resulting in the stability of food prices (Hanjra et al., 2009). Water is vital to food security and sustainable livelihoods, resulting from increased income, improved health and nutrition, and a diminished gap between food production and demand (Rosegrant et al., 2002). However, continued demand for water for non-agricultural uses, such as urban and industrial uses, and the associated environmental quality issues have resulted in limited availability of irrigation water. Worldwide, the volume of water used by industries is estimated to rise significantly from 752 billion cubic metres (BCM) in 1995 to 1170 BCM by 2025 per year (UNESCO–WWAP 2003). Irrigation demands and practices caused changed water flows, and land clearing which have resulted in surface water and groundwater quality deterioration (Hanjra and Qureshi, 2010). Irrigation return-flow is rich in salt, nutrients, minerals and pesticides, which impact downstream catchments and drinking water. Urban water use and protection of natural ecosystems are providing competition for water resources previously dedicated to agriculture (Tilman et al., 2002).

The growing demand for water is impacting the current availability of water for irrigation. There are already very severe water crises in Western, Central and South Asia, which use major portion of their water resources for irrigation (Table 17.2). In Northern Africa, the situation is worse as groundwater withdrawal for irrigation exceeds renewable resources due to groundwater overdraft (FAO, 2011).

A global inventory of groundwater use in agriculture conducted by FAO (Siebert et al., 2010) indicates that about 40 per cent of the irrigated area in the world depends on

Table 17.2 Annual average renewable water resources and withdrawal for irrigation

Continent/region	Renewable water resources (BCM)	Irrigation water withdrawal (BCM)	Pressure on water resources due to irrigation (%)
Africa	3931	184	5
Northern Africa	47	80	170
Sub-Saharan Africa	3884	105	3
Americas	19238	385	2
Northern America	6077	258	4
Central America and Caribbean	781	15	2
Southern America	12380	112	1
Asia	12413	2012	16
Western Asia	484	227	47
Central Asia	263	150	57
South Asia	1766	914	52
East Asia	3410	434	13
Southeast Asia	6490	287	4

Source: FAO (2011).

Table 17.3 Major food producing countries dependent of groundwater

Country	Area equipped for Irrigation (ha)	Groundwater (ha)	Surface water (ha)	Dependence on groundwater (% of area equipped for irrigation)
Brazil	3149217	591439	2557778	19
China	62392392	18794951	43597440	30
Egypt	3422178	331927	3090251	10
India	61907846	39425869	22481977	64
Pakistan	16725843	5172552	11553291	31
Thailand	5279860	481063	4798797	9
USA	27913872	16576243	11337629	59

Source: Siebert et al. (2010).

groundwater sources. Regions affected include some of the world's major grain-producing areas, such as the Punjab in India and parts of China. India depends on groundwater for irrigating 64 per cent of the total irrigated areas (Table 17.3) (FAO, 2011).

Overexploitation of water resources to meet increased water demands is a serious problem all over the world. Freshwater withdrawals are expected to rise by 50 per cent in developing countries and by 18 per cent in developed countries by 2025 (WBCSD, 2009). In the United States, about 20 per cent of the irrigated land uses groundwater pumped in excess of recharge (Tilman et al., 2002). Excessive groundwater pumping in some parts of the Central Valley in California, for example, has resulted in land subsidence reducing the ability of the rainfall to fully recharge the groundwater sources (Bertoldi, 1992). Most countries in the Middle East and North Africa can be classified as being water scarce today. By 2025, Pakistan, South Africa and large parts of India and China will be added to this category. By then, an estimated 1.8 billion people will live in countries experiencing acute water scarcity. These countries will not have sufficient water resources to sustain their current food production level from irrigated agriculture and also to meet the water needs for domestic, industrial and environmental uses. To sustain the growing needs, water will have to be transferred from the agricultural sector to the other sectors, which will affect the agricultural production in these countries and regions (IWMI, 2005).

India accounts for 2.5 per cent of land area and 4.0 per cent of water resources of the world while representing 16 per cent of the world population. With the current annual population growth of 1.9 per cent, India's population is expected to reach 1.5 billion by the year 2050. The Indian Planning Commission estimates that India's total water demand will increase to 1180 BCM in 2050 from 710 BCM in 2010. This will put tremendous pressure on the water resources in India (Gupta, 2005).

At present, the per capita water availability in India is about 1050 m^3 designating India as a water-stressed country. India's per capita water availability is expected to fall to 700 m^3 by 2050, indicating acute water scarcity. Even if the total available (or maximum utilizable) water is taken into account, per capita water availability is estimated to be 1200 m^3 by 2050, implying that India would remain water-stressed even if all existing natural flows are taken into account (TERI, 2006). Figure 17.2 shows the temporal trends in water availability in India.

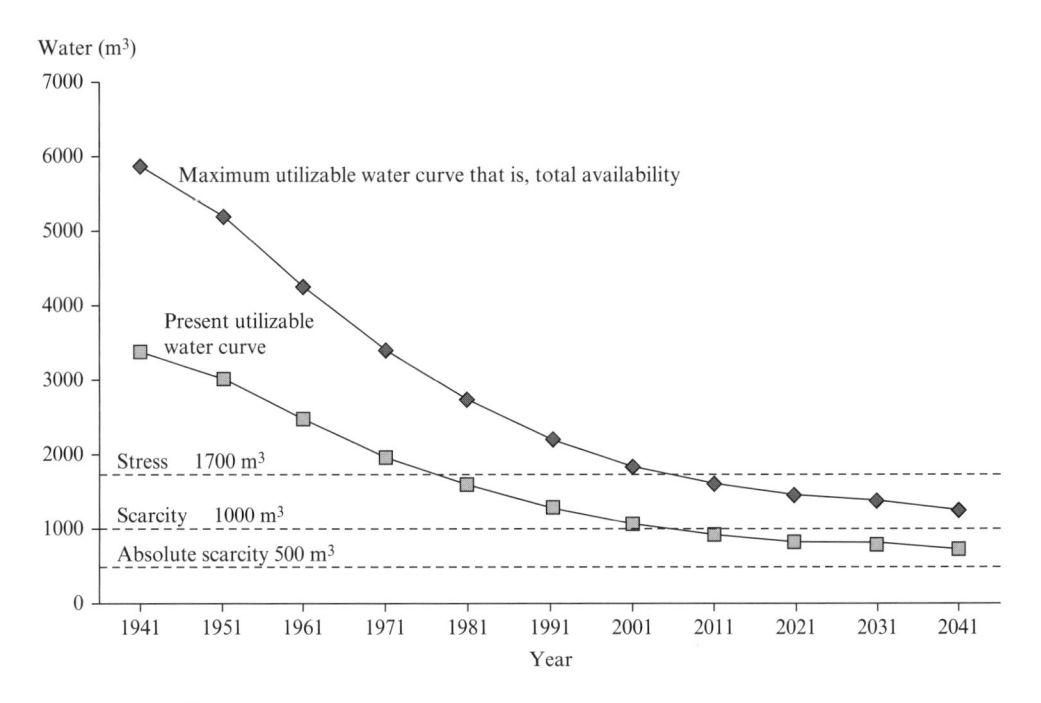

Source: TERI (2006).

Figure 17.2 Declining water resource availability in India

17.3 IMPACT OF LAND DEGRADATION AND WATER SCARCITY

17.3.1 Impact of Land Degradation

Land degradation leads to deterioration of ecosystem services and negative consequences for 2.6 billion people in more than 100 countries. An estimated loss of US$40 billion annually worldwide is directly or indirectly attributed to land degradation. With around 1 billion people being undernourished, shrinking water resources, increased land degradation and surmounting pressure on natural resources sustainable future seems a distant dream (GEF, 2009). The country rankings (first to fifth) based on severity of land degradation are presented in Table 17.4.

Food security

According to FAO's recent report, by 2050, the rising population and incomes will require 70 per cent increase in global food production and up to 100 per cent more in developing countries relative to 2009 levels. Over this time span, another 1 billion tonnes of cereals and 200 million extra tonnes of livestock products will need to be produced every year (FAO, 2011). In contrast, because of unsustainable land management practices that cause land degradation, the amount of productive land is declining. Consequently, it poses a serious threat to long-term food security. According to GLASOD, 40 per cent of the world's agricultural land is moderately degraded, and a further 9 per cent strongly degraded, reducing global crop yield by 13 per cent (Wood et al., 2000).

Substantial decline in productivity has been found in developing countries, especially cropland in Africa and Central America, pasture in Africa, and forests in Central America. Land areas of 5 to 8 million hectares become unproductive in each year. These are primarily lands at the margin of cultivation, especially at desert margins and in steeply sloping and high-altitude areas (Scherr, 1999). Tropical and sub-tropical countries, which have low physical resilience to land degradation, are associated with societies of poor people. About 42 per cent of the world's poor depend on degraded lands for nutrition and income. With such a large portion of the world's land and population being affected, the cost of

Table 17.4 The country rankings of severity of land degradation

Rank	Severity indicators			
	Per cent of global degrading area	Loss of NPP (million tonne C)	Per cent of country affected	Rural population affected (millions)
	Country (value)			
1	Russia (16.5)	Canada (94)	Swaziland (95)	China (457)
2	Canada (11.6)	Indonesia (68)	Angola (66)	India (177)
3	USA (7.9)	Brazil (63)	Gabon (64)	Indonesia (86)
4	China (7.6)	China (59)	Thailand (60)	Bangladesh (72)
5	Australia (6.2)	Australia (50)	Zambia (60)	Brazil (46)

Source: Bai et al. (2008).

land-based ecosystem degradation could amount to US$66 billion per year (Nkonya et al., 2011). In addition to this, they also have fewer resources for alleviating degradation, and are especially susceptible to the credit market failures and land tenure insecurity. These altogether, can raise time discount rates and reduce planning horizons, leading to faster soil mining (Coxhead and Oygard, 2007). The degradation of farmland, as a result of unsustainable use has often been abandoned and left as marginal grassland and forests, of which only part has been developed in secondary forest ecosystems. Due to this around 385–472 million hectares of farmland have been abandoned (Campbell et al., 2008).

Consequences of land degradation are more direct to subsistence farmers. As a producer, they get fewer yields with more efforts and hence either less food or less income. For consumers, degradation may also leads to increased cost of living due to higher food prices. So, household food security is affected in both ways. The relation between land degradation and food security is of enormous complexity due to the interactions between land, water, populations and wealth, and the rapid changes therein (de Vries and Molden, 2002).

Climate change

Land degradation has direct impact on services of ecosystems, in particular, nutrient cycling, the global carbon cycle and the hydrological cycle. The carbon pool in soil and above-ground vegetation of forests are quite large and disturbed. They are affected by unsustainable land management practices and also different forms of prevailing soil erosion (the most widespread form of soil degradation) processes such as water erosion, deforestation and soil compaction (GEF, 2006). Anthropogenic activities for conversion of natural to agricultural ecosystems lead to a reduction in the amount of root and litter biomass returned to the soil, distribution in cycles of elements and water, and change in the energy balance. Consequently, the soil organic carbon (SOC) pool is declined by acceleration in oxidation (C to CO_2) rate and losses due to erosion and leaching. It is estimated that most soils lose one half to two thirds of their SOC pool within 5 years in the tropics and 50 years in temperate regions. It is estimated that the total displacement of SOC pool may be 4.0–6.0 Pg/year (Pg = petagram = 10^{15} g = 1 billion metric ton) having a contribution of 0.8–1.2 Pg from erosion-induced emission (Lal, 2003). Such huge amount of carbon efflux (as CO_2) from soil to atmosphere has a very significant impact on climate, and future impacts are certain. Moreover, conversion of forest land to agricultural land also increases emission of other potential greenhouse gases such as CH_4 and N_2O into the atmosphere (GEF, 2006).

Land degradation also has significant impacts on hydrological cycle. Bare soil surfaces associated with land degradation increase the albedo (reflection of energy), which leads to cooling and suppression of local convection resulting in less precipitation. The reduction of local rainfall further reduces the vegetation cover and accelerates land degradation (Charney et al., 1975). However, most of the research has shown that alteration of soil moisture due to changes in vegetation cover plays an important role in altering local climate. Variation in soil moisture affects regional climate in three ways:

1. Inverse relation of soil moisture with albedo changes radiative regime;
2. Moist soils have higher thermal diffusivity, thermal conductivity and heat capacity which result in more energy transfer into the soil;

3. Soil directly provides moisture to atmosphere through evaporation or indirectly through transpiration (Entekhabi et al., 1992; Wainwright, 2009).

Thus, land degradation has multiple and complex impacts on the climate through a range of direct and indirect processes.

17.3.2 Impact of Water Scarcity

Agriculture and food security
Agricultural productivity is direly linked to food security. Agricultural water-use efficiency is low in India, The irrigation efficiency in India is barely 40 per cent compared to 80 per cent in Israel (Sharma, 2002). With judicious and efficient use of water, agricultural production can become sustainable. However, the freshwater resources become unsustainable due to mismanagement, over-pumping, and aquifer contamination. Human activities have already reached or exceeded renewable water limits in many regions (Gleick, 1998).

Agriculture in India is the source of income for almost two thirds of the work force. According to the Ministry of Agriculture, Government of India, Uttar Pradesh, Maharashtra, Rajasthan, Madhya Pradesh and Karnataka are the five states with the highest area under agriculture and Uttar Pradesh, Punjab, Andhra Pradesh, West Bengal and Haryana are the states with the highest agricultural production. Many of the Indian agricultural states are overexploiting groundwater to meet current irrigation needs (Postel, 2000). The total water deficit in those states amounts to an estimated 100×10^9 m^3 per year (Postel, 2000). Water scarcity reduces agricultural productions and jeopardizes food security. To feed an estimated 1.35 billion Indian population in 2025, agricultural production would have to be increased by about 25 per cent. Agricultural production in Punjab, Haryana, and western Uttar Pradesh, the major agricultural states of India, might not be sustainable unless appropriate water management plans are implemented (Hira, 2009).

Agricultural water efficiency needs to be enhanced both in irrigated and rainfed production using water-saving agricultural practices and better water management. Use of pressurized irrigation systems should be encouraged for reducing water consumption and enhancing agricultural water use efficiency. The potential of agricultural production system needs to be fully unlocked to resolve the world's water problems and to use limited water resources more efficiently. This will pave the way for producing 'more crop per drop'.

Water can be conserved in the agricultural fields by optimal and efficient water use by adopting efficient methods and farm practices. Various methods of water harvesting and groundwater recharging are being used all over the world to conserve water in areas with limited and low rainfall. In many regions, local people have used simple techniques that are suitable to specific regions to reduce the demand for water. For example, in India's arid and semi-arid areas, the 'tank' system is traditionally the backbone of agricultural production. Tanks are constructed either by bunding or by excavating the ground and collecting rainwater. Rajasthan, located in the Great Indian Desert, receives hardly any rainfall, but people have adapted to the harsh conditions by collecting whatever rain falls. Large bunds constructed to create reservoirs (locally called khadins), dams (locally called johads) and tanks are used to collect rainwater, which is used at the end of the monsoon (rainy) season (TERI, 2010). Agricultural practices such as mulching (application of organic or inorganic material such as plant debris, compost, etc., on land surface to slow down the surface run-off and reduce evaporation losses) and contour farming are established methods for soil and water conservation.

Human health and ecosystem
During the second half of the twentieth century, global food production increased significantly to cope with increased food demands for the growing world population. However, this increase in food production resulted in a significant pressure on the ecosystem. Increased use of fossil fuel, water and fertilizer has resulted in a considerable footprint on the environment (Khan and Hanjra, 2009). The negative environmental impacts of agricultural production include loss of natural habitats and freshwater fauna, loss of biodiversity, pollution in the agricultural catchments, depletion of groundwater aquifer and surface flows, and associated degradation of the ecosystems. As far as human health is concerned, water scarcity may result in malnutrition due to food insecurity (Berger and Finkbeiner, 2010). Groundwater contamination can cause disease to the biological system. In India, the exploitation of groundwater has altered the hydrogeochemical environment of the aquifers. This along with other geogenic reasons has caused synergistic impact to groundwater contamination with contaminants such as fluoride, arsenic, and nitrate beyond the permissible limits. These contaminants have resulted in the manifestation of diseases like fluorosis, arsenicosis, etc. in human beings. Microbiological contamination of the water sources have resulted in the proliferation of various water-borne and water-related diseases such as cholera, typhoid and diaorrhea (Gupta, 2005). According to the WHO, about 80 per cent of all diseases and one third of all deaths in developing countries are due to water-related diseases (Kundzewicz, 1997).

In India, there is evidence of contamination of water by heavy metals in some locations. Based on a study conducted by The Energy and Resources Institute (TERI) in the agricultural community in Delhi and Haryana states of India, the levels of nickel (Ni), manganese (Mn), and lead (Pb) in the water of river Yamuna were higher than the international aquatic water quality criteria for freshwater at some of the sampling sites (TERI, 2012). Levels of Ni, Mn, Pb and mercury (Hg) were above the permissible international standards in agricultural soil along the river at some of the sampling sites. High levels of these pollutants in the floodplains may be due to the treated and untreated effluents and sewage flowing into the river. Vegetables grown in this section of the flood plain of Yamuna area show higher levels of heavy metals contamination than those cultivated in rural areas, thus acting as an entry point for toxic metals into human food chain. Yamuna River serves as a source of drinking water and irrigation for agricultural fields that exist along its course. This is an alarming situation given the dangerous consequences of the consumption of these contaminants.

Water security in a climate change scenario
The earth's ecosystem will experience most direct impacts of climate change in the form of increased precipitation in some parts and severe dry conditions in some other parts of the world. It is projected that climate change will increase water scarcity in the coming decades (Lobell et al., 2008) in some regions and the water might not be sufficient to

meet increased food demands (Brown and Funk, 2008). Climate change will result in changes in mean precipitation, with wet extremes becoming more severe in many regions of the world where mean precipitation increases, and dry extremes becoming more severe where mean precipitation decreases (Bates et al., 2008).

Rosegrant and Cline (2003) reported that in the tropical conditions, climate change may cause more intense rainfall events between long dry periods resulting in reduced or more variable water resources for irrigation. These conditions may promote pests and diseases in crops and result in soil erosion and desertification in some region (Rosegrant and Cline, 2003). Rainfed food production systems will be severely affected due to erratic rainfall patterns resulting from climate change. Climate change may have serious negative effects on the irrigated agricultural production system, which provides about 40 per cent of global food production from just 18 per cent of cropland (Khan and Hanjra, 2009). Climate change will result in the increase in irrigation demand in most parts of the world due to the combined effect of decreased rainfall and increased evaporation arising from increased temperatures (Bates et al., 2008). Many studies conclude that agriculture will be affected due to global warming and climate change particularly in tropical countries, like India (Dasgupta and Sirohi, 2010). The climate change simulation models predict that climate change will impact temperatures, and rainfall pattern around the world, involving more intense and frequent flood and drought events (Eckstein, 2009). The severity of water crisis has prompted the United Nations (United Nations, 2007) to conclude that water scarcity will be the major issue related to food production to feed the world's population in the decades to come (Rosegrant and Cline, 2003).

Both domestic and international water laws and policies are inadequate to meet the challenges posed by global climate change to adapt to the consequences that seem to be unavoidable. According to the IPCC, freshwater resources are vulnerable and have the potential to be strongly impacted by climate change, with wide-ranging consequences on human societies and ecosystems (Bates et al., 2008). This conclusion is easily understood given that the hydrological cycle is inextricably connected to virtually all sectors of the natural and human environments (Eckstein, 2009).

17.4 INTEGRATED MANAGEMENT FOR SUSTAINABLE RESOURCE USE

17.4.1 Sustainable Land Management Practices

Overexploitation and degradation accelerated by climate change leads to reduced availability of natural resources and declining land productivity which directly affect food security and increase poverty. Sustainable land management (SLM) is the antidote which helps to increase average productivity, reduce seasonal fluctuations in yields, underpins diversified production and improved incomes. SLM is about looking after the land for the present and the future, and integrating the long-term coexistence of people with nature so that provisioning, regulating, cultural and supporting services of ecosystems are ensured (Liniger et al., 2011). There are certain principles in SLM and proper implementation of the same can bring about a significant improvement in food security and land's resilience to the various environmental threats.

Principle 1: increased land productivity

Efficient water uses, integrated soil fertility management, improvement of microclimate are the basic requirements for increment of land productivity. Water harvesting, prevention of water loss through evaporation and run-off, and management of surplus water are the key components of efficient water management. Soil fertility can be improved by controlling nutrient loss through leaching, erosion and emission to atmosphere; application of nutrients through crop rotation, intercropping, compost through integrated crop–livestock systems, supplementation with inorganic fertilizer; and also trapping of sediment and nutrients. Use of windbreaks and shelterbelts, agroforestry and multi-storey cropping practices are the efficient measures that can be taken to improve microclimate in dry areas. Protection of soil from heavy rainfall is very much important in humid areas (Liniger et al., 2011).

Principle 2: improved livelihoods

Higher net returns, low risks or a combination of both are prime factors in the adoption of SLM by land users. They are more willing to adopt practices that provide rapid and sustained pay-back in terms of food or income. However, based on the existing scenario, land users may require additional inputs related to machinery, labour, market and knowledge before taking any SLM practices. Those SLM practices that are easy to learn and thus require minimal training and capacity building are easier to promote (Liniger et al., 2011).

Principle 3: improved ecosystems: being environmentally friendly

SLM practices should be environmentally friendly and capable of reducing current land degradation; they should improve biodiversity and increase resilience to climate variation and change. Efficient water use, integrated soil fertility management, control of microclimate and diversification of production are the key issues in SLM and properly addressing these issues can provide better protection against natural disasters and increased resilience to climate variability and change (Liniger et al., 2011).

17.4.2 Integrated and Efficient Water Management for Sustainable Use

Integrated and efficient water resource management is essential for its sustainable use. Water resources management involves quantitative and qualitative aspects of surface water and groundwater, demand and supply, water use efficiency, water conservation and wastage minimization. Sustainable use of water needs an integrated approach and a holistic perspective, involving the hydrology and other components, such as the environment, economy, society, demography and institutional framework (Kundzewicz, 1997). Water resources management should also aim at the prevention of soil degradation in irrigated areas, groundwater depletion, water pollution and ecosystem degradation (Rosegrant and Cline, 2003). Exploiting the full potential of rainfed agriculture will involve an integrated approach involving water-harvesting technologies, crop breeding and extension services, as well as good access to markets, credit and supplies (Khan and Hanjra, 2009). There is no single solution to alleviate the environmental footprints of food production. Loss of soil fertility and water holding capacity, salinization, waterlogging and alkalinization of irrigated land, and depletion of groundwater affect the irrigated land, causing losses in crop productivity and jeopardizing food security (Khan and Hanjra, 2009).

17.4.3 Requisite Policies and Programs

To meet the expected food demand by 2050, International Water Management Institute's projections show that without water productivity gains, South Asia would need 57 per cent additional water for irrigated agriculture. Given the existing scarcity of water, and growing water needs, this level of productivity is not achievable unless adequate measures are undertaken (FAO, 2009a). This situation requires increase in water productivity, which can only be achievable with complete rejuvenation of the irrigation infrastructure, and adoption of appropriate management and policy (FAO, 2009b). Water policy should aim at protecting the water resources against the irreversible activities like improper management of the watersheds (Gleick, 1998). New water management policies should be developed to discourage wasteful use of already developed water supplies and to encourage rainfed agriculture (Rosegrant and Cline, 2003). To prevent groundwater depletion and contamination, groundwater pumping should be done considering the recharge capacity of the aquifers by the rainfall. In the irrigation fields, pressurized irrigation using sprinkler or drip technology should be used, where appropriate, to conserve water.

Agricultural water has been diverted to other sectors like domestic and industrial to meet the increasing water demands in those sectors making agriculture unsustainable. This justifies the need for a suitable agricultural policy in addition to the water policy for judicious allocation of water to various sectors including the agricultural sector, without affecting the environment and the economy of a region (FAO, 2012). For the efficient use of agricultural water at the watershed scale, FAO supports an increasingly important role for new financing mechanisms, including payment for environmental services, more inclusive and participatory approach in watershed management. FAO (2012) suggests adoption of the following actions in the agricultural sector to cope with water scarcity and unsustainability:

1. Importing water by inter-basin transfer, desalination;
2. Reducing variability of river flow by adopting on-farm water conservation;
3. Enhancing groundwater supply capacity through aquifer recharge;
4. Recycling and re-using urban wastewater for crop production;
5. Pollution control adopting integrated plant production and protection, pollution control in the agricultural fields (including payment for environmental services);
6. Reducing water loss by pressurized conveyance and application of water (drip), improved irrigation scheduling, moisture control and canal lining;
7. Increasing water productivity through better water control by improved water delivery in irrigation, and precision irrigation, adoption of improved agricultural practices;
8. Reallocating water by shifting to higher value crops in irrigation and minimizing evapotranspiration.

Proper policies and programs need to be developed for the success of such actions.

17.5 FUTURE VISION AND RECOMMENDATIONS

In spite of having different methods to address different forms of land degradation, persuading land users to adopt these methods remains a challenge. To involve and get a meaningful response from land users, policies and programmes should focus on addressing and changing the behavioural patterns that lead to land degradation. The poor are heavily dependent on land and there should be provision of proper incentives for those who invest their limited capital into preventing or mitigating land degradation. Access to basic services for land users such as rural roads, extension services, communication infrastructure, markets and other rural services should be facilitated as they link land users to market and reduce transaction cost, which in turn increases returns on land investment by the users. Limited resource availability and a neglectful attitude of institutions in playing a fundamental role in adaptation are the prime bottlenecks in translation of international policies and agreement on land degradation into national policies and programmes. Implementation of international policies guiding the national and regional policies is the long-term need for the affected countries (Nkonya et al., 2011).

Recently, in a policy brief on 'Zero Net Land Degradation (ZNLD), A Sustainable Development Goal for Rio+20', a list of elements was described as a prerequisite for a successful ZNLD (UNCCD, 2012). Some important elements include:

1. In the government sector there are requirements to set up national goals and targets, and to provide support for setting goals and targets at a regional level; rewarding progress on ZNLD through national, and even international resources and schemes; funding from different funds including Green Climate fund, the Adaptation fund and other existing funds.
2. The private sector should be engaged in investment on R&D that emphasizes SLM to increase land use efficiency and resilience of related ecosystem functioning and services and reduce risks.
3. Incorporation of economic instruments like 'payment for ecosystem services' should be facilitated to prevent degradation of non-degraded land as well as supporting the restoration of existing degraded land.
4. There is a need for development of policies, measures, guidelines and mechanisms for the implementation of ZNLD.
5. A comprehensive assessment of the economics of land degradation is needed to increase public awareness on the cost and benefits of individual and collective decisions affecting land and land-based ecosystem and their services.

Increasing the efficiency of water use and enhancing agricultural water productivity for increased food production should be a priority. This requires actions at all levels, ranging from implementation of suitable agricultural and irrigation schemes, to rejuvenation of national and international economic systems for improved water productivity and proper allocation of water to all sectors.

The finite source of water should be preserved and used judiciously and for this, a change in philosophy about water use is needed. It is the duty of humanity to work towards increasing the efficiency of water use by conserving it. Application of cutting-edge interdisciplinary science coupled with water governance and management practice is the need of the hour. Water must be a priority on all political agendas. It is possible to meet the food demand of the projected world population in 2050 within realistic rates for yield development, water-use efficiency and land expansion, provided adequate investments are made (FAO's baseline projection) and suitable policies are adopted. Good governance at all levels is the key to achieving food security. This will ensure essential public goods, including political stability, rule of law, respect for human rights, control of corruption and government effectiveness. Effective institutions are a particular feature of good governance. Priority should be given to institutional reforms that ensure that all members of society are represented in the policy process (FAO, 2009). Additionally, the projected scenarios of future water resource as a result of climate change should prompt the implementation of water governance and policy reforms, and adoption of effective integrated water resources management practices.

Here are some of the recommendations for water conservation and sustainability:

1. Institutional reforms for integrated watershed and river basin management;
2. Optimal and efficient water use in agriculture sector using efficient technologies and farm practices (explained in section 17.3.2);
3. Regular water audits of water storage and distribution systems in agricultural, rural, and urban water systems;
4. Efficient water delivery system in the agriculture sector to enhance water-use efficiency (regular maintenance of the drainage and water conservation structures etc.);
5. Use of information and communication technologies and risk (flooding and drought) management techniques for water management, and the benefits from these should trickle down to the grass root level farming communities;
6. Training and capacity building activities for the farmers and water managers;
7. Appropriate valuation (pricing) of water to promote efficient use and conservation;
8. Regulation of groundwater overexploitation through effective monitoring and penalties;
9. Incentives for water conservation interventions and promotion of policies encouraging efficient water use. In an effort to promote judicious use of water, the government should offer incentives, such as tax breaks, to big industrial users if they are able to reduce wastage of water and enhance water use efficiency. To make this move effective, the incentives should be included in the National Water Policy of the country. Such policies will encourage sustainable use of water by reducing wastage of water and promoting recycling.

Land and water are essential for the existence of humankind, and are intimately interrelated and interdependent natural resources. Therefore, there should be, not only, separate land and water specific conservation programs and policies, but also programs and policies that integrate land and water in a very effective way for sustainability and productivity of these two fundamental resources.

REFERENCES

Baartman, J.E.M., G.W.J. van Lynden, M.S. Reed, C.J. Ritsema and R. Hessel (2007), Desertification and land degradation: origins, processes and solutions: a literature review. Scientific Report # 4, ISRIC, Netherlands.

Bai, Z.G., D.L. Dent, L. Olsson and M.E. Schaepman (2008), Proxy global assessment of land degradation. *Soil Use and Management*, **24**, 223–34.

Bates, B.C., Z.W. Kundzewicz, S. Wu and J.P. Palutikof (eds) (2008), Climate change and water. Technical Paper of the Intergovernmental Panel on Climate Change, IPCC Secretariat, Geneva, 210 pp.

Berger, M. and M. Finkbeiner (2010), Water footprinting: how to address water use in life cycle assessment? *Sustainability*, **2**(4), 919–44.

Bertoldi, G.L. (1992), Subsidence and consolidation in alluvial aquifer systems. In *Proceedings of the 18th Biennial Conference on Groundwater*. Washington DC: US Geological Survey, pp. 62–74.

Brown, M.E. and C.C. Funk (2008), Food security under climate change. *Science*, **319**(5863), 580–81.

Campbell, E., D.B. Lobell, R.C. Genova and C.B. Field (2008), The global potential of bioenergy *Environmental Science and Technology*, **42**(15), 5791–5794.

Charney J., P.H. Stone and W.J. Quirk (1975), Drought in the Sahara: a biogeophysical feedback mechanism. *Science*, **187**(4175), 434–5.

Coxhead, I. and R. Oygard (2007), Land degradation. Available at: http://www.aae.wisc.edu/coxhead/papers/CCC-April7.pdf (accessed 13 October 2012).

Dasgupta, P. and S. Sirohi (2010), Indian agricultural scenario and food security concerns in the context of climate change: a review. MPRA Paper 24067, University Library of Munich, Germany.

Dean, W.R.J., M.T. Hoffman, M.E. Meadows and S.J. Milton (1995), Desertification in the semiarid Karoo, South Africa – review and reassessment. *Journal of Arid Environments*, **30**, 247–64.

de Vries, F.P. and D. Molden (2002), Implications of land and water degradation for food security, with particular reference to Asia and Africa. at International Symposium on Sustaining Food Security and Managing Natural Resources in Southeast Asia – Challenges for the 21st Century, January 8–11, Chiang Mai, Thailand.

Eckstein, G. (2009), Water scarcity, conflict, and security in a climate change world: challenges and opportunities for international law and policy. *Wisconsin International law Journal*, **27**(3), Texas Tech Law School Research Paper No. 2009–01.

Entekhabi, D., I. Rodriguez-Iturbe and R.L. Bras (1992), Variability in large-scale water balance with land surface-atmosphere interaction. *Journal of Climate*, **2**, 798–813.

EPA (2013), Ecosystems Research. Available at http://www.epa.gov/AthensR/sustainability.html (accessed 13 February 2013).

Falkenmark, M. and C. Widstrand (1992), Population and water resources: a delicate balance. *Population Bulletin*, Population Reference Bureau, Washington DC.

FAO (1996), *Our Land Our Future*. Rome and Nairobi: Food and Agriculture Organization and United Nations Environment Program.

FAO (2003a), *Trade Reforms and Food Security: Conceptualizing the Linkages*. Rome: FAO.

FAO (2003b), *World Agriculture Towards 2015/2030: An FAO Perspective*. London: Earthscan Publications Ltd.

FAO (2009a), IWMI–FAO report: revitalizing Asia's irrigation: to sustainably meet tomorrow's food needs. Available at: http://www.fao.org/nr/water/docs/iwmi-fao-report-revitalizing-asias-irrigation-to-sustainably-meet-tomorrows-food-needs.pdf (accessed 14 November 2012).

FAO (2009b), Feeding the World, Eradicating Hunger. Available at http://www.fao.org/fileadmin/templates/wsfs/Summit/WSFS_Issues_papers/WSFS_Background_paper_Feeding_the_world.pdf (accessed 9 April 2012).

FAO (2011), *The State of the World's Land and Water Resources for Food and Agriculture: Managing Systems at Risk*. New York: FAO and Earthscan.

FAO (2012), Coping with water scarcity: an action framework for agriculture and food security. FAO Water Reports 38, Food and Agriculture Organization of the United Nations, Rome.

Fedoroff, N.V., D.S. Battisti, R.N. Beachy, P.J.M. Cooper, D.A. Fischhoff, C.N. Hodges, V.C. Knauf, D. Lobell, B.J. Mazur, D. Molden, M.P. Reynolds, P.C. Ronald, M.W. Rosegrant, P.A. Sanchez, A. Vonshak and J.K. Zhu (2010), Radically rethinking agriculture for the 21st century. *Science*, **327**(5967), 833–4.

Foley, J.A., N. Ramankutty, K.A. Brauman, E.S. Cassidy, J.S. Gerber, M. Johnston, N.D. Mueller, C. O'Connell, D.K. Ray, P.C. West, C. Balzer, E.M. Bennett, S.R. Carpenter, J. Hill, C. Monfreda, S. Polasky, J. Rockstrom, J. Sheehan, S. Siebert, D. Tilman and P.M. Jakes (2011), Solutions for a cultivated planet. *Nature*, **478**, 337–42.

GEF (2006), Land degradation as a global environmental issue. A synthesis of three studies commissioned by the global environment facility to strengthen the knowledge base to support the land degradation focal area. GEF/C.30/Inf.8., 1–15.

GEF (2009), Investing in GEF's efforts to combat land degradation and desertification globally land stewardship. GEF, 1-40.

Gleick, P.H (1995), *Human Population and Water: To the Limits in the 21st Century*, Oakland, CA: Pacific Institute for Studies in Development, Environment, and Security.

Gleick, P.H. (1998), Water in crisis: paths to sustainable water use. *Ecological Applications*, **8**(3), 571–9.

Gupta, P. (2005), Underground water development in India – trends, crops. Kellogg School of Management, Northwestern University. Available at: http://www.gopio.net/india_development/ Water_Study_NU_2005.pdf.

Hanjra, M.A. and M.E Qureshi (2010), Global water crisis and future food security in an era of climate change. *Food Policy*, **35**, 365–77.

Hanjra, M.A., T. Ferede and D.G. Gutta (2009), Pathways to breaking the poverty trap in Ethiopia: investments in agricultural water, education, and markets. *Agricultural Water Management*, **96**(11), 2–11.

Hira, G.S. (2009), Water management in northern states and the food security of India. *Journal of Crop Improvement*, **23**(2), 136–57.

Holling, C.S. (1986), The resilience of terrestrial ecosystems, local surprise and global change. In W.C. Clark, and R.E. Munn (eds), *Sustainable Development of the Biosphere*. Cambridge: Cambridge University Press, pp. 292–317.

Holling, C.S. (2001), Understanding the complexity of economic, ecological, and social systems. *Ecosystems*, **4**, 390–405.

IPCC (2001), *Climate Change 2001: The Scientific Basis*. J.T. Houghton, Y. Ding, D.J. Griggs, M. Noguer, P.J. van der Linden, X. Dai, K. Maskell, C.A. Johnson (eds). Cambridge, UK: Cambridge University Press.

IWMI (2005), The global PODIUM. Interactive water and food security planning scenario tool. Available at: http://podium.iwmi.org/podium (accessed 14 November 2012).

Jägerskog, A. and T.J. Clausen (eds) (2012), Feeding a thirsty world: challenges and opportunities for a water and food secure future. Report No. 31. Stockholm International Water Institute, Stockholm, Sweden.

Kasperson, J., R. Kasperson and B. Turner (1995), *Regions at Risk*. Geneva: United Nations University Press.

Khan, S. and M.A. Hanjra (2009), Footprints of water and energy inputs in food production: global perspectives. *Food Policy*, **34**(2), 130–140.

Kundzewicz, Z.W. (1997), Water resources for sustainable development. *Hydrological Sciences*, **42**(4), 467–80.

Lal, R. (2003), Soil erosion and the global carbon budget. *Environment International*, **29**, 437–450.

Liniger, H., R.M. Studer, C. Hauert and M. Gurtner (2011), *Sustainable Land Management in Practice. Guidelines and Best Practices for Sub-Saharan Africa*. Rome: FAO.

Lobell, D.B., M.B. Burke, C. Tebaldi, M.D. Mastrandrea, W.P. Falcon and R.L. Naylor (2008), Prioritizing climate change adaptation needs for food security in 2030. *Science*, **319**(5863), 607–10.

Nkonya, E., N. Gerber, J. von Braun and A. De Pinto (2011), Economics of land degradation. The costs of action versus inaction. IFPRI Issue Brief 68, September 2011.

Oldeman, L.R., R.T.A Hakkeling and W.G. Sombroek (1991), *World Map of the Status of Human induced Soil Degradation: An Explanatory Note*, 2nd edn. Wageningen, the Netherlands, and Nairobi: ISRIC and UNEP.

Postel, S.L. (2000), Entering an era of water scarcity: the challenges ahead. *Ecological Applications*, **10**(4), 941–8.

Rosegrant, M.W. and S.A. Cline (2003), Global food security: challenges and policies. *Science*, **302**(5652), 1917–1919.

Rosegrant, M.W., X. Cai and S.A. Cline (2002), *World Water and Food to 2025: Dealing with Scarcity*. Washington DC: International Food Policy and Research Institute.

Scherr, S.J. (1999), Soil degradation: a threat to developing country food security in 2020? Food, Agriculture and the Environment Discussion Paper 27. IFPRI, Washington DC.

Sharma, U.C. (2002), Managing the fragile hydrological ecosystem of the northeast hilly region of India for resources conservation and improved productivity. In H.A. Van Lanen and S. Demuth (eds), *Regional Hydrology: Bridging the Gap Between Research and Practice*, Publication no. 274. Wallingford, UK: IAHS Press.

Shiklomanov, I.A. (2000), Appraisal and assessment of world water resources. *Water International*, **25**(1), 11–32.

Siebert, S., J. Burke, J.M. Faures, K. Frenken, J. Hoogeveen, P. Döll, and F.T. Portmann (2010), Groundwater use for irrigation: a global inventory. *Hydrology and Earth System Sciences*, **14**, 1863–1880. Available at: http://www.hydrol-earth-syst-sci.net/14/1863/2010/hess-14-1863-2010.html.

TERI (2006), Looking back to change track. *GREEN India 2047*, The Energy and Resources Institute, New Delhi, India.

TERI (2010), Water conservation. Available at: http://edugreen.teri.res.in/explore/water/conser.htm (accessed 9 April 2013).
TERI (2012), Living in a cleaner environment in India: a strategic analysis and assessment. Project report No. 2008 EE 06. The Energy and Resources Institute, New Delhi, India.
Tilman, D., K.G. Cassman, P.A. Matson, R. Naylor and S. Polasky (2002), Agricultural sustainability and intensive production practices. *Nature*, **418**, 671–7.
UNCCD (2012), Zero net land degradation, a sustainable development goal for Rio+20 to secure the contribution of our planet's land and soil to sustainable development, including food security and poverty eradication. United Secretariat Policy Brief, Germany.
UNEP (2011), *Towards a Green Economy: Pathways to Sustainable Development and Poverty Eradication: A Synthesis for Policy Makers*. Nairobi: United Nations Environment Programme.
UNESCO-WWAP (2003), Water for people-water for life. World Water Assessment Program. The United Nations World Water Development Report. Paris.
United Nations (2007), *Millennium Development Goals Report*. New York: United Nations. Available at: http://www.un.org/millenniumgoals/pdf/mdg2007.pdf (accessed 12 November 2013).
United Nations Conference on Trade and Development (UNCTAD) (2010), Agriculture at the crossroads: guaranteeing food security in a changing global climate. United Nations Conference on Trade and Development (UNCTAD) Policy Briefs 18 (December 2010).
UN-Water (2006b), Coping with water scarcity: a strategic issue and priority for system-wide action. UN-Water Thematic Initiatives. Geneva, Switzerland.
Wainwright, J. (2009), Desert ecogeomorphology. In A.J. Parsons and A.D. Abrahams (eds), *Geomorphology of Desert Environments*. Dordrecht, the Netherlands: Springer. pp. 33–4.
WBCSD (2009), *Water, Energy and Climate Change*. Geneva, Switzerland: World Business Council for Sustainable Development.
WMO (2005), Climate and land degradation. Climate information – resource conservation – sustainable management of land. WMO No. 989, p. 4.
Wood, S., K. Sebastian and S.J. Scherr (2000), *Pilot Analysis of Global Ecosystems: Agroecosystems*. Washington DC: International Food Policy Research Institute and World Resources Institute.

18. Viability of small-scale farms in Asia
Keijiro Otsuka

18.1 INTRODUCTION

The inverse relationship between farm size and productivity is oftentimes found in South Asia, which indicates that small farms are more efficient than large farms (e.g. Heltberg, 1998). In sub-Saharan Africa, too, the inverse relationship seems to have emerged with the gradual intensification of farming systems (Larson et al., 2013). In the cultivation of commercial crops, such as sugarcane and pineapples, in Asia the production grows faster under the peasant mode of production (e.g. Thailand) than under the plantation system (e.g. the Philippines), according to Hayami (2001, 2009). Such observations also indicate the higher efficiency of small farms over large farms. Furthermore, it is well-known that Green Revolution technology was rapidly adopted by small farmers in tropical Asia, which contributed to income growth, poverty reduction and food security (David and Otsuka, 1994; Pingali et al., 1997; Otsuka et al., 2009). In consequence, small-scale farms dominate throughout Asia with a very few exceptions.[1]

The high production efficiency of small-scale farming in the past, however, does not guarantee the equally high efficiency at present and in the future. Indeed, according to a recent study of Foster and Rozensweig (2010), large farms have become more productive than small farms in India with the introduction of farm machinery responding to rising labor costs, indicating that small farms are no longer more productive in this country. In high income economies in Asia, such as Japan, a positive relationship is found between farm size and productivity (Hayami and Kawagoe, 1989). Large-scale corporate farms have emerged in land-abundant countries in Latin America, Eastern Europe and Central Asia, where scale economies are observed (Key and Runsten, 1999; Rozelle and Swinnen, 2004; Gorton and Davidova, 2004; Helfand and Levine, 2004; Eastwood et al., 2009; Deininger and Byerlee, 2012). Thus, larger farms are more efficient than smaller farms at least in some parts of India, Japan and land-abundant countries.

In order to understand the diverse and seemingly contradictory observations on the effects of farm size on productivity and profitability in farming, this chapter attempts to identify the determinants of optimum farm size based on the literature review, economic theories and empirical evidence. The basic hypothesis is that the optimum farm size increases with an increase in wage rates. If farm size is small, the farming system is of necessity labor intensive. This is clearly the case for subsistence farming where major staples, such as rice, maize, sorghum and millet, are grown by using primarily manual methods. The dominance of small-scale farms does not cause any problem of production efficiency as long as wage rates are low. Indeed, the inverse relationship has been found because of the difficulty large farmers have in supervising wage workers in spatially dispersed and ecologically diverse farming environments (Feder, 1985; Hayami and Otsuka, 1993). As the economy develops, however, wage rates increase, so that labor-intensive small-scale farming systems become costly. At this stage, farm size must expand so as to introduce labor-saving production methods, such as large mechanization, in order to be competitive in international markets.

Farm size, however, does not expand smoothly with the economic development in many countries in Asia, because of the land tenure insecurity and land reform regulations. This is likely to be the serious problem in middle- and high-income countries in East Asia, where farm size has traditionally been small and wage rates have been rising sharply. In this chapter, I would like to argue that small-scale farms in Asia will become increasingly inefficient as production organization in agriculture (Otsuka, 2013).

I provide a conceptual framework to explain the changing optimum farm size in section 18.2. Then I show an overview of the farm size and land tenure systems in Asia in section 18.3, which will be followed by a review of literature on the inverse relationship between farm size and productivity in section 18.4. I examine the increasing inefficiency of small farms in Japan in section 18.5, and discuss the implications of the Japanese experience for the future of agriculture in China and other high-performing countries in Asia in section 18.6. I conclude the chapter in section 18.7.

18.2 A CONCEPTUAL FRAMEWORK

18.2.1 On the Dominance of Family Farms

Theoretically, it is well known that if one of the three markets, viz., land tenancy, land sale and labor markets, is perfectly competitive, an equally efficient allocation of resources among farming households can be achieved in equilibrium under the assumption of constant returns to scale in production, because land–labor ratios are equalized among farms (Kevane, 1996). In the real world, it is unlikely that labor market transactions lead to the efficient resource allocation, because it is generally costly to supervise and enforce hired labor in certain critical tasks in agricultural production. According to the theory of labor employment in agriculture formulated by Feder (1985) and Eswaran and Kotwal (1986), large farmers employ hired labor because of the limited endowment of family labor relative to owned land. Hired wage laborers, however, do not have strong work incentives, as they receive the same wage regardless of how hard they work.[2] Thus, it is not possible to enforce their work effort without explicit supervision. Furthermore, it is likely that the supervision cost of hired labor increases more than proportionally with farm size. Therefore, the high enforcement cost of hired labor will lead to lower production efficiency of large farms, even though those farms would have the advantage of better access to the credit market owing to the ownership of land that can be used as collateral for credit. Theoretical models of Feder (1985) and Eswaran and Kotwal (1986) assume that tenancy does not exist, because the landless laborers or near landless farmers do not have sufficient access to the credit market to pay for family consumption and purchased inputs and, hence, cannot undertake tenant cultivation. But landlords can and often do provide credit to their tenants, particularly under share tenancy. Therefore, the imperfection of credit market cannot justify the choice of labor contract over tenancy contract.

High enforcement costs of hired labor does not imply that casual labor markets are inactive. Since it is easy to observe work effort or inspect the outcome of work in such simple tasks as weeding, transplanting and harvesting, daily-wage labor is widely used for these activities. It is, however, costly to employ hired labor for the tasks that require care and judgment, such as land preparation, fertilizer application, supervision of a group of hired laborers, and water and pest control in spatially dispersed agricultural environments. Imperfect supervision and labor enforcement in these activities lead to shirking of hired wage labor, which leads to inefficiency of farm operation dependent on hired labor employment. These tasks therefore are usually carried out by family labor on small farms (Hayami and Otsuka, 1993).[3]

Even if the labor market fails to function, an efficient outcome can be achieved, if the land sales market functions well. If productivity of land is lower on larger farms, there must be an agreeable land price, at which the sellers (i.e. large landowners) and the buyers (small cultivators) can gain through market transactions. It is well known, however, that the land sales market is inactive in many places. To our knowledge, the most plausible explanation for this problem is offered by Binswanger and Rosenzweig (1986) and Binswanger and Elgin (1989), who take into account the role of collateral value of land. They argue that since land can be used as collateral for obtaining credit, the price of land exceeds the present value of future agricultural profits accrued to land by the amount of benefit accrued from the collateral value. Thus, the buyer of land cannot cover the cost of land purchase solely from the future agricultural profits. In order for the land transaction to take place, the buyer must have their own funds or additional savings to purchase land. If potential buyers are poor small farmers or the landless laborers, they would not possess such extra funds.

Actually, the land tenancy transaction is the most common way of adjusting the allocation of land among rural households with different factor endowments. This can be attributed to relatively less efficient functioning of land sales and labor market transactions than those of land tenancy market (Skoufias 1995). This does not imply, however, that there is no transaction cost of land tenancy; on the contrary, the search for contracting partners, negotiations about the terms and conditions, their monitoring and sanctions against the breach of contractual agreements all require some transaction costs. Thus, there are many self-sufficient owner–cultivator households which neither rent out nor rent in land (Skoufias 1995; Holden et al., 2008, 2013). So far as the endowment of owned land relative to family labor is substantially different among farming households, however, resource allocation in the rural economy will be significantly inefficient, unless the land tenancy market functions effectively (Bliss and Stern, 1982; Sadoulet et al., 2001). In practice in Asia, the majority of farms are family-based owner–cultivator supplemented by the relatively small areas of rented land.

18.2.2 Changing Optimum Farm Size

When labor is abundant relative to land and capital, a labor intensive method of cultivation is socially optimum. In Figure 18.1, the two types of farming system are portrayed; the labor-intensive system whose iso-quants are denoted by 'q', and the capital-intensive system whose iso-quants are denoted by 'Q'. For simplicity, I implicitly assume that land input, another major factor of production, changes with capital service more or less proportionally. In the case of the labor-intensive system, no major indivisible inputs are used and, hence, there is no major source of scale economies. Because of the high

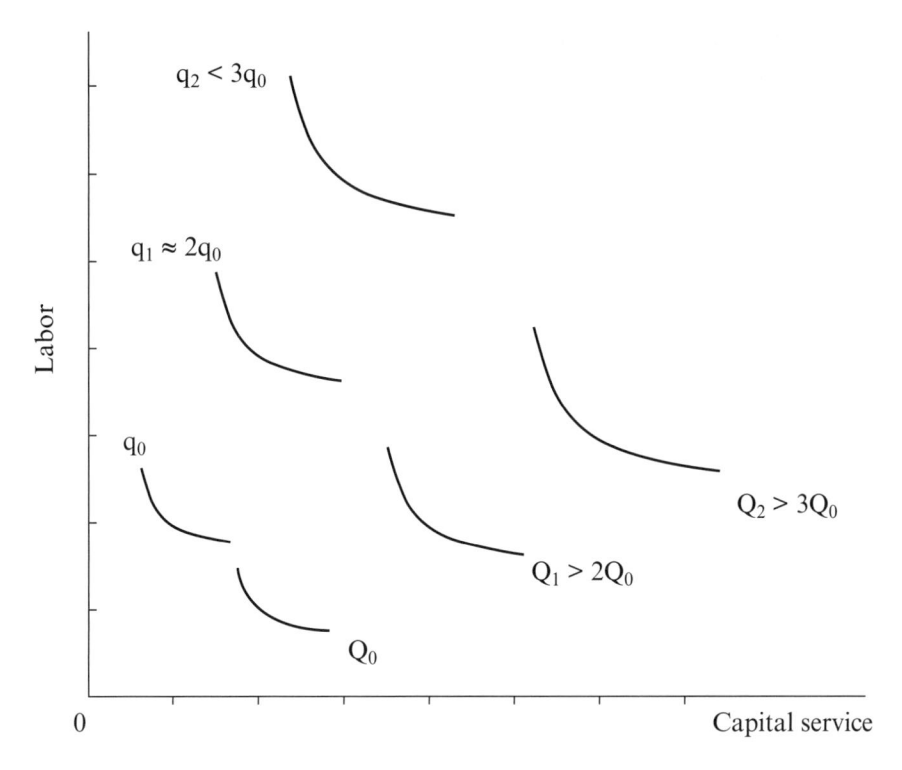

Figure 18.1 An illustration of decreasing-returns-to-scale labor-intensive farming system and increasing-returns-to-scale capital-intensive farming system, using a set of iso-quant curves

[Figure 18.1: Iso-quant curves with Labor on vertical axis and Capital service on horizontal axis. Curves shown from lower-left to upper-right: Q_0, q_0, $Q_1 > 2Q_0$, $q_1 \approx 2q_0$, $Q_2 > 3Q_0$, $q_2 < 3q_0$.]

monitoring cost of hired labor associated with the operation of large farms, there are scale diseconomies. Roughly speaking, a farm of 1–2 ha can be managed efficiently by family labor consisting of a few workers, if no machines are used. Thus, output increases less than three times when inputs increase three times (shown by $q_2 < 3q_0$), even though output may double when inputs increase only two times (shown by $q_1 \cong 2q_0$).

In the case of the capital-intensive, as well as land-intensive, system, output increases more than proportionally with increases in inputs due to scale economies, which are indicated by $Q_1 > 2Q_0$ and $Q_2 > 3Q_0$. Since large machines are indivisible, such scale advantage arises.[4]

The optimum farm size in low-wage economies would be small, because of the intensive use of labor. Substitution of capital for labor is costly, because labor is cheap relative to capital. As the real wage rate increases, however, labor cost increases, particularly if labor intensive production methods are employed. In order to reduce production costs, labor must be substituted for by machines and land. In order to operate machines efficiently, particularly the large ones, farm size must expand. Otherwise, output Q_2 is not attainable in terms of Figure 18.1.

Large-scale corporate farms have emerged in Latin America, Eastern Europe and Central Asia, and scale economies arising from large-scale mechanization prevail (Key and Runsten, 1999; Gorton and Davidova, 2004; Helfand and Levine, 2004; Rozelle and Swinnen, 2004; Eastwood et al., 2009; Deininger and Byerlee, 2012). In this capital-using farming system, the monitoring cost of hired labor is not high. In this situation, larger farms are more efficient than smaller farms, so that the land must be transferred from the latter to the former for the sake of production efficiency.

Renting is a practical way to transfer land to the hands of a smaller number of large farms. In fact, typically landlords are small farmers and tenants are large farmers in high-income economies such as the United States and Europe. When farm size is adjusted optimally by land renting as well as land sales transactions over time, we will not observe 'scale economies', as all the existing farms are more or less equally large and efficient. Scale economies tend to be observed clearly when small inefficient farms and large efficient farms coexist (Hayami and Kawagoe, 1989), which may be illustrated by production of q_0 by small farms and Q_2 by large farms in Figure 18.1.[5] This will be observed in the dynamic process of farm-size adjustment and also when the institutional constraints prevent the farm-size adjustment.

If a high-wage economy fails to achieve farm-size expansion, comparative advantage in agriculture will be lost and this country is likely to become a major importer of food grains. Furthermore, higher income will increase the demand for livestock products, which, in turn, will increase the demand for feed grains. If many of the high-performing Asian countries become major importers of grains, world grain prices will shoot up and poverty is expected to rise, thereby creating a scenario which is unfavorable to the attainment of the first of the Millennium Development Goals: to eradicate extreme poverty and hunger.

18.2.3 Changing Nature of Family Farms

Owner cultivation is the most common form of production organization in agriculture worldwide (Berry and Cline, 1979). In Asia, farming is dominated by small-scale owner–farmers whose cultivation is supplemented by tenancy transactions that facilitate land transfers from relatively land-abundant households to households with little land to make the ratio of operational farmland to family labor more equal (Otsuka et al.,1992a; Hayami and Otsuka, 1993; Otsuka, 2007). This is consistent with the analysis of scale-diseconomies under the labor-intensive farming system illustrated in Figure 18.1. This view stands in sharp contrast to the traditional view that tenancy is inefficient. Also, it is noteworthy that tenancy transactions improve the production efficiency not only by transferring land from less to more productive farmers but also from those who want to migrate to urban areas or to work off farm to those who want to continue farming.

Data from different countries in the world compiled by Eastwood et al. (2009) demonstrate that larger farms tend to employ more hired labor. The use of family labor, however, will be more efficient because family workers have a stronger tendency to elicit conscientious work effort, while hired laborers tend to shirk in the absence of supervision (Hayami and Otsuka, 1993). The monitoring cost of hired labor, however, decreases with mechanization, as less care and judgment is required in mechanized tasks. For example, the use of tractors to replace draft animals and the use of a thresher to replace threshing labor would simplify the monitoring tasks.

It is difficult to predict whether family labor will continue to comprise a large share of total farm labor when optimum farm size increases. In North America, for example, the importance of family labor survives even in recent years, despite the large and growing farm size because of labor-saving mechanization (Eastwood et al., 2009). Family labor's contribution to rice-farming activities in Central Luzon in the Philippines, declined significantly from 1966 to 1994 (Estudillo et al., 1999), as the opportunity cost of family labor increased with the increasing availability of nonfarm labor employment opportunities. In rice-growing villages in Central Luzon and Panay Island in the Philippines, the younger generation, who are more educated and have more skills, are found to be involved primarily in nonfarm activities, where returns to education are higher than in farming (Estudillo et al., 2009; Takahashi and Otsuka, 2009). In China, Yang (1997) finds that the better-educated household members participate in nonfarm wage activities while simultaneously contributing to agricultural management decisions. In Pakistan, Fafchamps and Quisumbing (1999) find that farm households with better-educated males earn higher off-farm income and divert family labor away from farm activities toward nonfarm work. Cherdchuchai et al. (2009) observe that the more educated members of rice-growing households in the Central Plain and Northeast Thailand tend to choose nonfarm employment either in nearby rural towns and cities, whereas the less educated members oftentimes migrate to Bangkok and other main cities to participate in casual nonfarm jobs such as construction and domestic work.

Thus, the optimum farm size and the use of family labor will be determined by real wage rate and monitoring costs of hired labor under mechanized and non-mechanized conditions.

18.3 AN OVERVIEW OF FARM SIZE STRUCTURE IN ASIA

In this section, I provide an overview of the agrarian structure in terms of average farm size and inequality of operational landholdings in selected developing countries of Asia (i.e. Bangladesh, India, Indonesia, the Philippines and Thailand), using agricultural census data from the 1970s, 1990s and 2000s.[6] Specifically, I examine how the average farm size has been changing and whether the dominance of small-scale farms has been strengthened or weakened over time in tropical Asia.

In Asia, the average operational farm size was small, ranging from about 1 ha in Indonesia to 3–4 ha in the Philippines and Thailand in the 1970s (Table 18.1). In the high-performing Southeast Asian countries, such as Indonesia and Thailand, reduction in farm size has been relatively modest over time due to rapid labor absorption in nonfarm sectors. In contrast, average farm size significantly declined in other economies due partly to rapid population growth in rural areas and partly to stagnant growth of nonfarm sectors. Particularly conspicuous is Bangladesh, where the average farm size declined from 1.4 ha in 1976–77 to 0.6 ha in 1996.[7] In this country, about 50 percent of farms were smaller than 1.0 ha in 1976/77 and this proportion increased to more than 80 percent in 1996. Large farms above 10 ha are very few, suggesting the absence of scale economies in agricultural production in this country.

While about 50 percent of farms were smaller than 1.0 ha and their total cultivation area amounted to only 9 percent of total farmland in India in 1970–71, large farms larger than 10 ha accounted for 3.9 percent of farm households and cultivated as much as 31

Table 18.1 Distribution of farms and farmland by operational farm size and the extent of tenancy in selected countries in Asia

Country	Year of survey	Average operational farm size (ha)	Percentage of farms and farmland[a]			
			Below 1 ha		Above 10 ha	
			Farms	Area	Farms	Area
Bangladesh	1976/77	1.4	49.7	28.8	n.a.[b] (9.4)[c]	n.a.[b] (1.6)[c]
	1996	0.6	80.8	41.1	0.1 (32.4)[c]	1.4 (16.5)[c]
India	1970/71	2.3	50.6	9.0	3.9	30.9
	1995/96	1.4	71.1	33.1	1.4	24.1
Indonesia	1973	1.0	70.4	30.0	5.9	10.3
	1993	0.9	70.8	29.8	0.2	3.4
Philippines	1971	3.6	13.6	1.9	4.9	33.9
	2002	2.0	40.1	8.3	2.0	20.5
Thailand	1978	3.7	16.4	2.5	6.0	23.6
	1993	3.4	21.5	3.6	4.5	23.2
	2003	3.1	13.1	n.a.	2.1	n.a.

Notes:
a. Since farm size classes differ from country to country, interpolations were made.
b. n.a.– not available.
c. Farm size above 3 ha.

Sources:
Bangladesh, *Report on the Agricultural Census of Bangladesh, 1977; 1978 Land Occupancy Survey of Bangladesh; Census of Agriculture 1996.*
India, *National Sample Survey, No. 215, 26*th *Round, 1971–72; All India Report on Agricultural Census 1980/71; Agricultural Census 1990-91.*
Indonesia, *1973 Agricultural Census; 1993 Agricultural Census.*
Philippines, *1971 Census of Agriculture; 1991 Census of Agriculture.*
Thailand, *1978 Agricultural Census Report; 1993 Agricultural Census.*

percent of total farmland in the same year. Similarly in the Philippines, large farms above 10 ha cultivated 34 percent of total farmland in 1971, 1 year before the initiation of the land reform program that was applied primarily to paddy areas characterized by a favorable production environment (Otsuka, 1991). There is, therefore, no wonder that the redistributive land reform programs were seriously implemented in these two countries among the five countries examined here. Possibly as a result of land reform implementation, the proportion of large farms and their relative share of the operational landholdings declined significantly from the 1970s to the 1990s or 2000s in these two countries.

Although unreported in Table 18.1, the proportion of tenant households including both pure tenant and owner-cum-tenant households was relatively high in Bangladesh (in the order of 40–45 percent) and the Philippines (30–50 percent) in the 1970s and 1990s, modestly high in Indonesia (about 20 percent) and low in India (5–9 percent) and Thailand (7–15 percent). In India, in all likelihood, this could be due to replacement of formal tenancy by informal or concealed tenancy to evade land reform regulations (e.g. Radhakrishnan, 1990; Ray, 1996; Thorat, 1997; Thimmaiah, 2001). In Thailand, tenancy is less important than in other countries because there had been uncultivated forest areas that could be opened up for cultivation by poor farmers in this country until recently. Thus, except in India and Thailand, cultivated land areas seem to have been reallocated substantially by tenancy transactions between rural households in Asia.

The proportion of pure tenant households was comparatively low except in the Philippines, implying that the majority of tenants were part owners holding own land rather than the landless. It is also indicated in the literature that the landless households do not have much access to land through land tenancy, particularly in South Asia (e.g. Sharma and Drèze, 1996; Sarap 1998). Why this is the case, however, is not clear from the existing studies. One possible explanation is the existence of the minimum size below which the efficiency of farming declines drastically.

Overall, it is clear that the average farm size has been declining in both Southeast and South Asia for the last few decades, during which the share of large farms has also been declining. These observations indicate that scale economies in farming are largely absent in tropical Asian countries.

In China, since the late 1970s, and in Vietnam, since the mid-1980s, collective farms have been transformed into small units of household-operated farms, which are largely similar to owner-cultivated farms in other Asian countries. This agricultural reform has dramatically improved agricultural productivity by enhancing work incentives to farmers (Lin, 1988; McMillan et al., 1989; Pingali and Xuan, 1992). In consequence, small-scale farms dominate throughout Asian countries. It is noteworthy that the average farm size is very small in China; it was 0.70 ha in 1985, declined to 0.55 ha in 2000 and recovered to 0.60 ha in 2010 (Huang et al., 2012). It will take 10 years to increase the farm size by 0.05 ha, if the current trend continues. Unless major reforms are implemented, small-scale farms dominate in China in foreseeable future.

18.4 THE INVERSE CORRELATION BETWEEN FARM SIZE AND PRODUCTIVITY

A large number of empirical studies have been conducted in Asia to analyse the relationship between farm size and yield or value added per unit of area or input use intensity (see Lipton, 2009, for the most recent and comprehensive review). While the significant inverse relation is seldom found in Southeast Asia (David and Otsuka, 1994),[8] it is found in South Asia, especially in India (Berry and Cline, 1979; Dyer, 1996/97; Heltberg, 1998). The observed inverse correlation is largely explained by differences in land quality and crop mix; large farmers tend to cultivate less fertile land and grow crops of lower output value (Verma and Bromley, 1987; Bhalla and Roy, 1988; Newell et al., 1997).[9] Yet, a significant inverse correlation remains even after controlling for land quality and other differences associated with farm size (Carter, 1984; Heltberg, 1998). It is often pointed out that the inverse correlation disappeared in India after the Green Revolution because larger farmers apply larger amount of purchased inputs.[10] According to Newell et al. (1997), the inverse relation between farm size and value added per hectare disappeared within a village after the Green Revolution, but the inverse relation between farm size and labor input per hectare remains significant even within a village in India. Ramasamy et al. (1994) also obtain similar results from their village study in Tamil Nadu in India.

These findings strongly indicate the larger use of family labor and lower use of purchased inputs by smaller farmers, reflecting the advantage of relatively abundant family labor endowment and disadvantage of unfavorable access to credit. Heltberg's (1998) careful analysis of household panel data in Pakistan clearly supports our interpretation.

If the inverse relationship exists, the transfer of land from larger farmers to smaller farmers will result in higher production efficiency as well as more equitable distribution of income. The question is why inefficient large farms do not lease out their land to smaller farmers and the landless to wipe out the inverse relationship.

In India, the land reform program applied to tenant-cultivated land with the exemption of owner-cultivated land using hired labor (Khusro, 1973; Dantwala and Shah, 1971; Appu, 1975; Ladejinsky, 1977; Herring, 1983; Holden et al., 2013). Since regulated land rent was set at a level significantly lower than the market rate, landlords were motivated to evict tenants in order to undertake owner cultivation. According to Bhalla (1976), Dantwala and Shah (1971), Ladejinsky (1977) and Bardhan (1989), many landlords actually evicted tenants and converted them to permanent laborers. At the all-India level the percentage of farm area under tenancy declined from about 20 percent in the pre-reform period of the mid-1950s to about 12 percent in the mid-1960s, at least partly because of the implementation of the land reform program (Narain and Joshi, 1969). Thus, it is likely that large farms employing permanent labor are less efficient than small farms based on family labor. It is also noteworthy that tenant eviction and land-reform-induced tenancy suppression are widely observed in Nepal, where the land-to-the tiller program similar to that in India has been implemented (Holden et al., 2013).

In the Philippines, more concrete evidence is available. According to Otsuka (1991), 20–50 percent of tenants were evicted at the time of land reform implementation in selected villages in Central Luzon and Panay Island. At the same time, a large number of share tenants have been converted to leaseholders and amortizing owners, and these beneficiaries received significantly higher income than the remaining share tenants (Otsuka et al., 1992b). Because of the prohibition of new tenancy and sub-tenancy, however, those land reform beneficiaries, who cultivate large areas relative to the endowment of family labor, began to employ permanent labor (Hayami and Otsuka, 1993). Cultivation of large farms by permanent labor, however, is revealed to be significantly inefficient (Otsuka et al. 1993). In this way, the inverse correlation was newly created by land reform implementation in rice-growing areas of the Philippines.

In China, where tenancy transaction was discouraged due to the weak tenure security of cultivators, Benjamin and Brandt (2002) find a significant inverse relation between farm size and labor intensity. As in Carter's (1984) study in India, their finding suggests the emergence of inefficiency in resource allocation.[11] This may pose serious problem in future of Chinese agriculture, because farmers are actively seeking nonfarm jobs in China (Yao, 2000), which requires the efficient reallocation of land among farm households to maintain the productivity of the farm sector (Kimura et al., 2010). Using household data, Dong (2000) finds from the estimation of Cobb–Douglas production function that agricultural production is subject to significant diseconomies of scale in China, which suggests the inverse correlation between farm size and productivity.

In sum, as far as low-income countries in Asia are concerned, there is fairly strong evidence that the suppression of land tenancy transactions leads to the inverse relationship between the farm size and productivity, due primarily to the scale diseconomies associated with the difficulty in the supervision of hired labor.

18.5 THE INEFFICIENCY OF SMALL-SCALE FARMS IN JAPAN

In industrial economies, where the wage rate is high relative to prices of other factor inputs, extensive mechanization becomes profitable, creating scale advantages and hence enlarging the optimum size of farm operation. Yet in Japan the average farm size had remained at around 1.0 ha or slightly above until the mid-1970s (less than one-tenth of the level in European countries and one-hundredth of that in the United States) despite the remarkable growth in wages. A part of the explanation for the dominance of small-scale farms in Japan is likely to lie in the regulation of tenancy transaction by land reform law.

18.5.1 Land Reform Regulations

Land reform in Japan was carried out from 1946 to 1950 under the firm direction of the general headquarters of the US occupation forces (Dore, 1958; Ogura, 1963). The most important reform was the land-to-the-tiller operation, and there is no question that the reforms significantly contributed to the equalization of income and wealth distribution in rural areas. However, tenancy transactions were suppressed to prevent the former landlords from re-accumulating land. As the wage rate increased due to the miraculous growth of the economy for more than a decade from the late 1950s, relaxation of the tenancy regulation was urgently needed for farm size expansion, but this was recognized only gradually by the government. Actually the tenancy regulation was largely removed in 1980, even though the government still set the standard rent, to which the negotiated rent is supposed to conform.

Despite a series of liberalization measures, however, the tenancy market has remained inactive. It is often pointed out that farmers are still reluctant to lease out their lands because they lack confidence that they will be able to get them back. In short, the common perception was that the ownership right in land was not perfectly secure.

18.5.2 Farm Size and Production Efficiency

Land reform in Japan did not change the identity of the cultivators of land and, consequently, average operational farm size and distribution were largely the same in 1940 and 1960 (Table 18.2), partly because the land reform did not directly affect the structure of farm size and partly because the land reform regulations restricted its changes (Hayami, 1988). It is also noteworthy that the average farm size did not change appreciably even from 1960 to 1980; it increased from only 1.0 to 1.2 ha, despite continuous and rapid increases in wages and substantial progress in mechanization. There is, however, some indication that the share of very small farms (less than 0.5 ha) decreased and that of relatively large farms (more than 3 ha) increased particularly in recent years. Such a tendency seems to reflect what Hayami and Kawagoe (1989) call the 'polarization' of farm

Table 18.2 *Percentage distribution of farms by size of cultivated area (ha) in Japan: 1940, 1960, 1980 and 2005*

	Less than 0.5	0.5–1.0	1.0–3.0	3.0–5.0	Larger than 5.0	Average size (ha)
1940	33.3	32.8	30.2	2.2	1.4	1.3
1960	38.5	31.7	27.4	1.5	1.0	1.0
1980	41.3	28.1	26.6	2.2	1.5	1.2
2005	22.3	34.4	33.8	5.0	4.5	1.8

Source: Ministry of Agriculture, Forestry and Fisheries (Japan), *Census of Agriculture and Fisheries*, various issues.

structure in Japan, in which large farmers accumulate land through renting, as well as purchase of land from small farmers.

The driving force behind this structural change has been the emergence of scale advantages associated with large-scale mechanization since the late 1960s, including the introduction of riding tractors and combines. This is illustrated by revenue and production costs per hectare of rice production by farm size in 1960 and 2007 (Table 18.3). In 1960 there was no appreciable difference in revenue and costs among farms of different sizes. Mechanization in this period was characterized by the widespread adoption of threshers and the introduction of small power-tillers. Since around 1970, however, a significant gap in production costs emerged with the introduction of large machinery; the total cost of rice production per hectare became substantially higher on small farms than on larger ones, primarily because both labor and machinery costs were much higher on the former. This tendency was further strengthened in 2007 – the total cost as well as labor and machinery costs on farms of less than 0.5 ha doubled on farms larger than 5 ha even though the revenue per hectare remained largely the same across different farm sizes. Thus, the increased share of large farms in recent years, observed in Table 18.2, is consistent with the emergence of the scale advantage associated with large-scale mechanization. Estimation of the translog production function by Kuroda (1987) confirms the emergence of scale economies. Yet the question remains of why small farms continue to be so dominant in Japan.

Small farmers are mostly part-time farmers, particularly type II, who have smaller farm income than off-farm income (Table 18.4). Many of the farmers work on their farms primarily on holidays, while holding regular jobs outside agriculture. Type II part-time farms accounted for 80–90 percent of small farms of less than 1.0 ha in 1979 and 72 percent in 2005. Full-time farms, on the other hand, as well as type I part-time farms with farm income larger than off-farm income, were larger in terms of farm size in both years. Indeed, full-time farmers are mostly found on large farms.

The increased share of part-time farming may represent reallocation of labor from agriculture to non-agriculture through labor market adjustments, corresponding to the increasing labor demand in the nonfarm sector during the process of rapid economic growth. Similar patterns are also found in Southeast and South Asian countries where the younger generations of the farming households are engaged in nonfarm work (Otsuka et al., 2009). But it is obvious that small part-time farmers are less efficient than large full-time farmers in farming because of the emerging scale economies in Japan. As

Table 18.3 Comparison of revenue and production costs per hectare of rice production by size of cultivated area (ha) in Japan: 1960 and 2007 (average = 100)

	Less than 0.5	0.5–1.0	1.0–3.0	Larger than 3.0	Larger than 5.0	Average size
1960						
Revenue	98	97	103	104	n.a.	100
Labor costs	111	105	96	88	n.a.	100
Machinery cost	86	97	106	96	n.a.	100
Total cost	105	102	99	94	n.a.	100
2007						
Revenue	98	102	97	101	100	100
Labor costs	159	127	99	65	63	100
Machinery cost	119	132	97	71	66	100
Total cost	147	127	96	71	69	100

Note: n.a. – not available.

Source: Ministry of Agriculture, Forestry and Fisheries (Japan), *Survey of Rice Production Costs*, various issues.

Table 18.4 demonstrates, the ratio of rented-in land was particularly high among the largest farm size category already in 1979 and increasingly so in 1989 and 2005.[12] In 1989, however, the average ratio of rented-in land was still as low as 5.9 percent due to the land reform regulations, which were still largely in effect. Thus, small farmers who might have wished to withdraw from the farm sector continue to farm on a part-time capacity, while full-time farmers who were willing to expand the scale of their farm operations failed to accumulate land through renting.[13]

Since legal barriers to renting were largely removed in 1980, the average ratio of rented land nearly doubled from 1979 to 1989 (from 5.9 to 10.9 percent), as well as from 1989 to 2005 (from 10.9 to 22.3 percent). The ratio of rented-in land increased sharply among farms exceeding 3 and 5 ha, which reached 32–33 percent in 1989 and 2005. In contrast, the ratio of land rented out in this year was negatively and strongly associated with farm size.[14] Thus, there were some farm size adjustments in accordance with the emerging scale economies.

Since the agricultural sector based on small-scale farming in Japan was incapable of competing with foreign producers, the Japanese government strictly controls the imports of agricultural products, notably rice, despite increasing pressures for trade liberalization from other countries. If tenancy regulations had been effectively relaxed, farm size in Japan would have been much larger. Accordingly, the efficiency of Japanese agricultural production would have been much higher and agricultural trade liberalization in Japan would not have aroused the fierce opposition from the Japanese farmers.

In this process, the grain self-sufficiency ratio declined from 69 percent in 1961 to 25 percent in 2008, which clearly indicates that Japan has lost comparative advantage in agriculture (Table 18.5). Japan, however, is not an exception: both Korea and Taiwan

Table 18.4 Percentage of full-time and part-time farms and rented areas by farm size in Japan: 1979, 1989 and 2005

	Less than 0.5	0.5–1.0	1.0–3.0	Larger than 3.0	Larger than 5.0	Average
1979						
Full-time[a]	8.0	8.9	18.7	29.9	48.8	11.7
Part-time[b]	2.1	12.2	42.1	66.3	48.3	17.4
Part-time[c]	89.9	78.9	39.2	3.8	2.9	70.9
Ratio of area rented in	5.7	5.1	5.7	7.6	18.1	5.9
1989						
Full-time[a]	12.9	11.1	16.0	27.5	36.0	13.8
Part-time[b]	1.8	8.9	28.9	58.2	58.4	13.1
Part-time[c]	85.2	80.0	55.1	14.3	5.6	73.1
Ratio of area rented in	7.0	7.3	10.4	17.5	33.4	10.9
Ratio of area rented out	24.0	6.2	2.4	1.4	0.8	5.8
2005						
Full-time[a]	22.3	20.2	22.0	33.6	41.0	22.6
Part-time[b]	5.6	8.9	21.0	45.0	49.1	15.7
Part-time[c]	72.1	70.8	56.9	21.4	9.9	61.7
Ratio of area rented in	6.1	7.7	13.6	33.0	32.0	22.3
Ratio of area rented out	26.9	10.6s	4.4	1.3	1.5	4.6

Notes:
a. Farms with no family member primarily working off-farm.
b. Farms with farm income larger than off-farm income.
c. Farms with farm income smaller than off-farm income.

Source: Ministry of Agriculture, Forestry and Fisheries (Japan), *Report on the Results of Agricultural Survey*, various issues.

Table 18.5 Changes in grain self-sufficiency ratios in selected countries in Asia

	South Asia		Southeast Asia			Northeast Asia		
	Bangladesh	India	Indonesia	Philippines	Thailand	China	Japan	Korea	Taiwan
1961	92.8	92.8	89.7	87.5	140.6	93.2	69.3	90.8	128.9
1971	89.6	96.7	96.2	84.0	142.5	97.8	45.0	69.4	109.7
1981	93.9	100.3	92.0	89.7	155.5	92.3	29.2	50.0	79.0
1991	92.2	100.9	91.6	87.8	141.8	96.5	25.4	37.1	66.2
2001	89.9	103.0	88.3	75.1	137.9	95.7	24.4	30.4	60.2
2008	93.5	103.0	90.5	80.5	134.0	90.7	24.7	26.2	59.3

Notes:
Grain here refers to rice, wheat, maize, and soybean. The Korean case includes coarse grains, and the Taiwan case includes cereals and pulses.

Source: FAOSTAT data.

(China) have reduced the grain self-sufficiency ratios considerably. Thus, it may well be that maintaining comparative advantage in agriculture in high-wage economies in East Asia is not a simple task. According to the estimation results of the food self-sufficiency ratio function by major region, which uses the country and year fixed-effect model from 1980 to 2010 by Otsuka et al. (2013), purchasing power parity (PPP) adjusted per capita gross domestic product (GDP) has a positive and decelerating effect on food self-sufficiency in Asia up to $7000, beyond which it has a negative effect. Thus, their results indicate that increases in per capita GDP tend to reduce comparative advantage in agriculture in Asia.

18.6 IMPLICATIONS FOR CHINA AND OTHER ASIAN COUNTRIES

Following the introduction of the household responsibility system, household farming now prevails in China, which is similar to owner farming in other Asian countries. In China, however, land is collectively owned. Therefore, the land market does not operate freely and in view of the increasing number of migrants from rural to urban areas, differences in factor endowments among farm households are bound to arise. Thus, tenancy transactions must play a role in transferring land from land-abundant to labor-abundant households. Although the Chinese government has strengthened the individual land rights (Kung, 1995; Yao, 2000), it appears that the provision of land rights is insufficient to achieve efficient resource allocation (Kimura et al. 2010), even though land renting has been becoming common over time (Huang et al., 2012).

China has been rapidly growing over the last three and a half decades and the wage rate has been rising sharply, particularly since around the turn of the century. Although its real GDP per capita based on the PPP is still one fifth of the Japanese level as of 2005, it is comparable to the Japanese level in the late 1960s. Given the existing income gap with Japan and other developed countries, it is likely that the Chinese economy will continue to grow rapidly for many years to come based on technology transfer from abroad, which may be similar to the Japanese experience (Hamada et al., 2011). Since agricultural wage rate or opportunity cost of family labor has increased, mechanization has taken place. Indeed, the use of riding-tractor and combine-harvester services are becoming common in a number of provinces (Yang et al., 2013). In these circumstances, production inefficiency of large farms will increase, as has been happening in Japan, even though the provision of machinery services mitigates handicaps in the use of machines by small farms. In China, appropriate adjustment of farm size through tenancy transaction is badly needed.

As is reported in Table 18.6, the import ratio of soybean (i.e. import divided by the sum of domestic production and import) has been increasing in China particularly since the late 1990s. The high ratio of imports of soybeans is explained mainly by the increasing demand for feeds for livestock. But potentially also important is the preservation of small farm size, with an average as small as 0.6 ha, which must be less efficient. The production cost of such small farms will certainly increase in the production of all major grains including rice, maize and wheat, which will lead to increased imports of these grains in future and a rise in world grain prices.

Table 18.6 Percentage of imports to total domestic consumption in China by grain, 1990–2010

Year	Rice	Maize	Wheat	Soybeans
1990	0.1	5.3	12.1	15.3
1995	1.3	9.4	11.0	17.6
2000	0.2	4.5	2.1	45.2
2005	0.5	3.5	4.8	64.0
2010	0.3	3.4	2.0	79.1

Source: FAOStat online.

Thus, extremely small farm size presents a major challenge for Chinese agriculture.[15] For example, in order to establish a 10 ha farm, a typical farmer must rent in land from, at least, as many as 16 other farmers. Such tenancy transactions are likely to be very costly. Also if rented fields are scattered, scale advantages potentially arising from large mechanization will not be fully realized. Thus, renting is unlikely to be the major means to create large farms in China. Since 2008 the Chinese government has allowed the consolidation of village farmlands, which is managed by a small number of selected full-time farmers. In this arrangement, ex-farmers who now work at the nonfarm sectors own shares, from which they receive certain amount of dividends from farming. Whether and to what extent such new arrangements work to create new efficient large farms remains to be seen.

Farms in Southeast and South Asia are also predominantly family farms, which are generally small consisting of 1–2 ha, except in Thailand (Table 18.1). These Asian countries have experienced a decrease in farm size due to population pressure, even though the absolute number of the rural population may begin decreasing. At the same time, many countries in the region have entered the phase of high economic growth that should have led to increases in wage rates. Many members of farm households are engaged in nonfarm jobs and continue to manage farms as part-time farmers without transferring land to full-time farmers. Thus, farm size expansion seldom takes place in these Asian countries (Otsuka et al., 2009; Hazell, 2013). Unless farm size expansion takes place, however, these countries sooner or later will face the problem of losing comparative advantage in agriculture and increasing food imports. As Hazell predicts, some small farms may specialize in labor-intensive production of high-value crops, such as vegetables and fruits, for domestic markets.

18.7 CONCLUDING REMARKS

This chapter attempted to demonstrate that the optimum farm size changes as the economy develops and, hence, wage rate increases. In most developing countries in Asia where wage rates are relatively low, the optimum farm size is small. Thus, the central land tenure issue is to transfer land from large to small farmers so as to equate the land–labor ratio. If such land transfer is not realized, the inverse correlation between farm size and production efficiency emerges. In all likelihood, the optimum farm size increases as wage rates increase. Then the critical land tenure issue becomes the transfer of land from small to large farmers to reap the benefits of scale economies. Farm size expansion, however, may not take place because of the distortion in the land markets and also because of the lack of skill of the farm population useful for nonfarm jobs.

Judging from the fact that high-wage advanced economies such as the United States and European countries are exporters of grains and low-wage economies such as African countries are net importers, it is clear that high wages do not imply the weak comparative advantage in agriculture. This is because labor can be substituted for by capital as well as land, which is less expensive than labor in advanced economies. Such substitution is possible only when the farm size becomes sufficiently large.

In general, Asian countries are handicapped in farm size expansion because of the small endowment of land relative to labor. This would imply that as the wage rate increases, these countries are likely to lose comparative advantage in agriculture in any event. The extent the comparative advantage is lost, however, will depend on the pace of the farm size expansion. If the farm size does not expand sufficiently fast, as in the case of Japan, the comparative advantage in agriculture will be lost precipitously and such countries will become major importers of food grains. China is likely to face this problem, if the economy continues to grow, as it certainly will. Hence, wage rate increases. If Chinese agriculture as well as agriculture in other Asian countries follows the path that Japanese agriculture has taken, the world may experience food shortages, because Asia is a populous continent and its imports are likely to affect grain prices on the world market.

In order to avoid the massive imports of food grains to Asia, land policies in many Asian countries must be reformed so as to facilitate both land sales and land rental transactions. Granting secure private landownership rights and protecting them are essential (Holden et al., 2013). Second, technology must be developed to enhance scale advantages, which should be intensive not only in the use of machines but also in the use of scientific knowledge, because the scientific knowledge is the fixed-factor within a farm, so that the scale advantages are strengthened. Third, policy measures should be taken to facilitate out-migration of farm population. The major constraints on rural to urban migration are the lack of useful skills in nonfarm jobs among rural population as well as the lack of entrepreneurship. Training programs for entrepreneurship, management skills and technology are known to be useful for nonfarm sector development (Sonobe and Otsuka 2011). Unless these measures are taken, small-scale part-time farms may continue to dominate in Asia, which cannot compete with imports of food grains from other countries.

NOTES

1. To my knowledge, farm size is large and expanding in Central Thailand, Punjab in India and the Mekong Delta in Vietnam.
2. In practice, piece-rate labor contracts, e.g. based on area plowed and amount of products harvested, are common, rather than daily wage contracts, in order to provide work incentives. Piece-rate contracts, however, may induce 'quality' shirking, as the quality of work is not counted.
3. Monitoring costs of hired labor may not be very high under highly mechanized systems on large and sometimes super large farms, which prevail in Latin America and Central Asia (Deininger and Byerlee, 2012).
4. The development of the machinery rental market will lessen the scale disadvantages, but the use of large machines in a number of small farms will be more costly than in the small number of large farms.

5. In our discussion of scale economies, we follow the conventional use of 'farm size' instead of 'field size' (Eastwood et al., 2009; Otsuka, 2007) while recognizing that fields located closer to one another could potentially realize a greater degree of economies of scale.
6. The census data in the 2000s for Bangladesh, India and Indonesia are not yet available online.
7. Agricultural landless households are excluded from the estimation of average farm size except in India. In Bangladesh, the average size declined to 0.46 ha in 1996, if the landless households are considered.
8. This is likely due to active land tenancy markets in this region.
9. See also Benjamin (1995) for the case of Java and Barrett et al. (2010) for the case of Madagascar.
10. Empirical evidence, however, is not necessarily strong. See, for example, literature reviews by Dyer (1996/97) and Heltberg (1998).
11. Benjamin and Brandt (2002), however, do not observe the inverse relation between farm size and yield. This may well be due to greater access of larger farmers to cheap credit markets, as in the case of India (Newell et al. 1997).
12. Since renting was uncommon until the late 1970s, data on the ratio of rented areas by farm size in early years was not available.
13. See Hayami (1988) for other reasons for the prevalence of part-time farming in Japan.
14. Data on land area rented out by farm size are not available for early years. Also, note that the average ratio of rented-in land was substantially higher than the ratio of rented-out land mainly because of those who have completely withdrawn from farming also rented out some land.
15. The Chinese government recognizes that in China farm sizes are too small to reap the economies of scale necessary for domestic production to satisfy increasing domestic demand for food grains. The Chinese proposed construction of new dams and roads in Mozambique and elsewhere in sub-Saharan Africa in exchange for favorable land leases to run mega-farms and cattle ranches primarily to boost food production to facilitate the rapid export of foodstuffs to China. The operation of such mega-farms resembles a plantation system which is less efficient than family farms because of the high cost of labor supervision or excessive mechanization (Hayami, 2009). Furthermore, mega-farms may create social conflict between the capitalist and native people.

REFERENCES

Appu, P.S. (1975), Tenancy reform in India, *Economic and Political Weekly*, **10**(33–5), 1339–1375.
Bardhan, P.K. (ed.) (1989), *The Economic Theory of Agrarian Institutions*. Oxford: Clarendon Press.
Barrett, C.B., M.F. Bellemare and J.Y. Hou (2010), Reconsidering conventional explanations of the inverse productivity size relationship. *World Development*, **38**(1), 88–97.
Benjamin, D. (1995), Can unobserved land quality explain the inverse productivity relationship?. *Journal of Development Economics*, **46**(1), 51–84.
Benjamin, D. and L. Brandt (2002), Property rights, labor markets, and efficiency in a transition economy: the case of rural China. *Canadian Journal of Economics*, **35**(4), 689–716.
Berry, R.A. and W.R. Cline (1979), *Agrarian Structure and Productivity in Developing Countries*. Baltimore, MD: Johns Hopkins University Press.
Bhalla, Sheila (1976), New relations of production in Haryana agriculture. *Economic and Political Weekly*, **11**(13), 23–30.
Bhalla, S.S. and P. Roy (1988), Mis-specification in farm productivity analysis: the role of land quality. *Oxford Economic Papers*, **40**(1), 55–73.
Binswanger, H.P. and M. Elgin (1989), What are the prospects for land reform? In P.P. Mazumder and R. Valdes (eds), *Agriculture and Government in an Interdependent World*. Sudbury, MA: Dartmouth Publishing, pp. 739–54.
Binswanger, H.P. and M.R. Rosenzweig (1986), Behavioral and material determinants of production relations in agriculture. *Journal of Development Studies*, **22**(3), 503–39.
Bliss, C.J. and N.H. Stern (1982), *Palanpur: The Economy of an Indian Village*. New York, NY: Clarendon Press.
Carter, M.R. (1984), Identification of the inverse relationship between farm size and productivity. *Oxford Economic Papers*, **36**(1), 131–45.
Cherdchuchai, S., K. Otsuka and J.P. Estudillo (2009), Income dynamics, schooling investment, and poverty reduction in Thai villages, 1987–2004. In K. Otsuka, J.P. Estudillo and Y. Sawada (eds), *Rural Poverty and Income Dynamics in Asia and Africa*. London: Routledge, pp. 69–93.
Dantwala, M.L. and C.H. Shah (1971), *Evaluation of Land Reforms*. Bombay: University of Bombay Press.
David, C.C. and K. Otsuka (1994), *Modern Rice Technology and Income Distribution in Asia*. Boulder, CO: Lynne Rienner.

Deininger, K. and D. Byerlee (2012), The rise in large farms in land abundant countries: do they have a future? *World Development*, **40**(4), 701–14.

Dong, X.Y. (2000), Public investment, social services, and productivity of Chinese household farms. *Journal of Development Studies*, **36**(3), 100–22.

Dore, R.P. (1958), *Land Reform in Japan*. London: Oxford University Press.

Dyer, G. (1996/97), Output per acre and size of holding: the logic of peasant agriculture under semi-feudalism. *Journal of Peasant Studies*, **24**(1/2), 102–31.

Eastwood, R., M. Lipton and A. Newell (2009), Farm size. In P. Pingli and R.E. Evenson (eds), *Handbook of Agricultural Economics*, Volume 4. Amsterdam: Elsevier, pp. 3323–3397.

Estudillo, J.P., M. Fujimura and M. Hossain (1999), New rice technology and comparative advantage in rice production in the Philippines. *Journal of Development Studies*, **35**(5), 162–84.

Estudillo, J.P., Y. Sawada and K. Otsuka (2009), The changing determinants of schooling investments: evidence from the villages in the Philippines, 1985–1989 and 2000–2004. *Journal of Development Studies*, **45**(3), 391–411.

Eswaran, M. and A. Kotwal (1986), Access to capital and agrarian production organization. *Economic Journal*, **96**(382), 482–98.

Fafchamps, M. and A.R. Quisumbing (1999), Human capital, productivity, and labor allocation in rural Pakistan. *Journal of Human Resources*, **34**(2), 369–406.

Feder, G. (1985), The relationship between farm size and farm productivity: the role of family labor, supervision, and credit constraints. *Journal of Development Economics*, **18**(2/3), 297–313.

Foster, A.D. and M.R. Rosenzweig (2010), Barriers to farm profitability in India: mechanization, scale and credit markets. Mimeo.

Gorton, M. and S. Davidova (2004), Farm productivity and efficiency in the CEE applicant countries: a synthesis of results. *Agricultural Economics*, **30**(1), 1–16.

Hamada, K., K. Otsuka, G. Ranis and K. Togo (2011), *Miraculous Growth and Stagnation, Lessons from the Experience of Postwar Japanese Economic Development*. London: Routledge.

Hayami, Y. (1988), *Japanese Agriculture under Siege: The Political Economy of Agricultural Policies*. London: Macmillan.

Hayami, Y. (2001), Ecology, history, and development: a perspective from rural southeast Asia. *World Bank Research Observer*, **16** (Fall 2001), 169–98.

Hayami, Y. (2009), Plantations agriculture in P. Pingli and R.E. Evenson (eds), *Handbook of Agricultural Economics*, Volume 4. Amsterdam: Elsevier, pp. 3305–3321.

Hayami, Y. and T. Kawagoe (1989), Farm mechanization, scale economies, and polarization. *Journal of Development Economics*, **31**(2), 221–39.

Hayami, Y. and K. Otsuka (1993), *The Economics of Contract Choice: An Agrarian Perspective*. Oxford, UK: Clarendon Press.

Hazell, P.B.R. (2013), Comparative study of trends in urbanization and changes in farm size in Africa and Asia: implications for agricultural research. Paper prepared for the ISPC.

Helfand, S.M. and E.S. Levine (2004), Farm size and the determinants of productive efficiency in the Brazilian center-west. *Agricultural Economics*, **31**(2–3), 241–9.

Heltberg, R. (1998), Rural market imperfections and the farm size-productivity relationships: evidence from Pakistan. *World Development*, **26**(10), 1807–1826.

Herring, R.J. (1983), *Land to the Tiller The Political Economy of Agrarian Reforms in South Asia*. New Haven, CT: Yale University Press.

Holden, S., K. Otsuka and F. Place (2008), *The Emergence of Land Markets in Africa: Assessing the Impacts on Poverty, Equity, and Efficiency*. Baltimore, MD: Resources for the Future.

Holden, S., K. Otsuka and K. Deininger (2013), *Land Tenure Reforms in Asia and Africa: Assessing Impacts on Poverty and Natural Resource Management*. Hampshire, UK: Palgrave Macmillan.

Huang, J., X. Wang and H. Qui (2012), Small-scale farmers in China in the face of modernization and globalization. London: International Institute for Environment and Development.

Kevane, M. (1996), Agrarian structure and agricultural practice: typology and application to western Sudan. *American Journal of Agricultural Economics*, **78**(1), 236–45.

Key, N. and D. Runsten (1999), Contract farming, smallholders, and rural development in Latin America: the organization of agroprocessing firms and the scale of outgrower production. *World Development*, **27**(2), 381–401.

Khusro, A.M. (1973), Farm size and land tenure in India. *Indian Economic Review*, **4**(2), 123–45.

Kimura, S., K. Otsuka, T. Sonobe and S. Rozelle (2010), Efficiency of land allocation through tenancy markets: evidence from China. *Economic Development and Cultural Change*, **59**(3), 485–510.

Kung, J.K.-S. (1995), Equal entitlement versus tenure security under a regime of collective property rights: peasants' preference for institutions in post-reform Chinese agriculture. *Journal of Comparative Economics*, **21**(1), 82–111.

Kuroda, Y. (1987), The production structure and demand for labor in postwar Japanese agriculture, 1952–82. *American Journal of Agricultural Economics*, **69**, 328–37.
Ladejinsky, W. (1977), *Agrarian Reform as Unfinished Business: Selected Papers of Wolf Ladejinsky*, Louis J. Walinsky (ed.), Oxford, UK: Oxford University Press.
Larson, D.F., T. Matsumoto, T. Kilic and K. Otsuka (2013), Should African rural development strategies depend on smallholder farms? An exploration of the inverse productivity hypothesis. *Agricultural Economics*, forthcoming.
Lin, J.Y. (1988), The household responsibility system in China's agricultural reform: a theoretical and empirical study. *Economic Development and Cultural Change*, **36**(2), 199–224.
Lipton, M. (2009), *Land Reform in Developing Countries: Property Rights and Property Wrongs*. Oxford, UK: Routledge.
McMillan, J., J. Whalley and J.Z. Li (1989), The impact of China's economic reforms on agricultural productivity growth. *Journal of Political Economy*, **97**(4), 781–807.
Narain, D. and P.C. Joshi (1969), Magnitude of agricultural tenancy. *Economic and Political Weekly*, **4**(39), A139–A142.
Newell, A., K. Pandya and J. Symons (1997), Farm size and the intensity of land use in Gujarat. *Oxford Economic Papers*, **49**(2), 307–15.
Ogura, T. (1963), *Agricultural Development of Modern Japan*. Tokyo: Fuji Publishing.
Otsuka, K. (1991), Determinants and consequences of land reform implementation in the Philippines. *Journal of Development Economics*, **35**(2), 339–55.
Otsuka, K. (2007), Efficiency and equity effects of land markets. In R.E. Evenson and P. Pingali (eds), *Handbook of Agricultural Economics*, Volume 3. Amsterdam: Elsevier, pp. 2672–2703.
Otsuka, K. (2013), Food insecurity, income inequality, and the changing comparative advantage in world agriculture. *Agricultural Economics*, forthcoming.
Otsuka, K., H. Chuma and Y. Hayami (1992a), Land and labor contracts in agrarian economies: theories and facts. *Journal of Economic Literature*, **30**(4), 1965–2018.
Otsuka, K., V.G. Cordova and C.C. David (1992b), Green revolution, land reform, and household income distribution in the Philippines. *Economic Development and Cultural Change*, **40**(4), 719–41.
Otsuka, K., H. Chuma and Y. Hayami (1993), Permanent labor and land tenancy contracts in agrarian economies: an integrated analysis. *Economica*, **60**(237), 57–77.
Otsuka, K., J. Estudillo and Y. Sawada (2009), *Rural Poverty and Income Dynamics in Asia and Africa*. London, UK: Routledge.
Otsuka, K., Y. Liu and F. Yamauchi (2013), Factor endowments, wage growth, and changing food self-sufficiency: evidence from country-level panel data. *American Journal of Agricultural Economics*, forthcoming.
Pingali, P. and V.T. Xuan (1992), Vietnam: decollectivization and rice productivity growth. *Economic Development and Cultural Change*, **40**(4), 697–718.
Pingali, L.P., M. Hossain and R.V. Gerpacio (1997), *Asian Rice Bowls: The Returning Crisis?* Wallingford, UK: CAB International.
Radhakrishnan, P. (1990), Land reforms: rhetoric and reality. *Economic and Political Weekly*, **25**(47), 2617–2621.
Ramasamy, C., P. Paramasivam and A. Kandaswamy (1994), Irrigation quality, modern variety adoption, and income distribution: the case of Tamil Nadu in India. In C. David and K. Otsuka (eds), *Modern Rice Technology and Income Distribution in Asia*, Boulder, CO: Lynne Rienner, pp. 323–73.
Ray, S.K. (1996), Land system and its reforms in India. *Indian Journal of Agricultural Economics*, **51**(1), 220–37.
Rozelle, S. and, J.F.M. Swinnen (2004), Success and failure of reforms: insights from transition agriculture. *Journal of Economic Literature*, **47**(2), 404–56.
Sadoulet, E., R. Murgai and A. de Janvry (2001), Access to land via land rental markets. In A. de Janvry, G. Gordillo, J.-P. Platteau and E. Sadoulet (eds), *Access to Land, Rural Poverty, and Public Action*. Oxford, UK: Oxford University Press.
Sarap, K. (1998), On the operation of the land market in backward agriculture: evidence form a village in Orissa, eastern India. *Journal of Peasant Studies*, **25**(2), 102–30.
Sharma, N. and J. Drèze (1996), Sharecropping in a north Indian village. *Journal of Development Studies*, **33**(1), 1–39.
Skoufias, E. (1995), Household resources, transaction costs, and adjustment through land tenancy. *Land Economics*, **71**(1), 42–56.
Sonobe, T. and K. Otsuka (2011), *Cluster-Based Industrial Development: A Comparative Study of Asia and Africa*. Hampshire, UK: Palgrave Macmillan.
Takahashi, K. and K. Otsuka (2009), Human capital investment and poverty reduction over generations: a case from the rural Philippines, 1979–2003. in K. Otsuka, J. Estudillo and Y. Sawada (eds), *Rural Poverty and Income Dynamics in Asia and Africa*. London: Routledge, pp. 47–68.

Thimmaiah, G. (2001), New perspectives on land reform in India. *Journal of Social and Economic Development*, **3**(2), 179–98.
Thorat, S. (1997), Trends in land ownership, tenancy, and land reform. In B.M. Desai (ed.), *Agricultural Development Paradigm for the Ninth Plan under New Economic Environment*. New Delhi: Oxford & IBH Publishing, pp. 684–711.
Verma, B.N. and D.W. Bromley (1987), The political economy of farm size in India: the elusive quest. *Economic Development and Cultural Change*, **35**(4), 791–808.
Yang, D.T. (1997), Education and off-farm work. *Economic Development and Cultural Change*, **45**(3), 613–32.
Yang, J., Z. Huang, X. Zhang and T. Reardon (2013), The rapid rise of cross-regional agricultural mechanization services in China. *American Journal of Agricultural Economics*, **95**(5), October, 1245–1251.
Yao, Y. (2000), The development of land lease market in rural China. *Land Economics*, **76**(2), 252–66.

19. Food entitlements, subsidies and right to food: a South Asian perspective
Simrit Kaur

19.1 INTRODUCTION

Hikes in global food prices have been a cause of grave concern in recent years, especially since 2007–08. Compared to the recent past, cereal prices have increased the most amongst all food commodities and are expected to remain high particularly in import-dependent developing countries. A recent study shows that the average world market price, relative to the 2010 level, of processed rice will rise by 31 per cent by 2020 and by 73 per cent by 2030 (Willenbockel, 2011). The corresponding figures for maize are 33 per cent and 89 per cent, respectively. Further, rise in prices has been accompanied by rising food price volatility. The Food and Agriculture Organization (FAO) predicts that high and volatile prices are likely to persist in the coming years on account of uncertainties surrounding output production in major food producing countries and a sharp run down of inventories (FAO, 2011).

In South Asia, food inflation varied widely in 2007–08, ranging from relatively moderate in India (about 7 per cent) to high in Nepal and Bangladesh (about 15 per cent), to very high in Pakistan (about 20 per cent) and in excess of 30 per cent in Sri Lanka and Afghanistan. Further, food price inflation exceeded nonfood inflation throughout South Asia (except India). Though food price inflation fell after reaching a peak in 2007–08, once again in 2010 food price inflation became the main factor driving general inflation.[1] South Asian countries responded to the food price hike by adopting a range of policies, including extension of social protection measures (World Bank, 2010).

Higher food prices mean higher spending to meet normal daily dietary needs. Countries of South Asia are expected to be hit hard as food represents a much larger share of their total spending. In addition, demand for food is highly priced and inelastic in these lower-income countries as compared to developed countries. Understandably, the large farmers and countries that are net exporters of food grain stand to gain from the price rise. Unfortunately, the majority of farms in South Asia are small and fragmented, which makes most of their farmers net buyers of food grains. Thus, they do not reap benefits from food price rise. Rather, they are net losers. Further, amongst all the South Asian countries, India is the only net exporter of food grain. While it stands to gain foreign exchange reserves, India has had to adopt contractionary macro-economic policies to curtail its food inflation in the recent past. This adversely impacted its GDP growth rate. A recent Asian Development Bank (ADB) study estimated that a 30 per cent rise in food prices might shave off 0.6 percentage points of GDP growth rate of low-income countries, including countries of South Asia (ADB, 2011). The other South Asian countries are in food deficit and are primarily net food importers. Global food inflation has led to widened trade deficits and domestic inflation in several Asian economies. In

Table 19.1   Food price surge and South Asian policy responses, 2010–11

I	Domestic Food Price Reduction	
1	Reduce Food Taxes	Bangladesh, Pakistan, Sri Lanka
2	Increase Supply of Grain Stocks	Afghanistan, Bangladesh, India, Pakistan, Nepal, Sri Lanka
3	Export Restriction	Bangladesh, India, Pakistan
4	Price Controls & Consumer Subsidies	Bangladesh, India, Pakistan, Nepal, Sri Lanka
II	Safety Net Programs	
1	Food for Work	Bangladesh
2	Food Aid	Afghanistan, Bangladesh, India, Pakistan
3	Feeding Programs	India
4	Cash Transfer	None
III	Stimulate Production	Afghanistan, Bangladesh, India

Source: ADB (2011), Global Food Price Inflation and Developing Asia.

addition, the food crisis has thrown millions of South Asians into poverty. With more people becoming poorer, higher food prices also mean higher probability of hunger and malnutrition (HLPE, 2011; Ivanic et al., 2011). It also slows down progress in achieving the Millennium Development Goals (MDGs). Amongst the 'Triple F' crises the world has experienced in recent years, South Asia has been impacted by *food* crisis the most. While the *fuel* and *financial* crises also impacted these economies, the consequence of rising food prices has been severe on state of food security in economies of this region.

Policy responses in South Asia have been immediate and primarily focused on (short-term) reduction of food prices to consumers. A wide range of policy instruments was used to ease the impact of the renewed food crisis. These include food price reduction, strengthening safety net programmes and stimulation of production. Table 19.1 summarizes the policy responses of the respective governments in South Asia to food price surge.

The present chapter has six sections. Section 19.1 discusses food insecurity in countries of South Asia. Aspects such as food consumption patterns; food prices and their impact on poverty; and prevalence of undernourishment and progress towards meeting Millennium Development Goals are analysed here. Section 19.2 delineates the rationale for government intervention to promote freedom from 'want and abject poverty'. Motivation for state intervention has been discussed from two perspectives: the *welfarist approach* and the *social justice approach*. The link between 'efficiency wages' and the 'poverty–nutrition trap' is briefly discussed to strengthen the argument. Additionally, the role of government in reducing risks and vulnerability of the affected population reinforces our argument for state intervention/targeted transfers. A brief description of the economic and social costs associated with such transfers is also provided. Section 19.3 follows critically analysing India's public distribution system (PDS). Thereafter, in section 19.4 we discuss the ongoing debate on right to food security as an aspect of rights-based development. As this aspect has figured prominently in the context of food policy reform in India, we have carried out a critical review of right to food in India as an illustrative case study. It is, we believe, amenable to extension to other developing countries where the state is directly involved in providing food to the poor and vulnerable. Section 19.5 tests a specific hypothesis, i.e. whether the PDS has a significant price-dampening effect. As theoretical predictions of the price effects of PDS are ambiguous, an empirical investigation of the same has considerable policy significance – especially in the context of the ongoing food crisis and proposed Food Security Ordinance. Using data from 1990 to 2011, our econometric results suggest that inflation in India is driven more by external than domestic factors. Further, within domestic factors it is driven more by supply-side bottlenecks than excess demand, although the two are not unrelated. In all our specifications, share of PDS in food availability, and also the revamping of PDS in 1997 has no significant price-dampening effect. Finally, section 19.6 concludes from a broad policy perspective.

19.2 FOOD SECURITY IN SOUTH ASIA

Food security is defined as the state in which people at all times have physical, social and economic access to sufficient and nutritious food that meets their dietary needs for a healthy and active life. This encompasses four criteria of food security: availability, access, utilization and stability. Using this definition adapted from the 1996 World Food Summit, the Global Food Security Index considers the core issues of affordability, availability and utilization. *Affordability* measures the ability of consumers to purchase food, their vulnerability to price shocks, and the presence of programmes and policies to support consumers when shocks occur. *Availability* measures the sufficiency of the national food supply, the risk of supply disruption, national capacity to disseminate food and research efforts to expand agricultural output. *Utilization as measured by Quality and Safety* is estimated by looking at the variety and nutritional quality of average diets, as well as, the safety of food. As stated in the Economist Intelligence Unit's (EIU's) Global Food Security Index (GFSI, 2012)[2] report, South Asia is the second most undernourished, malnourished and food insecure region in the world, next only to sub-Saharan Africa (Figure 19.1). Prevalence of underweight children (under 5 years) is also high in countries of South Asia. Within South Asia, India has the largest proportion (and number) of undernourished.

Additionally, the extent of social protection, as measured by the Social Protection Index (SPI[3]) in countries of South Asia is also very low at 0.061 (ADB, 2013). This implies that total social protection expenditure (per intended beneficiary) represents 6.1 per cent of poverty-line expenditures.[4] The depth and breadth of each of these programmes is also low for the region, with corresponding index values of 0.360 and 0.198.[5] This implies that the average benefits for social protection represent 36 per cent of poverty-line expenditures, and that these quite small benefits reach only about 20 per cent of all potential beneficiaries. While these ratios remain important in understanding the extent of social protection, they remain subject to a few shortcomings. For instance, the fraction of poor who benefit from food subsidies is subject to measurement errors. Also, the indirect effect through impact of food subsidies on regular market and wholesale prices may well be large but ignored in these ratios. Consequently, in this chapter, we try to estimate not just the benefit received by the target group, but also the impact

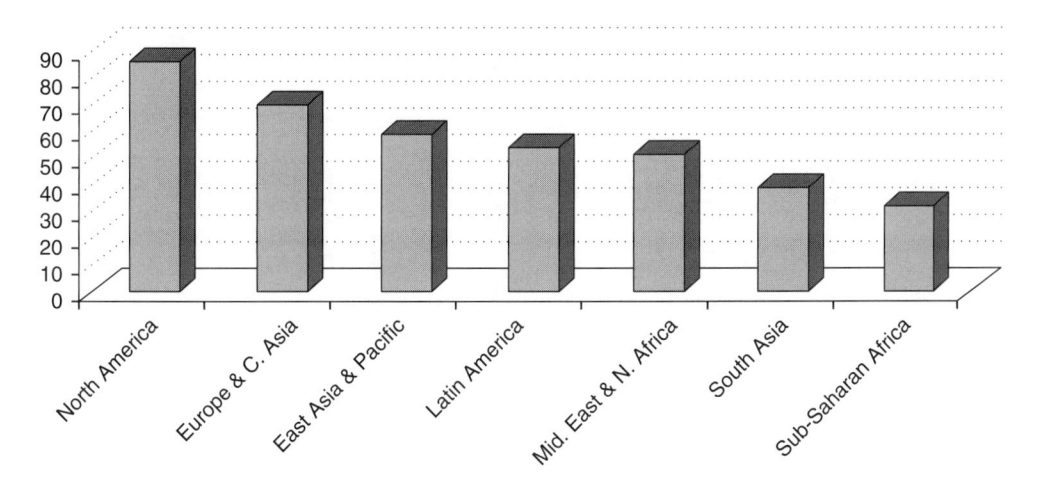

Source: GFSI (2012) Report, The Economist Intelligence Unit.

Figure 19.1 Food Security Index in regions of the world (score out of 100)

of social programmes (such as food subsidy) on the non-target group through changes in wholesale and market prices that may occur on account of food subsidies.

This section discusses four aspects of food security:

- Food insecurity in south Asia with respect to affordability, availability and utilization;
- Prevalence of undernourishment and progress towards the World Food Summit (WFS) and MDG in South Asia;
- Food consumption patterns in South Asia; and
- Food prices and impact on poverty from a South Asian perspective.

Each of these is now discussed below.

19.2.1 Food Insecurity in South Asia: Affordability, Availability and Utilization

Addressing food insecurity through the categories of 'affordability', 'availability' and 'quality and safety' (with respective weights as 40 per cent, 44 per cent and 16 per cent) shows that, in general, affordability is the most serious concern in countries of South Asia (see Figure 19.2). The problem of affordability is most grave in Nepal, followed by Pakistan, Bangladesh, Myanmar and India. Despite Asia having enjoyed substantial reductions in poverty rates since 1990, South Asia is not better off. While the percentage of people living on less than US$1.25 a day fell in South Asia from 61 per cent to 36 per cent between 1981 and 2008, this region is home to many of the developing world's poor. According to the World Bank's most recent poverty estimates (World Bank, 2013), about 571 million people in the region survive on less than US$1.25 a day, and they make up more than 44 per cent of the developing world's poor.

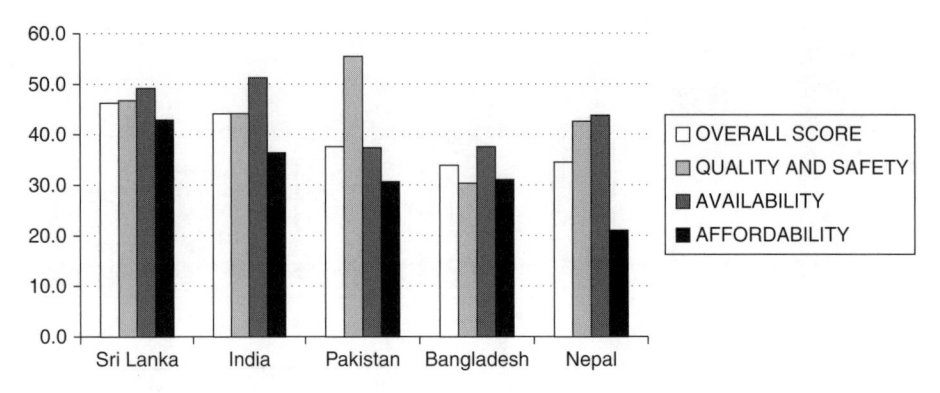

Source: GFSI (2012) Report, The Economist Intelligence Unit.

Figure 19.2   Food insecurity in South Asia: availability, affordability and utilization

The indicators for each of the sub-components of 'affordability', 'availability' and 'quality and safety' are discussed next (see Table 19.2).

Affordability
This is based on components such as GDP per capita, food consumption as a percentage of household expenditure, percentage of population below the poverty line, access to financing for farmers and presence of food safety net programmes. Food consumption as a percentage of household expenditure remains high for all South Asian countries. It varies from a high of over 70 per cent in Nepal to about 50 per cent in Bangladesh, India and Pakistan. Food safety net programmes[6] measure the public initiatives to protect the poor from food related shocks. The GFSI (2012) report categorizes India's food safety nets as having a national coverage, with very broad, though not deep coverage of these programmes (rating of 3 out of 4). Bangladesh and Sri Lanka come next, with ratings of 2 out of 4. These countries have moderate prevalence and depth of food safety net programmes run by the government, multilaterals, or NGOs. Nepal, Pakistan and Myanmar are categorized as countries with moderate presence of food safety net programmes, which are mainly run by NGOs or multilaterals. Further, the depth and/or prevalence of these programmes are considered to be inadequate. These countries have been assigned a rating of one.

Availability
This is based on components such as average food supply (kcal/capita/day), public expenditure on agricultural R&D and volatility of agricultural production. In terms of average food supply, Sri Lanka tops the list (2361 kcal/capita/day), while Bangladesh and Pakistan are at the lower end (2281 and 2293 kcal/capita/day respectively). Volatility of agricultural production has been estimated to be highest for Pakistan and Sri Lanka. Further, all five South Asian countries spend about 1 per cent of GDP on agricultural Research and Development.

Table 19.2 Food security indicators: sub-components of affordability, availability and utilization

	Bangladesh	India	Nepal	Pakistan	Sri Lanka
OVERALL SCORE	33.9	44.2	34.5	37.6	46.3
1 AFFORDABILITY (Weight: 40%)	31.2	36.4	21.1	30.7	42.9
1.1 Food consumption (% of household expenditure)	53.81	49.5	70.8	47.6	39.6
1.2 % of population under global poverty line ($2/day)	76.5	68.7	57.3	60.2	29.1
1.3 Gross domestic product per capita (US$)	1600	3740	1300	2560	5620
1.4 Agricultural import tariffs %	17.6	31.8	14.1	17	26.3
1.5 Presence of food safety net programs (0–4)	2	3	1	1	2
1.6 Access to financing for farmers (0–4)	3	3	1	2	2
2 AVAILABILITY (Weight: 44%)	37.6	51.3	43.8	37.4	49.2
2.1.1 Average food supply kcal/capita/day	2281	2352	2360	2293	2361
2.1.2 Dependency on chronic food aid (0–2)	0	1	1	1	1
2.2 Public exp on agricultural R&D (as % of Agri GDP)	1	1	1	1	1
2.4 Volatility of agricultural production (std. dev.)	0.045	0.058	0.034	0.068	0.068
2.5 Political stability risk (Rating 0–100; 100=highest risk)	70	25	65	65	45
3 QUALITY AND SAFETY (Weight: 16%)	30.4	44.2	42.6	55.5	46.8
3.1 Diet diversification %	19	38	27	52	42
3.3.1 Dietary availability of vitamin A (0–2)	0	1	1	2	1
3.3.2 Dietary availability of animal iron mg/person/day	0.9	0.6	1	1.4	1.1
3.3.3 Dietary availability of vegetal iron mg/person/day	7.2	10.2	14.2	7.5	10.7
3.4 Protein quality Grams	33.75	36.97	36.96	47.38	37.88
3.5.1 Agency to ensure safety and health of food (0–1)	1	1	1	1	1
3.5.2 % of population with access to potable water %	80	88	88	90	90
3.5.3 Presence of formal grocery sector (0–2)	1	1	1	1	1
4 BACKGROUND VARIABLES					
4.1 Prevalence of undernourishment %	26	19	17	25	20
4.2.1 Percentage of children stunted %	43.2	47.9	49.3	41.5	19.2

Table 19.2 (continued)

	Bangladesh	India	Nepal	Pakistan	Sri Lanka
OVERALL SCORE	33.9	44.2	34.5	37.6	46.3
4 BACKGROUND VARIABLES					
4.2.2 Percentage of children underweight %	41.3	43.5	38.8	31.3	21.6
4.3 Intensity of food deprivation kcal/person/day	290	240	220	280	250
4.4 Human Development Index Rating 0–1	0.5	0.547	0.458	0.504	0.691
4.5 EIU Women's Economic Opportunity Index Rating 0–100; 100=most favorable for Women	39.2	41.9	41.1	35.5	47.6
4.6 EIU Democracy Index Rating 1–10; 10=most democratic	5.87	7.28	4.24	4.55	6.64

Source: GFSI (2012) Report, The Economist Intelligence Unit.

Quality and safety

This is based on components such as diet diversification, intake of protein, safety and health of food, and percentage of population with access to potable water. Diet diversification is highest for Pakistan (52 per cent). Sri Lanka and India follow next (42 and 38 per cent, respectively). Bangladesh and Nepal have least diet diversification (19 and 27 per cent, respectively). A similar ranking is observed with respect to protein intake.

19.2.2 Prevalence of Undernourishment and Progress towards WFS and MDG in South Asia

Food insecurity and price instability affect hunger and malnutrition. Though the state of hunger in South Asia has improved as compared to the level in 1990, it is still high. According to the Global Hunger Index (2010),[7] hunger in Bangladesh and India has changed from extremely alarming to alarming, and, in Pakistan and Sri Lanka, from alarming to serious. The state of hunger in Nepal, however, has remained the same: alarming. Overall, hunger in South Asia is alarming and worse than in sub-Saharan Africa (von Grebmer et al., 2010).

To make matters worse, the food and economic crises are challenging our efforts to achieve the WFS[8] and MDGs[9] of reducing the number and proportion of people who suffer from hunger by half by 2015. Even if the MDG were to be achieved by 2015, some 600 million people in developing countries would still be undernourished. Higher food prices also affect nourishment intake by households. Even temporary reductions in disposable income due to price shocks can lead families to draw down on their capital (both physical and human). For example, sometimes, families sell household assets such as livestock in order to maintain food intake in the face of an economic shock. Alternatively, families may make fewer visits to the doctor, or remove children

Table 19.3 Prevalence of undernourishment and progress towards the World Food Summit (WFS) and the Millennium Development Goal (MDG) targets in South Asia

Region/ Country	Total Population (2006–08) (Million)	Number of Undernourished (Million)		Change so far (%)	Progress Towards WFS Targets	Proportion of Undernourished (%)		Change so far (%)	Progress Towards MDG Targets
		1990–02	2006–08			1990–02	2006–08		
Africa	962.9	170.9	223.6	30.8	Decline in Progress	26	23	−11	Progress Insufficient
Asia	3884.3	607.1	567.8	−6.5	Progress Insufficient	20	15	−27	Progress Insufficient
L. America	528.2	46.7	38.6	−17.2	Progress Insufficient	11	7	−35	Progress Insufficient
East Asia	1410.8	215.6	139.4	−35.3	Progress Insufficient	18	10	−44	Target will be met
South Asia	1642.8	267.5	330.1	23.4	Decline in Progress	22	20	−8	Progress Insufficient
Bangladesh	157.7	44.4	41.4	−6.8	Progress Insufficient	38	26	−30	Progress Insufficient
India	1164.6	177.0	224.6	26.9	Decline in Progress	20	19	−4	Progress Insufficient
Nepal	28.3	4.2	4.7	13.3	Decline in Progress	21	17	−22	Progress Insufficient
Pakistan	173.2	29.5	42.8	45	Decline in Progress	25	25	−1	No Progress or Decline
Sri Lanka	19.9	4.8	3.9	−18.4	Progress Insufficient	28	20	−28	Progress Insufficient

Source: FAO (2011), The State of Food Insecurity in the World: How Does International Price Volatility affect Domestic Economies and Food Security?

from school in order to save on school fees. These responses may result in a loss of human capital in the affected households. Such episodes can result in poverty traps, whereby a onetime shock has longer-term effects. In Table 19.3, we report the progress made by South Asian countries in meeting the targets as set under the WFS and the MDGs.

The main highlights of Table 19.3 are as follows:

1. South Asia fairs poorly in terms of meeting its obligations towards the WFS and MDGs. In none of the South Asian countries, have the targets for both already been met or are expected to be met by 2015. This may be contrasted with efforts made by some of the African countries which have done extremely well in meeting these targets. For instance, Ghana, Mali and Nigeria achieved these targets by 2008. Within Asia, China, Vietnam and Georgia are the countries that have already met these targets.
2. Within South Asia, Bangladesh and Sri Lanka are better performers than India, Nepal and Pakistan. The percentage of population that is undernourished in

Table 19.4 Expenditure elasticities of staples and high value food commodities in South Asia

Food Item	Bangladesh	India	Nepal	Pakistan	Sri Lanka
Rice	−0.078	−0.016	0.016	0.025	−0.071
Wheat	0.004	−0.109	−0.111	−0.121	−0.027
Coarse Grains	−0.129	−0.147	−0.152	−0.172	−0.170
Roots and Tubers	0.250	0.336	0.300	0.282	0.371
Pulses	0.227	0.214	0.263	0.189	0.224
Vegetable Oil	0.191	0.176	0.199	0.186	0.128
Vegetables	0.500	0.673	0.599	0.565	0.748
Fruits	0.666	0.702	0.698	0.710	0.556
Milk	0.581	0.589	0.634	0.575	0.689
Meat, Fish and Egg	0.822	0.892	0.860	0.670	0.866
Income Elasticity of Calories	0.440	0.500	0.048	0.047	0.058
Food	0.448	0.399	0.424	0.342	0.402

Source: Joshi et al. (2007).

Bangladesh, India, Nepal, Pakistan and Sri Lanka is 26, 19, 17, 25 and 20, respectively. Similarly, a large proportion of children under five years remain underweight.
3. Pakistan is the only country in the region which has made no progress (maybe a deterioration) in terms of meeting commitments towards either WFS or MDGs.
4. While South Asia fairs poorly in meeting the MDG targets, South East Asia, by contrast, has performed rather well. Its MDG targets were met by 2008.

19.2.3 Food Consumption Patterns in South Asia

Food consumption patterns in South Asia are of special interest because India in this region (accounting for more than 70 per cent of the South Asian population), together with China, is experiencing rapid transformation with implications for changing food demand patterns. With reference to South Asia, small inter-country differences in expenditure elasticities are observed (see Table 19.4). The expenditure elasticities for high-value commodities, such as vegetables, fruits, milk, meat, fish and eggs are much higher than for staples, such as rice and wheat, in all the South Asian countries. The expenditure elasticities of coarse grains throughout South Asia are, in fact, negative. Wheat and rice too have negative expenditure elasticities, except for wheat in Bangladesh and rice in Nepal and Bangladesh. Thus, Bennet's Law, which states that the proportion of expenditure on non-cereals increases as income increases, holds throughout the region. Further, the commodities with cheapest source of calories have been estimated to have lowest expenditure elasticities. The value of income elasticity of demand for cereals in Asia is the lowest among the regions of the world, a reflection of the importance of cereals in Asian diet.

Undoubtedly, the food basket in South Asia has diversified in recent years with increasing per capita consumption of milk, fruits and meat products (Gaiha et al., 2013).

Nevertheless, the point remains that these countries still spend substantial proportion of their expenditure on food.

19.2.4 Food Prices and Impact on Poverty: A South Asian Perspective

South Asia is arguably the most vulnerable region to increasing food inflation given the large segment of the population living below or near the poverty line. Additionally, the high proportion of income spent on food worsens the situation. A spike in the cost of food staples like rice and wheat could push millions of additional people into extreme poverty in South Asia. However, food subsidies targeted at the very poorest in the region would help them cope with still-high prices (ADB, 2012). ADB (2012) estimates the impact of food price increases on poverty for South Asia. Change in *percentage* of poor with increase in food prices and change in *number* of poor with increase in food prices by 10, 20 and 30 per cent, respectively, is reported in Table 19.5.

A few observations based on Table 19.5 are as follows:

Inter- and intra-country variations

Effects of food price increases on poverty vary across countries and within countries. For instance, India and Bangladesh would be most affected by increases in food prices. Sri Lanka, on the other hand, would be least affected. To illustrate, a 20 per cent increase in food prices in India would lead to a 5.4 per cent increase in poverty, making 59 million additional Indians poor. The corresponding figures for Sri Lanka are 2.4 per cent and fewer than half a million. Similarly, a 10 per cent rise in price could push almost

Table 19.5 Impact of food price increases on poverty for South Asia vs. developing Asia (25 countries), $1.25-a-day poverty line

	Change in *percentage* of poor with increase in food prices by			Change in *number* of poor (in millions) with increase in food prices by		
	10%	20%	30%	10%	20%	30%
Bangladesh	2.5	5	7.5	3.8	7.7	11.5
Bhutan	1.8	3.5	5.3	0.01	0.02	0.03
India–Rural	2.9	5.8	8.8	22.8	45.6	68.5
India–Urban	2.1	4.3	6.4	6.7	13.4	20.0
All India average	2.7	5.4	8.1	29.5	59.0	88.5
Nepal	2.0	4.1	6.1	0.6	1.1	1.7
Pakistan	2.2	4.5	6.7	3.47	6.9	10.4
Sri Lanka	1.2	2.4	3.6	0.24	0.47	0.71
South Asia Average/sum	2.1	4.1	6.2	37.6	75.2	112.8
Contribution of South Asia to Developing Asia's Poverty				58.40	58.40	58.40
Developing Asia	1.9	3.9	5.8	64.4	128.8	193.2

Source: Asian Development Bank (2012).

30 million more Indians and nearly 4 million more Bangladeshis into extreme poverty. Within India, rural areas are more sensitive to price rise.

South Asia versus Developing Asia
Data suggests that the poor in South Asia are on average more vulnerable to food price increases at 10, 20 and 30 per cent increases than other regions in developing Asia. For instance, while an additional 6.2 per cent of South Asians become poor with a 30 per cent food price rise, the corresponding figure for developing Asia is only 5.8. This re-affirms South Asia's relatively higher proportion of food in the consumption basket.

Contribution of South Asia to Developing Asia's poverty
Almost 60 per cent of the total increase in number of poor in developing Asia would be caused by increases in headcount ratios of poor in South Asia if food prices rise by 10, 20 or 30 per cent.

Notwithstanding the rising levels of poverty because of surge in food prices, one also needs to account for supply side effects of food price hikes that may dampen rising poverty levels. Recent evidence suggests that in response to rising food prices, major cereal producers, including both consumer nations and exporter nations, responded positively to spiralling food prices in 2007–08. For instance, Headey and Fan (2010) report that output of maize, rice and wheat increased by about 10 per cent in South Asia post the 2007 food price hike. Specifically, in Pakistan output of rice increased by as much as 20.7 per cent, while India's production of wheat increased by 14.2 per cent. Similar evidence is also available in Imai et al. (2011) and IFAD (2013). Imai et al.'s paper examines how commodity and input prices affect the supply of key food commodities in ten Asian economies. Their results also corroborate earlier evidence whereby own prices have been found to positively affect supply of rice, maize, wheat, fruits and vegetables. They also find that key input prices of oil and fertilizers have a negative impact on food supply. However, in *all* cases the own-price effects have been estimated to be larger than those of inputs (in absolute terms). Consequently, the authors believe that alarmist predictions of rise in poverty and hunger because of food price hike are exaggerated and contentious.

19.2.5 Freedom From 'Want and Deprivation' and the Role of the State

Current estimates suggest that there are approximately 925 million hungry people in the world, despite current per capita global food production, being at 2796 kcal/person/day – well in excess of 2100 kcals/person/day needed to provide sufficient energy for most daily activities. Given that, there is more than enough food in the world to feed its inhabitants, global hunger is not an insoluble problem. *Deprivation* in a *world of plenty* is an intrinsic rationale for state intervention to invest in programmes that reduce hunger and undernutrition.

Answers to questions such as when, where and how governments should intervene depend on the perspective from which one approaches the issue. For our purposes, it is useful to separate the existing perspectives into two categories: the *welfarist approach*[10] and the *social justice approach*. Arguably, the more influential, the *welfarist approach* identifies two motivations for government intervention. First, governments should intervene to address market failures and bring about a more efficient allocation of scarce resources. Second, governments should intervene to improve the distribution of resources and reduce poverty. Economic theory also provides guidance on the range of policy instruments that could be used to address these market failures and to reduce poverty, as well as, on the likely trade-offs between equity and efficiency inherent in each.[11] The *social justice approach* involves justifying government intervention based on various concepts of social justice. Two such approaches that have gained prominence over the past three decades are the *basic needs approach* and the *capabilities approach*.[12] Both of these distinguish between income as a 'means' or an 'end', and they often highlight the lack of correlation between income and other outcomes that enter into one's concept of development. State intervention is, therefore, often justified by appealing to some concept of a just society. Libertarians tend to focus more on preventing the government from restricting free choice than on the equally important role of government in promoting such freedoms (Sen, 1992).

Sen's concept of development as freedom shifts focus from 'income inequality' to the 'inequality in the distribution of *substantive freedoms* and *capabilities*' (Sen, 2000). This is due to the possibility of some 'coupling' of income inequality with unequal advantages in converting incomes into capabilities. He emphasizes that protective security is needed to provide a social safety net from preventing the affected population from (say, famines) being reduced to abject misery and in some cases even starvation and death. The overarching implication is that state actions and social arrangements are needed to secure and expand the freedom of individuals, especially in the context of developing countries. Sen emphasized this promotional role as distinct from the protective role. Studies by Kaur (2007, 2009) also corroborates Sen's view. Her findings indicate that while higher economic freedom (as measured by the Fraser Institute's economic freedom index) promotes growth, it does not necessarily expand *larger freedoms*, as measured by freedom from want and deprivation. On the other hand, big governments with large subsidies and transfers as a proportion of GDP (which by definition lowers the economic freedom index) have been instrumental in providing freedoms, such as, lowering poverty, inequality, infant mortality and malnutrition.

The link between 'efficiency wages' and the 'poverty–nutrition trap' reinforces the need for government intervention. For long, economists have analysed the links between nutrition and poverty. The notion that poverty causes undernutrition dates back at least to Adam Smith. Economists have also suggested the reverse causation: that inadequate nutrition is the reason for low productivity and poverty. This idea, captured in the notion of 'efficiency wages', dates back to Leibenstein (1957) and was subsequently given a stricter formulation by Mirrlees (1975), Stiglitz (1976) and Bliss and Stern (1978). The backbone in these models is the so-called efficiency–wage function. It postulates that the poor are doubly disadvantaged since:

> Being poor, the nutrition level is low. Therefore, the chances of being rationed out of the labour market are high. Further, since the poor do not own assets (both human and capital), non-wage income is low. This accompanied by a low wage income implies that the total income is low. Hence, the nutrition level is low. Thus, the chances of being rationed out are high. (Ray, 2004; Kaur, 2007)

In order to break the vicious cycle of deprivation, while economic growth is essential, evidence suggests that this happens at a modest rate. Thus targeted interventions, say, in the form of direct investments in nutrition are desirable (Alderman, 2005). The United Nations (2003, 2005) has also supported the role of government in reducing the risks and vulnerability of the affected population. *Risk-mitigating and coping policies* require targeted transfers to the elderly, the disabled, and protection of human capital of the poor (e.g. withdrawal of children from schools may be discouraged by providing snacks for attending school). Self-targeted rural public works, community-based services and subsidized food grain help reshape the development strategy and lead to larger freedoms such as amelioration of poverty and reduction of income inequality.

However, government intervention in the form of providing subsidies is often criticized on several grounds. Select arguments against subsidies are provided below:[13]

Price subsidies reduce allocative efficiency by distorting relative prices
Consumer price subsidies often are associated with overconsumption or underprovision of the subsidized item, while producer subsidies are associated with excess production. However, Čajanov's (early 1900s) view is contrary. According to him, producer subsidies make peasants work less hard. How peasants behave once their needs are satisfied, was the basic question addressed by him. During the early 1900s Čajanov formulated a theory[14] stating that peasant productivity was a function of the conflicting forces of the subjective marginal utility of labour and of the marginal disutility of effort. In his view, effort on the 'family labour farm' was designed to satisfy a locally homogeneous acceptable standard of consumption; when that was achieved,[15] the 'self-exploitation' of the peasant labourer ceased. Thus, peasants worked no harder than they had to and stopped when consumption demand was satisfied. They neither saved nor invested (Čajanov et al., 1966). To the extent that that idea can be replicated even today, provision of food subsidies to a peasant family will make them work less hard on farms, thereby having adverse production consequences.[16] Sahn and Alderman (1996) also studied the impact of food subsidy on labour supply in Sri Lanka. Their results indicate that for both men and women in rural and urban areas, the receipt of the subsidy had a marked adverse impact on the days worked, although, it had a little effect on the decision as to whether or not to work. On this basis, it is often argued that since subsidies induce perverse behavioural response by reducing labour supply, these should be avoided. However, it may be argued that even if it happens, it reflects rational consumer choice. In today's times when countries are estimating Gross Happiness Index, why should the national governments not want to make their people richer and happier as well? This argument is well developed by political scientists who demonstrate that a more generous welfare state contributes to higher levels of life satisfaction, and does so to rich and poor alike.[17] Notwithstanding their view, it is pertinent to state that if food subsidy lowers labour supply, it is then, not just a matter of individual satisfaction or happiness but also loss of efficiency that affects the entire society. Therefore, the choice is a lot more complex.

Rent-seeking activities and high costs associated with subsidies
Price subsidies have been associated with smuggling, black marketing (e.g. in India, wheat and rice distributed under the PDS have often been diverted and sold in the open market at a much higher price) and waste (e.g. subsidized wheat flour was used to mark soccer fields in Peru!). The inefficiency of this policy is also reflected in its high cost; as estimated by the Planning Commission (2008), 58 per cent of subsidized food grains in

India do not reach targeted families because of identification errors, non-transparent operations and unethical practices in the implementation of the public distribution programme.

Poverty and nutritional impact of food subsidies

Many developing countries use food-price subsidies to enhance purchasing power and/or improve nutrition. However, subsidizing goods on which households spend a high proportion of their budget can create large wealth effects, thereby making consumers switch towards foods with higher non-nutritional attributes (e.g. taste), but lower nutritional content per unit of money spent, weakening or perhaps even reversing the subsidy's intended impact. Additionally, in some cases, subsidizing of inappropriate commodities leads the poor to consume a less nutritious diet (e.g. in the Dominican Republic, the poor's intake of calories and protein fell when they substituted less nutritious subsidized chicken for rice, beans and oil plantains). Further, in India, despite the relatively large size of the subsidy provided under the PDS, evaluations of the programme based on data for the late 1980s and early 1990s found its effect on the poor to be minimal. Svedberg (2012) also corroborates the view and states that the impact of the PDS on outcome variables, such as poverty and malnutrition, are practically nil. The subsidy to the average poor household has been estimated at Rs 30 per month or Rs 6 per person,[18] which is equivalent to a 1.5–2 per cent increase in their monthly per capita expenditure (MPCE). This implies that the Government of India spent about 1 per cent of national income to boost the purchasing power of the average poor household by less than 2 per cent. The meagre subsidy as received by poor households in relation to high budget costs undoubtedly reflects malfunctioning across several dimensions.

Radhakrishna et al.'s (1997) analysis of 1986–87 (NSS 42nd round) household data reveals that transfers under the PDS programme represented an exceedingly small component of household expenditures.[19] They estimated the per capita income gains to the rural poor from all consumer subsidies (food and nonfood) to be only Rs 2 per month, or 2.7 per cent of per capita expenditures. These low-income gains generated correspondingly low effects on poverty and nutritional status. Similar results were found for the urban poor. A study by Jensen and Miller (2011) estimates the subsidy impacts on poor to be low for two Chinese provinces, Gansu and Hunan. Kochar (2005) also reports negligible effects of such subsidies on nutrition in India. However, a study by Zhou et al. (2001) reveals that the cereal consumption and nutritional intake of the poor has improved over time, due to India's PDS. It is believed that targeting was achieved because the relatively rich voluntarily sidestepped the programme. Studies by Jha et al. (2013a, b) have also found that PDS significantly increased the intake of calories, proteins and iron for the PDS participants in the states of Andhra Pradesh, Maharashtra and Rajasthan. An elaborated version of few of these studies is provided in the next section.

Substitution effects of food price subsidy

In countries that provide different types of safety nets for upliftment of the poor and vulnerable (for instance, food subsidy and rural work programmes), there might be a similar substitution effect at work. In other words, in the wake of availing one subsidy (say, food subsidy) the rural poor may not want to avail themselves of the other (say, to work at public works programme). A case in point is the workfare scheme, namely, the Mahatma Gandhi National Rural Employment Guarantee Act (MNREGA) and the direct food subsidy programme named the Targeted Public Distribution Scheme (TPDS) of India. They represent two alternative social safety nets instituted as anti-poverty measures. In their paper, Jha et al. (2013c) try to understand whether, from the point of view of individual households, the two programmes are substitutes or complements, as this sheds light on the appropriateness of the design of the two programmes. Based on primary data collected from the Indian states of Rajasthan and Madhya Pradesh, the results show that in Rajasthan, a large percentage of households consider TPDS and MNREGA programmes to be substitutes for each other, while in Madhya Pradesh, the households often perceive the two programmes as complements.[20] They conclude by discussing important policy implications of this finding.

Despite these shortcomings, interventions are considered beneficial, especially micronutrient interventions as they have a high benefit–cost ratio. The Copenhagen Consensus held in 2008[21] considered 30 options and ranked the provision of micronutrients as the world's best investment for development. Food-based approaches such as integrating micronutrient interventions with existing health, nutrition and food security programmes have often been ranked highly (Copenhagen Consensus papers by Behrman et al., 2004; Horton et al., 2008; Hoddinott et al., 2012). For instance, Hoddinott et al. (2012) have estimated the economic benefits of reduced stunting in India and their results indicate that the benefit–cost ratio is as high as 44.5.

In a study conducted by Micronutrient Initiative and UNICEF (2004), Afghanistan loses as much as 2.3 per cent of its GDP to all forms of vitamins and mineral deficiencies (VMD). Pakistan, Nepal and Bhutan also lose over 1.5 per cent of GDP due to VMD. India loses 1 per cent, while Bangladesh loses a little under 1 per cent. Given the average GDP per annum over the period 2006 to 2010 (as reported in column 3, Table 19.6), in India, VMD represent an annual GDP loss of US$12.5 billion. In Pakistan, they may be costing the country around US$2.5 billion annually.[22]

Thus, from a longer-term perspective, South Asian countries need to move away from

Table 19.6 Estimated percentage of GDP lost to all forms of vitamins and mineral deficiencies (VMD)

Country	GDP lost due to VMD (%)*	Average GDP per annum over the period 2006–2010 (USD Billion)	Average GDP lost per annum over the period 2006–2010 (USD Billion)
Afghanistan	2.3	12.17	0.28
Bangladesh	0.9	79.92	0.72
Bhutan	1.6	1.23	0.02
India	1	1291.46	12.91
Nepal	1.5	12.17	0.18
Pakistan	1.7	154.65	2.63

Source: Author's estimates.
*Data as reported in Vitamin and Mineral Deficiency, Global Damage Assessment Report (2004), by The Micronutrient Initiative and UNICEF.

the present bias towards calorie based food security programmes to ones that address the issue of nutritional deficiency.

We now move to the ongoing debate on right to food as an aspect of rights-based development. As this aspect has figured prominently in the context of food policy reform in India, we have carried out a critical review of right to food in India as an illustrative case study. We believe it is of relevance to other developing countries as well where the state provides food assistance to the poor and vulnerable. It is in this regard, that a discussion on India's PDS becomes imperative. This is the focus of our study in the next section.

19.3   INDIA'S PDS: IMPLICATIONS FOR FOOD SECURITY

An important food subsidy programme of India is its PDS. It distributes wheat and rice and also edible oils, kerosene and sugar at subsidized prices to rural and urban households. Under PDS, the allocation is made on a scale of issue which is 35 kg per family below poverty line (BPL)[23] and Antyodaya Anna Yojana (AAY)[24] categories and is variable based on food grain availability for the above poverty line (APL) category. It is currently one of India's largest social programmes, as also the largest distribution network of its kind in the world. Faced with budgetary difficulties, the government redesigned the PDS in 1997 and introduced the TPDS. The system changed from providing subsidies to *all in poor areas* towards extending targeted subsidies to *poor in all areas*. The TPDS is operated under the joint responsibility of the Central and the State Governments. While the Central Government is responsible for ensuring *availability*, *acceptability* and *affordability*, the states are to ensure *accessibility* of food grains to the poor through a network of Fair Price Shops (FPS).

PDS off-take and PDS procurement in the pre- and post-TPDS period is presented in Figure 19.3. Analysis shows that the average PDS off-take as a proportion of total food

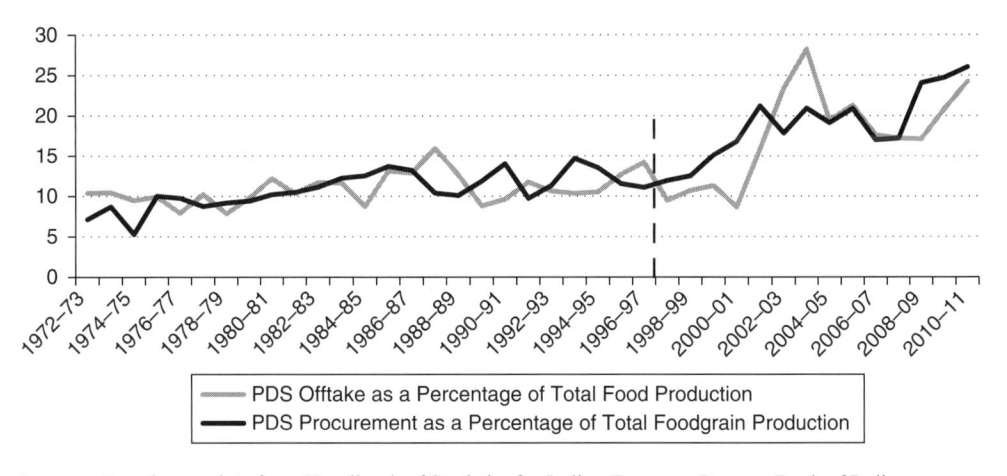

Source: Based upon data from Handbook of Statistics for Indian Economy, Reserve Bank of India.

Figure 19.3   DS off-take and PDS procurement

grain production in the pre-TPDS period was 11.61 per cent (18.42 million tonnes per year), while in the post TPDS period it rose to 17.54 per cent (about 40 million tonnes per year). Similarly, the average PDS procurement as a percentage of total food grain production went up from 11.99 per cent during the pre TPDS period to 18.97 per cent for the post TPDS period.

Despite the noble intention of targeting subsidized food grains, the TPDS is plagued with controversies (Jha et al., 1999, 2013a; Jha and Srinivasan, 2001; Kochar, 2005; Bhattacharyya and Rana, 2008; Khera, 2008, 2011; Planning Commission, 2008; Kumar, 2010; Svedberg, 2012). A few of these are discussed next.

Ineffective targeting, substantial exclusion, and low off-take
According to the NSSO 2004–05 survey, only 37.6 per cent of rural households below the poverty line have BPL cards (the corresponding figure is 25.7 per cent per cent for urban areas). Additionally, Svedberg (2012) draws attention to the fact that while cardholders are allowed to buy 35 kg of subsidized grains per month, the actual purchase is just 14.7 kg in rural areas and 17.4 kg in urban areas. Khera (2011) also finds that among those households with access to the PDS (the BPL households or BPL + AAY cardholders), utilization levels are low, both in terms of proportion of households buying some grain from the PDS as also in terms of quantities purchased. The reasons include ineffective targeting, long distances, and/or long waiting time to/at FPS, irregular availability of grains in FPS, cardholders not being allowed to purchase in small installments, low quality of grains offered and preference for local grain variety, amongst others. Consequently, the poverty impacts have also been considerably low.

Low nutrition, poverty and income transfer effects
It is often reported that PDS has negligible poverty and nutritional impact on the recipients. In her study, Kochar (2005) estimates that the effect of TPDS on calorie intake of the poor has been marginal. She finds that the elasticity of caloric intake with respect to the value of food subsidies is very low at 0.06.[25] The reasons for this have been attributed primarily to (1) the very small proportion of the poor who availed themselves of the TPDS, and (2) the substantial shortfall in the quantities of subsidized food grains actually purchased relative to entitlements.[26]

Gaiha et al. (2013) examine the reasons for low real income transfers (RIT) through TPDS in three states: Andhra Pradesh, Maharashtra and Rajasthan. Yet again, real income transfers have been estimated to be rather low. In Rajasthan, about 48 per cent of the households have no RIT from TPDS, while in Maharashtra about 34 per cent of the households have no RIT. Similarly, for rice in Rajasthan, about 63 per cent of the participating households have no RIT, while in Maharashtra, 33 per cent obtained no real income transfer. Their analysis focuses on variation in real income transfers to be associated with poverty of households, demographic characteristics, transaction costs of buying from PDS, food price subsidy and (proximate) measures of supply constraints. In Andhra Pradesh, for instance, the authors find that poorer households have larger real income transfers with respect to subsidized rice. The effect of land Gini on RIT is negative, implying that in villages with higher inequality in land distribution, the benefits are restricted which may be on account of greater diversion of rice to open markets from such villages. Further, the lower the ratio of PDS to market price of rice, the greater is the real income gain (either because the quantity bought is higher or the same quantity bought translates into higher income gain because of a higher price subsidy). Distance to FPS has been estimated not to influence real income gain as they are well dispersed. Further, household size has a significant positive effect through higher rice demand, though the effect weakens among larger households. However, the overall positive effect on RIT is substantial.

Extensive corruption
According to Khera (2011), the earnings of honest FPS are very low, sometimes close to a meagre Rs 100 per month. Under TPDS, low margins are compounded by shrinkage of volumes. Hence, the incentive to cheat is strong. Wheat diversions for FPS are very profitable. The shopkeeper gets a paltry margin of 7 paise[27] per kilogramme of wheat sold to a BPL household, as compared with a margin of Rs 1.97[28] for selling this amount in the open market and a much higher margin of Rs 4.50[29] per kilogramme of Antyodaya wheat. Furthermore, corruption is rampant[30] in obtaining a licence; commissions are paid to FCI officials for expediting supplies; and amounts supplied are frequently lower than recorded. BPL consumers are often turned away on grounds of inadequate supplies; the quality sold is abysmal; and buying quotas in installments is discouraged.

Leakages and diversions
A study by Planning Commission (2008) reports that 58 per cent of subsidized food grains issued from the central pool do not reach BPL families because of identification errors, non-transparent operations and unethical practices in the implementation of TDPS. Including handling costs, the government ends up spending Rs 8.5 to transfer 1 Rs to the poor, indicating that 1 Rs of budgetary consumer subsidy is worth only 12 paise to the poor. Khera (2011) also estimates that 67 per cent of the wheat meant for poor is diverted elsewhere. In other words, for every 1 kg of wheat that reaches the poor household, the government transfers 3 kg of wheat to them. Himanshu and Sen (2011) also state that between 1993–94 (a universal PDS) and 2004–05 (TPDS), the leakages grew enormously – that of rice from 19 per cent to 40 per cent and that of wheat from 41 per cent to 73 per cent. Jha et al. (2013a) state that with the shift to TPDS and extremely low margins on sales to BPL households, FPSs have a weak incentive to maintain adequate stocks, or when the stocks are adequate, large supplies are diverted to the open market at much higher margins.

Leakages and diversions in TPDS take place in two distinct ways. One is at the FPS level and the other is through leakages because of ghost BPL cardholders. At the FPS level, when the actual off-take of subsidized food grains by active BPL cardholders is less than their entitlement, the quantity of grains not issued to consumers is diverted by the FPS to make extra money. In addition, it may be noted that many poor families, particularly the daily wage earners, do not draw their full ration quota because they receive payment of wages in kind in particular seasons and due to seasonal migration to work places. Thus, in most states, the average off-take by a cardholder is less than their entitlement (Khera, 2011; Svedberg, 2012; Jha et al., 2013a). Based on trends in monthly PDS purchase, Khera (2011) categorizes the Indian states into three groups: 'functioning,'[31] 'reforming'[32] and 'languishing'.[33]. Based on data available in Khera (2011), we estimate the correlation coefficients between diversion of PDS food grain and monthly per capita

Table 19.7 Correlation between Diversion of PDS food grain and PC Purchase of PDS food grain

Rural/Urban	Commodity	Classification	1999–00	2007–08
Rural	Rice	Functioning	−0.9256**	−0.6467
		Reforming	−0.8926	−0.6044
		Languishing	−0.3638	0.2356
		All India	−0.6751***	−0.723***
	Wheat	Functioning	−0.2602	0.1556
		Reforming	−0.9586**	−0.1879
		Languishing	−0.9838***	−0.6785*
		All India	−0.6662***	−0.0846
Urban	Rice	Functioning	−0.7424*	−0.7179*
		Reforming	−0.9191*	−0.5009
		Languishing	−0.2224	0.5500
		All India	−0.6011**	−0.6390***
	Wheat	Functioning	−0.8717**	0.1196
		Reforming	0.8552	−0.0985
		Languishing	−0.6707*	−0.3792
		All India	−0.7720***	−0.0916

Notes:
* represents level of significance; *** significant at 1%, ** significant at 5%, * significant at 10%.

Source: Author's estimate.

purchases of food grain in the functioning, reforming and languishing states for rural and urban households. These are reported in Table 19.7. An analysis of Table 19.7 reveals the following.

The correlation coefficient between per capita (PC) purchases and diversion of PDS grains is negative. Several of these negative coefficients have been estimated to be significant. In the few cases where the correlation coefficient is positive, the relationship is non-significant. Over the period 1999–00 to 2007–08, in general, the relationship between diversions and PC purchases has weakened, though it has remained negative. For urban rice consumers at the all-India level, the negative relationship between diversion and monthly per capita purchase has not only increased but strengthened too. However, for wheat, the relationship is no longer estimated to be significant. It is also interesting to note that for the urban households in functioning states, the inverse relationship between purchase and diversion of PDS rice has remained significant over the period 1999–00 to 2007–08. Since these are primarily rice-consuming states, a closer examination of this is warranted. However, for rural households, the estimated relationship between the two has reduced or weakened (in both value and level of significance).

In the above correlation analysis, the direction of causality remains unknown. However, it is important to know whether higher diversions are due to low per capita monthly purchases or alternatively, are low purchases due to higher diversions. To test for causality between food diversion and food purchase, we run the Granger causality test on our data of 20 Indian states for five rounds of NSS. Our objective here is to gauge

Table 19.8 Granger causality estimates

Null Hypothesis	F statistic	Probability	Number of panel observations
Fp does not Granger cause fd (1 lag)	36.6132*	4.9E-08	80
Fd does not Granger Cause fp (1 lag)	0.70389	0.40408	80
Fp does not Granger cause fd (2 lags)	5.29179*	0.00791	60
Fd does not Granger cause fp (2 lags)	1.44495	0.24457	60

Source: Author's estimates.

whether changes in food diversion (fd) predict changes in food purchase (fp) and/or vice versa. For this, we use the test developed by Hurlin and Venet (2004) that is suitable for testing causality in panel data with a short time-series dimension.[34] The following equations are estimated:

$$fd_{it} = \alpha_i + \sum_{i=1}^{p} \beta_i^k fd_{i,t-k} + \sum_{i=0}^{p} \gamma_i^k fp_{i,t-k} + \varepsilon_{it}$$

$$fp_{it} = \alpha_i + \sum_{i=1}^{p} \beta_i^k fp_{i,t-k} + \sum_{i=0}^{p} \gamma_i^k fd_{i,t-k} + \varepsilon_{it}$$

We test for homogenous non-causality and use both single and double lag estimations. From the results (Table 19.8), it is apparent that the statistic is significant indicating that fp Granger causes fd for both 1 and 2 lags. However, the causality does not run the other way round, implying that fd does not Granger cause fp. This indicates that most FPS owners are likely to divert only that part of food grain that is not purchased by ration cardholders. This implies that diversion is more demand driven (households not lifting entire entitlements) than supply driven (incentives for FPS owners to divert). Not negating Khera's claim that incentive for diversions are high due to low margins, we nevertheless state that this motive may not be paramount.

19.4 PDS AND THE RIGHT TO FOOD IN INDIA

To counter food and hunger issues, the National Advisory Commission in 2011 proposed the National Food Security Bill (NFSB). It is defined as: 'An Act to ensure public provisioning of food and related measures to enable assured economic and social access to adequate food, for all persons in the country, at all times, in pursuance of their fundamental right to live with dignity.' As on 4 July 2013, 'The Bill' has been enacted as an ordinance (referred to as the National Food Security Ordinance, NFSO). This marks a paradigm shift in addressing the problem of food security, from the current welfare approach to a rights-based approach. The Ordinance targets food grain entitlement for up to 75 per cent of the rural population and 50 per cent of urban population. The percentage of eligible households in a particular state is to be determined by the centre and identified by the states. States have been given up to 6 months to identify the beneficiaries. The NFSO proposes 5 kg of subsidized food grain per person per month to eligible households, with the respective prices of rice, wheat and coarse grain not exceeding Rs 3, Rs 2 and Rs 1 per kilogramme.[35] However, the current entitlement of AAY households (the poorest of the poor) will continue at 35 kg of subsidized food grain every month.[36] The NFSO also proposes to take special care of specific groups such as pregnant women and lactating mothers, children between the ages of 6 months and 14 years, malnourished children, disaster-affected persons and destitute, homeless and starving persons.

However, the Ordinance suffers from major operational and financial challenges. Based on analytical and policy issues, we comment upon few contentious issues. For instance, the Ordinance seeks to ensure food security through TPDS, which is already plagued with huge aberrations. Several administrative and logistical challenges associated with TPDS remain un-addressed. To begin, we discuss the targeting errors. The panel's recommendation to demarcate households between 'eligible' and 'non-eligible', while seemingly sound on theoretical grounds remains flawed in practice. It is well documented that targeting remains inherently inefficient. Identification errors plagued by large *errors of exclusion* (of BPL families) and *errors of inclusion* (of APL) remain rampant. With India ranked poorly (95/182) in Transparency International's Corruption Perceptions Index 2011, it is a common fact that even the poor pay a bribe to get a BPL card. It is primarily on these grounds that Himanshu and Sen (2011) consider alternatives that are universal and less targeted. Further, effective targeting in a country where poverty is not static (since few households keep moving in and out of poverty over time) is an added challenge. From a policy perspective, it is important to identify and differentiate between the transient and persistently poor. Monitoring each household on a regular basis is almost impossible. While unique identification may help, by itself it does not ensure effective targeting over time.[37]

Diversion and leakages of food grains is the second issue. Under-purchase by households remains high. The NFSO does not take adequate measures to circumvent this problem. Thus, the proportion of 'diverted' food grains also remains high. Himanshu and Sen (2011) remain emphatic that universal food subsidies would lower both diversions and leakages. However, Gaiha et al. (2013) state that whether or not subsidies reduce leakages to the market has little to do with their being universal and more to do with the wedge between market and PDS prices. If procurements are higher, market price is likely to rise relative to the PDS price, and market diversions are expected to be larger. As far as wastage is concerned, with larger procurements and given storage facilities, wastage is also likely to be larger under a universal scheme.

Expanded budgetary provision is another aspect. According to the government's calculations, the Centre's total food subsidy bill is expected to be Rs 124747 crore[38] in 2013–14, with the additional annual food subsidy burden (over and above the food subsidy under the existing PDS and other welfare schemes) being Rs 23800 crore. However, this concern should not form the thrust of our arguments. Undoubtedly, India's fiscal deficit is high. However, the government needs to work on composition of this deficit rather than its size per se. The indirect benefits that India may reap through better nourished and less hungry population also needs to be accounted for. Improving nutrition contributes to productivity and economic development by improving physical work capacity, cognitive development, school performance and health by reducing disease and mortality. The economic costs of malnutrition are estimated to be high. This makes government intervention more an issue of *desirability* and *priority* rather than *fiscal feasibility*. Fully appreciating that *food security* and *nutrition security* do not have a one-to-one correspondence, we nevertheless argue that to the extent food subsidy reduces undernourishment, GDP will increase thereby promoting tax collections to partially finance the additional food subsidy. Reaping such benefits reinforces the need for effective targeting and better distribution network.

The NFSO is also criticized for having a cereal-centric supply-based approach, rather than a demand-based approach. Though cereals are central to the issue of food security, diversifying demand patterns to protein rich items also needs to be appreciated (Gaiha et al., 2013). In this context, it is worth noting that cash transfers might have been a better option. However, the food security ordinance is being operationalized by providing assistance in 'kind', while internationally, conditional cash transfers (CCTs), rather than physical distribution of subsidized food, are being considered a better option.[39] Evidence shows that 'income policy' approach rather than 'price policy' is much more efficient in achieving equity ends and this has been adopted successfully by many countries across the world such as Brazil, Mexico and the Philippines. In this context, Gulati and Saini (2013) state that the policy of cash transfers for 29 schemes – excluding food and fertilizers' subsidy – in select districts from 1 January 2013 and the 'Dilli Annashree Yojana' announced by the Delhi Government are initiatives in the right direction. However, in light of inconclusive theoretical arguments in favour of either type of subsidy provision (cash or kind); we recommend that the decision of the delivery mechanism be left to the states. Since states such as Chhattisgarh and Tamil Nadu have efficient PDS, it does not make sense to dismantle the system and introduce cash subsidies everywhere. While the NFSO may fix the household's food entitlement, the delivery mechanism should be at the discretion of the states.

The rights-based approach requires adequate food supplies with the government at all times. In addition to increasing production of food grain in the country, it also implies additional procurement and stocking of grains, to meet the distributional commitments. With procurement levels already as high as one third of cereal production in states like Punjab and Haryana, additional procurement is likely to not only crowd out private initiative, but the virtual monopsonistic powers of government will also adversely affect the overall efficiency of the system. This would affect production of non-cereals, thereby slowing down the process of overall diversification in agriculture, negating the changing patterns of diet diversification.

Next, we discuss how the 'right to food' for targeted households may affect the non-targeted households through change in open market prices. Understandably, the NFSO aims to protect the poor from the inflationary effect of food prices. However, to the extent that market prices of food grains get impacted due to its implementation, the consequences may be felt even by the non-poor (as well as by the poor, who rely on market purchase to supplement food supplies). With the NFSO passed, market prices of food grains can move in either direction. This is because the demand for food grains by the poor from the open market is likely to shrink with the possibility for market prices to dampen. However, in order to cater to large sections of society, the procurement levels will also increase. With shrinking grain availability in the open market, price dampening is unlikely to take place. In addition, with rising subsidy levels, the inflationary impact of expansionary fiscal policy remains undisputed. To the extent that market prices get impacted because of food security ordinance, inflationary expectations will be modified. The direction though remains ambiguous.

Thus, a strong link exists between implementation of the NFSO and market prices. While a few forces tend to dampen market prices, others work in the opposite direction. Thus, the direction of the impact remains ambiguous, at least on theoretical grounds, thereby necessitating an empirical investigation of the same. This is the subject matter of next section.

19.5 GOVERNMENT'S INTERVENTIONIST POLICIES AND FOOD PRICES: AN ECONOMETRIC ANALYSIS

The continuous rise in the consumer price index (CPI) for agricultural labour (food and all commodities) is shown in Figure 19.4. There are understandable concerns about the effects on India's poor of higher food prices (Saith, 1981; Gaiha, 1995; Sen, 1996; Ravallion, 1998), irrespective of whether this price rise is on account of PDS or otherwise. This is pertinent as the food group even today accounts for substantial weight in the CPI.

Notwithstanding the shortcomings of PDS,[40] our hypothesis is that a programme should be evaluated not just in terms of what it does to the targeted group but also what happens to the non-targeted group. For instance, if PDS has a significant price dampening effect, then the benefits to both the non-poor and the poor would be large. Theoretically, the effect of procurement and distribution policies on market prices is ambiguous (Schiff, 1993). Empirical analysis, on the other hand, at best is not only scant but dated too. Few studies (Dantwala, 1967, 1993; Mellor, 1968; Hayami et al., 1982) have shown that that the two-tier producer and consumer food-pricing policies raise the open market price so much that it ultimately increases the average price received by farmers. They thus argue that farmers gain from such procurement policies, while the non-poor lose. However, Schiff (1993) states that their conclusion is in contradiction

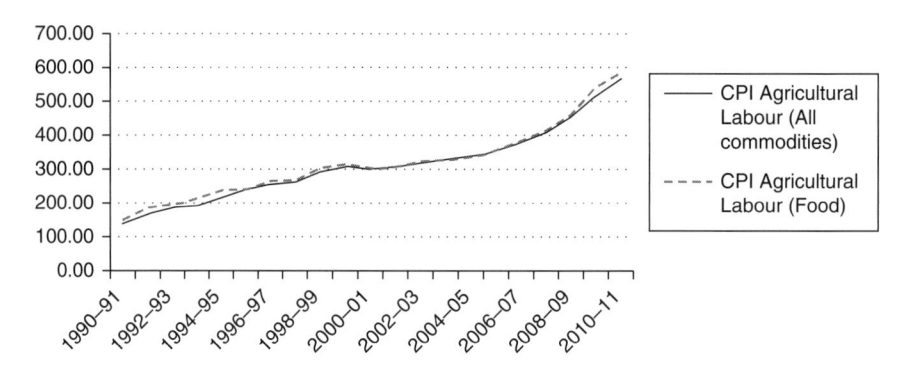

Source: Handbook of Statistics on Indian Economy, Reserve Bank of India.

Figure 19.4 Consumer price index agricultural labour (1990–91 to 2010–11)

with the behaviour of wheat farmers who resist selling their output to the procurement agencies stating low procurement prices and severe restrictions on the selling of wheat to other states. In light of the contradiction, in this section we attempt to empirically analyse the effect of PDS on market prices. To the extent the NFSO is to be implemented via PDS, we believe the results are amenable to extension once the food security ordinance is implemented.

19.5.1 Econometric Analysis

Given the ambiguity regarding market prices and government policies, the present section attempts to analyse the effect of PDS on prices in a macro formulation. In light of existing literature, we have delineated various hypotheses about the plausible factors that could be influencing Indian food price inflation, including distribution of food grain through the PDS. These hypotheses need to be tested with econometric tools to see their statistical significance in explaining Indian inflation.

In the analysis that follows, we consider two dependent variables, i.e. inflation based upon wholesale price index (WPI) and CPI. Additionally, regressions have been run for both *food inflation* and *overall inflation*. Further, the inflation rates are explained through five independent variables that capture both, the domestic and global factors. Changes in prices are expected to depend on factors such as:

Domestic policy variables comprise money supply, gross fiscal deficit of the centre and share of food grains distributed through the PDS. Domestic supply variables comprise share of food production in total agricultural production[41] and global factors as captured by the global food price index. Gulati et al. (2013a) state that Indian agriculture has been gradually integrating with the global agri-markets since the adoption of new economic policies in 1991. They estimated that the agri-trade (exports plus imports) as a percentage of agri-GDP, which was about 5 per cent in 1990–91, increased to three times of that, touching 18 per cent in 2011–12. Thus, it is not wrong to conclude that greater integration with rest of the world (in terms of larger exports and imports of goods and services) also makes the domestic economy more vulnerable to export and import of international price fluctuations. According to Raj et al. (2008), imported price inflation, on an average, accounts for about 1 to 2 percentage points increase in domestic inflation.

Specifically, changes in prices are posited to depend on:

$$\Delta \ln (Price)_t = \alpha + \beta_1 \Delta \ln (M_3)_{t-1} + \beta_2 \ln (Food)_{t-1} + \beta_3 \ln (GFD)_{t-1} + \beta_4 \ln (PDS)_{t-1} + \beta_5 \ln (GFPI)_{t-1} + \beta_6 D_t + \beta_7 T$$

Where:

- 'Price' represents either of the following:
  1. Wholesale price index for food articles (WPI_{FA})
  2. CPI for agricultural labour (CPI_{AL}), or
  3. CPI for industrial worker (CPI_{IW})

- Additionally, regressions have been run for both *food inflation* and *overall inflation*.
- 'M_3' is money supply.

- 'Food' is share of food production in total agricultural output.
- 'PDS' is food grain distributed through the PDS as a percentage of total food grain production (in an alternate specification, this variable has been replaced by 'procurement' as a percentage of total food grain production).
- 'GFD' is the gross fiscal deficit as a proportion of GDP.
- 'GFPI' is the Global Food Price Index.
- 'D' is a dummy variable, taking a value of 1 for post 1997 period – the year in which TDPS was introduced.
- 'T' is time period from 1990 to 2011.
- 't' is time subscript, and the error term is omitted, and
- All variables (except T and the Dummy) are in logarithms.[42]

The data have primarily been collected from various issues of the *Economic Survey*, the *Handbook of Statistics on Indian Economy* (Reserve Bank of India) and FAO's website.

Following a modified version of the specification used by Gaiha (2003), the results based on GLS (Prais–Winsten) formulation[43] are presented in Table 19.9.[44]

Based on our econometric results, following conclusions are warranted:

Table 19.9 *Determinants of inflation, 1990 to 2011 (based on GLS Prais–Winsten)*

	ΔWPI Food Articles	ΔCPI Industrial Workers (Food)	ΔCPI Industrial Workers (Overall)	ΔCPI Agricultural Labour (Food)	ΔCPI Agricultural Labour (Overall)
Δ Ln Broad Money (t-1)	0.00857 (0.02)	0.475 (1.40)	0.315 (1.52)	0.0377 (0.06)	0.466 (1.32)
Ln Food (t-1)	−0.0265 (−0.14)	−0.150 (−0.63)	−0.0146 (−0.10)	−0.0359 (−0.09)	0.00958 (0.05)
Ln GFD (t-1)	0.103** (2.46)	0.0358 (1.28)	0.0510** (3.04)	0.0509 (0.84)	0.0770* (1.90)
Ln PDS (t-1)	−0.0287 (−0.55)	−0.00210 (−0.05)	0.00858 (0.32)	−0.0104 (−0.13)	0.0115 (0.23)
Ln GFPI (t-1)	0.235* (2.10)	0.281** (3.99)	0.214*** (5.05)	0.255 (1.65)	0.184 (1.69)
D	−0.0646 (−1.58)	−0.0214 (−0.87)	−0.00660 (−0.45)	−0.0327 (−0.58)	−0.0392 (−0.99)
t	0.00405 (0.72)	0.000730 (0.15)	−0.00184 (−0.60)	0.00123 (0.13)	−0.000615 (−0.11)
Constant	−0.979	−0.573	−0.990	−0.995	−1.044
Number of Observations	20	20	20	20	20
Adj R^2	0.4212	0.7000	0.7829	0.3487	0.3204

Notes:
t statistics in parentheses. *p, 0.1, **$p < 0.05$, ***$p < 0.01$.
Here PDS is one period lagged value of Log of PDS off-take of rice and wheat as a proportion of total food grain production.

1. PDS and prices:
   - PDS, in general, has a negative (though non-significant) impact on food inflation. The results are robust and remain similar irrespective of whether food inflation based on WPI, CPI_{AL}, or CPI_{IW} is considered.
   - Revamping of the PDS in 1997 also has a similar effect. This is because the coefficient of 'D' is negative and non-significant across specifications.
   - The effect of PDS on overall inflation (both CPI_{AL} and CPI_{IW}) though positive remains non-significant.

2. Food production is estimated to have a negative impact on inflation, though the effect remains non-significant across specifications.
3. Expansionary monetary policy too has been estimated to have a non-significant (though positive) impact on inflation, both for the food group, as well as, for overall grouping. This result reinforces the belief that contractionary monetary policies, as adopted by the RBI (India's Central Bank) in recent months, curtail food inflation (a demand management approach) have been inappropriate measures.
4. Gross fiscal deficit has been estimated to increase inflation significantly, especially *overall* inflation for both industrial workers, as well as, agricultural workers. However, its impact on *food* inflation, though positive, remains non-significant for both classes of workers (industrial and agricultural). Interestingly, expansionary fiscal policies have been estimated to have maximum impact on 'food article' inflation based upon WPI.
5. Global food price index has been estimated to have a positive and significant impact on 'food article' inflation based on WPI. Similarly, it also impacts inflation based upon CPI positively and significantly for industrial workers (both food and overall). However, its impact on inflation for agricultural workers though positive, is non-significant.
6. Empirical results show that the five variables together explain more than 70 per cent of the variation in inflation based on CPI for industrial workers (both food and overall). However, the overall degree of variation explained by these factors for inflation based on CPI_{AL} and WPI_{FA} remains lower.

To conclude, our results indicate that PDS off-take (or procurement as a percentage of food grain production[45]) does not impact inflation. Thus, it may be stated that increase in PDS off-take, on account of implementation of NFSO is unlikely to affect India's inflation. Results also indicate that food production has no significant impact on food inflation. This makes us understand that it is the inadequacy of food supplies in the market (say, on account of inadequate infrastructure, inadequate storage facilities and poor supply-chain management) rather than inadequacy of food grain production per se that may have influenced food inflation. These supply bottlenecks do not allow the economy to store and distribute the produce at the desired pace. As a consequence, supply to the market place falls short of demand, resulting in higher inflation. Therefore, it is important that steps are taken at the policy level to remove impediments on such supply side constraints. Following Reddy (2013), there are primarily three types of supply reasons causing inflation and each needs an appropriate policy action. One is a *supply shock*, which is like an exogenous factor, not permanent in nature; the second is a *supply bottleneck*, which is endogenous to a system and can be addressed by catering to the supply-side logistics and other support mechanisms; and the third is *supply inelasticity*, which requires substantial investments. Thus, structural bottlenecks need to be tackled in the economy as a long-term solution to control food inflation. Controlling fuel price remains an added challenge. Our results also corroborate the view that Indian food inflation is not insulated to changes in the global food markets. To the extent that this inflation is imported, Indian policy makers have less control of it. The only way to negate its adverse effects, especially in the short run, is by adopting effective safety net programmes, such as, distribution of food grain through PDS and providing employment opportunities through programmes such as MNREGA.[46]

19.6 CONCLUSION AND POLICY IMPLICATION

To put the analysis in perspective, few basic conclusions emerge. First, the state of food security in South Asia is rather poor. It is the second most undernourished, malnourished and food-insecure region in the world. Amongst affordability, availability and utilization, the region is most insecure in terms of affordability. Second, in terms of coverage and depth of food safety nets, Nepal, Pakistan and Myanmar rank lowest. Even Bangladesh and Sri Lanka have only moderate prevalence and depth of food safety net programmes. Third, South Asia fairs poorly in meeting its obligations towards WFS and MDGs. In fact, Pakistan has made no progress until now in meeting its commitments towards either of the two. Fourth, South Asia is the most vulnerable region to increasing food inflation, given its relatively higher proportion of food in the consumption basket. Within South Asia, India and Bangladesh are most affected by food price increase.

Such a pessimistic food-security scenario reinforces the need for strong government support in the form of subsidies, despite its shortcomings that undermine their effectiveness. The present study, in addition to analysing several dimensions of a food subsidy programme in India (namely, the PDS), tests a specific hypothesis, i.e. whether PDS has a significant price dampening effect. Using data from 1990 to 2011, our econometric analysis suggests that share of PDS in food availability, as also the revamping of PDS in 1997, has had no significant price dampening effect. Results also indicate that inflation in India is driven more by external than domestic factors. Within domestic factors, supply side infrastructural bottlenecks, as opposed to food production, drive prices more than excess demand. Therefore, it is recommended that appropriate action be taken on priority basis to address supply side concerns.

We now ask, would the situation of food insecurity in South Asia be any different if every individual had the right to food? The responsibility for the implementation of the right to food rests mainly with the national authorities. In recognition of this responsibility, many countries have enshrined the right to adequate food in their national constitutions. Several developing countries have either adopted or are in the process of adopting a framework law on providing food security to its residents. However, it is disappointing that barring India, no other South Asian country is even proposing to implement it in the near future.[47] As the issue of right to food has figured prominently in the context of food-policy reforms in India, we carried out a critical review of the NFSO as an illustrative case study. It is, we believe, amenable to extension to other developing countries

Food entitlements, subsidies and right to food in South Asia 509

where the state is directly involved in providing food to the poor and vulnerable. Several issues relate to India's food security ordinance. Amongst others, the chapter reviewed apprehensions related to its operational and financial challenges, targeting concerns, and its likely impact on food inflation. Providing such a security cover, though laudable, awaits testing

On an alternate note, economic arguments aside, the political dividend that the governments in South Asia and elsewhere could reap, makes the case for right to food strong. If schemes such as *loan waivers* (as in India) have made political sense (with no economic sense), then why not schemes likely to promote *hunger waiver*? Undoubtedly, effective enforcement and implementation of the 'right-based approach' to food security, will supplement political dividends with economic gains.

NOTES

1. However, few economists have argued that the real price of food has not gone up by as much. Nevertheless, the fact that several of these economies continue to spend a large part of their income on food, the impact of rising food prices on food security remains relevant. For instance, as per NSSO 2009–10, though the share of expenditure on food in India has declined, the fact remains that these proportions continue to remain high (48.6 per cent in rural India and 38.5 per cent in urban India).
2. The Global Food Security Index (GFSI) is a comprehensive assessment of the drivers of food security. The index analyses the issue across three internationally designated dimensions: affordability, availability and utilization – the last of which the Economist Intelligence Unit calls 'quality and safety'. The three issues of food security are addressed for a set of 105 countries, constructed from 25 unique indicators. It is a dynamic, qualitative and quantitative benchmarking model, which adjusts for the monthly impact of global food prices. Three category scores are calculated from the weighted mean of underlying indicators and scaled from 0 to 100, where 100 represents most favourable. The overall score for the GFSI (from 0 to 100) is calculated from a simple weighted average of the category and indicator scores. The category weights are: 40 per cent, 44 per cent and 16 per cent respectively for affordability, availability, and quality and safety. The indicator scores are normalized and then aggregated across categories to enable a comparison of broader concepts across countries. The indicators where a higher value indicates a more favourable environment for food security, such as gross domestic product per capita or average food supply, have been normalized on the basis of:

$$x = (x - \text{Min}(x)) / (\text{Max}(x) - \text{Min}(x))$$

  Where $\text{Min}(x)$ and $\text{Max}(x)$ are respectively, the lowest and highest values, in the 105 economies for any given indicator. The normalized value is then transformed from a 0–1 value to a 0–100 score to make it directly comparable with other indicators. Data for the quantitative indicators are drawn from national and international statistical sources. However, some qualitative indicators have been created by the EIU specifically for this index, based on information from development banks, government websites, and range of surveys.
3. SPI is an indicator that divides total expenditures on social protection by the total number of intended beneficiaries of all social protection programmes. For assessment and comparison purposes, this ratio of expenditures to beneficiaries is compared with poverty-line expenditures. The SPI of each country can be expressed as: [Total Social Protection Expenditures/Total Intended Beneficiaries] *divided by* [0.25 (GDP/Total Population)]. Hence, if the SPI were 0.100 in country X, this index number would mean that total social protection expenditures (per intended beneficiary) represents 10 per cent of poverty-line expenditure. The higher this index, the better a country's performance.
4. For purposes of consistency, each country's poverty-line expenditures are set at one quarter of its gross domestic product (GDP) per capita. Because of this stipulation, the SPI can also be expressed directly as a percentage of GDP per capita. For example, South Asia's SPI of 0.061 would be equivalent to 1.5 per cent of its GDP per capita.
5. Depth means the average size of benefits received by actual beneficiaries, and breadth means the proportion of intended beneficiaries who actually receive benefits.
6. Presence of food safety net programmes is a qualitative indicator that measures public initiatives to

protect the poor from food-related shocks. This indicator considers food safety net programmes, including in-kind food transfers, conditional cash transfers (i.e. food vouchers), and the existence of school feeding programmes by the government, NGOs (nongovernmental agencies) or multilateral sectors. It takes a value between 0 and 4.
7. The hunger index is derived from estimates and indexing of indicators such as proportion of undernourished, prevalence of underweight in child under five years, and mortality.
8. World Food Summit goal: halve, between 1990–92 and 2015, the number of undernourished people.
9. Millennium Development Goal 1, target 1C: halve, between 1990 and 2015, the proportion of people who suffer from hunger.
10. But welfarist theory also recognizes that what governments can achieve is limited by information and administrative constraints, both of which must be understood in order to determine whether and how to intervene. For example, where firms or individuals have more information on the costs and benefits of their decisions, the theory suggests that decentralized market-based instruments are preferable.
11. It is also important to recognize that equity–efficiency trade-offs are not always present. Where market failures are more pervasive among the poor (for example, where the poor are poor because they are disproportionately affected by market failures), 'win–win' possibilities arise, where government intervention leads to both a more efficient and a more equitable allocation of resources. Poverty itself may be the source of the market failure, for example, where lack of access to credit and the absence of savings prevent poor households from accumulating income-generating assets. In this case, the poor are caught in a 'poverty trap' that gives rise to persistent poverty. Strategies for alleviating poverty that address both the market failure and the resource constraint dimensions of persistent poverty may thus give rise to a self-reinforcing 'virtuous cycle' whereby public policy enables the poor to pull themselves out of poverty through their own actions (Hoff, 1996; Banerjee and Somanathan, 2001; Ravallion, 2002).
12. Also, note that under both of the social justice approaches considered, the exact form of action required is still an open question and, from this perspective, the insights from the welfarist approach may, therefore, still be valid.
13. For a detailed exposition on the efficiency and welfare effects of consumer subsidies, refer to Gaiha (1993).
14. His theory was based upon observing behaviour of Russian peasants.
15. At the intersection of the curves of marginal utility of labour and marginal disutility of effort.
16. Dasgupta and Ray (1987) argue that undernutrition rations out sections from participating in rural labour markets when wages are efficiency wages.
17. Pacek and Radcliff (2008); Alvarez Diaz et al. (2010).
18. US$1 equals Rupees 60, approximately.
19. Many also believe that the poor were better served by the universal programme (Swaminathan, 2000, 2001; Drèze, 2001; Bunsha, 2002).
20. This holds irrespective of household size, education level, size of land-holding, social group, transaction costs and poverty status.
21. The Copenhagen Consensus exercise started as a simple idea of prioritizing global opportunities. The Copenhagen Consensus Center (CCC) is a think-tank that publicizes the best ways for governments and philanthropists to spend aid and development money. Similar to the Olympics, the exercise is conducted every four years, starting in 2004.
22. Countries with a GDP > US$15 000 are assumed to be free of vitamin A deficiency.
23. BPL households are entitled to purchase rice from fair price shops (FPS) for Rs 5.65 per kg and wheat for Rs 4.15.
24. Under AAY, the poorest of the poor are given the option to buy food at even more subsidized prices. The prices for AAY households are Rs 3 per kg of rice and Rs 2 per kg of wheat, respectively.
25. The low estimated elasticity of caloric intake with respect to food subsidies provides support for the hypothesis that a substantial improvement in nutrition may not be possible with a universal programme. These estimates, therefore, provide theoretical support for targeted programmes, which use available government funds to provide substantial transfers to poor households only.
26. Indeed, the discrepancy between intended and actual benefits under the TPDS exceeds that under the PDS. To explain this, the author suggests that the quantity of PDS food grains provided to BPL households, and hence their take-up rates, will vary positively with the value of the programme to the non-poor, reducing the effectiveness of targeted poverty programmes that limit benefits to the non-poor.
However, Gaiha et al. found that TPDS significantly increased the intake of protein, carbohydrates, calories, phosphorous, iron, thiamine and niacin in AP, Maharashtra and Rajasthan.
27. One rupee equals 100 paise. Average current exchange rate is US$1 = 60 Rupees. Thus 7 paise equals US$0.001.
28. US$0.032 at an average current exchange rate of US$1 = 60 Rupees.
29. US$0.075 at an average current exchange rate of US$1 = 60 Rupees.

30. On 10 January 2013, Justice D. P. Wadhwa Committee (formed by the Supreme Court of India) said there is undoubtedly a nexus between the FPS owners, transporters, bureaucrats and politicians.
31. Per capita purchase of PDS grain has been greater than 1 kg/month throughout the period 1999–2000 to 2007–08 and has improved over time. These states are primarily rice-consuming states (South: Andhra Pradesh, Karnataka, Kerala and Tamil Nadu; West: Maharashtra; North: Jammu and Kashmir and Himachal Pradesh).
32. Per capita purchases were roughly 1 kg/month at the beginning of the period, i.e. 1999–2000, but have risen since then (North: Uttar Pradesh and Uttarakhand; Central India: Chhattisgarh and Madhya Pradesh; East: Orissa).
33. Per capita purchases have remained below 1 kg/month over the period 1999–2000 to 2007–08 (North: Haryana, Punjab, Rajasthan; East: Assam, Bihar, Jharkhand and West Bengal; West: Gujarat).
34. The autoregressive coefficients β_i^k are assumed constant along with the regression coefficients γ_i^k.
35. US$0.05, US$0.033 and US$0.016 per kilogramme, respectively (at an average current exchange rate of US$1 = 60 Rupees).
36. The right, however, cannot be claimed if supply is affected by war or natural calamities.
37. Also, unique identification does not help as it is only biometric with no information on socioeconomic status.
38. One Crore equals 10 million.
39. It is, however, debatable (Basu, 2011; Ghosh, 2011; Himanshu, 2011; Kapur, 2011; Kotwal et al., 2011) whether cash transfers should replace the public provision of essential goods and services. Also, the question still remains – who will receive the cash transfers? Unique identification is also unlikely to help here as it is only biometric with no information on socioeconomic status.
40. On 16 September 2007 food riots occurred in West Bengal in India over a shortage of food and widespread corruption in the PDS. The riots initially occurred in Burdwan, Bankura and Birbhum, but later spread to other districts. Police shot and killed three villagers during the riots and more than 300 villagers were injured. At least three ration distributors committed suicide. The state government took damage-control measures, suspended 113 dealers, and served show-cause notices to 37 food inspectors.
41. Effect of rainfall deviation (from the long period average rainfall) on foodgrain production (including droughts) is partially captured by using this variable. However, study by Gulati et al. (2013b) found rainfall deviations to have no significant effect on food price index for the period analysed by them.
42. In order to take care of the problem of endogeneity, an extended formulation would have been desirable. However, to some extent this problem has been overcome (though not eliminated) by using the lagged values for RHS variables.
43. Between the Cochrane–Orcutt and Prais–Winsten estimators, the latter is preferred since loss of efficiency in discarding the initial observation in the former can be substantial.
44. Time series observations not being very large, stationarity tests were not conducted.
45. Results for 'procurement' available on request
46. However, Gulati and Saini (2013) have statistically shown that rising farm wages especially on account of MNREGA have contributed majorly to inflation.
47. As of 2011, only ten countries had adopted a framework law on food security or the right to food (Argentina, Bolivia, Brazil, Ecuador, El Salvador, Guatemala, Indonesia, Nicaragua, Peru and Venezuela), while nine countries were drafting a framework law on food security or the right to food (Honduras, India (Food Security Ordinance Passed in July, 2013), Malawi, Mexico, Mozambique, Paraguay, South Africa, Tanzania and Uganda). Additionally, three countries (El Salvador, Nicaragua and Peru) were drafting to update, replace or strengthen their framework law. Each country has adopted 'Right to Food' differently: by framework law, through constitutional means, for example explicitly as a right, implicit or as directive principle, or simply through international law

REFERENCES

ADB (2011), *Global Food Price Inflation and Developing Asia*. Manila: Asian Development Bank.
ADB (2012), Food Price Escalation in South Asia-A Serious and Growing Concern. South Asia Working Paper Series No. 10, February 2012.
ADB (2013), *Social Protection Index: Assessing Results for Asia and the Pacific*. Manila: Asian Development Bank.
Alderman, H. (2005), Linkages between poverty reduction strategies and child nutrition: an Asian perspective. *Economic and Political Weekly*, November 12, 4837–4842.

Alvarez-Diaz, A., L. Gonzalez and B. Radcliff (2010), The politics of happiness: on the political determinants of quality of life in the American states. *The Journal of Politics*, **72**(3), 894–905.

Banerjee, A. and R. Somanathan (2001), Caste, community and collective action: the political economy of public good provision in India. Available at: http://time.dufe.edu.cn/wencong/banerjee/download19.pdf.

Basu, K. (2011), India's foodgrain policy: an economic theory perspective. *Economic & Political Weekly*, EPW January 29, **xlvi**, 5.

Behrman, J., H. Alderman, and J. Hoddinott (2004). Hunger and malnutrition. In B. Lomborg (ed.), *Global Crises, Global Solutions*. Cambridge, UK: Cambridge University Press, pp. 363–420.

Bhattacharyya, D. and K. Rana (2008), Politics of PDS ANGER in West Bengal. *Economic and Political Weekly*, 2 February 2008.

Bliss, C. and N. Stern (1978) Productivity, wages and nutrition. Part I: the theory. *Journal of Development Economics*, **5**(2) 331–62.

Bunsha, D. (2002), The human face of adjustment. *Frontline*, **19**(1), 5–18.

Čajanov A.V, D. Thorner, B.H. Kerblay and R.E.F. Smith (1966), *The Theory of Peasant Economy*. Manchester, UK: Manchester University Press.

Dantwala, M.L. (1967), Incentives and disincentives in Indian agriculture. *Indian Journal of Agricultural Economics*, **22**, 1–25.

Dantwala, M.L. (1993), Agricultural policy: prices and public distribution system. A review. *Indian Journal of Agricultural Economics*, **48**, 173–86.

Dasgupta, P. and D. Ray (1987), Inequality as a determinant of malnutrition and unemployment: policy. *Economic Journal*, **97**, 177–88.

Drèze, J. (2001), Right to food and public accountability. *The Hindu*, 5 December 2001.

FAO (2011), *The State of Food Insecurity in the World 2010: How Does International Price Volatility Affect Domestic Economies and Food Security?* Rome: FAO.

Gaiha, R. (1993), Design of poverty alleviation strategy in rural areas. FAO Economic and Social Development Paper 115, Rome.

Gaiha, R. (1995), Does agricultural growth matter to poverty alleviation? *Development and Change*, **26**(2), 285–304.

Gaiha, R. (2003), Does the right to food matter? *Economic and Political Weekly*, 4 October 2003.

Gaiha, R., R. Jha, V. Kulkarni and N. Kaicker (2013), Diets, nutrition and poverty in India. In R. J. Herring (ed.), *Handbook on Food, Politics and Society*. New York: Oxford University Press.

GFSI (2012), Global Food Security Index. The Economist Intelligence Unit.

Ghosh J. (2011), Cash transfers as the silver bullet for poverty reduction: a sceptical note. *Economic and Political Weekly*, **XLVI**, No. 21.

Global Hunger Index (2010), *The Challenge of Hunger: Focus on the Crisis of Child Undernutrition*. Washington DC: International Food Policy Research Institute.

Gulati, A. and S. Saini (2013), Taming food inflation in India. Discussion Paper No. 4, Commission for Agricultural Costs and Prices, Department of Agriculture and Cooperation, Ministry of Agriculture, Government of India, New Delhi.

Gulati A., S. Jain and A. Hoda (2013a), Farm trade tapping the hidden potential. Discussion Paper No. 3. Commission for Agricultural Costs and Prices, Department of Agriculture and Cooperation, Ministry of Agriculture, Government of India, New Delhi.

Gulati A., S. Jain and N. Satija (2013b), Rising Farm Wages in India – the pull and the push factors. Discussion Paper No. 5, Commission for Agricultural Costs and Prices, Department of Agriculture and Cooperation, Ministry of Agriculture, Government of India, New Delhi.

Hayami, Y., K. Subbarao and K. Otsuka. (1982), Efficiency and equity in the producer levy in India. *American Journal of Agricultural Economics*, **64**(4), 654–63.

Headey, D. and S. Fan (2010), Reflections on the global food crisis: how did it happen? How has it hurt? And how can we prevent the next one?. IFPRI Research Monograph 165, Washington DC.

Himanshu (2011), A flawed approach to food security. *Live Mint*, 19 January.

Himanshu and A. Sen (2011), Why not a universal food security legislation? *Economic and Political Weekly*, **46**(12), 19 March.

HLPE (2011), Price volatility and food security. A report by the High Level Panel of Experts on Food Security and Nutrition of the Committee on World Food Security, Rome, 2011.

Hoddinott J., M. Rosegrant and M. Torero (2012), Investments to reduce hunger and undernutrition. Copenhagen Consensus 2012 Challenge Paper, Copenhagen Consensus Center, Copenhagen.

Hoff, K. (1996), Market failures and the distribution of wealth: a perspective from the economics of information. *Politics and Society*, **24**(4), 411–32.

Horton, S., H. Alderman and J. Rivera (2008), Hunger and malnutrition. Copenhagen Consensus 2008 Challenge Paper, Copenhagen Consensus Center, Copenhagen.

Hurlin, C. and B. Venet (2004), Granger causality tests in panel data models with fixed coefficients. Working Paper Eurisco 2001–09, University of Paris Dauphine.
IFAD (2013), *Agriculture-Pathways to Prosperity in Asia and the Pacific*. Asia and the Pacific Division, Occasional Papers 17, Rome.
Imai, K.S., R. Gaiha and G. Thapa (2011), Supply response to changes in agricultural commodity prices in Asian countries. *Journal of Asian Economics*, **22**(1), 61–75.
Ivanic, M., W. Martin and H. Zaman (2011), Estimating the short-run poverty impacts of the 2010–11 surge in food prices. World Bank Policy Research Working Paper Series, 5366.
Jensen, R.T. and N.H. Miller (2011), Do consumer price subsidies really improve nutrition? *The Review of Economics and Statistics*, **93**(4), 1205–1223.
Jha, S. and P.V. Srinivasan (2001), Taking the PDS to the poor: directions for further reform. *Economic and Political Weekly*, September 29.
Jha, R., K.V.B. Murthy, H.K. Nagarajan and Ashok Seth (1999), Real consumption levels and public distribution in India. *Economic and Political Weekly*, 10 April.
Jha, R., R. Gaiha, M. Pandey and N. Kaicker (2013a), Food subsidy, income transfer and the poor: a comparative analysis of the public distribution system in India's states. *Journal of Policy Modeling* (in press).
Jha, R., R. Gaiha and M. Pandey (2013b), Body mass index, participation, duration of work and earnings under the National Rural Employment Guarantee Scheme: evidence from Rajasthan. *Journal of Asian Economics*, **26**(2013), 14–30.
Jha, R., S. Kaur, R. Gaiha and M. Pandey (2013c), National Rural Employment Guarantee Scheme and Targeted Public Distribution Scheme in Rajasthan and Madhya Pradesh: complements or substitutes? *Journal of Asian and African Studies* (in press).
Joshi P.K., A. Gulati and R. Cummings (eds) (2007), *Agricultural Diversification and Smallholders in South Asia*. New Delhi, India: Academic Foundation.
Kapur, D. (2011), The shift to cash transfers: running better but on the wrong road. *Economic and Political Weekly*, 21 May, **XLVI**, 21.
Kaur, S. (2007), Economic freedom, inequality and poverty: re-examining the role of government. *Indian Economic Journal*, 55(2), July–September.
Kaur, S. (2009), Economic freedom, larger freedoms and public policy. The forum of public policy, *Journal of the Oxford Round Table*. Available at: http://forumonpublicpolicy.com/archivespring08/kaur.pdf.
Khera, R. (2008), Access to the Targeted Public Distribution System: a case study in Rajasthan. *Economic and Political Weekly*, November 1.
Khera, R. (2011), India's Public Distribution System: utilisation and impact. *Journal of Development Studies*, **47**(3), 1–23.
Kochar, A. (2005), Can targeted foodgrain programs improve nutrition? An empirical analysis of India's Public Distribution System. *Economic Development and Cultural Change*, **54**, 203–35.
Kotwal, A, M. Murukar and B. Ramaswami (2011), PDS Forever? *Economic and Political Weekly*, May 21, **XLVI**, 21.
Kumar, P. (2010), *Targeted Public Distribution System: Performance and Inefficiencies*. Delhi: Academic Foundation and NCAER.
Leibenstein, H. (1957), *Economic Backwardness and Economic Growth: Studies In the Theory of Economic Development*. New York: Wiley and Sons.
Mellor, J.W. (1968), Functions of agricultural prices in economic development. *Indian Journal of Agricultural Economics*, **23**, 23–37.
Mirrlees, J.A. (1975), A pure theory of underdeveloped economies. In L. Reynolds (ed.), *Agriculture in Development Theory*. New Haven, CT: Yale University Press, pp. 84–108.
Pacek, A. and B.F. Radcliff (2008), Assessing the welfare state: the politics of happiness. *Perspectives on Politics*, **6**, 267–77.
Planning Commission (2008), *Eleventh Five-Year Plan*, New Delhi.
Radhakrishna R., K. Subba Rao, S. Indrakant and C. Ravi (1997), India's Public Distribution System: a national and international perspective. World Bank Discussion Paper No. 380, World Bank, Washington DC.
Raj, J., S. Dhal and R. Jain (2008), Imported inflation: the evidence from India. Reserve Bank of India Occasional Papers Vol. 29, No. 3, Winter 2008.
Ravallion, M. (1998), Poverty lines in theory and practice, living standards measurement study. Working Paper 133. World Bank, Washington DC.
Ravallion, M. (2002), On the urbanization of poverty. *Journal of Development Economics*, **68**(2), 435–42.
Ray, D. (2004), *Development Economics*. New Delhi: Oxford University Press.
Reddy, Y.V. (2013), *Economic Policies and India's Reform Agenda: A New Thinking*. Himayatnagar, India: Orient Blackswan.

Sahn, D.E. and H. Alderman (1996), The effect of food subsidies on labour supply in Sri Lanka. *Economic Development and Cultural Change*, **45**(1), 125–45.
Saith, A. (1981), Production, prices, and poverty in rural India. *Journal of Development Studies*, **19**(2) 196–214.
Schiff, M. (1993), The impact of two-tier producer and consumer food pricing in India. Working Paper Series, WPS1236.
Sen, A. (1992), *Inequality Re-examined*. Oxford: Clarendon Press.
Sen, A. (1996), Economic reforms, employment, and poverty: trends and options. *Economic and Political Weekly*, **31** (September), 2459–2478.
Sen, A. (2000), *Development as Freedom*. Oxford University Press.
Stiglitz, J.E. (1976), The efficiency wage hypothesis, surplus labour, and the distribution of incomes in LDCs. Oxford Economic Papers, 28.
Svedberg, P. (2012), Reforming or replacing the public distribution system with cash transfers? *Economic and Political Weekly*, **18**(7), 53–62.
Swaminathan, M. (2000), *Weakening Welfare: The Public Distribution of Food in India*. New Delhi: LeftWord Books.
Swaminathan, M. (2001), A further attack on the PDS. *Frontline*, **18**(2), 20 January–2 February.
Transparency International (2011), Corruption Perceptions Index 2011. Available at: http://www.transparency.org/cpi2011.
UNICEF (2004), Vitamin and mineral deficiency, global damage assessment report (2004). The Micronutrient Initiative and UNICEF.
United Nations (2003), *Human Security Now, Commission on Human Security*. New York: United Nations.
United Nations (2005), *In Larger Freedom: Towards Development, Security and Human Rights for All*. New York: United Nations.
von Grebmer, K., H. Fritschel, B. Nestorova, T. Olofnbiyi, R. Pandya-Lorch and Y. Yohannes (2010), Global Hunger Index Report, 2010. Welthungerhilfe, International Food Policy Research Institute, and Concern, Bonn, Washington DC and Dublin.
Willenbockel, D. (2011), Exploring food price scenarios towards 2030 with a global mutliregional model. Oxfam Research Reports. Available at: http:// http://www.oxfam.org/sites/www.oxfam.org/files/rr-exploring-food-price-scenarios-010611-en.pdf.
World Bank (2010), *Food Price Increases in South Asia: National Responses and Regional Dimensions*. Washington DC: World Bank.
World Bank (2013), South Asia Regional Brief, 17 April. Available at: http://www.worldbank.org/en/news/feature/2013/04/17/south-asia-regional-brief (accessed 25 June 2013).
Zhou, Z.Y., X.A. Liu and N. Perera N. (2001), Nutritional poverty and the role of PDS in India: an inter-state analyses. In S.S. Acharya and D.P. Chaudhri (eds), *Indian Agricultural Policy at the Crossroads*. New Delhi: Rawat Publications, pp. 515–69.

20. Global middle class and dietary patterns: a sociological perspective
Vani S. Kulkarni

20.1 INTRODUCTION

The phenomenon of dietary consumption patterns among the middle class constitute three key elements: class, middleclassness and eating or dietary consumption. In analysing the dietary consumption patterns, the present chapter, therefore, explores the relationship among these elements.

Eating has two major aspects – scientific/medical and social. Concerns with nutrients/nutrition and health status constitute the scientific dimension but there is also a social element associated with it. Class is one such key social element. The class phenomenon, however, for most part represented a limited social element as it focused dominantly on the economic aspect. This is because historically, class as a theoretical category, has been studied from two key perspectives, Marxian and Weberian, both of which emphasize the importance of market capacities in shaping life chances and the relationship to the means of production. These theories of social class have been influential perspectives on the middle class. Lately, class itself is being defined in non-economic terms, thus expanding not only the meaning of class but thereby also the implications of class for everyday life of populations. The non-economic dimension has given rise to what is called the *new middle class*. This is defined in ways beyond economic and includes issues of politics and lifestyles and consumption. Consumption of food and dietary patterns is one important aspect of the middle class that has gained increased attention in the past few years. Shifts in food preference, consumption and dietary patterns among middle classes have been quite dramatic so much so that the meaning of middleclassness is traced through the *ontology of diet consumption*.

Although consumption patterns, including dietary consumption patterns, are a reflection of life styles and perceptions, and a certain habitus (Bourdieu, 1984[1979], 1990[1980]; Wacquant, 2004), like the class phenomenon, dietary consumption among middle classes is also dominantly analysed in terms of the scientific model and the economic perspective. Economic affluence and implications for nutrition are certainly important drivers of dietary consumption pattern, and hence necessary to analyse. Nevertheless, these analyses are not *sufficient* to gain a comprehensive understanding of diet behavior of the middle class. This is because the consumption patterns of middle classes are embedded within a much broader social context that influence dietary consumptions and are influenced by it. As dietary patterns become increasingly diversified and size and nature of the middle class becomes ever more heterogeneous, a more detailed inquiry is necessary into the relationship between dietary patterns of the middle class and the economic, social and cultural processes. This chapter is just such an enquiry. It underscores that the economic conditions and nutrition concerns represent the husk of dietary choices of the middle class, not the kernel. The latter constitutes the informal, unofficial and nuanced social, psychological and cultural processes embedded in the dietary consumption patterns. It includes the phenomenon of symbolized identities, psychological and emotional conditions, memories, historical traditions and 'the local configuration of social relations which comprise social structures such as class, race, and gender; institutional practices, collective and individual behaviour, and intersecting personal biographies' (Poland et al., 2006: 60). It also emphasizes why and how the various aspects of dietary patterns of the middle class are relationally connected. The chapter, therefore, proposes a sociological approach to the study of dietary consumption patterns of the middle class.

It is important here to clarify that there is good amount of research that focuses on various domains of the middle-class practices, such as economic, political, social, cultural and religious, arguing how these are transformed and transform the middle class experience. In this analysis, the consumption patterns, including diets, form the economic and more materialistic, commodity-centered, public dimension. Although consumption patterns, including dietary consumption and middle-class phenomenon, are intrinsically related, there is a distinction to be made between multidimensionality of the middle-class practices, on the one hand, and multidimensionality of dietary consumption pattern itself, on the other. In middle-class studies, consumption patterns are but one domain – the materialistic and economic domain of middle-class characteristics, whereas in consumption studies, the multidimensionality is explored by asking the following question: how the largely analysed commodity-centered consumption itself has a political, social, cultural and symbolic meaning? Of course, this distinction constitutes an analytical framework for the study. Empirically, the various dimensions of the middle class are all related and expressed through each other. Thus, although the dietary consumption of the middle class is dominantly analysed in relation to economic affluence or lack of it, the cultural values and political ideologies of the middle class *shape* the eating practice – quantity and quality and make it a non-economic enterprise. Hence, in seeking to answer the question how the largely analysed commodity-centered consumption itself has a political, social, cultural and symbolic meaning, the chapter will bring to light the impact of the relational connection between these various aspects on the middle-class diets. The distinctiveness of the middle class in its dietary patterns is thus rooted in the impact of this relational connection on the dietary consumption.

The chapter is organized around the themes discussed above. It first gives a conceptual overview of the existing literature on middle-class dietary consumption with particular focus on Asia and then offers a sociological perspective to the study of middle class diet consumption by reconceptualizing the role of culture in middle-class dietary patterns in Asia. It begins with discussion of definitions of class, middle classness, size, profile and measurement of the middle class globally and in Asia that the literature records. In the second section, the chapter discusses the consumption behavior of the middle class in Asia and nature of dietary consumption – dietary shifts in Asia with an emphasis on India and Vietnam. Based upon the discussion in the first three sections, the third, and the final section analyses middle-class dietary consumption within a non-economic framework. It is divided into two parts. The first part highlights the significance of sociology of middle-class consumption patterns. The second part titled 'Toward sociology of middle-class dietary consumption' spells out the sociological dimension by reconceptualizing the role of culture and proposing a sociological research agenda for middle-class patterns of dietary consumption that emphasizes the usefulness of the social relational perspective for understanding eating behavior of the middle classes.

20.2 CLASS, MIDDLE CLASS AND MIDDLECLASSNESS

Understanding of the phenomenon of class and class structure is integral to any discussion of the middle class. Theoretically, two perspectives on class have been very influential – neo-Marxist and neo-Weberian. While neo-Marxists see class structure in terms of relationship to the means of production, both these perspectives 'emphasize the importance of market capacities in shaping life chances' (Fitzgerald, 2012). In other words, historically the economic–materialistic dimension has been a key dimension to understanding class and class structure. In this categorization, classes were usually classified into two categories – those who owned the means of production and had access to property and those who did not.

It is important to clarify here that although Marxian analysis of class is attributed to simple polarization of classes – proletariat and bourgeoisie, yet there is clear evidence in the *Communist Manifesto* that both Marx and Engels recognized the salaried groups of managers, overseers and other capitalist functionaries, all of whom belonged to the intermediate class. For Marx, the middle class included horde of flunkeys, soldiers, sailors, police, lower officials as well as ill-paid lawyers, artists and physicians. The reason why the Marxian view of middle class does not have the same significance as his theory of class is because although he recognized the existence of middle, intermediate class, he did not consider them to be economically and politically significant as proletariat and bourgeoisie and, therefore, 'not part of his general model of capitalist society as a class on par with the proletariat or the bourgeoisie' (Burris, 1986: 20).

In addition to these two perspectives, a third influential approach to studying class structure emerged that focused on the role of social reproduction, cultural boundaries and the everyday practices such as tastes, including consumption patterns, skills, expertise and internalized behaviors and values (Bourdieu, 1984 [1979]). These defining features of class relations went beyond the economic dimension and began to be identified with not class structure per se but with middle class structure. The theoretical perspective on the middle class thus speaks to the non-economic and cultural dimension of the class. These dimensions shift the analysis of class from objective category to a subjective category. Conceptually, therefore, middle classes are to be judged by a plurality of criteria. They are as much a product of the internalized values and tastes and subjectivities as they are of objective economic capital and relations of production.

In the history of social thought, whether in politics or literature middle classes have been thought of in terms of ethics and morality. For instance, Aristotle in one of his writings stated,

> The most perfect political community must be amongst those who are in the middle rank, and those states are best instituted wherein these are a larger and more respectable part, if possible, than both the other; or, if that cannot be, at least than either of them separate. (Excerpt from *Politics: A Treatise on Government*)

Similarly, George Bernard Shaw said, 'I have to live for others and not for myself: that's middle-class morality.'

Middle class has also occupied a special place in the history of economic thought especially since the late fourteenth century when the Bourgeoisie class ventured into the capitalist market economy (Kharas, 2010: 7). Toward the early twentieth century, scholars recognized a decay of the middle class or the Marxian intermediate class that consisted of the small merchants and shopkeepers. However, since the late twentieth century, scholars have argued for an emergence of a 'new middle class and uncovered ways in which members of this class differ from other classes in terms of political orientations and activities' (Fitzgerald, 2012). Although there are differences between middle class and new middle class, for the purpose of this chapter, both will be used interchangeably.

In contemporary times, the empirical literature on the middle class addresses, among other issues, the structural forces that shape the emergence of the middle class in different national contexts and how the political, economic, and social trends of the time shape the experiences of the middle class such as increasing their debts and bankruptcies, and downward mobility; the issue of social reproduction – about how values and resources are reduced in middle classes in a way that their advantage (vis-à-vis the working class) is perpetuated through generations (Fitzgerald, 2012).

20.2.1 Middle Class is Defined in Several Different Ways

The simplest and straightforward definition is something that is in the middle. Middle class is a class that is between the classes that have access to valued resources comprising aristocrats, rich bourgeoisie or nobility or upper classes, on the one hand, and those who have very little of these resources including working class, proletariats, peasants and manual laborers, on the other.

'Middle class is a heterogeneous layer, a notoriously elusive category, defined almost by default as what is-in-the-middle, between upper layers of society and the plebian masses' (Jafferlot and van der Veer, 2008: 11).

Middle class formation and identities can be defined along the lines of both objective indicators such as their size, education, occupation, income/wealth, network, power and their relationship to means of production. They can be defined on subjective categories that are not based on economic assets per se but accumulation of social and cultural capital that includes life styles, everyday practices, tastes, perceptions that give birth to middle-class subjectivities.

Middle class is defined in terms of the occupation they are engaged in and the occupation associated with the middle class is that of entrepreneurial activities that is differentiated from feudal economy consisting of the nobility and the peasants (Acemoglu and Zilibotti, 1997).

Another understanding of the middle class is that it contributes to the human capital and saving (Doepke and Zilibotti, 2007) and to growth (Banerjee and Duflo, 2007). Banerjee and Duflo link middle class to democracy and then growth by arguing that middle class contributes to democracy and democracy causes growth and so middle class contributes to growth.

A major characteristic that is now being increasingly associated with the middle class is its consumption patterns – both quantity and quality. This is related to the absolute and relative consumption rates. Hence, middle classes are also defined in absolute and relative terms. The relativity of middle classes makes middle class a heterogeneous class. For instance, middle classes are defined as those classes that fall between the 20th and 80th percentiles of consumption distribution (Birdsall et al., 2000; Easterly, 2000). In contrast, middle classes are also defined in absolute terms where, for instance, they constitute a class which earns more than US$3900 annually in purchasing power parity (Bhalla, 2009).

The other major defining feature of middle class moves beyond economic and income and occupation assets and includes social and cultural capital. Middle classes are defined on the basis of access and achievement of higher, tertiary education, professional jobs including professors, doctors, academics, lawyers, chartered engineers and politicians. They are defined also on the basis of life-style choices, beliefs and values like education, hard work and thrift regardless of their leisure or wealth. Middle classes are also defined on the basis of certain cultural practices like adoption of pop culture, eating culture.

The various definitions point to the fact that middle classes are hard to define, are heterogeneous and not fixed. This then becomes problematic for an empiricist approach to the study of the middle class. Recently, however, consumption patterns have become a principal feature of the middle class. It is the 'new consumerism' that defines the middle class (Schor, 1999). It includes a 'constant, up scaling of lifestyle norms; pervasiveness of conspicuous, status goods and of competition for acquiring them; and the growing disconnect between consumer desires and incomes' (Schor, 1999). Consumption of middle class is also understood what Murphy, Shleifer and Vishny (1989) say as the 'willingness of the middle class consumer to pay a little extra for quality as a force that encourages product differentiation and thereby feeds investment in production and marketing of new goods' (Kharas, 2011: 7).

Two aspects of feature of consumerism of the middle class deserve mention. One, the consumerist dimension of the middle class has been brought to light in a big way in recent years owing to, among other reasons, the conspicuously unique and large consumptions by populations in Asia – particularly India and China. The consumer demand, which has so far been concentrated in the rich economies of the OECD is now being increasingly shifted to Asia and thus contributing to the increasing growth of the middle classes in Asia – especially India and China. It is believed that the new Asian consumerism or the 'shifting wealth' that is emerging is sufficient to replace the forecast shortfalls in the US consumer demand growth . . . and lead to long-term institutional changes' (Kharas, 2011: 8).

Two, an important question in the context of consumption is what exactly are the consumer goods? Among other things, the consumption of food and dietary patterns is one important aspect of consumption by the middle class that has gained increasing attention. Shifts in food preference, consumption and dietary patterns – eating out, ordering in of food among middle classes-have been quite dramatic so much so that the meaning of middleclassness is traced through the *ontology of diet consumption*.

The analysis below, therefore, will focus on the dietary consumption patterns of the middle classes with special focus on Asia. It will first present a few figures and facts of size, measurement of middle classes in Asia, followed by figures and facts of dietary shifts in the Asian context. An explanation and interpretations of the dietary shifts will be the focus of the final section.

20.3 MEASUREMENT OF THE SIZE OF MIDDLE CLASS

There is no unanimity on the measurement criteria and, as illustrated in Table 20.1, the size of the middle class in selected Asian Countries varies with the criterion used.

China has the highest share of the middle class on all criteria except ownership of motor vehicles. On the latter, Indonesia has the highest share. The lowest share of the middle class is in Cambodia, followed by Bangladesh. India, Pakistan and Nepal too have low shares. If we go by mobile cellular subscriptions, the shares are relatively high in: the Philippines (40.66 per cent), China (30.09 per cent), and Indonesia (20.64 per cent). Among South Asian countries, Sri Lanka has the highest share of the middle class if we go by this criterion.

20.3.1 Dietary Shift

Rapid economic growth, urbanization and globalization have resulted in dietary shifts in Asia, away from staples and increasingly towards livestock and dairy products, fruits and vegetables, and fats and oils. Current consumption patterns seem to be converging towards a Western diet (Pingali, 2004, 2006; Popkin et al., 2012).

These dietary changes reflect the interaction of demand and supply factors.

Demand factors include: rapid income growth and urbanization, bringing about new dietary needs; and, more generally, growing affluence and lifestyle changes. Expansion of the middle class, higher participation by women in the workforce, the emergence of nuclear two-income families, and a sharp age divide in food preferences (with younger age groups more susceptible to new foods advertised in the media) underlie the demand.

Table 20.1 Size of middle class in selected Asian countries in 2005

Country/Criterion	Telephone lines (per 100 people)	Internet users (per 100 people)	Motor vehicles (per 1000 people)	Mobile cellular subscriptions (per 100 people)
Bangladesh	0.82	1.80	2.00	6.40
Cambodia	0.27	0.49		7.95
China	27.67	16.04	32.00	30.09
India	3.34	3.95	15.00	7.91
Indonesia	8.40	5.79	70.00	20.64
Nepal	2.47	1.41	5.00	0.83
Pakistan	2.92	6.80	12.00	8.05
Philippines	4.44	5.97	32.00	40.66
Sri Lanka	13.53	3.93	45.00	16.94
Vietnam	13.13	20.95	13.00	11.54

Source: Computed by the author from Economist Intelligence Unit (2012).

As incomes rise, exposure to global 'urban' eating patterns increases. Recent evidence also points to greater reliance of smaller and poorer households on street food. Urban slums often mimic the branded products of fast-food outlets (Pingali, 2004). On the supply side, the main factors associated with availability of food are: closer integration of global economies, severing the link between local production and availability of food; liberalization of foreign direct investment, with a new role for multinational corporations – especially supermarkets and fast-food outlets, and a sharp reduction in freight and transportation costs (Pingali, 2006).

Two illustrative sets of evidence on the food consumption pattern of the middle class (the median group) in India and Vietnam are given below.

India

There was a sharp reduction in cereal consumption between 1993 and 2009 – 15 per cent in rural areas and 12 per cent in urban areas.[1] While the reduction was more drastic in the first period (1993–94 to 2004–05) in rural areas, as compared to the second (2004-05 to 2009–10), in urban areas, the rate of reduction was almost equal in both the periods.[2]

In both rural and urban areas, pulses/nuts/dry fruits recorded a sharp drop between 1993 and 2004. While this group of food commodities continued to decline in urban areas (although at a lesser rate), it increased substantially in the rural areas. The consumption of sugar decreased too, in both the periods and in both the sectors – rural and urban.[3] By contrast, intakes of vanaspati oil rose sharply in both rural and urban areas, especially in the first period. The consumption of milk and milk products increased, and, more substantially, for urban areas (by about 10 per cent between 1993 and 2009), especially in the second period. Intakes of meat/fish/poultry increased slightly in rural areas (by 2 per cent) and declined in urban areas (by 5 per cent) between 1993–2009. Vegetable intakes increased moderately in the first period in both rural and urban areas, but declined by an equal amount in the second, leaving the intakes largely unchanged between 1993 and 2009. Fruit consumption increased substantially in the urban areas, especially in the second period. There are marked differences in the intakes of various food commodities among various income classes too, as illustrated below in Table 20.2.

If we compare changes in consumption of various food commodities between the 20th percentile and median households, we find that the consumption of cereals was higher by 7.87 per cent among the former relative to the 20th percentile; that of milk and milk products was higher by 126 per cent; that of vanaspati oil by 30.71 per cent; of sugar by 42.6 per cent; of poultry, fish and meat by 47.45 per cent; and finally of fruits by 64.47 per cent. In brief, the shares of most non-cereal commodities in the consumption basket of the median households were considerably higher than those of the 20th percentile.

A similar pattern is observed in urban India in 2009. Cereal consumption was higher among median households by 4.58 per cent relative to the 20th percentile; milk and milk products' consumption was higher by 76.06 per cent; of vegetable oil by 32 per cent; of sugar by 30.19 per cent; of meat by 34 per cent; and finally of fruits by 82.25 per cent. So in urban India too, the middle class had a significant role in shaping food consumption behavior (Table 20.2).

Table 20.2 Per capita consumption of food commodities (g), 2009–10 by decile of monthly per capita expenditure

Deciles of MPCE	Cereals	Milk Products Ghee/ Butter	Vanaspati- Oil	Sugar	Eggs	Meat/ Fish/ Poultry	Pulses/ Nuts/ Dry Fruits	Fruits	Vegetables
Rural India									
1	339.1	25.4	11.2	10.9	0.7	4.0	14.4	4.5	110.6
2	354.1	41.4	14.0	15.0	1.1	5.9	17.9	7.6	132.4
3	368.4	62.4	15.2	17.3	1.3	7.0	19.4	9.2	139.3
4	371.2	78.3	16.6	19.1	1.5	8.3	19.9	10.7	148.5
5	382.2	93.9	18.3	21.4	1.6	8.7	22.1	12.5	156.5
6	380.5	111.9	19.1	23.5	1.8	10.1	23.2	15.3	159.9
7	390.7	131.1	20.6	25.7	2.1	11.7	24.6	17.0	167.5
8	391.7	159.5	21.7	28.3	2.3	12.6	27.7	21.5	171.4
9	401.8	194.5	23.6	32.6	2.4	15.3	29.8	25.1	185.6
10	402.4	275.0	27.1	40.9	3.5	23.6	36.8	41.6	205.9
Urban India									
1	314.5	50.9	14.5	16.6	1.2	5.9	17.3	7.3	115.7
2	318.3	77.7	18.1	21.2	2.0	9.7	20.9	12.4	134.8
3	315.7	100.9	20.4	23.4	2.2	10.2	22.3	15.6	141.6
4	320.3	121.1	22.4	25.4	2.6	11.2	25.3	19.9	155.2
5	322.9	136.8	23.9	27.6	2.9	12.1	28.0	22.6	158.3
6	317.2	164.6	25.2	29.6	3.1	14.0	30.2	27.4	171.8
7	315.1	183.3	27.0	30.8	3.7	14.8	33.2	33.0	176.3
8	311.7	210.6	28.6	32.6	3.5	14.7	35.7	38.8	189.7
9	307.6	241.5	29.5	33.5	4.0	17.8	37.7	48.5	203.6
10	285.6	292.2	31.6	36.8	5.6	21.1	43.1	77.8	230.5

Note: Calculations based on various rounds of the NSS.

Source: For details, see Gaiha et al. (2013a)

Vietnam

The evidence for Vietnam is considerably restricted, as shown below in Table 20.3. Hence the comments are brief.

The food consumption patterns differ somewhat over a short period, 2002–04, but are in line with the dietary transition delineated above. Although the median households continued much larger amounts of cereals and pulses than the 25th percentile, this difference narrowed between 2002–04, from 71 per cent to 50 per cent, as the 25th percentile's consumption increased more. The difference in consumption of eggs/meat/fish was about 82 per cent higher among the median households in 2002 and remained just as high in 2004. The difference in the consumption of fruits and vegetables grew from 66.66 per cent in 2002 to 74.07 per cent in 2004, as the consumption of the median households increased more. There was a small reduction, however, in the intake of sugar, from 114.28 per cent in 2002 to 100 per cent in 2004.

Table 20.3 Food consumption pattern of different expenditure groups in Vietnam (dong), 2002–04

Year/Food item/percentile	p25	p50	p75
2002			
Cereals and Pulses	131	224	371
Milk and Products	0	0	8
Eggs/Meat/Fish/Poultry	93	169	303
Fruits and Vegetables	66	110	174
Sugar	7	15	29
2004			
Cereals and Pulses	334	501	746
Milk and Products	0	1	21
Eggs/Meat/Fish/Poultry	256	464	812
Fruits and Vegetables	81	141	245
Sugar	9	18	38
*at 2002 prices			

Note: p denotes per capita expenditure percentile.

Source: For details, see Imai et al. (2013).

20.4 THE RISE OF ASIA'S MIDDLE CLASS, ADB 2010

20.4.1 Definition and Measurement

The middle class is not easily defined as it is not a distinct group in society. It represents a range along the income continuum (a group that lies between the poor and the rich) and social class (an intermediate group between the working class and upper class).

Most definitions and measures are all based on consumption expenditure or income. ADB (2010) uses the per capita daily expenditure range of $2 to $20, and divides it into three groups. The lower middle class – in the range $2–4 – is slightly above the World Bank poverty line of $1.25. The 'middle' middle class – in the range $4–10 – lives above subsistence level and able to save and consume non-essential goods. The upper middle class consumes $10–20 per day.

20.4.2 The Size and Growth of Developing Asia's Middle Class

Asia's middle class ($2–20) has grown rapidly in the last two decades. While its share in Asia's population was only 21 per cent in 1990, it more than doubled to 56 per cent by 2008; up more than three times from 565 million in 1990 to 1.9 billion in 2008 in absolute terms. The five countries with the largest middle class shares are: Azerbaizan, Malaysia, Thailand, Kazakhstan, and Georgia; the five smallest are Bangladesh, Nepal, Laos, Uzbekistan and India. In absolute terms, however, India has a large middle class, second to that of China.

Armenia, China and Vietnam have exhibited very rapid growth in the middle class share in the total population in recent years, with the shares increasing 60–80 percentage points. China, of course, stands out as it added more than 800 million to the middle class during 1990–2008 and increased annual middle class spending by more than $1.8 trillion. India comes a second, with 250 million joining the middle class and $256 billion in additional middle class annual expenditure (ADB, 2010).

In China, the most rapid increase in the relative size of the middle class occurred in the rural areas, where the middle class rose from 28 per cent of the population in 1995 to 87.5 per cent in 2007. By 2007, the relative size of the middle class in the rural areas (87.5 per cent) was close to that in urban areas (91.3 per cent).

In India, the population share of the middle class rose from about 29 per cent in 1993–94 to 38 per cent in 2004–05. The NSS data suggest that in 2004–05 the middle class comprised 418 million people out of a total population of 1.1 billion. The increase was roughly similar in rural and urban areas. Most of the increase occurred in the expenditure interval $2–4.

In Indonesia, the population share of the middle class rose from 25 per cent in 1999 to 43 per cent in 2009. The increase was roughly similar in rural and urban areas. In absolute terms, the middle class population doubled in the 10 years from 45 million to 93 million.

20.4.3 Perception

Whether one belongs to the middle class is also subjective in as much as perception matters. The World Value Surveys (WVS) have collected information on whether respondents consider themselves as belonging to one of five classes: lower, working, lower middle, upper middle or upper. The surveys also enquire where the individuals place themselves in the country's income distribution.

There is a marked variation across countries in this subjective measure. At one extreme is India, where 20 per cent of the (self-identified) middle class placed itself in the third income decile of the income distribution and only 4 per cent in the 8th decile. At the other extreme is Vietnam, where 2 per cent of the middle class placed itself in the third income decile and as many as 17 per cent in the 8th decile (ADB, 2010).

An important point, however, is that no matter what definition is used, there is a sizable middle class in India and that has grown rapidly in the last two decades.

20.4.4 Profile

Based on household surveys in 11 Asian countries, it is generally the case that average middle class household size is smaller than among the poor (but larger than among the rich). But there is cross-country variation. In the $4–10 expenditure group, for instance, Bangladesh, Cambodia, Nepal and Pakistan have unusually large average family size, while China, India and Thailand lower than average household size.

The middle class is also better educated. In China, for instance, while less than 1 per cent of the poor belonged to a household with a high-school-educated head, this number was 5.5 per cent among the lower middle class, 22 per cent among the middle class, and 40 per cent among the upper middle class. A similar pattern is observed in India. While only 3–4 per cent of the poor in rural areas (and 5–12 per cent in urban areas) in 2004–05 had a chief wage earner with higher secondary or more education, as many as 25 per cent of the upper middle class in rural areas (and 54 per cent in urban area) did (ADB, 2010).

Another important distinguishing attribute is employment and occupation.

Middle class individuals in rural India are less likely than the poor to be farmers and fishermen, and more likely to be professional and technical workers. In urban areas, they are less likely to be production workers and laborers and more likely to be administrative, executive, professional and technical workers. A similar pattern is observed in the Philippines where middle-class individuals are more likely to be involved in government and corporations. In China, middle-class households in rural areas are less likely to be involved in agriculture and more likely to be involved in production enterprises, whether privately owned or government run units. Urban middle class households are more likely to have office, professional, or technical occupations compared to poor households.

20.4.5 Consumption Behaviour

Asia's middle class is driving the market sales of refrigerators, television sets, mobile phones and automobiles.

More pertinent in the context of the present study is change in diet associated with the growth of the middle-income class and related health concerns.

There has been a shift towards foods rich in fat and low in fiber and micronutrients. At the same time, the urban middle class has become more sedentary as it has come to rely more heavily on motorbikes and cars, and watching TV in its leisure hours.

This is partly a result of greater availability of and lower prices for processed foods, leading to increased fat consumption in low income countries. The transition from a complex-carbohydrate, low-fat diet to an energy-dense, high-fat diet now occurs at much lower levels of income than previously and has been further accelerated by rapid urbanization so that larger sections of the middle class are exposed to more unhealthy diets (ADB, 2010; Popkin et al., 2012; Gaiha et al., 2013a). In China, for example, upper income groups consuming a relatively high-fat diet (>30 per cent of daily energy intake) rose from 22.8 per cent in 1989 to 66.6 per cent in 1993. The middle-income class consuming a high fat diet also rose (from 19.1 per cent to 51 per cent). India's NSS data show similar changes. Average fat intake rose sharply from 1972–73 to 2004–05 even as average fat intake per person calorie intake fell. This implies that the ratio of fat to calorie intake almost doubled over the period.[4]

The rise in obesity is connected to diabetes which has risen to alarming levels in many Asian countries. For example, India and China have now the largest number of diabetics in the world (51 million and 43 million, respectively). The incidence of diabetes in Malaysia, Sri Lanka and South Korea is now as high as in developed countries such as the United States, Germany and Canada (ADB, 2010).

In developing countries, cardiovascular disease accounts for three quarters of the mortality from all non-communicable diseases. So without better health care and dietary choices, cardiovascular deaths are likely to rise as affluence increases.[5]

20.5 SOCIOLOGICAL ANALYSIS

Although the affluence and economic dimension continues to be dominant in the understanding of consumption patterns including diet consumption, in the last decade, the emphasis on the multidimensional nature of middle-class dietary consumption patterns constitutes an extremely important shift in the research on consumption. By stressing the different dimensions, scholars have rightly moved beyond the economic domain that dominated research a few decades ago. A notable shift can be deciphered in the focus on the (1) class, particularly middle class is now understood not just as an economic category but defined in relation to political, cultural and historical conditions; (2) dietary shifts as representing and as a consequence of not just economic affluence and material conditions but also as a result of and an expression of ideas, values, identities, social network and capital, emotions, knowledge, skills and historical memories.

Despite the fact that the focus on a non-economic model of dietary consumption and middle class has served to challenge the mainstream perspective on dietary consumption, there remains an unhinged focus of research on the subject. Missing particularly is a comprehensive sociological perspective on middle-class dietary-consumption patterns. While significant research exists on the sociology of the middle class, on the one hand, and on the sociology of food and eating, on the other, these research agenda, however, cannot be equated with sociological approach on the middle-class dietary consumption. In this section, an attempt is made to combine the two research agenda by *bringing sociology back* into the study of middle-class eating patterns. Two issues will guide the discussion: (1) Why is it important to view middle-class dietary shifts from a sociological perspective and (2) what kind of research agenda accomplishes the use of sociological lens.

20.5.1 Significance

Middle-class dietary patterns connect the individual behavior with the collective practice, the micro with the macro, the agency with the structure. This connection constitutes the *sociological imagination* (Mills, 1959). Being a middle class means 'practices and values that constitute a social field and agency derived from it' (Donner and De Neve, 2011:7). The very *essence* of dietary consumption of middle classes thus is as much sociological as it is economic.

Second, middle class dietary patterns constitute a social structure as well as a social process. Sociological perspective has the potential to capture this phenomenon by bringing to light the fact that dietary patterns are affected by the social context and then affect the social context that constitutes culture, family and kinship institutions religion, social norms and values, gender, race and ethnic affiliations. Middle classes are affected by social context in the sense that middle classes – the meaning, uses, functions – are all constituted in the process of social interactions with other members of the middle class and with the populations of other classes. Just as identity is not stable (Roth et al., 2004), middle class identity does not have an a priori existence as is often perceived. Thus, class identities, practices and 'lived experience' are not 'afterthoughts' tacked on to preexisting classes. They enter into the very making of these classes (Bourdieu and Wacquant, 1992: 51).

Once constituted through the social process, middle class impacts, among other things, the consumption behavior which itself is shaped and shapes existing relationships and institutions such as culture, family and gender. This mutual, cyclical influence indicates middle class consumption as a social structure and social process.

Middle class dietary consumption is also a social phenomenon because of the *consequences* for social processes such as social mobility, social capital formation, collective memory, history, social cohesion and conflict.

Third, while economic capital is core to consumption of middle classes, dietary consumption of middle classes is as much a *social phenomenon*. This is because dietary consumption of middle class is a plural concept and thus constitutes various interpretations and meanings. It reflects process of globalization, insecurities and anxieties about food systems, food technologies, food supply and costs, health concerns and healthy life styles, ethical concerns, construction of identities and memberships to cultural groups. It also reflects power relationships between different classes and between professional groups of nutritionists and practicing dieticians and lay middle-class populations. It also indicates gender power relations as cooking is a predominantly female activity and with increasing labor force participation of women in middle classes, middle class food consumption is reflective of consumption as much as of changing gender relations within and outside the society. The power relationships between different classes is embedded in the food consumption in that through dietary consumption middle classes do not just reproduce their class identities and reaffirm their belongingness to the fixed middle class but these consumption patterns also produce contestations between different classes and within middle classes and engage in 'local reproduction of inequalities' (O'Dougherty, 2002: 12). They also produce contestations and tension and competitiveness between different levels of providers – markets, government, inter- and intra-class groups and even household members. Consumption of any kind, including food, thus not only indicates desire and hunger and agency but such a desire and hunger produces an 'emotive imagery of the starving, the exploited and the Third World' (Itulua-Abumere, 2013: 82). The desirable and the power and exploitative dimension of consumption, scholars have argued, results in a dual, and often contradictory, nature of consumer society (Edwards, 2000). Consumption is a political activity and to 'consume is to participate in a field of disputes over goods that the society produces and over the ways of using them' (Garcia-Canclini, 1995: 18). Food consumption patterns hence are embedded in such power relationships as well. So the political relevance of the existence of middle classes may not be only in the public, visible areas – protests in the civil sphere (Alexander, 2006) – but also in everyday practices, in private sites and acts of consumption itself.

Middle-class diet consumerism is also a social phenomenon because just as all social identities such as caste, race, ethnic affiliation, religion, region, gender and language are central to formulation of middleclassness (Kaviraj, 1997; Fernandez, 2006; Derne, 2008), they are also central to middle class dietary consumerist patterns. Thus, middle class diets of Brahmins from the southern region of a nation will be different from non-Brahmins from the same region. In other words, middle class dietary patterns embody a social form in the sense that they are embedded within the social matrix that consists of social institutions such as, family, kinship, marriage and identities such as gender, religion, ethnic groups, social networks.

These reasons make middle class a strong candidate for an in-depth sociological analysis.

20.5.2 What Constitutes and Should be Included in a Sociological Research Agenda for Middle Class Dietary Pattern?

Based upon the discussion of various studies of middle-class dietary patterns, the analyses below discuss what the sociological research constitutes and should focus on.

While sociological analyses of middle classes have been in existence for a long time, sociology of food and eating behavior has received increased attention in the recent years. The work of Jack Goody (1982) *Cooking, Cuisine, and Class: A Study in Comparative Sociology* is seen as the watershed in the social analysis of food. In recent years the focus has been on issues of globalization of food supply, food insecurities, food ethics, and health concerns (Ward et al., 2010).

An emphatic focus on social aspect of food can be discerned in Patricia Crotty's observations that 'the act of swallowing divides nutrition's 'two cultures', the post-swallowing world of biology, physiology, biochemistry and pathology, and the pre-swallowing domain of behaviour, culture, society and experience' (1993: 109). It will be useful to briefly summarize the sociological research on the subject of food and eating behavior.

Broadly, food systems, including eating behavior 'have been used to illuminate broad societal processes' (Mintz and Du Bois, 2002:100). These processes include political–economic value-creation (Mintz, 1985), symbolic value creation (Munn, 1986), and the social construction of memory (Sutton, 2001). Similarly, studies have pointed to the collective character of dietary patterns among social groups (Douglas, 1984; Murcott, 1988), in contrast to behavioral approaches, to explain eating patterns in relation to their sociocultural contexts (Mennell et al., 1992; Murcott, 1996).

Whether cultural materialism or structural and symbolic explanations are important to understand food behavior has also been a subject of interest to scholars (Harris, 1998 [1985]; Simoons, 1994, 1998; Gade, 1999).

While relationship between consumption and identity formation has been analyzed in great depth (Warde, 1994), the relationship between eating patterns and social identity has also gained attention in extant research. Studies indicate how issues of symbolic identities are shaped and represented by dietary patterns and have dominated the field (Lee, 1993; Lasch, 1978; Warde, 1997). While identities are an important subject of food consumption, scholars have argued that by the end of the millennium the topic of food symbolizing identities had become old and vague and singular, and static (MacClancy, 2004: 63–64). Holtzman (2009: 60) argues it is difficult to say whether identities are produced by food qualities themselves that make it an especially cogent means of identification or whether it is imposed by westerners. Studies have also focused on how food consumption, particularly middle-class consumption, produces networks and connects most unlikely populations across the globe (Fischer and Benson, 2006). They show that export of Guatemalan broccoli that indicated American middle-class concerns with 'eating right' represented a new, export crop for Mayan farmers. In another study, Wilk's (2006) finds that Belizian foodways and food consumption culture indicated a connection of global and local forces in that global processes produced local culinary traditions among Belizinas and also their food preference and appreciation for foods from other countries.

Household arrangements, government policy, community organization and industrial conflict (Fine and Leopold, 1993; Warde, 1997), all shape consumption activity including food consumption. Research has illuminated broad societal processes such as political–economic, value creation, (Mintz, 1985), symbolic value creation (Munn, 1986) in food systems. Food and eating is also associated with the social construction of memory (Sutton, 2001). Sutton (2001: 170) tries to understand how food conveys memories and how eating and drinking engender and maintain historical consciousness. Holtzman's (2009) study supports this finding when he demonstrates that food practice among Samburu of Northern Kenya indicated that because food and dietary changes among the Samburu were a result of economic development, a decreasing commitment to a pastoral lifestyle, and an increasing dependence on 'town food', food for Samburu indicated their predicament and historical consciousness.

According to the sociology of consumption analysis, 'food is a most enlightening critical case study. Food, its preparation and consumption, is intricately connected to many other central processes of social life. Food preparation also absorbs huge amounts of time: Shopping, planning, storing, cooking, serving and clearing up are the regular activities necessary to sustain the habit of almost everyone eating several times a day. Food is also a significant means of cultural expression and is often used as a general means of commentary on contemporary culture (Itulua-Abumere, 2013: 79). That food is a cultural marker is indicated in research that focuses on varied perceptions and experiences with regard to food choice and the practice of eating out (Warde and Martens, 1998; 2000).

Additionally, food is also a matter of considerable psychological and emotional significance as a whole range of phenomena, from the meaning of Mother's cooking to illnesses like anorexia nervosa (Warde, 1997). Due to this polyvalent significance, food practices can easily be used as a laboratory for the understanding of social relations. For instance, in one short essay, Furst (1988) describes ways in which food generates and reinforces gender divisions in the household, how food preferences are generation related, the symbolic and ritual significance to the preparation of 'traditional' meals at the weekend if quickly prepared supermarket food is used during the week, how different cultures preserve a sense of identity through their food practices (like eating rotting trout in Norway, for instance), how meals structure daily time, and also how they express emotion and caring (Itulua-Abumere, 2013: 79).

While social aspect is integral to food systems defined broadly, impressive research exists on the relationship between non-economic, social factors and the *dietary shifts and changes in eating patterns*. Food shifts are associated, for instance, with a variety of economic and political changes, such as male out-migration, interclass rivalry and imitation, and market integration (Lentz, 1999; Mintz and Du Bois, 2002: 104). In the context of rural India, changing caste relations have been linked with village foodways (Mayer, 1996). Government policies and social transformations have shaped dietary habits of children in China (Jing, 2000). Mennell (1985) and Levenstein (1993) have noted that historically culinary changes have been one consequence of changing social processes. Studies have brought to light the roles of cultural institutions such as advertising and marketing (Cwiertka, 2000), artistic and refined presentations of food (Hine, 1995), movement of organic foods (Campbell and Liepins, 2001), incorporation and inspiration of different ethnic cuisines within communities (Belasco, 1987; Lockwood and Lockwood, 2000) in understanding changes in dietary patterns.

The above studies point to the role of larger social structural processes affecting dietary changes. The powerful role of social dimension of dietary change, however, can be discerned through the structure and agency and social practice framework (Delormier et al., 2009). Hence, the focus is not just on how larger social structural changes have affected dietary patterns among populations but how food and eating behavior also has an agency in that eating behavior also fosters social change. For instance, choice of organic food has given rise to not just changes in food industry like new measures of food security but broader social changes such as poverty alleviation and sustainable development and social identities. The agency of dietary patterns includes not only the financial ability to make food choices but also 'a frame of reference that includes knowledgeability (skills, beliefs, experiences), and what is most adequate at the moment of food choice' (Delormier et al., 2009: 220). These rituals and beliefs surrounding food choices can also affect social relations as they reinforce religious and ethnic boundaries (see e.g. Mahias, 1985; Bahloul, 1989; Fabre-Vassas, 1997) and reproduce older caste, religious boundaries, family values, intergenerational links and middle-class identities (Donner and de Neve, 2011). Food consumptions also represent and reinforce gender relationships within household (Furst, 1988; Donner and de Neve, 2011).

The studies discussed above provide robust evidence of the correlations of patterns of dietary consumption and changes with different dimensions of the social and sociological framework. In recent years, the examination of the role of one aspect of the social processes and framework viz., social class, particularly middle class, in dietary consumption patterns has been gaining attention. These studies focus on the understanding of the relationship between class positions and differences including middle class positions and dietary patterns (Holgado et al., 2000; Hulshof et al. 1991, 2003; Smith et. al., 1992; Hupkens, 2000; Mishra et. al., 2002; Darmon and Drewnowski, 2008; Donner and de Neve, 2011).

This research on the relationship between middle class and dietary pattern is indeed very significant as it moves beyond the individual behavioral and nutrition science perspective on dietary consumption and brings to light the role of social class processes. The dominant focus of the class analysis, however, is on its materialistic dimension. Delormier et al. (2009: 217–218) note that the 'social processes include both the symbolic aspect – *meanings* of food and the material conditions and aspects of food – to explain eating patterns of groups of people'. In this sense then class as a social process has both the materialistic and the symbolic dimension. The eating pattern of the middle classes, for instance, is not only a function of their materialistic resources – income and occupation but also of symbolic meanings attached to food choices. 'Healthy' or 'junk' food characterizes food categories that convey health-related properties which stem from signification structures or meanings related to discourses about food and health in society. Social structures, through interpretive schemes, shape food choice practices; for example, food practices categorized as 'traditional' come to hold meanings which are distinguished from food practices involving store bought foods (Delormier and Kuhnlein, 1999). The non-materialistic and cultural dimension of social class impact on eating patterns is revealed in Coveney's (2004) study. Coveney 'examined lay knowledge and showed how meanings of food and health involved in decision making around feeding children differed among social classes. Working class families tended to express health and food in terms of the outward appearance and functional capacity of children, whereas the tendency in middle-class families was to express this relationship in scientific and nutrition informed terms. Interpretive schemes expressed in food choice patterns assist in identifying structures of significance that come into play during social interaction related to family food choices. Decision making power for what family members eat is an authoritative resource conferring onto actors the capacity to make food choices for family members or limiting this power when resources are lacking' (Delormier et al., 2009: 222).

Findings of another study on the food consumption patterns and changes among the middle class Bengalis in Kolkata, India, support this perspective. Donner (2011) indicates that changing food patterns and choices are related not so much to consumption per se but 'closely related to the gendered roles in the domestic sphere and women's work at home.' Donner notes that despite women's labor force participation, their role in the domestic sphere – cooking/feeding and responding to dietary changes of the sons and daughters – continues to be their primary identity. Middle-class dietary shifts are also closely related to family values, intergenerational links and middle class identities (Donner, 2011).

The aforementioned discussion reveals that the middle-class dietary consumption is not a function only of individual behavior and nutrition and health concern. It is closely associated with the social processes broadly construed. Social class, including middle-class structure is one such central social process that impacts pattern of dietary consumption. Indeed, studies have examined the connection of middle class – defined in terms of education, occupation and income – with dietary consumption. Such a connection is what I refer to as materialist linkage. In contrast, the chapter proposes a sociological perspective that emphasizes the symbolic and cultural linkage of middle class with diets. Few studies have emphasized such non-materialistic linkage. What is missing, however, is an in-depth sociological approach. A robust sociological perspective is useful and much needed given intrinsic features of middle class diets. The analysis below proposes few directions for future research in this field.

1. Sociological perspective/approach on middle class dietary consumption can be conceptualized at two levels: (a) sociology in middle-class diets and (b) sociology of middle-class diets. The former emphasizes sociological factors such as gender, caste, class identities that shape middle-class-diet experience in terms of eating out, ordering in, cooking food, and choice of food. If middle class dietary policies decide to take into account sociological variables then in this approach policy makers would select/ identify these sociological variables, along with other factors, while designing, implementing and evaluating middle-class policies. Here the social variables are tangible and more or less mechanically incorporated in the list of factors that influence or have potential to influence middle-class eating. Also, these factors are seen as impacting dietary pattern as isolated factors, existing independently of one another.

    While this is useful, the attention to socio-cultural factors is not as comprehensive. In recent years, there has been a conspicuous emphasis on the role of culture in dietary patterns and indeed the socio-cultural component discussed above has emerged as a prominent dimension. Culture, however, is a nuanced concept and raises questions such as, how exactly is culture located/present in dietary pattern of middle class? How should it be identified/captured while designing and implementing middle-class dietary policies? The approach calls attention to the role of sociology/sociological lens as cultural broker between policy makers and food consumers. Consequently, the sociology of middle class consumption pattern elaborated here reconceptualizes culture in a study of middle-class dietary consumption.

One, it emphasizes the necessity of distinguishing the socio-cultural mechanisms and agents from socio-cultural structures and groups. The mechanisms constitute the process and the groups constitute the structure. In other words, dietary pattern of middle classes constitute a social structure and social process, a phenomenon as discussed above. Thus when family, gender, and religious class identities are treated in the cultural analysis of middle-class diet patterns, it is not a complete cultural analysis. A robust sociological approach to middle class diets, by contrast, identifies those mechanisms, often not easily observable, through which social institutions and categories such as families, caste, gender, and class influence remittance experience. For instance, what exactly impacts the families' food choices and changes – is it values regarding money or values regarding family? What causes women's empowerment or disempowerment through dietary shifts and demands by family members – is it affluence or ideology of patriarchy? What leads to exclusion or inclusion of certain members of middle class as they attempt to shift their patterns of eating? What makes families and communities in case of middle class as a collective group to invest in certain kinds of food more than in others? Why do different religious groups belonging to same middle class consume differently? The argument here is that just including or acknowledging categories such as family, religion and gender is not enough for a socio-cultural approach to middle-class eating patterns. What is needed is a deeper understanding of the social mechanisms that propel religious identities, gender and family institutions to influence middle class diets and generally the food experience. These socio-cultural mechanisms include but not confined to, patriarchal values, biases and prejudices of social groups, perceptions of identity, cultural beliefs about food, beliefs about how money should be spent, skills of preparation of food preparation and knowledge-base of middle class and dietary policies.

2. From a *substantialist* perspective, another gap of socio-cultural analysis in evaluating middle-class diets is that the focus on socio-cultural factors is one where culture is seen as isolated from, say, structural factors such as income and education. Culture and structure are seen as two discrete, isolated, independent variables shaping collective action (Bourdieu, 1984 [1979]). A robust sociological analysis thus is one that recognizes the different forms of cultural factors and also seeks to capture what Bourdieu (1984 [1979]) refers to as the relational nature of socio-cultural factors. In other words, cultural factors shape and are shaped by dietary experience of the middle class, not as isolated independent factors but in relation to and in interaction with structural factors. This is because the properties that make up both structure and culture are developed in relation to one another. For instance, different perceptions regarding healthcare are developed in the process of interaction with the structural element – levels and kinds of education. Thus, the cultural and structural factors derive their significance from the relations that link them rather than

from intrinsic features of individual elements (Swartz, 1997). Culture and structure are related in a cyclical fashion, where the structure-cultural interaction produces another distinct form of structure, which we refer to as quasi-normative structure.

Such cultural analysis is useful in understanding middle class diets in the following way: multidimensionality of middle class diet pattern that focuses on identity, beliefs, gender roles and class positions that research has focused on is certainly useful. However, in emphasizing the multidimensionality, studies have not addressed how these dimensions are relationally related to one another and to the economic dimension in particular and how that shapes the dietary experience of the middle class. In other words, diets of middle class are impacted through an interaction of various dimensions rather than as independently of one another. For instance, studies which have recorded that the income effects on middle class diets or how education and occupation contribute to the quality of dietary shifts (economic aspect) cannot be explained only in economic terms because the shifts in eating patterns is not just an economic act. Rather, it is the cultural values of gender identities and family values that oblige and guide how the affordability of new kinds of food and different patterns of eating can be realized. Without the recognition and practice of patriarchal value that women are responsible for feeding or without the shared meanings related to discourses about food and health in society, the dietary shifts that are bought by paying money cannot be sustained. So it is the intersection of cultural framework supporting dietary shifts with the economic act of being able to buy food that produces the outcome that sustains the dietary shifts and also produces new patterns for the middle classes.

3. Research on the middle-class dietary patterns has focused at the macro level. Thus the focus has been on the impact of the changes in urbanization, globalization and economic conditions at the national and global level on the ever-growing middle class consumption patterns, including diets. According to the key findings particularly in the Asian context, the middle class consumption levels have increased very rapidly. I argue that this finding is perhaps more a result of how the impact has been studied. It has been studied predominantly in economic terms because the dominant paradigm of middle class consumption including diets has been economic. However, if the consequences of these processes on middle class dietary consumption are studied in non-economic terms, such as impact on family relationships, social capital, social networks and even value that money may carry, one can hope to discover nuanced impact of these macro processes on middle-class dietary consumption. This would mean doing ethnographic case studies focusing on the individual and household level. This would also allow capturing a more complex and subtle understanding of development. For instance, while urbanization's impact on dietary consumption with high-level consumption may indicate positive impact of macro processes, if women's continue to experience the burden of double-shift, it will indicate at best lop-sided development.

4. The focus on macro and micro level of consumption of middle class is related to the phenomenon of the publicness and privateness of the middle-class consumption. Scholars note that there has been an obsessive public concern with the middle class (Mazzarella and Dwyer, 2005), that is, people have been publicly identifying themselves as belonging to the middle, between the poor and rich class. In the context

of consumption, scholars also suggest the need to study alternative sites – more private sites where middleclassness is constructed and thus exists. Appadurai and Breckenridge (1995) suggest that middleclassness needs to be understood in terms of consumption but the consumerist identities should not be confined to media representations and youth culture, films, fashion and advertising as they dominantly are and should include less obvious practices and activities that are found in domestic spheres. In the context of diet consumption of middle classes, the research focus should thus shift to more private sites, such as the domestic sphere.

5. Although the non-materialistic dimension of the middle class with focus on values and identities has been emphasized in research and the non-materialistic dimension of food consumption is also emphasized, there are very few studies that focus on the cultural dimensions of middle class dietary consumptions. In other words, the extant evidence of distinctiveness of middle classes is in terms of materialistic dimensions – income, education and occupational levels and hence distinctiveness in their food pattern is measured by relating it to these dimensions. Questions such as, how are the middle class values different from working class values in relation to food consumption? What is the nature of middle class identities shaped by dietary shifts that are distinct from working class identities? How is the gender roles and gender relations in middle classes dietary patterns distinct from gender roles among working class food patterns? What are the structural constraints experienced by working and middle classes and the agency and power experienced by each class when it relates to food choice patterns, have not been researched upon in great depth. As middle class consumption levels rise and dietary options diversify, it will not only be the income level that will determine the dietary patterns. Factors such as symbolic identities, traditional practices, and 'the local configuration of social relations which are comprise social structures such as class, race, and gender; institutional practices, collective and individual behaviour, and intersecting personal biographies' (Poland et al., 2006: 60) of the middle classes will become ever more important. Sociological and socio-cultural framework is thus intrinsically linked to the middle-class dietary patterns. The absence of these linkages is made significant by the gaps.

NOTES

1. This draws upon Gaiha et al. (2013a).
2. The rural areas were hit by a drought in 2009.
3. It is well documented that sugar content of beverages is underestimated. See, for example, Popkin et al. (2012).
4. For an updated analysis up to 2009–10, see Gaiha et al. (2013b).
5. For an analysis with India's household data, see Gaiha et al. (2013b).

REFERENCES

Acemoglu, D. and F. Zilibotti (1997), Was Prometheus unbound by chance? *Journal of Political Economy*, **105**(4), 709–51.
Alexander, J.C. (2006), *The Civil Sphere*. New York: Oxford University Press.
Appadurai, A. and C. Breckenridge (1995), Public modernity in India. In C. Beckenridge, *Consuming*

Modernity: Public Culture in a South Asian World. Minneapolis, MN: University of Minnesota Press, pp. 1–21.
Aristotle (trans. 1928), Politics: A Treatise on Government. Available at: http://www.gutenberg.org/files/6762/6762-h/6762-h.htm.
Asian Development Bank ADB (2010), The rise of Asia's middle class. In *Key Indicators for Asia and the Pacific*. ADB: Manila, special chapter.
Bahloul, J. (1989), From a Muslim banquet to a Jewish seder: foodways and ethnicity among North African Jews. In M.R. Cohen and A.L. Udovitch (eds), *Jews Among Arabs: Contacts and Boundaries*. Princeton, NJ: Darwin, pp. 85–96.
Banerjee, A. and E. Duflo (2007), What is middle class about the middle classes around the world? MIT Department of Economics Working Paper 07-29, Cambridge, MA.
Belasco, W.J. (1987), Ethnic fast foods: the corporate melting pot. *Food Foodways*, **2**, 1–30.
Bhalla, S. (2009), *The Middle Class Kingdoms of India and China*. Washington DC: Peterson Institute for International Economics.
Birdsall, N., C. Graham and S. Pettinato (2000), Stuck in tunnel: is globalization muddling the middle? Working Paper 14, Brookings Institution, Washington DC.
Bourdieu, P. (1984 [1979]), *Distinction: A Social Critique of the Judgment of Taste*. Cambridge, MA: Harvard University Press.
Bourdieu, P. (1990 [1980]), *The Logic of Practice*. Cambridge, MA: Polity Press.
Bourdieu, P. and L. Wacquant (1992), *An Invitation to Reflexive Sociology*. Chicago, IL: The University of Chicago Press.
Burris, V. (1986), The discovery of the new middle class. *Theory and Society*, **15**(3), 317–49.
Campbell, H. and R. Liepins (2001), Naming organics: understanding organic standards in New Zealand as a discursive field. *Journal of Rural Social Sciences*, **41**(1), 21–39.
Coveney, J. (2004), A qualitative study exploring socio-economic differences in parental lay knowledge of food and health: implications for public health nutrition. *Public Health Nutrition*, **8**(3), 290–97.
Crotty, P. (1993), The value of qualitative research in nutrition. *Annual Review of Health and Social Sciences*, **3**, 109–18.
Cwiertka, K.J. (2000), From Yokohama to Amsterdam: Meidi-Ya and dietary change in modern Japan. *Japanstudien*, **12**, 45–63.
Darmon, N. and A. Drewnowski (2008), Does social class predict diet quality? *American Journal of Clinical Nutrition*, **87**, 1107–1117.
Delormier, T. and H. Kuhnlein (1999), Dietary characteristics of Eastern James Bay Cree women's diets. *Arctic*, **52**(2), 182–7.
Delormier, T., K.L. Frohlich and L. Potvin (2009), Food and eating as social practice: understanding eating patterns as social phenomena and implications for public health. *Sociology of Health & Illness*, **31**(2), 215–28.
Derne, S. (2008), *Globalization on the Ground: New Media and the Transformation of Culture, Class, and Gender in India*. New Delhi, India: Sage.
Doepke, M. and F. Zilibotti (2007), Occupational choice and the spirit of capitalism. NBER Working Paper 12917, National Bureau of Economic Research Inc., Cambridge, MA.
Donner, H. (ed.) (2011), *A Way of Life: Changing Middle-class Identities in Postliberalisation India*. London: Routledge.
Donner, H. and G. de Neve (2011), Introduction. In *Being Middle-class in India: A Way of Life*, Oxon: Routledge, pp. 1–22.
Douglas, M. (1984), *Food in the Social Order: Studies of Food and Festivities in Three American Communities*. London and New York: Routledge.
Easterly, W. (2000), The middle class consensus and economic development. Policy Research Working Paper 2346, World Bank, Washington DC.
Edwards, T. (2000), *Contraditions of Consumption: Concepts, Practices and Politics in Consumer Society*. Buckingham, UK: Open University Press.
Fabre-Vassas, C. (1997), *The Singular Beast: Jews, Christians, and the Pig*. New York: Columbia University Press.
Fernandez, L. (2006), *India's New Middle Class: Democratic Politics in an Era of Economic Reform*, Minneapolis. MN: University of Minnesota Press.
Fine, B. and E. Leopold (1993), *The World of Consumption*. London: Routledge.
Fischer, E.F. and P. Benson (2006), *Broccoli and Desire: Global Connections and Maya*. Stanford, CA: Stanford University Press.
Fitzgerald, S.T. (2012), Middle Class. In J. Manza (ed.), *Oxford Bibliographies in Sociology*. New York: Oxford University Press.
Furst, E. (1988), The cultural significance of food. In P. Otnes (ed.), *Sociology of Consumption: An Anthology*. Oslo: Solum Forlag, pp. 89–100.

Gade, D.W. (1999), *Nature and Culture in the Andes*. Madison, WI: University of Wisconsin Press.
Gaiha, R., N. Kaicker, K. Imai, V.S. Kulkarni and G. Thapa (2013a), 'Has dietary Transition slowed in India? An analysis based on the 50th, 61st and 66th rounds of the National Sample Survey. Occasional Paper 16, Asia and the Pacific Division, IFAD.
Gaiha, R., R. Jha and V.S. Kulkarni (2013b), *Diets, Malnutrition and Disease in India*. New Delhi: Oxford University Press, forthcoming.
Garcia-Canclini, N. (1995), *Consumidores y Ciudadanos: Conflictos Multiculturales de la Globalizacion*. Mexico: Grejalbo.
Goody, J. (1982), *Cooking, Cuisine and Class: A Study in Comparative Sociology*. Cambridge, UK: Cambridge University Press.
Harris, Marvin. (1998 [1985]), *Good to Eat: Riddles of Food and Culture*, 2nd edition. Prospect Heights, IL: Waveland.
Hine, T. (1995), *The Total Package: the Secret History and Hidden Meanings of Boxes*. New York: Little, Brown and Company.
Holgado, B., J.D. Irala-EsteÂvez, J.A. MartõÂnez-Gonzaâlez, M. Gibney, J. Kearney and J.A. MartõÂnez (2000), Barriers and benefits of a healthy diet in Spain. *European Journal of Clinical Nutrition*, **54**(4), 453–59.
Holtzman, J. (2009), *Uncertain Tastes: Memory, Ambivalence and the Politics of Eating in Samburu, Northern Kenya*. Berkeley, CA: University of California Press.
Hulshof, K.F., M.R. Lowik, F.J. Kok et al. (1991), Diet and other life-style factors in high and low socio-economic groups (Dutch Nutrition Surveillance System). *European Journal of Clinical Nutrition*, **45**, 441–50.
Hulshof, K.F., J.H. Brussaard, A.G. Kruizinga, J. Telman and M.R. Lowik (2003), Socio-economic status, dietary intake and 10-year trends: the Dutch National Food Consumption Survey. *European Journal of Clinical Nutrition*, **57**, 128–37.
Hupkens, C.L., R.A. Knibbe and M.J. Drop (2000), Social class differences in food consumption. *European Journal of Public Health*, **10**, 108–13.
Imai, K.S., R. Gaiha and G. Thapa (2013), Dietary transition in Vietnam. Draft. Asia and the Pacific Division, IFAD, Rome.
Itulua-Abumere, F. (2013), Concepts and practices of food consumptions in modern society. *Open Journal of Social Science Research*, **4**, 78–85.
Jafferlot, C. and P. van der Veer (eds) (2008), *Patterns of Middle Class Consumption in India and China*. New Delhi: Sage Publication.
Jing, J. (ed.) (2000), *Feeding China's Little Emperors: Food, Children, and Social Change*. Stanford, CA: Stanford University Press.
Kaviraj, S. (1997), The general elections in India. *Government and Opposition*, **32**(1), 3–24.
Kharas, H. (2010), The emerging middle class in developing countries. Working Paper No. 285, OECD Development Center, Paris, January.
Kharas, H. (2011), *Catalyzing Development: A New Vision for Aid*. Washington DC: The Brookings Press.
Lasch, C. (1978), *The Culture of Narcissism: American Life in an Age of Diminishing Expectations*. New York: Norton.
Lee, M.J. (1993), *Consumer Culture Reborn: The Cultural Politics of Consumption*. London: Routledge.
Lentz, C. (ed.) (1999), *Changing Food Habits: Case Studies from Africa, South America, and Europe*. Amsterdam: Harwood Acad.
Levenstein, H. (1993), *Paradox of Plenty: A Social History of Eating in Modern America*. Oxford: Oxford University Press.
Lockwood, W.G. and Y.R. Lockwood (2000), Continuity and adaptation in Arab American foodways. In N. Abraham and A. Shryock (ed.), *Arab Detroit: From Margin to Mainstream*. Detroit, MI: Wayne State University Press, pp. 515–59.
MacClancy, J. (2004), Food, identity, identification. In H. Macbeth and J. MacClancy (eds), *Researching Food Habits*. New York: Berghahn Books, pp. 63–74.
Mahias, M.C. (1985), *Delivrance et Convivialite: le Systeme Culinaire des Jaina*. Paris: Ed. Maison Sci. l'Homme.
Mayer, A. (1996), Caste in an Indian village: change and continuity 1954–1992. In C.J. Fuller (ed.), *Caste Today*. Delhi: Oxford University Press, pp. 32–64.
Mazzarella, W. and R. Dwyer (2005), Indian Middle Class. In R. Dwyer (ed.), *South Asia Keywords*. Available at: http://www.soas.ac.uk/csasfiles/keywords/Mazzarella-middleclass.pdf.
Mennell, S. (1985), *All Manners of Food*. Oxford: Blackwell.
Mennell, S., A. Murcott and A.H. van Otterloo (1992), *The Sociology of Food: Eating, Diet and Culture*. London: Sage.
Mills, C.W. (1959), *The Sociological Imagination*. New York: Grove Press.
Mintz, S.W. (1985), *Sweetness and Power: the Place of Sugar in Modern History*. New York: Penguin.

Mintz, S.W. and C. Du Bois (2002), The anthropology of food and eating. *Annual Review of Anthropology*, **31**, 99–119.

Mishra, G., K. Ball, J. Arbuckle and D. Crawford (2002), Dietary patterns of Australian adults and their association with socioeconomic status: results from the 1995 National Nutrition Survey. *European Journal of Clinical Nutrition*, **56**, 687–93.

Munn, N.D. (1986), *The Fame of Gawa: a Symbolic Study of Value Transformation in a Massim (Papua New Guinea) Society*. Cambridge, UK: Cambridge University Press.

Murcott, A. (1988), Sociological and social anthropological approaches to food and eating. *World Review. Nutritional Diet*, **55**, 1–40.

Murcott, A. (1996), Food as an expression of identity. In S. Gustafsson and L. Lewin (ed.), *The Future of the National State: Essays on Cultural Pluralism and Political Integration*. Stockholm: Nerenius & Santerus, pp. 49–77.

Murphy, K.M., A. Shleifer and R. Vishny (1989), Income distribution, market size, and industrialization. *The Quarterly Journal of Economics*, **104**(3), 537–64.

O'Dougherty, M. (2002), *Consumption Intensified: The Politics of Middle-Class Daily Life in Brazil*. Durham: Duke University Press.

Pingali, P. (2004), Westernisation of Asian diets and the transformation of food systems: implications for research and policy. ESA working Paper No. 04-17, FAO, Rome.

Pingali, P. (2006), Westernisation of Asian diets and the transformation of food systems: implications for research and policy. *Food Policy*, **32**, 281–98.

Poland, B., K. Frohlich, R.J. Haines, E. Mykhalovskiy, M. Rock and R. Sparks (2006), The social context of smoking: the next frontier in tobacco control? *Tobacco Control*, **15**(1), 59–63.

Popkin, B., L. Adair and S. Ng (2012), Global nutrition transition and the pandemic of obesity in developing countries. *Nutrition Review*, **70**(1), 3–21.

Roth, W.-M., K. Tobin, R. Elmesky, C. Carambo, Y. McKnight and J. Beers (2004), Re/making identities in the praxis of urban schooling: a cultural historical perspective. *Mind, Culture, and Activity*, **11**, 48–69.

Schor, J. (1999), The new politics of consumption. *Boston Review*, Summer.

Simoons, F. (1998), *Plants of Life, Plants of Death*. Madison, WI: University of Wisconsin Press.

Simoons, F. (1994), *Eat Not this Flesh: Food Avoidances from Prehistory to the Present*. Madison, WI: University of Wisconsin Press.

Smith, A.M. and K.I. Baghurst (1992), Public health implications of dietary differences between social status and occupational category groups. *Journal of Epidemiology and Community Health*, **46**, 409–16.

Sutton, D. (2001), *Remembrance of Repasts: an Anthropology of Food and Memory*. Oxford: Berg.

Swartz, D. (1997), *Culture and Power: The Sociology of Pierre Bourdieu*, Chicago, IL: University of Chicago Press.

Wacquant, L. (2004), Habitus. In J. Beckert and M. Zafirovski (eds), *International Encyclopedia of Economic Sociology*. London: Routledge, pp. 315–9.

Ward, P., J. Coveney and J. Henderson (2010), Editorial. A sociology of food and eating: why now? *Journal of Sociology*, **46**(2) 347–51.

Warde, A. (1994), Consumption, identity formation and uncertainty. *Sociology*, **28**(4), 877–98.

Warde, A. (1997), *Consumption, Food and Taste*. London: Sage.

Warde, A. and L. Martens (1998), A sociological approach to food choice: the case of eating out. In A. Murcott (ed.), *The Nation's Diet*. London: Longman.

Warde, A. and L. Martens (2000), *Eating Out: Social Differentiation, Consumption and Pleasure*. Cambridge: Cambridge University Press.

Wilk, R. (2006), *Home Cooking in the Global Village: Caribbean Food from Buccaners to Ecotourists*. Oxford: Berg.

Index

AAY (Antyodaya Anna Yojana) category 497, 502
Abbott, P. 211
'acid rain' 391
ADB (Asian Development Bank) 2, 3–4, 19, 20, 72, 76, 87, 89, 91, 96, 97, 218, 242, 483, 484, 482, 491, 511, 523, 524, 525, 535
Adda, J. 313, 314, 316
ADF (Augmented Dickey–Fuller) test 130, 156, 158, 173
Adholeya, Alok 17–18, 443
Anshuman 17–18, 443
AFOLU (agriculture, forestry and other land use) sectors 17, 422–3, 428, 433, 436, 438–9
agency coordination 58–9
agricultural growth 238–9
agricultural mismanagement 446
agricultural productivity improvement 16, 363, 365–9
agricultural subsidies 237–8, 240
agricultural trade 325, 326, 328–34, 332, 334, 335–7, 339–48, 350
Aguero, J. 294, 316
AIC (Akaike Information Criterion) 135, 144, 162
Aksoy, M. 326, 351
alcohol 66, 86, 190, 212, 215, 219, 225–6, 241, 296–7, 298, 313–14
Alderman, H. 222, 238, 242, 243, 494, 512
Al-Eyd, A. 86, 97
American Heart Foundation 296
amino acids 268, 273, 381, 384, 388, 397–9
Andean-crop report (1989) 409
Anderson, K. 83, 92–3, 97, 339, 370
Antman, F. 253, 257
APL (above poverty line) category 497, 502
Appadurai, A. 534
ARCH (Autoregressive Conditional Heteroscedasticity) 138, 158–9, 162, 164–5
Aristotle 517, 535
Atkinson, Edward 262–3, 271, 275
atmospheric CO_2, increased 392–3, 416–17
Atwater, Wilbur O. 262–3, 271, 274
Aulerich, N. 135, 136, 145, 152
AUM (assets under management) 128

Bai, J. 221, 242
Baicker, K. 315, 317
Balcombe, K. 336, 349
Balisacan, A. 21, 117, 119
Banerjee, A. 252, 510, 512, 518, 535
Bank for International Settlements 124
Bardhan, P. 254, 257, 470, 478
'Barker's hypothesis' 313
Barrett, C. 42, 61, 117, 119, 249, 349, 478
'basic needs approach' 493
Behrman, J. 188–9, 192, 250, 254, 257, 496, 512
Benjamin, D. 470, 478
Bennet's Law 490
Bhalla, S. 469, 470, 478
Bhandari, R. 218, 242
Bhore Committee 267
Bicchetti, D. 139, 145
Bill and Melinda Gates Foundation (BMGF) 406, 407
BIMARU (Bihar, Madhya Pradesh, Rajasthan and Uttar Pradesh) region 184, 185, 186, 187, 196, 254
Binswanger, H. 248, 251, 252, 257, 259, 464, 478
biofuel 1–2, 13, 19, 20, 46, 73, 77–9, 93–4, 96, 98, 142, 146, 151, 175, 335, 337, 381, 440, 442
biomass-flow optimization 432
Bliss, C. 248, 257, 478, 493, 512
Block, S. 20, 32, 39, 54, 57, 59, 61, 68, 115, 119
blood pressure 290, 296, 298, 300, 301, 306, 309, 310, 314, 318
Bloom, D. 173, 178, 191, 192, 294, 311, 317
BMI (Body Mass Index) 224, 248, 255, 267–8, 297, 300–309, 312–13, 513
Bobenrieth, E. B. 146, 151, 174
Bonds, M. 250–51, 257
border price transmission 328, 340–41
Borlaug, Norman 385
Bourguignon, F. 251, 257
BPL (below poverty line) category 497–9, 502
Brandt, L. 470, 478
Breckenridge, C. 534
Bretton Woods system 84, 327
British dietary studies 261–2
Brooks, C. 130, 145
Brunetti, C. 138, 146
bubbles, food price 129–33, 143, 151–2

Buffie, E. F. 341, 343, 344, 349
Büyükşahin, B. 138, 139, 146, 150–51

Caballero, R. 7, 20, 129, 146
Čajanov, A. 494, 512
calorie deprivation simulations 45–6
calorie intake
    and crop options 381, 382
    and dietary allowances 261, 262, 265, 266–74
    and dietary transition 185–7, 188–9, 190, 197–8, 217–18, 219–20, 222
    and food security 359
    and NCDs 298
    and PNTs 248, 249–50
    and poverty reduction 375–6
cancers
    age-adjusted statistics 281–2, 284–6 , 287, 293
    causal factors 293–9
        studies on 300–309
    and competing risks 293–4, 315
    and economic status 286–7, 288–93, 295–9, 310–15
    and income levels 280–81, 282–4, 287, 293, 299, 310–16
    inter-regional variations 281–2, 287, 293
    and life expectancy 280–82, 287, 293–4, 297
    and longevity 294–5
    and nutrition 294
    and public health interventions 282–3, 294
    and risk factors 295–9
        evidence of 299, 310–15
        studies on 300–309
    and YLL 283–4, 287
Canning, D. 279, 294, 317
'capabilities approach' 493
Capelle-Blancard, G. 134, 146
capital-intensive farming system 464–6
Carter, C. 208, 211, 212,
Carter, M. 469, 470, 478
Case, A. 294–5
Cashin, P. 335–6, 349
CBT (Chicago Board of Trade) 80, 123, 125–9, 134, 136, 175–6
CCTs (conditional cash transfers) 97, 322, 503, 510
CDF (cumulative distribution function) 359–61
CFTC (Commodity Futures Trading Commission) 125–6, 128, 134–5, 152
CGE (Computable General Equilibrium) model 329
CGIAR (Consultative Group on International Agricultural Research) programs 400–402, 404, 415

Chapman, C. 261, 262, 275
CHD (coronary heart disease) 8, 290, 292, 295–6, 310, 315
Chen, Xiwen 239, 241
Cherdchuchai, S. 467, 478
child mortality 90, 246, 293, 295
CHNS (China Health and Nutrition Surveys) 217–18, 220, 222–3, 298, 313, 321
Christiaensen, L. 252, 332, 350
CIMMYT (International Maize and Wheat Improvement Center) 400, 401
CIP (International Potato Center) 400, 410
CIT (commodity index traders) 128–9, 133, 134–6, 138
climate change
    and crop options 386–7, 394
    and food security 368–9
    and GHG emissions 422–3, 433–5, 439
    and land degradation 451–2
    and natural disasters 76
    and sustainability of food output 10
    and water scarcity 453–4
Climate Commission report (2012) 394
CO_2 fertilization 392, 411
'collapse regime' 130
collective farms 469
Collier, P. 251, 258
'commodity development trap' 332
commodity markets
    financialization of 122–9, 133–9, 143–4, 149, 172–3
    and food price bubbles 129–33, 143, 151–2
    and food price co-movement 139–42, 143
    and food price inflation 149
    and food price volatility 336–7
    and food security 332, 335–7, 340–41
    impact of macroeconomic factors 160–72
    price movements 150–55
    speculators in 122–3, 149
    study data/methodology 155–60
    study results 160–72
    and trade policy 332, 335–7, 340–41
commodity prices 73–4, 78–81
Common Agricultural Policy (EU) 333
Cooking, Cuisine, and Class: A Study in Comparative Sociology (book) 528
COP/MOP (Conference of the Parties/Meeting of the Parties) 423
Copenhagen Consensus (2008) 496
Corden, W. 344, 349, 350
corruption 499, 502
COT (Commitments of Traders) reports 125–6, 152
Coulibaly, D. 134, 146
Coveney, J. 530–31, 535

CPI (consumer price index)
  and commodity markets 155, 158, 160–69, 175
  and food price inflation 85–6, 95
  and government intervention 504, 505–7
  and price transmission 100
C-reactive protein 295, 296
crime 251
crop options
  alternatives to staple crops 406–12, 416
  and calorie intake 381, 382
  CGIAR programs 400–402, 404, 415
  and climate change 386–7, 394
  and commodity markets 412–13
  and crop efficiency 385–6
  cultural expectations 412
  current food staples 396–400
  CWR project 402–4, 415
  and diseases 407–8
  and food quality 383–4
  and food security 381–2, 412–13
  future study recommendations 417–18
  and global connectedness 383
  and 'Green Revolution' 385–6, 416
  and increased food demand 407
  investment in current crops 404, 408, 415–16
  limiting factors 413–14
  and native crops 408–12, 416
  and nutrition 381, 382, 383–4, 397–400, 414, 415
  and photosynthesis 387–96, 397, 406, 411, 414–15, 416–17
  R&D 382, 387, 390, 404, 415
  and 'right to food' 413
  and urbanization 413
  urgency/feasibility of solutions 382–3
crop yields 75–6, 90–91
cultural expectations 412
current food staples 396–400
Cutler, D. 282, 294, 295, 314, 315, 318
CVD (cardiovascular disease)
  age-adjusted statistics 281–2, 284–6, 287, 293
  causal factors 293–9
    studies of 300–309
  and competing risks 293–4, 315
  and economic status 286–7, 288–93, 295–9, 310–15
  and income levels 280–81, 282–4, 287, 293, 299, 310–16
  inter-regional variations 281–2, 287, 293
  and life expectancy 280–82, 287, 293–4, 297
  and longevity 294–5
  and nutrition 294
  and public health interventions 282–3, 294
  and risk factors 295–9

  evidence of 299, 310–15
  studies on 300–309
  and YLL 283–4, 287
CWR (Crop Wild Relatives) project 402–4, 415
Czeck, B. 392, 418

DALYs (disability adjusted life years) 279, 280–82, 287, 297
Dandekar, V. 269, 275
Dang, T. N. 88, 98
Dantwala, M. 470, 478
Das, Manab 17–18
Dasgupta, P. 222, 242, 249, 250, 252, 257, 258
Dawe, D. 13, 83–4
DCC (Dynamic Conditional Correlation) 139
De Brauw, A. 220, 242
de Hoyos, R. 41, 47, 48, 49, 51, 60, 61
Deaton, A. 41, 44, 46, 61, 63, 116–17, 120, 191, 192, 217, 222, 244, 250, 255, 258, 259, 272, 276, 294, 295, 311, 318, 329, 350, 376, 379
deforestation 423, 431, 438, 445
Dehn, J. 88, 97, 332, 350
Delormier, T. 530, 531, 535
Demeke, M. 105, 120, 327, 350
Deolalikar, A. 1, 8, 20, 36, 184, 188–9, 190, 191, 192, 196, 217, 242, 248, 250, 257, 258
Dercon, S. 44, 61, 251, 252, 257, 350
Dessus, S. 46, 47
diabetes 296, 297
Diao, X. 345, 350
dietary allowances
  and calorie intake 261, 262, 265, 266–74
  emergence of nutritional science 260
  inter-war nutritional standards 264–7
  post-war hypotheses 267–73
  pre-war dietary studies 260–64
dietary consumption patterns
  future research propositions 531–4
  in India 521–2
  and middle classes 515–17, 519–21, 525–34
  social aspects of 515–16, 527–31
  in Vietnam 522–3
dietary diversity
  and economic shocks 44, 45, 52, 57, 58
  and FDI index 178–9, 183–8, 196–7, 203
  and nutrition 177–8
dietary transition
  and agricultural growth 238–9
  changes in food item consumption 181–3, 189, 194–5, 208–11, 216–17, 225–9
  demand elasticity 211–15, 217
  and eating out 179–81, 220–21
  of emerging economies 7–8, 177, 204
  and FDI index 178–9, 183–8, 196–7, 203

and food consumption expenditure 205–8, 211
and food market interventions 232–8, 240
and food quality 217–18
and food security 204, 225–38, 240–41, 490–91
and imports/exports 229–31
and income inequality 218–20
and IV regression 184–5, 196–203
and labour migration 220
and NCDs 7, 8, 178, 189, 190, 224–5, 298
and nutrition 177–8, 217–18, 222–5, 238
and obesity 189–90, 223, 224
slowing down of 188–9, 189–90
and supply and demand 177, 225–32, 520–21
survey results/explanation 184–9
Dinsa, G. 300, 312, 318
direct crop breeding 390–91
Dirks, R. 263, 276
disposable income 46, 90, 205, 338, 488
Dokken, B. 296, 319
Dollex Index 155, 157–8, 160–9, 171–2, 175
domestic staple food prices 100–105
Dong, F. 211, 217, 243
Dong, X. 470, 479
Donohue, R. 393, 418
'dormant regime' 130
Dorosh, P. 117, 119
'double burden' 7
Drèze, J. 191, 192, 255, 258, 272, 275, 276, 376, 379
Du, S. 298, 313, 314, 319

Eastwood, R. 462, 466, 467, 478, 479
eating out 179–81, 220–21
Ecker, O. 12, 41, 47, 52, 59, 62, 222, 243
economic shocks
 behavioral responses to 42–4
 and elasticities of demand 43–4
 and food crises 42–3
 and food price inflation 76, 80–81, 86–7
 and food security 41–2, 54, 325–6, 335–6
 impact simulations 44–50
 and nutrition 41, 54, 57
 survey-based impact evidence 50–57, 59–60, 64–71
 and welfare 42–50
economic status 279–80, 286–7, 288–93, 295–9, 310–15
education 312, 314–15, 314–16
efficiency wage hypothesis 6, 90, 248, 255, 493–4
Efficient Market Hypothesis 152

E-GARCH (Exponential Generalised Autoregressive Conditional Heteroscedasticity) 159, 162, 164–5
EIU (Economist Intelligence Unit) 484
El Niño 52
elasticities of demand 43–4
Elbers, C. 252, 258
Elgin, M. 464, 478
emergency stock maintenance 373
Engel curves 205, 223, 255
enteric fermentation 427, 436
Erb, C. 150, 174, 432, 440
Erten, B. 88, 97
Eswaran, M. 251, 258, 463, 479
European dietary studies 260–61
evapo-transpiration 434
expenditure (in food crises impact simulations) 46–50
'explosive regime' 130
exports see imports/exports
extreme weather events 394, 416–17
Eyjafjallajökull (volcano) 391

'factor proportion' prediction 331
Fafchamps, M. 467, 479
FAFH (food away from home) 220–21
Fahri, E. 129, 146
family farms 463–4, 466–7
Fan, S. 47, 50, 60, 62, 79, 97, 492, 512
Fantel, J. 395, 419
FAO (Food and Agriculture Organization of the United Nations)
 and dietary allowances 267–8, 273
 and food price inflation 482
 food production estimates 445
 and food security 329
 and FPI (Food Price Index) 361
 and GHG emissions 423–4, 425–6, 428–31, 436, 438
 GPV forecasts 403
 and high frequency surveys 59
 and imports/exports 337, 338
 and minimum calorie requirements 45
 and NCDs 298
 nutritional deficiency estimates 1
 and trade policy 347
 and water resource management 456
FAOSTAT Emission database 423–4, 425–6, 428–31, 436
farm prices 110–14
fat intake 188, 201–2, 217–18, 223
FCS (food consumption score) 51–2, 58
FCVI (Food Security Vulnerability Indices) 361

FDI (food diversification index) 178–9, 183–8, 196–7, 203
FDI (foreign direct investment) 368
Feder, G. 462, 463, 479
fertilizer prices 110–12
FEVD (forecast error variance decomposition) 168
Figuerola-Ferretti, I. 131–3, 146
Fogel, R. 25, 38, 279, 294
Foley, J. 407, 418
food access 325, 357
food affordability 484, 485–8
food availability 325, 484, 485–8
'food balance sheets' 298
food crises
  behavioral dimensions of 27–30
  and economic shocks 42–3
  and food security 22–3, 26, 27–30, 327
  impact simulations 44–50
  preventing 31–4
  and trade policy 327
food price bubbles 129–33, 143, 151–2
food price co-movement 139–42, 143
food price inflation
  and biofuel 1–2
  and commodity markets 73–4, 78–81, 149
  and crop yields 75–6, 90–91
  in developing Asia 72, 82–95
  and domestic markets 2–3, 81–5
  and economic growth 85–8
  and economic shocks 76, 80–81, 86–7
  and food price volatility 72, 73, 84–5, 88, 93, 95–6, 482
  and food production 9
  and food security 325–7, 345–6, 353–4
  and fuel prices 77–9, 93–4
  and GDP growth 3–4
  and general inflation 3, 85–8
  and government intervention 505–7
  and imports/exports 92–3, 482
  and livestock production 76–7
  and nutrition 6–7, 72
  and obesity 6–7
  and oil prices 1–2
  and policy choices 91–5, 96, 483
  and poverty 3–5, 88–91, 483, 491–2
  and real factor incomes 5–6
  resurgence of 73–81
  and rice production 2, 3, 80–81, 82
  in South Asia 482–3, 491–2
  and supply and demand 73, 75
  and trade policy 325–7, 345–6
  and weather 2
food price regulation 232–6
food price subsidies 494–7, 502, 503

food price volatility
  and commodity markets 136–9, 143, 152–5, 336–7
  and food price inflation 72, 73, 84–5, 88, 93, 95–6, 482
  and food security 22–4, 26–7, 28–30
  and poverty 34
  and price transmission 109
'food problem' 87–8
food security
  and agricultural trade 325, 328–34, 339–48
  and calorie intake 359
  and climate change 368–9
  and commodity markets 332, 335–7, 340–41
  and crop options 381–2, 412–13
  definitions of 41, 325, 357–9, 384, 444, 484
  and dietary transition 204, 225–38, 240–41, 490–91
  and economic shocks 41–2, 54, 325–6, 335–6
  empirical estimates of 361–3
  enhancing 353–6
    through international trade 369–74
    through poverty reduction 355, 374–6
    through productivity improvement 363, 365–9
    through social food safety nets 355, 376–8
  and food affordability 484, 485–8
  and food availability 325, 484, 485–8
  and food crises 22–3, 26, 27–30, 327
  and food price inflation 325–7, 345–6, 353–4
  and food price volatility 22–4, 26–7, 28–30
  and food utilization 325, 484, 485–8
  framework for 24–6
  and GHG emissions 437–8
  and global connectedness 383
  and government intervention 483, 493–508
  and imports/exports 325–6, 330–31, 338–9, 340–7, 369–73
  improving measurement of 58–60
  and income levels 328
  and land degradation 450–51
  levels of 358–61
  'mechanism design' 34–5
  meaning of 356–63
  and nutrition 41, 54, 57, 359
  and political economy 22, 35–6
  and poverty 346, 355, 374–6, 492–7
  quantifying 359–61
  and rice prices 26–7, 28–31, 114–15
  right to 483, 504–8
  in South Asia 483, 484–509
  and trade policy 325–34, 339–48, 348–9
  and undernourishment 488–90
  and water scarcity 452–3
food self-reliance 330, 331

food self-sufficiency 26–7, 329–30, 331
food stability 325
food supply chain losses 434–5
food utilization 325, 484, 485–8
Foster, A. 462, 479
FPI (Food Price Index) 361–2
FPS (Fair Price Shops) 497–9, 501
FRA (Forest Resource Assessment) 424, 431
Framingham Study (US) 286
Frankenberg, E. 54, 57, 60, 61, 62
free trade 330–31, 332–4, 341, 343
Freire, C. 96, 97, 119, 120
Friedman, J. 46, 54, 61, 62, 64
FSI (Food Security Index) 361
fuel prices 77–9, 93–4
fuel wood consumption 446
Fuller, F. 211, 217, 243
Furst, E. 529, 535

G20 (Group of 20) 92
Gaiha, Raghav 7, 8, 12, 13–14, 15, 20, 21, 36, 98, 120, 173, 178, 191, 193, 220, 243, 252, 255, 258, 272, 276, 298, 319, 375, 379, 490, 498, 502, 503, 506, 536
Galtier, F. 370, 379
GARCH (Generalized AutoRegressive Conditional Heteroscedasticity) 138, 139, 150, 158–9
Garcia, P. 135, 145, 173
GCDT (Global Crop Diversity Trust) 402
GDP (Gross Domestic Product) 3–4, 278, 280–1, 282, 482
GEF (Global Environment Facility) 444
Gelos, G. 86–7, 97
gender relationships/divisions 527, 529, 530, 531
GFSI (Global Food Security Index) 484–5, 488
GHG (greenhouse gas) emissions
  agriculture emission trends 424, 427–31
  analysis discussion 436–7
  and climate change 422–3, 433–5, 439
  and deforestation 431, 438
  and enteric fermentation 427, 429, 436
  and food security 437–8
  increase in 422–3, 437
  land-based mitigation 431–3
  manure emissions 428–30, 436
  materials/methods of analysis 423–4, 425–7
  mitigation for 422, 431–5, 437–9
  and population growth 422
  results of analysis 424, 427–35
  and rice cultivation 430–31
  and supply and demand 432–5, 438–9
GHI (Global Hunger Index) 246, 247, 361

GIDD (Global Income Distribution Dynamics) database 119
Gilbert, Christopher L. 13, 19, 38, 76, 80, 93, 97, 100, 120, 123, 129, 131–3, 135, 136, 138, 139, 142, 145, 146, 336
Giovino, G. 298, 319
GLASOD (Global Assessment of Soil Degradation) 445, 450
Gleick, P. 444, 452, 456, 460
Glewwe, P. 245, 294, 319
Glied, S. 314, 319
Global Burden of Disease 2010 Study (2013) 283
global level food security 358–9
GM (genetically modified) crops 387, 390–91, 405–6
Godfray, H. 407, 414, 419
'Golden Rice' initiative 405–6
Goletti, F. 116, 120
Goody, Jack 528, 536
Gopalan, C. 268–9, 271, 273, 276
Gorton, G. 150, 174
Gorton, M. 466, 479
Goswami, Debashish 17–18
Gould, B. 208, 211, 213–15, 217, 221, 243
Gourinchas, P. 129, 146
GPV (gross production values) 403
Grain for Green programmes (China) 240
grain self-sufficiency ratios 473–5
Granger causality analysis 79, 134–6, 138, 143, 152, 159, 168, 172, 500–501
Gready, Jill 16–17, 390, 391, 419
'Great Moderation' 129
Green Climate Fund 423, 457
'Green Revolution' 17, 365, 385–6, 416, 462, 469
Greer, R. 150, 174
GRiSP (Global Rice Science Partnership) 402, 405
Gross Happiness Index 494
groundwater 447–8
Guenther, P. 218, 243
Gulati, A. 503, 505, 511, 512
Guo, X. 217–19, 224, 243
Guy, William 261, 276
GWP (Gallup World Poll) data 51

Hall, S. 130, 146
Hallal, P. 302, 303, 312, 320
Hamilton, J. 134, 147, 159, 160, 174
Hartini, T. N. S. 54, 62
Havlík, P. 434, 435, 440
Hayami, Y. 462, 464, 466, 470, 471–2, 478, 479
Hazell, P. 62, 345, 350, 476, 479

Headey, Derek 1, 2, 12, 19, 21, 41, 47, 50, 51, 60, 62, 79, 350, 379, 492, 512
Heckman self-selection procedure 253
HEI (healthy-eating index) 218
Heltberg, R. 462, 469, 470, 478, 479
Henneberry, S. 213–15, 219, 245
Hernandez, M. 79, 97
Herrera, S. 47, 48
Herring, J. 258, 395, 419
HIES (household income and expenditure survey) 119
'high food drain' 87–8
high frequency surveys 59–60
Himanshu 375, 379, 499, 502, 511, 512
HIV/AIDS 279
hoarding (of food) 28, 29, 30–31, 106–8, 149
Hoddinott, J. 496, 512
Holtzman, J. 528, 529, 536
Honore, B. 285, 320
Horton, S. 193, 249, 258, 420, 496, 513
household level food security 358, 359–60
Household Responsibility System (China) 204, 475
household surveys
 and dietary transition 179–81, 184–9
 and food security 329
 and impact of economic shocks 50–57
 and NCDs 286–7, 293
 and PNTs 253–6
Hovhannisyan, V. 208, 211, 213–15, 217, 243
Huang, J. 229, 231, 237
Hurlin, C. 501
hypertension 296, 298, 316

ICARDA (International Center for Agricultural Research in the Dry Areas) 400, 401
ICAs (International Commodity Agreements) 372–3
ICMR (Indian Council of Medical Research) 273
ICRISAT (International Crops Research Institute for the Semi-Arid Tropics) 400
IFAD (International Fund for Agricultural Development) 1, 362
IFLS (Indonesian Family Life Surveys) 53, 54, 55, 57, 66–7
IFPRI (International Food Policy Research Institute) 246, 345, 361, 386, 394
IHDS (India Human Development Survey, 2005) 179–81
Imai, Katsushi S. 13–14, 15, 19, 21, 110, 112, 120, 244, 247, 255, 256, 257, 258, 319, 492, 513, 523, 536
IMF (International Monetary Fund) 94, 124

import/exports
 and commodity markets 151
 and dietary transition 229–31
 and food price inflation 92–3, 482
 and food security 325–6, 330–1, 338–9, 340–47, 369–73
 and price transmission 105–8
 and rice production 26, 28, 30, 116–17
 and trade policy 325–6, 330–31, 337–9, 340–47
income inequality 218–20
income levels
 and food security 328
 and NCDs 280–81, 282–4, 287, 293, 299, 310–16
 and trade policy 328
Indian National Movement 266
Indonesian financial crisis (1998) 42, 43, 46, 52–7, 64–71
infant industries 333
informed traders 133–4
instrumental variable (IV)regression 184–5, 196–203
Inter-Departmental Committee on Physical Deterioration 272
International Emergency Food Reserve 93
International Labour Conference (1935) 264
International Water Management Institute 456
IPCC (Intergovernmental Panel on Climate Change) 17, 368, 422, 423, 428, 430–1, 436
IRFs (impulse response functions) 168, 170–71
iron deficiency 249, 250
IRRI (International Rice Research Institute) 400, 402, 406
irrigation 447–8, 452
Irwin, S. 125, 134, 135, 138, 144, 147, 336, 350
Isgut, A. 119, 120
Ivanic, M. 41, 46, 47, 48–9, 62, 90, 98, 116, 117, 118–19, 120, 329, 337, 350, 483, 513

Jalan, J. 252, 258
Jayne, T. 346, 350
Jensen, R. 272, 276, 495, 513
Jha, Raghbendra 5, 6, 15, 20, 21, 36, 88, 90, 96, 98, 173, 190, 191, 193, 222, 224, 243, 244, 250, 253–5, 257, 258, 495, 496, 498, 499, 512, 513, 536
Jha, Shikha 13, 73, 80, 85, 98, 377, 379, 498, 513
Johnson, R. 313, 320

Kaicker, Nidhi 13–14, 21, 191, 193
Katan, M. 296, 322
Katsaris, A. 130, 145
Kaur, Simrit 18, 493, 513

Kawagoe, T. 462, 466, 471–2, 479
KCBT (Kansas City Board of Trade) 135, 155, 176
Kenkel, D. 314, 320
Keynes, J. 331–2, 350
Khan, M. 88, 98
Khan, S. 453–6
Khera, R. 499–500, 501, 513
Kim, B. 312, 314, 320
Kingsbury, N. 386, 396, 408, 415–16, 419
Kleiman–Weiner, M. 238, 244
Knox, J. 368, 379
Kotwal, A. 251, 379, 463, 479, 495
Krakatoa (volcano) 391
Krishna, A. 256, 258
Krueger, A. 346, 351
Kulkarni, Vani S. 14, 18–19, 20, 379, 512, 536
Kurkure, A. 287, 288, 320
kwashiorkor 268–9

labor-intensive farming system 464–5
Ladejinsky, W. 470, 480
Lakdawalla, D. 254, 259, 299, 310, 311, 314, 320
land degradation
　and climate change 451–2
　current challenges 445–7
　definition of 443–4
　and food security 450–51
　future recommendations 457–8
　impact of 443, 446–7, 450–52
　and sustainable land management 454–5, 457
Land Reform Regulations (Japan) 471
'larger freedoms' 493
LDCs (Least Developed Countries) 326, 343, 346–7
League of Nations 264–6
Leibenstein, H. 248, 493, 513
Levenstein, H. 263, 276, 529, 536
Levinsohn, J. 46, 54, 62, 64
LIFDCs (low-income food-deficit countries) 337, 338
life expectancy 278–9, 280–82, 287, 293–4, 297
livestock production 10, 76–7, 225–6, 228–9, 239
Lleras-Muney, A. 285, 295, 314, 318
LNHO (League of Nations Health Organisation) 266–7
longevity 294–5
long-run food security measures 24–5
'loose money' 129
'Lost Crops of the Incas' report (1989) 408, 411

low birth weight 313
LSMS–ISA (Living Standards Measurement Surveys–Integrated Surveys on Agriculture) project 47
Lubotsky, D. 311, 318

Ma, H. 211, 212–15, 217, 221, 244
macro food policies 33–4
Mahal, Ajay 15–16, 178, 191, 311, 315, 321, 324
Maizels, A. 133, 147
malnutrition *see* nutrition
Malthus, Thomas 353
manure emissions 428–30, 436
market failures 32–4, 251, 279, 341, 344, 371–2, 492–3
market uncertainty/unpredictability 331–2, 335–7
marketing margins 112–14
market-oriented approach (to preventing food crises) 31–2, 33–4
Markov-switching approach 130
'Marmot Review' (2010) 279
Marmot, M. 279, 295, 310–11, 317
Martin, W. 46, 47, 92–3, 116, 117, 118–19, 329, 337, 341, 350, 351, 370
Marx, Karl 517
Marxian/Weberian class perspectives 515, 517, 518
'Masters Hypothesis' 134
Masters, Michael 122, 138, 336
'Masters Volatility Hypothesis' 138
Masters, W. 344
maternal mortality 90
maternal thinness 57
Mathur, Kritika 13–14, 20, 21
Mayer, J. 123, 134, 145, 152
Maystre, N. 139, 145
McCrorie, J. 131–3, 146
McCulloch, N. 116, 117, 120, 352
McDermott, C. J. 335–6, 349
McKenzie, D. 253, 257
MDGs (Millennium Development Goals) 72, 362, 483, 485, 488–90, 508
Meara, E. 294, 295, 318
'mechanism design' 34–5
Medicaid 315
Medvedev, D. 47, 49, 51, 60, 61
Mennell, S. 528, 529, 536
MGE (Minneapolis Grain Exchange) 155, 176
Micronutrient Initiative 496
middle classes
　definitions of 518–19, 523
　and dietary consumption patterns 515–17, 519–21, 525–34

and dietary transition 180–81, 184, 185, 186, 196, 218, 520–21
future research propositions 531–4
Marxian/Weberian class perspectives 515, 517, 518
measuring size of 520–3, 523–4
and 'middleclassness' 517–20, 527, 534
perception of 524
profile of 524–5
rise of (in Asia) 523–5
and social aspects of food consumption 515–16, 527–31
'middleclassness' 517–20, 527, 534
Miller, N. 272, 276, 495, 513
minimum calorie requirements 45
Minot, N. 21, 83, 102, 116, 120
Mirrlees, J. 248, 259, 493, 513
Mirzaei, M. 284–5, 321
Mishra, G. 530, 537
Mishra, P. 86, 98
mixed cropping 412
MNREGA (Mahatma Gandhi National Rural Employment Guarantee Act) 496
Morgan, C. 136, 146, 336
Morley, R. 313, 321
MOU (memorandum of understanding) 108
MPCE (monthly per capita expenditure) 495
MSCI (Morgan Stanley Commodities Index) 155, 157–8, 160–70, 172, 175
Mu, R. 220, 243
Mueller, N. 437, 441
Mugera, H. 139, 142, 146
Mullainathan, F. 252, 257
Murphy, K. 519, 537

National Academies Advisory Panel 408, 411, 416
National Food Security Bill 11
national level food security 358, 360–61
National Longitudinal Survey among Youth (US) 310
National Sample Survey (NSS) 11
native crops 408–12, 416
natural crop climate range 393
natural disasters 76
NBR (net benefit ratio) 46
NCDs (non-communicable diseases)
  age-adjusted statistics 281–2, 284–6, 287, 293
  and alcohol 296–7, 298, 313–14
  causal factors 293–9
    studies on 300–309
  and competing risks 293–4, 315
  and dietary transition 7, 8, 178, 189, 190, 224–5, 298

and economic status 279–80, 286–7, 288–93, 295–9, 310–15
and education 312, 314–16
and GDP 280–81, 282
and income levels 280–81, 282–4, 287, 293, 299, 310–16
inter-regional variations 281–2, 287, 293
and life expectancy 279, 280–82, 287, 293–4, 297
and longevity 294–5
and nutrition 294
and obesity 7, 296, 297, 310, 312–13
and physical activity/inactivity 297–8, 310, 312
and public health interventions 282–3, 294
and risk factors 295–9
  evidence of 299, 310–15
  studies on 300–309
and YLL 283–4, 287
'neighbourhood effects' 316
Nelson, D. 159
Nelson, G. 368, 386
NERICA (New Rice for Africa) 404–5
Neufeld, L. 359
New Cooperative Medical Scheme (China) 224
Newell, A. 469
NFHS (National Family Health Survey) 255, 256
NFIDCs (net food importing developing countries) 327
NFSO (National Food Security Ordinance) 501–4, 507, 508–9
Ng, F. 326
Ng, N. 298
Ngwenya, E. 54, 61, 62
Nissanke, M. 133, 147, 151–2
nitrogen 395
No. 1 Central Document (2012) 226, 237, 239–40
noise traders 133–4
NPC (National Planning Committee) 266–7
NRA (Nominal Rate of Assistance) 339–40
NREGS (National Rural Employment Guarantee Scheme) 255–6
NSS (National Sample Survey) 53–7, 59, 68–9, 178, 184, 255, 298, 500–501, 524, 526
'nuclear winter' 391
Nurses' Health Study (US) 286
nutrition
  and crop options 381, 382, 383–4, 397–400, 414, 415
  and dietary allowances 260–74
  and dietary diversity 177–8
  and dietary transition 177–8, 217–18, 222–5, 238

and economic shocks 41, 54, 57
and food price inflation 6–7, 72
and food security 41, 54, 57, 359
and NCDs 294
and poverty 493, 495, 498
and rice prices 115
see also PNTs (poverty–nutrition traps)

OBCs (Other Backward Castes) 179–80
obesity
   and diabetes 296, 297
   and dietary allowances 263–4
   and dietary transition 189–90, 223, 224
   and food price inflation 6–7
   and NCDs 7, 296, 297, 310, 312–13
Ocampo, J. 88, 97
ODCs (other developing countries) 326
Oddy, D. 261, 272, 277
oil prices 1–2, 139–42, 143–4
open economies 16, 325, 333–4, 348
optimum farm size 464–6, 476–7
'optimum tariffs' 333
Ortega, D. 208, 244
Otsuka, Keijiro 18, 462, 463, 464, 466, 467, 470, 475, 476, 477, 478, 479
overgrazing 445

Panel Study of Income Dynamics (US) 313
Pardey, P. 20, 379, 407, 420
Patnaik, U. 255, 259, 375, 379
Paxson, C. 295, 318
Payne, P. 267–8, 277
PDF (probability density function) 359–60
PDS (Public Distribution System) 11, 94, 255, 375, 377, 483–4, 494–5, 497–508
pensions 294–5
Pfuderer, Simone 13, 135, 136, 145, 146
Philipson, P. 299, 310, 311, 314, 320
Phillips, P. 130, 133, 145, 147
phosphorus 395–6
photosynthesis 387–96, 397, 406, 411, 414–15, 416–17
physical activity/inactivity 297–8, 310, 312
'planetary boundaries' 393, 395, 416
PNTs (poverty–nutrition traps)
   and calorie intake 248, 249–50
   and 'efficiency wages' 493
   and food price inflation 6, 90
   implications of undernutrition 246, 256
   in India 253–6
   overview of 247–50
   and wage rates 248–9, 250, 253–5
Poapongsakorn, N. 115, 117, 121
Polaski, S. 91, 98, 116, 121
political economy 22, 35–6, 260–73

pollution 391
Popkin, B. 177, 190, 191, 193, 196, 224, 225, 243, 298, 322
population growth (global) 8, 422
post-harvest productivity 368
potato crops 409–11
Poulton, C. 345, 351
poverty
   and crime 251
   and food crises impact simulations 46–50
   and food price inflation 88–91, 483, 491–2
   and food price volatility 34
   and food security 346, 355, 374–6, 492–7
   and geographical locations 251–2
   and health 250–51
   impact of rising food prices 3–5
   and land degradation 445
   and market failure 251
   and nutrition 493, 495, 498
   reducing 355, 374–6
   and rice prices 114–18
   and risk 252
   and trade policy 327–8, 329, 346
   traps 250–53
   undernourishment statistics 362–4
   see also PNTs (poverty–nutrition traps)
PP (Phillips–Perron) test 156, 158
PPP (purchasing power parity) 280, 283–4, 475
Prakash, A. 332, 351
Preston, S. 282, 295, 322
price transmission
   and domestic farm/retail prices 100–105, 118–19
   and farmgate prices 110–12
   and trade policy 105–9, 328, 340–41
prisoners' diets 261
productivity improvement 363, 365–9
protein intake 187–8, 199–200, 220, 268–9, 359
Psaradakis, Z. 130–31, 146
public health interventions 282–3, 294

quinoa crops 397–8, 400, 411–12
Quisumbing, A. 467, 479

Radhakrishna, R. 495, 513
Raj, J. 505, 513
Rao, Jaya 269, 271, 276
Rashid, S. 116, 121
Raskin program (Indonesia) 32, 377
Rath, N. 269, 276
Ravallion, M. 116, 121, 204, 232, 239, 242, 244, 252, 258
Ray, R. 54, 57, 61, 62
real factor incomes 5–6
Reardon, T. 26, 38, 62, 368, 379, 481

Reddy, K. 296
Reddy, Y. 507
Redfern, S. 405
relative food prices, reducing 355
reliability of supplies 337–9
rent-seeking 494–5
rice production/prices
   and crop options 396–7, 402, 404–6, 415
   and dietary transition 229–31
   and food price inflation 2, 3, 80–81, 82
   and food security 26–7, 28–31, 114–15
   and GHG emissions 430–31
   and hoarding 28, 29, 30–31
   and imports/exports 26, 28, 30, 116–17
   and international trade 370
   and marketing margins 113–14
   and nutrition 115
   and poverty 114–18
   and price transmission 100–102
   and supply and demand 29
   and 'supply of storage' model 29
'right to food' 11–12, 413, 501–4
risk 252
RIT (real income transfers) 498–9
Robertson, L. 295, 322
Robles, M. 37, 38, 102, 117, 121
Rosegrant, M. 368–9, 379
Rosenzweig, M. 248, 252, 257, 462, 464, 478
Ross, J. 249, 258
Rouwenhorst, K. 123, 146, 150, 174
Roy, D. 86, 98
Royal Society report (2009) 389
RTF Act (Right to Food, 2013) 11–12
Rubisco 387–90, 393
Rubner, Max 260, 261, 275
RUE (radiation use efficiency) 389, 397, 406, 416
Ruel, M. 58, 62, 177, 191, 192, 193, 238, 244
Ruhm, C. 310, 314, 315, 320

Sahn, D. 117, 121, 494, 514
Sanders, D. 125, 134, 138, 144, 145, 147
Sanogo, I. 51–2, 53, 57, 63
Sarkozy, Nicolas 122
Sarris, Alexandros 16, 37, 147, 331, 332, 336, 337, 346, 349, 351
Sathyamala, C. 15, 275, 277
SBIC (Schwartz Bayesian Information Criterion) 162, 168
SBP (systolic blood pressure) 298
Schaller, H. 130, 147
Schiff, M. 351, 504–5, 514
Schmidhuber, Josef 17, 422, 441,
Schoeni, R. 313, 320
Schultz, T. W. 87–8, 98

Schwandt, H. 314, 323
SCs (Scheduled Castes) 179–80, 185, 186, 187
SCS (staple calorie share) measure 272
SEAP (South East Asia and the Pacific) sub-region 9–10
Seckler, D. 270, 277
Sen, A. 493, 499, 502, 504, 512
Senhadji, A. 88, 98
Shah, C. 470
Shah, K.T. 267
Shaw, George Bernard 518
Sheehy, John 406
Shi, S. 133, 147
Shimokawa, S. 217, 218, 238, 241, 244
Shleifer, A. 519, 537
short-run food security measures 24–5
Silvennoinen, A. 150, 173
Singh, Manmohan 23
SLM (sustainable land management) 454–5, 457
'small but healthy' hypothesis 269–71
small-scale farms
   in China 475–6, 477
   comparisons with larger farms 462, 466, 469–70, 471–6
   conceptual framework 463–7
   and economic growth 462–3
   efficiency of 462–3, 471–5, 476
   and family farms 463–4, 466–7
   farm size structure (Asia) 467–9
   grain self-sufficiency ratios 473–5
   in Japan 471–5, 477
   and optimum farm size 464–6, 476–7
   and productivity 462, 469–71
Smith, D. 253, 259
Smith, Edward 261–2, 275
Smith, F. 218, 242
Smith, L. 45, 63
smoking 296, 298, 313–14
SOC (soil organic carbon) pool 451
social aspects of food consumption 515–16, 527–31
social food safety nets 355, 376–8
'social justice approach' 492–3
social protection 484
soil moisture 451–2
Sokhey, Col. S.S. 266–7
Sola, M. 130–31, 146
Sombilla, M. 363, 365, 379
Sozialistengesetz (Socialist law) 261
Spagnolo, F. 130–31, 147
SPI (Social Protection Index) 484
Srinivasan, P.V. 13, 85, 98, 498, 513
SSA (sub-Saharan Africa) 345–6

stabilization approach (to preventing food crises) 31
'State of Food Insecurity in the World' report (2011) 329, 362, 489
stationarity tests 155–8
Steptoe, A. 295, 310–11, 323
Stern, N. 248, 257, 464, 478, 493, 512
Stiglitz, J. 259, 493, 514
Stoll, H. 133, 134, 145, 147
Strauss, J. 248, 250, 257, 259
Stringhini, S. 311, 323
strokes 295–6
STs (Scheduled Tribes) 179–80, 185, 186, 187
stunting 55–7, 67, 223, 269, 271, 359, 496
Sub-Committee on Colonial Territories 266–7
Subramanian, S. 60, 63, 217, 222, 244
'substantialist perspective' 532–3
'substantive freedoms' 493
Sukhatme, P. 269–71, 275, 277
supply and demand
 and dietary transition 177, 225–32, 520–21
 and food price inflation 73, 75
 and GHG emissions 432–5, 438–9
 and oil prices 1
 and rice production 29
'supply bottleneck' 508
supply chains 10–11
'supply inelasticity' 508
'supply of storage' model 29
'supply shock' 507–8
SUSENAS (National Socio-Economic Surveys) 53, 54, 55, 64–5
sustainability of food output 9–11
Sutton, Lainie 15–16, 528, 529, 537
Svedberg, P. 45, 63, 249, 250, 257, 259
Swamy, A. 248, 259
swap positions 124–5
synthetic fertilizers 430, 438

Tan, Jean-Francois Trinh 12
Tang, K. 139, 142, 148, 150, 157, 174
taxation 237, 346
'technology capital' 9
TERI (The Energy and Resources Institute) 453
TFP (total factor productivity) growth 4, 8–9, 365–6
Thapa, Ganesh 13–14
The Economist (newspaper) 381
The State of Food Insecurity in the World, 2012 (report) 362
Thomas, D. 248, 250, 257, 259
Thorp, S. 150, 173
Tilman, D. 407, 413, 415, 420, 437, 441
Timmer, C. Peter 1, 2, 8, 12, 19, 21, 23, 24, 25, 26, 27, 28, 29, 31, 79–80, 98, 100, 107, 109, 112, 119, 121, 178, 191, 193, 299, 323, 353, 369, 379
Tiwari, S. 60, 63, 118, 121
Torero, M. 79, 117, 121
TPDS (Targeted Public Distribution Scheme) 496, 497–9, 502
trade policy
 and commodity markets 332, 335–7, 340–41
 and economic shocks 325–6, 335–6
 and food crises 327
 and food price inflation 325–7, 345–6
 and food security 325–34, 339–48, 348–9
 and imports/exports 325–6, 330–31, 337–9, 340–47
 and income levels 328
 and poverty 327–8, 329, 346
 and price transmission 105–9, 328, 340–41
 and reliability of supplies 337–9
Tubiello, Francesco N. 17, 422, 423, 424, 440

UNCCD (United Nations Convention to Combat Desertification) 443
under tree cropping 412
undernourishment statistics 362–4
UNICEF (United Nations Children's Fund) 246
uninformed traders 133–4
UN-REDD (United Nations Collaborative Programme on Reducing Emissions from Deforestation and Forest Degradation) 423
urban dietary transition 177, 182, 208, 211, 217, 219–20
urbanization 413, 446
US dietary studies 262–4
US Senate Subcommittee (2009) 122
USDA (United States Department of Agriculture) trade model 44–5
USDA National Nutrient Database 397–9
Ustyugova, Y. 86–7, 97

van Noorden, S. 130, 147
VAR (value at risk) 158–9, 160, 162, 168, 172
Venet, B. 501, 513
Villarreal, H. 213–15, 221, 243
Vishny, R. 519, 537
VMD (vitamins and mineral deficiencies) 496

wage rates 248–9, 250, 253–5
Wang, H. 213–15, 221, 245
'want and deprivation' 492–7
Warr, Peter 16, 116–17, 355, 358, 365, 379, 380
Washington Consensus 327

water scarcity
  and climate change 453–4
  and crop production growth 444–5
  current challenges 447–9
  definition of 444
  and food security 452–3
  future recommendations 457–8
  and health 453
  impact of 443, 448–9, 452–4
  and sustainable land management 455, 457
  and water resource management 455–6
Waters, H. 54, 63
Webbink, D. 312, 323
Weinberger, K. 250, 259
'welfarist approach' 492–3
WFP (World Food Programme) 1, 51–2, 58, 59, 362
Whaley, R. 134, 145, 147
White, A. 154, 174, 336
Whitehall Study (UK) 286, 310
WHO (World Health Organization) 268, 281–2, 297, 357, 358, 453
Wilk, R. 528, 537
Winters, L. 202, 327, 328
Wodon, Q. 48–9, 62, 117
Wood, B. 116, 117, 121
World Bank
  and agriculture lending 354
  and food security 339–40
  and high frequency surveys 59
  and LSMS–ISA project 47
  and NCDs 281–2
  and PNTs 251
  poverty estimates 4
  report (2011) 149

World Food Conference (1974) 271
World Food Summit (1996) 22, 357, 358, 444, 484, 485, 488–90, 508
WPI (wholesale price index) 505–7
Wright, B. 151
WTI (West Texas Intermediate) 155, 157–8, 160–69, 171–2, 175
WTO (World Trade Organization) 223, 331, 372
Wu, C. 134, 147
Wu, Y. 130, 147
WVS (World Value Surveys) 524

Xiong, W. 139, 142, 147, 150, 157
Xu, Z. 240, 243

Yang, D. 313, 321, 467, 481
Yang, J. 234, 245
Yeole, B. 287, 288, 320
YLL (years of life lost) 283–4, 287
You, Jing 14–15, 220, 245
Yu, J. 130, 133, 147
Yu, X. 233, 235, 239, 245
Yudhoyono, Susilo Bambang 23

Zaman, H. 47, 49, 60, 62, 63, 98, 118, 513
Zezza, A. 46, 116, 117, 220, 245
Zhao, M. 218, 245
Zhen, L. 232, 245
Zheng, Z. 219, 245
Zhong, F. 208, 211, 245
Zhou, Z. 495, 514
Zhoug, G. 288, 324
Zhu, X. 389, 397, 408, 421
Zhuang, R. 211, 245
ZNLD (Zero Net Land Degradation) 457